A HISTORY OF AMERICAN MAGAZINES

Volume V: Sketches of 21 Magazines
1905–1930

FRANK LUTHER MOTT

This picture was taken in 1961 after a graduate-student seminar in his study at home in Columbia, Missouri. He died in 1964. Photograph by George W. Gardner.

A History of
AMERICAN MAGAZINES

Volume V: Sketches of 21 Magazines
1905–1930

BY THE LATE
FRANK LUTHER MOTT

With a cumulative index to the five volumes

THE BELKNAP PRESS OF
HARVARD UNIVERSITY PRESS
Cambridge, Massachusetts
1968

St. Mary's College Library
Winona, Minnesota

© COPYRIGHT 1968
BY THE PRESIDENT AND FELLOWS OF HARVARD COLLEGE

All rights reserved

DISTRIBUTED IN GREAT BRITAIN BY
OXFORD UNIVERSITY PRESS, LONDON

LIBRARY OF CONGRESS CATALOG CARD NUMBER 39-2823
PRINTED IN THE UNITED STATES OF AMERICA

050
M92
v.5

CONTENTS

106676

Foreword by Howard Mumford Jones ix

Editorial Note by Mildred Mott Wedel xv

Sketches of Magazines

1. *The American Mercury* 3
2. *Appleton's Booklovers Magazine* 27
3. *Better Homes and Gardens* 36
4. *Current History* 49
5. *Editor & Publisher* 59
6. *Everybody's Magazine* 72
7. *The Freeman* 88
8. *The Fugitive* 100
9. *The Golden Book Magazine* 117
10. *Good Housekeeping* 125
11. *Hampton's Broadway Magazine* 145
12. *House Beautiful* 154
13. *The Little Review* 166
    (Portion by John T. Frederick, 172–178)
14. *The Midland* 179
15. *The New Republic* 191
16. *Poetry* 225
    (Portion by John T. Frederick, 231–235)
17. *The Smart Set* 246
18. *The South Atlantic Quarterly* 273
19. *Success* 286
20. *Time* 293
21. *The Yale Review* 329

Unfinished Story; or, The Man in the Carrel (Mott's account of *A History of American Magazines*) 341

Bibliography of Mott's Writings on American Magazines . . 351

Index to the Five Volumes 353

ILLUSTRATIONS

Frank Luther Mott . . . *frontispiece*
The American Mercury, 1927 . . . 2
Listerine advertisement, 1927 . . . 16
Appleton's Booklovers Magazine, 1905 . . . 31
Victor Talking Machine advertisement, 1908 . . . 34
Coca-Cola advertisement, 1906 . . . 35
Fruit, Garden and Home, 1924 . . . 39
Better Homes & Gardens, 1928 . . . 40
Better Homes and Gardens, 1965 . . . 41
Current History, 1915 . . . 52
Current History, 1967 . . . 53
The Editor and Publisher, 1901 . . . 60
Editor & Publisher, 1967 . . . 61
James Wright Brown of *Editor & Publisher* . . . 65
Everybody's Magazine, 1904 . . . 77
The Golden Book Magazine, 1927 . . . 120
Good Housekeeping, 1885 . . . 127
Good Housekeeping, 1908 . . . 128
Good Housekeeping, 1967 . . . 129
A fashion column of 1919 . . . 135
Broadway Magazine, 1899 . . . 144
The House Beautiful, 1908 . . . 160
House Beautiful, 1967 . . . 161
The Little Review, 1915 . . . 170
The Midland, 1915 . . . 181
John T. Frederick of *The Midland* . . . 189
Herbert David Croly of *The New Republic* . . . 194
The New Republic, 1914 . . . 198
The New Republic, 1967 . . . 199
Harriet Monroe of *Poetry* . . . 227
Poetry, 1919 . . . 232
Poetry, 1967 . . . 233
The Smart Set, 1908 . . . 252
Henry L. Mencken . . . 253
The South Atlantic Quarterly, 1905 . . . 279
Success Magazine, 1906 . . . 289
Time, 1923 . . . 299
Time, 1945 . . . 300
Time, 1967 . . . 301
Henry R. Luce of *Time* . . . 310
The Yale Review, 1918 . . . 334
The Yale Review, 1967 . . . 335

CREDITS

The following persons and periodicals have granted permission for the use of the illustrations on the pages indicated:

George W. Gardner, the frontispiece.

Better Homes and Gardens, pp. 39, 40, 41.

Current History, pp. 52, 53.

Editor & Publisher, pp. 61, 65 (supplied photograph for p. 65).

Good Housekeeping, pp. 129, 135. Illustration on p. 129 reprinted by permission from February 1967 issue of *Good Housekeeping* magazine, © 1967 by the Hearst Corporation. Illustration on p. 135 reprinted by permission from March 1919 issue of *Good Housekeeping* magazine.

House Beautiful, p. 161. Reprinted by permission of *House Beautiful,* © 1967 by the Hearst Corporation.

John T. Frederick, pp. 181, 189 (supplied photograph for p. 189).

The New Republic, pp. 194, 198, 199 (supplied photograph for p. 194).

Poetry, pp. 227, 232, 233 (supplied photograph for p. 227).

Time, pp. 299, 300, 301, 310. Illustration for p. 299, courtesy *Time,* copyright Time Inc. 1923. For p. 300, courtesy *Time,* copyright Time Inc. 1945. For p. 301, courtesy *Time,* copyright Time Inc. 1967. Photograph for p. 310 supplied by *Time* and reproduced with permission of Time Inc.

The Yale Review, pp. 334, 335.

FOREWORD BY HOWARD MUMFORD JONES

SOME books have an air of having existed forever. The mind accepts the historical truth that there must have been a date when the world did not contain them, but this fact receives only notional acceptance, not what Newman would call real assent. Such titles are Bartlett's *Familiar Quotations,* the Anglican Prayer Book, the *Encyclopaedia Britannica,* and Webster's *Dictionary*. Their titles become, as it were, common nouns and categorize a whole species. "To look it up in Webster" means to look it up in any competent dictionary, an area of publishing in which Noah Webster is simply *primus inter pares,* the most powerful ghost in American lexicography. When in 1930 Frank Luther Mott issued his *A History of American Magazines, 1741–1850* and announced that other volumes were to follow, he not only entered into his kingdom, he became one of these inevitable names. Others have written more fully about particular periodicals, others have been more detailed about particular eras in magazine publishing, but Mott is like Gibbon. You cannot think of the history of the Roman empire without thinking of Gibbon, and you cannot think of the history of the magazine in our country without thinking of Mott, the first book you turn to, the latest you consult.

Alas, as Longfellow wrote of Hawthorne,

> The unfinished window in Aladdin's tower
> Unfinished must remain.

The present Volume V, incomplete but majestic, is all we shall have from the Master of the Magazines, who died October 23, 1964. With affectionate care his daughter, advised and assisted by Theodore Peterson and John T. Frederick, has smoothed out a few rough spots, got rid of inconsistencies, and added some recent facts to the "biographies" of the magazines in the present volume. No one has attempted to write the judicious yet sweeping survey of the years 1905–1930 that only Mott could do.

Frank Luther Mott was born near What Cheer, Iowa, a felicitous name that still adorns the map, and his father published a weekly newspaper called *The Patriot*. Both names were good omens. The multivolume *History of American Magazines* from 1741 forward is the work of an American who believed in scholarship and who believed that scholarship had something to do with the national intelligence. His modesty led him to argue in the introduction to the first volume that the history of American periodicals might be a valuable addition to the stock of national intelligence. It is in 1968 difficult to think back over about four decades to a time when somebody as good as Mott was a little defensive on his topic. He pointed out that in the United States, magazines have contributed to the democracy of literature without necessarily lowering its tone, and were an important element in the economics of publishing and invaluable records of contemporaneous history. The creation of American Studies programs has not merely validated these modest assumptions but made Mott more and more useful to American historians as the decades drift by.

As for What Cheer, Iowa, a name that escaped the condescension of Matthew Arnold and the bewilderment of Henry James, that, too, was a good omen. No one who has read, or read in, any of the five volumes but must be aware of an author happy in his work and happily conscious of the comic side of men, matter, and opinions. By this I do not mean that Frank Luther Mott was a merry fellow only. In the hands of somebody else a compilation about the whole great body of American periodical publishing might have had the deadly impersonality of the telephone book. I can think of other vast surveys of this dull character. Endlessly patient, never tired, never disillusioned (or if he was, he concealed the fact), Frank Luther Mott displayed the same happy interest in the vagaries of his subject, whether he was dealing with a general magazine or a specialized periodical. He had an unquenchable thirst for the anecdote that illumines, the phrase that reveals. Who but he would have dredged up from the dusty closets of time the stern judgment of the Illinois Federation of Women's Clubs that the use of the female figure in advertising "corrupts the youth of the land"? Or noted a clothing store advertisement in *Browning's Magazine:* "the best fin de siècle clothing at moderate cost"? Or dryly quoted the judgment of the *American Quarterly* in 1834: "There is scarcely anything more remarkable in the character of the last five or six years than their sterility in literary production," and then noted that Poe, Bryant, Whittier, Irving, Paulding, George Bancroft, Davy Crockett and others had brought out important titles in this "lustrum"? The real turning of the knife in the wound, however, is in the next sentence: "But there was also a poem by a dentist on diseases of the teeth, and Dr. McHenry spent some space on it." Never was solemn stupidity more neatly pinned to the wall.

I think Mott brought to his gigantic enterprise some other salient characteristics. One of these was a function of his life as a newspaperman. He was at one time or another a practising newspaper editor; he wrote (incredible!) in the midst of his *History of American Magazines* a reliable history of American journalism, which he twice revised; he was chief of the journalism section of the American Army University of Biarritz; he was sent to Japan to advise General MacArthur's staff about newspapers and newspaper ways; he taught journalism at the State University of Iowa and became dean of the School of Journalism at the University of Missouri, a post influential in both academic and newspaper circles. I think this rich and varied knowledge of the newspaper world helped him make the *History of American Magazines* the judicious, accurate, and sympathetic work it is.

In the first place the newspaperman has to write—endlessly, fluently, and immediately. In the next place he has to be accurate if he and his paper are to avoid quarrels, protests, and libel suits. In the third place, though his style may lack high distinction, it must have clarity, and it can be a style, as contemporary columnists demonstrate, of considerable range. Much is to be said about the *mot juste,* but much is also to be said against it, especially in the academic world and in certain provinces of the world of literature. Paralysis ensues when the writer feels he must pat every syllable into place or when the scholar becomes a devotee of perfection and ends by writing nothing. The successful newspaperman, however much he may respect the styles of great poets and novelists, comes by and by to realize that an exercise in transcendental art is not for him. His business is to get the thing down on paper, responsibly, clearly, succinctly. Mott was a supreme journalist—a term likely to lead some artists and academicians to look upon his writing with profound suspicion. But a newspaperman cannot die of a rose in aromatic pain. To carry the burden of five large volumes, chronicles not merely of the vagaries of the publishing world but also of scores of individual periodicals, required an attitude towards writing the thing down that Mott clearly had. Some pages are of course better than others. It would be difficult for anybody to get up much warmth about faded theological reviews and obsolete agrarian magazines important in their time and therefore to be included. Whatever these and other obstacles, one never has to wonder what Mott is saying. He developed a style flexible, responsible, accurate, and tough enough to stand up under the strain of about 3,000 pages (perhaps more) of closely packed print. Moreover, he had to verify the details as he went along. How he found time to do all these things I do not know. There are slips in these volumes, but they are minor.

A second quality in newspaper writing at first sight looks like derogating the writer but on second thought will, I trust, be taken as the compliment I intend. The intelligent newspaperman makes his material, his judgment, and his style appeal to the average reader, a person of sense and some education to whom most publishing is intended to appeal. It would have been possible for somebody to write a history of American magazines that would deplore their banality, condemn the low level of the commercial world which supports them, and point with scorn to the venality of editors, hack writers, and others who live in the half-world that is neither journalism nor literature. It would also be possible to reverse this valuation, to insist that if highbrows had only got off their high horses, the history of magazine publishing and the history of the American mind would have been oh! so much better. One can hear the same argument today about television.

Mott refused to join either camp. When a good highbrow periodical swims into his ken, he notes its excellencies and its appeal—an example in this volume is his treatment of *The New Republic.* When a lowbrow magazine exhibits long life and exerts influence, he tries to estimate its virtues and defects —an example is the history of *Leslie's Weekly* in Volume II. He can be interested in eccentric publications like *Brann's Iconoclast* (Volume IV) and revel in the history of *The National Police Gazette* (Volume II). In the present volume nothing is more absorbing than his accounts of *The Smart Set* and *The American Mercury.* Specialized periodicals aside (that is, scientific, theological, agricultural or other publications restricting themselves to a particular public), Mott assumes that the editor and the publisher of a general magazine want circulation and must therefore appeal to that elusive yet powerful personage, the general reader. His judgments on a magazine *qua* magazine tend to rest upon the success or failure of editorial and publishing policies. I think this is a sound approach. Even books have to sell, but the problem of selling magazines is complex and was seldom solved among the periodicals of the colonial period, the Revolution, and antebellum America. The weakness of the criterion is not that there is something wrong about good business judgment; the weakness lies in the inescapable difficulty that Mott, who had done so much, could not (among other reasons, for lack of data) deal as richly with problems of advertising intake and circulation build-up as a total history would theoretically require.

I have spoken of Frank Luther Mott as if he were "only" a journalist. He taught courses in English, he co-edited an influential mid-Western literary periodical, he wrote critical essays, and he wrote fiction. One short story by him, "The Man with the Good Face," got into O'Brien's *The Best Short Stories of 1921* and continues to live the peculiar life of anthologized short stories; I find it a little stagey, but somebody has written in a copy of this anthology "A regular Hawthorne story set in New York," and the unknown commentator may be a wiser critic than I am. The point, however, is that Mott's sensibilities were literary no less than journalistic, a quality in him that raises him above the merely colloquial, the merely contemporary. It is this side of him that gives us the sympathetic account of the Fugitive group in the present volume that balances the just estimate of the commercial success of *Good Housekeeping,* which he also chronicles. But when was there a really competent historian without some literary sense? Among the silly things said about the first volume the silliest was probably a phrase that appeared in the *Times Literary Supplement:* "No interest to the general reader." Few there are who sit down to read through Gibbon or Bartlett, Webster or the *Encyclopaedia Britannica,* and I doubt that the general reader ever dreamed of reading Mott all the way through. When a reviewer of the 1957 volume said the whole work was "a sort of syllabus of our cultural history," he was nearer the center of the target; and those who begin by consulting Mott for a particular point commonly find themselves reading on and on. Higher tribute cannot be paid to a standard history or a standard book of reference.

EDITORIAL NOTE BY MILDRED MOTT WEDEL

WHEN my father, Frank Luther Mott, died in 1964, he was hard at work on Volume V of *A History of American Magazines.* Volume I had appeared in 1930. It was followed in 1938 by Volumes II and III for which he was awarded the Pulitzer Prize in History the following year. In 1957 Volume IV was published, bringing the running history of magazine development up to the year 1905, and earning for him the Bancroft Prize in 1958.

Volume V was to deal with the next twenty-five years, 1905 to 1930. Like the previous volumes it would have consisted of (1) a general discussion of magazine publication in the period, with emphasis on the ways in which magazines reflected the history of the times, and (2) a series of historical sketches of certain magazines which were important and flourishing within this span of years (not necessarily begun in or limited to the period). There were to be thirty-one of these sketches. The author had planned for a sixth volume which would have brought the history up to the present.

At the time of Dr. Mott's death, the completed portion of the manuscript for Volume V consisted of twenty of the separate magazine histories, with another substantially written. These twenty-one sketches are being published here. He had not made final revisions, and the stories of those magazines which are still publishing ended with the late 1950's or early 1960's, according to the date of writing. He had planned to update them just before publication.

Harvard University Press and I agreed we did not want to ask anyone else to write the uncompleted parts of the volume, with two exceptions. I asked John T. Frederick to complete the history of the *Little Review* which Dr. Mott was in process of writing in the late summer of 1964, and to supply a section for the *Poetry* sketch which my father had indicated he intended to insert. The *Poetry* insertion is enclosed in brackets and indicated by an asterisk footnote; the other and longer section is also plainly footnoted.

The ten magazines for which individual sketches were planned but not written are: *Christian Century, Field and Stream, Liberty, Masses, Physical Culture, Pictorial Review, Reader's Digest, Red Book, Saturday Review,* and *True Story.*

Harvard University Press and I also agreed that changes were not warranted in the manuscript except where accuracy or clarity was concerned. Relatively few changes have been made, probably fewer than the author himself would have felt desirable in certain of the early-draft sketches. Although some of the current magazines which are treated in the volume are still pursuing the even tenor of their course as set down at the time the sketch was written, others have experienced notable expansion or change in editorial outlook. Such developments have been noted and other information presented in asterisk footnotes, for all of which I am responsible. Material in brackets in numbered footnotes was inserted by me, and I have updated the first footnote for each sketch. I also selected the illustrations and wrote the captions for them.

It is hoped that the inclusion (page 341) of a bit of personal history from Dr. Mott's book of autobiographical essays will not seem merely a sentimental gesture but will be of genuine interest to those who have used and enjoyed the volumes composing *A History of American Magazines.* The cumulative index, made by Robert J. Palmer, includes many more subject headings than appear in the earlier volume indexes. The bibliography is, of course, only one part of Dr. Mott's entire publication record which would include writings in the wider field of journalism and in American literature, as well as his short stories.

Theodore Peterson, Dean of the College of Journalism and Communications at the University of Illinois and author of *Magazines in the Twentieth Century,* kindly consented to read the entire manuscript when plans were first set up for its publication. His suggestions touching on various aspects of the book have been valued and often followed. For updating information I am particularly grateful to Robert S. Clark, public relations department, *Better Homes and Gardens;* to Guy Henle, executive editor, *House Beautiful;* to Henry Rago, editor, *Poetry* magazine; and to Frank R. Shea, assistant to the managing editor, *Time* magazine. I appreciate also the generous help of Lawrence Spivak on certain matters relating to the sketch of the *American Mercury*.

In the preface to Volume II, my father composed a historians' addition to the Litany, which went as follows: "From mistakes of omission and commission, from slips in dates, from transposition of citations, from blunders obvious and recondite, Good Lord, deliver us!" To this I emphatically add, "Amen!"

Washington, D.C.
February 1968

SKETCHES OF MAGAZINES

MENCKEN'S *MERCURY* IN 1927

This same handsome cover, in dark green ink on light green paper, was used, little changed, from the magazine's beginning in 1924 until 1930, that is, during most of H. L. Mencken's editorship. For picture of Mencken see sketch of the *Smart Set*.

1

THE AMERICAN MERCURY[1]

BY 1923 H. L. Mencken and George Jean Nathan were tired of their connection with the *Smart Set* and hopeful of something better. For some fifteen years they had written critical articles for that magazine, and during the last half of that term they had been in editorial charge. They had won a wide reputation and an enthusiastic following, especially among the young and skeptical; and Mencken, through his forthright and biting essays collected in a series entitled

[1] TITLES: *The American Mercury.* (*The New American Mercury,* Dec. 1950–Feb. 1951 only.)

FIRST ISSUE: Jan. 1924. Current.

PERIODICITY: Monthly, 1924–62. 3 vols. yearly, 1924–40 (1–51); 2 vols. yearly, 1941–61 (52–93); 1 vol. yearly, 1962–current. Monthly, 1962 except for Summer (May, June, July) and Sept.–Oct.; quarterly, 1963–current (Fall, 1965, omitted).

PUBLISHERS: Alfred A. Knopf, Inc., 1924–35 (Samuel Knopf, business manager, 1924–32, Lawrence Edmund Spivak, 1933–35); L. E. Spivak, 1935–36; Paul Palmer, 1936–39; L. E. Spivak, 1939–50 (Joseph W. Ferman, bus. man., 1940–50); Clendenin J. Ryan, 1950–51; J. Russell Maguire, 1952–60 (Robert C. Hodgson, bus. man., 1953–56; Leslie J. Yarbrough, 1956–60); all New York. Defenders of the Christian Faith, Inc. (Gwynne W. Davidson, chairman; M. L. Flowers, bus. man.), 1960–62; Oklahoma City. The Legion for the Survival of Freedom, Inc. (E. Wiltsie Platzer, chairman, 1963–66; Bruce Holman, chairman, 1966–current), 1963–66. The Legion name is missing from Fall and Winter, 1966, but Holman is still listed as "Chairman of the Board." (Edwin A. Walker states in the Sept. 1965 issue that he was publisher Dec. 1964—Sept. 1965.) McAllen, Texas, 1963–65; Houston, Texas, 1966; Torrance, Calif., 1966–current.

EDITORS: Henry Louis Mencken and George Jean Nathan, 1924–25; H. L. Mencken, 1925–33; Henry Hazlitt, 1934; Charles Angoff, 1934–35; Paul Palmer, 1935–39; Eugene Lyons, 1939–44; L. E. Spivak, 1944–50; William Bradford Huie, 1950–53; John A. Clements, 1953–55; J. R. Maguire, 1955–57; William La Varre, 1957–58; Maurine Halliburton, 1958–60; Gerald S. Pope, 1960–62; Marcia C. J. Matthews, 1963; Jason Matthews, 1963–64; Edwin A. Walker (man. ed.), Dec. 1964–65; La Vonne Doden Furr, 1966–current.

INDEX: *Readers' Guide* to 1961.

REFERENCES: Anon., "The Importance of Charles Angoff," *Little Review,* v. 4, August 1917, pp. 37–48; M. K. Singleton, *H. L. Mencken and the American Mercury Adventure* (Durham, N.C., 1962); Johnny L. Kloefkorn, "A Critical Study of the Work of H. L. Mencken As Literary Editor and Critic of *The American Mercury,*" Emporia State Research Studies, v. 7, no. 4 (Kansas State Teachers College, 1959); Stephen E. Fitzgerald, "The Mencken Myth," *Saturday Review,* Dec. 17, 1960, pp. 13–15, 71; Lawrence E. Spivak and Charles Angoff, eds., *The American Mercury Reader* (Philadelphia, 1944).

Prejudices, had become a prophet of modern apostasy. They were ready for a more impressive and dignified forum than that afforded by a magazine with the cheap name and rather sleazy tradition of the *Smart Set.*

Thus, when Alfred A. Knopf offered to set up a monthly review, giving them a one-third working interest in it as editors, they were quick to accept. Such titles as "The Blue Review," "The Twentieth Century," and "The Portfolio" were suggested; that of *The American Mercury* was adopted when Knopf and Nathan outvoted Mencken.[2]

The first number was dated January 1924 and came out early in the preceding month. It made an impressive appearance as a whacking big octavo with 128 double-column Garamond-set pages bound in green covers. Elmer Adler was the designer. It was clearly planned for the more thoughtful reader of a free-thinking sort who had fifty cents to spend on a magazine in these inflationary years. For such a reader the contents of the new review were both intellectually exciting and to the last page entertaining.

And so it caught on. The original print order was for ten thousand copies; and two reprints were called for, bringing the total to 15,500. By the time the second number was in press, Vol. I, No. 1 was selling to collectors for ten dollars.[3] By the end of its first year, the *Mercury* was printing 55,000 copies, which was pretty good for a magazine whose projectors had counted on a circulation of 20,000.[4] Of this total, more than two-thirds were newsstand sales. Average net paid circulation went on climbing until it reached, in the magazine's second year, about 75,000.[5]

That first ten-dollar number is worth examining, since it set the pace that the magazine followed rather consistently for

[2] William Manchester, *Disturber of the Peace: The Life of H. L. Mencken* (New York, 1951), pp. 148–49. The author is indebted to this work for many facts pertaining to the Mencken editorship of the *Mercury,* which Mr. Manchester derived from personal communication with his subject.

[3] *New Republic,* v. 37, Feb. 6, 1924, p. 274.

[4] Mencken, in *American Mercury,* v. 30, Dec. 1933, p. 387.

[5] See circulation figures month by month, *Mercury,* v. 6, Dec. 1925, pp. xlii–xliv; also *N. W. Ayer & Son's Directory of Newspapers and Periodicals* (Philadelphia, 1925–current). Circulation figures given later in this chapter are based chiefly on *Ayer.*

more than five years. It opens with a "debunking" article by Isaac R. Pennypacker on "The Lincoln Legend," which emphasizes the prominence of the family from which he sprang on the one hand, and his shortcomings as a military leader on the other. A later article in the number, by Harry Elmer Barnes, "The Drool Method in History," attacks the historians for their capitulation to school boards and legislatures that forbid any disrespect to established idols and mores. A good little chapter on Stephen Crane by Carl Van Doren, a collection of personal letters to various friends from the late James Huneker, and a literary colloquium between George Moore and Samuel C. Chew (more notable for its novel form and its badinage than for any new ideas) constitute the literary criticism of this initial number. "Santayana at Cambridge," by the daughter of Hugo Münsterberg, is more a character sketch than a philosophical dissertation; and Woodbridge Riley's "The New Thought" is a rather muddled, satirical account of that school and its connection with Christian Science, which is called "Eddyism." "Aesthete: Model 1924," by Ernest Boyd, is a satire on editors of the "little magazines." The two political articles are a satirical sketch of Hiram Johnson by John W. Owens and a factual analysis of "The Communist Hoax" in the United States by James Oneal. Two pieces dealing with military matters are anonymous—one a sober and statistical review of actual disarmament since the adoption of the Anglo-Japanese-American Treaty of 1922; and the other a short essay, "On a Second-Rate War," in which "the struggle of 1914–1918" is discussed in a summary studded with words like "jumble," "childish," "unpreparedness," and "strategic error."

The only poems in the number are an undistinguished group by Theodore Dreiser. There are three short stories—Ruth Suckow's fine genre piece from Iowa entitled "Four Generations," Leonard Cline's funny and fanciful satire on "cops" called "Sweeny's Grail," and John McClure's sketch of Cairo street-life, "The Weaver's Tale."

Of departments there are six scattered through the book. The first is a four-page "Editorial." "The Editors," writes Mencken, "are committed to nothing save this: to keep to common sense as fast as they can, to belabor sham as agreeably as possible, to give a civilized entertainment." He provides a little advance list of his bêtes noires in this passage:

The ideal realm imagined by an A. Mitchell Palmer, a King Kleagle of the Ku Klux Klan or a Grand Inquisitor of the Anti-Saloon League, with all human curiosity and enterprise brought down to a simple passion for the goose-step, is as idiotically utopian as the ideal of an Alcott, a Marx, or a Bryan. . . . It will be an agreeable duty to track down some of the worst nonsense prevailing and to do execution upon it—not indignantly, of course, but nevertheless with a sufficient play of malice to give the business a Christian and philanthropic air.[6]

Ah, that is the authentic Mencken! Turn on twenty pages and you come to the second department—one which became, as the months passed, perhaps the most popular feature of the magazine—"Americana." Herein are gathered bits of this "worst nonsense," geographically classified. This first batch begins as so many later ones did, with Alabama, wherein it is noted that Birmingham's Commissioner of Safety W. C. Bloe had ordered the city's "exclusive clubs" to cease and desist allowing the playing of Sunday golf, billiards, and dominoes; and it ends with the state of Washington, in which Bellingham's Garden Street Methodist Church had come up with a report, printed in a national publishers' journal, that "$100 worth of advertising had brought in more than $1,700 in silver plate collections."

The department called "Clinical Notes" is edited in this number by Mencken and Nathan jointly; later Nathan carried it on alone. Here are short expressions of "prejudices," opinions, comment on social and artistic matters, mostly heterodox, sometimes calculated to shock, occasionally sophomoric, often commonsense without conventional camouflage. "The more the theologian seeks to prove the acumen and omnipotence of God by His works, the more he is dashed by evidences of divine incompetence and irresolution." Mencken is displeased by "such dreadful botches as the tonsils, the gall-bladder, the uterus, and the prostate gland." [7]

"The Arts and Sciences" is one of the best of the magazine's

[6] *American Mercury,* v. 1, Jan. 1924, pp. 27–28.

[7] *Ibid.,* v. 1, Jan. 1924, pp. 75–76.

departments. In this first number, it dips into "Architecture" with a short piece by C. Grant La Farge about the new city skylines, into "Medicine" with a sensible little article about glands and rejuvenation by L. M. Hussey, and into "Philology" with an admirable essay by George Philip Krapp about acceptability of language usages. Later nearly all categories of human knowledge were tapped in the short pieces in this department—the various sciences, law, theology, economics, pedagogy, the fine arts, poetry, radio, and so on. The other two departments are Nathan's "The Theater," with his always incisive and informed commentary on current plays and the affairs and personalities of the playhouse; and "The Library," with reviews of new books by Mencken and others. In this initial issue, the "others" were James Branch Cabell, Ernest Boyd, and Isaac Goldberg; later Mencken did them all himself, and there was also a "Check List of New Books" including brief notices. Most of these departments were carried over from the old *Smart Set,* where they had made much of the success of that magazine—"Americana," Mencken's reviews and Nathan's theatrical criticism, and the "Clinical Notes." These last fortunately lost, in the transition, their former heading "Répétition Générale."

Readers of this first number of the *American Mercury* found that all of its articles were short, most of them running from four to seven pages. They also noted that the review was preoccupied with American topics; if they did not, they were reminded in the "Editorial": "In general *The American Mercury* will live up to the adjective in its name. It will lay chief stress at all times upon American ideas, American problems, and American personalities because it assumes that nine-tenths of its readers will be Americans and that they will be more interested in their own country than in any other." [8]

Further, readers must have been impressed with the prominence of satire in the magazine—a satire that often ran into iconoclasm and "debunking," as the term went in those days. Said the *New Republic,* a severe critic from the first: " 'Iconoclastic' is a word which one fears will be frequently applied to our *Mercury.* A better word will have to be invented to describe

[8] *Ibid.,* v. 1, Jan. 1924, p. 30.

someone who loves to hear the crash of empty bottles quite as much as that of ikons, who often can't tell the difference between them, and who always uses the same crowbar on both. The resulting noise is so loud as almost to sound like a philosophical system, and many people have been fooled accordingly." [9]

This leaves unanswered the question as to whether the *New Republic* considered Hiram Johnson, for example, an ikon or an empty bottle; but indisputable ikons in the *Mercury's* range were Lincoln and Whitman. The Lincoln article, noted above, presented views which have since had wide acceptance; the one on Whitman, by Ernest Boyd, expressed opinions even then out of date and destined with passing years to seem more and more unperceptive. Boyd saw Whitman as "the first of the literary exhibitionists whose cacophonous incongruities and general echolalia are the distinguishing marks of what is regarded as poetry in aesthetic circles today. . . . With the lapse of time, his false position has reached the last degree of unreality." [10] According to Assistant Editor Angoff, this article was "the subject of heated controversy in the office," and "Mencken himself eventually admitted that the author was overstating his case." [11] A number of other pieces in early numbers of the *Mercury,* it must be added, treated Whitman and his work more tenderly.

But, ikons or empty bottles, there is no doubt that Mencken had great fun smashing what he considered to be "frauds," and most of his readers enjoyed the game no less. In the magazine's fifth anniversary number, he wrote a paragraph that is worth quoting for its catalogue of the objects of Mercurial attack:

> In this benign work [of exposing frauds] it has covered a considerable range, and tried to proceed with a reasonable impartiality. The chiropractors and the Socialists, the Holy Rollers and the homeopaths, the pacifists and the spiritualists have all taken their turns upon its operating table. It has exhibited, mainly in their own words, the dreams and imbecilities of the prophets of high-powered salesmanship, vocational guidance, osteopathy, comstockery, and pedagogy. It has brought to notice, in the chaste, dispassionate

[9] *New Republic,* v. 37, Feb. 6, 1924, p. 274.
[10] *American Mercury,* v. 6, Dec. 1925, pp. 451, 458.
[11] *New Republic,* v. 131, Sept. 13, 1954, p. 19.

manner of the clinic, the hallucinations of Rotary, the Gideons, the D. A. R., the American Legion, the League of American Penwomen, the Methodist Board of Temperance, Prohibition, and Public Morals, and a multitude of other such klans and sodalities, many of them highly influential and all of them amusing.[12]

But in the same editorial, Mencken points out that his review has done much more than expose "frauds": "It has given a great deal more space to something quite different, namely, to introducing one kind of American to another." And he mentions such articles as those of the lumberjack James Stevens, later famous for his "Paul Bunyan" stories; the convict Ernest Booth, whose series about bank-robbing and such were cut short by prison authorities; and the musician Daniel Gregory Mason, who, in his stories of the Chautauqua, poked fun at the yokels whose favor he had once courted on the platform. There were also Jim Tully, who wrote of "hobo" life; George Milburn, with his Oklahoma sketches; Mary Austin, who told Indian tales, and so on.

Other favorite topics in Mencken's *Mercury* were the American newspaper, often treated with understanding, sometimes with severity; advertising and press-agentry, usually assailed; folk literature, superstitions, and anthropology; the American Negro, his progress and his problems; philology, with emphasis on American usages; American history, particularly unswept corners and picturesque personalities and events; and literary figures such as Poe, Whitman, and Melville.

George S. Schuyler was a leading writer on the racial problem, and his article "A Negro Looks Ahead" created a sensation not only in the South but throughout the country. It concluded: "The Aframerican, shrewd, calculating, diplomatic, patient and a master of Nordic psychology, steadily saps the foundation of white supremacy. Time, he knows, is with him. . . . By 2000 A.D. a full-blooded American Negro may be rare enough to get a job in a museum, and a century from now our American social leaders may be as tanned naturally as they are now striving to become artificially."[13]

All regions came in for occasional lashings in the pages of the *Mercury*—the Midwest's "Bible Belt," puritanical New Eng-

[12] *American Mercury,* v. 15, Dec. 1928, pp. 407–8.

[13] *Ibid.,* v. 19, Feb. 1930, p. 220.

land, the culturally arid West—but the South perhaps caught it hardest. Wrote W. J. Cash in "The Mind of the South": "There *is* a new South, to be sure. It is a chicken-pox of factories on the Watch-Us-Grow maps; it is a kaleidoscopic chromo of stacks and chimneys on the club-car window as the train rolls southward from Washington to New Orleans. But I question that it is much more. For the mind of that heroic region, I opine, is still basically and essentially the mind of the Old South."[14]

Political articles of a serious nature were rare in the *Mercury*. Most of those about contemporary political figures and most of Mencken's editorials in this field were designed to puncture the balloons of popular reputations. The most famous of such pieces was the mercilessly contumelious editorial about Bryan, published in the October 1925 number, shortly after that statesman's death. It is still amusing reading, the real, distilled Mencken. There was really not much politics in it; it was a postscript to what Mencken had written (chiefly for the Baltimore *Sun*) about the Scopes trial. One astute critic of Mencken's total work has written: ". . . It was significant that one of the cruelest things he ever wrote, his essay on Bryan, was probably the most brilliant."[15]

Though contemporary literature was often treated in the *Mercury's* articles, it was in Mencken's own book reviews that the heart of the magazine's comment on the writing of the day appeared. These reviews were, indeed, one of the most interesting features of the *Mercury*. In them Mencken expressed, in striking and exuberant style, his devotion to basic actualities and his contempt of gentility and sentimentality, his stout support of writers who defied conventionality and popular inhibitions, and his scorn for the idols of mass culture. Carefully discriminated and qualified book reviews are often dull; Mencken's never were, partly at least because he usually condemned or praised, and no nonsense about it. Let us take two examples more or less at random. In the second number of the *Mercury*, a review of *The Great Game of Politics*, by Frank R. Kent, a colleague of the reviewer on the Baltimore *Sun*, began:

[14] *Ibid.*, v. 18, Oct. 1929, p. 185.
[15] Alfred Kazin, *On Native Grounds* (New York, 1942), pp. 203–4

Astonishingly enough, this is the first book ever written in America which describes realistically and in detail the way in which the mountebanks and scoundrels who govern 110,000,000 free and brave people obtain and hold their power.[16]

And a year or more later appeared the following succinct review of Ernest Hemingway's second book, *In Our Time:*

The sort of brave, bold stuff that all atheistic young newspaper reporters write. Jesus Christ in lower case. A hanging, a carnal love, and disembowellings. Here it is, set forth solemnly on Rives handmade paper, in an edition limited to 170 copies, and with the imprimatur of Ezra Pound.[17]

Like a good journalist, Mencken did give his readers much information about the new books; but many read his reviews more for the Mencken in them than for anything else. They were always readable, sometimes amusing. Mencken was "at least half Puck," observed a later critic, and added, "He loved to hear the rumble of his own hyperboles." [18]

"Menckenism" became a common word to describe a compound of prejudices, hyberbole, and a kind of free-wheeling diction just this side of rant. Certain words were overused: imbecile, mountebank, oaf, nincompoop, rascal, wowser, swine, pusillanimous, perfidious, fraudulent. To this "Menckenese" must be added two invented terms which have gained a considerable acceptance in the language: *booboisie* and *Homo Boobus,* the latter corrected by the more learned Boyd, we are told, to *Homo Boobiens.*[19] Contributors had to submit their copy to editing which, if it did not include "a proper salting of Menckenese," at least brought it into harmony with the tone of the magazine.[20]

"Mencken was always eager to print authors for the first time," according to his assistant editor, "and to that end he

[16] *American Mercury,* v. 1, Feb. 1924, p. 248.

[17] *Ibid.,* v. 5, Aug. 1925, p. xxxviii. This appeared in the "Check List," a department of brief notices, but I have the word of Mr. Angoff, then assistant editor, that Mencken wrote it (Angoff to Mott, June 13, 1959).

[18] Eric F. Goldman, *Rendezvous With Destiny* (New York, 1952), p. 316.

[19] H. L. Mencken, *The American Language,* 4th ed. (New York, 1936), p. 560, n. 1.

[20] Manchester, *Disturber of the Peace,* pp. 153–54. For comment on this assimilative process in contributions to the *Mercury,* see Oscar Cargill, *Intellectual America* (New York, 1941), p. 494.

carried on a huge correspondence with young men and women in all parts of the country." [21] This was a practice he had brought from the *Smart Set;* in the two magazines, he introduced to a larger public many writers virtually unknown before. Such a list would include Ruth Suckow, James Stevens, Jim Tully, and many others.

But the *Mercury's* table of contents was loaded with plenty of names well known to the reading public. In addition to those mentioned in other places in this chapter, we may list here a few representative frequent contributors: Gerald W. Johnson, Chester T. Crowell, Robert L. Duffus, Fred Lewis Pattee, Henry F. Pringle, C. Hartley Grattan, Louis Adamic, Duncan Aikman, Marquis W. Childs, Margaret Mead, Nelson Antrim Crawford ("A Man of Learning," August 1925), Benjamin deCasseres, Lewis Mumford, Louis Untermeyer, and William E. Dodd.

The *Mercury* printed many short stories of considerable distinction. Some of them had regional settings, like those of Ruth Suckow, Winifred Sanford, James Stevens, George Sterling, Idwal Jones, and William Faulkner. It is said that Mencken did not like Faulkner, and accepted "That Evening Sun Go Down" (March 1931) under protest.[22] Sinclair Lewis provided both non-fiction and fiction ("The Man Who Knew Coolidge," January 1928) from his busy typewriter.

Mencken looked upon his own early book of verse as a youthful indiscretion, and had little respect for contemporary poetry.[23] In his *Mercury* salutatory, he promised "some verse (but not much)." [24] This meant, apparently, a poem or two in each number. Some of them were very good, indeed. Favorites were the Midwesterners Vachel Lindsay, Edgar Lee Masters, and Carl Sandburg; the Negroes Countee Cullen and James Weldon Johnson ("Go Down, Death!" April 1927); and the

21 Charles Angoff in the *New Republic,* v. 131, Sept. 13, 1954, p. 21.

22 Charles Angoff, *H. L. Mencken: A Portrait From Memory* (New York, 1956), pp. 107–8.

23 Angoff, *Mencken,* p. 83 and chap. vii. Angoff says Mencken in later life bought up any stray copies of his *Ventures Into Verse* when he found them, and destroyed them. No wonder: see quotations from the volume in Cargill, *Intellectual America,* p. 484.

24 *American Mercury,* v. 1, Jan. 1924, p. 30.

Westerner George Sterling; as well as Joseph Auslander, Grace Stone Coates, and Gwendolen Haste.

The *Mercury* also published some works in dramatic form, notably Eugene O'Neill's "All God's Chillun Got Wings" (February 1924), and several short pieces in dialogue by James M. Cain. Incidentally, Mencken was "violently" opposed to publishing the O'Neill play, but Nathan is said to have "threatened to resign" if it was rejected.[25]

The most dramatic episode of the magazine's early history was the result of the publication in the issue for April 1926 of a sketch by Herbert Asbury entitled "Hatrack." This was one of a series presenting the author's recollections of the religious life of a small town, later published as *Up From Methodism;* and since evangelists sometimes preached realistically against sexual misdemeanors, Asbury found an opportunity here to bring in a little character sketch of a village prostitute. It was all in the best tone of stag-party hilarity. That it exaggerated and gibed a phase of the religious and social life of the small town, and that it offended tastes more refined than those of Asbury and Mencken there can be no doubt; but surely there were few readers of the *Mercury* who considered it obscene or corrupting to morals. Harlotry doubtless has its humorous phases, and "Hatrack" followed a not unfamiliar literary tradition.

That was not the attitude of Boston's Watch and Ward Society. It seems clear that Mencken courted some overt action by this unofficial organization; his biographer says that he had anticipated it.[26] He had baited the society in September of the preceding year by publishing an article entitled "Keeping the Puritans Pure," by A. L. S. Wood of the *Springfield Union,* in which Jason Frank Chase, then secretary of the society, was ridiculed. So when the "Hatrack" number appeared, Chase notified the dealers' trade agency in Boston that it was "objectionable"; and the dealers, accustomed to unquestioned yielding to the threat of prosecution implied in a Chase edict, stopped the sale of the April *Mercury*. Thereupon Mencken and Knopf

[25] Statement made to Lawrence E. Spivak by Angoff, and reported in a letter (Feb 10, 1959) to Mott.

[26] Manchester, *Disturber of the Peace,* p. 187. The fullest accounts of the "Hatrack" episode are in chap vii of this book and in Arthur Garfield Hays, *Let Freedom Ring,* revised ed. (New York, 1937), pp. 157–85.

enlisted Arthur Garfield Hays, famous attorney of the American Civil Liberties Union, in behalf of the *Mercury;* and Hays suggested that Mencken make a clean-cut case of it by himself selling a copy of the banned periodical to Chief Watcher and Warder Chase within the pure precincts of Boston. Mencken agreed, Chase agreed. Wrote Hays in his recollections: "On April 5, 1926, a milling, enthusiastic, and hilarious mob of thousands gathered at the corner of Park and Tremont streets in Boston, the crowd running over onto the Boston Common. Word had leaked out that at two o'clock in the afternoon the April number of *The American Mercury* was to be sold. There was a huge demand for the magazine at almost any price. People were wildly waving one, five, and ten dollar bills." [27]

But only one copy was sold, and that to Chase by Mencken at fifty cents. The clowning Mencken tested the coin with his teeth. Immediately after the transaction Mencken was arrested and taken to the police station, where he furnished bail. The next morning there was a judicial hearing on the charge of selling "obscene, indecent, and impure literature . . . manifestly tending to corrupt the morals of youth." Somewhat to the surprise of the defendant,[28] the charge was dismissed. "I cannot imagine," said the judge, "anyone reading the article and finding himself or herself attracted toward vice." [29]

There were sequels to this hearing. The April *Mercury* was suppressed in many cities and towns throughout the country. A Cambridge dealer who had sold it to Harvard "youths" was actually fined a hundred dollars, which the *Mercury* paid. A week later an injunction was obtained to prevent further interference with the sale of the moot number of the magazine. But most embarrassing was the action of the United States Post Office Department in refusing to accept the April *Mercury* for mailing. Eventually Hays had to get a federal injunction to force acceptance; and then the case was carried to the Circuit Court of Appeals, which decided that the question was "academic," the April number being by that time far out of date.[30]

27 Hays, *Let Freedom Ring,* p. 160.

28 Manchester, *Disturber of the Peace,* p. 196.

29 Hays, *Let Freedom Ring,* p. 169.

30 *The American Mercury* v. *Kiely, Postmaster, et al.,* 19 Fed. (2d) 295 (1927).

The case cost the *Mercury* some ten thousand dollars, which nearly exhausted its reserve.[31] Newspapers generally disapproved the ribaldry of "Hatrack" and were inclined to sympathize with the censors. A leading editorial in the *New York Herald Tribune* began: "The incurable vulgarity of Mr. H. L. Mencken is mixed with a considerable amount of business acumen. In his latest escapade he has been alert to capitalize to the utmost the egregious bad taste of an article to which the Boston authorities took exception. The case is flagrant enough to urge a stocktaking of current standards of decency in print." The writer goes on to admit that "Hatrack" was "neither obscene nor suggestive," though vulgar and indecent; and after this exercise in semantics, he adds that Mencken "is scarcely worth his space in a good jail." [32]

According to Angoff, Mencken later regretted having printed "Hatrack." [33] Commercially, as the *Herald Tribune* suggested, it was probably good business. The *Mercury's* average net circulation for 1926 rose to about seventy thousand, and the next year it added some five thousand more. The years 1926–1928 brought the magazine's greatest prosperity.[34] Issues occasionally ran to 140 pages, of which 11 might be advertising. Book "ads" led; but clothing, foods, cosmetics, cigarettes, travel aids, and investment opportunities took much space. An amusing feature of the advertising section in these years was the series of full pages taken by manufacturers (such as the Lambert Pharmacal Company, distributors of Listerine) to criticize the *Mercury* itself and satirize its famous editor.

In July 1925, Nathan retired from his co-editorship to the position of contributing editor in charge of the departments "Clinical Notes" and "The Theater." He felt that the magazine

[31] Manchester, *Disturber of the Peace,* p. 207.

[32] *New York Herald Tribune,* April 7, 1926, p. 22, col. 1.

[33] Angoff, *Mencken,* p. 52.

[34] Lawrence E. Spivak, later business manager of the magazine, writes (Jan. 30, 1959): "According to my figures, the *Mercury* reached its highest volume of business—close to $415,000—in 1927, but it reached its highest profit of $16,000 on a volume of $373,000 in 1926. The profit in 1927 was only $6,000; in 1928 it was $8,500; and in 1929 the magazine lost about $15,000. It continued to lose money through 1939, with the exception of 1933, when it made $900 largely because of vigorous cuts in expenditures." Letter quoted with permission of the author.

BLESSED BE THE BOOBS!

It has always seemed to us that the boobery is divided into two classes:

1. The grade B boobs, (of which we are one,) whom Mencken attacks, and who do not read him.

2. The grade A boobs, whom he praises and who believe everything he says.

Of the two, the grade B boobs are, of course, the lesser evil. Great is their patience. And when they suffer, they suffer in silence.

We actually look upon them with considerable respect. Granted they have a certain type of stupidity, it is the type that is largely and unconsciously responsible for these United States being the pleasant and profitable place they are.

So long as the grade B boobs remain as they are, so long will our country remain a merry spot where one may live, labor, sin and pass out 'mid pleasant surroundings.

On the other hand, if Old Doctor Mencken could wave his wand (which falls some several thousand miles short of being magic) and commit us to the dominion of the boobs of the second class, how much worse off we would be!

For, given a little power and turned loose, the intellectual boob can raise hell in a grand manner; our little world, now somewhat astigmatic, would be downright cock-eyed—and that, too, quickly. Let this never come to pass, Jehovah!

And in the meantime, to the boobs of today—prosit! They all use Listerine. And a special prosit to the grade A boobs, because they use more of it.

LAMBERT PHARMACAL COMPANY
St. Louis, Mo., U.S.A.

LISTERINE ADVERTISEMENT SATIRIZING MENCKEN

Appearing in the *American Mercury* for September 1927, this was one of an amusing series of Listerine advertisements that criticized the *Mercury* and Mencken.

was losing the esthetic and cultural tone that he valued most, and in 1930 he severed his connection with it entirely and sold his stock to Knopf.[35] Charles Angoff, a young Harvard graduate with a brief experience on Boston newspapers, joined the *Mercury* in 1925 as assistant editor, and eventually outstayed his chief on the staff.

The early thirties marked the end of an era of American life, and they also marked the end of the Mencken *Mercury*. The magazine's circulation dropped from 62,000 in 1930 to a little more than half of that in 1933. Relations between editor and assistant editor were often strained.[36] Samuel Knopf, the publisher's father and a heavy stockholder, died in 1932. In the probation of his will, the value of the magazine was placed at zero; [37] and this was supported by a comptroller's affidavit which declared that the *Mercury* was "a one-man magazine catering to a very selective class of readers who are followers of its editor," and that it must be reorganized to survive.[38]

The fact was that the beginning of the depression had coincided with a marked recession in the popularity of H. L. Mencken. In 1926 Walter Lippmann had called Mencken "the most powerful personal influence on this whole generation of educated people," though he had added the observation that "the man is bigger than his ideas," which are "sub-rational" —that is, he appeals to "those vital preferences which lie deeper than coherent thinking." [39] But the "vital preferences" of the twenties were not those of the thirties. Wrote Angoff many years later: "The world was leaving him behind. Even the college boys had begun to sneer at him. . . . The clippings from the [college] newspapers were becoming more and more unfavorable, and one literary editor on the West Coast referred to him as 'The Late Mr. Mencken.' " [40]

The sober counsel of the more "coherent" thinkers was be-

[35] Manchester, *Disturber of the Peace,* pp. 219–20.

[36] Angoff, *Mencken,* pp. 217–18.

[37] *Newsweek,* v. 8, Sept. 26, 1936, p. 48.

[38] Manchester, *Disturber of the Peace,* p. 266.

[39] *Saturday Review of Literature,* v. 3, Dec. 11, 1926, p. 413. This article was reprinted in pamphlet form by Knopf.

[40] Angoff, *Mencken,* p. 225. Manchester, a much more sympathetic biographer, agrees about the decay of Mencken's popularity; *Disturber of the Peace,* pp 266–67.

ginning to prevail under the stresses of the thirties. The *Mercury* formula was no longer so acceptable, even to the young intellectuals. Norman Cousins, trying to account for the failure of the review under Mencken, once wrote:

> There was something wrong with its basic diagnosis. America was not the home of the fools and the land of the boobs they [the editors of the *Mercury*] thought it was. There was plenty of surface stuff that made us look silly, but there was also solid stuff far more significant that had to be recognized. The items that appeared in the *Mercury's* Americana were part of the froth and not of the essence. . . . The pulsebeat of historical America failed to come through in the *Mercury*. . . . To be totally without respect for the mechanism of hope in man as were the editors of the *Mercury* was to live in the wrong century.[41]

Doubtless the decline of Mencken's popularity had something to do with his growing wish to retire from the editorship of the *Mercury,* but there were other reasons. Because of the magazine's financial straits, he was drawing no salary.[42] He was tired and unwell. When he visited Upton Sinclair in California in the late twenties, that worthy, always a severe critic of the review "with the arsenical green covers," remarked upon his tiredness. Sinclair argued with Mencken over the *Mercury's* emphasis on "the absurdities of democracy," and later said: "If you ask Mencken what is the remedy for these horrors, he will tell you they are the natural and inevitable manifestations of the boobus Americanus. If you ask him why then labor so monstrously, he will say that it is for his own enjoyment, he is so constituted that he finds his recreation in laughing at his fellow boobs. But watch him a while, and you will see the light of hilarity die out of his eyes, and you will note lines of tiredness in his face, and lines of not quite perfect health, and you will realize that he is lying to himself and to you; he is a new-style crusader, a Christian Anti-Christ, a propagandist of no-propaganda." [43]

41 *Saturday Review of Literature,* v. 37, June 12, 1954, p. 22.

42 Letter from Spivak, Jan. 30, 1959. Spivak adds: "According to my recollection Mencken never drew more than $9,000 a year." Letter quoted with permission of the author.

43 Upton Sinclair, *Money Writes!* (New York, 1927), pp. 131–32. Chaps. viii and xxvi in this volume are devoted to criticisms of Mencken.

Mencken retired as editor of the *American Mercury* at the end of 1933. He was succeeded by Henry Hazlitt, who had been literary editor of the *Nation,* but who had spent most of his professional life as a financial writer for newspapers. The retiring editor wrote of his successor: "He is the only competent critic that I have ever heard of who was at the same time a competent economist . . . one of the few economists in human history who could really write." He would continue the review's established policy, playing "a bright light over the national scene, revealing whatever is amusing and instructive."[44] But Hazlitt's ideas, it soon developed, did not fit with the *Mercury* pattern, and after a few months he resigned the editorship to Angoff.[45]

Changes in editorship, however, did not restore prosperity. The magazine continued to decline both in the zestful and uninhibited spirit that had once been its fundamental elixir and, more alarmingly, in circulation. And so, in 1935, Knopf sold the *Mercury*[46] to Paul Palmer and Lawrence E. Spivak, the former coming from the newspaper field, and the latter from magazine work. Palmer took over the editorship and Spivak the publisher's chair. A new policy was proclaimed: the review would renounce its left-wing tendencies and become a kind of combination *Forum-New Yorker-Collier's*. Lombard C. Jones was managing editor briefly; he was succeeded by Gordon Carroll. Angoff, offered an associate editorship, declared that he "would rather go out and shovel manure . . . than associate myself with the publication they have in mind."[47]

Whatever Angoff preferred to shovel, the *Mercury* handled

[44] *American Mercury,* v. 30, Dec. 1933, pp. 385, 386.

[45] Hazlitt joined the editorial staff in the fall of 1933, and announcement of the change was made in the papers on October 5; but his name did not appear as editor until January 1934. Angoff took over with the May 1934 issue, though he was not given the title of editor until August.

[46] This statement oversimplifies a complicated deal by which Business Manager Spivak bought the magazine in January 1935 for its debt ($38,000) to be paid out of problematical profits; but, as Spivak remembers it, Palmer a little later advanced some cash and he and Spivak divided the stock equally. In April, under this ownership, Spivak became publisher and Palmer editor. A year later the company needed money and Spivak gave up his half of the stock when Palmer put up more cash. Spivak then resigned as "publisher," but continued as business manager (Spivak letter, Jan. 30, 1959).

[47] *Newsweek,* v. 5, Feb. 2, 1935, p. 26.

much excellent and well-written material under the new management. Laurence Stallings wrote the book reviews in "The Library." "The Clinic" had some resemblance to the old "Arts and Sciences" department; it contained short articles on social, scientific, and economic matters. Among contributors were Katharine Fullerton Gerould, William Henry Chamberlin (on Russia), Ralph Adams Cram, Ford Madox Ford, and Anthony M. Turano. Mencken contributed two articles attacking Roosevelt in 1936.

But circulation continued on the downward curve. A strike of the office staff called by the Office Workers' Union in June 1935, which triggered picketing for fourteen weeks, did not help matters.[48] Advertising had fallen off dangerously and circulation had dropped below thirty thousand when, in the fall of 1936, radical changes in format, price, and editorial policy saved the magazine. The pocket, or "digest," size was adopted, with 128 double-column pages. The old fifty-cent price was cut in half. The magazine took a strong conservative stand—anti-New Deal, pro-capitalism. "President Roosevelt," declared an editorial in 1938, "no longer desires recovery under the present Capitalist system." [49] A strong drive against Stalinism and against Soviet infiltration in America was initiated; Eugene

[48] Much attention was given to the issues of this labor contest by the *New Republic,* v. 83, July 10, 1935, p. 254, and the *Nation,* v. 140, June 26, 1935, p. 741, and v. 141, July 31, 1935, pp. 128–29. [The strike was called by the Office Workers' Union after the dismissal of two employees from the *Mercury* staff, which had joined the union only a few days before. The union chose to interpret the dismissal as reprisal for union affiliation, which would have been against the law according to NRA regulations; Spivak and Palmer disavowed previous knowledge that the staff had been unionized, and insisted the cause of firing was "inefficiency." The dispute was taken to the Regional Labor Board which, in May, handed down a decision favorable to the strikers. However, the Supreme Court decision of that same month voided the NRA, resulting in the National Labor Relations Board dropping the *Mercury* case. Palmer had ignored the decision anyway, and tried to ignore the continued picketing and to carry on as usual. Mass picketing which developed in mid-June continued into July, with rough behavior causing many police problems. After fourteen weeks, the strike was called off in August, although a boycott continued. Spivak in the June 26 *Nation* attributed the trouble to a "radical group" which disapproved of the recent editorial change in the *Mercury* from an extreme left position of the previous editor to that of "liberalism" which was "always its tradition." It is of interest to note that in 1949 the C.I.O. took action to expel the Office Workers' Union from its membership because of Communist domination.]

[49] *American Mercury,* v. 45, Nov. 1938, p. 257.

Lyons was the chief contributor in this field. Topics related to sex were common in the magazine for a few years. Havelock Ellis wrote on "Studies in Sex: A History" (January 1936) and Mencken on "Utopia by Sterilization" (August 1937); but the articles that provoked the most scathing replies in the "Open Forum" were two by anonymous women—"I Believe in the Double Standard," by "A Wife" (April 1937) and "Chastity on the Campus," by "A Co-Ed" (June 1938). A rather plaintive reply to the latter by a Brooklyn girl declares her intention to remain chaste in spite of everything.[50]

Departments were reshuffled. "Americana" was retained, of course, though shrunken to two or three of the smaller pages. John W. Thomason, Jr., reviewed books in "The Library"; and "The Check List," repository of brief reviews, was eventually taken out of the advertising section to appear in the body of the book. "Open Forum," a revival of "The Soap Box," which had appeared toward the end of the Mencken regime, invited short letters from irate or pleased readers; it occasionally ran to nearly twenty pages. "Book Preview," giving extracts from forthcoming books, and "The Other Side," in which prominent liberals were given their say, were short-lived departments. A little nature essay by Alan Devoe appeared each month under the heading "Down to Earth." "Poetry" was a departmental heading for a few years; later the poems were again distributed through the magazine. Perhaps the best of the new departments was one in which Albert J. Nock for a few years discussed public affairs, speaking for the editorial board. And, finally, Nathan came back in 1938 to do a theater department for the ensuing twelve years.

Among leading contributors during the Palmer editorship were Harold Lord Varney, Benjamin Stolberg, and Stewart H. Holbrook. An article by Varney in the number for December 1936 accusing the American Civil Liberties Union of undue sympathies for Russia brought on a libel suit. When Mencken entered the picture by protesting that the suit was a threat to the freedom of the press, for which the A. C. L. U. had always stood, Director Arthur Garfield Hays of the Union suggested that Mencken act as arbitrator. The idea of Mencken the ex-

[50] *Ibid.,* v. 45, Sept. 1938, p. 117.

tremist judicially weighing the matters in dispute was ludicrous, but he did just that. The printing of his report in the *Mercury* was supposed to settle the whole matter; but inasmuch as he found against both contestants, there was an aftermath of replies. "I am substantially right," Mencken concluded, "and decline to change a word." [51]

The new *Mercury,* in the smaller size and at the smaller price, more than doubled its circulation in a short time, but it lost advertising. American Mercury Books—reprints of popular books in soft covers at twenty-five cents—proved to be a money-maker, however. It began in 1937, with James M. Cain's "The Postman Always Rings Twice," advertised as "a classic of the tough school of American fiction"; and the series developed into the extensive business of Mercury Publications, Inc., publishers of mystery and science fiction magazines and books.[52] This was the first successful modern paperbound series in America. It was a Spivak idea, and it furnished the profits to keep the *Mercury* going during the Spivak administration.

Lawrence E. Spivak, son of a New York dress manufacturer, was a Harvard graduate and had been assistant publisher of *Hunting and Fishing* before he came to the *Mercury* as business manager in 1933. When he purchased complete control of the magazine in 1939, he installed Eugene Lyons as editor. Russian-born Lyons had been brought to New York as a child and there, after some work at City College, he had become very interested in Communism. He edited *Soviet Russia Pictorial 1922–1923,* and became an assistant director of Tass, the Russian news and propaganda agency; but he never joined the Communist Party. A term of six years as United Press correspondent in Russia brought him into close touch with events and situations and broke the spell that the Soviet ideology had held over him; and after his recall in 1934 at the demand of the U.S.S.R. authorities, he became one of the most prominent anti-Soviet writers in America. Under Lyons' editorship and Spivak's management, the *Mercury* became a leader in the attack on Stalin and in exposing Communist "penetration" in the

51 *Ibid.,* v. 45, Oct. 1938, p. 240.

52 See Frank L. Schick, *The Paperbound Book in America* (New York, 1958), pp. 62–65.

United States. In this crusade he was assisted by John Roy Carlson, whose *Under Cover* was a sensational and controversial best-seller in 1943; Jan Valtin, whose *Out of the Night* scored a similar success in 1941; and others.

Another cause strongly and repeatedly presented in the *Mercury* in these years was that of the importance of the air force in our military system. Major Alexander P. de Seversky wrote many articles about the superiority of air attack and defense in the early forties. These were supported by several contributions of Colonel Hugh J. Knerr in 1942.

Articles were usually short, as they had been since the change to the smaller size, and content was varied. An outstanding article of Lyons' editorship was Thomas Wolfe's "The Anatomy of Loneliness" (October 1941). Mary M. Colum had charge of "The Library" for a year or two; thereafter the reviewing was shared by several hands. Associate editors for short terms were Allen Churchill, William Doerflinger and John Tebbel; in 1943 Angoff dropped his shovel and came back to the *Mercury* to serve first as literary editor and then as managing editor as long as Spivak remained as publisher.

With the number for July 1944, Lyons retired from the editorship to take charge of the new magazine *Pageant;* and Spivak became both editor and publisher. He and Angoff filled the *Mercury* with stimulating articles on lively questions. Kingsbury Smith's series about the workings of the State Department was outstanding. The magazine, on the whole, took a more liberal position than it had once occupied. Norman Angell and Russell Davenport were contributors, along with many writers comparatively unknown. Nathan and Devoe continued their departments, and in 1948 Bergen Evans started a new one on popular superstitions headed "Skeptic's Corner." More attractive covers than the magazine had ever known were supplied by Al Hirschfield; they carried colored caricature-portraits of public figures.

In the years 1943–1945, the *Mercury* gradually increased its circulation, reaching an average of eighty thousand per issue, the highest of its history; then it began to slide down again. In a day of mass circulations, the *Mercury* was a midget. Spivak was losing about $100,000 a year on the magazine, making up its deficits out of the profits of Mercury Publications, Inc.[53] In 1949 the price per copy was raised to thirty-five cents, and circulation declined to forty thousand. The absorption of *Common Sense,* an anti-Communist monthly, did not help much. In the fall of 1950 Spivak sold the magazine to Clendenin J. Ryan for about $50,000,[54] and thereafter devoted himself to "Meet the Press," which had started on radio in October 1945 and moved to television in November 1947. Four years later Spivak sold Mercury Publications, Inc., to Joseph W. Ferman, who had been associated with him for several years on the magazine and in the publishing concern.

Ryan, the new owner, was the son of Thomas Fortune Ryan, and a man of wealth who could afford to experiment with a magazine of famous name and lively spirit. He had once been an assistant to Mayor La Guardia of New York City, and was interested in political reform. He now associated himself with William Bradford Huie, lecturer, author, and air-power devotee, who was given "complete autonomy of policy and action" in the conduct of the magazine. Huie at once declared his intention to "re-create the magazine in the Mencken tradition," but with a difference: "The boobs," he said, "have become bureaucrats; the censors have become commissars; the yahoos have been marshaled into pressure groups." But he added, "We are more interested in manners, morals, and the arts than in politics."[55] Angoff was succeeded as managing editor by Susie Berg. The price was again placed at twenty-five cents.

Manners and morals did indeed occupy much space in what was for a short time called *The New American Mercury*. The editor found time, between lecture engagements and television broadcasts, to write much for the magazine himself, including a fiction serial of 1951 entitled "The Revolt of Mamie Stover," which was announced as "a serious book about a whore."[56] Alfred Towne's "Homosexuality in American Culture" ran in the fall of 1951. And so on. Lee Mortimer, author of *Washing-*

53 Correspondence with Spivak, Jan. 30, 1959.

54 About half in cash and half in subscription liabilities (Spivak correspondence).

55 All quotations in this paragraph are from the editor's statement, *American Mercury,* v. 71, Dec. 1950, pp. 665–68.

56 *Ibid.,* v. 72, March 1951, p. 280.

ton Confidential and such classics, was a steady contributor.

But the magazine was not all sex. Huie hated Truman, and in an open letter to General Eisenhower advised him to break with the President and announce himself openly as a candidate for the Republican nomination for the presidency.[57] The magazine was now throughly conservative in politics. Too much of its literary criticism was on the level of one writer's dismissal of Irving Howe's analysis of Sherwood Anderson: "The silliest damn statement I've heard in years."[58] But the *Mercury* retained as contributors such writers from the Spivak regime as Nathan, Holbrook, Devoe, Tebbel, Stolberg, and Evans.

Two years of paying deficits were enough for Ryan, and in 1952 he sold the magazine to J. Russell Maguire, multimillionaire oil man and munitions-maker. The new owner was not as complaisant toward his editor's policy as Ryan had been; and beginning February 1953 Huie was supplanted by John A. Clements, who had been promotion director of the Hearst magazines, with Joseph B. Breed as managing editor. The price went to thirty-five cents.

The emphasis on sex now disappeared, and the anti-Red theme was resumed with vigor. The *Mercury* defended Senator Joseph McCarthy in his drive against Soviet "infiltration"; and, in general, it took a strong right-wing Republican position. J. B. Matthews was chief editorial writer, assisted, especially in the crusade against Communism, by the indefatigable Lyons and Varney, as well as by Ralph de Toledano and Alan Set. George Fielding Eliot, John T. Flynn, and Harry T. Brundidge were frequent contributors. There were many short departments. Variety and brevity were watchwords; forty or more articles might appear in a single number, each from one to four pages in length. There were a few full-page cartoons.

A clean sweep changed the editorial management of the magazine in the fall of 1955. Editor Clements and his chief associates and contributors went out, and owner Maguire carried on until the appointment of William La Varre to the editorship in 1957. La Varre, explorer and feature writer, had the assistance of Natasha Boissevain, who had become managing

[57] *Ibid.,* v. 73, Dec. 1951, pp. 3–8.
[58] *Ibid.,* v. 72, May 1951, p. 616.

editor on Clements' retirement; and Maguire continued to write editorials. Maurine Halliburton succeeded to the editorship in the summer of 1958.

The editorial policy was now very clear: the *Mercury* was an organ of rather extreme right-wing Republicanism. It published short contributions by United States senators, members of Congress, and governors belonging to that faction; and its editorials supported that school of thought. Many of its articles dealt with international affairs, but there was still a wide variety in its offering outside of politics. The "Forum" departments for readers' letters were lively and interesting. Articles on the popular religious movement had some prominence; Billy Graham, J. Howard Pew, and James Hargis wrote in that field. Circulation advanced gradually in the fifties to some seventy thousand.

It is impossible to measure such an intangible as the "influence" of a magazine. One cannot doubt, however, that the *American Mercury* under most of Mencken's editorship had a considerable effect on the thinking of many people—chiefly, perhaps, in the younger and more literate groups. Also, it seems evident that the magazine under the Spivak management in the forties had a notable impact on public opinion. Its later advenures in sex problems and "McCarthyism" were less impressive. In the fifties it was in some ways a spokesman for conservatives in politics. But in 1960, when one sees the magazine on a newsstand, one is likely to exclaim, "Oh, is the *American Mercury* still published?" *

* This historical sketch was written in 1960. In 1966 the *American Mercury* was not likely to be seen on a newsstand, but it was still published, presumably by the Legion for the Survival of Freedom, Inc. (see n. 1). In the issue for June 1966, it was stated that *Western Destiny, Folk,* and *Northern World* had merged with the *Mercury*.

The magazine proclaims it has been "published continuously since it was founded by H. L. Mencken and George Jean Nathan," but certainly the only continuity is in name and volume numbering. It is now a vehicle for severe criticism by the ultra-conservatives.

In 1959 Lawrence Spivak wrote that if he had known what was going to happen to the *Mercury* when he sold it in 1950 to Clendenin J. Ryan, he "would have buried it. . . . It is a shame that the magazine that contributed so much and earned a great name in its day, should come to its present low state" (Spivak to Mott, Jan. 30, 1959, quoted with permission of author). Since 1960 the magazine has shifted ever further to the right in its editorial policy.

2

APPLETON'S BOOKLOVERS MAGAZINE [1]

IT was at the very end of the nineteenth century that Seymour Eaton, journalist and promoter, founded a successful lending-library system international in scope. The Booklovers Libraries in the United States and England were the basis of this business; and a little later the Tabard Inn Libraries, in which the customer bought the initial book and then traded it for another for a small fee, spread throughout America.

The *Booklovers Magazine,* a monthly miscellany selling at twenty-five cents, was founded by Eaton in January 1903. It was published in Philadelphia by the Library Publishing Company, which was a subsidiary of the Tabard Inn Corporation. It was something more than a house organ for the circulating library business,[2] however; Eaton had ambitions in the direction of both book and magazine publishing, and the magazine advertised all his projects. He was president of the publishing company and editor of the magazine.

The *Booklovers* was different from other magazines. Its uniqueness consisted in the combination of three kinds of content: (1) short, signed "editorials" on all kinds of subjects by famous and near-famous people; (2) a lot of brief eclectic miscellany clipped from periodicals; and (3) copious illustration, much of it in color. It was of the same size as other standard magazines, whether they sold for ten cents or twenty-five—double-column royal octavo—but one had only to glance inside

[1] TITLES: (1) *The Booklovers Magazine,* Jan. 1903—June 1905; (2) *Appleton's Booklovers Magazine,* July 1905—June 1906; (3) *Appleton's Magazine,* July 1906—June 1909.

FIRST ISSUE: Jan. 1903. LAST ISSUE: June 1909.

PERIODICITY: Monthly. Regular semiannual vols., 1–13.

PUBLISHERS: Library Publishing Company, Philadelphia, 1903–5; D. Appleton & Company, New York, 1905–9.

EDITORS: Seymour Eaton, 1903–4; Ellery Sedgwick, 1905; Trumbull White, 1906–9.

INDEXES: *Poole's Index, Annual Library Index.*

[2] Eaton published a weekly house organ for his business from October 21, 1901, through May 1, 1903. It was called *Booklovers Weekly* for about four months, and its title was then changed to *Booklovers Bulletin.*

the cover of the *Booklovers* to see how different it was. What Eaton was doing was plain enough: he was attempting to capitalize on the popular magazine trends toward concise brevity and bright illustration.

The "editorials," for which the magazine paid "cash and good prices," were little essays of about five hundred words each, signed, in the facsimile of his autograph, by the author. In the first volume these short pieces were written by such contributors as Goldwin Smith, Hamilton W. Mabie, Julian Ralph, Henry Cabot Lodge, Norman Hapgood, Brander Matthews, Amelia E. Barr, Edgar Saltus, Theodore Dreiser, and others less well known. After the first year, the tendency was to abandon these brief essays for longer articles, particularly in the fields of art, travel, education, and literature. Personality sketches, in both the longer and the shorter forms, were favorites. Essays on contemporary literary movements early became common, and they were occasionally by foreign critics. In June 1903 Paul Bourget wrote on "The Evolution of the Modern French Novel," and his article was printed in both French and English in parallel columns; in March 1905 Hall Caine wrote on "Religion in the Novel." But when Joseph Conrad wrote for the *Booklovers* (May 1905) it was on "Sailing as a Fine Art."

The brief miscellany, gathered together in a department called "The Best Things from the Periodicals of the World," was an amusing and sometimes informative section which at first bulked large in the magazine. Newspapers, magazines, and the foreign satirical weeklies were laid under tribute. Cartoons, paragraphs of comment, anecdotes, verse, and bits of information were found in this department—the result in a considerable degree of the complaisance of copyright owners who considered brief quotations good publicity for the larger works.

The pictures were the expensive part of the magazine. The art reproductions in full color were attractive to many readers. Chief emphasis was on the contemporary and minor artists. If the artistic judgment and the excellence of the color printing were not quite first class, the brilliant pictorial displays in the *Booklovers Magazine* were at least interesting and instructive. Besides the art studies, portraits and picturesque foreign scenes were prominent in the magazine's illustration.

In its second year the *Booklovers Magazine* absorbed another monthly of very similar name, Warren Elbridge Price's New York *Book-Lover*.[3] Born in San Francisco, this had been a rather faddish journal of curious and interesting matter of a literary sort. But it had been unsuccessful, and it may be doubted whether the *Booklovers* gained much in acquiring it.

By its third year, the *Booklovers* had grown more like other magazines. A short story appeared in each issue, by Robert Barr, Susan Glaspell, or some other good fictioneer. Full length articles were much more common, especially some dealing with public affairs and famous personalities. The editing was less amateurish, and the magazine had a somewhat less casual air.

Apparently, however, it had grown rather out of proportion to Eaton's other enterprises; and it clearly needed more attention, more money, and more experienced management if it was to develop into a great national magazine. Eaton therefore sold it in the early summer of 1905 to the New York book-publishing firm of D. Appleton & Company. Appleton's was by no means inexperienced in the publishing of magazines. Their *Popular Science Monthly* was outstanding in its field, and the *New York Medical Journal* was scarcely less so.[4] They had published other class journals, and this was the second general literary magazine which they had attempted, *Appleton's Journal* having once enjoyed a career of considerable value and importance, ending in 1881.[5] Joseph H. Sears, the new president of Appleton's, had been connected with the *Youth's Companion* and *Harper's Monthly* and was convinced that a magazine was

[3] Price was also editor and publisher of the *Book and News Dealer* (1890–1906), also begun in San Francisco and moved to New York in 1903. The *Book-Lover* was subtitled: *A Magazine of Book Lore, Being a Miscellany of Curiously Interesting and Generally Unknown Facts About the World's Literature and literary people; now newly arranged, with Incidental Divertissement, and All very Delightfull* [*sic*] *to Read*. Volumes ran as follows: 1, Autumn, Winter 1899, Spring, Summer 1900; 2, Autumn, Winter 1900, Spring, Summer, Nov.–Dec. 1901, Jan.–Feb. 1902; 3, March–April 1902 through Jan.–Feb. 1903; 4, March–April 1903 through Sept.–Oct. 1903, Nov., Dec. 1903; 5, Jan. through June 1904. Thus it was quarterly, 1899–1901; bimonthly, 1901–3; monthly 1903–4. It began at a dollar, ended at two dollars yearly.

[4] See F. L. Mott, *A History of American Magazines*, v. 3 (Cambridge, Mass., 1938), pp. 495–99 (*Popular Science Monthly*) and p. 140 (*New York Medical Journal*).

[5] Mott, *American Magazines*, v. 3, pp. 417–21.

a necessary adjunct of a publishing business.[6] The new owners declared: "A huge publishing house, like the Appletons', with its varied publications—more varied than those of any other publishing house in the world . . . manifestly, in order to complete its universal significance, must have a magazine."[7]

Completing universal significance was grandiloquence for what Appleton's proceeded to do, but they did at once bring new quality and maturity into the pages of what was now called *Appleton's Booklovers Magazine.* Edward S. Martin of *Life* wrote an editorial department full of charm and wisdom called "Current Reflections." Serial publication of a historical novel by Robert W. Chambers, *The Reckoning,* was immediately begun. Rex Beach, Booth Tarkington, Harry Leon Wilson, and other short story writers were introduced. The magazine came to look very much like other "quality" monthlies—particularly like *Scribner's.* Ellery Sedgwick, later famous as editor of the *Atlantic Monthly,* headed the staff of *Appleton's* for a short time, and other editors followed in quick succession; [8] but in 1906 Trumbull White, a resourceful and experienced man, was hired away from the *Red Book* to conduct what had become virtually a new magazine. In its second year under the Appleton management, it dropped the word *Booklovers* from its title and became simply *Appleton's Magazine.*

Appleton's under Trumbull White was a high-class monthly in both form and content. There were pictures by such illustrators as George Brehm and John Cassel, reproduced by line-cut or halftone, with one occasionally in color. The type was readable, and the page was wider than in most octavo magazines. Among *Appleton's* writers of serial fiction were Lloyd Osbourne, Frederic Jesup Stimson, Maxim Gorky, John Oxenham, Elizabeth Duer Miller, and Joseph C. Lincoln. Short fiction was contributed by James Branch Cabell, Zona Gale, Emerson Hough, Myra Kelly, Marie Van Vorst, Porter Emerson Browne, and others. Hall Caine's autobiography was a fea-

6 Samuel C. Chew, ed., *Fruit Among the Leaves: An Anniversary Anthology* (New York, 1950), pp. 52–53. The editor supplies a history of Appleton's as an introduction to this volume, pages 53–55 being given to *Appleton's Booklovers Magazine.*

7 *Appleton's Booklovers Magazine,* v. 6, Aug. 1905, p. 259.

8 Chew, *Fruit Among the Leaves,* p. 54.

APPLETON'S BOOKLOVERS MAGAZINE, 1905 COVER

This name was used for one year after D. Appleton & Company bought the *Booklovers Magazine.* Then it became simply *Appleton's Magazine.* In the cover shown here the border was in brown, simulating tooled leather; the rectangular center area was blue.

ture in 1908-1909. John T. McCutcheon's articles, illustrated by his own drawings, were amusing. The Reverend Charles F. Aked's series in 1908 on contemporary religion attracted much attention. There were some good travel articles, and others about industry, public affairs, and politics. A series on prohibition by different writers appeared in 1908. Literary discussions, so prominent in the earlier phase of the magazine, were now infrequent; there were some, however, about art, music, and the stage. John Philip Sousa's "The Menace of Mechanical Music" brought some sharp replies from defenders of the phonograph. Verse was comparatively infrequent and undistinguished.

An unusual feature was the editorial comment which White wrote for the first few pages of each issue. This was on various topics, but in general it reflected the conservative tendency of the magazine. *Appleton's* came just at the close of the muckraking era, and it fell in with the reaction against that movement. True, the magazine did print Rex Beach's series on "The Looting of Alaska" in 1906. But the closing paragraph of the editorial for the October 1908 number read:

> Great combinations have come in the natural course of evolution. They came as a necessity because it is better to work together than to struggle against one another. They have come to stay. Their evils are temporary and incidental. Their benefits are permanent and inherent. This is where this magazine stands.[9]

In the next issue the lead article was entitled "Unjust Attacks on Business Must Cease," by Senator Albert J. Beveridge, timed to appear just before the national election in which Bryan opposed Taft. In its last year or two *Appleton's* seemed to be making an effort to interpret industry, big business, and transportation to the people.

The magazine's circulation never exceeded 100,000, and that was too low to compete successfully in the field of popular general magazines, though it sold for fifteen cents. Advertising was sold at one hundred dollars a page, and it did not often exceed twenty pages.[10] For a magazine of 128 pages of "quality" text,

[9] *Appleton's Magazine,* v. 12, Oct. 1908, p. 389.

[10] See N. W. Ayer & Son's *Newspaper Annual and Directory* (Philadelphia, 1908), p. 1259; also the volume for 1909, p. 593, quoting the only circulation statement the magazine ever made.

this was far from enough. The June 1909 number was the last of *Appleton's Magazine;* it ended abruptly with the misleading line "To be continued" at the close of an installment of a serial by Florence Morse Kingsley. It had consistently lost money for its publishers.[11]

In its first form, the *Booklovers* was a curious and interesting periodical with little real significance. In its latter phase, it cannot be said to have completed the "universal significance" of D. Appleton & Company, but for three or four years it was a "quality" magazine reflecting credit upon that publishing house.

[11] Chew, *Fruit Among the Leaves,* p. 55.

THE NEWFANGLED "TALKING MACHINE"

Advertisement in the April 1908 issue of *Appleton's Magazine,* two years after John Philip Sousa had contributed an article on "The Menace of Mechanical Music."

COCA-COLA, AN AID TO SUCCESS

This advertisement appeared in *Success Magazine* in September 1906 when that periodical was living up to its name and ads cost $800 a page. See p. 288.

3

BETTER HOMES AND GARDENS [1]

IN the summer of 1922, Edwin Thomas Meredith was forty-five years old and had retired as Secretary of Agriculture—a post that he had filled during the last year of Woodrow Wilson's presidency. His vigor, ambition, business ability, and social responsibility had made him an outstanding figure. The agricultural monthly *Successful Farming,*[2] which he had founded when he was a young man, was helping its readers to succeed on their farms and at the same time making a substantial financial success for its publisher. Released from his duties at Washington by the change of administrations, Meredith turned to new projects, and especially to one he had long cherished.

As early as 1913, a small advertisement of a proposed magazine for town and city home-owners had appeared in *Successful Farming;* but the response had not been immediately encouraging, no major promotional effort followed, and eventually such

[1] TITLES: (1) *Fruit, Garden and Home,* July 1922—July 1924; (2) *Better Homes and Gardens,* Aug. 1924–current [*& Gardens,* 1927–45].

FIRST ISSUE: July 1922. Current.

PERIODICITY: Monthly. Vol. 1 (14 numbers), July 1922—Aug. 1923; 2–28 (annual vols. Sept.–Aug.), Sept. 1923—Aug. 1950; 29, Sept. 1950—Dec. 1951; 30–current (regular annual vols.), Jan. 1952–current.

PUBLISHERS: Edwin Thomas Meredith, 1922–28; Meredith Publishing Company (Frederick O. Bohen, pres., 1929–65; Gordon Ewing, 1965–66; Darwin Tucker, 1966–current; Fred Bohen, chief executive officer, 1965–current), 1928–current. George H. Allen, publisher, 1964–66; Robert A. Burnett, 1966–current. Des Moines, Iowa.

EDITORS: Chesla C. Sherlock, 1922–27; Elmer T. Peterson, 1927–37; Frank Wheatley McDonough, 1938–50; Joe E. Ratner, 1950–52; Hugh Everett Curtis, Jr., 1952–60; Berthold Dieter, 1960–67; James A. Riggs, 1967–current.

INDEX: *Readers' Guide* since 1930.

REFERENCES: Anon., *This is Merediths* (Des Moines, 1947; rev. 1957); Anon., *Edwin T. Meredith: A Memorial Volume* (Des Moines, 1931); Robert P. Crossley, "Family Men Edit Big Home Magazine," *Quill,* June 1949, pp. 6–7, 20; Peter Ainsworth, "The Meredith Publications," *Palimpsest,* v. 11, June 1930, pp. 256–65; F. L. Mott, "Iowa Magazines for Women and the Home," *Palimpsest,* v. 44, Aug. 1963, pp. 361–63; [Mitchell V. Charnley and Blair Converse, *Magazine Writing and Editing* (New York, 1938).]

[2] F. L. Mott, *A History of American Magazines,* v. 4 (Cambridge, Mass., 1957), p. 340.

money as had been received for advance subscriptions was returned.[3] Now Meredith again took up the idea, and in July 1922, a trial number of *Fruit, Garden and Home* was issued from his printing and publishing plant in Des Moines, Iowa. It was a fifty-two-page quarto, well printed and illustrated, with full-color cover. Nearly half its space was filled with advertising of good quality. Publisher Meredith had a folksy letter on the first page; this he continued in subsequent issues except when he was absent from the office on one of his advertising-selling tours, when the editor filled in for him.

The first editor was Chesla C. Sherlock, whom Meredith lured from the *Iowa Homestead,* a farm journal.[4] He was then twenty-seven years old; he was a graduate of Drake University's law school, an indefatigable writer, and a man of wide interests. He served as editor during the magazine's initial and formative lustrum, later joining the staff of the *Ladies' Home Journal.* His most notable printed contribution to *Better Homes and Gardens* was a series of articles on "Homes of Famous Americans," begun in January, 1923, and eventually collected and published in two volumes.

Early numbers of *Fruit, Garden and Home* contained many short articles of a practical nature on the subjects indicated by its title. Leading off the first issue was one telling of the Delicious Apple and its origins; it was supported by a cover-page advertisement placed by the promoters of the new fruit. This happened to be an Iowa theme, though the magazine was fully national in scope and never emphasized its home state. In the first issue, too, was a piece entitled, "What $50 Will Do in The Backyard"—the forerunner of many articles in the early volumes dealing with the use of that area for fruit and flower gardens, chicken-raising, apiaries, and so on. Two pages of fashions, furnished by New York designers, appeared in early numbers of the magazine; but this feature was soon dropped, and fashion articles never again formed any part of the magazine's offering. "Mrs. Bohen's Shopping Suggestions," presenting articles available from Chicago stores, was another trial run that was of short duration, though a similar mail-order project

[3] *Edwin T. Meredith,* p. 11.

[4] Mott, *American Magazines,* v. 2 (1938), pp. 89–90, n. 200.

found favor ten years later. In fact, the first thirty monthly issues of the magazine were devoted to careful experimentation; reactions were checked constantly, and letters from readers were solicited. The magazine, declared Meredith in its first number, was to be a "forum" for exchanges of "experiences," "ideas," "practical information";[5] and such close reader-relationship at once became the policy—and eventually the tradition—of the periodical.

The experimental nature of its first two or three years is emphasized by the early price of the magazine. The first two numbers—excellent though they were—came free to the subscriber, whose term of subscription (at thirty-five cents a year or three years for one dollar) began with the September issue. This low annual rate continued through 1924, when it was raised to sixty cents, or two years for a dollar. This, with the change of title, marked the end of the experimental period. In August, 1924, the original name disappeared and the magazine was titled *Better Homes and Gardens*. By this time it was a handsome periodical of fifty pages or more, with larger illustrations, carrying liberal advertising, and boasting a circulation of about half a million.[6]

The increase in the subscription rate did not halt circulation growth. The magazine was well worth any householder's money, with its monthly treasury of practical suggestions for house and home, garden and kitchen. Its landscape planning service, initiated in 1924; its money-back guarantee of articles advertised, first printed in the magazine in 1925; and its test kitchen for food recipes, set up in 1928, were notable advances that followed shortly upon the changes in name and price. It took an active part in the movement which led to the formation of the American Homes Congress, sponsored by the General Federation of Women's Clubs. When Meredith died in 1928, *Better Homes and Gardens* was a prosperous looking monthly, with some issues of more than 150 pages, and it had reached the one million mark in circulation—the first magazine in history to achieve that goal without the aid of fiction or fashions.[7]

[5] *Better Homes and Gardens,* v. 1, July 1922, p. 3.

[6] *Ibid.,* v. 3, Dec. 1924, p. 3.

[7] Ainsworth, "Meredith Publications," p. 262.

FRUIT, GARDEN AND HOME, 1924

Bright colors enhanced this pleasant cover. In August of this same year the title was changed to *Better Homes & Gardens,* marking the end of the initial experimental period.

BETTER HOMES & GARDENS, JANUARY 1928

This was the year of E. T. Meredith's death. In only six years he brought the magazine to a million circulation.

BETTER HOMES AND GARDENS, JANUARY 1965

By this time the circulation was 6,500,000. The reduction of the words "and Gardens" to a smaller size had taken place in November 1945.

Immediately after Meredith's death, his son-in-law, Fred Bohen, who had been appointed general manager in 1927, became publisher also, and in 1929 he was named president of Meredith Publishing Company. E. T. Meredith, Jr., joined the company shortly after his father's death, becoming vice-president in 1937, and serving as vice-president and general manager from 1938 to 1957.* Bohen had a newspaper background and had joined Meredith's the year before *Fruit, Garden and Home* was founded. His drive, foresight, and versatility were admirably suited to responsibilities with which he was already familiar. The first years of the Depression Thirties were difficult, but in 1937 *Better Homes and Gardens* put out an April issue of 186 pages. By 1940 circulation had passed the two million mark, and a decade later it was averaging nearly three and a half million a month.

Bohen recruited new staff members as needed through an efficient personnel department, and he showed good judgment in his selection of men for top positions. Shortly before Meredith's death, Sherlock had been succeeded as editor by Elmer T. Peterson, a writer of ability and a hard-working and imaginative staff member, who served the magazine for a full decade.

The hardships of the 1930's seem to have stimulated the management to enterprise in developing new projects. Cookery had been important in the magazine from the first, but the publication of *My Better Homes and Gardens Cook Book* in 1930 gave Meredith's a new distinction in that field. Cookbooks have always ranked high among non-literary best sellers in the United States; but it is safe to say that the *Better Homes and Gardens Cook Book,* with its various revisions, has attained a greater sales figure at this date (about ten million in 1964) than any other American hard-cover book; among top long-term best sellers in the United States, it has been exceeded only by the Bible.[8] It has been kept up-to-date, and since 1937

* E. T. Meredith, Jr., remained an important officer of the company until his death in June, 1966.

8 It has been said that Webster's dictionary occupies second place in such a list; but many publishers have issued dictionaries under the Webster name, and since they are different books, their sales cannot be combined for comparison with individual works. They are not revisions of the Merriam-Webster or of each other. The only individual dictionary that could be considered as

punched pages of recipes (with illustrations) have been included in the monthly issues of the magazine, suitable for removal and insertion in the *Cook Book*.

It was also in 1930 that the magazine campaigned for a comprehensive national home-building plan, including the establishment of standards, long-time amortization of costs, and a national association to determine loan risks for such projects. These editorials were an important factor in forming the policies of the National Conference on Building set up by President Hoover, which led eventually to the enactment of the National Housing Act. By 1930 the Junior Garden Clubs, which had been promoted by *Better Homes and Gardens* the preceding year, were flourishing; they later reached a membership of half a million. In 1930 the magazine's "More Beautiful America" contests, with awards to communities that could show special accomplishments in eliminating ugly features, were initiated. Two years later came a contest on home-remodeling, conducted on the basis of cash prizes for articles (with before-and-after pictures); in five years this contest drew 150,000 entries. Still another project of the early 1930's was the "Bildcost Home Plan," by which lists of materials available for building the homes described and pictured monthly in the magazine were furnished to readers on request, and plans and specifications supplied at nominal prices. By the middle 1950's *Better Homes and Gardens'* promotion department was estimating that 65,000 homes had been built with such aids.[9]

Among regular features in the 1930's were Harry R. O'Brien's pleasant and helpful "Diary of a Plain Dirt Gardener" and Harlan Miller's "The Man Next Door," a relaxed paragraphic commentary on manners and living in home and community. Miller's page began in 1935, and he continued it until 1949, when he transferred his notes to the *Ladies' Home Journal*. Later the page carried the signature of "Burton

---

among the topmost long-term best sellers would be *Webster's Collegiate Dictionary,* first issued in 1898. G. & C. Merriam, its publishers, refuse to divulge its sales figures; but it seems highly doubtful that they have topped the 10,000,000 mark. [The *Better Homes and Gardens Cook Book* reached total sales of twelve million copies in 1967.]

[9] Figures and much data in this paragraph are derived from a promotional memorandum in Meredith files, "Selling Through Service."

Hillis." Articles on child care were a regular feature, most of them written by Gladys Denny Schultz, the magazine's Child Care and Training Editor until 1945.

In 1938 Peterson was succeeded as editor by Frank W. McDonough, who held the position through the 1940's.[10] The years of World War II brought shortages of paper and also a reduction in advertising caused by the use for the armed services of materials commonly employed in the manufacture of goods offered to the public. *Better Homes and Gardens* became a leader in the Victory Gardens movement. In 1943 it helped to meet the "war baby" surge and the shortage of doctors by issuing its *Baby Book,* which was to sell a million and a half copies within the next decade.

But advertising revenue dropped off about a million dollars in the first year of America's participation in the war, which meant a 25 percent loss. It came back in the next year or two, largely with the aid of liberal food-advertising—a field in which *Better Homes and Gardens* had always done well. And then, immediately after the war, through vigorous efforts largely centered upon techniques of cooperation with dealers in construction materials, department stores, and house furnishing retailers (most of them originated in earlier years but now pursued with increased energy), *Better Homes and Gardens* recovered from its slump and thereupon proceeded to overtake the *Woman's Home Companion, McCall's, Good Housekeeping,* and finally the *Ladies' Home Journal* in total advertising receipts by the beginning of the 1950's. Though it kept this primacy for a few years, it lost it eventually in the shifts and hurly-burly of competition; but it continued to retain a position near the top of the magazines published for women and the home in both circulation and advertising.[11]

When McDonough died in 1950, he was succeeded for two years by J. E. Ratner, a specialist in business research. When Ratner resigned to go into advertising agency work, Hugh Curtis took over. Curtis had come to Meredith's in 1931 di-

10 For a period from September 1937 to July 1938, no editor was listed, Peterson having moved to the West Coast.

11 See annual reports of Publishers Information Bureau, Inc., for statistics on advertising revenue of the various magazines.

rectly from college, and he had worked on both of the company's periodicals. He was editor of *Better Homes and Gardens* until 1960, and his constructive ideas and industry were important in the magazine's continuing growth. In 1960 Curtis went to the Webb Publishing Company of St. Paul as director of their Service Division and two years later became dean of the School of Journalism at Drake University. He was succeeded as editor by Bert Dieter, who had come to the magazine twenty-six years before as a graphic designer. He had become art editor in 1940, and art and content editor in 1953.

In 1951 the magazine began the presentation of its advertising guarantee in a characteristic graphic form recognizable as a symbol. Though later changed somewhat in shape, it has continued to carry virtually the same wording as when printed in 1926. In 1963 the symbol was made available to *Better Homes and Gardens'* advertisers for use in general promotion and advertising. It was prominently displayed by this time in connection with the magazine's mail order advertising—an attractive department of small illustrated "ads" begun in 1933 under the heading "It's News to Me" and later entitled "Gift Shopping by Mail."

The emphasis given by *Better Homes and Gardens* to various topics has shifted somewhat. As the magazine increased in size—with occasional issues over four hundred pages in the late 1950's—the number of building, remodeling, and home furnishing articles increased, while the space given to gardening seems to have remained the same. As early as 1945 the words in the cover title *and Gardens* began to appear in smaller type. This directly reflected the proportionately smaller advertising support for gardening articles. Yet the cultivation of flowers (if not that of vegetables, now so available in supermarkets) remained a characteristic topic. "Home Management" grew in importance as a department, and by the early 1960's "Family Money Management" was listed first in the table of contents. Budgets, accounting, taxes, and insurance received much attention.

But foods and their preparation were perennial interests. As color came to illumine the magazine more and more, the food sections, under Myrna Johnston's skillful direction, became increasingly attractive. The cookery suggestions were accompanied by pictures luscious enough to tempt any gourmet or any ambitious cook. Also, articles were published that were ingeniously designed to lure men into the kitchen. This was in line with the magazine's established and frequently stated policy to appeal to men as much as to women; it has always been classified not as a "woman's magazine" but as a "home magazine."

Articles were always practical. Hints for the "handyman" appeared along with those for easier housecleaning. Advice on such subjects as "How to Get Dinner in 30 Minutes," with each of the nine simple operations fully illustrated, and "How to Be a Great Hostess!" with recipes and color pictures,[12] were combined with house and room designs in monthly *"Better Homes* Project Plans" for which blueprints were procurable, and with down-to-earth home and family management suggestions. *Better Homes and Gardens* did not deal much with generalities, but chiefly with facts and figures, materials and measurements. Moreover, it did not spare expense in acquiring and testing its data.[13]

The great distinguishing characteristic of this magazine was this precise practicality, this usable service for house, home, and family. Of course, this was not a new concept for home magazines, but *Better Homes and Gardens* worked harder at it than had any of the others. Men leaving the staff of the Des Moines magazine carried this policy and its techniques to other publications, and thus Meredith's exerted a special influence on the entire field of home magazines at the mid-century.[14]

Members of *Better Homes and Gardens'* staff have always felt at home with the matters with which they have dealt. The magazine has sometimes boasted that most of its editorial staff "live pretty much like their average reader—in 'single-family detached dwellings.' "[15] That mutuality helps to explain the magazine.

12 *Better Homes and Gardens,* v. 28, Feb. 1950, pp. 72–73; v. 43, Feb. 1964, pp. 74–77.

13 *Time,* v. 53, April 4, 1949, p. 53.

14 See Theodore Peterson, *Magazines in the Twentieth Century,* revised ed. (Urbana, Ill., 1964), p. 383.

15 Crossley, "Family Men," p. 6.

When mass-circulation periodicals generally adopted the split-run technique in the latter 1950's, in order to meet the needs of advertisers who did not require total coverage, *Better Homes and Gardens* began publishing regional editions. In 1963 it refined the system of standard editions by issuing what it called "custom regionals," designed to help advertisers "to tailor campaigns to match their distribution and sales patterns." This quickly brought to 22 the number of custom and standard regional editions of the magazine.[16]

By this time Meredith's was issuing six *Better Homes and Gardens* "idea annuals." The oldest were *Home Building Ideas* (1937), *Garden Ideas* (1940), and *Home Furnishings Ideas* (1941); begun in the 1950's were *Christmas Ideas, Kitchen Ideas,* and *Home Improvement Ideas*. In the aggregate, these books had a circulation each year of over a million and a half copies.

In 1957–1961 Meredith's undertook a physical expansion program that cost over $10,000,000. The publishing plant in Des Moines had been extended and remodeled from time to time in preceding years. Now a new printing plant was built, covering about ten acres and equipped with modern high-speed six-color presses. Its facilities enabled the company to publish not only *Better Homes and Gardens* and *Successful Farming* but other magazines on a contract printing basis.

Like other publishing concerns of its times, Meredith's entered competing communications fields in the 1950's and 1960's. Beginning in 1948, it erected or purchased several radio and television stations scattered over the country from Syracuse, New York, to Phoenix, Arizona. In 1960 and 1961 respectively, it purchased the well-known New York book publishing houses of Appleton-Century-Crofts and Duell, Sloan & Pearce. The textbook firm of Lyons & Carnahan, Chicago, was also acquired in 1961. This book-publishing expansion was not unnatural for a company that had been producing for many years such popular manuals as the *Better Homes and Gardens Cook Book, Baby Book, Handyman's Book, Diet Book, Junior Cook Book,* the "idea annuals," and so on. In

16 Memorandum in files of *Better Homes and Gardens,* Sept. 27, 1963. [With the May 1967 issue there were 78 regional editions.]

the early 1960's Meredith's published a dozen or more new *Better Homes and Gardens* books, ranging in subject matter from a *First Aid Book* to a *Money Management Book*.

On the second anniversary of its birth the editor of the magazine wrote: "When *Better Homes and Gardens* was launched, we had in mind that it must be a magazine that would attract and be helpful to at least one million American homes—1,000,000 subscribers." [17] In 1964 it numbered over six million circulation at thirty-five cents a copy, or three dollars a year (with approximately half-price introductory offers by mail); and it was receiving about $25,000,000 annually in advertising revenue.* This success over a term of little more than forty years had been due to resourceful business management, as well as to the fact that the magazine had been consistently faithful editorially to its original ideals of practical service and emphasis on quality for the middle-class American home and family.†

[17] *Better Homes and Gardens,* v. 3, Sept. 1924, p. 3.

* The guaranteed circulation of *Better Homes and Gardens* reached seven million with the February, 1967, issue. Advertising revenues totaled $33.9 million in 1966.

† This sketch was written in 1964. In May 1967, Dieter became editorial director of the magazine and James A. Riggs was made editor. He had joined the Meredith Company in 1950, was made managing editor of *Better Homes and Gardens* in 1955, and five years later became its executive editor. See n. 1 for other post-1964 staff changes.

4

CURRENT HISTORY[1]

CURRENT HISTORY was begun as a kind of supplement to the *New York Times*. It was intended to provide, in a form better adapted to leisurely reading and study than that of the newspaper, some extensive articles and public documents, as well as matter somewhat obliquely related to the news of the day. Here was news as history, to be considered and remembered. Here were the footnotes and commentaries on the news. And the news was the news of the great European War of 1914, for it was the overflow from material produced by that great event, or series of events, that called forth the new magazine.

It was at first a big square octavo of more than two hundred double-column pages. The first number, issued in December

[1] Titles: (1) *The New York Times Current History of the European War,* Dec. 1914—Jan. 1915; (2) *The New York Times Current History: A Monthly Magazine: The European War,* Feb. 1915—Jan. 1916; (3) *Current History: A Monthly Magazine of the New York Times,* Feb 1916—Sept. 1923; (4) *Current History: A Monthly Magazine,* Oct. 1923—June 1940; (5) *Current History and Forum,* July 1940—June 1941; (6) *Current History,* 1941–current.

First issue: Dec. 1914. Current.

Periodicity: Semimonthly, Dec. 1914—Jan. 1915; monthly thereafter except Nov. 1940—Jan. 1941, when it was issued twice a month at irregular intervals. Vol. 1, Dec. 1914—March 1915; 2–46, April 1915—Sept. 1937, semiannual vols. April–Sept. and Oct.–March; 47, Oct.–Dec. 1937; 48, Jan.–June 1938 (July–Aug. 1938 omitted); 49, Sept. 1938—Feb. 1939; 50, March–Aug. 1939; 51, Sept. 1939—Aug. 1940; 52, Sept. 1940—May 1941; 53, June 1941 (July–Aug. 1941 omitted). [New Series] 1–4, Sept. 1941—Aug. 1943, semiannual vols. Sept.–Feb. and March–Aug.; 5, Sept.–Dec. 1943; 6–current, Jan. 1944–current, regular semiannual volumes.

Publishers: *New York Times,* Dec. 1914—April 1936; Current History, Inc. (M. E. Tracy, publisher), May 1936—Feb. 1939; Current History Publishing Corporation, March 1939—June 1941 (Joseph Hilton Smyth, publisher, March–Nov. 1939, and E. Trevor Hill, pres., Dec. 1939—June 1941); Events Publishing Company, July 1941–59 (Spencer Brodney, president, 1941–43; Daniel G. Redmond, 1943–55; D. G. Redmond, Jr., 1955–59); Current History, Inc., 1959–current (D. G. Redmond, Jr., publisher, 1959–current).

Editors: George Washington Ochs-Oakes, 1915–31; Spencer Brodney, 1931–36, 1941–43; Merle Elliott Tracy, 1936–39; E. Trevor Hill and John T. Hackett, 1939–41; Daniel George Redmond, 1943–55; Carol L. Thompson, 1955–current.

Index: *Readers' Guide.*

1914, was captioned *The New York Times Current History of the European War;* but its main title was "What Men of Letters Say," and it was filled with contributions of famous authors to the controversy over the great conflict—a paper war begun by Bernard Shaw's comments and replies to them. In this number we have not only English but European (including a few German) utterances, all illustrated by full-page portraits in roto. That was a good beginning, and later that month there was a second issue titled "Who Began the War and Why?" This gave both sides, but an anti-German element came in when the number was filled out with some accounts of reported "atrocities" in Belgium.

There were two issues in the next month also, but the supplement was becoming more magazinish. That is, although the numbers had special titles indicating emphasis in content, they were much more varied and miscellaneous than their predecessors. They contained many shorter pieces, including a few poems; and a section reproducing current cartoons was introduced.

In the issue for February 1915, *Current History* had for a subtitle the words, *A Monthly Magazine.* It carried forty-eight pages of war pictures produced by rotogravure, as well as maps, an enlarged section of cartoons, and a continuation of thc day-by-day chronicle of the war begun the preceding month. These became fixtures in the magazine, except for the war pictures, which were soon reduced to a minimum by the founding of another *Times* auxiliary, the *Mid-Week Pictorial.* Some of the most brilliant of the *Times* correspondents abroad were represented by articles reprinted from the newspaper or written especially for the magazine; and the by-lines of Philip Gibbs, Perceval Gibbon, and Cyril Brown were common. J. B. W. Gardiner was the leading armchair military analyst.

Current History's chief competitors in the news-magazine field were the monthly *Current Opinion* and the weekly *Literary Digest,* both of them devoted mainly to extracts from the newspapers, and the well-edited *Review of Reviews* and *World's Work.* But by mid-1915 the new magazine had created a modest following of its own among newsstand purchasers and subscribers; and on July 1, 1915, Adolph S. Ochs, publisher of the *Times,* appointed his brother George W. Ochs editor of both *Current History* and the *Mid-Week Pictorial.*[2] George Washington Ochs-Oakes, as he was soon to call himself,[3] had recently returned from a thirteen-year term as publisher of the Philadelphia *Public Ledger,* then owned by his elder brother, and was glad to take on the somewhat different job of managing a monthly magazine.

As the war developed, the magazine continued to be highly eclectic, reprinting much from English and continental newspapers and reviews, analytical accounts of military actions by *Times* staffmen, public addresses, and documents. At first, there was much exposition of the German point of view; but this declined rapidly, especially after the sinking of the "Lusitania." *Current History* continued, however, to quote pro-German pieces from the *New Yorker Staats-Zeitung* until after the United States entered the war, and after that it offered translations from German periodicals occasionally.

In November 1915, *Current History* initiated a front-of-the-book department of chronicle and comment entitled "World Affairs of the Month," soon to be followed by a second department called "Interpretations of World Events." These were combined in 1917–1918, then abandoned for a time, and later reinstated in a different form. This initial department of commentary was of the same type as "The Progress of the World" in the *Review of Reviews* and "The March of Events" in *World's Work.* Also a section of reviews of "Important War Books" was carried for a time.

In addition to the eclectic content of the magazine, there were some important contributed articles, such as "The Peace of the World," by H. G. Wells (April 1915), Gilbert Parker's "The War to Date" (September 1915), a debate between Hugo Muensterberg and Albert Bushnell Hart on the position of German-Americans in the United States (November 1915), and Rudyard Kipling's stories of submarine adventure entitled "Tales of 'The Trade' " (August 1916). Norman Angell wrote

[2] William M. Schuyler, ed., *The Life and Letters of George Washington Ochs-Oakes* (New York, 1932), p. 40.

[3] *Ibid.,* pp. 42–44. Adding Oakes to his name was an act of repudiation of his German ancestry in the heat of the war feeling.

VOL. II No. 3 JUNE 1915

The New York Times

PRICE 25 Cents

CURRENT HISTORY

A MONTHLY MAGAZINE

THE EUROPEAN WAR

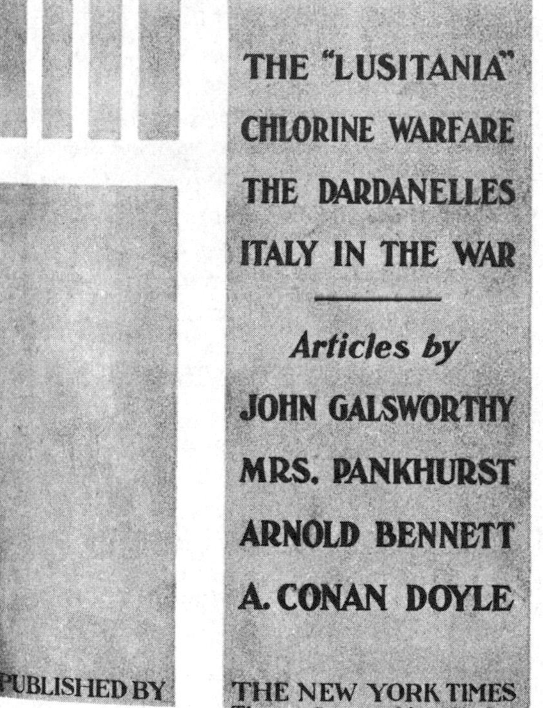

THE "LUSITANIA"

CHLORINE WARFARE

THE DARDANELLES

ITALY IN THE WAR

Articles by

JOHN GALSWORTHY

MRS. PANKHURST

ARNOLD BENNETT

A. CONAN DOYLE

PUBLISHED BY THE NEW YORK TIMES

COMPANY

JUNE 1915 COVER OF *CURRENT HISTORY*

The articles by Galsworthy, Conan Doyle, and others were on subjects related to World War I.

CURRENT

History A MONTHLY MAGAZINE OF WORLD AFFAIRS

FEBRUARY 1967

THE MIDDLE EAST TODAY

CHANGING OF THE GUARD IN THE MIDDLE EAST .... *Halford L. Hoskins* 65

THE SOVIET UNION IN THE MIDDLE EAST .... *Benjamin Shwadran* 72

ISRAEL: THE UNRELENTING BATTLE ...... *Dwight J. Simpson* 78

POLITICAL TRENDS IN IRAQ AND KUWAIT..*Majid Khadduri* 84

THE NEW EGYPT AFTER 1952 ....*Christina Phelps Harris* 90

TRADITION AND REFORM IN SAUDI ARABIA .... *George Lenczowski* 98

NEW REGIME IN TURKEY .... *Ruth C. Lawson* 105

REGULAR FEATURES

MAPS • *The Middle East: A Broad View* 67

BOOK REVIEWS 111

CURRENT DOCUMENTS • *United Nations Censure of Israel* 113

Secretary Rusk on the Middle East .. 113

THE MONTH IN REVIEW 117

FOR READING TODAY...FOR REFERENCE TOMORROW

HALF A CENTURY LATER—FEBRUARY 1967

The cover lists the contents, but now blocks of eye-catching color enliven the page.

on "America and a New World State" in April 1915; and from 1918 onward there was much about the League of Nations, including pronouncements by statesmen at home and abroad.

By 1918 *Current History* had reached a circulation of 76,000. In November of that year it initiated the frontispiece picture gallery, soon to occupy sixteen pages, an imitation of a *World's Work* feature. In 1920 it also followed the example of that magazine in raising its price to thirty-five cents a copy. The circulation dropped off by one-half in the next two years, and the twenty-five-cent price was restored in 1923; thereupon circulation went up to 80,000, the highest point of its history.

But it was not the price change alone that brought increased popularity to *Current History* in 1924; it was a new editorial plan, and an advertising campaign to support the new plan. For the first few years after the war, the magazine had clearly been groping and hoping. It had been composed chiefly of summaries of news, divided by countries, with important documents and some special articles, nearly all foreign. By-lines were rarer, but Gustavus Myers, Frank Parker Stockbridge, Stephen Bonsal, Charles H. Grasty, and Admiral William S. Sims were frequent contributors. Illustration by roto had been abandoned, and halftones grew fewer and fewer. Then by 1922 there was a noticeable tendency to draw on university professors as contributors—Eliot of Harvard, Hadley of Yale, and many others. This crystallized in November 1923 into a system of reviewing world events, of which Ochs-Oakes was very proud and which seemed to give the magazine a new lease on life.

By this system twelve professors of history from colleges and universities in the United States and Canada were assigned each to a country or a region, and together they furnished a "Monthly Survey of World Events." These "associates in *Current History*" were headed by Albert Bushnell Hart, of Harvard. There were many changes in succeeding months and years both in the personnel of this board of editors and in the way their reports were handled. In February 1926, the "Historians' Chronicle of the World" became Part II of the magazine, and James Thayer Gerould became the leading commentator on general international affairs. Hart did the United States section until 1931, when E. Francis Brown took over. In the thirties the formal pattern was considerably broken up, and special features became more prominent; but many of these were contributed by professors of history—Charles A. Beard on the New Deal, Allan Nevins on European affairs, Henry Steele Commager on American issues, and so on. The magazine still carried "A Month's World History" by countries when it was sold by the *Times* in 1936.

In these years there were sporadic attempts to conduct a science department, notably one by Watson Davis in 1924 through 1932. Waldemar Kaempffert was a frequent contributor. Too many things in the magazine were "sporadic," and there was an impression of experimentation by inexperienced staff.

The prohibition issue occupied much space. The magazine was sympathetic with the "noble experiment." In national presidential campaigns, issues were presented objectively, platforms were printed in full, and there were accounts of the conventions of all parties. In June 1928 there appeared an unusual symposium, with nine different writers presenting various angles of the questions at issue in the campaign of that year.

By the mid-thirties journalists tended to crowd the professors in the pages of the magazine; representative contributors were William Hard, Bruce Bliven, Ernest K. Lindley, Ralph Thompson, and Raymond B. Clapper. Some book reviews in the fields of history and biography were carried in the advertising section.

The early thirties were challenging years for the reviews, but they were difficult times financially for all of them. The *Review of Reviews* absorbed *World's Work* in 1932; the *Literary Digest* was merged in 1937 with the remains of the other two (it had taken over *Current Opinion* in 1924), but the resulting publication lasted only a short time.[4] *Current History's* circulation declined slowly but steadily through these years, reaching 61,000 in the panic year of 1930. There was some advertising, but usually not more than ten or a dozen pages of it. Cheaper paper was adopted in 1931, and all illustrations abandoned ex-

[4] See F. L. Mott, *A History of American Magazines,* v. 4 (Cambridge, Mass., 1957), pp. 578–9, 663–64; and Theodore Peterson, *Magazines in the Twentieth Century,* revised ed. (Urbana, Ill., 1964), pp. 152–54.

cept the cartoons and some maps. Editor Ochs-Oakes died in 1931, and Spencer Brodney, who had been a member of *Current History's* staff for several years,[5] became its editor. But five years more of the depression, with circulation down to 42,000, persuaded the *Times* to sell the magazine.

The purchaser was the nearly blind journalist, Merle Elliott Tracy, who had been a columnist for the Scripps-Howard papers, and who now became editor and publisher of *Current History* for three years. Better paper, better illustration, and eventually a larger page characterized the new magazine. A "Log of Major Currents," composed of short commentary, occupied some thirty of the magazine's 132 pages. "They Say" was a twelve-page department of quotations and clippings. "The World in Books" was conducted by Norman B. Cousins, literary editor from February 1937, while Vernon F. Calverton had charge of "The Cultural Barometer." There were other departments, and the magazine was more attractive than ever before.

Tracy wrote an editorial page, decidedly anti-New Deal. Gradually such well-known names as those of Bernard M. Baruch and Rexford Guy Tugwell came into the tables of contents. Nearly half the magazine was devoted to foreign affairs, and Winston Churchill and Leon Blum were added to the list of contributors. The professors were not neglected; and Charles A. Hodges (politics, New York University), David S. Muzzey (history, Columbia), and Harry A. Overstreet (psychology, City College) were on a new editorial board organized in 1937.

But the new *Current History* did not prosper; indeed, it continued its slow decline in circulation. Early in 1939 it was sold to interests represented by Joseph Hilton Smyth—who was later to be convicted of spreading Japanese propaganda in America for a price, through the medium of another magazine. Smyth's control lasted only nine months. The editorial policy was isolationist, Senator Robert A. Taft's "Let's Mind Our Own Business" (June 1939) setting the tone. The magazine tended to become more and more eclectic; characteristic was the "Town Meeting" department edited by George V. Denny

[5] *New York Times,* July 24, 1941, p. 13, col. 1.

of radio fame, giving cross sections of public opinion on various issues.

In December 1939 appeared the first number of the magazine under a new ownership and management headed by E. Trevor Hill, with John T. Hackett as joint editor. That issue contained a symposium on "The War in Europe: 1939," by Hugh S. Johnson, Henry C. Wolfe, Ernest Dimnet, Alfred Duff Cooper, and others. Next month the magazine declared its neutrality and its strong opposition to United States participation in the war. Vincent Sheean, Lindsay Rogers, and James Truslow Adams became frequent contributors.

The Hill organization purchased the *Forum and Century* [6] and combined it with *Current History* in July 1940 under the name, *Current History and Forum.* Eleanor Van Alen succeeded Cousins as literary editor, and Robert Strausz-Hupé and Roger W. Straus, Jr., became associate editors. The monthly debate on a current issue, characteristic of the *Forum,* was retained for a few months and then dropped; "They Say" and the chronology were retained, and new departments were added. On the whole, the magazine was livelier than before, but there was no adequate coverage of World War II comparable to that given World War I by the original *Current History.* The magazine under Hill abandoned its isolationism and in its last number (June 1941) urged that the United States should take up the burdens of world leadership.

This was the last number of the original series. The merger had brought the circulation up, but the gain had not been held. So *Current History* was sold in the summer of 1941 to Spencer Brodney, who had been its editor when it had passed out of the hands of the *New York Times,* and who had shortly thereafter founded a magazine of his own called *Events.* He claimed that *Events* had all along been the true successor of the *New York Times Current History;* [7] and now he made a clean break with the management that had been operating *Current History and Forum* and with the number for September 1941 started a new *Current History* with new numbering, format, staff, and policy. For a year and a half he carried the subtitle, "Incorporating

[6] Mott, *American Magazines,* v. 4, p. 522.

[7] *Current History,* N.S., v. 1, Sept. 1941, Back-cover page.

Events, Forum and Century," but after that it was simply, "A Monthly Magazine of World Affairs."

The new *Current History* page was in between the pocket size and the regular magazine size—a squarish five by seven and a half page carrying two columns. Six years later it was to enlarge this page to a small quarto, raising the price at the same time from twenty-five to thirty-five cents. It dispensed entirely with illustration. Brodney was editor until 1943, when he was succeeded by Daniel George Redmond, whose term of service lasted for twelve years. Carol L. Thompson, long-time associate editor, took over on Redmond's death in 1955, and D. G. Redmond, Jr., became publisher.

The magazine with its new numbering, conducted first by Brodney and then by the Redmonds, was designed largely for students and libraries. A "Study Plan" and monthly tests were furnished for a while at reduced cost to students, and free copies to teachers. It raised its price in 1951 to fifty cents. Its content, largely concerned with foreign and international matters, was consistently nonpartisan, intelligent, and of a high analytical quality. Special numbers, common for several years, became the rule in the mid-fifties; the first six numbers in 1956, for example, dealt with "The Soviet Union Since Stalin," "Report on India," "Problems of American Foreign Policy," and "Reports" on Germany, Africa, and the Middle East. These "Reports" later became "Area Studies," which coordinated much valuable information on vital areas.

In the best tradition of the magazine, its contributing editors have been drawn from college and university faculties. Prominent in the pages of *Current History* for many years have been Frederick L. Schuman (politics, Williams), Sidney B. Fay (history, Harvard, Yale), Alzada Comstock (economics, Mt. Holyoke), Colston E. Warne (economics, Amherst), and others.

Though bibliographically a separate periodical from the *Current History* of 1914–1941, the later magazine is historically a sequel to it, and carries in each issue the statement: "Founded in 1914 by the *New York Times*." *

* This historical sketch was written in the late 1950's. The price of an issue rose in 1960 to eighty-five cents, in 1965 to ninety cents, and in 1967 is ninety-five cents and $8.50 a year. Circulation is slightly over 26,000.

5

EDITOR & PUBLISHER [1]

JAMES B. SHALE, publisher of the *News* at McKeesport, Pennsylvania, was one of a group of newspaper owners who organized the Publishers' Press Association at the time of the collapse of the old United Press in 1897. Shale became president and general manager of the new wire service, which at first served chiefly Pennsylvania and New York papers. But other eastern papers soon joined, and the agency expanded rapidly—perhaps too rapidly, for in 1904 Shale and his chief partner in the venture were willing to sell out to the Scripps-McRae Press Association for $150,000. A few years later Scripps merged the Publishers' Press in his new United Press Associations.[2]

In the midst of all this activity, Shale took time to found, in New York, a periodical that he named *The Editor and Publisher: A Journal for Newspaper Makers*. It might seem that

[1] TITLES: (1) *The Editor and Publisher,* 1901–15; (2) *Editor & Publisher,* 1915–current. ("The" was dropped in 1918.) SUBTITLES: (1) *and Journalist* (with variants), 1907–16; (2) *The Fourth Estate,* 1927–current; (3) *The Oldest Publishers' and Advertisers' Newspaper in America,* 1916–current.

FIRST ISSUE: June 29, 1901. Current.

PERIODICITY: Weekly. Annual volumes, 1–14 (usually July–June; sometimes mid-June to mid-June), 1901–15; 15–46 omitted, vol. numbers changed March 15, 1915, to take over founding date of merged *Journalist* (1884): thus vol. for June 1914—June 1915 began as 14, ended as 47; 48–50, June 1915—June 1918; 51, July 1918—May 1919; 52–54 (May–June), 1919–22; 55–67, (June–May), 1922–35; 68, May–Dec. 1935; 69–current (Jan.–Dec.), 1936–current.

PUBLISHERS: James B. Shale, 1901–12; Editor & Publisher, Inc. (James Wright Brown, pres., 1912–47, 1948–53; James Wright Brown, Jr., 1947–48; Robert Utting Brown, 1953–58, publisher, 1958–current), 1912–current. New York. Chairman of the Board, James Wright Brown, 1953–59.

EDITORS: James B. Shale, 1901–02, 1909–12; Frank LeRoy Blanchard (managing ed.) 1901–02, 1908, 1911–16; Philip R. Dillon (man. ed.) 1908–09; J. W Brown, 1916–24, 1936–38, 1943–44; Marlen Edwin Pew, 1924–36; Arthur T. Robb, 1938–43; R. U. Brown, 1944–current.

INDEXES: Semiannual, 1935–61.

REFERENCES: *Editor & Publisher,* "Golden Jubilee Number," v. 67, July 21, 1934, pp. 34–35, 308–9; 65th anniversary number, v. 82, April 23, 1949, pp. 25–28, 32B–32D, 76–102; "75th Anniversary Edition," v. 92, June 27, 1959, sec. 2, pp. 107–18.

[2] Victor Rosewater, *History of Coöperative News-Gathering in the United States* (New York, 1930), pp. 342–44.

THE EDITOR AND PUBLISHER

A JOURNAL FOR NEWSPAPER MAKERS.

VOL. 1., NO. 4. | NEW YORK, JULY 20, 1901. | $1 A YEAR, 5 CENTS A COPY.

THE KING OBJECTS

EDWARD DISLIKES AND RESENTS THE ESPIONAGE OF THE NEWSPAPER MEN.

Thinks that His Movements Should Not Be Reported Except When They Concern Matters of State—Much Amazed by the Report that He Was Going to Sail on Shamrock II.

The Prince of Wales and King Edward are two different personalities. When the King was the Prince he treated the newspaper representatives with great consideration, and often went out of his way to assist them in obtaining news. Since the Prince became King his attitude, so a correspondent of the New York Sun says, has changed.

It seems that the King objects to his movements being reported except where they concern matters of State. He thinks that then the newspapers should be contented with the official record as supplied by the court news man.

ANNOYED BY REPORTS.

His majesty was much annoyed a couple of months ago when the newspapers announced that he was going to sail on the Shamrock II., and that certain ladies would be of the party, and he was irritated last week when his intention to go to Windsor Castle in a motor car was made known by the same means.

This week he has been exasperated by the publication of a harmless paragraph stating that Lord Rosebery had an interview with him lasting a full hour. Apparently the gravity of the offense lay in the statement regarding the duration of the visit. It is showed, said his majesty's private secretary, that Marlborough House was being watched and such an intolerable state of things would have to be stopped.

EJECTED FROM MARLBOROUGH.

An unhappy coincidence was that the day following the report of the visit a wholly irresponsible newspaper announced that Lord Rosebery was about to be married to the Duchess of Albany, the King's sister-in-law

When a reporter called at Marlborough House to inquire as to the truth of the report, he was ordered out, and orders were issued to the servants that he never again be permitted to pass the threshold.

The private secretary scornfully refused to say a word of confirmation or denial of what was described as a monstrous assertion. Inquirers were left to guess whether the adjective applied to the idea that Lord Rosebery was engaged to the Duchess of Albany or to the unauthorized and unofficial publication.

New Paper at Nashville.

The Nashville (Tenn.) Daily News is the newest venture in Southern journalism. It made its appearance July 15, and promises to make a place for itself as a profitable venture in short order.

The News is equipped with an eight-page Scott perfecting press and five linotypes. The paper is backed with $45,000 in cash and $55,000 more available.

The backers are prominent men, who intend that the paper shall become a political power in the State and nation.

MELVILLE E. STONE,

GENERAL MANAGER OF THE ASSOCIATED PRESS.

CENSORSHIP REMOVED.

Manila Editors Take Advantage of Their Freedom to Make Charges.

Recent dispatches from Manila indicated that the abolition of the severe military press censorship has resulted in the publication of some severe criticisms of military and civil officials.

The Daily American, of which Franklin Brooks, now in this country, is the editor, recently accused Prof. Worcester, of the Philippine Commission, of exploitation. It subsequently apologized, however.

An article in the Federal organ, signed by the party president, openly instructed the provincial committees to institute demonstrations against the friars. Then the latter vilified the Federals.

Last week the Freedom recklessly attacked Gov. Whitmarsh and Secretary Speerer, of Banguet. The American devotes its first page to reproducing in its largest type an article from the Liberta of Thursday, which it holds up for execration, but as a matter of fact the article is no worse than some that are printed daily in the United States.

It violently attacks President McKinley's policy and the Philippine Commission. The Liberta, however, is owned and edited by friars, and it frequently indulges in spasms of venom and filth, attacking persons without reserve.

Gov. Taft recently stated that the newspapers would have every opportunity to obtain the fullest justice, but the publication of libels or other lawbreaking articles would be severely punished. A special translator reviews the newspapers daily, but the situation is steadily becoming aggravated.

Verdict Against London Mail.

Hettie Chattell, the actress, a single woman, brought suit against the London Daily Mail for libel because that paper printed a paragraph on Feb. 25 to the effect that Rosie Boote, the actress, who married the Marquis of Headfort, was a daughter of Miss Chattell.

The libel suit was based on the ground that this suggested that Miss Chattell was immoral.

The jury awarded Miss Chattell £2,500 damages.

Receiver for St. Paul Paper.

Eli S. Warner has been appointed receiver of the St. Paul (Minn.) Saturday Evening News and directed to sell the property. This was brought about by the suit of H. M. Kalscheuer against A. E. Donaldson et al., the latter being the proprietors of the paper in question. It was claimed that the concern was insolvent and unable to pay its obligations.

MELVILLE E. STONE.

CHARACTERISTICS OF THE ASSOCIATED PRESS'S GENERAL MANAGER.

The Part He Has Played in the Newspaper History of Chicago—His Success—How He Got Even with a Milwaukee Man Who Objected to an Article.

Chicago, the city marvelous, has enlisted in its newspaper field some of the strongest intellects in the nation—men of broad mental grasp, cosmopolitan ideas and notable business sagacity. Conspicuous among those who have given the city prestige in this direction must be placed Melville E. Stone. His identification with "the art preservative of all arts" has been one of distinctive predilection, and, though he has intermittently turned his attention to enterprises of different nature, still, true to the instinct said to characterize every newspaper man, he has invariably returned to the work, strengthened and reinforced by the experiences which have been his.

Mr. Stone was born in the village of Hudson, McLean County, Ill., on the 22d of August, 1848, being the son of the Rev. Elijah Stone, a member of the Rock River Methodist Episcopal Conference, and afterward pastor of what is now the Centenary Church, Chicago.

He obtained his first newspaper experience on the old Chicago Republican, and when that paper was merged with the Inter-Ocean he became the city editor.

CONSOLIDATED THE POST AND MAIL.

About eighteen months later he aided in bringing about the consolidation of the Post and Mail, and became managing editor of the new paper, in whose interest he repaired to Washington as correspondent some months later.

While in the Federal Capital he became a member of the Congressional staff of the New York Herald.

He returned to Chicago and resumed his former position as managing editor, but he soon tendered his resignation for the purpose of concentrating on a new journalistic venture. The nucleus of the great enterprise which brought to Mr. Stone both success and renown was shown forth on Christmas day, 1875, when the first issue of the Chicago Daily News, the original one-cent paper of the city, made its appearance.

The inception of this enterprise, whose success is now a part of the history of Chicago journalism, was of most modest order, Mr. Stone's associates having been William E. Dougherty and Percy Neggy. In 1883 a stock company was formed, all the stock being retained by Mr. Stone and Mr. Lawson.

HIS TEMPORARY RETIREMENT.

Mr. Stone remained in the business until 1888, when, having accumulated a fortune, he temporarily retired from journalism. He passed two years abroad in company with his family. On his return home in 1890 he became the prime factor in bringing about the organization of the Globe National Bank, which was recognized as one of the solid financial institutions of the city. In 1893 Mr. Stone became general manager of the Associated Press, in which capacity his talents

FOURTH ISSUE OF THE *EDITOR AND PUBLISHER*

The date: July 20, 1901. Until 1915, the first page of the paper characteristically featured a portrait of someone prominent in journalism or advertising—in this case Melville E. Stone, general manager of the Associated Press.

APRIL 15, 1967
Twenty cents

Editor & Publisher

SPOT NEWS AND FEATURES ABOUT NEWSPAPERS, ADVERTISERS AND AGENCIES

SDX Awards

Supreme Court views P&G's ad power

Gannett buys 2 newspapers in Rockford

Federated adds 2 on West Coast

Bias or halo for tv group ownership?

Knight papers' top executives move up

Readers stormed the newsstands for the Chicago Tribune's 32-page "Big Snow" magazine.

The great snow of '67 was one of the biggest stories ever to hit—and bury—Chicago.

To capture all the drama, desolation and occasional humor of the storm and its aftermath, the Tribune gave its readers something memorable. While Chicago was still digging out, the Tribune delivered a two-color, 32-page rotogravure magazine in every copy of its Sunday edition on February 19.

Reader response broke all records. Despite a greatly increased press run, the Sunday Tribune was completely sold out by early morning. To meet the demand, more than 100,000 extra copies of the "Big Snow" magazine were reprinted and sold.

The Tribune serves Chicago in many ways. Covering big stories in a memorable way is one of them.

Chicago Tribune

P.S. Chicago's big snow was something to see—as is our "Big Snow" magazine. For a free copy (while our short supply lasts) write: Chicago Tribune, Rm. 770, 435 N. Michigan Ave., Chicago, Ill. 60611

MODERN APPEARANCE OF *EDITOR & PUBLISHER*

The date: April 15, 1967. An advertisement now is typically printed on the cover, often an ad for one of the Chicago papers. The ampersand in the periodical's title has been a sort of trademark since 1915. "The" was dropped in 1918.

three other papers serving the same industry which were in course of publication in the same city at that time [3] would have been a deterrent to this undertaking; but the newspaper business was booming, and Colonel Shale looked covetously upon the advertising columns of the *Fourth Estate, Newspaperdom,* and the *Journalist.* He promised in his first issue that: "As an advertising medium, the paper will be the best in its special field, because it will reach weekly the men with whom the manufacturers of printing inks and presses, the paper makers, the stereotype and linotype metal producers, dealers in oils, desire to do business. It will be of special value [as an advertising medium] to the publisher because it will be placed in the hands of a selected list of general advertisers and the agents who handle large contracts." [4]

Shale sometimes listed himself as "editor" of his journal, but was interested in the business side chiefly, and left the editorial work to others. Frank LeRoy Blanchard, who had worked for four or five New York newspapers and had also held for some years a staff position on the *Fourth Estate,* was Shale's "managing editor" during part of his ownership, as were Paul Lodge, Philip R. Dillon, and W. D. Showalter.

The first *Editor and Publisher* was an eight-page paper without cover. It was attractive in appearance, well printed on good paper, and illustrated by excellent portraits of men prominent in journalism and advertising. The picture of a boyish-looking William R. Hearst was prominent on page one of the first issue, which was dated June 29, 1901.

The paper supplied a good quota of news from its chosen field, with sketches of journalistic personalities. It had a widespread interest geographically; notable, for example, were its reports from "Breezy Chicago." Also, it was surprisingly good at reporting the leading events related to magazine publishing.

From the very first, *Editor and Publisher* was a practical journal. One sentence from its salutatory is worth quoting because it announced a policy that the journal has followed throughout its long career:

[3] F. L. Mott, *A History of American Magazines,* v. 4 (Cambridge, Mass., 1957), pp. 243–44.

[4] *Editor and Publisher,* v. 1, June 29, 1901, p. 4.

> It will be our purpose from time to time to present papers of a practical nature by experienced men on circulation schemes, the preparation and display of advertisements, the production and printing of half-tones, the cost of running daily newspapers in large and small cities and kindred topics.[5]

The "topics" have changed somewhat in the last sixty-odd years, as the newspaper picture has changed, but the journal's general policy has remained the same.

On the whole, Shale and Blanchard conducted a good newspaperman's newspaper. It did not dodge disputes, but it tried "to give both sides of every controversy, and to maintain equipoise and good nature in all circumstances."[6] In 1907 it absorbed the *Journalist,*[7] whose owner was by that time ready to give up because of ill health and ill success; and two years later it enlarged its size to sixteen pages. But circulation and advertising responses were both discouraging. The paper was never fat with "ads," even for the numbers reporting the great newspapermen's conventions; and though it claimed two thousand circulation by 1911, it probably had less than half that much—at a dollar a year, along with a yearly advertising revenue of about $16,000.[8] So when Colonel Shale, who had become involved in mining projects in the West, found a buyer for his paper, he was glad to get out of the publishing business for good. The buyer was "Jim" Brown, who enlisted seven minor stockholders to help him make the purchase, while retaining the controlling interest himself.

James Wright Brown had begun his newspaper career when, a boy of eighteen, he had found a job as reporter on the *Tribune* in his home city of Detroit. In the latter 1890's he worked on Chicago newspapers in various capacities; from there he went to Louisville, Kentucky, to serve as general manager of the *Herald* from 1903 to 1911. He was thirty-eight years old and in his prime when he accepted an offer to move on to New York, the nation's newspaper capital, and take over the management of the *Fourth Estate,* a weekly published for news-

[5] *Editor and Publisher,* v. 1, June 29, 1901, p. 4.

[6] Seventh birthday number of *Editor and Publisher,* v. 8, July 4, 1908, p. 4.

[7] Mott, *American Magazines,* v. 4, p. 243.

[8] Marlen Pew, "Story of the Rise of *Editor & Publisher,*" *Editor & Publisher,* v. 67, July 21, 1934, p. 34.

papermen. Then the very next year he had the opportunity to buy a majority interest in a competing journal and find out what he could do on his own. The first number of *Editor and Publisher* under his ownership was issued April 6, 1912.

Brown was a man of unusual capacities and character. He possessed business sense in a high degree, but he also had high ideals and a sense of public responsibility. Distinguished in appearance, he commanded respect wherever he went. He made acquaintances easily, and for many years he was the center of an increasingly large circle of friends who held him in affectionate regard. His influence was not limited to his own country; he was a participant in many international organizations, a Chevalier of the Legion of Honor of France, and an honorary member of the Company of Newspaper Makers of London and of the International Circulation Managers' Association. He joined with Walter Williams, of the University of Missouri School of Journalism, in the organization of the first Press Congresses of the World.

In his introductory editorial statement, Brown declared his intention "to maintain the best traditions of American journalism," and he promised to "fight the evils within and without the trade." [9] He crusaded from the first against bad advertising, press agentry abuses, attempts to undermine the freedom of the press, and frauds in the news. But Brown was not conducting a paper devoted mainly to crusading or muckraking. He retained Blanchard as editor for the first four years of his ownership, continuing good coverage of the newspaper field. In fact, such reporting could now be more thorough with the added space available in issues of twenty pages a week. A country-wide staff of regional and metropolitan correspondents furnishing occasional stories was set up and has been continued ever since. A striking increase in advertising and in size was notable as soon as Brown assumed management of the paper. Before nine months were up, he gave it a firmer financial foundation by doubling the subscription price; thus he met the two-dollar rate of the *Fourth Estate*—with a better paper.

Editor and Publisher had from the first issued special numbers when the country's newspapermen gathered in New York

[9] *Editor and Publisher,* v. 11, April 6, 1912, p. 8.

JAMES WRIGHT BROWN, 1873–1959

Brown purchased *Editor & Publisher* in 1912 and made it indispensable to editors, publishers, and advertisers. His sons now carry on the tradition. Photograph by Jean Raeburn.

to attend the annual conventions of the American Newspaper Publishers' Association and the Associated Press. But the first such number planned under Brown's ownership was amazing, running to 126 pages, and overflowing with interesting contents. Among other things, it contained what was called "A General History of American Journalism," printed and illustrated in de luxe style to occupy thirty-nine pages.[10] This was followed by histories of the Associated Press and the United Press by Melville E. Stone and Roy W. Howard respectively, and then sixteen pages devoted to sketches of "A Few Newspapers of Today." In succeeding years the journal's large special numbers for the May conventions in New York became an important part of its service to its readers. After 1922, when the American Society of Newspaper Editors was founded, its Washington meetings received attention in special editions; and coverage of the conventions of advertising and circulation organizations and other groups was also important.

In 1915 the founding date of the merged *Journalist* was adopted as *Editor and Publisher's* own, and in its issue for March 15 it jumped its volume numbering from 14 to 47. Two months later the "and" in its title was changed to an ampersand, which has become a kind of trademark of *Editor & Publisher*. The journal was flourishing, with consistent increases in advertising, circulation, and number of pages. In 1925 it absorbed *Newspaperdom,* then being issued semimonthly.[11] Two years later it took over its lagging rival, the *Fourth Estate*. Circulation had now reached nine thousand.

James Wright Brown had a native gift for surrounding himself with a cooperative and able staff. In 1922 he recruited

[10] April 26, 1913. The first sixteen pages dealt with ancient hieroglyphics and the like, Greek and Latin writing, and early German and English news-sheets and newsbooks. Unfortunately, the whole performance contained many errors of fact, implication, and conclusion. The representation of the front page of *Publick Occurrences* was faked. Editor Blanchard's note under the portrait of the author contained a fairy story about extensive travels in Europe undertaken to produce the first sixteen pages, but it is obvious that the compiler need have traveled no farther than to the New York Public Library at Fifth Avenue and Forty-second Street.

[11] *Newspaperdom* had been started as a monthly, had at times been a weekly, and had experienced various changes in ownership. When Brown bought it, he issued it for six months under the title *Advertising,* before merging it with *Editor & Publisher*. See Mott, *American Magazines,* v. 4, p. 244.

Marlen Edwin Pew, then serving as general manager of the International Press Service, and two years later made him editor of *Editor & Publisher*—a position he held until his death in 1936. Pew was an excellent man for the post. Experienced in all departments of newspaper work, high-minded, enterprising, forthright in comment, he gave the journal to which he had been called both the tone and the extension in service that Brown desired. Pew began his "Shop Talk at Thirty" in October 1926; this was and has remained an informal commentary department relegated to the last page of the magazine, but often read first by its subscribers. Originally designed as a supplementary editorial page, the pungency and force of Pew's writing soon made it a leading feature.

Another department initiated by Pew soon after he became editor was "Our Own World of Letters," a book review section by James Melvin Lee, head of the journalism department at New York University. Lee's work under this heading constitutes the most consistently excellent reviewing of books related to journalism that has appeared in any periodical. Upon his death in 1929, reviews for the department were written by various staff members for a few years. In 1946 Professor Roscoe Ellard of Columbia University began contributing book reviews, at first weekly and then less frequently. Since Ellard's death in 1960, Ray Erwin, staff feature writer, has provided notices about books in the journalism field.

Another distinguished contribution by Lee was a series of six articles on "The Growth and Development of American Journalism," published every other week beginning November 10, 1917, which formed the basis for Lee's *History of American Journalism,* first of the "modern" works in this field. Brown's travels abroad opened sources of information about the foreign press, and in the twenties and thirties *Editor & Publisher* was especially rich in such materials. The first of its International Numbers appeared May 22, 1919; it ran to 172 pages and was truly worldwide in scope. The number for June 19, 1926, included two handsome supplements with special covers, one entitled "Greater France" and the other "Britain and Progress." Both were well patronized by foreign advertisers.

Many columns, departments, and series have appeared as

features of *Editor & Publisher* for longer or shorter periods. "Hunches" and "Dollar Pullers" were back-of-the-book departments of practical hints in the 1920's. "Romances of American Journalism" was the overall title of a series of attractive stories about leading newspaper figures by different writers; it appeared irregularly for two or three decades, beginning in the early 1920's. Much more recent have been "Ray Erwin's Column" of amusing and curious miscellany and Roy H. Copperud's "Editorial Workshop," dealing with the proper use of words and phrases. The quadrennial polls of newspaper preferences for presidential candidates have been a feature since the 1936 campaign.[12]

One of the great *Editor & Publisher* services initiated by James Wright Brown and consistently expanded by those who have followed him in the conduct of the paper has been the collection and presentation of statistics and other data of the newspaper industry. Such compilations have supplemented the regular editorial matter in such a way and to such an extent as to make this journal not only unrivaled but indispensable in its field.

From its beginning *Editor & Publisher* was a strong advocate of honest circulation statements.[13] In 1908 it was printing weekly a "Roll of Honor" listing the names of newspapers allowing the Association of American Advertisers to make circulation audits of their books. Only twenty-four papers were listed at the beginning, but the number grew steadily. The organization of the Audit Bureau of Circulations in 1914 and its gradual acceptance led to the substitution of a list of ABC members for the "Roll of Honor," and then to a semiannual listing of circulations and advertising rates of newspapers, be-

[12] It should be noted that in figuring percentages of support for each candidate, *Editor & Publisher* used as the base, not the total number making a partisan declaration of alignment, nor the total number of papers published, but the number of dailies responding in its polls (including the "independents"). It is not improbable that most of those that did not respond should be added to the "independents." See F. L. Mott, *American Journalism, 1690–1960* (New York, 1962), p. 719, nn. 2, 3; p. 858, n. 1.

[13] It is sad to state, however, that as long as Shale owned *Editor and Publisher,* he never furnished a sworn statement of his own circulation for the Ayer directory.

ginning in the number for June 1, 1918. On the following January 11, *Editor & Publisher* was able to present what it declared was "the first complete list of advertising rates [of American newspapers] ever compiled," including over two thousand English-language papers. Such lists were continued at the midyear for some time even after the big annual directories were begun.

The first of these directories appeared as a supplement to the number for January 28, 1922. It was called the "Seventh Semi-Annual Listing," but it was much more comprehensive than its predecessors, containing not only circulations and rates, but a directory of advertising agencies, one of syndicates, and lists of British, Cuban, Mexican, Japanese, and Chinese papers. Next year the data were even more extensive, and the compilation was called *International Year Book.* It was issued as a separate section to regular subscribers and was offered in hard binding for an extra payment. This was only a beginning; successive *Year Books* gave more personnel information, lists of papers in more foreign countries, more data about associations, the faculties of schools of journalism, bibliographies of books in the field, and so on and on. In 1945 the *International Year Book* became a separate annual publication included in the regular subscription price, a "53rd issue." Finally it was completely divorced from the weekly in 1959, carrying its own price tag.

Somewhat the same course was followed by *Editor & Publisher's Market Guide,* which was designed to furnish advertisers data for their study of potential markets. It had its beginning in analyses of markets in various states and the larger cities presented in special numbers through 1918–1923, and the first comprehensive report appeared in the issue of December 3, 1924. It was furnished as an annual supplement, until it achieved separate publication in 1942. The "Annual Syndicate Directory" also began in 1924, to continue as the "Second Section" of a summer or fall number. For many years extensive tables of page and paper sizes of newspapers were printed semiannually. The first linage report covered the advertising of five hundred papers for the first six months of 1922; these tabulations became a semiannual feature. By 1930 *Editor & Publisher* was buying such data from Media Records, Inc., and eventually published them more frequently. And finally, a monthly "Equipment Review" section began in 1933.

In the meantime, the journal maintained its policy of excellent news coverage of its field. It gave increased attention in the 1940's and 1950's to developments in the advertising world, and by the 1960's the line under its cover nameplate read: "Spot News and Features About Newspapers, Advertisers and Agencies." In 1956 it recognized the increasing use of color in newspapers by bringing out a "Spring Color Issue," which has become an annual feature. It contains a compilation of color linage data, color advertisers, and has general articles on color-printing in newspapers.

Marlen Pew died in 1936, to be succeeded by Arthur T. Robb, who had been managing editor since 1924. Charles T. Stuart came to *Editor & Publisher* from a varied career in promotion and finance to become its advertising director in 1931; ten years later he became general manager, and for a full decade before his death in 1959 his title was "publisher." James Wright Brown, Jr., who had studied at the University of Missouri's School of Journalism, joined the staff in 1925, serving as circulation manager, as business manager, and then president and publisher. In 1948 he withdrew from the organization, but returned a few years later as vice-president and general manager. His brother, Robert U. Brown, a Dartmouth graduate, joined *Editor & Publisher* in 1936, holding various editorial positions until 1944 when he followed Robb as editor. In 1953 he became president of the publishing company as well. Their father, "full of honor and years," died in 1959. Bob Brown's aggressive policy of continuing and increasing service to newspaper publishing and his ability in organization sustained the position and prestige of *Editor & Publisher*. He has been national president of Sigma Delta Chi, the great association of city press clubs and school of journalism societies, and has held other positions of honor and responsibility.

By mid-century *Editor & Publisher* had become more definitely a "special pleader" for the newspaper industry than in its early years. It strongly resented criticisms of the newspapers and of advertising practices; it was deeply antagonistic to radio and television (the latter it always called "tv" in lower-case even in headlines); and the Republican party leanings of a large majority of metropolitan publishers may be assumed to have prompted its frequent attacks on Democratic policies and activities. *Editor & Publisher's* founder had been a friend of both Woodrow Wilson and Herbert Hoover and had kept his paper nonpartisan; the breakdown of the tradition seems to have come with Roosevelt and his NRA, when newspapers fought hard and with some success to get out from under the wings of the Blue Eagle.

In 1944 *Editor & Publisher* page and type sizes were slightly decreased, but the number of pages continued to grow. It stated in its 75th edition, 1959, that its gross annual revenue even then exceeded $1,250,000.[14] The subscription rate was raised to $5.00 in 1947, to $6.50 in 1954, and as of 1964 was unchanged. The *Market Guide* price had risen, by this time, to $10.00 a copy and that of the *International Year Book* to $8.00. By 1964 *Editor & Publisher* had a circulation of over twenty thousand and a remarkably steady renewal rate.

In its early years the journal's offices were in the Pulitzer Building on Park Row, the great newspaper street of New York City; then for many years it occupied the seventeenth floor of the Times Tower at 42nd Street and Broadway, where it was a mecca for visiting journalists. In 1961 its business offices were moved to 850 Third Avenue.

Few large industries have been so faithfully served by a single journal as newspaper publishing has long been by *Editor & Publisher*.*

[14] *Editor & Publisher,* "75th Anniversary Edition," June 27, 1959, sec. 2, p. 114.

* This historical sketch was written in 1961, and updated somewhat in 1964.

6

EVERYBODY'S MAGAZINE [1]

JOHN WANAMAKER, the famous Philadelphia merchant, had been Postmaster General under President Harrison and was interested in many public and philanthropic activities. In 1896 he purchased the great A. T. Stewart department store in New York, and three years later this New York branch of Wanamaker's founded *Everybody's Magazine*.

John Wanamaker himself seems to have had little or nothing to do with the magazine, leaving it to Robert C. Ogden, his New York partner. More than half of the contents of *Everybody's* in its first year was purchased directly from the Pearson Publishing Company, of London, and consisted of serials, short stories, articles, and poems, with illustrations, which had already appeared in the *Royal Magazine* of that city. Most of the writers were little known in the United States, though some of them—like Rafael Sabatini and Ethel M. Dell—were later to win American popularity. The Baroness Emmusca Orczy was the leading serialist the first year or two. Among contributions from this side of the Atlantic were potboilers by Theodore Dreiser and Rupert Hughes. There were series on new technological developments and great American industries by George

[1] TITLES: (1) *Everybody's Magazine,* 1899–1923; (2) *Everybody's,* 1923–29. (The word "Magazine" was dropped in the half-title and captions in 1921, but retained on the cover until 1923.)

FIRST ISSUE: September 1899. LAST ISSUE: March 1929.

PERIODICITY: Monthly. Vol. 1, Sept.–Dec. 1899; 2–59, regular semiannual volumes, 1900–1928; 60, three numbers, Jan.–March 1929. Merged into *Romance.*

PUBLISHERS: John Wanamaker, Sept. 1899—May 1903 (under name North American Company, Sept. 1899—Nov. 1900); Ridgway-Thayer Company (Erman Jesse Ridgway, John Adams Thayer and George W. Wilder), June 1903—Sept. 1906; Ridgway Company (E. J. Ridgway, pres. 1906–16; James H. Gannon, 1916–26; Joseph A. Moore, 1926–29), Oct. 1906—March 1929.

EDITORS: Chauncey Montgomery M'Govern, 1899–1900; John O'Hara Cosgrave, 1900–1903, 1906–11; E. J. Ridgway, 1903–6; Trumbull White, 1911–14; William Hard, 1915; Howard Wheeler, 1916–18; S. V. Roderick, 1919–21; Sewell Haggard, 1921–25; Frank Quinn, 1925–26; Oscar Graeve, 1927; William Corcoran, 1928–29.

INDEXES: *Poole's Index, Annual Library Index.*

H. Perry and others, and much emphasis on camera pictures illustrating American scenes and situations of current interest. Printing and illustration were attractive, and the magazine sold for ten cents a monthly number, or a dollar a year.

The editor for the first year was Chauncey Montgomery M'Govern. Then, with the intention of reducing the amount of English material, the editorial management was turned over to the new firm of Doubleday and Page, who were beginning periodicals of their own, but who capitalized on Walter H. Page's skill and prestige in the field by undertaking advisement and consultation with other magazines.[2] Page first suggested Joel Chandler Harris for the editorship of *Everybody's Magazine*,[3] and when he refused, named John O'Hara Cosgrave. The new editor had been born in Australia, educated in New Zealand, and trained as a journalist in San Francisco. Better known names now began appearing in the by-lines of *Everybody's* stories and articles—Rudyard Kipling and S. R. Crockett from overseas; Frank Norris, O. Henry, Charles Major, Owen Wister, Justus Miles Forman, Mary E. Wilkins, and James Whitcomb Riley from the United States.

More attention was now paid to news events and to current political and economic problems. The capture of the Filipino chieftain, Aguinaldo, was featured through his own story (August 1901) and the narrative of General Funston, his captor (September 1901). Pointing a prophetic finger toward the magazine's future muckraking was a series by David Graham Phillips beginning with an article on David B. Hill (November 1902).

Some departments and series were designed to appeal to women readers. The earliest was entitled "How to Make Money," and consisted of practical suggestions for pin-money projects. Bessie Van Vorst began a series on "The Woman That Toils" in October 1902, and this was followed the next

[2] *World's Work* was the first of the Doubleday-Page periodicals; *Country Life in America* and *Garden Magazine* came a little later. Page was advising *Frank Leslie's Magazine*. Also the firm had just taken in hand the American publication of the new *Monthly Review*, of London. See *Publishers' Weekly*, v. 58, Nov. 3, 1900, p. 1234.

[3] Julia C. Harris, *Life and Letters of Joel Chandler Harris* (Boston, 1918), p. 433.

year by Lillian Pettingill's articles on domestic servants titled "Toilers of the Home." Meantime Mary Manners was writing on "The Unemployed Rich." "Little Stories of Real Life," a department of short short stories, for years one of the magazine's most popular features, began in October 1902 with two stories by Sidney Porter (O. Henry).

By 1903 *Everybody's Magazine* had achieved 150,000 circulation, largely by dint of low clubbing rates and direct mail advertising; but it needed more intimate management and better promotion. The public was too prone to regard it as merely "one of the departments of the big department store of John Wanamaker" [4]—which is what it was, of course. When the magazine was sold in May 1903, devoted management and bold promotion were precisely what it got. The selling price was $75,000.

Head of the new firm was Erman Jesse Ridgway, who had learned magazine publishing in the Munsey organization, where he had served for nearly nine years. His active partner was John Adams Thayer, primarily an advertising man, who had won his spurs on the *Ladies' Home Journal.* Third man in the organization was George Warren Wilder, president of the Butterick Publishing Company, which published the *Delineator* [5] and other periodicals. Wilder was, in the main, a silent partner, though he occasionally made helpful suggestions to Ridgway and Thayer; [6] his chief function was to furnish the capital necessary for purchase and promotion. Though Ridgway was editorial director, Cosgrave, who now had a financial interest in the magazine, was retained as managing editor. In fact, Cosgrave held the job which Thayer designated as "acting editor" [7] for more than ten years—much the longest of *Everybody's* editorships. He was managing editor for three years under Page and for an equal term under Ridgway; then after Ridgway had started his *Weekly* and was giving it his full attention, Cosgrave was called editor-in-chief.

[4] *Journalist,* v. 33, May 23, 1903, p. 73.

[5] See F. L. Mott, *A History of American Magazines,* v. 3 (Cambridge, Mass., 1938), pp. 481–90.

[6] *Everybody's* v. 26, Jan. 1912, p. 56. See also John Adams Thayer, *Astir* (Boston, 1910), pp. 229–30, 250–51.

[7] Thayer, *Astir,* p. 254.

The new management increased the number of pages in the magazine by a third, and made it very attractive with copious and varied illustration. About a third of the content was fiction (by O. Henry, Holman F. Day, Juliet Wilbor Tompkins, Will Irwin, and others); and there were timely articles on politics, history, and national affairs (by Alfred Henry Lewis and Bailey Millard), descriptive pieces about places at home and abroad, a monthly stage section, a department called "With the Procession," which took the liberal side in politics and also commented on art and literature, and a back-of-the-book section, "With *Everybody's* Publishers," in which Thayer and Ridgway boasted about the magazine's progress.

They had something to boast about, for November 1903 showed not only a substantial circulation increase, but 160 pages of advertising, and a small net profit.[8] But it was Thomas William Lawson, the Boston stockmarket speculator, who really put the magazine on what appeared to be Easy Street: later it was found that the street sign had been misread—it was Uneasy Street. At any rate, Wilder, hearing that Lawson had resolved to turn informer and acquaint the American people with the wiles and manipulations and skulduggery of Standard Oil, Amalgamated Copper, *et al.*, suggested to Ridgway and Thayer that this might be the sensational series for which they had been praying. After a campaign of persuasion, Lawson was induced to use *Everybody's Magazine* as his medium of exposure. He agreed to contribute the articles without remuneration, but he required Ridgway-Thayer to agree to spend $50,000 in advertising them.[9]

"Frenzied Finance" was one of the four or five most famous contributions to the journalistic genre later known as "muckraking." It ran for twenty months, beginning in July 1904, and was followed by supplementary chapters, including some fiction, through 1906 and 1907. These chapters and articles dealt with many financial operations, gave details of many "deals," and brought the reader behind the scenes to meet famous and infamous financial and industrial leaders. Their aim appeared

[8] *Everybody's*, v. 9, Dec. 1903, p. 850.

[9] Thayer, *Astir*, chap. xiii, "The Discovery of Tom Lawson." At first Lawson demanded that this money should be offered as a prize for an essay on the series, but he was later dissuaded.

to be to expose the "system" by which the people were robbed to swell the fortunes of the rich. In the penultimate chapter of "Frenzied Finance," Lawson expresses this aim in a kind of vision:

Then the scene changed to the great banquet-hall at Sherry's, with Jimmy Hyde in his white satin breeches, his violets, and his foreign decorations, the center of a gay throng of bediamonded women in silks and tulles and men in strange apparel. And as I remembered that this sumptuous scene, this matchless luxury, were paid for out of dollars, blood- and tear-soaked, wrung cent by cent from the honest toilers of the land—that these dollars meant sacrifice and abstinence, chilled bodies and scant food, fireless hearths and dreary days—all that there might be [of] a widow's mite or an orphan's livelihood—a fierce rage rose within me.[10]

But more genuine was the author's fierce rage against his opponents in some of his own financial contests, and his wish to pay off old scores. Sincere also was the desire of the publishers to build up the circulation of their magazine.

Tom Lawson's style was melodramatic, highly colored, spectacular, feverish. If the finance he was describing was "frenzied," so was the manner of the author. He wrote on the run, without the restraints of literary discipline, factual exactitude, or space limitation. His verbosity habitually led him to overrun the space allotted; and since he always furnished copy at the last possible minute, his contributions frequently had to be continued into the advertising section. Cosgrave practically lived in Boston, acting as monitor, editor, and chore-boy for the great man, during the entire period of Lawson's contributorship. In choosing a passage to stand as an example of Lawsonism, we take, more or less at random, the introduction to Part III of "Frenzied Finance." It begins with one of those little romantic anecdotes of which the author was fond: an African explorer who, having escaped many perils of attack by the savages and wild animals and all the dangers of the forest, was finally engulfed and swallowed up in a soft and insidious quicksand. The application:

Among men, it is as in the wilds. Silent craft is as dangerous as brute strength. More to be dreaded in the world of finance than the

[10] *Everybody's,* v. 14, Feb. 1906, advertising p. 67.

HUNTING THE TIGER WITH *EVERYBODY'S*

This cover appeared on *Everybody's Magazine* for October 1904 while Thomas William Lawson's muckraking series, "Frenzied Finance," was scorching the pages of the magazine.

daring plunger is the "unco quid" [sic] banker, whose gold bricks are served out to unwary investors from under a cloak of sanctity. In the course of this incidentful story my readers have been shown many strange men in dark places. With the pirates of finance and their ways there has been opportunity to establish an intimate acquaintance. It is now the turn of another and more subtle contingent, the disguised buccaneers, a group of whom at this juncture come into my chronicle. I refer to the "smug men of frenzied finance," those "O-Lord,-we-are-all-that-we-should-be,-thanks-to-Thy-having-created-things-for-our-special-benefit" creatures of the dollar world.

When these white-wax-plated warriors of the golden highway are marshaled for the easel, the inkpot must be discarded and the quill reversed lest their immaculately glazed hides should be stained or punctured. So with the feather end of my weapon, I shall run over their enameled-for-inspection surface and lay-in their outlines in a solution of smudge juice and pansy extract.[11]

The reaction to the Lawson romance was mixed. Readers apparently welcomed it, though $300,000 (Lawson is said to have added over $250,000 to Ridgway-Thayer's $50,000 to promote "Frenzied Finance")[12] would have made any well-selected feature a big circulation builder. It may have exerted a reformatory effect in various directions, as its author and publishers frequently claimed but never proved. There is no doubt that many of the crooks attacked deserved all the excoriation Lawson administered, and for a time the lash in his hand made him a great man. Ridgway was an awed admirer of his leading contributor. At a public dinner in Lawson's honor, Ridgway, as a climax to his eulogy, uttered the following orotund sentence: "When God needed a father of his country, He raised a Washington; when He needed an emancipator for the country, He raised a Lincoln; when He needed a savior of the country, He raised a Lawson." William Travers Jerome, who followed Ridgway, rather spoiled the effect by remarking that in his opinion, when God created Lawson He needed someone to raise hell.[13]

"Frenzied Finance" certainly got a "play" in the press, espe-

[11] *Ibid.,* v. 14, Jan. 1906, p. 73.
[12] *Ibid.,* v. 18, March 1908, p. 432.
[13] Thayer, *Astir,* pp. 284–85.

cially through the personal attacks involved. A western mining operator named Greene stated in page advertisements in his home paper that he was going east to "settle with" his maligner, Lawson, but the Boston crowds who assembled to witness Colonel Greene's arrival were disappointed that he did not emerge from his Pullman shooting. The expected duel proved to be a verbal one. Various lawsuits were brought against Lawson, including a criminal libel action by C. W. Barron, the financial journalist; but he emerged unscathed from these ordeals in the courts. Another financial editor, Denis Donohoe, wrote a series of articles entitled "The Truth about Frenzied Finance" for *Public Opinion,* exposing or purporting to expose the Lawson operations.[14] Norman Hapgood, editor of the liberal *Collier's,* carried on a controversy with Lawson in May and June 1905. "We have shown entire disbelief in Mr. Lawson's honesty," wrote Hapgood.[15] In a little history of *Everybody's* which the advertising man George French wrote some time later, there is an acute comment: "People never found out what 'Frenzied Finance' was all about, or what it was for. Lawson promised to tell, but never did. But it was great fun to read the excoriating stuff Lawson furnished." [16]

Finally Lawson tired of the game. On December 7, 1907, Ridgway was shocked when he read in the papers a statement by Lawson which ended with the following paragraph:

> I have devoted three and a half years of my time and some millions of my fortune to reform work in the interests of the public. Beginning January 1st, I shall allow the public to do their own reforming, and I shall devote my time and capital exclusively to my own business of stock "gambling" in Wall and State Streets—particularly Wall Street—for the purpose of recouping the millions I have donated to my public work. P.S.—One of the oldest of human laws and as immutable is "the devil take the hindmost." [17]

A few days later, Ridgway wrote Lawson a long, sad letter. "I can't help feeling, Mr. Lawson," he said, "that this is an awful thing you have done." Lawson retorted: "You talk of

[14] *Public Opinion,* v. 38, Jan. 19–Feb. 18, 1905.

[15] *Collier's* v. 35, May 13, 1905, p. 8.

[16] *Twentieth Century,* v. 6, July 1912, p. 49.

[17] *Everybody's,* v. 18, Feb. 1908, p. 287. Ridgway's reply and Lawson's rejoinder are on the following pages.

what I owe the people. What do I owe to the gelatine-spined shrimps? What have the saffron-blooded apes done for me or mine that I should halt any decisions to match their lightning-change ten-above-ten-below-zero chameleon-hued loyalty?"

In the course of Ridgway's protest, he said: "While I cannot but regret the damage your announcement must inevitably do to the prestige of *Everybody's* Magazine, you gave it its prestige, and if anyone has a right to take it away, you have." This was a very handsome acknowledgment, but it ignores the fact that while Tom Lawson's opus was running in the magazine, its general content had been brought to a level comparing favorably with that of any current fifteen-cent magazine.

Thayer tells with some amusement, in his autobiography, of Hall Caine's remark when he heard of *Everybody's* big gain in circulation in 1904–1905: "Yes, I expected it. That is the American magazine which is publishing my new story." [18] But it is by no means impossible, or even improbable, that Hall Caine, long a best seller in America, did make an important contribution to the magazine's growing prosperity. The publishers surely expected this, for they paid $10,000 for the serial: it was *The Prodigal Son.*[19] Other popular serials followed—Rex Beach's *The Spoilers,* Jack London's *Before Adam,* Booth Tarkington's *The Quest of Quesnay,* and so on. Dorothy Canfield, Stewart Edward White, Charles G. D. Roberts, Joseph C. Lincoln, and Zona Gale contributed short fiction, and there were still O. Henry stories. A rather good department of anecdotes called "Under the Spreading Chestnut Tree" began in 1905 and ran for many years. The "Little Stories of Real Life" continued to be excellent.

General nonfiction was interesting and well illustrated—articles on the San Francisco disaster by James Hopper and Will Irwin, features from Europe by Vance Thompson, Leroy Scott's sketches of the Russian revolution, nostalgic home-town recollections of Eugene Wood and Hugh Pendexter (the former a long time contributor to *Everybody's*), Hamlin Garland's psychic observations entitled *The Shadow World,* and so on. President Theodore Roosevelt opened an exciting literary

[18] Thayer, *Astir,* p. 257.
[19] *Everybody's,* v. 11, July 1904, p. 144.

and scientific controversy when he went after the "nature fakirs" in an interview given to Edward B. Clark and published in the number for June 1907. Carrying a strong chorus to Tom Lawson were Charles Edward Russell, Will Payne, Upton Sinclair, William Hard, Edwin Lefèvre, and others. Russell especially, with his series on the beef trust and a later one on social conditions abroad entitled "Soldiers of the Common Good," and still another called "Where Did You Get It, Gentlemen?" wrote literature of exposure on a comparatively high level.

Circulation, kicked high by the boot of the newspaper advertising of "Frenzied Finance," soared in late 1904 to something less than a million, more than half of it from newsstand sales. During most of the run of "Frenzied Finance" the magazine printed about 750,000 copies. The issue for May 1905 had 120 pages of advertising at the ruinously low price of $350 a page,[20] but soon rates caught up with a somewhat more stable circulation; and by 1907 the magazine, with a little over half a million circulation at fifteen cents a copy, was carrying liberal advertising—sometimes as much as 180 pages in an issue—at $500 a page. Thayer had excluded, from the time of his first connection with *Everybody's,* all patent medicine advertising. In 1913 the magazine published a list of its heaviest advertisers during the decade just closed: Postum Cereals (Post Toasties, Grape Nuts, Postum) was first, with about $111,500; Victor Talking Machine second, with $86,300; and Eastman Kodak third, with $72,400.[21]

At the height of the monthly's success, Ridgway conceived a grandiose plan for a national weekly; Wilder agreed with the proposal, but Thayer opposed it. Finally, in 1906, Thayer sold out to his partners rather than join in the risks of the new periodical. It was rumored that Thayer received "several hundred thousand dollars" when he left the company; [22] at any rate, he was well paid for his three years' work, and was probably the luckiest of all the men who put effort and money into *Everybody's.*

Ridgway's Weekly lasted only a few months, but the monthly

20 *Ibid.,* v. 12, June 1905, p. 857.
21 *Ibid.,* v. 29, July 1913, p. 144.
22 *Critic,* v. 49, Sept. 1906, p. 198.

continued to prosper, in spite of the panic of 1907. In that year it cleared over $200,000.[23] In that year also, it offered to the public bonds amounting to $200,000 of a new half-million issue; it gave as its reason for the new financing its plan to erect a new plant—a project never carried out. In 1908 it offered $150,000 more of its stock, since "one of our largest stockholders was caught in the panic." [24] The next year the Ridgway Publishing Company was purchased by the Butterick Publishing Company. Wilder had major holdings in both. Butterick was capitalized at $12,000,000 and Ridgway at $1,000,000; Butterick issued $3,000,000 of new stock and exchanged it for Ridgway stock three for one. Tom Lawson was not the only one who could play at stock deals.

Lawson's defection had by no means ruined the magazine; indeed, during the four years following that event it was probably a better moneymaker than at any other time during its existence. In that quadrennium, 1908–1911, with a circulation over half a million, *Everybody's* led the field of American general monthlies in its volume of advertising. In 1909 it averaged over 150 pages of paid matter per month. Thayer had been a genius as an advertising manager; but Robert Frothingham, who followed him, was even more successful. Another factor in the magazine's prosperity during these years was its secession from the American News Company, which for many years had exercised a dictatorship over the distribution of magazines to newsstands the country over. Circulation Manager John F. Bresnahan devised in 1906 a system of distributing *Everybody's* and *Ridgway's* through newspaper wholesalers who were independent of the American News Company. Six years later, Bresnahan consolidated his successes by organizing Ridgway's, Butterick's, and other periodicals into the Publishers News Company.[25]

Fiction writers in these years, besides such familiar contribu-

[23] *Everybody's,* v. 18, June 1908, advertising section insert between pp. 24 and 25.

[24] *Ibid.,* v. 25, Aug. 1911, p. 287. This was Charles W. Morse, a banker, who was sentenced to a term in a federal prison. See *Twentieth Century,* v. 6, July 1912, p. 51.

[25] Roy Quinlan, "The Story of Magazine Distribution," *Magazine Week,* v. 1, Oct. 19, 1953, pp. 4–5.

tors as Beach, Tarkington, and Zona Gale, were William J. Locke, Leonard Merrick, E. W. Hornung, Lloyd Osbourne, Eleanor Hallowell Abbott, Harvey J. O'Higgins, Arthur Train, Kathleen Norris, and Dorothy Canfield. In 1912 the magazine offered $10,000 in prizes for the best solutions to Mary Roberts Rinehart's mystery, "The Case of Jennie Brice." But despite changing trends, *Everybody's* still emphasized nonfiction, and still stuck to muckraking. Judge Lindsey's autobiography, *The Beast and the Jungle,* was a feature of 1909 which the magazine advertised to the tune of $50,000.[26] Richard Washburn Child contributed two series in 1910—one on the railways, and another on the tariff on wool. In the same year, Lincoln Steffens wrote a series called *It* on the political power of organized business, and in the closing months of 1911 he engaged in a remarkable debate on free speech versus censorship with Publisher Ridgway. Ex-Senator Frank J. Cannon had a notable series in 1911 called *Under the Prophet in Utah.* C. P. Connolly wrote on *Big Business and the Bench* in 1912.

Then, in 1912–1913, Tom Lawson reappeared with *The Remedy,* a disquisition which he had promised his readers seven years before, but for which he had later claimed the people were not yet ready. Now, presumably, they were ready; but the great solution turned out to be only "a crusade to rout the sinister forces of the underworld of Wall Street"—in short, the abolition of stock exchange gambling. There was as much frenzied prose as ever, and more frenzied blackface capitals, but readers did not rally 'round as they once had. A big advertising campaign brought an average increase of less than a hundred thousand in the circulation of the Lawson numbers, which ended in July 1913. Some months later, Ridgway wrote frankly that muckraking was no longer a paying business. He thought government had reformed, anyway, and said *Everybody's* would thenceforth be "constructive." He added, however, that since circulation responded to fighting and attack, the magazine would now take up arms against the Demon Rum.[27] This it did through prize letters on the subject, but there is no evidence that Ridgway received the help he hoped for by this campaign.

26 *Everybody's,* v. 21, Dec. 1909, p. 863.
27 *Ibid.,* v. 30, April 1914, p. 505.

And he was beginning to need help. Circulation, which had taken a small spurt in 1911, bringing it over six hundred thousand, dropped off slowly but steadily thereafter. An advertising decline began in 1911.[28]

In that year Trumbull White, an experienced magazine man, came from *Adventure* to take Cosgrave's place on *Everybody's*, with the valuable assistance of Gilman Hall, who had come from *Ainslee's*. The magazine was as attractive as ever—more attractive, indeed, with color and the illustrations of such artists as Jay Hambidge, S. J. Woolf, N. C. Wyeth, May Wilson Preston, Oliver Herford, James Montgomery Flagg, and others. Departments included Franklin P. Adams' "Everybody's Almanac," John Parr's financial section (begun 1913), Clayton Hamilton's "The Players," the perennial "Little Stories of Real Life," Coningsby Dawson's (it had been J. B. Kerfoot's) "A Row of Books," and "Under the Spreading Chestnut Tree." But in May 1915 all departments except the "Chestnut Tree" were abandoned in favor of one devoted to editorial comment on current events called "Keep Posted," which ran for almost two years.

A feature of 1913 was a series of excerpts from Captain Robert F. Scott's diary, entitled *The Uttermost South*, and one of the next year was the debate on socialism by Morris Hillquit and Father Ryan. In 1914 also came William Hard's "constructive" series *Better Business*.

By 1914 *Everybody's* was keeping close to war developments. Frederick Palmer wrote a series on the occupation of the city of Vera Cruz by United States naval forces, and later was *Everybody's* correspondent on the European front. A prize contest for letters on the question, "What Is a Christian?" in 1914–1915 resulted from what was conceived to be a popular interest in the morality of war. But soon theorizing gave place to a more martial spirit. Theodore Roosevelt's "America—On Guard!" in January 1915 was a clarion call to military preparedness. The magazine favored compulsory military training. In January 1916 appeared a notable symposium entitled, "America's Neutrality as England Sees It," to which Lord Bryce, H. G. Wells, G. B. Shaw, G. K. Chesterton, and other

[28] *Ibid.*, v. 30, June 1914, p. 865.

famous Britons contributed. By 1917 all the leading articles pertained to the war, as did much of the fiction. "The Poetry of the War" was an interesting department. Lincoln Steffens and William G. Shepherd wrote on the Russian revolution, and Samuel Hopkins Adams had a series on German propaganda and American disloyalty. The great feature of 1918 was Brand Whitlock's *Belgium.* In 1919–1920 the magazine published two notable biographical serials—Irving Bacheller's life of Lincoln called *A Man for the Ages* and Vernon Kellogg's *The Story of Hoover.*

Fiction offerings in these years continued to be attractive; and there was a good deal about the theater, including articles by Alexander Woollcott. In late 1914, Shaw's *Pygmalion* was published in the pages of *Everybody's,* and *Great Catherine* in early 1915. Honoré Willsie's *Still Jim* and Owen Johnson's *Making Money* in 1915 were popular continued stories, Ernest Poole's *His Family* in the next year, and Joseph Hergesheimer's *Linda Condon* in 1919. Other fictioneers in the magazine were George Randolph Chester, Talbot Mundy, Henry Kitchell Webster, Edgar Wallace, and Ben Ames Williams.

Popular fiction was a fighting question with *Everybody's* in these years. In 1914, when Ridgway had to acknowledge at last that muckraking was played out, he apparently took a good long look at his chief competitor, *Cosmopolitan,* which was just then soaring toward a million circulation on the wings of Robert W. Chambers' sex-in-society serials. Ridgway claimed that *Everybody's* had lost circulation by refusing to use "tainted fiction." [29] In 1914 it conducted something of a crusade against such fiction and "the indecent stage."

Nevertheless, *Everybody's* kept to its half-million figure pretty steadily for a few years. Trumbull White gave up his editorial chair to William Hard in 1915, and Hard resigned it to Howard Wheeler in 1916. Wheeler developed an interesting page layout which emphasized margins by line illustrations and subheads. In November 1917, *Everybody's*—hitherto royal octavo in size—followed other magazines in adopting the quarto form. Ridgway withdrew from the publishing company, which continued to bear his name, in 1916.

[29] *Everybody's,* v. 30, June 1914, p. 865.

These changes indicated that all was not well with the magazine. Its content seemed well balanced and attractive during the First World War, but circulation declined to less than three hundred thousand. During S. V. Roderick's editorship, 1919–1921, there was a slight recovery, but in 1921 Sewell Haggard, whose creed was stated in the dictum, "Sheer entertainment is the ingredient essential to success,"[30] became editor, and *Everybody's* became an all-fiction magazine, with the motto, "If it's in *Everybody's* it's a good story." Page size came back to the old royal octavo, but with an increase in number of pages to 180, and the price was raised to twenty-five cents.

There were some distinguished contributors to the all-fiction *Everybody's.* A. S. M. Hutchinson's best-selling *If Winter Comes* was the leading serial in 1921. Hugh Walpole, Rafael Sabatini, Michael Arlen, E. Phillips Oppenheim, Achmed Abdullah, Mrs. Wilson Woodrow, and Samuel Merwin may be named as leading writers for the magazine in the twenties. Beginning in 1925 under Frank Quinn (there was a new editor nearly every year now) two "old" short stories were reprinted each month. Woodpulp paper for part of the magazine came in about that time; by 1927 it was all woodpulp.

In the mid-twenties some miscellaneous articles were used, especially sports stories; but from December 1926 contents were strictly limited to fiction, and even the old "Chestnut Tree" was chopped down. During the next three years each number carried two novelettes, two serial installments, and seven short stories. Circulation steadily declined to about fifty thousand. The last number was issued for March 1929, after which the magazine was merged into another Ridgway fiction periodical called *Romance,* under the title *Everybody's Combined with Romance;*[31] and thus it did its last ten-months' stretch ingloriously as a species of confession magazine.

Everybody's reminds one of the lady with a record, whose career was rather checkered. It would be pleasant to think that its reformatory zeal during the decade beginning in 1903 was

30 Doris Ulmann, *A Portrait Gallery of American Editors* (New York, 1925), p. 68.

31 The first number after the merger was called *Romance Combined with Everybody's.*

entirely sincere, but certain utterances of Ridgway, Thayer and Lawson convince us that it was not. However, *Everybody's* did publish a spate of readable material in its thirty years—some of it literature, and a lot of it good entertainment and information.

7

THE FREEMAN [1]

FRANCIS NEILSON was born in Birkenhead, England, with the surname of Butters, but later he took his mother's maiden name.[2] Both his father and mother were professional cooks. "Butters" might be all right for a cook, but the son was aiming for a stage career; and "Neilson" was obviously better for the theater. While playing in New York in the nineties, Neilson became much interested in Henry George's economic and political theories. When he returned to England, he went into politics himself and was elected to Parliament 1910–1915.

In 1915 Albert Jay Nock was in England, occupying himself, among other things, with making unofficial contacts that might be useful to Secretary of State William Jennings Bryan.[3] Nock was the son of a clergyman, and himself served in an Episcopal pastorate for several years; but for the five years preceding this visit to England, he had been a kind of associate member of that famous group of muckrakers that had just given up control of the *American Magazine*.[4] Brand Whitlock, United States Minister to Belgium, had given Nock a note of introduction to Neilson, and the two found they had many ideas and enthusiasms in common. Neilson had a book manuscript, anti-state in character, for which he had not been able to find a publisher. Nock convinced him that he could get it printed in the United

[1] TITLE: *The Freeman*.

FIRST ISSUE: March 17, 1920. LAST ISSUE: March 5, 1924.

PERIODICITY: Weekly. Semiannual volumes.

PUBLISHER: Freeman Corporation, New York, B. W. Huebsch, general manager.

EDITORS: Francis Neilson and Albert Jay Nock. Associate editors: Van Wyck Brooks (1921–24), (Clara) Suzanne La Follette (1921–24), Geroid Tanquary Robinson (1921–24), Walter G. Fuller (1921–22), Harold Kellock (1923–24).

INDEX: *Readers' Guide*.

[2] Francis Neilson, *My Life in Two Worlds* (2 vols.; Appleton, Wis., 1953). Parts of this work are valuable for *Freeman* backgrounds.

[3] Francis Neilson, *The Story of 'The Freeman,'* Supplement to the *American Journal of Economics and Sociology*, v. 6, Oct. 1946, p. 6. Issued separately.

[4] See F. L. Mott, *A History of American Magazines*, v. 3 (Cambridge, Mass., 1938), pp. 513–14.

States, and that he could find a literary career more easily in the newer land. So in that same year Neilson moved to New York, bringing his wife and two daughters.

His book, *How Diplomats Make War,* was published by young B. W. Huebsch anonymously, ("By a British Statesman"), with a signed introduction by Nock; and during the next winter Neilson lectured in a number of cities on "imperialist causes" of the war. In Chicago he encountered again Mrs. Helen Swift Morris, whom he had previously met in England. The year after, 1917, he was divorced, and Mrs. Morris proposed marriage to him.[5] Helen Swift had been a packing-house heiress, and she had married Edward Morris, who represented another meat-packing fortune; she was now a very wealthy widow with four grown children. She and Neilson were married that same year. One of the things made possible by Neilson's new affluence was his placing Nock on the staff of the *Nation* in 1918–1919 by paying his salary. In fact, Mrs. Neilson tried to buy the *Nation* for her husband and Nock to conduct, but Villard would not sell. She then decided to found a new weekly for them.

This was the *Freeman,* and the Neilsons and Nock agreed to disregard Chicago's literary pretensions and take it to New York. Perhaps the meat-packing capital's literary boom was waning by that time; at any rate, the founders of the new magazine set up headquarters at New York's Ritz-Carlton and began to organize staff, enlist contributors and make publishing arrangements.[6]

A notable staff was brought together. At the head of it were the two editors, Neilson and Nock. Neilson, fifty-three years old, with all his stage background, was a student by nature and largely self-educated. However, he lacked intellectual subtlety and charm of style. As the chief student of the *Freeman* history and file has observed, Neilson was "a simple man and something of a dupe." [7] Eventually, the rigors of editorship weighed

[5] Neilson, *My Life in Two Worlds,* p. 23.

[6] Neilson, *Story of 'The Freeman,'* p. 20.

[7] Susan Jane Turner, "A Short History of *The Freeman,* a Magazine of the Early Twenties, with Particular Attention to the Literary Criticism," unpub. diss. Columbia University, 1956. [See also, Turner, *A History of The Freeman, Literary Landmark of the Early Twenties* (New York, 1963).]

too heavily in the scale against the pleasures of travel, fishing, and golf. In a singularly revelatory sentence, Neilson later wrote of himself as "a man who at first agreed to send in [to the *Freeman*] only a few ideas because he wanted time to enjoy a life of leisure with his wife." [8] After the first year and a half of the *Freeman's* life, he did not do even that much. In contrast, Nock, forty-seven years old, was devoted to his job. To Neilson's growing resentment,[9] Nock came to be considered by many as the head and front of the weekly—which he was. His stylistic skills, which included happy phrasing, verbal ingenuity, clarity, and wit, had much to do with making the *Freeman* what it was. At the same time, Nock's highly cultivated self-esteem and glibness were offensive to some. His account of the *Freeman* in his autobiography is mostly arrogant nonsense.[10]

The literary editor was Van Wyck Brooks, who came to the *Freeman* from the short-lived but brilliant *Seven Arts*. He was a leader of the literary radicals, often called "the young intellectuals," and he now became the chief guide of the new weekly in its extensive literary criticism. He remained in that position throughout the *Freeman's* four years, except for six months in 1923, when Nock relieved him so he could work on his study of Henry James. Chief lieutenants of Brooks among the magazine's contributors were Lewis Mumford and Harold Stearns.

Suzanne La Follette, who had been secretary for her famous relative, Senator Robert M. La Follette, and had later performed the same services for her father, Congressman William L. La Follette, of Washington, came to the magazine with an intense interest in the Russian experiment and in reform in general. Hard-working and intelligent, she made a good assistant for Nock. From the *Dial* staff was recruited young Geroid Tanquary Robinson, who was later to become professor of history at Columbia and a specialist in Slavic affairs. Walter

8 Neilson, *Story of 'The Freeman,'* p. 42.

9 Neilson's *Story of 'The Freeman'* is mainly an arraignment of Nock, whom the author accuses of ignorance, of claiming credit due Neilson and others, and of exploitation of the Neilson wealth.

10 Albert Jay Nock, *Memoirs of a Superfluous Man* (New York, 1943), Chap. ix.

G. Fuller was an Englishman with a special talent for paragraphing, "rewrite," and general office editorship. B.W. Huebsch, the publisher, was occasionally a contributor. For more clerical work, the staff enjoyed the services of Lucy Taussig and Emilie McMillan, who came to the magazine from Wellesley and Smith respectively.

The first number of the *Freeman,* issued March 17, 1920, met a friendly reception from all except those who found it rather too "radical." One of the most enthusiastic welcomers was the *New Republic,* which waxed poetic in comparing the new weekly to Shelley's west wind, "tameless and swift and proud." [11] True, there was some criticism of the anglicism of the new paper, which used such spellings as "labour" and which looked like the *Spectator* of London. In a letter to the editor published in the second number, Lewis Mumford alleged that Number One was "not American" but "a bland mixture of the best elements in each" of the six English weekly journals of opinion.[12]

The *Freeman* was not immediately recognized by all as a single-tax, no-state paper; but these were its two great causes throughout its life. It was devoted to "the simple expedient of confiscating rent," as it stated in an early number; and on this principle it took its stand in discussing all economic issues. This made it, the editors claimed, a genuinely radical journal (in the etymological sense of the word), and it often twitted the *New Republic* and *Nation* with being, not "radical," but merely "liberal." George Santayana took them to task for this position:

> The editors of the *Freeman* say they are radical because at the root of things is the fact that man is a land animal and has *a natural right* to the source of his subsistence. This is not radical at all: the notion of "right" is as derivative, complicated and conventional as that of "duty." Man has no more right to possess land than mosquitos have to possess the air. Nothing has a right to exist. . . . Not only is the logic of the word "right" sophistical, but the temper of it is wrong. We exist on sufferance. Wisdom is to enjoy life, not to claim it.

11 *New Republic,* v. 22, March 24, 1920, p. 105.
12 *Freeman,* v. 1, March 24, 1920, p. 34.

To which Nock replied:

> Mr. Santayana is, on one point, quite right. Man has no natural right to possess land. We have never said that he had. We said that he had a natural right to *use* land, and we still maintain that he has. There is a school of philosophers to which Matthew Arnold belonged, which denies that man has any natural rights of any kind. Perhaps Mr. Santayana belongs to this school. If so, he is in excellent company, and for all except philosophical reasons we are sorry we can not join him.[13]

The reply is amusing, but not quite satisfying, and a little too glib. It illustrates Nock's qualities as a writer.

The *Freeman's* advocacy of philosophic anarchism fell in with an international movement of the twentieth century to explore the origin and nature of sovereignty, and owed much to writings on the state by Franz Oppenheimer, Harold J. Laski, and others. Perhaps it reached its climax so far as the *Freeman* was concerned in Nock's series entitled "The State," published in June and July 1923 and revised and extended later in his book, *Our Enemy the State.*

But the *Freeman* never advocated violent overthrow of the government; revolution, to be sure, but a revolution in which reason will conquer injustice and the common sense of mankind consign to the limbo of useless, worn-out things the machinery of political government. "A peaceful revolution is still possible and practicable," wrote Suzanne La Follette in the first number of the *Freeman,* "and such is the eager hope of enlightened minds."[14]

Not only was this journal opposed to violent revolution, it rejected direct political action as well. This gave its commentary on all political matters a negativist cast; it was a mildly cynical spectator of the political scene. After April Fool's Day of 1920, it could remark that "The first prize in the great All-Fools' Day free-for-all was this year awarded" to the New York Assembly for disfranchising and unseating the Socialist party in that state, with a second prize "to President Wilson for his inimitable animadversion upon the relations between the

13 *Freeman,* v. 3, March 30, 1921, p. 65. But Mumford's review of Santayana's *The Life of Reason* calls the author "a star of the first magnitude" in the "firmament of philosophy"; *Freeman,* v. 7, May 23, 1923, p. 260.

14 *Freeman,* v. 1, March 17, 1920, p. 1.

Soviet Government of Russia and the 'civilized world' " contained in a note to the Allied Powers.[15] This superior attitude the *Freeman* rarely abandoned, though it was often submerged in the charm or force of essays on various subjects.

Some of its friends found an inconsistency in the journal's opposition to direct political action (including socialism as a party movement) and its open-mindedness to labor unionism and all forms of industrial organization that might circumvent state controls—syndicalism, strikes, guild socialism, even the Soviets. One good example of the general strike in Britain, Italy, or the United States, it once asserted, "would be enough to win economic freedom for labor." [16] Norman Thomas was among those who objected to the *Freeman's* "blessings for the economic action of the class-conscious labour organizations, and cursings for the class-struggle theory on which these organizations operate." [17]

Many political, economic and social topics engaged the attention of the *Freeman;* its variety of interests was remarkable. Charles and Mary Beard remarked approvingly that its mission seemed to be "to scatter acid on many a sacred convention." [18] It was against all parties, all corporations, all newspapers, all politicians. In the earlier part of the file, political criticism seemed dominant; later the paper was more literary, Nock's adherence to Henry George's single-tax views seemed more stylized and mechanical, and even his anti-statism was less aggressive. He did not trouble to keep the paper consistent, but sometimes admitted articles that ran counter to the single-tax and anarchistic beliefs of himself and Neilson. Brooks, the literary editor, not only was a Socialist but was not a Georgist.

In the journal's first year and a half, Brooks, with Mumford and Stearns, made the *Freeman* the organ of the Young Intellectuals in current American literature. They adopted the Whitman idea of the artist as leader and prophet, and looked to the new writers for social interpretation and criticism. This position pitted the *Freeman* against the chief organ of the esthetic experimentalist, the *Dial,* which spoke so often and shrilly for

[15] *Ibid.,* v. 1, April 14, 1920, p. 97.

[16] *Ibid.,* v. 2, Oct. 27, 1920, p. 150.

[17] *Ibid.,* v. 1, Sept. 1, 1920, pp. 590–91; quotation on p. 591.

[18] Charles A. and Mary R. Beard, *The Rise of American Civilization* (New York, 1930), v. 2, p. 765. Quoted in Nock, *Superfluous Man,* p. 171.

Ezra Pound, T. S. Eliot, and James Joyce. Nock, taking the place which he loved as critic of the critics, scolded the young intellectuals for their complaints about the victimization of the artist by American society—"the wholly imaginary predicament so vividly conjured up by Mr. Mumford"—and urged them to deal less with such childishness and more with the problems of a work of art.[19] Thus the editor sided with the enemy. But Stearns was especially concerned with the barrenness of America so far as art and the appreciation of art were concerned. "Limbo, the place of lost souls; the world of the magazines, of this accepted American literature of ours, is nothing or less," he wrote.[20] Later he had much about the expatriates, climaxed by his famous advice to the American artist: "GET OUT!"[21] This negativistic criticism tended to increase in the *Freeman's* pages; and as Brooks's own attitude became less aggressive in 1922, turning more to general evaluations and historical reviews, the journal seemed to fail a little in its original critical vigor.

If the *Freeman* lost some sharpness of point in its political-economic and literary-critical attacks in its last year or two, it gained in variety and urbanity. Originally it had only a few departments of editorial comment and criticism; by 1923 it had developed ten such sections. These may be reviewed here, in order to give a picture of the journal's variety.

Each number throughout the file opened with about three pages of short, unheaded editorials grouped under the title of "Current Comment." These dealt with all facets of the contemporary scene, were contributed by various staff members, and were always lively and well written. "In our humble opinion, if there is one thing more obscene than printed indecency, it is the uproar of the professional moralists," wrote Harold Kellock, and went on to prophesy the "bootlegging" of literature, and packaging such as would make it suitable to be carried on the hip, like illicit liquor.[22]

"Topics of the Times" contained editorials of somewhat

19 *Freeman,* v. 3, March 16, 1921, p. 11.

20 *Ibid.,* v. 1, July 28, 1920, p. 463.

21 *Ibid.,* v. 1, Aug. 4, 1920, p. 491. These articles reappeared in Harold Stearns' *America and the Young Intellectual* (New York, 1921).

22 *Freeman,* v. 7, March 21, 1923, p. 27.

greater length and occupied three or four pages. They dealt chiefly with politics and economics in the first half of the file, and more with art and literature, education, religion, and so on, in the latter half.

"Miscellany" carried further editorial commentary—much like "Current Comment," but dealing more with music, the theater, and variegated social phenomena. "Charles Beard, the historian, has mentioned to me the humorous idea of potting a lot of obituary-notices from the daily press and working them up into a kind of anthology of vacuity and blather," wrote Nock, and then went on with curious talk about obituaries.[23]

Then came the section called by the staff "the middle articles"—headed and signed pieces of great variety, many of them written by contributors rather than staff.[24] Nock's several serial disquisitions appeared in this department. A serial in April–May 1922 was signed "Somnia Vana" and was entitled "College Education: An Inquest"; it took American higher education apart. Here also appeared some of the most important articles by Brooks, Mumford, and Stearns; Daniel Gregory Mason's musical criticism, Walter Pach's studies of contemporary art, and Alexander Harvey's rather heavy series on classical literature (1920) and another on theological history (1922). Here were the various critiques of the small town, including Thorstein Veblen's series "The Country Town" (July 1923)—all supplemented by reviews in the later book section discussing the work of Sinclair Lewis, Sherwood Anderson, Floyd Dell, and Waldo Frank. Nock took occasion to compare the work of this school to Gogol's *Dead Souls* (January 26, 1921).

Also among the "middle articles" were short fiction, sketches, light essays, and verse, which the *Freeman* published sparely at first, but later somewhat more plentifully. This work definitely was not of the experimental schools. Some of it consisted of translations from the German and Russian. Gerhart

23 *Ibid.*, v. 8, Feb. 27, 1924, p. 584.

24 The publisher kept a file in which each piece, however small, bore the annotated name of the author; and in *The Freeman Book* (New York, 1924), Huebsch and Miss McMillan gathered together what they called "typical editorials, essays, critiques, and other selections from the eight volumes of *The Freeman,*" noting the author of each.

Hauptmann's "Phantom" (September–December 1922) was the journal's only fiction serial. There were two short stories and a few other pieces by the owner, Mrs. Neilson; the stories were character take-offs of the "natives" who lived near the Neilson summer home in northern Michigan (September 1923). There were one-act plays by Laurence Housman, short stories by J. D. Beresford, "Vignettes of City Life" by Walter Prichard Eaton. And there was also some poetry; James Weldon Johnson's "The Creation" was first printed in the *Freeman* (December 1, 1920), and Carl Sandburg, Leonora Speyer, Witter Bynner, Alfred Noyes, Jeannette Marks, and Howard Mumford Jones were occasional contributors of verse.

Eaton was not only a contributor of sketches from city streets, but he was also the journal's chief critic of the New York theater. Current plays and published drama came in for treatment also at the hands of the editors and the various book reviewers. Reviews of the current theater commonly occupied only one page. "Letters to the Editor" was also a one-page department—often a very spicy single page.

"Books," consisting of five or six pages of reviews, was one of the best of the magazine's sections. Some of the best book-reviewing done in any American journal in the twenties appeared in the *Freeman.* Charles A. Beard, Newton Arvin, Mary M. Colum, John Gould Fletcher, and Edwin Muir were only a few of the many brilliant writers of book reviews who, drawn from many fields, supplemented the work of the regular editors. In conformity with the general policy of the journal, the work of the experimental-esthetic school of the decade did not fare so well at the hands of the *Freeman's* reviewers as that of the writers who bore the social, economic, and political burdens of the day. But on the whole, this group of critics seems to have been singularly competent and enlightened.

"Literary Notes," later called "Ex Libris," was for a long time written by John Macy; when he went to the *Nation* as its literary editor, this commentary about writers and publishing projects was furnished by Percy Boynton and others. "A Reviewer's Notebook" appeared irregularly and contained evaluations of writers old and new; Brooks did most of these articles.

Both Neilson and Nock were well acquainted with England

and the European countries. The English influence on the very spelling and format of the *Freeman* has been noted, and several English contributors have been mentioned. The names of G. D. H. Cole, Llewellyn Powys, and Henry W. Nevinson may be added as frequent contributors. Neilson himself wrote on English politics with all the background of a former Member of Parliament. He opposed British policy in Ireland and India; he was anti-Churchill and pro-Labour.

There were three roving correspondents who wrote series for the journal: Gilbert Cannan's "Letters from a Distance" were mostly about England and often dull; Charles R. Hargrove's "Letters from Abroad" were more varied and interesting; and Harry W. Frantz's "University of the World" began his long-popular "vagabonding" writings.

Translations from the German have been mentioned. Nock's sympathy with Germany is evident in his editorials and in his serial "The Myth of a Guilty Nation" (1921), later published in book form.

But it was the *Freeman's* sympathy with the Russian Soviets that formed the most conspicuous element of its foreign policy. Its very first number carried a sympathetic discussion of Soviet government, in which Cole considered it (1) as political expediency and (2) as political theory. A month later the journal carried the first of Robinson's sympathetic but critical essays on the Soviet experiment. And another month later William Leavitt Stoddard noted happily the increasing influence of the Soviet idea on American labor. Hiram K. Moderwell wrote of the growing power of the Soviets in Italy (October 1920). And so the *Freeman* went on with the U.S.S.R. polemic. In an editorial on "Lenin's Purge," Nock wrote editorially: "Lenin is forging—or rather, the Third Internationale is forging—a compact, revolutionary minority, sure of its end, seeking and giving no quarter, and ready to fight with weapons of the flesh as well as of the spirit the revolutionary fight for the power and dictatorship of the proletariat." [25] A notable series on Russia was the one by William Henry Chamberlin in 1923. On the literary side were two important serials—Maxim Gorky's fragmentary "Reminiscences of Tolstoy" (July–August 1920) and

[25] *Freeman,* v. 2, Nov. 3, 1920, p. 175.

Alexander Kuprin's "To Chekhof's Memory" (August 1921).

In a brief survey of the content of such a varied journal as the *Freeman,* it is inevitable that important items and writers should be neglected. It would be a pity not to mention the posthumous anti-state articles of Randolph S. Bourne; or the literary criticism of Ernest Boyd, Louis Untermeyer, Howard Mumford Jones, John Gould Fletcher, and Gorham B. Munson. Among the "discoveries" of the *Freeman* were John Dos Passos and Constance Rourke. Amos Pinchot, William S. Bullitt, Arthur Gleason, and Robert H. Lowie were brilliant writers in varied fields.

The *Freeman* was throughout its history a twenty-four-page, self-covered, small quarto with double columns, typographically chaste, and well printed. It sold for six dollars a year, or fifteen cents a number. It never passed seven thousand circulation. It carried no advertising except its own announcement on page 24. Its deficits cost Mrs. Neilson in the neighborhood of $7,000 a year,[26] about a dollar a year per subscription.

In his autobiography, Nock made the manifestly absurd statement that the *Freeman's* "character and quality were maintained at an exact level throughout the four years of its existence."[27] As a matter of fact it began to lose some of its aggressive attack and probably some of its influence after its first eighteen or twenty months; it seemed less affirmative and more negative than ever. Neilson, as has been pointed out, lost most of his interest in the conduct of the journal after the first year and a half. In the fourth year, Nock himself took an extended holiday in Europe, leaving the editorship in the hands of Miss La Follette. Brooks, the literary editor, had lost some of the critical drive that distinguished the early *Freeman.* Editors wrote less of the journal, and contributors more. It was still admirably written, and to some, pleasanter reading than in its earlier phases. But as a radical journal, it was running down, and its editors and its owner were losing interest. Moreover, much ill feeling had developed between Neilson and Nock.[28]

Mrs. Neilson had originally agreed to support the paper for

26 Turner, "Short History," p. 38.

27 Nock, *Superfluous Man,* p. 168.

28 Neilson, *Story of 'The Freeman,'* pp. 32–53.

three years; but when that time was exhausted she added another year, and then quit. In announcing the end of the *Freeman,* it was said editorially: "The paper was a gift to the American people, a gift as real as hospitals, laboratories, colleges, and other public services supported by wealthy citizens, and more valuable from the point of view of civilization than many of these." [29]

"We produced what was quite generally acknowledged to be the best paper published in our language," declared Nock with characteristic braggadocio several years later.[30] The *Nation's* epitaph was also one of eulogy, but more measured: "The best written and most brilliantly edited of the weeklies of protest." [31] Nock once modestly suggested that Socrates would have liked the *Freeman,*[32] and in another place he exclaimed: "How the millennium would be hastened if 100,000 new readers were added to our list in 1921!" [33] But quips and exaggerations aside, it may be said that the pages of the weekly *Freeman* were filled for four years with well-written commentary and disquisition, thought provoking, and charged with wit and argument about important matters.

Six years after the discontinuance of the *Freeman,* a *New Freeman* was founded, also in New York, with Suzanne La Follette as editor.[34] Nock was a "contributing editor," and Boyd was literary editor. The new journal attracted many of the same contributors who had given character to the original *Freeman,* which it resembled. Its extreme pro-Russian attitude was less acceptable in 1930 than it would have been earlier, and it perished after fourteen months of publication.

29 *Freeman,* v. 8, Feb. 6, 1924, p. 508.

30 Nock, *Superfluous Man,* p. 168.

31 *Nation,* v. 118, Feb. 6, 1924, p. 131.

32 *Freeman,* v. 8, Jan. 30, 1924, advertisement, p. 504.

33 *Ibid.,* v. 2, Jan. 5, 1921, advertisement, p. 408.

34 It began at $4.00 a year but was soon raised to $5.00. Peter Fireman was president of the publishing company. Clifton Fadiman and George Jean Nathan were among the new contributors. The fortnightly *Freeman* begun in 1950 by John Chamberlain, Henry Hazlitt, and Suzanne La Follette was in most respects a very different periodical.

8

THE FUGITIVE[1]

IN 1914 a group of men in Nashville, Tennessee, most of them connected with Vanderbilt University, were drawn together by a common interest in philosophical and literary subjects and began a series of informal evening meetings that led, several years later, to the publication of a magazine of poetry called the *Fugitive*.

At the center of this group was Sidney Mttron[2] Hirsch, who belonged to a cultivated Jewish family in Nashville. Hirsch had traveled widely in Europe and the Orient, had been a model in Paris and a playwright in New York, had formed acquaintances in eastern literary and artistic circles, and was now fre-

[1] TITLE: *The Fugitive.*

FIRST ISSUE: April 1922. LAST ISSUE: Dec. 1925.

PERIODICITY: Quarterly 1922, 1925; bimonthly 1923–24. Vol. 1, April, June, Oct., Dec. 1922; 2, Feb.–March, April–May, June–July, Aug.–Sept., Oct., Dec. 1923; 3, Feb., April, June, Aug., Dec. (double number), 1924; 4, March, June, Sept., Dec. 1925. In vols. 1–2 issue number and paging are continuous.

EDITORS and PUBLISHERS: Walter Clyde Curry, Donald Grady Davidson, James Marshall Frank, Sidney D. Mttron Hirsch, Stanley Phillips Johnson, John Crowe Ransom, Alec Brock Stevenson, John Orley Allen Tate (withdrew Feb. 1925). Added June 1922, Merrill Moore; Dec. 1922, William Yandell Elliott and William Frierson "in absentia"; and Ridley Wills and Jesse Ely Wills. Added Feb. 1924, Robert Penn Warren; March 1925, Laura Riding Gottschalk; Sept. 1925, Alfred Starr. (Managing editors: Davidson, 1923–24; Ransom and Warren, 1925. Associate editors: Tate, 1923—April 1924; Jesse Wills, June 1924—Dec. 1924. Business Manager: Jacques Back, Oct. 1923—Dec. 1924.)

INDEX: Contents for all issues are given in Cowan (see below), pp. 258–67.

REFERENCES: Louise Cowan, *The Fugitive Group: A Literary History* (Baton Rouge, La., 1959); John M. Bradbury, *The Fugitives: A Critical Account* (Chapel Hill, N.C., 1958); Merrill Moore, ed., *The Fugitive: Clippings and Comment* (Boston, 1939); Allen Tate, *"The Fugitive,* 1922–25," *Princeton University Literary Chronicle,* v. 3, April 1942, pp. 75–84; Donald Davidson, "The Thankless Muse and her Fugitive Poets," *Sewanee Review,* v. 66, Spring 1958, pp. 201–28; Rob Roy Purdy, ed., *Fugitives' Reunion: Conversations at Vanderbilt,* May 3–5, 1956 (Nashville, 1959); Frederick J. Hoffman, Charles Allen and Carolyn F. Ulrich, *The Little Magazine: A History and a Bibliography* (Princeton, 1946), pp. 116–24, 265–66.

[2] The name Mttron is said to be derived from the Kabbalah, in which the angel representing Deity is given that cognomen. It is pronounced Me-tát-tron. For interesting characterizations of Hirsch, see Purdy, *Fugitives' Reunion,* pp. 124–29.

quently back in his native city making his home with his half-brother Nat. This home extended a warm welcome to a remarkable group of young men, who found Sidney Hirsch's eclectic interests in philosophy, mysticism, and poetry, as well as his fancies in etymology and language in general, fascinating and stimulating.

John Crowe Ransom had been graduated from Vanderbilt, had spent three years at Oxford as a Rhodes scholar, and was now invited by Edwin Mims, recently appointed head of Vanderbilt's English Department, to become an instructor at his alma mater. In this same year of 1914, Donald Davidson returned to Vanderbilt to resume his work as an undergraduate and, incidentally, to take courses under Ransom. About the same time, Walter Clyde Curry, a South Carolinian who had just received his doctorate at Stanford and whose special interest lay in the field of literary esthetics, joined the Vanderbilt faculty.

Two other young men who were still undergraduates in 1914 but were eventually to become members of what was later to be called the Fugitive group were Stanley Johnson and Alec Stevenson. The former was a native of Nashville, majoring in philosophy and modern languages; the latter was the bookish son of Vanderbilt's professor of Semitic languages.

These young men and some others frequented the Hirsch home, gathering informally for an afternoon or an evening of discussions dealing mainly with philosophical matters. Some met also in other groupings at other places, and eventually there came to be a strong feeling of kinship among them. "It was as if we had been cousins all the time," wrote Davidson many years later.[3]

The First World War broke up these associations. Hirsch and Curry remained in Nashville, but the others were soon drawn into the armed services. When Ransom and Davidson found each other at the Ft. Oglethorpe Officers' Training Camp in 1917, their talk was more of poetry than war; and Ransom read to his friend some of the poems that were to be published later in his first volume of verse, *Poems about God*. By the fall of 1919, the war over, Ransom had returned to Vanderbilt; and

[3] Davidson, "Thankless Muse," p. 207.

in the following year the original group was completely reassembled in Nashville.

Its members now formed the custom of meeting every other Saturday evening at the home of James M. Frank, brother-in-law of Sidney Hirsch. Frank, a prosperous shirt manufacturer, a graduate of Peabody College, and a man of culture and learning, found pleasure in offering hospitality to the talented men who gathered at his house. Hirsch, now a semi-invalid as the result of an old injury received during his wanderings in the Far East—or perhaps a valetudinarian by inclination—was living in the Frank home. Allen Tate, the last man to join the group before the magazine was begun, was to write thus of Hirsch: ". . . a man of vast if somewhat perverse erudition . . . a mystic and I think a Rosicrucian, a great deal of whose doctrine skittered elusively among imaginary etymologies. . . . He was a large man, an invalid who never moved from his *chaise longue,* and he always presided at our meetings. . . . Shining pince-nez stood up on his handsome nose, and curled Assyrian hair topped a massive brow." [4]

Tate himself was a student in his senior year at Vanderbilt at this time. He was then strongly under the influence of Herbert Charles Sanborn, professor of philosophy, and the interest in esthetic criticism acquired in the classes of that able teacher was to mean much to him. He brought to the discussions that took place in the Frank home modern "abstractionist" views that eventually became rather unsettling to some of his elders.

As these discussions turned more and more to poetry, largely under the influence of Ransom and Davidson, it became the custom for members to bring poetical "offerings" to the meetings. Louise Cowan, in her admirable history of the *Fugitive,* tells what the meetings were like:

There, with the Franks' comfortable living room and dining room thrown open and a log fire crackling, the poems were read without apology and were given honest, detailed criticism. Carbon copies of individual pieces were customarily furnished by the authors, so that the audience might mark special points during the reading. Usually, after all the poems were read, a more general topic of discussion emerged naturally from the specific criticisms; and this long debate

[4] Tate, "Fugitive," p. 76.

on an aesthetic question would last well into the next morning.

Mrs. Frank never joined in the conversation; she was self-effacing, leaving the men to themselves except for talking with them affectionately before the meeting and putting out food for them—usually hot chocolate, cake, and fruit, but sometimes more elaborate concoctions, such as steaming hot dishes of creole eggs, cold meats, little sandwiches, butter cookies, and various relishes.[5]

These activities led surely to the establishment of a "little magazine." The 1920's saw a remarkable flowering of small journals, many of them devoted chiefly to poetry; the South had two or three such periodicals before the *Fugitive* was begun. Generally these adventures in publication were edited and published either by one man or by a group of two or three; the *Fugitive* was written, edited and published at its beginning by a group of eight, and it continued throughout its four years to be produced under group management. In the past, associations of gentlemen had occasionally supported magazines at various times and places and under varying arrangements for management.[6] Indeed, the "steaming hot dishes of creole eggs" recall in fragrant memory the suppers of "widgeon and teal" with which the members of the Monthly Anthology Club regaled themselves in Boston in the early years of the nineteenth century.[7] But the Fugitives, as they came to call themselves, regarded their "cousinship" in poetry and criticism as something very special and precious, as indeed it was.

Apparently Hirsch and Frank were the first to suggest the publication of a magazine, though if they had not done so another of the group would soon have ventured the proposal.[8] Davidson and Tate differ as to who named it—Stevenson or Hirsch;[9] but certainly it was Hirsch, with his flair for walking over philology "on high stilts,"[10] who had fun explaining the meaning of the word settled upon as a title for the fledgling. "A

[5] Cowan, *Fugitive Group,* p. 41.

[6] See F. L. Mott, *A History of American Magazines,* v. 1 (Cambridge, Mass., 1930), p. 194.

[7] *Ibid.,* p. 256.

[8] "Fugitives Add to Literary Honors of Tennessee," *Nashville Tennesseean,* May 27, 1923, reprinted in Moore, *The Fugitive,* p. 32.

[9] Davidson, "Thankless Muse," p. 217; Tate, "Fugitive," p. 79. But see also Purdy, *Fugitives' Reunion,* p. 125.

[10] Davidson, "Thankless Muse," p. 212.

Fugitive was quite simply a Poet: the Wanderer, or even the Wandering Jew, the Outcast, the man who carries the secret wisdom around the world." [11] Less erudite and poetical scoffers, however, commonly thought that the title reflected a foreboding of the editors that their magazine was more or less ephemeral. Such a feeling was frankly stated, indeed, in the foreword to the first issue, in which three to five numbers were promised. Beyond that point, readers were told, "the editors, aware of the common mortality, do not venture to publish any hopes they may entertain for the infant as to a further tenure of this precarious existence."

The first number of the *Fugitive* appeared in April 1922, with thirty-two well-printed small quarto pages enclosed in a blue cover. All eight editors were represented save Frank, who reserved his first contribution for the second number. Ransom wrote the foreword and four of the seventeen poems in Volume I, Number 1. Some whimsy led the contributors to sign their poems with pen-names; Ransom was "Roger Prim," Davidson "Robin Galivant," Tate "Feathertop," and so on. This masquerade was abandoned after the second issue.

The decision to sign their own names to their work was forced upon them by the assumption of some critics (including H. L. Mencken)[12] that the entire magazine was written by one man. There is no doubt about the "cousinship" of the group, but only the most casual examination of the poems of those early issues would mistake the binding sympathy of the group for identity of ideas and style. This sympathy, which was to withstand bitter clashes of critical theory, was apparently based upon three principles, two of which were stated explicitly by Ransom in editorials appearing in the early numbers of the magazine: (1) "The group mind is evidently neither radical nor reactionary, but quite catholic, and perhaps excessively earnest, in literary dogma"; [13] and (2) "The *Fugitive* flees from nothing faster than from the high-caste Brahmins of the Old South." [14] The third canon in the creed of the Fugitives

[11] Tate, "Fugitive," p. 79.
[12] Moore, *The Fugitive,* p. 17.
[13] *Fugitive,* v. 1, June 1922, p. 34.
[14] *Ibid.,* v. 1, April 1922, p. 1.

was based upon resentment of the growing industrialism about them—of the false gospel of the "New South" as preached by Henry W. Grady and others.

But disunity in critical theory was almost a rule of the group; they appear to have been in complete agreement on only one principle—that complete agreement was not only impossible but undesirable. Yet such were the bonds of tolerance and friendship among them that they published—in concert, as it were—nineteen numbers of a distinguished poetry magazine. Ransom's initial poem in the first number, "Ego," is as near to a literary manifesto as anything the *Fugitive* ever published. Its last lines run:

And if an alien, miserably at feud
With those my generation, I have reason
To think to salve the fester of my treason:
A seven of friends exceeds much multitude.[15]

Whether the treason was toward the Old South, or the New South, or the traditional rationale of poesy is not clear—possibly toward all three.

The greatest editorial outburst against what was popularly regarded as the southern literary tradition to appear in the *Fugitive* came as a reply to "Aunt Harriet" Monroe's advice to southern poets to interpret appropriately "a region so specialized in beauty, so rich in racial tang and prejudice, so jewel-weighted with a historic past." The *Fugitive* greeted with "guffaws" the idea that "the southern writer of today must embalm and serve up an ancient dish." [16] Nevertheless, the eight founders were all southern born except Stevenson, who was brought to Nashville as a child; all received their early education in the South; and one of the strongest bonds that united them was a deep-seated regional devotion. Even Tate, chief exemplar in the group of the "modern" cerebral, highly individualized verse, appeared to join with his fellows in a regional rebellion against incursions of the North into the industry, education, and cul-

[15] *Fugitive,* v. 1, April 1922, p. 4. Reprinted with permission of the author.

[16] *Fugitive,* v. 2, June–July 1923, p. 66. Miss Monroe's statement appeared in a review of *Carolina Chansons,* by DuBose Heyward and Hervey Allen, in *Poetry,* v. 22, May 1923, p. 91.

ture of the South.[17] The southern traditions the Fugitives really served were those that survived from an English culture imported in Colonial times. As Davidson later wrote:

Whatever the temporary concern of the poet, the main direction of the poetry follows the principle so casually uttered by Tate: that "the form requires the myth." Or, in other terms, that the images and symbols, in fact the total economy of the poem, require the support of a tradition based upon a generally diffused belief. . . . And since a tradition could not flourish without a society to support it, the natural step was to remember that after all we were Southerners and that the South still possessed at least the remnants, maybe more than the remnants, of a traditional believing society.[18]

The "clashes of critical theory" referred to grew mainly out of differences among members of the group over degrees of adherence to the more traditional forms and ideas of English poetry and, on the other hand, of acceptance of the "modernistic" modes best represented, perhaps, by the work of T. S. Eliot.

Professor Mims, who felt some responsibility for the literary activities of members of his English department at Vanderbilt and of students working under them, made some attempt to dissuade the projectors of the magazine from the venture in early 1922; [19] it may be surmised that he had some fears of "modernistic" follies. But after two numbers of the magazine had appeared, Mims spoke before a Nashville literary club in praise of the work of the *Fugitive* poets. "They keep in line with tradition," he was reported in the local newspaper to have said. "They are not writers of free verse. Their writings have a certain freshness and individuality, and yet maintain the traditions of English verse." [20] Writing much later about those early attitudes of the Fugitives as a group, Davidson explained:

Except for Tate, we were not as yet admirers of Eliot. Yet we were perfectly ready to concede some merit to modern experimenta-

17 See Alfred Kazin, *On Native Grounds* (New York, 1942), p. 442; also Tate's own statement, in "Fugitive," p. 83.

18 Davidson, "Thankless Muse," p. 228.

19 Tate, "Fugitive," p. 79.

20 *Nashville Tennesseean,* Oct. 13, 1922, reprinted in Moore, *The Fugitive,* p. 20.

tion—even to "free verse"—on two conditions: (1) the experiment must stand as severe a test as to form and technique as any other of the rhetorics of poetry; the mere novelty of experimentalism allowed no immunity from such criticism; (2) mastery of traditional forms was a prerequisite to valid experimentalism; to deviate from traditional forms without first practising them was to ignore the total resources of the art and engage in irresponsible dilettantism.[21]

All of this sounds like good doctrine on a rather academic level. But as one number of the magazine succeeded another, as the group expanded, and as the critical debates at the Frank home went on late into many a night, a rift developed among the cousins. There was no unfriendliness, but differences in critical judgment became more marked. Tate's influence grew. Davidson admired the work and valued the criticism of his younger associate.[22] And when Ridley Wills and Robert Penn Warren joined the group, they reinforced the modernists. Wills had distinguished himself by a revolt against authority in Vanderbilt's student newspaper and later by writing a novel and finding a publisher for it. Warren was a young Kentuckian who had come to Vanderbilt to study chemistry but had found Ransom and Davidson such stimulating teachers of English that he was swept into the dominant literary current of the time and place. Tate tells of his first meeting with Warren:

He was tall and thin, and when he walked across the room he made a sliding shuffle, as if his bones didn't belong to one another. He had a long quivering nose, large brown eyes, and a long chin—all topped by curly red hair. He spoke in a soft whisper, asking to see my poem; then he showed me one of his own—it was about Hell, and I remember this line: "Where lightly bloom the purple lilies . . ." He said that he was 16 years old and a sophomore. This remarkable young man was "Red," Robert Penn Warren, the most gifted person I have ever known.[23]

Tate, Warren, and Wills shared a room in a Vanderbilt dormitory intended for theological students and called Wesley Hall; they also shared critical discussions, horseplay, and

[21] Davidson, "Thankless Muse," p. 222.
[22] *Ibid.*, p. 220.
[23] Tate, "Fugitive," pp. 81–82.

poetical experimentation. Tate and Wills collaborated on a series of parodies dedicated to the *Fugitive,* in which Wills wrote eleven poems in conventional style, each of which was followed on the next page by one on the same subject by Tate using all the 'modernistic' techniques and devices. Both writers, of course, exaggerated their patterns, like good parodists; but the prank showed an awareness of the distinct cleavage that had grown up in the group.

The entire series was written in one evening, but when the two wits showed it to Merrill Moore the next day, he wanted to have a part in the travesty. When the little book was privately published a little later,[24] it carried an introduction by Moore, a short poem by him addressed to R.W., one to A.T., and a third "Panegyric to the Entity."

Moore was a pre-medical student, the son of a Tennessee writer of some note; he later became a psychiatrist in Boston but never entirely abandoned the Muse. His form was the sonnet, and he was probably the most prolific sonneteer in the history of literature. It is said that he invented a shorthand of his own to get his lines on paper quickly between less poetic but more demanding employments. Moore himself stated eight years before his death that his three volumes (one of them entitled *M* to indicate the thousand sonnets it contained) and his several smaller collections published as brochures "don't represent one percent of my output."[25] If one may apply simple arithmetic to poetry, this surely means that he produced over one hundred thousand sonnets during his lifetime. Yet Moore was far from a freak. He had many admirers among perceptive critics; and his poems, though not often profound, showed a pleasant fancy, wit, and sharpness of perception.

Though Moore was not much inclined, apparently, to take sides in the controversies that came to divide the Fugitives, he was definitely a conservative himself. And so were William Yandell Elliott and William Frierson, each of whom won

24 [Ridley Wills and Allen Tate], *The Golden Mean and Other Poems* (Nashville, 1923). Privately printed.

25 Merrill Moore, *M: One Thousand Autobiographical Sonnets* (New York, 1938); *New York Times Book Review,* Jan. 23, 1949, p. 8.

Rhodes scholarships at Oxford and were listed as editors *in absentia* during most of the life of the magazine.

The conservative-modernistic differences make the successive numbers of the *Fugitive* a fascinating study. As early as December, 1922, Tate declared editorially, "Yes, we *are* experimentalists, but perhaps not too bold"; and he goes on to approve abstraction in modern art and the break with representation.[26] But in the same number, Frierson rails at the modern themes (rather than the forms) of recent *Fugitive* verse:

> I am tired of being bitter.
> I am weary of the disillusionists,
> . . . the sinister sterility of irreverence.[27]

And in the next number Stanley Johnson wrote editorially, rebuking the "modern poets," who, he says, "have pointed out from time to time that there is no God, that pessimism is the end of knowledge . . . that garbage heaps and dunghills are subject matter of poetry. . . . [They] have prepared for themselves a freedom which looks tragically like slavery, a courage which smacks of cowardice, and in their creedless night have committed themselves to a creed of spiritual anarchy." [28]

But modernism in both form and idea (especially in idea) was not to be denied in the *Fugitive*. A year or two later Tate wrote in his "Credo: An Aesthetic":

> Good manners, madam, are had these days not
> For your asking nor mine, nor what-we-used-to-be's.
> The day is a loud grenade that bursts a smile
> Of comic weeds in my fragile lily plot;
> Comic or not, heterogeneities
> Divert my proud flesh to indecisive guile.[29]

Even outside the Frank drawing-room and the *Fugitive's* pages, the group carried on an earnest but friendly contro-

[26] *Fugitive,* v. 1, Dec. 1922, p. 99.

[27] "Reactions on the October *Fugitive,*" *Fugitive,* v. 1, Dec. 1922, p. 106. Reprinted with permission of Mrs. William C. Frierson.

[28] *Fugitive,* v. 2, Feb.–March 1923, p. 2.

[29] *Ibid.,* v. 3, June 1924, p. 87. Reprinted with permission of the author.

versy. When Ransom attacked Tate's article, "Waste Lands," in the *Literary Review,* Tate wrote a reply, to which Ransom made a rejoinder.[30] Tate withdrew from the *Fugitive's* editorial board early in 1925. He was then living in New York, though he continued to make occasional contributions to the magazine; indeed, he had a poem in its last issue.

About the time of Tate's withdrawal, Davidson was writing to Laura Riding: "The Fugitives are not a unit in their literary beliefs and practice. I believe they represent all varieties of poetical creed and practice, from the wholly traditional to the more or less radical. Nevertheless we are prevailingly 'modern' in tone, I am sure, occupying perhaps a middle position between the extreme conservatives and the extreme radicals." [31]

Laura Riding Gottschalk, wife of a history professor at the University of Louisville (later at the University of Chicago), had won a prize in a poetry contest sponsored by the *Fugitive* and had later contributed some other poems. She was energetic in her promotion of the magazine and eventually came down to Nashville to meet with the group. But a woman could scarcely adapt herself to this unusual fellowship of gentlemen. Mrs. Gottschalk quarreled with Grand Master Hirsch; and though she was made a member of the board of editors, she was never a real Fugitive.

Another very late comer to the group was Alfred Starr, a mathematician who had been a student of Ransom's and a classmate of Tate and Wills. But the Fugitives generally were living up to their name by 1925. Tate was deeply engaged in his New York activities. Ridley Wills was in newspaper work in that city; and though his cousin Jesse, who had also become a member of the magazine's editorial staff, was still in Nashville, he was devoted more to his insurance business than to poetry. Warren was at the University of California as student and graduate assistant. Elliott had just left that institution to join the faculty of the department of government at Harvard.

30 *Literary Review of the New York Evening Post,* July 14, Aug. 4, Aug. 11, 1923, quoted in Cowan, *Fugitive Group,* pp. 123–25.

31 Cowan, *Fugitive Group,* p. 182. See also Purdy, *Fugitives' Reunion,* pp. 120–21.

Frierson was an English professor at the University of Alabama. Curry was busy finishing his authoritative study of Chaucer and science,[32] and Davidson was finding his spare time occupied by the editorship of a distinguished book page for the *Nashville Tennesseean.* Moore was in medical school, though never too busy to dash off a sonnet between laboratory and lecture room. Meetings were still held at the Frank home; but much of the magic of the early "cousinship" had vanished, and nobody seemed to want to perform the inevitable detailed labors of production.

In the third issue of the *Fugitive* an interesting note about the conduct of the quarterly had appeared. After expressing gratification over the success of the two numbers already published, the writer promised that "The magazine will run through another year at any rate, and indefinitely, so far as appears now, until the present group is no longer intact."[33] Obviously, that time had now arrived.

In this same issue, a fantastic statement of the magazine's production was presented: "The procedure of publication is simply to gather up the poems that rank the highest by general consent, and take them down to the publisher." The publication of even a "little magazine" was of course more complicated than that: such chores as copyreading, page layout, and proofreading had to be performed by someone; and since the *Fugitive's* editors were also its publishers, a business side demanded attention. The group might heave a communal sigh of relief because "Our books are not complicated by revenues from advertising matter nor payments to contributors";[34] nevertheless, some of the group had to keep subscription records, look after a bank account, pay the printers, and attend to mailing out the successive issues.

Davidson and Stevenson were the chief chore-men during the magazine's first year.[35] The former was named as "managing editor" in an official statement of ownership dated March 20, 1923, and he was listed on the contents page as

[32] Walter Clyde Curry's Study was *Chaucer and the Mediaeval Sciences* (New York and London, 1926).
[33] *Fugitive,* v. 1, Oct. 1922, p. 66.
[34] *Ibid.*
[35] Cowan, *Fugitive Group,* p. 74.

St. Mary's College Library
Winona, Minnesota

editor throughout 1924. In 1925, the magazine's final year, Ransom and Warren were so listed. Tate's name was printed as "associate editor" in several issues of 1923–1924, to be followed by that of Jesse Wills when Tate left for New York. There were also "editorial committees" and editors of individual issues from time to time, though the "cousins" insisted loudly now and then and here and there that the editorship of the magazine was a total group activity—as, of course, in general it was.

Even poetry has usually required, alas, dollar support. The printer's bill for a single number was only $100, to be sure; but when only twenty-seven renewals and eighteen new subscriptions had dribbled in by mid-January of the second year,[36] special efforts (chiefly by mail solicitation) were undertaken for both new subscribers and "patrons" who were willing to contribute five dollars or more to culture. More than a dozen such philanthropists were rounded up, some paying ten dollars a year.[37] At the same time the magazine raised its price to $1.50 and promised six numbers in 1923. Also the group members dug down into their pockets—a resource, said one of their circulars, "which we contemplate at all times with reasonable alarm."[38]

Thus the *Fugitive* got through its second year, after which a minor miracle happened. An "angel" appeared unto the brethren and said unto them: "I'll take over the entire financial responsibility of this operation—receipts, expenditures, profits up to twenty-five percent, losses up to one hundred percent, printing, mailing, what not—and all you have to do is to write the poetry for it." This dispensation lasted only for one year, at the end of which time an editorial writer referred to their rescuer as a "rare spirit" and recorded the injunction: "When the annals of *The Fugitive* are written, let the chronicler pause here, and write the name of Jacques Back into his record."[39] Selah.

When Back, who ran a local advertising agency, took over, the group agreed to pro-rate the debt to the printers among its

36 Cowan, *Fugitive Group,* p. 95.
37 Davidson, "The Thankless Muse," p. 204.
38 Moore, *The Fugitive,* p. 8.
39 *Fugitive,* v. 3, Dec. 1924, p. 131.

members; but at the beginning of 1925, some of that indebtedness was still outstanding.[40] During its last two years the magazine resumed quarterly publication at a dollar a year, with black covers imprinted with gilt. Its circulation probably never exceeded five hundred.

The inevitable announcement of discontinuance appeared in the number for December 1925, with the explanation:

> This action is taken because there is no available Editor to take over the administrative duties incidental to the publication of a periodical of even such limited scope as the *Fugitive*. The Fugitives are busy people, for the most part enslaved by Mammon. . . . No financial exigency was the joint in our armor, the vulnerable heel in our anatomy. The *Fugitive* from the beginning has solved its financial problem without undue effort.[41]

No joint in the armor or vulnerable heel perhaps; but, more prosaically, an occasional drain on pocketbooks, however "undue."

Local commercial interests had not been unaware of the little magazine, however, and had rallied 'round in support of Nashville culture to a modest extent. The Retailers' Association of the city offered prize money for poetry contests outside the group; this adventure, though obviously at variance with the original plan of limited authorship, had been welcomed by the Fugitives. It brought in a flood of entries, which were judged by Jessie B. Rittenhouse, William Alexander Percy, and Gorham B. Munson. Most of the prize-winning poems were rather below the *Fugitive* level of excellence; but the contests did bring in work by Robert Penn Warren and Laura Riding, who were to become members of the group, and a contribution from Hart Crane. They doubtless had some value as promotion among poetry lovers. Other "guest contributors" from time to time were Louis Untermeyer, Witter Bynner, W. A. Percy, David Morton, John Gould Fletcher, Joseph Auslander, and the Englishmen, Robert Graves and L. A. G. Strong.

What was the *Fugitive* "level of excellence," all in all? The term is too mathematical, of course. But it may be noted that criticism has ranged from the "extremely mediocre" judgment

[40] Cowan, *Fugitive Group*, pp. 118, 182.

[41] *Fugitive*, v. 4, Dec. 1925, p. 125.

of the *New York Times* writer who discussed the poems of the magazine's first number [42] to the prediction of a much later critic: "In the future history of American letters, the Fugitive group almost certainly will occupy a position analogous to that of the Transcendental Group of the mid-nineteenth century." [43] Truth must lie between these extremes; but it is not likely to be denied by any unprejudiced reader who undertakes the pleasant task of reviewing the nineteen numbers of the *Fugitive* that here is, on the whole, good poetry, provocative in ideas and interesting in the many techniques displayed. It would be gratifying if one could point a finger at two or three poems in the file and say, "Here are great works, sure of permanent place in American literature." But much as one may like certain poems, no great ones emerge.

Among the men of talent in the group, Ransom stands out as the leader in poetical achievement.[44] He had more maturity as an artist in 1922–1925 than had his "cousins," and he apparently had more influence upon them than they or he realized. Poems such as "Necrological" (June 1922), "Judith of Bethulia" (October 1923), "Bells for John Whiteside's Daughter" (February 1924), and "Eclogue" (March 1925) are memorable partly because of their reappearance in anthologies. Ransom's frequent use of the allegorical ballad and his occasional ironical thrust or wry observation are recognizable characteristics. Interested as he was in experimentalism, he never held with the abstractionists. In a two-page editorial on "The Future of Poetry" in the latter years of the *Fugitive,* he insisted on the duty of poets "to conduct a logical sequence with their meanings on the one hand," and "to realize an objective pattern with their sounds on the other"—a lucid statement of a point of view that was generally, though not always, accepted by the Fugitives.[45]

Pointing out individual poems of note would be of doubtful value if continued at length, but a few of special significance should be mentioned. Davidson, romanticist by nature and

[42] Moore, *The Fugitive,* p. 16, reprints an article from "a Nashville paper of June 1922" which quotes the *Times* without date.

[43] Bradbury, *The Fugitives,* p. vii. Bradbury's observation was not limited to the work of the group that appeared in the *Fugitive.*

[44] Cowan, *Fugitive Group,* p. 93; Purdy, *Fugitives' Reunion,* pp. 86–94.

[45] *Fugitive,* v. 3, Feb. 1924, pp. 2–4.

inclination, but sensitive to modernistic trends, is probably best remembered by *Fugitive* readers for a poem not quite characteristic—his satiric "Ecclesiasticus" (February–March 1923). Tate's growing commitment to the abstract and cryptic tended to separate him somewhat from the fellowship before the end of the file; perhaps the best of his early *Fugitive* poems was his "Horation Epode to the Duchess of Malfi" (October 1922). Warren's "To a Face in The Crowd" (June 1925) was probably his most distinguished contribution to the *Fugitive*. But perhaps the most frequently reprinted of all the poems that appeared in the magazine was Merrill Moore's "The Noise That Time Makes," which appeared in the last number. The critical reader, however, must choose the best poems himself, and the *Fugitive* anthology [46] published a few years after the magazine was suspended conveniently affords poems for such a diversion.

Varied though the offerings of the *Fugitive* were, a few characteristics of its verse were more or less general. Irony, used with greater or less delicacy, was common, whether applied, stiletto-like, to type characters, or used more philosophically. Vocabulary was a preoccupation of the Fugitives, from Hirsch to Tate; esoteric, invented, foreign-language terms tended to give an academic, and sometimes even an occult, tone to many of the poems. This is related to the quality of much of the verse in the *Fugitive* that often has been called "metaphysical." Doubtless most of the Fugitives, students of the history of English literature as they were, did discover an agreeable fellowship with the seventeenth-century poets—Donne, Marvell, Carew, and others of that "metaphysical school"—with their metaphors extended to conceits and with their short, sometimes cryptic phrases memorable for remarkable content of wisdom. Such wits, such philosophers, were sure to appeal to the Fugitives and perhaps to influence their own work.

A pithy characterization of the *Fugitive* verse is that of the author of the short introduction to that curious farrago of recorded conversations between Fugitives who returned to

[46] *Fugitives: An Anthology of Verse* (New York, 1928). Davidson wrote a foreword to this volume; he and Tate were its editors for the group then scattered.

Nashville in 1956 to hold one more (and doubtless the last) of their long series of conversations. Rubin writes: "During a time of considerable caprice and striking of attitudes in verse, the poetry of *The Fugitive* was characterized for the most part by a serious and hard-wrought dignity." [47]

Davidson, with his unmatched understanding of the whole *Fugitive* episode, has pointed out that a growing realization that the Fugitives were southerners, with responsibilities to southern society, had much to do with the ending of their magazine. He wrote: "The Dayton 'anti-evolution trial' of 1925, with its jeering accompaniment of large-scale mockery directed against Tennessee and the South, broke in upon our literary concerns like a midnight alarm. It was not the sole cause of change, but from that time Ransom, Tate, Warren, and I began to remember and haul up for consideration the assumptions that, as members of the Fugitive Group, we had not much bothered to examine. They were, as it turned out, of the greatest relevance to poetry itself, but discussion of them in the closed and intimate circle of the Fugitive Group was hardly appropriate. From that moment publication of *The Fugitive* ceased to be attractive, and in fact became a burden we did not wish to carry. The defense of poetry and with it the 'New Criticism' were in the making. The defense of the South, for which we were to seek new friends and allies, lay only a few years ahead." [48]

The "defense of the South" here referred to was undertaken by a group rather badly named "Agrarians." Ransom, Davidson, Tate, and Warren were members. They attacked industrialism as a way of life and rejected the theory that the growth of commercial prosperity was *ipso facto* true progress. The essays of this group [49] may be considered in a sense a postscript to the critical views expressed and inherent in the *Fugitive*.

[47] Louis D. Rubin, Jr., Introduction to Purdy, *Fugitives' Reunion,* p. 15.

[48] Davidson, "Thankless Muse," p. 228.

[49] Allen Tate, ed., *I'll Take My Stand: The South and the Agrarian Tradition,* by Twelve Southerners (New York, 1930). Other members of the Agrarians were Andrew Lytle, Stark Young, John Gould Fletcher, Frank Lawrence Owsley, Lyle Lanier, H. C. Nixon, John Donald Wade, Henry Blue Kline.

9

THE GOLDEN BOOK MAGAZINE[1]

"AMONG the Christmas magazines at the news-stalls there lay a newcomer, a monthly fiction magazine, with a creamy cover, a big golden moon, a golden skirted lady and gold stars. You stared at this magazine because there, beside the lady's skirt, in big red letters, the list of contributors looked so extraordinary. You had heard all the names before, but for a moment you could in no way connect them with a news-stall. It was like running across a bishop in a saloon or seeing your wife about to play quarterback for the Varsity. 'Hullo, what are you doing here?' you said, as you read: 'Heine, Dumas, Kipling, Gaboriau, Tolstoy, de Alarçon, Anatole France, Robert Louis Stevenson. . . .' "[2]

Thus *Time,* itself rather new, handsomely introduced to its readers the new *Golden Book Magazine,* published by the Review of Reviews Corporation. Volume I, Number 1 of the magazine, dated January 1925, reached the newsstands in time for the 1924 Christmas trade.

The title was a good one, though the magazine had but slight connection, connotative or otherwise, with the medieval Venetian caste-register known as *Libro d'oro,* which it fancied as a kind of godmother. The new magazine carried about 150 small quarto double-column pages (a little over six by nine

[1] TITLE: *The Golden Book Magazine.*

FIRST ISSUE: Jan. 1925. LAST ISSUE: Sept. 1935.

PERIODICITY: Monthly. Semiannual vols.: Jan.–June and July–Dec., except 13 (Jan.–July 1931), 14 (Aug.–Dec. 1931), and 22 (July–Sept. 1935).

PUBLISHER: Review of Reviews Corporation, New York.

EDITORS: Henry Wysham Lanier, 1925–28; Edith O'Dell, 1929–30; Frederica Pisek Field (literary editor, 1929–30), 1930–33; Ralph Rockafellow, managing editor, 1930–31; Mary Letha Elting, managing editor, 1931–35. Editorial Board: William Lyons Phelps, 1925–26; Stuart P. Sherman, 1925–26; J. Cotton Dana, 1925–28; Charles Mills Gayley, 1925–28; Henry Seidel Canby, 1930–33; Hugh Walpole, 1930–33; Albert Shaw, 1930–33; Edwin Mims, 1930–33; Blanche Colton Williams, 1931–33.

INDEXES: *The Golden Book Magazine Author-Index,* 1925–34, with *Addenda 1935* (mimeographed), comp. by F.P.; *Readers' Guide.*

[2] *Time,* v. 4, Dec. 29, 1924, p. 23.

inches) and was well printed, without illustration but with attractive typography, on a good quality of rough-finish (wood-pulp) paper. It sold for twenty-five cents at the newsstands, or three dollars annually by subscription. Its content consisted of reprinted material, with emphasis on the short story.

Time's little write-up gives only an inkling of the richness of content in that first *Golden Book* number. O. Henry was also represented, and so were Richard Harding Davis, Owen Wister, Bret Harte, H. C. Bunner, Sir Richard F. Burton, Sir Harry Johnston, and James Ohio Pattie. The poets included Sir Thomas Wyatt, Robert Burns, François Villon, Emily Dickinson, Ben King, and Walter Malone. There was a page of "Sayings That Have Made Men Immortal," another of "Sayings That Are Portraits," two pages of bits by famous men about "Some Women I Have Met," and three pages of extracts showing "How Men Make Love in Novels." There was a little piece by Don Marquis on "Loneliness," and a comic strip by A. B. Frost. Two pages were given to a musical composition by Brahms (an experiment never renewed), and three pages to a "Booklover's Calendar," with quotations for each day in the month (a feature that lasted throughout most of the magazine's history).

Freighted with such treasures, the new *Golden Book* made a distinct hit, and the early numbers were completely sold out. Within two years it reached a circulation of 165,000—the highest it ever attained.

The true founder of the magazine was Henry Wysham Lanier, son of the poet. He had in previous years been employed in the publishing houses of Scribner and Doubleday, but for some time he had been freelancing. He had now persuaded his brother, Charles Day Lanier,[3] a New Yorker who had made a success in industrial and mining ventures, to put some money into a new monthly eclectic that should specialize in reprinting the best short stories of the past; and the two of them had induced Albert Shaw's Review of Reviews Corporation to undertake the publication of the magazine. Henry W. Lanier, of course, became the editor. He set up an advisory board on which J. Cotton Dana and Charles Mills Gay-

[3] *Time,* v. 26, Sept. 16, 1935, p. 33.

ley served for four years, and William Lyon Phelps and Stuart P. Sherman for two.

Leaders among the older American writers drawn upon were Hawthorne, Harte, Bynner, and Bierce. From the end-of-the-century crop there were many stories by Stephen Crane, Richard Harding Davis, Chester Bailey Fernald, Jack London, O. Henry, Mark Twain, and Owen Wister. Among contemporary short story writers, Achmed Abdullah, Sherwood Anderson, Willa S. Cather, Irvin S. Cobb, Theodore Dreiser, and Stewart Edward White were most often seen in the pages of the *Golden Book*. The chief English short story writers were Stacy Aumonier, Joseph Conrad, Charles Dickens, W. W. Jacobs, Katherine Mansfield, Leonard Merrick, "Saki," Rafael Sabatini, and Robert Louis Stevenson.

One has only to glance at this catalog to realize what a variety of fare the magazine was providing for its readers. But this was by no means all. Translations from the Russian and French were also furnished plentifully—Averchenko, Chekhov, Turgeniev; Daudet, Balzac, Maupassant, Dumas, France, Merimée. And stories came from other European countries as well, though not in such quantities: contributors ranged from Boccaccio to Bojer, from Petronius to Pirandello.

The *Golden Book* liked two-part stories: Stevenson's "Prince Otto" was reprinted in its first two numbers. But it also came to like, increasingly, serial stories running through three to six numbers. It printed twenty of these in its ten years of existence. Among its fiction serials were two each by Willa Cather and Joseph Conrad, Donn Byrne's "Messer Marco Polo" (1932), and Owen Wister's "The Virginian" (1927–1928). The magazine was publishing H. Rider Haggard's "She" at the time of its demise; readers who wished to follow Ayesha to her doom had to do it elsewhere.

Somewhat more than a fourth of the *Golden Book* was usually given over to nonfiction miscellany, including poetry and plays. The poets down the ages were drawn upon, as well as contemporary writers of verse; thus we have them all the way from Sappho to Sarett, Horace to Hovey. There was much of the older English poets, but de la Mare and Masefield also ap-

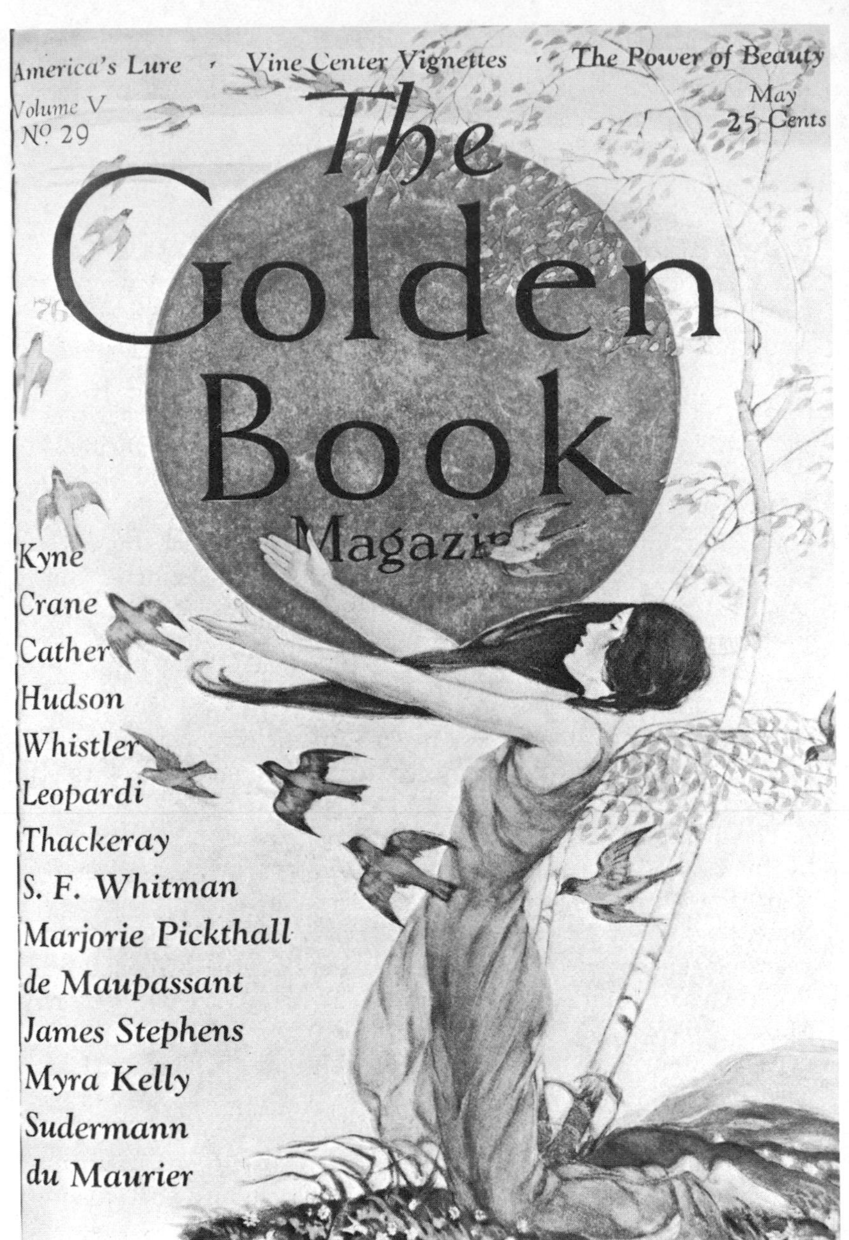

THE *GOLDEN BOOK MAGAZINE,* MAY 1927

The golden sun, the bluebirds, and the wind-blown maiden, perhaps symbolic of spring, form a characteristic romanticized cover picture. The golden disk was on every cover.

peared frequently. Frost and Lindsay, among current American poets, were occasionally represented; and there were many of the older favorites. The playwrights, too, had a great range—from Euripides to O'Neill. The Irish dramatic school —Lady Gregory, Synge, Dunsany—were favorites; another group was composed of von Kotzebue, Sudermann, Schnitzler. One-act plays by such writers as Chekhov, Maurice Baring, and W. S. Gilbert were on the preferred list; full-length plays were less frequent.

There was a little nonfiction from the first—occasional bits of true adventure and travel and reminiscence. Several pieces by Henry Adams appeared in 1927–1928. John B. Watson wrote on "What Is Behaviorism?" in April 1928. The year 1930 saw more of such nonfiction ventures than any other twelve months in the file: there was a debate between Aldous Huxley and Robert E. Sherwood over the talking motion pictures in April, O. W. Holmes's "Natural Law" in August, and Harry Emerson Fosdick's "The Old Savage in the New Civilization" in November—as well as other less notable pieces dealing with contemporary thought.

Humor was a mainstay in the *Golden Book*. Besides the older, accepted humorists like Mark Twain, Artemus Ward, and Bill Nye, there was a long list of contemporaries: George Ade, John Kendrick Bangs, Ellis Parker Butler, Stephen Leacock, Ring Lardner, and Dorothy Parker—to mention but a few. The magazine had a fashion of using collections of bits from writers like Lewis Carroll, Max Beerbohm, or G. K. Chesterton. This was by no means limited to the wits; Amiel received that kind of treatment as well as Thackeray.

Indeed, a kind of jackdaw-like picking out of shining bits of literature was a characteristic of the *Golden Book*. An episode might be excerpted from a novel, a scene taken from a play, or a memorable paragraph lifted from any book. This led to the magazine's "hors d'oeuvres pages." Taking the number for July 1930 from the middle of the file as a sample, we note thirteen pages of such material—the familiar "Booklover's Calendar," with its literary quotations (three pages); "So They Say," an equally familiar collection of contemporary "quotes" from newspapers, magazines, and books (two pages); "The Jolly Angler," bits about fishing from many books (four pages); "The Tenth Muse—*Advertisia,*" another favorite of these collections, relating to advertising facts and foibles (one page); "Love, Life and Laughter," epigrams by Anatole France (one page); and "Hors d'Oeuvres from the Newest Books," a usual *Golden Book* department, sometimes strung through the advertising pages. Such were the contents, in general and particular, of the *Golden Book* throughout its entire life. But there were changes.

At the end of 1928, Charles D. Lanier withdrew as the magazine's "angel" and his brother resigned as editor. It had done well at the start, but 1927 and 1928 had shown successive declines in circulation; [4] and it now seemed clear that the magazine's gold was to remain chiefly in its title and cover-page. The Shaws wished to make some changes, but the Laniers were doubtful and decided to quit.

The *Golden Book* of January 1929, edited by Edith O'Dell, was larger in page size, to conform to the new fashion dictated by the advertisers. But it was a handsome, readable page. There was more nonfiction: "Of Fiction and True Stories," said the subtitle, but soon the thoughtful article made its appearance. However, the essential nature of the magazine was not changed much. The chief improvement was in a more open page and greater illustration.

At the start, the *Golden Book* had carried no illustration except some ornamental figures and an occasional page of comic drawings—plus the ever-present facsimile signatures of its authors. A break was made when "Trilby" was serialized with the original du Maurier pictures in 1926–1927. Then in September 1928 "The Rime of the Ancient Mariner" was reprinted with the great Doré illustrations. Of course the covers were pictorial and in color, usually a stylized romantic scene including a big golden moon. Amy Hogeboom did many of these covers. When the 1929 change in editors came, there were attractive line drawings; and when smooth-finish paper largely supplanted the accustomed woodpulp of the magazine, there were halftones. Color appeared in the advertising pages

[4] Circulation recorded in *N. W. Ayer & Son's Directory of Newspapers and Periodicals.*

and on the covers by Artzybasheff, but none in the body of the book.

Advertising had followed the circulation curve, accumulating to seventy-five pages a month in 1926, but slowly declining thereafter. Books and travel were the chief topics of the advertising pages, but there was also a considerable offering of household "luxuries"—silver, pianos, fine furniture.

Again in 1930–1933 there was a board of advisory editors —Henry S. Canby, Hugh Walpole (who wrote a short-lived monthly letter from England), Albert Shaw (the chief owner), Edwin Mims, and Blanche Colton Williams. To the sympathetic reader of today, as to many readers of the thirties, it seems that such an attractive magazine, in which basic literary values were so well combined with the passing interests of intelligent persons, deserved to succeed. In fact, circulation did rise a little; but it never quite reached 140,000 during the publication of the full-quarto series, from January 1929 through July 1931. By that time the financial crash had ruined the magazine's slender chances. The page size was reduced to an octavo, smaller than the one with which it had begun life, and smaller print in order to offer equivalent, or (as it claimed) a larger amount of material. But the country was now fully in the grip of the Great Depression, and circulation went down rapidly.

Frederica Pisek Field, who had edited the magazine for four years after Miss O'Dell's brief incumbency, gave way to Mary Letha Elting in 1933. There were now a few original stories—one a month for a while. Various straws were grasped at, giving the magazine's editorial policy a curious inconsistency. In its last few months it even tried over-emphasis on sex: it carried what its table of contents called "a spicy yarn" from the *Arabian Nights* and the story of "The False Courtesan" from Balzac's *Droll Stories* in the number for May 1935; and in the following issues offered "Don Juan's Greatest Love" by Jules Barbey d'Aurévilly, Nietzsche on "Chastity," and an excerpt from Rousseau's *Confessions*. Casanova, Rabelais, and the others were laid under tribute.

The magazine's owners, in serious trouble with their chief property, the *Review of Reviews,* ever since the end of the

World War,[5] were forced to give up the fight for the *Golden Book* in the fall of 1935. Its early success had stimulated the establishment of a group of imitators—one of which, *Famous Stories Magazine* (1925–1927), it had absorbed—and now it was itself merged in a very new periodical of the same character. *Fiction Parade* had begun in May 1935; in October of that year, it became *Fiction Parade and Golden Book*. It lasted until February 1938.

Throughout its short life, the *Golden Book* was conducted with bookish fervor and literary enthusiasm, not only by Lanier but by the lady editors who followed him. It was a victim of the depression, but it was also the victim of lack of general public response to the spirit of literary eclecticism in which the magazine was from the first conducted.

[5] See F. L. Mott, *A History of American Magazines,* v. 4 (Cambridge, Mass., 1957), p. 663.

10

GOOD HOUSEKEEPING[1]

CLARK W. BRYAN, founder of *Good Housekeeping,* was a man of energy, versatility, and talent. He began his professional career as editor and publisher of the *Berkshire Courier,* of Great Barrington, Massachusetts. In addition to conducting his own paper, he acted as regional correspondent for the *Springfield Republican.* In those years, before the telegraph network covered such backwoods areas as western Massachusetts, gathering election returns in the Berkshire towns and getting them to the *Republican* promptly was a task requiring great effort and ingenuity. Bryan made a strong impression at the *Republican* office by his accomplishments in this field and also by his ability as a writer, as displayed in the *Courier.* He was surprised in late 1854 to receive an offer of a position on the editorial staff of the great Springfield paper, and he accepted without hesitation.

On the *Republican* he found himself associated with two

[1] TITLES: (1) *Good Housekeeping,* 1885–1909, 1916–current; (2) *Good Housekeeping Magazine,* 1909–16. Various subtitles, including *Conducted in the Interests of the Higher Life of the Household,* 1885–1911; *The Magazine America Lives By,* 1941–59.

FIRST ISSUE: May 2, 1885. Current.

PERIODICITY: Biweekly, May 1885—Dec. 1890; monthly, Jan. 1891—current. Vols. 1–10, semiannual (May–Oct., Nov.–April), May 1885—April 1890; 11, May–Dec. 1890; 12–current, semiannual (Jan.–June, July–Dec.), Jan. 1891—current.

OWNERS: Clark W. Bryan & Co., Holyoke, Mass., 1885–86, Springfield, Mass., 1887–98; John Pettigrew, Springfield, Mass., 1898; George D. Chamberlain, Springfield, Mass., 1898–1900; Phelps Publishing Company, Springfield, Mass., 1900–1911; American Home Magazine Company (renamed International Magazine Company, 1914; Hearst Magazines, 1936; Hearst Corporation, 1952), 1911–current. New York.

EDITORS: Clark W. Bryan, 1885–98; James Eaton Tower, 1899–1913; William Frederick Bigelow, 1913–42; Herbert Raymond Mayes, 1942–58; Wade Hampton Nichols, Jr., 1959–current.

INDEXES: Volume indexes, 1885–1922; *Readers' Guide,* 1909–current.

REFERENCES: W. F. Bigelow, "Now That We Are Forty," *Good Housekeeping,* v. 80, April 1925, p. 4; 50th anniversary number, v. 100, May 1935, especially pp. 4, 80–83, 224–26; Amos Stote, "*Good Housekeeping* Lives Up to Its Name," *Magazine World,* v. 3, Feb. 1947, pp. 10–12, 27.

remarkable personalities—young Samuel Bowles, whose independent discussion of political questions had already made him an important editorial voice throughout the nation, and Dr. Josiah G. Holland, who was later to attain wide popularity as novelist, poet, and essayist. Partly because Bowles was at the time more or less incapacitated by eye trouble and partly because of his own terrific energy, Bryan nearly worked himself to death in his first year on the *Republican.*

When he returned to duty after his recovery from a physical collapse, Bryan was made a partner in the firm of Samuel Bowles and Company and placed in charge of business operations. Soon he set up an auxiliary job-printing shop, which prospered and later expanded into the book-publishing field. But in 1872 Bowles decided upon a separation of the *Republican* from the printing and publishing operation. Bryan thereupon retired from the newspaper firm and organized his own company to conduct the business he had built up. Shortly afterward Clark W. Bryan and Company purchased the *Republican's* evening competitor, the *Union,* and brought over to its staff some of the *Republican's* best men. This was easy to do at the moment because Bowles's business had fallen off as a result of the offence he had given to many old-line Republicans by refusing to support Grant's current candidacy for a second term.[2] But the *Union's* popularity declined after the campaign was over, and Bryan soon disposed of the paper and moved his printing business to the nearby town of Holyoke. There he prospered moderately, especially after he established his lively trade journal, the *Paper World.*[3]

Under the date of May 2, 1885, Bryan published, from Holyoke, the first number of *Good Housekeeping: A Family Journal Conducted in the Interests of the Higher Life of the Household.* It was a thirty-two-page quarto, with stout green cover, to be issued fortnightly at $2.50 a year.

The periodical clearly represented Bryan's tastes and talents. It was literary in tone; perhaps "subliterary" is the bet-

[2] For Bryan's relations with Bowles and the *Republican,* see George S. Merriam, *The Life and Times of Samuel Bowles* (New York, 1885), v. 1, pp. 103–4; v. 2, pp. 201–9.

[3] See F. L. Mott, *A History of American Magazines,* v. 3 (Cambridge, Mass., 1938), p. 128.

Vol. II.—No. 1. NOVEMBER 14, 1885. Whole No. 14.

FOR THE HOMES OF THE WORLD.

Good·Housekeeping

BILL OF FARE.

Ten Dollars Enough, I, ... *Catharine Owen.*
Our Daily Bread, ... *Helen Campbell.*
How I Learned Housekeeping, II. . . . . . *Arel Lane.*
What we Eat for Breakfast, ... *Rose Terry Cooke.*
How Elnathan and I went to Housekeeping, VI, *H. Annette Poole.*
The Fashions, ... *Georgiana H. S. Hull.*
The Bruntons' Family Problem Again, . *Lucretia P. Hale.*
Scrap Books, ... *Sara J. Blanchard.*
Recreation for Leisure Hours, ... *Eva M. Niles.*
The Cozy Corner. . . . .
In Pursuit of Knowledge Under Difficulties, .
A Page of Fugitive Verse. . . . .
Autumn Beauties, Winter Duties, Poetry, . *Clark W. Bryan.*
The Broken Thread, Poetry, ... *J. K. Ludlum.*
A November Day, Poetry, ... *Ione L. Jones.*
The Squire's Decision, ... *Mrs. Ellis L. Mumma.*
Summer Gone, Poetry, ... *Mrs. J. H. Meech.*
Sandwiches of Various Kinds, . . . *Prepared by the Editor.*
With an Editorial Dessert Embracing:
"Around the Family Table,"
"Conversational Resources,"
"For Thanksgiving and Christmas."
Etc., Etc., Etc.

PUBLICATION OFFICES,
HOLYOKE, MASS.
AND
111 Broadway, NEW YORK.

CLARK W. BRYAN & CO.,
PUBLISHERS.

$2.50 A Year. Single Copies 10 Cents.

HOW *GOOD HOUSEKEEPING* LOOKED IN 1885

For its first five years the magazine's covers were drab gray-green with no illustration. The number shown here is dated November 14, 1885, when the magazine was in its seventh month and was being published biweekly at Holyoke, Massachusetts.

GOOD HOUSEKEEPING IN OCTOBER 1908

By this time the cover of the magazine featured bright colors and pictures of children and lovely young women.

GOOD HOUSEKEEPING IN FEBRUARY 1967

The Seal of Approval, visible here just above the title, does not appear on every cover. Photograph on this cover was taken by Jerome Ducrot.

ter word, for its contributors during its first five or ten years were generally writers without brilliance or originality. Nevertheless it was not an unattractive magazine, comparing favorably enough with other family journals of its times. Usually it gave its first page to a single poem, hand-lettered and decorated; its leading articles were introduced by an illustrative type of factotum initial; and other small woodcuts came to be used in connection with its discussions of fashions, embroidery, and the like. The poems and short stories, though they gave the little magazine much of its special character, were subordinate to the articles of advice on household affairs, cookery, dressmaking, house-designing and furnishings, and such miscellany as puzzles, quiz games (with small prizes for the best answers), query departments, and so on. The general effect was scrapbookish, lower middle class, and "homey."

Good Housekeeping adopted at the very first a policy that was to characterize it throughout its long life: it kept very close to its readers. It invited contributions from them and set up modest contests in which they were invited to participate. One of the earliest of these offered $250 for the best series of six articles, of 2,000 words each, on "How to Eat, Drink and Sleep as Christians Should." This was won by Margaret Sidney (Mrs. Daniel Lothrop), author of the best-selling *Five Little Peppers* stories for juveniles. A contest for articles on the making and eating of bread was won by Helen Campbell, later well known as a writer on the socio-economic position of women and for a time editor of *Good Housekeeping's* own department entitled "Woman's Work and Wages." In the issue of April 28, 1888, appeared an offer of $25 each for "the best Buffalo Bug Extinguisher, the best Bed Bug Finisher, the best Moth Eradicator, and the best Fly and Flea Exterminator."

As a result of this reliance on reader-written articles, few distinguished names appeared in the magazine, though the editor took pride in paying, however meagerly, for all contributions. Of course, Margaret Sidney's name was well known; and so was that of "Marion Harland," who had been an indefatigable writer for nearly all the home journals for a generation, but who appears to have been abducted from what Bryan liked to call "the *Good Housekeeping* family" by the *Ladies' Home Journal* after a few years. Rose Terry Cooke was a writer of some reputation when she contributed "Tom and Sally: How They Loved and Lived Life Worth Living" as *Good Housekeeping's* first serial in 1886. Maria Parloa, of cooking-school and cookbook fame, edited a department entitled "Gustatory Thought and Suggestions." Catherine Owen, whose serial of 1885–1886 in narrative form headed "Keeping House Well on $10 a Week" introduced such factual material as cooking recipes, was later added to Houghton Mifflin's list of authors. E. C. Gardner, editor of the *Philadelphia Builder,* wrote on "Model Houses for Model Housekeeping" in early numbers of the magazine.

Clark W. Bryan and Company moved its operations back to Springfield in 1887. There it continued to publish *Good Housekeeping* and the *Paper World,* and a few years later began *Amateur Gardener,* a weekly designed to supplement the older monthly, and also two local periodicals.[4]

In 1891 *Good Housekeeping* was changed from fortnightly to monthly publication, at two dollars a year. It now offered about fifty pages of somewhat smaller size and seemed moderately prosperous. It carried a few pages of advertising, most of it consisting of small "mail-order ads"—not a high-class lot, but the kind that supported most home magazines of the period. Circulation was probably less than 25,000.[5]

The change to monthly publication had little effect on the character of the magazine. Halftone illustrations began to appear in the mid-nineties. An "Eclectic Department" emphasized the growing tendency to use selections from books, magazines, and newspapers. The many departments, ranging from the older "Cozy Corner" and "Fugitive Verse" to the newer "Domestic Economy" and "Sunday Song and Sermon," occupied the latter half of the magazine.

From the first, Bryan had written much for his own magazine. He was a prolific poet, and during his thirteen-year term

[4] *Progressive Springfield,* sponsored by the local Chamber of Commerce, and a *Bulletin* for the City Library, both monthlies.

[5] The report given to N. W. Ayer and Co. for their 1891 directory set the figure at 28,500; ten years later it was quoted at 25,000. These were not sworn statements.

as editor he printed hundreds of his own poems. Occasional contributions to other publications were strays to be gathered immediately into his own pages. In the last six months of his editorship of *Good Housekeeping,* Bryan used no less than thirty-four of his own poems, all signed by his name. In an early issue of 1898, eight of his poems appeared, including "A Family Picture Gallery," which was given fancy display on the first page, and another set full-width in pica type to occupy five pages, entitled "Nothing New in the Paper." [6] Bryan sometimes attempted, with rather lamentable effect, the higher flights of poesy; he was at his best in homely verse about homely matters.

Three months after this outburst of song in March 1898, Clark Bryan, plagued by illness and financial worries, took his own life. Though his other publishing ventures were promptly discontinued, a purchaser was found for *Good Housekeeping*—one John Pettigrew, who soon turned it over to his printer, George D. Chamberlain, who in turn conducted it for less than two years before disposing of it to the Phelps Publishing Company. This firm was headed by E. H. Phelps, a former associate of Bryan's in the *Springfield Republican* organization, and had offices in both Springfield and New York; it published four agricultural papers designed to serve the interests of farmers in different regions of the country.[7]

James Eaton Tower, who had been editor of one of these papers, was drafted to edit *Good Housekeeping* under the new management. For a few years he followed much the same lines as those to which readers had become accustomed. But the appearance of the magazine improved, with illustrations in two colors and more of them. Maud Tousey's drawings were especially attractive. Soon covers were printed in full color. The price per copy was reduced to ten cents, but raised again to fifteen cents in 1905.

By 1908 *Good Housekeeping* had a sworn circulation of over two hundred thousand and between twenty and thirty pages of advertising of good quality. The rise in circulation

[6] *Good Housekeeping,* v. 26, March 1898, pp. 110–14.

[7] *American Agriculturist, Orange Judd Farmer, New England Homestead,* and *Farm and Home.* See Mott, *American Magazines,* v. 3, p. 731.

was due to four factors—general prosperity, more aggressive and informed management, the improved appearance of the magazine, and a greater emphasis (beginning about 1904) on fiction by well-known writers.

This was a literary period characterized by great popular interest in fiction; nearly all the best sellers were novels, many of which dealt with domestic and community life.[8] Tower brought to the pages of *Good Housekeeping* such notable writers of the time as Thomas Nelson Page, Margaret Deland, Mary Stewart Cutting, Joseph C. Lincoln, Mary Heaton Vorse, and Selma Lagerlöf. Humor lightened many issues (especially the August "Fun Number"); Ellis Parker Butler, Tom Masson, Marietta Holley, and Wallace Irwin were prominent contributors. Among the poets were Richard Le Gallienne and Edwin Markham.

The magazine was by no means all fiction, however. Under the Tower editorship it placed much emphasis on household management, and especially on domestic economies. In the December 1907 number, for example, appeared articles entitled "Living on a Little," "Inexpensive Christmas Gifts," and "Not Much, But Something." Standards of excellence in foods were first given systematic attention in 1905. Domestic service and women's work outside the home were much discussed.

By 1911 *Good Housekeeping* was a handsome magazine of 125 pages with a circulation of over 300,000 at $1.25 a year and good advertising patronage. In that year it was purchased by the Hearst interests and added to their group of magazines. Two years later Tower resigned his editorship; his successor was William Frederick Bigelow, who came over from Hearst's *Cosmopolitan* and served *Good Housekeeping* for almost thirty years.

Now a period of major development began. Bigelow followed Tower's editorial pattern but expanded it in all departments. *Good Housekeeping* became popular as a fiction magazine; eventually each number contained installments of two or three serials and four or five short stories. Most of the fiction

[8] See F. L. Mott, *Golden Multitudes: The Story of Best Sellers in the United States* (New York, 1947), chap. xxxii and pp. 312–13.

was by "name authors," and some by the first-class writers of the time. Somerset Maugham, William J. Locke, James Hilton, and I. R. Wylie were among English authors occasionally represented. Galsworthy's "The Apple Tree" was a serial of 1917. But the popular American writers were prominent, too. Mary Roberts Rinehart's "The Confession," illustrated by James Montgomery Flagg, ran in 1917, and Kathleen Norris serials appeared in 1917–19. In 1923 Gene Stratton-Porter (sic), Coningsby Dawson, and James Oliver Curwood had serials appearing at the same time. All of this fiction was illustrated by the best magazine artists.

The short stories were as notable as the serials. Ellen Glasgow's remarkable "The Past" appeared in the number for October 1920. Wilbur Daniel Steele and Irvin S. Cobb contributed some of their best work to *Good Housekeeping* during the Bigelow editorship. But much of the short fiction was lighter in tone—Booth Tarkington's "Penrod" pieces, George Ade's "Fables in Slang," Wallace Irwin's amusing "Togo" sketches, George Randolph Chester's "Get Rich Quick Wallingford" stories, and those matchless Ring Lardner tales of the times.

The nonfiction interest also grew in importance. Frances Parkinson Keyes, a talented writer and the wife of Senator Henry W. Keyes, of New Hampshire, wrote a monthly article from Washington headed "Letters from a Senator's Wife," later gathered into a popular book. They were chatty epistles dealing much with leading personalities in the capital (and their wives and families), but also occasionally touching upon real issues of government. In 1923 Mrs. Keyes covered the International Women's Suffrage Alliance meeting in Rome for *Good Housekeeping*. "The Real Calvin Coolidge," by his widow "and others" was a serial of 1935. Among the writers of scientific articles were Hugo Münsterberg, Woods Hutchinson, and Harvey W. Wiley. Dr. Wiley's contributions were a part of the editorial content that grew out of the magazine's "Institute"; it became an important feature of the magazine in the 1920's. "Discoveries" had long been a popular department of household hints. *Good Housekeeping's* poets included

I Have Found Out For You

At the beginning of the war in Europe, America was dependent on Germany for all of the dyes used in the American manufacture of textiles. Now America is making her own dyes and making them in dependable colors and shades. The new American dye-makers have provided ably for the needs of our textile manufacturers and are making twenty different standard colors—among them good blacks and blues—in sufficient quantities for all needs. There are, in addition, seventy colors which have been produced satisfactorily in smaller quantities, many of which are available for spring frocks.

Any one of the following smart spring colors may be chosen with the assurance that the garment should not become faded and shabby from sun and weather: Bark, dust, parchment, reindeer, and doe are among the cool brown tones which will be particularly smart this spring—these are the tan shades by other names. Henna, rust, and Titian are among the warm browns. Peony red, dandelion yellow, and marine blue will be good for sports garments.

Not only the dye-makers, but the great woollen, silk, and cotton manufacturers have played a very splendid part in meeting a trying situation, and in pushing America onward to seek a world market for its products. Mr. Cheney, a recognized leader of the silk industry, who operates great mills, states:

Progress of American Dye Manufacturing

"In our opinion the progress made by the American dye industry is in many ways remarkable, both for the rapidity of its development and for the amount of products produced. We are using American dyes to the fullest extent possible, and as a general thing find them very satisfactory. In many cases they are better than the old German dyes of the same types. Of course there are many dyes which have not yet been produced in this country, but now that the war is over, and the dye manufacturers have the unrestricted opportunity of supplying themselves with raw materials and intermediates, we feel confident that in the reasonably near future practically all types of dyes will be satisfactorily produced in this country. This is provided we have the sense and foresight to see that this industry has adequate protection, which is imperative not only as a peace measure but also as a war measure, because the dye industry and the explosive industry go hand in hand."

It is only fair to our own new industries to realize that there is no necessity for any manufacturer or retailer to try to evade the responsibility of merchandise by apologizing for American dyes. Such apologies as one finds in the little tags bearing the statement, "On account of the dye situation, we can not guarantee colors in fabrics to be absolutely fast," are unconscious propaganda for keeping open the market for German dyes in America, for after-the-war trade. Let such tags disappear.

Other able merchants who have done much to evolve the dye and textile industries are Haas Brothers. Mr. Benjamin Haas spoke enthusiastically of a new spirit which, since the war, has brought the country together. "We know each other better and can no longer be considered provincial," he said. "During the past six months American goods have been exploited in different parts of the world to an extent never before attained." The, splendid (*Continued on page 86*)

Helen Koues

The first tendency of spring fashions is the "boxed" line, as in this dress of blue serge with black satin vest embroidered in henna red; $49.50

The second tendency of the new fashions is the tunic and tight underskirt, as in this frock of navy blue, black, or taupe taffeta, and a rarely good dress for $27.50; there is an embroidered yoke

The third tendency of the spring is the short, bell sleeve, as in this dress of gray, henna red, or navy blue Georgette crêpe with heavy, dyed lace trimming: $40.50

64

SPRING FASHIONS FOR MILADY, 1919

A page from the March 1919 issue of *Good Housekeeping*. Three fashion "tendencies" are noted, "cool brown tones" are designated as "particularly smart," and dyes made in America are praised. The signature is that of Helen Koues.

Amy Lowell, Edna St. Vincent Millay, Alfred Noyes, Ogden Nash, and Ella Wheeler Wilcox.

In 1916 *Good Housekeeping's* page size was increased to quarto, about that with which it had begun. By the end of Bigelow's editorship in the mid-thirties, 250-page numbers were common, glowing with color, distinguished by the drawings of such artists as Charles Dana Gibson and Jessie Willcox Smith, and presenting a great variety of attractive and helpful articles and service features, fiction, verse, and entertainment for children (such as Rose O'Neill's "Kewpies"). Circulation had passed the million mark in the mid-twenties and doubled in the next dozen years in spite of the Great Depression. Its success was no less than phenomenal. For 1938, the magazine showed an operating profit of $2,583,202—more than three times the profit of Hearst's other eight magazines combined.[9] This was a recession year, in which magazine advertising as a whole dropped off 22 percent from the 1937 figure, and many small periodicals died.[10] At that time *Good Housekeeping* was probably the most profitable monthly published. Four years later Bigelow retired from the editorship after a long and successful career with the Hearst magazines.

Herbert R. Mayes came to *Good Housekeeping* from *Pictorial Review,* which the Hearst organization was about to discontinue. He was well aware of the declining interest in magazine fiction, and he soon began to reduce *Good Housekeeping's* traditionally generous offerings in that field. In the early 1940's two-part stories began to replace long serials; novelettes and condensed novels complete in one issue came along in the next decade; and eventually the fictional fare in each issue commonly consisted of one such longer story plus three short ones. Among contributors about mid-century were Sinclair Lewis, Christopher Morley, William March, Evelyn Waugh, Daphne du Maurier (her terrifying story, "The Birds," appeared October, 1952), and John P. Marquand.

A tremendous variety continued to characterize the magazine. Hollywood, building and furnishing, babies, books, food, hairdos, fashions; the table of contents in these years ran a

9 *Printers' Ink,* v. 186, March 16, 1939, p. 16.
10 *1939 Britannica Book of the Year,* p. 17.

wide gamut. But with all its diversity, *Good Housekeeping* remained definitely a home magazine; world affairs, politics, economics, and social problems were generally put aside except as they directly affected the home. Nor were gardening topics, horticulture, landscaping, and the like given much attention.

Although the extraordinary offering of popular fiction during Bigelow's editorship had been one of the reasons for the ascending spiral of *Good Housekeeping's* prosperity, that factor had been supplemented not only by the home service feature articles in the magazine but by the *Good Housekeeping* Institute and Bureau of Foods, with their Seal of Approval. This operation was integrated with both the editorial and advertising departments of the magazine.

Early in its second year, *Good Housekeeping* entered the fight against misrepresentation of products with an editorial entitled "Guard Against Adulteration."[11] This was twenty years before the enactment of the National Food and Drug Act of 1906. The magazine continued its testimony against abuses in the sale of foods, but throughout Bryan's ownership its own advertising pages were by no means free from fault, especially in the fields of proprietary medicines and cosmetics. When Phelps took over, however, a new era began.

In 1900 *Good Housekeeping* set up its own Experiment Station to test various methods and practices to be recommended to housewives in the magazine. This was only a beginning, for it soon became apparent that reliable materials and equipment were necessary to good practice; and in 1902 the Station began testing such products, accepting advertising only for those that won its approval, and printing in each issue "An Inflexible Contract Between the Publisher and Each Subscriber" that included a money-back "guarantee" of the reliability of every advertisement printed in *Good Housekeeping*.[12]

The Experiment Station was conducted for several years by the editorial staff; but in 1909 Richard H. Waldo, then

[11] *Good Housekeeping*, v. 3, Sept. 18, 1886, p. 250.

[12] The early development of the Station and the Institute is described in *Good Housekeeping's* 50th anniversary number, v. 100, May 1935, p. 8.

publisher of the magazine, set up the *Good Housekeeping* Institute on a laboratory basis under the direction of Helen Louise Johnson. Three years later the Institute gained prestige by adding to its staff Dr. Harvey W. Wiley, who, as chief chemist of the United States Department of Agriculture for thirty years, had become famous as a leader of the crusade against food adulteration that had resulted in the Food and Drug Act of 1906. In the Institute, Wiley conducted his own Bureau of Foods, Sanitation and Health, as well as serving as a contributing editor of the magazine. His "Question Box" was a popular department for many years. He died in 1930 and was succeeded in the bureau by Dr. Walter H. Eddy. For a time in the 1940's the Bureau was represented in the magazine only by a "Question Box"; but Albert A. Schaal made it more prominent during the years 1947–1963, and by the time of his retirement it had a staff of nine workers.[13]

Beginning with a "Beauty Clinic" in 1932, other departments were added to the Institute from year to year—a "Needlework Room," a "Baby's Center," and departments of "Engineering," "Foods and Cookery," "Appliances and Home Care," and "Special Projects." Such older departments of the magazine as those devoted to fashions, patterns, and "The Decorating Studio and Building Forum" were also related to *Good Housekeeping* Institute. Some of these divisions—notably the Bureau—functioned as testing laboratories for advertised products; others, though experimental in spirit, were designed mainly to produce editorial copy. But all had the double purpose of testing products and processes and filling the magazine with helpful information for the consumer.

From the testing by the Experiment Station, "Our Roll of Honor for Pure Food Products" developed naturally in 1905, and products listed therein were distinguished in the advertising pages by a five-pointed star carrying the words, "Pure Food Assurance—*Good Housekeeping*." It was in 1909, when

[13] See "Who, What, Why, and Wonderful: The *Good Housekeeping* Institute," in the magazine's 75th anniversary number, v. 150, May 1960, pp. 116–24.

the Institute was set up, that the first seal, designating "examined apparatus and readily available products," was inaugurated; it was designed as an ellipse enclosing the words, "Tested and Approved by the Good Housekeeping Institute Conducted by *Good Housekeeping Magazine*."

This Seal of Approval eventually became the object of an acrimonious controversy having two more or less related motivations. When Rexford G. Tugwell became Assistant Secretary of Agriculture in 1933, he brought to his new job a strong conviction against what he considered the social and economic abuses of advertising.[14] Hoping to capitalize upon a popular sentiment already initiated by attacks on this industry in current books and periodicals,[15] and by such governmental agencies as the Consumer Services division of the Office of Price Administration (itself a bureau of the National Industrial Recovery Administration), Tugwell set out to push through Congress a new food and drug law that was to embody the principle of grade labeling. When the Food, Drug and Cosmetics Act of 1938 was at last made law, it did not include the grade-labeling provision, which many considered as opening the door to arbitrary decisions by government agencies and invading the consumer's right to free choice.

The Hearst Corporation fought arbitrary grade labeling with energy and even virulence. It was, of course, well aware that the *Good Housekeeping* Seal of Approval would be superseded by government grading. But its fight against the New Deal consumer agencies did not end with the passage of the act in 1938. Indeed, it published an eight-page tabloid monthly called *Consumers Information Service* (1936–1942), "Sponsored by the *Good Housekeeping* Club Service," as a propaganda organ attacking those agencies. "The slow strangulation of American industry with regulations and limitations,"

[14] See Arthur M. Schlesinger, Jr., *The Coming of the New Deal*, v. 2 of *The Age of Roosevelt* (Boston, 1959), pp. 354–61, for a sympathetic account of Tugwell's crusade against current advertising practices.

[15] Stuart Chase and F. J. Schlink, *Your Money's Worth* (New York, 1927); F. J. Schlink and Arthur Kallet, *100,000,000 Guinea Pigs* (New York, 1923); *Consumers' Research Bulletin* ("confidential" 1929–32; N.S. 1934–current); *Consumers' Union Reports* (1936–current; title since 1943, *Consumer Reports*).

this periodical averred, "is not the system of free enterprise known to this country." [16]

This feud probably furnished an important motivation for the action of the Federal Trade Commission against *Good Housekeeping* and its Seal of Approval. The FTC had been given certain powers to control advertising that appeared to violate the Food, Drug and Cosmetics Act of 1938 by the Wheeler-Lea Act of the same year; and in 1939 it filed a complaint charging *Good Housekeeping* with "misleading and deceptive acts and practices in the issuance of guarantys, seals of approval, and the publication in its advertising pages of grossly exaggerated and false claims." General Manager Berlin countered with a flat refusal to sign the cease-and-desist stipulation submitted by the FTC, declaring that "In no single case . . . was the Commission able to show that *Good Housekeeping* had failed to carry out its guaranty, which has been in existence for over 30 years. . . ." [17]

Hearings on this complaint continued over nearly two years, in New York, Chicago, and Washington. Suspicion that envy of competitors directed against the home magazine that had surpassed all others in prosperity during the depression was a second motivation for the FTC complaint was aroused by the fact that among the leading witnesses to testify that the *Good Housekeeping* Seal of Approval constituted unfair competition were Publisher Walter D. Fuller, of the *Ladies' Home Journal* and Editor Otis Wiese, of *McCall's*.

After the long series of hearings, which occasionally developed displays of ill temper on both sides, the commission issued an order on May 23, 1941, directing *Good Housekeeping* to cease and desist from the use of seals declaring that its advertised products had been "tested and approved." It declared that "while tests were made by . . . *Good Housekeeping* magazine, such tests were generally not sufficient to assure the fulfillment of the claims made for such products." It also found that the magazine was publishing advertising containing deceptive statements about "the therapeutic value of medicinal preparations" as well as "the effectiveness of cosmetic

[16] *Consumers Information Service,* v. 4, Dec. 1941, p. 2.
[17] *Time,* v. 34, Aug. 28, 1939, p. 44.

preparations" and the qualities of wearing apparel, food, and commercial services. Specific advertised products were named.[18]

The business of *Good Housekeeping* appears to have been little affected by these hearings. Circulation continued its steady advance, reaching 2,500,000 in 1943 and passing 3,500,000 in the mid-fifties. In the first half of 1955 the magazine's gross advertising passed all its previous records at $8,000,000. Four years later a similar period showed over $11,000,000.[19]

But the seal was changed following the commission's order; the words "tested and approved" were deleted, and the guarantee read: "Replacement or Refund of Money Guaranteed by *Good Housekeeping* if Not as Advertised Therein." Unquestionably the popular image of the Seal of Approval remained the same, however. In 1962 its guarantee was further altered: "If Product or Performance Defective, *Good Housekeeping* Guarantees Replacement or Refund to Consumer." It will be noted that this last guarantee makes no reference to advertising claims.

The relation of the seal to *Good Housekeeping* advertising has varied somewhat throughout its history. Immediately after the FTC order, the magazine made the editorial statement: "As a matter of fact of all the products that have received the Seal of Approval less than 30 percent have ever been advertised in *Good Housekeeping*."[20] Thereafter, however, the terms for use of the seal came to require some advertising in the magazine. Eventually the formal contract authorizing a distributor to use the seal granted such license only in connection with submission of advertising copy for the magazine and after "*Good Housekeeping* . . . has examined the product(s) and/or service(s) listed . . . and has examined the copy submitted for publication in the Magazine, and has satisfied itself that the product is a good product and that the advertising copy is acceptable. . . ." This contract covered a

[18] *Editor & Publisher,* v. 72, Nov. 18, 1939, p. 7. Curiously enough, these products were also being advertised in the *Ladies' Home Journal* and *McCall's* at the same time.

[19] *Magazine Industry Newsletter,* April 30, 1955 and May 23, 1959.

[20] *Good Housekeeping,* v. 113, July 1941, p. 6.

period of one year only, provided for re-examination in case of changes in the product, and authorized inspection of factory or product at any time during the term of the license.[21]

Once licensed, the advertiser might use the seal by affixing it to the product, or in any of its other advertising, including that appearing on the television screen or on billboards. *Good Housekeeping* outranked all other magazines in "advertiser tie-in linage"—that is, the amount of advertising in other media making some reference to the advertising of the product in a magazine.[22] The seal was not intended, however, to supplant the reputation and prestige of the product itself, its name, its label, or its own symbols. Indeed, by the early 1960's less than a third of the advertisements appearing in *Good Housekeeping* displayed the magazine's seal,[23] and it rarely appeared in the larger "ads" of the better known products. Why should it? On page six of every issue appeared a statement of approval covering all the advertising in the magazine, with specific exception of those for insurance, real estate, automobiles and the kind of promotion described as "institutional." "We satisfy ourselves," runs this statement, "that products and services advertised in *Good Housekeeping* are good ones, and that the advertising claims made for them in our magazine are truthful." Certain "points" are then specifically noted in the practical application of the *Good Housekeeping* guarantee, such as the impossibility of measuring taste, the necessity of proper installation of equipment, and so on.

Other magazines have followed *Good Housekeeping's* lead in the matter of emblems of approval; by the 1960's *Parents' Magazine, McCall's,* and *Better Homes and Gardens* had joined the parade of seals.

Meantime *Good Housekeeping* continued to prosper, al-

21 "Agreement Governing the Use of the *Good Housekeeping* Consumers' Guaranty by the Advertiser" (available on application). The author is indebted to Miss Susan Crumbaker for access to her collection of materials related to the backgrounds and present operation of Good Housekeeping, made in connection with a study performed at Syracuse University.

22 *Standard Rate and Data Service,* Consumer Magazine Section, March 27, 1963, p. 339.

23 Specifically, in the issue for Nov. 1963, 61 of the 209 advertisements displayed the seal, or 29 percent. The *Parents' Magazine* seal was displayed, along with that of *Good Housekeeping,* in 11.

though editors changed. Wade H. Nichols, Jr., coming from the editorship of *Redbook,* succeeded Mayes in 1959. *Good Housekeeping* passed the five million mark in circulation in 1962. It was then carrying about 125 pages of advertising in each issue, at approximately $20,000 for a black-and-white page and $25,000 for one in full color. It provided split-run printings covering eight regions for its advertisers.

Editorially, the magazine, having swung away from its former heavy emphasis on fiction, had become mainly a household service journal. Leading topics were family life and children, medical matters, cookery and foods, fashions and beauty hints, house building and landscaping, furnishings and decorations, appliances, budgeting, diet. Many of the articles came directly from the *Good Housekeeping* Institute. In its eightieth year, it was an attractive, colorful magazine of three hundred pages or more, full of interest and practical help for the moderate-income family.*

* This historical sketch was written in the early 1960's. *Good Housekeeping's* circulation was over 5,500,000 in 1966.

"RISKY" COVER OF *BROADWAY MAGAZINE,* 1899

The bathing girls illustrate this magazine's "shock-'em-and-sell-'em" technique. Theodore Dreiser became editor seven years later.

11

HAMPTON'S BROADWAY MAGAZINE [1]

TWO young New Yorkers, George A. Sherin and Roland Burke Hennessy, founded the *Broadway Magazine* in April 1898. Sherin put up most of the money required and became general manager. Hennessy put up his experience on the *Standard,* a Saturday weekly devoted chiefly to the theater, and on the *Metropolitan Magazine* in its initial experiments with sex sensationalism. He became editor of the new magazine.

The *Broadway* began as a ten-cent offering of text and illustration of the kind then called by its devotees "risky." Pictures of burlesque queens in tights and décolletage, art reproductions emphasizing the nude female figure, peeks at bathing girls in bloomers, and representations of "living picture" posing were prominent in the copious illustration. For text, the "Red Soubrette" told "saucy truths in a saucy way"; and other gossip departments combined to make the *Broadway* "absolutely the most unique, beautiful and satisfying monthly," according to one of its blatant and badly worded boasts.

[1] Titles: (1) *Broadway Magazine,* April 1898—Nov. 1907; (2) *The New Broadway Magazine,* Dec. 1907—Sept. 1908; (3) *Hampton's Broadway Magazine,* Oct. 1908—Jan. 1909; (4) *Hampton's Magazine: The New Broadway,* Feb.–April 1909; (5) *Hampton's Magazine,* May 1909—Sept. 1911; (6) *Hampton-Columbian Magazine,* Oct. 1911—Jan. 1912; (7) *The Hampton Magazine,* Feb.–May 1912.

First issue: April 1898. Last issue: May 1912.

Periodicity: Monthly. Vols. 1–19, semiannual vols., April 1898—March 1908; 20, April–June 1908; 20–26, regular semiannual vols., July 1908—June 1911; 27, July 1911—Jan. 1912; 28, nos. 1–4, Feb.–May 1912

Publishers: Broadway Publishing Company (George A. Sherin, general manager) 1898–1903; Broadway Magazine Company (C. H. Young, publisher) 1904–5; Broadway Magazine, Inc. (Benjamin Bowles Hampton, owner, 1906–11) 1905–11; Columbian-Sterling Magazine Company (Frank Orff, pres.) 1911–12. All New York.

Editors: Roland Burke Hennessy, 1898–1903; Courtland H. Young, 1904; Charles Edward Barns, 1904; Theodore Dreiser, 1906–7; B. B. Hampton, 1907–11; W. W. Young, 1911–12.

Indexes: *Bulletin of Bibliography Subject-Index,* 1906–7; *Readers' Guide,* 1910–12.

Broadway doubtless shocked many who found it on the newsstands in the closing years of the nineteenth century. Today, however, the abundantly clothed bathing beauties and the gals in tights seem funny rather than shocking; and the first few volumes of the *Broadway Magazine,* with their shock-'em-and-sell-'em technique, are amusing in a somewhat tawdry fashion.

By 1902 there were more articles, mostly about the stage and New York life. For a while Sherin published also the *Broadway Weekly* and a *Broadway Quarterly,* both containing pictures of stage beauties and notes on the New York theater, and thriftily using over and over some of the Broadway Publishing Company's plates.

In 1904, Courtland H. Young, who had been publishing *Young's Magazine,* which exploited "snappy stories," gained control of *Broadway*. He changed the policy of the magazine somewhat. Though it still emphasized the stage and the nude in art, and though it printed much about New York society, it now abandoned burlesque queens and "smart" gossip in favor of feature articles and what it called "storiettes"—short short stories. But the magazine, which had for a few years enjoyed a circulation of about one hundred thousand, went down rather than up, and its advertising was not impressive in either quantity or quality. Young sold the *Broadway* in 1905 to a company headed by Thomas H. McKee. It was early the next year that Theodore Dreiser wrote to the *Broadway,* offering to take over as editor at forty dollars a week and suggesting a nine-point editorial program embodying much of the former pattern, but with careful supervision of the art work "as to merit and purity", and addition of such features as "What Americans Are Thinking," occasional interviews with the famous, articles on the "Big Questions"—socialism, morality, spiritualism—and so on. His offer was accepted immediately.[2] Dreiser had been working at editorial jobs in the magazine field for a decade, and came to the *Broadway* from *Smith's,*

[2] Dreiser correspondence, University of Pennsylvania Library. Letter of application dated April 10, 1906. Letter from C. L. Litchfield, business manager, offering the job, dated April 18, 1906. Dreiser was warned that the job might not last long on account of the uncertainty caused by a probable sale of the magazine.

another specialist in female pulchritude. He was not yet famous as a novelist, though *Sister Carrie* had been published (if publication it could be called) six years earlier.

Dreiser's position was uncertain from the first, since the sale of the magazine was again being considered. The purchaser, later that year, was Benjamin B. Hampton, an advertising man. Hampton had been an Illinois newspaper publisher before he had come to New York at twenty-five to make his fortune in the advertising agency business. In six years he had accumulated some $200,000.[3] He bought the *Broadway* in 1906 at a low price as an investment, intending to dispose of it within a year; but he soon fell in love with the whole business of magazine editing and publishing and decided to put his entire fortune into promoting this venture.[4] Hampton was by nature a plunger, intolerant of advice, versatile, brilliant.[5]

He kept Dreiser on as editor. "The minute I set eyes on him," said Hampton many years later, "I figured the man was a genius. I said to myself, 'Jesus, here's a wow!' "[6] Dreiser was given the commission to do much more than he had been doing on *Smith's* and more than anyone had hitherto done on the *Broadway*. Dreiser later wrote that he took "an anemic 'white-light' monthly" and attempted "to recast it into a national or international metropolitan picture."[7] The price was raised to fifteen cents; and the literary content, the editing, the illustration and layout, and the printing were all improved.

The roll of the new magazine's authors now became impressive. Carl Van Vechten, Edgar Saltus, James L. Ford, Eugene Wood, and Harris Merton Lyon were constant contributors,

3 See George French, "The Damnation of the Magazines," in *Twentieth Century Magazine,* v. 6, June 1912, p. 9.

4 See obituary, *New York Times,* Feb. 1, 1932, p. 17, col. 3; also Theodore Dreiser, *Twelve Men* (New York, 1919), pp. 209–10.

5 French, "Damnation of Magazines," p. 8.

6 Dorothy Dudley, *Forgotten Frontiers* (New York, 1932), p. 209. Interviewed by Miss Dudley shortly before his death, Hampton got his facts as to how he met Dreiser confused; but the above quotation probably conveys something of the new owner's impression of his editor. Hampton also told Dreiser's biographer that he paid Dreiser $60 a week, with a promise of $100 when the circulation reached 75,000. It soon went over 100,000.

7 Dreiser, *Twelve Men,* p. 208.

and members of a small group which Dreiser rallied about the magazine. In the narrative which Dreiser later wrote about Lyon under the title "De Maupassant, Jr." in his *Twelve Men,* he told with gusto of bringing this group together. But he wrote also about his resentment against the interference of the owner in editorial matters. Hampton seemed to him "a small, energetic, vibrant and colorful soul, all egotism and middle-class conviction as to the need of 'push,' ambition, 'closeness to life,' 'punch,' and what not else . . . Hampton was accustomed to enter and force a conversation here and there, anxious of course to gather the full import of all these various energies and enthusiasms. One of the things which Lyon most resented in him at the time was his air of supreme material well-being, his obvious attempt and wish not to convey it, his carefully cut clothes, his car, his numerous assistants and secretaries following him here and there. . . ."[8] Dreiser and Hampton were incompatible,[9] and it is remarkable that they managed to work together for more than a year.

In 1907 Hampton took over the editorship himself, and soon changed the name to *Hampton's Broadway Magazine.* The table of contents now bristled with great names. There were such serials as Rex Beach's *The Silver Horde* (1910) and Harold MacGrath's *Carpet from Bagdad,* stories by Joseph Conrad, O. Henry, Jack London, F. Hopkinson Smith, Emerson Hough, Montague Glass, George Randolph Chester, and James Hopper; as well as the "Luther Trant" detective stories by Edwin Balmer and William B. MacHarg, and a department of "short shorts." Edmond Rostand's drama *Chantecler,* in Gertrude Hall's translation, was printed serially in the summer of 1910. In nonfiction, the offerings were quite as distinguished. Admiral Robley D. Evans' history of the American Navy (1908), Robert E. Peary's story of his discovery of the North Pole for which the author was said to have received $50,000 (1910),[10] and "Dr. Cook's Own Story" (1911) were

[8] Dreiser, *Twelve Men,* pp. 209–10, 215.

[9] He also had difficulties with "Kee," who had apparently stayed on in an executive position. Dreiser correspondence, including office memos, University of Pennsylvania Library.

[10] On Peary's fee, see *Putnam's,* v. 7, Feb. 1910, p. 627.

outstanding. A theater department and another called "Personalities" lent attraction to the magazine.

But the most notable articles published by *Hampton's* were certain series on public abuses which form a kind of postscript to the muckraking movement. Herbert N. Casson, writing on the railroads in the summer of 1908, was sympathetic with their problems; it was not until November that he adopted the tone of the muckraker in "The Wall Street Nuisance." John L. Mathews discussed the "power trust" and water resources in three articles in the summer of 1909, and later he contributed other articles on the preservation of natural resources for the public benefit. Judson C. Welliver wrote on the sugar trust in 1910. Eugene P. Lyle, Jr., discussed "The Guggenheims and the Smelter Trust" in the same year. Hampton himself wrote about Alaskan resources and the attempt to "steal" them. There were many other articles attacking "entrenched wealth" and "reactionary" statesmen.

Rheta Childe Dorr had a field all her own; she wrote about suffrage, the wrecking of the home by the employment of wives and mothers, "The Prodigal Daughter," public health and education, protective legislation for working girls. Though these articles fitted well with the exposé tone of the magazine, they were not precisely muckraking forays, but challenging discussions of important social problems, bolstered with facts.

Chief of the magazine's band of writers on economic questions was Charles Edward Russell, who attacked millionaires and capitalists right and left, wielding his muckrake like a claymore. An early piece was the bitingly satirical "Rational Plan for an American Peerage" (July 1908), in which Russell proposed his scheme to put American millionaires in a good trading position when they tried to marry their daughters to foreign noblemen. Some of his studies of socialistic movements abroad were published in *Hampton's*. But perhaps the strongest of his contributions were the series attacking the Southern Pacific Railroad in 1910, and the one which later arraigned the New Haven Railway.

Newspaper critics of *Hampton's* pointed out that it was now the only muckraking magazine left in the field. To which Hampton replied:

> Make no mistake. "Muck-raking" has not gone out of date. It really is just beginning to find itself, to make itself efficient . . . we know a great deal more about the temper of the American people than the politicians do. . . . For a while the "muck-raking" was sensational without accomplishing much good. . . . Nowadays, we know how to get results.[11]

The "efficiency" of *Hampton's* in obtaining reforms may be questioned, but it probably had a part in driving Secretary of Interior Ballinger out of office, and perhaps it helped to loose the hold of the Southern Pacific on California government and to promote other reformatory movements.[12] Many of its exposure articles were very much in the public interest.

But Ben Hampton had trouble financing the expansion of his magazine. He had owned it only a few months when he initiated a campaign to raise funds by selling stock to its readers, beginning with an issue of $100,000. In this he followed the pattern of *Everybody's* development, just as he had followed that magazine's formula of building circulation by sensational muckraking, and indeed its general policy as to content. In the spring of 1908, *Hampton's* was advertising that "*Everybody's*, the *Ladies' Home Journal*, and others represent wonderful money-making investments. Our offer of *Broadway Magazine* stock represents the same opportunity to you. . . . If you have fifty dollars, a hundred, or a thousand that you would like to invest where it will be *safe*, and earn unusually large dividends, you ought to send for the booklet immediately."

The first $100,000 came easily; but it also went easily, and Hampton thereupon sold additional stock until a total of about $700,000 worth was disposed of and Hampton's had some 4,500 reader-stockholders.[13]

With money to spend in newspaper advertising, with an increase to 140 pages in size, with a marked advance in quality of content, and with a series of sensational exposés of big business and corrupt politics, *Hampton's Magazine* was able to increase rapidly in circulation. In 1908 it reached 125,000,

11 *Hampton's*, v. 24, June 1910, p. 876.

12 C. C. Regier, *The Era of the Muckrakers* (Chapel Hill, N.C., 1932), pp. 203–4; also "Editorial Notes" in *Hampton's, passim.*

13 French, "Damnation of Magazines," p. 8.

the next year it doubled that, and by 1910 it touched its highest point at about 450,000. Suddenly it had plenty of advertising, and was publishing fat, prosperous-looking numbers each month.

But it was never stabilized. *Hampton's* shares fared badly on the stock exchange, thus stopping further sales of stock, and when the magazine "needed a few thousand dollars of capital to carry us through the summer," it could not raise the money either through stock sales or from banks. Hampton himself said the banks would lend nothing because "*Hampton's* fearless, aggressive editorial policy had offended the powers of Wall Street. . . ."[14] Editorial policy may have had something to do with it; undoubtedly the financial policy of Ben Hampton was scarcely reassuring. At any rate, when he found himself unable to borrow, at the end of his string in the stockselling game, facing a breakdown in health, Hampton was forced to give up. He took a much needed rest, and commissioned his brother, Jesse D. Hampton, to sell the magazine.

This was not easy to do, but a buyer was found in June 1911. He was Frank Orff, a St. Louis publisher who was at the time conducting four periodicals.[15] Orff announced that

[14] *Hampton's,* v. 27, Aug. 1911, p. 258.

[15] French, "Damnation of Magazines," p. 9. But before the sale to Orff, Hampton had made some kind of deal with the International Correspondence School, of Scranton, Pa., to save himself from bankruptcy. Later this deal got into the courts, but Hampton never recovered anything. As he later wrote, "Of course, the property in the meantime had been ruined." See interesting and picturesque (but often vague) statement made by Hampton about the latter months of his ownership in Upton Sinclair's *The Brass Check,* rev. ed. (New York, 1936), pp. 230–33. In Sinclair's ranting, *The Profits of Religion* (Pasadena, Calif., 1918), pp. 181–83, the author alleges that the New Haven Railroad wrecked the magazine in retaliation for the articles about it by Russell. Says Sinclair (p. 181): ". . . the story of its [*Hampton's*] wrecking by the New Haven criminals will some day serve in school text-books as the classic illustration of that financial piracy which brought on the American social revolution." See also, Russell's "The Magazine Soft Pedal," *Pearson's,* v. 31, Feb. 1914, pp. 179–89.

Orff's other periodicals were the *American Woman's Review,* formerly *Chaperone* (see F. L. Mott, *A History of American Magazines,* v. 4 [Cambridge, Mass., 1957], p. 361), the *Home, Orff's Farm Review* (1900–12), the *Sterling Magazine* (1909–11), and the *Columbian Magazine* (1909–11). They were all published in St. Louis except the last named, which was a New York general literary magazine edited by the Englishman Henry Mann.

Hampton would remain as "consulting editor" of all his publications; but this did not work out, and William W. Young was soon installed as editor of *Hampton's*. Mayor Tom L. Johnson's *My Nine Years' War With Privilege* was a 1911 serial. Russell, who had been Socialist candidate for governor of New York in 1910, was still a valued contributor, and his article on "Socialism: Just Where It Stands Today" (January 1912) was a significant document. Robert W. Chambers had some short stories, and Mrs. Dorr continued her excellent studies. Interest was continued in two fields much cultivated by *Hampton's*—psychic research and the progress of aviation.

Orff combined *Hampton's* and his other New York magazine, the *Columbian,* in October 1911, under the name of *Hampton-Columbian Magazine.* He had purchased the Winthrop Press, a New York printing plant, from which the merged magazine was issued; and he had made other combinations and expansions in connection with his St. Louis ventures.[16] Orff's operating capital had come from the sale of stock to readers on the *Everybody's-Hampton's* plan, and his company had 24,000 stockholders when it bought *Hampton's*.[17] But over-expansion brought increasing need for capital; and the stockholders, hungry for dividends, received only appeals for more activity in selling subscriptions and more and bigger investment of savings. The collapse came at the end of 1911. The *Hampton Magazine,* as it was now renamed, was then sold to a committee of preferred stockholders for about $10,000.[18] Orff and some other officers of his company were later indicted for using the mails to defraud, by misrepresenting the financial condition of the Columbia-Stirling Company and the circulation of the magazines in selling stock. After a trial in June 1913, they were acquitted.[19]

The *Hampton Magazine* was an attractive quarto of eighty pages, of which less than twenty were filled with advertising. It lasted only four months. Its editorials were progressive, but

[16] *Hampton-Columbian,* v. 27, Oct. 1911, pp. 557–64.

[17] *Hampton's,* v. 27, Aug. 1911, p. 268.

[18] French, "Damnation of Magazines," p. 9.

[19] *New York Times,* June 7, 1913, p. 6, col. 2; June 10, 1913, p. 7, col. 4; June 29, 1913, sec. 2, p. 6, col. 1; July 1, 1913, p. 7, col. 7.

there was no more muckraking. Such leftist observers as Sinclair and Russell agreed that the magazine was forced by "Wall Street" to use the "soft pedal" at the time Ben Hampton was squeezed out. As has been noted, however, Russell's impassioned defense of Socialism appeared as late as January 1912. At this distance it would seem that neither Hampton nor Orff was a convinced Socialist or even a sincere economic reformer. They seem to have been unsuccessful entrepreneurs who skated frantically over thin ice toward their private visions of wealth and power.

12

HOUSE BEAUTIFUL[1]

THE title of this magazine was derived from Robert Louis Stevenson's charming little poem, "The House Beautiful," and affectionate remembrance of this origin caused the article *The* to be retained in its nameplate throughout its first thirty years. The poem begins:

A naked house, a naked moor,
A shivering pool before the door,
A garden bare of flowers and fruit,
And poplars at the garden foot;
Such is the place I live in,
Bleak without and bare within.

[1] TITLE: *The House Beautiful* (the article *The* was dropped in 1925). On mergers with *Indoors and Out* (1908), *Modern Homes* (1909), *American Suburbs* (1912), *Home and Field* (1934), their names appeared in subtitles for brief periods.

FIRST ISSUE: Dec. 1896. Current.

PERIODICITY: Monthly. Vols. 1–43 (semiannual, Dec.–May, June–Nov.), Dec. 1896—May 1918; 44, June–Dec. 1918; 45–current (semiannual, Jan.–June, July–Dec.), 1919–current.

OWNERS: Klapp & Company (Eugene Klapp and Henry Blodgett Harvey), Chicago, 1896–97; Herbert S. Stone & Company, Chicago, 1897–1906; House Beautiful Company (H. S. Stone, pres.), Chicago, 1906–11; House Beautiful Company (H. S. Stone, pres., 1911–12; G. Henry Stetson, Wallace S. Peace, Stuart W. Buck, and others, officers and stockholders, 1912–13), New York, 1911–13; House Beautiful Company (Atlantic Monthly Co., MacGregor Jenkins, pres.), New York, 1913–15, Boston, 1915–34; International Magazines Company (renamed Hearst Magazines, 1936; Hearst Corporation, 1952), New York, 1934–current.

EDITORS: Eugene Klapp and H. B. Harvey, 1896–97; Eugene Klapp, 1897–98; Herbert Stuart Stone, 1898–1913; Virginia Robie, 1913–15; Mabel Kent, 1915–16; Grace Atkinson Kimball, 1916–18; Mabel Rollins, 1918–20; Charlotte Lewis, 1921; Ellery Sedgwick, 1922; Ethel B. Power, 1923–34; Arthur H. Samuels, 1934–36; Kenneth K. Stowell, 1936–41; Elizabeth Gordon (Norcross), 1941–64; Sarah Tomerlin Lee, 1965–current.

INDEXES: Semiannual for each volume; *Readers' Guide,* 1909–current.

REFERENCES: Virginia Robie, "How We Did It in the Old Days," *House Beautiful,* v. 88, Dec. 1946 (50th anniversary number), pp. 153, 243–50; Amos Stote, "The Quality Quartette of the Hearst Collection," *Magazine World,* v. 3, March 1947, pp. 11–13; Herbert E. Fleming, "The Literary Interests of Chicago-V," *American Journal of Sociology,* v. 11, May 1906, pp. 803–4 (this series of papers was reissued in paper binding by the University of Chicago Press, 1906, with the title, *Magazines of a Market-Metropolis*).

The verses go on to develop their theme:

> God's intricate and bright device
> Of days and seasons doth suffice.[2]

This appears to suit, to a degree, the idea followed by this magazine throughout its long career—simplicity combined with beauty in the home. For many years *The House Beautiful* boasted that it was "The Only Magazine in America Devoted to Simplicity, Economy and Appropriateness in the Home." And yet, viewed more critically and less poetically, Stevenson's lines did not express fully the aims of this magazine; it wished for no naked house nor garden bare, but rather for one well provided with good furniture and a tended garden—all within a frame of beautiful simplicity.

The House Beautiful was begun in December 1896, by Eugene Klapp, a Chicago engineer who had a flair for architecture and literature, with the assistance of his friend Henry Blodgett Harvey, who also had a liking for such things along with some available cash. The first monthly number carried twenty-eight royal octavo pages of text, illustrated by ten pages of good halftones representing houses and interiors, plus sixteen pages of advertising. It sold for ten cents and quoted a subscription price of a dollar a year. Its articles were short and readable, and were obvioul y designed for the average householder rather than for the rich home owner or the professional builder or decorator. The series "Successful Homes," written by the senior editor, was begun in the first number; and there, on the very first page of the magazine, this principle was laid down: "A little money spent with careful thought by people of keen artistic perception will achieve a result which is astonishing."[3] Also in this first issue—typical of many that followed—were articles on Satsuma ware, Oriental rugs, and "A Plea for the Amateur." An essay entitled "The Moral Side of Beauty" emphasized a concept that was to reappear again and again in the magazine.

After less than a year on their own, Klapp and Harvey

[2] Reprinted from Stevenson's *Poems and Ballads* in *The House Beautiful,* v. 15, Dec. 1903, p. 1.

[3] *The House Beautiful,* v. 1, Dec. 1896, p. 1. The series was reprinted in book form under the same title by Herbert S. Stone & Co., Chicago, 1898.

found a good publisher in Herbert S. Stone & Company, though they remained as editors until the end of 1897. Indeed Klapp continued in the chief editorial position through May of the next year, after which he joined the army as a volunteer in the war in Cuba. Later he was a faithful contributor for many years, usually writing under the pen-name of Oliver Coleman.

Stone had first attained prominence in the world of letters when he and his partner Ingalls Kimball, while they were still Harvard undergraduates, had begun publication of the *Chap-Book*,[4] a pioneer in the "little magazine" movement. As soon as their college days were over, Stone and Kimball moved their operations, which already included a small book-publishing business, to Chicago. That city was then becoming a lively literary center; and it was the home of the senior partner's father, Melville E. Stone, general manager of the Associated Press and a prosperous banker. But by 1896, Kimball wanted to move to New York, and so Stone sold his share of the book business to his partner and stayed behind in Chicago to run the *Chap-Book*.

That periodical, though undeniably a *succès d'estime*, showed no signs of yielding a financial profit, and in 1897 Stone purchased *The House Beautiful* and the next year disposed of the *Chap-Book* to the Chicago *Dial*[5] in order to devote himself to publishing and editing the new magazine. He was well fitted by talent and inclination to conduct such a periodical as *The House Beautiful*. He had an almost religious devotion to simple beauty, an abhorrence of display and blatancy in modern life, and a special interest in the development of new art forms and the revival of old ones as he found them within the framework of beauty and suitability. Stone remained as editor after the magazine removed to New York, serving in that capacity for sixteen years in all. Returning from a European holiday on the "Lusitania" in 1915, he was drowned when the ship was sunk by a German submarine.

[4] See F. L. Mott, *A History of American Magazines*, v. 4 (Cambridge, Mass., 1957), pp. 450–52.

[5] *Ibid.*, v. 3 (1938), pp. 539–43.

The House Beautiful continued on much the same lines under Stone as it had begun under Klapp, the only marked changes being the use of calendered paper, so that the halftones could be scattered more freely throughout the text; an increased attention to country homes and to French, Swedish, and Oriental houses and furnishings; and the addition of some departments, such as one for housekeeping advice and another for inquiries and comments from readers. In 1900 the size of the magazine was increased to sixty-four pages, the price was doubled, and Stone was claiming a circulation of seven thousand. The cover subtitle was "A Monthly Magazine of Art and Artisanship."

An episode in the early history of the magazine that illustrated better than any other its crusading spirit was the publication in 1904–1905 of several essays under the general title, "The Poor Taste of the Rich: A Series of Articles Which Show That Wealth Is Not Essential to the Decoration of a House, and That the Homes of Many of Our Richest Citizens Are Furnished in Execrable Taste." These severely critical pieces were not only illustrated by halftones from actual photographs of the homes discussed, but the names of the rich men with bad taste were not withheld. The series attracted much attention, and the rich men may have felt some resentment; if so, none invited further publicity by suing for damages to his injured feelings. Shortly before this series began, *The House Beautiful* had published a two-part article (July–August, 1904) by Ethel M. Colson and Anne Higginson Spicer entitled "Successful Furnishing and Decoration on an Income of $3,500 a Year." But the magazine was generally aimed at families enjoying about double that income[6]—in other words, at the upper middle class of those times.

Bêtes noires of the magazine were golden oak (and later, mission) furniture, overcrowded rooms, mansard roofs, multiple gables, and other "gingerbread" decoration in house design and furnishings. As early as 1898, *The House Beautiful* conducted its first competition for house plans; it was for the best design for a $3,000 house. These contests continued for many

[6] Fleming, "Literary Interests," p. 804.

years, though of course the price levels increased, especially in the inflationary 1920's. In the late 1930's actual blueprints were being folded into the magazine.

Apartment-house furnishing gained some attention by 1903, as did antiques, collections, fabrics, gardens, and so on. The magazine was growing, and the next year it was enlarged to a quarto of fifty pages, including advertisements. Then began such features as a household helps department, first conducted by Dean Marion Talbot, of the University of Chicago, and afterward by a long train of other specialists in the field of home economics; one on the home garden, edited by the well-known botanist and author, Clarence Moores Weed; "The Woman's Forum," dealing chiefly with social and industrial problems, edited by Ellen M. Henrotin, a former president of the General Federation of Women's Clubs; "Notes and Comments," by the faithful "Oliver Coleman;" as well as a department about household equipment and one dealing with the new-fangled automobile.

Much had been printed from the beginning of the magazine about good pictures and good floor and wall coverings, but soon after the turn of the century a more modern note began to appear in its art criticism. This was especially true in respect to architecture, and articles stimulated by the work of Frank Lloyd Wright, Howard Shaw, Alfred Granger, and others were notable.

Circulation and advertising responded to the enlargement and improvements of 1904, the former reaching twenty thousand and the latter reaching twenty pages or more the following year.[7]

Excursions into the fiction field were made more than once, only to be abandoned after brief experiments. George Barr McCutcheon's *Castle Craneycrow* was a serial of 1902–1903, and C. N. and A. M. Williamson's *The Motor Maid* ran in 1907–1908. A few short stories, by such writers as Grace Ellery Channing and "Octave Thanet," appeared; and some were reprinted from the *Chap-Book*. Dallas Lore Sharp's pleasant sketches of country life were a feature in 1915. Reprinted

[7] *The House Beautiful*, v. 17, May 1905, p. 50. Circulation checked in *N. W. Ayer & Son's Directory of Newspapers and Periodicals.*

verse occasionally found a place, and through 1909 a full page of each number was devoted to "Old Favorites."

Three-color covers began in 1906. As early as 1903, fine art reproductions in one color printed on manila sheets had begun to adorn the magazine, and a few full-color plates appeared from time to time after the turn of the century; but it was not until the late 1930's that *House Beautiful* really adjusted to the color cult of the magazines of the time, and it reached its full polychromous effulgence in the following decade.

In the meantime the magazine's basic financial and management structure had been undergoing changes. *Indoors and Outdoors* was absorbed in 1908, and two years later a merger with *Modern Homes,* of Memphis, brought in fresh management. In 1911, the magazine, still called *The House Beautiful* and still edited by Stone (who retained at least a minority interest) was moved to New York. But the New York climate was difficult, and a new purchaser was soon found in G. Henry Stetson and his associates, publishers of a monthly called *American Suburbs,* which they immediately consolidated with their new purchase. Again *The House Beautiful* kept its own name, its established character, and its long-time editor. Yet the very next year (1913), the ownership changed again, passing into the hands of the Atlantic Monthly Company. Under the enterprising and knowledgeable management of MacGregor Jenkins, who had already, in partnership with Ellery Sedgwick, achieved the rescue of the *Atlantic Monthly* from impending desuetude,[8] *The House Beautiful* was now given a fresh impulse to active and progressive life. New typographical designing, with initials and decorations by Bruce Rogers, improved its appearance, and in 1915 it was removed from New York to Boston.

Stone had resigned as editor when the Atlantic management took over, though he retained a financial interest until his untimely death. Virginia Robie, who had long been a staff member and a leading contributor, succeeded him, following the pattern of what she affectionately called the "Stone Age" during her brief editorship. She was the first of a line of six women who served successively as editors of the magazine

[8] Mott, *American Magazines,* v. 2 (1938), pp. 513–14.

COZY COVER OF *THE HOUSE BEAUTIFUL*, 1908

Because of Robert Louis Stevenson's poem, "The" was kept in the title until 1925.

FIFTY-NINE YEARS LATER

The cover for May 1967 is in the radiant color now used effectively throughout the magazine.

under Jenkins—a feminine procession interrupted only when Ellery Sedgwick had a try at it in 1922.

Jenkins broadened the magazine's scope thematically and geographically. Its specified fields were "Building, Furnishing, Planting." Its spring building numbers became comprehensive and important. Special issues dealing with homes in various states and cities attracted attention; in the 1920's, Indianapolis, Lincoln, and Pasadena (to name but three) were so treated. Though it continued to emphasize "modest homes," it talked no longer of $3,500 incomes during this carefree decade of larger earnings for nearly everyone, expansion of credit, and mass production by new technologies; the new upper middle class was interested not only in the magazine's traditional emphasis on simplicity and economy but also in more elaborate houses and furnishings.

The magazine joined in the general prosperity. Within a year after the removal to Boston, each number carried about sixty pages, at least half of them filled with advertising. And by the early 1930's *House Beautiful* (*The* had been dropped in 1925) was a high-class, well-produced monthly book, lavishly illustrated, consisting of about a hundred pages and having a circulation of 100,000 copies or more.

Then came the unhappy years of the Great Depression, and another change of ownership for *House Beautiful.* In 1934 the magazine was sold to the International Magazines Company, Richard E. Berlin, president. This was the magazine division of the William Randolph Hearst enterprises. The new owner merged its monthly *Home and Field* with its newly acquired magazine. The essential vitality of *House Beautiful* is attested by the fact that, though it changed hands repeatedly and three of its purchasers consolidated their own house-and-home periodicals with it, it kept its own name; and through all its vicissitudes of changing owners, editors, and places of publication, it maintained a reasonable consistency in editorial policy. It was now moved back to New York, and Arthur Hiram Samuels was installed as editor. Samuels had formerly held editorial positions on the *New Yorker, Home and Field,* and *Harper's Bazaar;* but he proved to be another short-term editor of

House Beautiful and was followed in 1936 by Kenneth K. Stowell.

It was in 1941 that *House Beautiful* found an editor so well fitted for the position that she was to continue to fill it with distinction for many years. Elizabeth Gordon had been a newspaper woman and an advertising agency worker before Hearst Magazines hired her for its *Good Housekeeping* staff. She was already writing a syndicated column on housing, and it was not long before she was moved over to the editorship of *House Beautiful.* No single individual could be credited with the success of such a complicated operation as *House Beautiful* became in the next two decades; but with the assistance of an able staff and the cooperation of ownership, Miss Gordon saw the magazine grow in that period from less than one hundred pages to over two hundred (sometimes over three hundred), from a circulation of about 200,000 to 750,000, crammed with advertising, scintillating with color, and still maintaining its original principle of sensible spending for good building and furnishing. By 1964 its circulation was over 900,000.

Common in later years had been a special theme for emphasis in each number, such as the "Three-Bedroom House With Two-Car Garage for $8,650" (April 1947), "Frank Lloyd Wright—His Contribution to the Beauty of American Life" (November 1955), "Three Houses Built by the Owner's Own Hands" (July 1960), and "Remodeling" (September 1963). As many as a dozen articles commonly centered upon the special theme.

A semiannual publication entitled *House Beautiful's Building Manual* was begun in 1935, reprinting articles on building from the magazine. In 1940 the predecessor of *House Beautiful's* current annual *Gardening and Outdoor Living* was begun. An annual *Houses and Plans Book* was established in 1957, followed in 1962 by the semiannual *Portfolio of Home Decorating,* and in 1964 by *Home Remodeling.**

An outstanding feature of the modern *House Beautiful* is its

* The first issue of *House Beautiful's Vacation Homes* annual appeared in 1967.

"Window Shopping" department. This was begun as "Shopping Guide (in Metropolitan Shops)" while the magazine was still published in Chicago; it then occupied four pages, with a supplementary "Real Estate Directory" of three pages. This was expanded after the moves to New York and Boston, but it was not until the early 1940's that it became a unique characteristic of the magazine's appeal.

In recent years the "Window Shopping" section has commonly consisted of more than fifty pages of small advertisements of retailers (mainly gift shops, specialty dealers, personal or small producers and manufacturers) offering their products for sale by mail delivery. These pages are divided into twelfths, though on nearly every page at least one advertiser takes two of these small spaces; thus there are many pages carrying eleven "ads." These pages are divided vertically into two halves, with small display "ads" on the left half, and on the other side six reading notices, each with an illustration of the product lined up to its left. All this adds up to a respectable typographical layout instead of the hodge-podge that might be expected in the presentation of so many small advertisements. Besides the big "Window Shopping" section, there are two other "product departments"—"Take It Easy," advertising household appliances and gadgets in quarter-page reading notices, and a similar "It's Worth Mentioning," with shorter "readers."

If all this sounds like a mail-order catalog—well, that is what it is. But the skillful typography, good printing, and interesting variety of offerings make these sections fascinating reading for any home owner. In a sense, this is a throw-back to the old mail-order journal technique that began in the late 1870's and lasted for three decades.[9] But there is a vast difference between those old cheaply printed periodicals and *House Beautiful,* so that any comparison seems a little absurd. In the first place, the contrast in quality of presentation is obvious; and in the second, *House Beautiful* is strict about the kind and quality of the products advertised. It accepts no objectionable patent medicine copy, and it requires its advertisers to refund purchase prices when dissatisfied patrons return

[9] Mott, *American Magazines,* v. 4 (1957), pp. 364–68.

merchandise and also when they are unable to make delivery within two weeks (unless the purchaser agrees to an extension of time).

The number of advertisements in any single issue of *House Beautiful* in the 1950's and 1960's is amazing—ranging from six to eight hundred. Of these, a hundred or so will carry double-page, full-page, or half-page announcements. In these larger spaces, full color is the rule. A single page in full color was quoted at $8,750 in 1964.

The combined facts that *House Beautiful* publishes so much highly practical editorial matter in the home building and furnishing fields ("more than any other national consumer magazine," it claims [10]) and that it presents such an amazing array of advertising for the home owner make its production an extraordinary industrial operation. And it may be added, incidentally, that the end result is an interesting and valuable magazine.*

[10] *Standard Rate and Data Service,* Feb. 27, 1960 (Consumer Magazine and Farm Publication Section, p. 157).

* This historical sketch was written in 1964. Elizabeth Gordon retired from the editorship at the end of 1964. She was succeeded by Sarah Tomerlin Lee in January, 1965. Prior to joining *House Beautiful,* Mrs. Lee was vice-president of Lord & Taylor, responsible for advertising, public relations, and promotion. She has held positions on the editorial staffs of *Harper's Bazaar* and *Vogue*. Circulation of *House Beautiful* in 1966 was slightly under 1,000,000.

13

THE LITTLE REVIEW[1]

THE *Little Review* was an outgrowth of a Chicago cultural movement which followed the Columbian Exposition and developed over two decades or more notable talents in art, music, and literature. Nevertheless, the editor was without the slightest doubt correct in claiming in her first number that the little magazine was her own "personal enterprise."[2]

Margaret Anderson escaped from her home town of Columbus, Indiana, in 1912 when she was nineteen. She had little family feeling, except perhaps for her father, who later died in a sanitarium. In her autobiography she wrote: "I am not a daughter: my father is dead and my mother rejected me long ago. I am not a sister: my two sisters find me more than a little mad, and that is no basis for a sisterly relationship."[3] In

[1] TITLE: *The Little Review.*

FIRST ISSUE: March 1914. LAST ISSUE: May 1929.

PERIODICITY: Monthly, March 1914—April 1920; irregular, July–Aug. 1920—May 1929. Vol. 1, March 1914—Feb. 1915 (Aug. number omitted); 2, March 1915—Feb. 1916 (Jan.–Feb., June–July combined); 3, March, April, May, June–July, Aug., Sept., Nov. 1916, Jan., March, April 1917; 4, May 1917—April 1918; 5, May 1918—April 1919 (Feb.–March combined); 6, May 1919—April 1920 (Feb. number omitted); 7, May–June, July–Aug., Sept.–Dec., 1920, Jan.–March 1921; 8, Autumn 1921, Spring 1922; 9, Autumn 1922, Winter 1922, Spring 1923, Autumn–Winter 1923–24; 10, Spring 1924, Autumn–Winter 1924–25; 11, Spring 1925, Winter 1926; 12, Spring–Summer 1926, May 1929.

EDITOR, PUBLISHER, OWNER: Margaret C. Anderson, 1914–29. Associate editor: Jane Heap, 1916–29. Foreign editors: Ezra Pound, 1917–19, 1921–24; Jules Romains, 1919–21; John Rodker, 1919–21; Francis Picabia, 1921–23. Business manager, Charles A. Zwaska, 1914–17. Chicago, March 1914—May 1916, November 1916—January 1917; San Francisco, June–July, August–September, 1916; New York, February 1917–1926; Paris, France, May 1929.

INDEX: *An Index to 'The Little Review' 1914–1929,* compiled by Kenneth A. Lohf and Eugene P. Sheehy, New York Public Library, 1961.

REFERENCES: Margaret Anderson, *My Thirty Years' War: An Autobiography* (New York, 1930); Frederick J. Hoffman, Charles Allen, and Carolyn F. Ulrich, *The Little Magazine: A History and a Bibliography* (Princeton, N.J., 1946), chap. iv; Harry Hansen, *Midwest Portraits* (New York, 1923), pp. 102–7; Margaret Anderson, ed., *The Little Review Anthology* (New York, 1953).

[2] *Little Review,* v. 1, March 1914, p. 2.

[3] Anderson, *My Thirty Years' War,* p. 4.

Chicago Margaret found employment working in a bookstore and writing reviews for Chicago's conservative literary weekly, the *Dial,* which took her on its staff for a time, and for the religious weekly, the *Interior,* for which she served briefly as literary editor.[4] She could not be happy long with either of these periodicals; but she learned something about magazine work from them, and soon she was projecting her own journal, to be called the *Little Review.*

"The thing I wanted—would die without," wrote Miss Anderson when she recounted in the magazine's last number the story of its founding, "—was conversation. The only way to get it was to reach people with ideas."[5] This "conversation" objective is restated again and again in the magazine and in the editor's autobiography. And the content of the *Little Review* itself, the mood, was that of animated conversation—informal, personal, unacademic. This was true especially in the early numbers, in which there was a larger proportion of criticism than in those that followed. There was sharp controversy, but in general the keynote was unrestrained praise. Miss Anderson wrote in the first number of "our perfectly inexpressible enthusiasm," and a correspondent in the "Reader Critic" department called the magazine "the official organ of exuberance."[6]

As soon as she decided to publish a magazine, she talked about it to all her acquaintances. She interested a young man whom she calls "Dick" in her autobiography; he was on the staff of an agricultural journal and promised to contribute a substantial share of his salary to the project for at least a year.[7] Then Margaret hastened to New York to sell advertising in the magazine of which not even a trial number had been issued. And she did it, too—about $450 worth to book publishers. Her charming personality,[8] her ability to talk with en-

[4] See F. L. Mott, *A History of American Magazines,* v. 3 (Cambridge, Mass., 1938), pp. 539–47.

[5] *Little Review,* v. 12, March 1929, p. 3.

[6] *Ibid.,* v. 1, March 1914, p. 2, and P.H.W. in v. 1, May 1914, p. 53.

[7] His first name was really Dewitt, she says; Anderson, *My Thirty Years' War,* pp. 39–43. DeWitt C. Wing was a contributor to the first number of the magazine.

[8] See Harry Hansen, *Midwest Portraits,* p. 105.

thusiasm (that "conversation" that she could not live without) won over the most hard-hearted publishers.

And so the first number of the *Little Review,* "A Magazine of the Arts, Making No Compromise with the Public Taste," appeared under the date of March 1914. It consisted of sixty-four pages (seventeen of them devoted to book advertising) measuring six by nine inches and bound in a brown cover. This initial issue contained several pieces by the editor, including an enthusiastic review of Galsworthy's *The Dark Flower* and one of Ethel Sidgwick's *Succession;* of the latter novelist, the reviewer declared, ". . . I enjoy her novels more than any novels I have ever read. . . ."[9] In an article entitled "Paderewski and the New Gods," Miss Anderson, who was herself a devoted pianist, struggles to express what seems to be almost an agony of admiration. Two midwestern poets who were later to be frequent contributors bow to the *Little Review* audience in this first number—Vachel Lindsay and Arthur Davidson Ficke; and Sherwood Anderson, who was to publish some of his *Winesburg* stories in this magazine, contributed a short article on writing. George Soule, who was to furnish a New York literary letter for early issues, made his first appearance. George Burman Foster, of the University of Chicago, who was also to be found frequently in later *Little Review* pages, always as an interpreter of liberal thought, contributed to the first number a four-page discussion of Nietzsche as "The Prophet of a New Culture"; and Llewellyn Jones, then literary editor of the *Chicago Evening Post,* wrote about Henri Bergson.

This initial number was typical of the *Little Review* in content and tone for the first year or two. It came gradually to devote more attention, however, to poetry; and the work of poets of various "modernist" schools became prominent. Eventually revolutionary movements in painting and sculpture were emphasized. Indeed, the history of the magazine is the story of a succession of enthusiasms for new ideas and forms, for the "marked," and the eccentric.

Margaret Anderson's first and abiding enthusiasm was for "beauty." That is a word not easy to define philosophically,

[9] *Little Review,* v. 1, March 1914, p. 34.

but Margaret did it emotionally in the introduction to the first issue of her magazine:

> If you've ever read poetry with a feeling that it was your religion, your very life; if you've ever come suddenly upon the whiteness of a Venus in a dim, deep room; if you've ever felt music replacing your soul with a new one of shining gold; if, in the early morning, you've watched a bird with great white wings fly from the edge of the sea straight up into the rose-colored sun—if these things have happened to you and continue to happen till you're left quite speechless with the wonder of it all, then you'll understand our hope to bring them nearer the common experience of the people who read us.[10]

Perhaps it is not fair to quote this passage without quoting also an observation made by Miss Anderson sixteen years later in her autobiography: "The first number betrayed nothing but my adolescence."[11] But despite editorial excesses in early numbers, the magazine found devoted friends in a limited circle. It was lively and exciting because of its "causes," and because its contributors represented new movements in writing.

Feminism was almost as persistent an interest of Miss Anderson's as "beauty" though it was not pursued with a crusading spirit, except perhaps in her defense of Margaret Sanger and her birth-control campaign. More definitely a crusade was the *Little Review's* stout support of anarchism, which began with an article by the editor in the third number on Emma Goldman, who had just delivered some lectures in Chicago. The editor and the propagandist for philosophical anarchism became personal friends, and the magazine published Miss Goldman's "Letters from Prison" in May 1916. But fifteen months later Margaret wrote of the tenets of anarchism: "I have long since given them up."[12]

Her support of anarchism had alienated Miss Anderson from some of her friends—notably from "Dick," who withdrew his financial support of the magazine.[13] She had no thought of giving up, however, but expected "miracles" to turn up to keep the magazine going. It kept going, if not by

[10] *Little Review,* v. 1, March 1914, p. 2.
[11] Anderson, *My Thirty Years' War,* p. 47.
[12] *Little Review,* v. 4, Aug. 1917, p. 20.
[13] Anderson, *My Thirty Years' War,* pp. 55–56.

THE LITTLE REVIEW

Literature Drama Music Art

MARGARET C. ANDERSON
EDITOR

SEPTEMBER, 1915

Reversals — *The Editor*
Moods: — *Ben Hecht*
  Sorrow
  Humoresque
  Rain
  An Invitation to Cheat Posterity
  My Island
Soul-Sleep and Modern Novels — *Will Levington Comfort*
Poems: — *Maxwell Bodenheim*
  Pastels
  Thoughts
  A Woman in the Park
Richard Aldington's Poetry — *Amy Lowell*
Café Sketches — *Arthur Davison Ficke*
Emma Goldman on Trial — *Louise Bryant*
Poetry versus Imagism — *Huntly Carter*
The New Idol — *George Burman Foster*
Book Discussion
The Poets' Translation Series
The Reader Critic

Published Monthly
MARGARET C. ANDERSON, Publisher
Fine Arts Building
CHICAGO

15 cents a copy **$1.50 a year**

Entered as second-class matter at Postoffice, Chicago

THE EXCITEMENT WAS INSIDE THE COVER

The date: September 1915. During the first half of the *Little Review's* existence the covers were plain. The title was on a kind of sticker glued to the brown sheet bearing the table of contents. Later the sticker appeared in various colors, and finally modernistic drawings on brilliantly colored paper shattered the earlier tradition.

miracles, by dogged persistence, self-sacrifice, begging, occasional omissions of regular issues, and all kinds of shenanigans with printers and owners of office and living quarters, over a period of no less than fifteen years. Eunice Tietjens donated a diamond ring to pay a printer's bill at one crisis; at another, Lawrence Langner, who had just sold a play to *Vanity Fair,* turned over the check to the *Little Review.*[14] In December of its first year Miss Anderson sent out an emotional appeal for funds, and from time to time friends were asked for donations of five dollars or more.[15] In 1918, after the magazine had moved to New York, a group of four wealthy persons, including Otto Kahn, contributed $400 each to supply the magazine's deficits for a year.[16]

The magazine's subscription price was $2.50 yearly at the beginning, reduced after six months to $1.50 but restored in 1918 to $2.50. It seems unlikely that circulation ever rose to much over a thousand,[17] and with advertising seldom or never exceeding $500 a year, it was hard to meet printers' bills, pay rent on offices or "studio," and find much left for the living expenses of the editor and her close associates who helped with the magazine. In the summer of 1914, announcing the change in price, the editor declared that the *Little Review* was "free of debt" and "we even have money in the bank."[18] Such a situation may have recurred from time to time, but in general, the magazine was chronically insolvent; in the third volume Miss Anderson laments "our eternal poverty."[19] There were times when she was half-starved, had only one presentable outfit of clothes, and, with her associate, Jane Heap, did her own cooking, housework, cleaning, and so on. They even cut each other's hair.[20]

Jane Heap was the most important and persistent of Miss

14 *Ibid.,* pp. 68, 142.

15 The appeal was included in the magazine's advertising section, December 1914, also see, for example, the issue for May–June, 1920.

16 Anderson, *My Thirty Years' War,* p. 208.

17 The "conjecture" of a circulation of 2,000 in Hoffman, Allen, and Ulrich, *Little Magazine,* p. 57, with its unreliable foundation, seems unacceptable. The magazine never furnished its circulation figures to the directories.

18 *Little Review,* v. 1, July 1914, p. 67.

19 *Ibid.,* v. 3, March 1917, p. 22.

20 Anderson, *My Thirty Years' War,* pp. 156, 205–6.

Anderson's associates in the conduct of the *Little Review.* None of these associates was hired; they just came. First was Charles A. Zwaska, a seventeen-year-old boy who was fascinated by the first number of the magazine and offered his services as office-boy by telephone. Wrote Miss Anderson later: "He joined the staff half an hour after his telephone call, he did all the practical work in the office for years, besides writing occasionally for the magazine, and he always insisted on calling himself the office boy. We called him Caesar." [21] Each of Margaret's sisters shared for a time in the hardships and editorial work of the staff. Harriet Dean came from Indianapolis to serve the magazine, drawn by much the same hypnotic force as that which had attracted Caesar; she shared the good and ill of the staff for about two years.[22]

Jane Heap was a Chicago art student who frequented the soirées where the "New Chicago Movement" was being nursed and its achievements celebrated. She and Miss Anderson were united by a natural magnetic attraction. "I felt in 1916," wrote Miss Anderson in her autobiography, "and I feel today that Jane Heap is the world's best talker." [23] Thus it was the integration and collision of ideas in the "conversation", of which both were so fond, that drew them together and soon made "jh" *de facto* associate editor of the *Little Review* for the remainder of its life. Through much of the file her name did not appear at all.

The rest of the sketch is by John T. Frederick. Dr. Mott was writing this history of the Little Review *at the time of his death. Professor Frederick was asked to complete the chapter, following the outline Dr. Mott had made for the entire sketch and using his notes. In addition, Professor Frederick reviewed for himself the entire file of the magazine.**

[21] *Ibid.,* p. 51. He was specified as "business manager" in the statement of ownership for 1917. Apparently he did not go with the magazine when it was moved to New York the next year.

[22] *Ibid.,* pp. 67–68.

[23] *Ibid.,* p. 103.

* Professor Frederick was editor of the *Midland,* a Midwest-oriented "little magazine" devoted to belles-lettres, which existed contemporaneously with the *Little Review* and outlasted it by a few years. For five years in the 1920's Dr. Mott was co-editor of the *Midland* with Professor Frederick. In an autobi-

In attempting to assess after five decades the achievement of the *Little Review,* one is compelled to recognize (as would be true of any magazine of the period) the substantial proportion of space devoted to the work of writers now largely forgotten. However, the chief impression is that of a very high proportion of significant discoveries and early recognitions. The *Little Review's* record for publication of important contemporary writers is not surpassed—if indeed it is equalled—by that of any other magazine of the period. Within its twelve volumes the *Little Review* presented work of Sherwood Anderson, Hart Crane, Theodore Dreiser, T. S. Eliot, Ford Madox Ford, Lady Gregory, Ernest Hemingway, Aldous Huxley, James Joyce, Wyndham Lewis, Marianne Moore, Ezra Pound, Dorothy Richardson, Gertrude Stein, Wallace Stevens, William Carlos Williams, and William Butler Yeats: a list which could be extended.

Though many of these names are those of American writers, the number is misleading. Actually the lion's share of the *Little Review's* space was given to British and European writers, and the expatriate Ezra Pound. The "episodes" from Joyce's *Ulysses* occupied over 300 pages, the varied contributions of Ezra Pound over 250, Dorothy Richardson's novel *Interim* nearly 150, and the works of Wyndham Lewis and Ford Madox Ford nearly 100 pages each. The only American writers represented in comparable extent were Sherwood Anderson with some 90 pages and Ben Hecht with 120.

The high incidence of British and continental European writers was due primarily to the efforts of Ezra Pound, foreign editor for most of the magazine's career. He was directly responsible for Joyce's sending the *Ulysses* material to the *Little Review,*[24] and for the interest of Eliot, Richard Aldington,

ographical essay written much later, touching on those years, Dr. Mott wrote: "Never was there a happier partnership. The editors agreed basically in theory and nearly always in taste. . . ." His relationship with Professor Frederick he described as "one of the most valued friendships of my life." *Time Enough* (Chapel Hill, N.C., 1962), chap. viii.

Author of two novels dealing with midwestern life, Professor Frederick is now teaching in the English Department of the University of Iowa.

24 Margaret Anderson, ed., *The Little Review Anthology* (New York, 1953), p. 175. References are made to this book when possible rather than to files of the magazine because of its greater availability. [J.T.F.]

Ford Madox Ford, and many others. Predictably, Pound was not easy to work with. Periodically he demanded money which the magazine did not have:

> My net value to the concern appears to be about $2350, of which over $2000 does not "accrue" to the protagonist. . . . Roughly speaking, either the *Little Review* will have to provide me with the necessities of life and a reasonable amount of leisure, by May 1st, 1919, or I shall have to apply my energies elsewhere.[25]

He tended to criticize severely editorial choices made by the American editors, and to use the pages of the periodical for airing of his personal controversies and grievances. However, to readers who objected to Pound's work and influence in the magazine, Jane Heap replied:

> As long as Mr. Pound sends us work by Yeats, Joyce, Eliot, de Boschere,—work bearing the stamp of originality and permanence—we have no complaint of him as an editor. If we are slightly jarred by his manner of asking for alms, or by any other personal manifestation, we can take care of that outside the magazine. We need no commiseration for our connection with Mr. Pound.[26]

Pound's greatest single service to the magazine was his suggestion to James Joyce that he send portions of *Ulysses* to the *Little Review*. Both Margaret Anderson and Jane Heap had praised Joyce's *A Portrait of the Artist as a Young Man* on its appearance, Miss Anderson declaring: "This James Joyce book is the most beautiful piece of writing and the most creative piece of prose anywhere to be seen on the horizon today;"[27] and when Pound made his suggestion, Joyce responded promptly. The subsequent prosecution and conviction of Margaret Anderson for the publication of certain allegedly obscene passages of *Ulysses* was the most dramatic incident in the *Little Review's* colorful history, and affords one of the most interesting passages in *My Thirty Years' War*.[28] Actually an earlier issue of the *Little Review* had been suppressed—also on the complaint of John Sumner of the New York Society for the Suppression of Vice—for publication of the

[25] *Ibid.*, pp. 185, 186.
[26] *Ibid.*, pp. 272–73.
[27] *Little Review*, v. 3, April 1917, p. 9.
[28] Anderson, *My Thirty Years' War*, pp. 214–22.

story "Cantelman's Spring-mate" by Wyndham Lewis (October 1917). One of the most revealing passages in Miss Anderson's autobiography is her sympathetic and almost affectionate portrayal of Sumner in connection with the *Ulysses* proceedings.[29]

Among the major editorial contributions of Pound were his "Henry James Number" (August 1918), most of which, he complained, he had to write himself,[30] and the "W. H. Hudson Number" (May–June, 1920). The issue for November 1918 was called an "Ezra Pound Number" and was largely by or about Pound. His long article, written with Ernest Fenollosa, on "The Chinese Written Character as a medium for poetry," appeared in four issues of the following year. In summary, it is clear that if the material written by or obtained by Pound were subtracted from the file of the *Little Review,* the magazine's historical importance would be greatly diminished. This is not at all to disparage the courage and judgment of Miss Anderson in accepting and publishing the material, nor her achievement in "getting along" with Pound as long as she did. At the end their relations were not cordial. When for the final number Jane Heap sent out a rather preposterous questionnaire asking broad questions about highly personal matters of purposes and convictions, Ezra replied:

> Print what you've got on hand.—Ezra Pound. P.S. This refers to mss. of mine suppressed by you or "jh", when I last assisted you in preparing a number of the L. R., and never returned to the author.

On which Miss Anderson commented:

> (Suppressed by me, dear Ezra, and conscientiously thrown into the wastebasket; and a very good thing for you. Such a lot of stale witticisms it has rarely been my lot to receive. You really couldn't have hoped to get away with them in a magazine published in New York City, U.S.A., in the year 1926.)—M.C.A.[31]

In addition to the abundant and usually distinguished work of British writers, contemporary French literature received much emphasis in the pages of the magazine. Pound contrib-

[29] *Ibid.,* pp. 218–19.
[30] Anderson, *Anthology,* p. 185.
[31] Anderson, *Anthology,* p. 366.

uted "A Study in French Poets" which occupied some sixty pages, and the work of some of these poets was published frequently, usually in French. French writers were consistently discussed in reviews and editorials, and other European literature was reviewed or sparingly represented.

That the editors were in a measure aware of the degree to which the *Little Review* was dominated by foreign material is suggested by their identifying two numbers—for June and December, 1918—as "American Numbers." Actually the earlier volumes (before Pound was named as foreign editor) were largely American in origin. The desire for "good conversation," which was Margaret Anderson's avowed primary motive in starting the magazine, led to her coming to know most of the members of the literary group then centered in Chicago; and the early volumes of the *Little Review* included representative work of Carl Sandburg, Edgar Lee Masters, Vachel Lindsay, Ben Hecht, Sherwood Anderson and others of that group in addition to the literary criticism most of which was written by Chicagoans.

Most of these American contributors, however, fell away before or soon after the advent of Pound. The only ones for whom mutual loyalty between writer and editor continued significantly were Sherwood Anderson, who was represented in all volumes of the *Little Review* but one, Ben Hecht, Arthur Davison Ficke, and Maxwell Bodenheim, who appeared in all volumes but three. Miss Anderson was totally antipathetic to the important regional movement in all parts of the United States during this period. With the exception of pieces by Anderson and a very few others, the only American life represented in the *Little Review* is that of the great cities. Further, Miss Anderson was not notably successful, if indeed she was sincere, in her proclaimed search for promising American writers. Highly significant is her comment in the *Little Review Anthology* that a certain piece of work was "one of the two or three unsolicited manuscripts we printed in all the years." [32]

Most of the important American writers mentioned earlier in this account had only minuscule representation—among these, Cummings, Dreiser, Hart Crane, Wallace Stevens, and

[32] Anderson, *Anthology,* p. 21.

Marianne Moore. Miss Anderson frankly disliked what she called the "intellectual" poetry of Miss Moore: "It is almost impossible for me to express, with moderation, my dislike of intellectual poetry. It is an anomaly. I can't read it without impatience. It can enrage me. My position needs no defense —the simplest statement defends it: INTELLECTUAL POETRY IS NOT POETRY." She also disparaged most of the work of Gertrude Stein, and included in the *Little Review Anthology* an example "as typical of why her work didn't interest me." [33]

Perhaps the only American writers of lasting importance to whom the *Little Review* gave really substantial aid and comfort through publication were Sherwood Anderson and William Carlos Williams; Williams' highly individual work occupies some seventy pages of the *Little Review* file. In addition to a few of the stories collected later in *Winesburg, Ohio* and *The Triumph of the Egg,* and some shorter pieces, Anderson contributed (to the sixth and seventh volumes) a series of twelve "Testaments" which include some of his most characteristic writing. Parts of these appeared in his *A New Testament* in 1927, labeled as "poems" and curiously fragmented and altered so that they are far less impressive than in their original form in the *Little Review.*

It is quite possibly true that in terms of actual influence on and participation in the cultural current of its times, the *Little Review* was more influential in the other arts than in that of literature. Margaret Anderson was throughout the career of the magazine intensely interested in and responsive to matters of music; and the early volumes of the *Little Review* display this interest very generously. The editorial pages tend to give as much emphasis to music and musicians as to books and writers. Articles about—and in some cases by—musicians are numerous. To a slightly less marked degree, the *Little Review* was devoted to the theatre—in the persons of its editors as playgoers, and in their comments in the magazine.

Perhaps even more substantial was the function of the *Little Review* in introducing new names and new work in painting and sculpture. From the beginning, in spite of her limited

[33] *Ibid.,* pp. 187, 317.

financial resources, Miss Anderson contrived to publish many excellent portraits of her contributors—among these Pound, Yeats, and many others. In the later volumes there was markedly increased presentation of reproductions of new painting and sculpture. Indeed, Miss Anderson herself commented:

> From this time on (1926) the virtue of *The Little Review,* to me, lay exclusively in its reproductions of modern painting and sculpture. There is not a name of international fame today, I believe, that was not included in our roster—Archipenko, Arp, Brancusi, Braque, Gaudier-Brzeska, Chagall, Chirico, Demuth, Ernst, Gabo, Gris, Grosz, Kandinsky, Klee, Léger, Wyndham Lewis, Lipchitz, Marcousis, Matisse, Miro, Modigliani, Moholy-Nagy, Pascin, Peuzner, Picabia, Picasso, Man Ray, Segonzac, Stella, Tchelietchev, Zadkine, etc., etc.
>
> As for the literature that filled the pages of these last years, I will give samples only. I "was not amused." [34]

The European orientation in this impressive list is of course manifest. The *Little Review* gave little attention to American painters and sculptors. Even more markedly than in the field of literature, the magazine's primary service lay in the introduction to America of foreign talent and tendencies.

The ultimate effect and value of the *Little Review's* emphasis on contemporary music, painting and sculpture I am not competent to assess. I have no doubt, however, of the importance of the magazine's service to literature. I count as its major contributions its publication of portions of Joyce's *Ulysses,* and of some of the best poems of Pound, Eliot, and Yeats; and its encouragement and extensive publication of Sherwood Anderson and William Carlos Williams.

[34] Anderson, *Anthology,* pp. 345–46.

14

THE MIDLAND[1]

WHEN Josiah Royce came out to the State University of Iowa from Harvard to deliver the annual Phi Beta Kappa address in 1902, he said some things about the "Higher Provincialism" that attracted wide attention;[2] but, as he clearly intended, he was planting some seeds of thought right there in Iowa City that he hoped might sprout and grow to some kind of practical fruition. What Royce wanted was a provincial spirit and culture to oppose the overweening power of our national industrialism. It is hard to pin down such an intangible activity as direct influence on social

[1] TITLE: *The Midland.*

FIRST ISSUE: Jan. 1915. LAST ISSUE: March–April, May–June 1933. Merged with the *Frontier* as *Frontier and Midland.*

PERIODICITY: Monthly, 1915–17; bimonthly, 1918–19; monthly 1920–24 (combinations Jan.–Feb.–March 1920, Sept.–Oct. 1921, Aug.–Sept. 1922, June–July–Aug. 1923, June–July–Aug. 1924); semimonthly, 1925 (combinations July, Aug.); monthly, 1926–27; bimonthly, 1928—March–April 1931; monthly, May–Oct. 1931; bimonthly, Nov.–Dec. 1931—Jan.–Feb. 1933; final combination number March–April, May–June 1933. Annual vols. 1–20, no. 2–3.

PUBLISHERS: John Towner Frederick (with Ival McPeak, 1916; Frank Luther Mott, 1926–30). Iowa City, Iowa, 1915–17 (Corning, Iowa, May–Aug. 1916), 1921–22, 1923–31; Moorhead, Minn., 1917–19; Glennie, Mich., 1919–21; Pittsburgh, Penna., 1922–23; Chicago, Ill., 1931–33.

EDITORS: J. T. Frederick, 1915–33, except Ival McPeak, May–Aug. 1916. Coeditors: F. L. Mott, 1925–30; Esther Paulus Frederick, 1930–33. Associate editors: Clarke Fisher Ansley, 1915–29; Raymond H. Durboraw, 1915–18; Roger L. Sergel, 1915–28; Ival McPeak, 1915–23; Edwin Ford Piper, 1915–30; Esther Paulus Frederick, 1915–30; Nelson Antrim Crawford, 1917–29; Hartley Burr Alexander, 1918–28; Mary Grove Chawner, 1918–28; Percival Hunt, 1918–20; Weare Holbrook, 1918–22; Roy A. Tower, 1921–28; Ruth Suckow, 1921–22; F. L. Mott, 1921–25, 1930–33; George Carver, 1923–28; Raymond Knister, 1923–24.

[2] Royce's *Provincialism* (Iowa City, 1910) was issued in pamphlet form by the university, and included in a collection of Royce's papers entitled *Race Questions, Provincialism, and Other American Problems* (New York, 1908). Charles A. Allen calls attention to the Royce address and its influence in his unpublished dissertation, "The Advance Guard: A Chapter in the History of the American Little Magazine," University of Iowa, 1942. Allen's work contains the best study yet made of the *Midland* (chap. vi); it is repeated in a shorter version in Frederick J. Hoffman, Charles Allen, and Carolyn F. Ulrich, *The Little Magazine: A History and a Bibliography* (Princeton, N.J., 1946), pp. 140–47.

ideas; and probably all that Royce's address really did was to help precipitate some elements in community thought into specific ideas for action over the years.

One of these was the idea of a midwestern magazine. Clarke Fisher Ansley, head of the English department at the university, doubtless heard Royce's address; but it was not until a decade later that a group of young men gathered about him and determined to found a non-commercial monthly journal of belles-lettres. There was some echo of Royce in the words of the magazine's first editorial,

> Possibly the region between the mountains would gain in variety at least if it retained more of its makers of literature, music, pictures, and other expressions of civilization. And possibly civilization itself might be with us a somewhat swifter process if expression of its spirit were more frequent.[3]

John Towner Frederick was the leader of the group of young men who met in Professor Ansley's classroom, office, and home to discuss the need for a midwestern magazine; and when the first number of the *Midland* appeared, he was listed as its editor. Though he had associates from time to time who shared the burdens of editing and publishing, during the eighteen years of its existence, John Frederick was the *Midland*. His fellow founders of the magazine were Raymond H. Durboraw, who died in 1918; Roger L. Sergel, novelist, later a Chicago publisher; and Ival McPeak, teacher and writer, who was associate editor of the *Midland* for its first year, and for part of its second took over from Frederick the chief direction of the magazine.

Virtually members of the founding group also were Edwin Ford Piper, poet, and assistant professor of English at the university; and Esther Paulus, fellow student, who later made the bond between herself and the *Midland* permanent by marrying the editor. A few years later the staff of associate editors was strengthened by the addition of Nelson Antrim Crawford, poet, who was to serve for many years as editor of the *Household Magazine,* of Topeka, Kansas; and Hartley Burr Alexander, poet and essayist, and at that time professor of philosophy at the University of Nebraska.

Frederick himself was born on a farm in southwestern Iowa,

[3] *Midland,* v. 1, Jan. 1915, p. 1.

The Midland

A MAGAZINE OF
THE MIDDLE WEST

JANUARY 1915

The First Person Plural........ 1
From The Midland Monthly to The Midland................ 3
JOHNSON BRIGHAM
The Masterpiece, a Poem....... 6
ARTHUR DAVISON FICKE
Silent Battle, a Story.......... 8
KEENE ABBOTT
The Authors' Homecoming of 1914.......................22
JAMES B. WEAVER
The Midland Library..........26
The Midland Chronicle.........30
Editorial Note...............32

PUBLISHED MONTHLY AT IOWA CITY, IOWA
$1.50 a Year *15 cents a Copy*
Application for entry as second class matter at the post office at Iowa City, Iowa, pending.

VOL. I, NO. 1 OF THE *MIDLAND*

The date: January 1915. Covers of the *Midland* remained essentially the same in style (and tan in color) through most of its life. In 1930, with a change in subtitle to "A National Literary Magazine," a drawing indicative of the national aspect was added to a bright cover-page.

educated at a small-town high school and at the state university. He grew up sensitive to beauty as he saw it in the Iowa countryside, in literature, and in art. His master's thesis was on William Morris, with emphasis on the fine printing at the Kelmscott Press. At the university he found a strong interest in the sincere interpretation of human life and environment in good prose and verse; this soon developed into a passionate desire to furnish a medium for the literature of his own Midwest which would be quite untouched by the all too obvious commercialism of the big-circulation magazines. What he was after, and what the entire eighteen-volume file of the *Midland* represents, was literature "strictly in the amateur spirit."[4] And he meant the word "amateur" in its etymological sense of what is done for love, not gain.

A survey of the first few volumes shows that not even at the beginning was the *Midland* wholly devoted to the depiction and interpretation of the Midwest. Several pieces are about the Far West, some stories are set even in the East, and much of the poetry is universal. Some articles and verse deal with foreign lands. As the country came closer to the verge of World War I, and finally entered the world conflict, no little poetry and fiction reflected army life and the war mood. Kate Buss's touching story of the war in France was in the number for May 1917, and Raymond Weeks' "Two Sketches of the War" in that for July 1921; but perhaps the most distinguished war contribution appeared some years later (Nov.–Dec. 1930)—a series of sketches by William March entitled "Fifteen From Company K," later elaborated in the author's novel, *Company K*. But the emphasis was always on the Great Valley, its people and its life.

The *Midland* soon won a reputation for its good short stories. In the same year in which it was founded, Edward J. O'Brien began the compilation of his annual *Best Short Stories* series. O'Brien shared with Frederick a dislike of formula stories and a respect for the sincere and indigenous. In the introduction to his first volume O'Brien wrote:

> One new periodical . . . claim[s] unique attention this year for . . . recent achievement and abundant future promise. A year ago a

[4] *Midland,* v. 1, Jan. 1915, p. 2.

slender little monthly magazine entitled the *Midland* was first issued in Iowa City. It attracted very little attention, and in the course of the year published but ten short stories. It has been my pleasure and wonder to find in these ten stories the most vital interpretation in fiction of our national life that many years have been able to show. Since the most brilliant days of the New England men of letters, no such white hope has proclaimed itself with such assurance and modesty.[5]

O'Brien went on to rate every story the new magazine had printed as "distinctive"—an honor bestowed on only one other magazine. Walter J. Muilenburg's "Heart of Youth" (November 1915) was reprinted. In succeeding volumes O'Brien continued to deal kindly with the *Midland,* sometimes reprinting as many as three of its stories from a single year's output. This was very helpful to the magazine. Writers were attracted to a medium with a superlative O'Brien rating; even though they knew it paid nothing in cash for contributions, they often sent in their manuscripts with dreams of a three-star O'Brien accolade. It was a great period for the short story, and O'Brien was its prophet; his annual combination anthology and yearbook was widely respected and eagerly awaited.

A list of the men and women who wrote short stories for the *Midland* would show that most of them were then and now unknown to fame. Frederick never collected big names, and he rejected many a manuscript with a by-line illustrious in the magazinedom of the twenties because it did not seem to him to meet the *Midland's* ideal of the sincere representation of life.

The *Midland* published the first magazine contribution of Ruth Suckow—a slight but charming quatrain—and it shared with the *Smart Set* the introduction of her short fiction. It printed three of her best short stories—"Uprooted" (February 1921), "Retired" (April 1921), and "A Rural Community" (July 1922). Another important short story writer for the magazine was Raymond Weeks, poet, scholar, humorist, whose "Arkansas" (June 1923) and other sketches and stories did much to enliven its pages. Still another notable short story writer was Leo L. Ward, whose "The Threshing Ring" (July

5 Edward J. O'Brien, ed., *The Best Short Stories of 1915 and the Yearbook of the American Short Story* (Boston, 1916), p. 9.

1930) and other contributions were vivid in representation, strong in mood, and sensitive to beauty. Father Ward later became head of the English Department of Notre Dame University.

Not less memorable were such stories as Agnes Mary Brownell's "Doc Greer's Practice" (January 1921), Raymond Knister's "Mist-Green Oats" (August 1922), Leonard Cline's "If There's Men There's Mermaids" (February 1926), Harry Hartwick's "Light" (April 1927), Paul F. Corey's "Onlookers" (May 1930), and Dudley Schnabel's "Load" (May 1931). During its whole career, the *Midland* published over 250 stories, most of which stand well the test of re-reading. It would be wrong not to mention, in addition to those writers already listed, such contributors as Jeannette Marks, Grant Showerman, Albert Halper, James T. Farrell, Nelia Gardner White, Thomas W. Duncan, and August W. Derleth.

In poetry, the magazine was strong also. William Stanley Braithwaite, who made a survey of American magazine verse every year for the *Boston Transcript,* and published an annual anthology 1913–1929, always placed the *Midland* high; in some years, as 1918, it topped the list. Among favorite *Midland* poets were Edwin Ford Piper, an associate editor who wrote much for the magazine and whose "Barbed Wire Poems" appeared in the first four numbers of 1917; Leland Huckfield, whose Canadian poems were features of some of the early volumes; Jay G. Sigmund, whose verses and prose pieces about Iowa country people were often memorable; and James Hearst, another Iowa poet, who wrote simply and satisfyingly of farm life. Other poets frequently found in the earlier volumes of the *Midland* were Arthur Davison Ficke, Hazel Hall, William Ellery Leonard, Hartley Burr Alexander, and Howard Mumford Jones.

The *Midland's* taste in verse was inclined to the conservative, but its catholicism was often shown. Piper and Sigmund wrote a rugged kind of blank verse suitable to their themes. Haniel Long's "Notes for a New Mythology" in rhythmic prose comprised the number for January 15, 1925. In the twenties also appeared the work of Helen Hoyt and Glenn Ward Dresbach. Throughout the file are sprinkled verses by many of the better known poets—John G. Neihardt, Witter Bynner, Lizette Woodworth Reese, Mary Carolyn Davies, Mark Van Doren, Clement Wood, and so on.

From time to time, the *Midland* carried some editorial notes in the back of the book; these observations by Frederick on literary matters, on his farm life at Glennie, Michigan, and on politics and art and life were always worth reading. Throughout most of its file, the magazine published short book reviews by the editor, which tended to be pleasant, personalized little essays.[6] Off and on there was a "Sketch Book" department, to which *Midland* writers contributed personal essays, sketches, and short short stories.

A word should be said about humor in the *Midland*. Frederick himself had a ready laughter. Once he wrote in an editorial:

> I hope the *Midland* is not thought to take itself too seriously. I do not want it to seem to assume the air of the Elect. Nor do I desire that its editor be thought of as a pale and serious Martyr to a Cause. I can say truthfully that of many amusing objects in the world, I have yet to find one so laughable as myself; and my sense of the ridiculous in my doings and person extends to my activities in connection with *The Midland*.[7]

The learned Raymond Weeks, of Columbia University, turned out to be one of the magazine's leading humorists; his "The Hound-Tuner of Callaway" (December 1926) became a minor classic, and his "Fat Women of Boone and Other Dialect Sketches" occupied the whole of the *Midland's* number for January 1, 1925. A delightful satire on university administration was Howard Mumford Jones' "Drigsby's Universal Regulator" (November 1920). Then there were the hilarious "Turtle" (December 1924) by Mary Wolfe Thompson, and Father Ward's "Balaam in Burrville" (July 1929).

The octavo-size *Midland* was printed throughout by the Economy Advertising Company, of Iowa City, whose president, Willis Mercer, took a personal interest in the magazine

[6] After F. L. Mott became co-editor in 1925, he did about half of the reviewing for the magazine. There were occasional reviews by Mrs. Frederick, and a few by other associate editors.

[7] *Midland*, v. 8, Oct. 1922, p. 295.

and was liberal in his dealings with it. John Springer, master printer, was responsible for its pleasant simple design. Printing was done at what now seems the incredibly low price of fifty dollars an issue for the first few years, though that figure doubled by the end of the twenties. Even with liberal printing arrangements, however, Frederick and his backers nearly always had a sizable deficit to make up during the *Midland's* first decade.[8] Before the move to Chicago it never had a circulation exceeding five hundred. Its subscription price began at \$1.50 a year, increased to \$2.00 in 1920, and to \$3.00 in 1924. For several years the magazine had the help of a small group of "guarantors," but receipts from this source never amounted to more than a few hundred dollars in any single year.

When Frederick left his instructorship in English at Iowa to join his friend Durboraw at Minnesota Teachers' College at Moorhead, he took the editorial and publication offices with him, though he kept the same Iowa City printers. Two years later he and his father bought a tract of land in the "cut-over" region of northeastern Michigan, near Lake Huron, and set about carving a farm out of it. By this time the *Midland* was the alter ego of John Frederick; and he and his wife Esther took it along with them to the wilds and gave it houseroom in their farm home. In 1921 the Fredericks came back to the State University of Iowa for a year, and later he spent a year as professor of English at the University of Pittsburgh, before returning once more to Iowa. In these changes the *Midland* followed him, adapting itself to the gypsy life. The printing base was always the Mercer plant at Iowa City; and the farm near Glennie was always a haven of refuge for the Fredericks in the summers and at other times when they could escape for a while from university life. To Glennie, also, many a writer of the *Midland* circle made a pilgrimage from time to time, some staying to live and work a while in the visitors' cottage. Walter Muilenburg took up a farm nearby.

Frederick maintained a close liaison with his contributors. An industrious letter writer, he criticized unacceptable work at length and with sympathy; and the kindliness of his per-

[8] A small circular issued in 1917 gave a balance sheet for the first three years. See also Allen, "Advance Guard," pp. 77–78.

sonality robbed his "I regret" letters of their sting. Thus those who could not visit him at Iowa City or Glennie came to know him through his extensive, handwritten correspondence.

Not only did the magazine change offices frequently during the first half of its existence, but it also shifted back and forth from monthly to bimonthly to semimonthly publication. When it was a semimonthly (1925) it often devoted all its pages to the presentation of the work of a single writer.

One of the conditions of Frederick's returning to Iowa City in 1923 was that the university should furnish modest office room and the part-time services of a graduate assistant for clerical work on the *Midland*. A procession of ambitious and talented young writers occupied this assistantship—Ruth Lechlitner, Harry Hartwick, Percy Wood, Charles Brown Nelson, and others.

In 1924 Frederick invited Frank Luther Mott, who had been an Iowa country journalist and was now a member of the English faculty at the university, to join him as co-editor of the magazine. Mott had already contributed fiction and criticism to the *Midland,* and the new partnership was a happy one; the two men agreed fundamentally in literary theory and taste, and differed enough to make them checks upon each other. After a year as co-editor Mott became also joint publisher, sharing equally not only in the editorial management but in the business responsibilities and the profits and losses. In this period of inflation in the latter twenties, the *Midland* for the first time managed to break about even by the end of each year.

In the optimistic climate of the late twenties, ideas and plans for the cultural development of the Midwest developed profusely. The region was prosperous industrially; why not artistically? Why should not Chicago be the cultural center of the nation, with pre-eminent art galleries, symphony orchestras and operas, book publishers, and magazines? In 1930 Edward J. O'Brien made this suggestion:

> The true remedy for this lagging behind of the better monthlies is probably the establishment of a new national monthly in the Middle West, which is nearer the present centre of population. If I may venture a suggestion, I think the time is now ripe for *The Midland*

to pool its interests with *The Prairie Schooner, The Frontier,* and perhaps one or two other regional periodicals such as *The Southwest Review,* and to issue a full-grown national monthly of belles-lettres in which short stories, poems, and essays should be given pride of place. . . .

If *The Midland* chooses to take the lead in this matter, I am convinced, after many years' reflection, that it has the same opportunity to crystallize the best expression of contemporary national life that *The Atlantic Monthly* was able to seize upon its foundation, and that *Harper's Magazine* enjoyed a generation ago. Two generations ago, Boston was the geographical centre of American literary life, one generation ago, New York could claim pride of place, and I trust that the idea will not seem too unfamiliar if I suggest that the geographical centre today is Iowa City.[9]

Months before this appeared, Frederick had been thinking along the same lines. He was not especially interested in mergers, however; and he was convinced that Chicago, which had supported *Poetry* so loyally, and which had recently developed an influential literary group, was a better center for a new experiment than Iowa City. In his editorial telling of his change of base, he concluded:

Finally, there is the immediate attractiveness of Chicago itself, with its vigor and turbulence, with the typical American contrasts and American problems intensified to their utmost dramatic concreteness and meaning. *The Midland* has been edited on real frontiers in Minnesota and Michigan, at the gateway between east and middle west at Pittsburgh, and in the relative quiet of a small university city in Iowa. Perhaps it needs Chicago in order to round out its reflection of the American scene.[10]

And so, ignoring the echoes of the crash of stocks in Wall Street and the tightening of credits, relying on the promises of Chicago friends of letters, Frederick in 1930 moved the *Midland* to Chicago. The next year the magazine, still printed by the Mercers in Iowa City, was given a quarto page. Typographically, and perhaps in content as well, it was livelier and more attractive than ever before. Esther Paulus Frederick became co-editor. But inexorably the Great Depression advanced, mowing down all struggling ventures in its path. Chi-

[9] O'Brien, *Best Short Stories of 1930,* pp. x–xi.
[10] *Midland,* v. 16, Nov.–Dec. 1930, p. 371.

JOHN TOWNER FREDERICK (TAKEN IN 1967)

Frederick was editor and publisher of the *Midland* from its beginning in 1915 to its demise in 1933. Photograph by Fred Kent.

cago friends who had pledged their generosity to the *Midland* if it would move to their city suddenly found they had nothing to be generous with. "The fourth year of the depression proves to be one year too many for *The Midland,*" wrote Frederick in the last number of the magazine, issued in June, 1933. "I shall miss *The Midland* for its own sake," he confessed, and then continued ruefully: "For nearly twenty years I have given to it money taken from my income as teacher and farmer, time taken from my work, as teacher and farmer, from my reading, from my family life; and though the money and time have been alike sometimes needed and hard to spare, my personal rewards have been great." [11]

Henry L. Mencken once wrote to Editor Frederick, in an enthusiastic moment, that the *Midland* was "probably the most important literary magazine ever established in America." "May I quote you?" Frederick wrote back. "Go ahead," replied Mencken. So those words of the Sage of Baltimore adorned the magazine's promotional leaflets for years. It was Menckenian hyperbole, of course; but it can scarcely be denied that the *Midland* had a very real importance in the encouragment of sincere authorship and good writing during almost two decades. This influence was doubtless strongest in the Midwest, but it was far from negligible in the nation at large.

[11] *Midland,* v. 20, March–April, May–June 1933, p. 56.

15

THE NEW REPUBLIC[1]

WILLARD STRAIGHT represented that combination of idealism and success in practical affairs that has occasionally produced such remarkable characters in American life. Although educated as an architect, he never followed that profession. He was a talented illustrator,[2] but he

[1] TITLE: *The New Republic: A Journal of Opinion.*

FIRST ISSUE: Nov. 7, 1914. Current.

PERIODICITY: Weekly. Vols. 1–100, 13 nos. each, 1–1300 (Nov. 7, 1914—Nov. 1, 1939); 101, 8 nos., 1301–8 (Nov. 8–Dec. 27, 1939); 102–27, semiannual vols., 1309–1987 (1940–52); 128, 30 nos. 1988–2017 (Jan. 5–July 27, 1953); 129, 22 nos., 2019–40 (Aug. 3–Dec. 28, 1953); 130–current, semiannual vols. Suspended Oct. 15–Nov. 5, 1919; 2018 omitted in numbering.

PUBLISHERS: Republic Publishing Company, New York, 1914–25 (Herbert Croly, pres.; Robert Hallowell, treas.); New Republic Publishing Company, New York, 1925–36 (Herbert Croly, pres., 1925–30; Bruce Bliven, pres., 1930–36; Daniel Mebane, treas.); Editorial Publications, Inc., New York, 1937–50, and Washington, D.C., 1950–51 (Michael W. Straight, publisher, 1946–51; Daniel Mebane, treas.); Westbury Publications, Inc., Washington, D.C., 1951–53 (Daniel Mebane, publisher); New Republic, Inc., Washington, D.C., 1953–current (Gilbert A. Harrison, publisher, 1953–63, 1966; Robert B. Luce, 1963–66; Garth Hite, 1966–current.)

EDITORS: Herbert Croly, 1914–30; Bruce Bliven, 1930–46; Henry Agard Wallace, 1946–47; Michael Whitney Straight, 1948–56; Gilbert A. Harrison, 1956–current. Managing editors: Helen Fuller, 1952–61; Selig S. Harrison, 1961–62; Alexander Campbell, 1963–current. Associate editors: Philip Littell, 1914–23; Walter Edward Weyl, 1914–16, 1918; Walter Lippmann, 1914–17, 1919–21; Francis Hackett, 1914–22; Alvin Saunders Johnson, 1915–26; George Soule, 1917–18, 1925–46; Charles Merz, 1917–20; Signe Toksvig, 1918–21; Robert Morss Lovett, 1921–40; Stark Young, 1922–24, 1929–46; Robert Littell, 1922–28; Bruce Bliven, 1923–30 (editorial director), 1946–52 (chairman editorial board), 1952–54; Edmund Wilson, 1926–31; Malcolm Cowley, 1930–45; M. W. Straight, 1941–46; Helen Fuller (Washington editor), 1946–52; William Harlan Hale, 1946–47; Robert Evett (often books, music, art editor), 1952–current; Selig S. Harrison, 1959–61; Christopher Jencks, 1962–63; Murray Kempton, 1963–64; James Ridgeway, 1963–current; Andrew Kopkind, 1965–67; David Sanford, 1967–current; Joseph Featherstone, 1967–current.

INDEX: *Readers' Guide.*

REFERENCES: Bruce Bliven, "The First 40 Years," *New Republic,* 40th Anniversary Edition, v. 131, Nov. 22, 1954, pp. 6–10; T. S. Matthews, *Name and Address: An Autobiography* (New York, 1960), pp. 186–215; [Richard Homer Gentry, "Liberalism and the *New Republic:* 1914–1960," unpub. diss., University of Illinois, 1960; Robert B. Luce, ed., *The Faces of Five Decades:* Selections from Fifty Years of the *New Republic* (New York, 1964)].

[2] A number of his sketches are reproduced in Herbert Croly, *Willard Straight* (New York, 1924).

sketched only for the amusement of himself and his friends. He early felt a strong attraction to the Orient, and he began his career as a customs inspector in Peking. Later he entered the consular service; but he was obsessed by dreams of improving economic and social conditions in China by exploitation of that country's resources based on American enterprise and capital, and eventually he became an agent of New York bankers and railroad magnates in northern China.

One of a tourist party in the Orient in 1909 was Dorothy Whitney, daughter of William C. and Flora P. Whitney, of New York. Her father had been Secretary of the Navy in Cleveland's cabinet, a sportsman in the expensive manner, and a traction magnate. The mother had inherited a large fortune from her father, Senator Henry B. Payne, of Ohio, once treasurer of the Standard Oil Company. But Dorothy was unspoiled by wealth and society; she was a humanitarian, with special interest in settlement house work, in crusades against sweatshops, and social reforms generally.[3] She was "a real angel," wrote one of the editors later associated with her on the *New Republic;* "not one person ever detected the faintest blot on the white purity of her spirit." [4]

Willard Straight fell in love with Dorothy Whitney when he first met her in Peking, followed her when her party went on to Europe, and continued his courtship amid the excitements of a grand tour; but it was not until two years later that the couple was married in Geneva, Switzerland.

The Straights returned to New York in 1912. While still in China they had read *The Promise of American Life,* a remarkable book by Herbert Croly. Wealthy, lively minded, anxious to play their part in bringing to pass such an ideal system as this book adumbrated, Willard and Dorothy Straight "hunted up" the author soon after they returned to America and employed him for some social and educational investigations.[5] There was no paradox here: wealth was interested in social reform, all within the capitalistic system; and confirmed imperialists had

[3] See Eric F. Goldman, *Rendezvous With Destiny* (New York, 1952), pp. 230–31.

[4] Alvin Johnson, *Pioneer's Progress* (New York, 1952), pp. 233–34.

[5] Croly, *Willard Straight,* pp. 472–74.

strong leanings toward the Progressive movement in contemporary politics.[6]

Herbert Croly was the son of David G. Croly, a journalist and a disciple of the positivist philosophy of Auguste Comte, and Jane Cunningham ("Jennie June") Croly, also a journalist, and founder of the women's club movement.[7] The father's belief in such Comtian theories as social regeneration, utilitarianism, and the religion of humanity undoubtedly had a strong effect on the son's thinking.[8] After some years of study, especially in history and philosophy, at the College of the City of New York and Harvard University, Herbert Croly became editor of the *Architectural Record* in 1900. He had grown up to be a shy person, an introvert and scholar, deeply earnest, a writer who took infinite pains and still did not always make himself clear.[9] Eventually the ideas that were to be set forth in *The Promise of American Life* had so taken possession of his mind that he retired to an assistant editorship on the *Record* in order to write the book.

The Promise had become "a political classic" by the time of Croly's death, wrote Walter Lippmann in a memorial number of the *New Republic.*[10] Whether or not this was true in a larger sense, it cannot be doubted that Croly's famous book was highly regarded by the group of writers that made the *New Republic;* and for that reason a few lines about it are necessary here. It is an essay in historical criticism, founded on the thesis

[6] See William E. Leuchtenburg, "Progressivism and Imperialism: The Progressive Movement and American Foreign Policy, 1898–1916," *Mississippi Valley Historical Review,* v. 39, Dec. 1952, pp. 483–504.

[7] See F. L. Mott, *A History of American Magazines,* v. 3 (Cambridge, Mass., 1938), pp. 325–27.

[8] See M. James Bolquerin, "An Investigation of the Contributions of David, Jane and Herbert Croly to American Life, With Emphasis on the Influence of the Father on the Son," unpub. diss., University of Missouri, 1948. See also pp. 10–25 of Charles Budd Forcey's admirable "Intellectuals in Crisis: Croly, Weyl, Lippmann, and the *New Republic,* 1900–1919," unpub. diss., University of Wisconsin, 1954. See also Forcey, *The Crossroads of Liberalism: Croly, Weyl, Lippmann and the Progressive Era, 1900–1925* (New York, 1961).

[9] Edmund Wilson, "H. C.," pp. 266–68; Waldo Frank, "The Promise of Herbert Croly," pp. 260–63; Walter Lippmann, "Notes for a Biography," pp. 250–52; and other articles in *New Republic,* v. 63, July 16, 1930, Part 2; see also Robert Morss Lovett, *All Our Years* (New York, 1948), p. 173.

[10] *New Republic,* v. 63, July 16, 1930, Part 2, p. 250.

HERBERT DAVID CROLY, 1869–1930

Croly was editor of the *New Republic* from its first issue in 1914 until his death in 1930.

that "the latent regeneracy and brotherhood of mankind" [11] will eventuate in a realization of democratic responsibility which, instrumented by heroic and intellectual leadership, will fulfill America's destiny as a "Land of Promise." On the issue on which, it seems, all our historians must take sides, Croly aligned himself frankly with Hamilton rather than Jefferson, though he was less a committed partisan than many, alleging that Hamilton "perverted the American national idea almost as much as Jefferson perverted the American democratic idea." [12] Hamilton's objective was to provide a stable government for the protection of property; Jefferson's, to achieve "automatically" the good life through as little government and as much individual freedom as possible; Croly's, to foster interdependence "between an efficient national organization and a group of radical democratic institutions and ideals." [13] This last program called for not only a "planned economy," but a carefully blueprinted social system as well—and all of this based on a rise in general education and a social morality that was essentially religious.

It was a political and social theory built on such a framework as this that drew the Straights and Herbert Croly together. One evening when Croly was a guest at the Straight home on Long Island, conversation touched upon the new status of *Harper's Weekly,* of which Norman Hapgood had just become editor.[14] Croly, who had expected much from the change, expressed his disappointment that Hapgood had not taken a bold, liberal stand as soon as he took over. "Why don't you start a weekly yourself, Herbert?" challenged Dorothy Straight. At least one answer was obvious: no funds. How much would it take? They estimated a hundred thousand dollars for the first

[11] This oft-quoted phrase of Croly's appeared first in a supplement to the issue of Dec. 6, 1922, entitled, "The New Republic Idea." The supplement was quoted at some length in *New Republic,* v. 63, July 16, 1930, Part 2, pp. 258–59; Groff Conklin, ed., *The New Republic Anthology, 1915–1935* (New York, 1936), pp. xxxv–xl; Doris Ulmann, *A Portrait Gallery of American Editors* (New York, 1925), p. 30.

[12] Herbert Croly, *The Promise of American Life* (New York, 1909), p. 29.

[13] Croly, *Promise,* pp. 33–34, chap. ii is devoted to the Hamilton-Jefferson controversy.

[14] Mott, *American Magazines,* v. 2 (1938), p. 486.

year, then less each year until it should be paying for itself in five years. "I'll find the money," said Mrs. Straight.[15]

Thus the *New Republic* was conceived. It was in gestation throughout a year of conferences and planning. Late in 1913 four prospective members of an editorial board were brought into the council—Walter Lippmann, Walter Weyl, Francis Hackett, and Philip Littell.[16] Lippmann was a brilliant young man of twenty-five. He had been a student assistant of Santayana's while at Harvard, and later private secretary of George R. Lunn, Socialist mayor of Schenectady, New York.[17] The year before he joined the *New Republic,* his first book, *A Preface to Politics,* had been published; it had made a success, and had made it mainly with an insistence on the kind of dynamic government that Croly had advocated in *The Promise of American Life.* Weyl, primarily an economist, had also recently written a book, *The New Democracy;* in it he had advocated a greater democratization of government and the socialization of industry. Hackett was an Irish-born critic and liberal who had attracted attention by his brilliant editorship of the *Chicago Evening Post Literary Review.* He was a wit, with a leaning toward satire, and a clever writer. Littell was a grandson of Eliakim Littell and a son of Robert S. Littell, successive editors for over half a century of *Littell's Living Age.*[18] He, too, was a good writer, though most of his contribution to the *New Republic* was confined to his "Books and Things" page.

Croly was not editor-in-chief by title or by any formal authority, but he was *de facto* leader of the group because he had organized it and because its members all held him in high respect. Charles B. Forcey, leading student of the early *New Republic* and its group, concludes that Croly's control was based on "a tyranny of sensitivity, a tyranny all the more effective for having the appearance of its opposite." [19] Ostensibly, there was no control, to say nothing of tyranny. Robert Morss Lovett, an editor during the twenties, wrote in his autobiography: "In

15 Johnson, *Pioneer's Progress,* p. 233.

16 Walter Lippmann, "Notes," p. 250.

17 David Elliott Weingast, *Walter Lippmann: A Study in Personal Journalism* (New Brunswick, N.J., 1949), pp. 5–13.

18 Mott, *American Magazines,* v. 1 (1930), pp. 747–49.

19 Forcey, "Intellectuals," p. 8.

Croly's conception of the journal the editorial board was a soviet. Its decisions were reached in conference and were presumed to be unanimous. Contributions from outside were submitted to all the editors. Each number was issued with the *nil obstat* of the entire group and carried the unique authority of an elite board. How long this condition endured in its pristine vigor I do not know. When I joined the staff there were rifts in the fabric." [20]

The system of getting things done quickly by unanimous concurrence was bound to break down from time to time even in the most agreeable group. Though there was much homogeneity among the members of the editorial board in education, ideas, and taste, all of them were independent thinkers. The Hamiltonian Croly, the Jeffersonian Weyl and Hackett, and the pragmatic Lippmann might be expected to disagree occasionally, especially when Weyl's Zionism and Hackett's Sinn Fein sympathies were mixed into the brew. Lippmann once complained that "Croly has the religious bug very badly and Hackett is simply Sinn Fein." [21]

Then there was Willard Straight, affiliated with the operations of J. P. Morgan and Company, who had one vote, and only one, on the editorial board.[22] Though he sometimes disagreed with *New Republic* policy (especially over its support of Wilson in the 1916 campaign), there was never any threat of withdrawing the subsidies that he and his wife contributed regularly to the magazine's support. This relation once led H. L. Mencken to refer to *New Republic* editors as "kept idealists." [23]

There were several factors that helped maintain that Quaker-like unanimous-consent procedure, or a semblance of it, throughout Croly's editorship. One was the common respect of his associates for their leader; another was their agreement in many matters, and especially in their disapprovals; and a third was a habit of conference. "Our editorial staff was in practically

[20] Lovett, *All Our Years,* p. 172.

[21] Mark DeWolfe Howe, ed., *Holmes-Laski Letters, 1916–1935* (Cambridge, Mass., 1953), v. 1, p. 231, Laski to Holmes, Jan. 4, 1920. These differences are noted in Goldman, *Rendezvous,* p. 231.

[22] Croly, *Straight,* pp. 473–74.

[23] Goldman, *Rendezvous,* p. 316; Charles Angoff, *H. L. Mencken: A Portrait From Memory* (New York, 1956), p. 189.

The New
REPUBLIC
Published Weekly
Saturday December 12th 1914

In this issue:

Pacifism vs. Passivism
Socialist Degeneration
In a Moscow Hospital
The Reformer

TEN CENTS A COPY
FOUR DOLLARS A YEAR

Published by THE REPUBLIC PUBLISHING COMPANY, Inc., 421 West 21st Street, New York, N.Y.

THE *NEW REPUBLIC* IN ITS FIRST YEAR—

Dated December 12, 1914, this was the periodical's fifth issue. Its black and white cover continued for many years in virtually this same style. In the 1940's a little color began to be used and an occasional drawing.

How Is Youth to Be Served? *Henry Fairlie*

THE NEW REPUBLIC

April 8, 1967, 35 cents

Chou En-lai

Kai-yu Hsu

Problem-Solvers — *James Ridgeway*

Money for the States — *Joseph Pechman*

Appeals to Reason — *The Editors*

"The Other Side" — *Ronald Steel*

Thornton Wilder — *Stanley Kauffmann*

—AND OVER HALF A CENTURY LATER

The date: April 8, 1967. *New Republic* covers are still in about the same pattern of the earlier issues. They continue to display a generalized table of contents, but a block background of bright color makes them more striking in appearance.

continuous consultation," wrote one of the editors later. "All our differences of opinion, however," he added, "ironed themselves out in the staff discussions." [24] In their office building they had a kitchen and dining room, and there the staff, often with visitors and contributors, commonly ate luncheon and sometimes dinner with all the intimacy of a big family.[25]

A member of the editorial staff who must not be forgotten was Charlotte Rudyard, invaluable office editor and copyreader, who had been associate editor of *Harper's Magazine.* In 1916 she married Robert Hallowell, who was the paper's business manager, but who "doubled in brass" as its art critic.[26] She was succeeded as office editor by Signe Toksvig, who also married within the *New Republic* editorial family. She wed Francis Hackett and in 1922 took him off to Denmark with her.[27] Alvin S. Johnson was a contributor to the *New Republic* from the first; he joined the editorial board in 1915 and served longer than any of the others except Croly himself. Johnson had been a professor of economics at Stanford and at other universities.[28] Also sharing in the planning for the new magazine and a frequent contributor to the early numbers was Felix Frankfurter,[29] newly appointed professor of law at Harvard. Prominently associated with the early numbers as contributors, if not as advisors, were John Dewey and Charles A. Beard.

And so, after long gestation, the *New Republic* was born November 7, 1914. It was a good-looking weekly of thirty-two pages quarto including self-cover, with typographic design by Ingalls Kimball.[30] The cover displayed the leading titles and authors of the issue. There were no illustrations. The journal opened with some three pages of fairly short editorial comment, and these were followed by four or five headed editorial articles that occupied five or six pages. Then came the signed articles

24 Johnson, *Pioneer's Progress,* pp. 241, 242.

25 Lovett, *All Our Years,* p. 174; Francis Hackett, *I Chose Denmark* (New York, 1940), p. 1.

26 Johnson, *Pioneer's Progress,* p. 234; Lippmann, "Notes," p. 250.

27 Hackett, *Denmark,* pp. 1–3, 38.

28 Johnson, *Pioneer's Progress,* pp. 233–34, 240–70.

29 Felix Frankfurter, "Herbert Croly and American Public Opinion," *New Republic,* v. 63, July 16, 1930, Part 2, pp. 247–50.

30 *New Republic,* v. 131, Nov. 22, 1954, p. 10.

known in the office as "light middles";[31] though by no means all of them were light, they had more variety in style and topic than the editorial section, and most of them were "outside" contributions. Each of these ran for a page or two in length, and there were five or six of them. "Communications" was the heading of an interesting and often distinguished department of two or three pages. Book reviews, including Littell's "Books and Things" department, commonly occupied four or five pages. Then there were a few pages of advertising, chiefly of books. The paper sold for ten cents on the newsstands, or four dollars a year by subscription.

The magazine was advertised by its subtitle as "A Journal of Opinion," and that it was. Its editorials and articles expressed the collective opinion of the editors, mainly on the political, economic, and social problems of the day. Music, art, and drama were occasionally touched upon; and somewhat later these subjects had their own departments. Poetry was introduced into the journal's pages auspiciously with Robert Frost's "The Death of the Hired Man," February 6, 1915; but it appeared rarely at first and never with regularity and abundance. William Faulkner's first published work, a poem—"L'Après-Midi d'un Faune"—was printed in August 1919.

The *New Republic* began with a circulation of 875.[32] At the end of the first year it had reached only about 15,000; some retrenchment in size seemed to be indicated, and for the next few years it was cut to about twenty-six pages an issue. The former size was restored, however, when a modest boom ensued upon the journal's support of the Wilson war policy—perhaps the most affirmative position of its early history. In 1917–1920 it circulated well over 30,000 and for some issues up to 43,000.[33]

At its highest point, this was a small distribution for a national

[31] Johnson, *Pioneer's Progress,* p. 242.

[32] Frederick L. Paxson, *American Democracy and the World War* (Boston, 1936), v. 1, p. 189.

[33] *New Republic,* v. 40, Oct. 29, 1924, p. ii. *N.W. Ayer & Son's Directory of Newspapers and Periodicals* is helpful for these early years. See also William H. Attwood, "Pathfinders of American Liberalism: The Story of the *New Republic,*" senior thesis in history, Princeton University, 1941, pp. 11–13. This is a good study, chiefly concerned with the magazine's political and economic policy, 1914–40.

magazine. It was, in fact, not truly national either in respect to its topical purview or the range of its contributors. Forcey's analysis brings him to the conclusion that "the *New Republic* for the first few years was largely an organ of eastern intellectuals and of the New York wing of the progressive movement." [34] Perhaps its influence was out of all proportion to its circulation. With its Hamiltonian theories of government, fired by Jeffersonian idealism, it undoubtedly aspired to affect political leadership; and we shall note presently its relations with Roosevelt and Wilson. But Bruce Bliven wrote, at the time of Croly's death: "I should be surprised if there were ever in the 14 years of his active editorship as many as 10 percent of the national House of Representatives and 20 percent of the Senate capable of following his discussion of public affairs. . . ." [35] Indeed, many critics felt a kind of "inspired vagueness" and "intellectual dilettanteism" in the *New Republic* editorials.[36] The more radical *Freeman* was whimsical but severe in its criticism: "The *chimaera bombinans in vacuo* is ten times more easily reconstructible from a cat's thigh-bone, as far as our poor abilities go, than Mr. Croly's ideas, or pseudo-ideas, are reconstructible from his phraseology." [37] And a satirist in the *New York Tribune* expressed his impressions "On Reading the *New Republic*," in verse:

> Ah, pause, Appreciation, here
> Sophistication doubly nice is,
> See polished paragraphs appear
> Anent some cataclysmic crisis.
>
> Note raw-boned, rude, impulsive thought
> Arrested here and subtly twitted;
> Note youth comporting as he ought,
> And naked truth correctly fitted.
>
> . . . .
>
> And here beyond the stir of strife,
> Where distant drones the blatant babble,

[34] Forcey, "Intellectuals," pp. 418–22.

[35] *New Republic*, v. 63, July 16, 1930, Part 2, p. 259.

[36] These epithets are taken from an article in the *Catholic World*, v. 116, March 1923, p. 787.

[37] *Freeman*, v. 2, Dec. 22, 1920, p. 344.

Ah, tread the promenade of life,
A pace behind the vulgar rabble.[38]

Even Justice Oliver Wendell Holmes was irked by this superior attitude. "It riles me," he wrote to Harold Laski, "to note the air of having it all for the first time that is so common in the contributors to that noble sheet."[39] And someone, perhaps Albert J. Nock of the *Freeman,* punned: "The paper always has a Crolier than thou air!"[40]

The early *New Republic* not only repelled the general reader by its style and its superior air, but it offended both the popular audience and many of the radicals by its failure to support current reform movements aggressively. Max Eastman, who had greeted the editors of the new journal on its first appearance as "mighty, young bronze beasts," soon changed his mind and, after two years of reading their essays, wrote in his *Masses:* "They still live in a world in which fundamental democratic progress comes by telling, and persuading, and showing how, and propagating reasonable opinions, and better social feeling. The *real* world is a world in which privilege can only be uprooted by power."[41] And the brilliant Amos Pinchot, aggravated because "the *New Republic* does not take sides on the fundamental issues in the larger struggle between privilege and democracy," burst out irascibly: "If the editors of the *New Republic* had been called upon to write the Book of Genesis, I believe that the story of the creation would have begun with the sixth day when God saw everything he had made, and, behold, it was very good—except the Sherman Law and the Democratic administration."[42]

The *New Republic's* real object, as Croly once said, was "less to inform and entertain its readers than to start little insurrections in the realm of their convictions." "Little insurrections" were not enough for the radicals, and they were too much for

[38] Seymour Barnard, in the *New York Tribune,* Dec. 7, 1917, p. 10, col. 3, reprinted in *Bookman,* v. 46, Jan. 1918, p. 554.

[39] *Holmes-Laski Letters,* v. 1, p. 114, Holmes to Laski, Nov. 30, 1917. Johnson, in *Pioneer's Progress,* p. 243, called Laski "almost a member of the staff."

[40] Lovett, *All Our Years,* pp. 178–79.

[41] *Masses,* quoted in *New Republic,* v. 3, May 29, 1915, p. 95, and *Masses,* v. 9, Dec. 1916, p. 12.

[42] *New Republic,* v. 3, May 29, 1915, p. 96.

the popular audience. Perhaps the best apologia for the *New Republic* negativism came not from the editors themselves but from a contributor, James Harvey Robinson, who wrote a letter for the magazine at the end of its first six months containing the following acute observations:

> [The editors] dreamed, I suspect, not of adhesion but of detachment; not of loyalty to principle but of serious and persistent criticism; not of conclusions but of discussion. . . . May it not be that the chief distinction and importance of the *New Republic* consists precisely in not "standing for" anything? . . . The great opportunity of the *New Republic* seems to be that it proposes to introduce scientific doubt into human affairs on a larger scale than any other journal of opinion. . . .[43]

It would be wrong, however, to give the impression that the *New Republic* was always general and vague, and that it was attached to no "causes." Its attachments were always critical and never quite stable; it was committed to independent examination, both on the plane of philosophical generalization and that of mere nipping. But it was not wholly negative, nor always in the clouds. Its adherence to the instrumentalism of pragmatic theory [44] led it to the aggressive support, from time to time, of definite policies.

Indeed, the *New Republic* was in some sense born of a reform movement. Though it came two years after the defeat of the "Bull Moose" party at the polls, it was a Progressive partisan. Lippmann wrote in the Croly memorial supplement: "The *New Republic* was founded to explore and develop and apply the ideas which had been advertised by Theodore Roosevelt when he was the leader of the Progressive party." [45] In the same issue Felix Frankfurter asserted that both Roosevelt's "New Nationalism" and Wilson's "New Freedom" were "derived from Croly." [46] In a contemporary issue of the *American Magazine* Croly was called "the man from whom Col. Roosevelt got his 'New Nationalism.'" [47] These may be overstate-

[43] *New Republic,* v. 3, May 8, 1915, pp. 9–10.

[44] See Forcey, "Intellectuals," pp. 27–37.

[45] Lippmann, "Notes," p. 250.

[46] *New Republic,* v. 63, July 16, 1930, Part 2, p. 247.

[47] *American Magazine,* v. 75, Nov. 1912, p. 23. The words appear in a "cutline" under a portrait of Croly.

ments, but most students of Roosevelt and the Progressive movement give Croly more or less definite credit for the ideas promulgated in the "New Nationalism" address at Ossawatomie, Kansas, in August 1910.[48] Certainly the two had exchanged laudatory compliments. Wrote Croly in *The Promise of American Life:* "More than any other American political leader, except Lincoln, his [Roosevelt's] devotion both to the national and to the democratic ideas is thorough-going and absolute."[49] Wrote T. R. in the *Outlook:* Croly's *Promise of American Life* is "the most profound and illuminating study of our National conditions which has appeared for many years. . . ."[50] Both Croly's *Promise* and Lippmann's *Preface to Politics* were accepted as manifestoes of Progressivism; they were part of that stream of thought and performed an important service in helping crystallize the ideas of the movement.

This alliance is writ large in the pages of the early *New Republic.* Readers became well aware of the journal's support of such specific "causes" as labor unionism, the eight-hour day, workmen's compensation, the nationalization of railroads, the short ballot, women's suffrage, birth control, prison reform, and academic freedom.[51]

It is true that political maneuvers in support of these reforms were often criticized by the *New Republic,* whose directors early laid down the axiom: "An editor too friendly with a politician has mortgaged his integrity."[52] From its very first number the journal began to print some strictures on Progressive Party measures, and it was not long before certain criticism of Roosevelt himself so angered that leader that he never forgave the editors of the magazine from which he had expected so much.[53] The criticism that caused the break with T. R. grew out of a debate on Wilson's foreign policy. *New Republic* editors had at first distrusted Wilson; he was not enough of an innovator or agitator to suit them.[54] But as the weeks wore on,

48 See Forcey, "Intellectuals," pp. 252–73, also see Bolquerin, "The Crolys," where there is a résumé of these commentaries.

49 Croly, *Promise,* p. 170.

50 *Outlook,* v. 97, Jan. 21, 1911, p. 97.

51 See Attwood, "Story of the *New Republic,*" pp. 31–32.

52 *New Republic,* v. 2, Feb. 13, 1915, p. 34.

53 Lippmann, "Notes," p. 251.

54 *New Republic,* v. 4, Sept. 4, 1915, p. 111.

they found more to approve and defend in his unfolding program.

The *New Republic* was first planned without prophetic intimations of approaching war. How impregnable seemed the American position of security and peace in 1913! But the day the staff of the proposed journal moved into its new offices, August 1, 1914, Germany declared war on Russia and touched off the European conflagration. Even then, wrote the editors later, they still saw nationalism, placed so high on the Crolian scale, "in innocent terms" and "unsaturated with the menace" that it carried later.[55]

Through the first year or more of the war, the editors advocated the policy of American neutrality. They took the sinking of the "Lusitania" calmly, heading their editorial about it, "Not Our War." [56] But later in 1915 they were printing pieces by Harold Laski and Norman Angell supporting the British cause, in December they were nagging Wilson over his "moral suasion" diplomacy,[57] and early the next year they urged American entry into the war. The "Communications" department was for a time a forum for pro-war and anti-war advocates; then after the editors were beating the war drums, groups of pacifists and the peace societies sometimes took paid advertising space to air their views. Thus the editors in their own columns and such publicists as Max Eastman, Amos Pinchot, Joseph H. Choate, Alton B. Parker, and Randolph S. Bourne in the advertising pages carried on a joint debate. Bourne, that brilliant mind in a distorted body, who had been happy to contribute to the initial numbers of the *New Republic,* was now especially bitter against it.[58]

The editors supported Wilson in the presidential campaign of 1916. As one critic observed, they had "arrived at the support of Wilson's policies by a long and painful exercise in logistics"; [59] but they did arrive. For more than two years the

[55] *Ibid.,* v. 4, Sept. 11, 1915, pp. 143–44.

[56] *Ibid.,* v. 3, June 5, 1915, pp. 108–10.

[57] *Ibid.,* v. 4, Sept. 4, 1915, pp. 128–30; v. 5, Dec. 11, 1915, p. 133, and Dec. 25, 1915, p. 198.

[58] Goldman, *Rendezvous,* pp. 220–22, 237–38; Lovett, *All Our Years,* p. 151.

[59] Beulah Amidon, "The Nation and the *New Republic,*" *Survey Graphic,* v. 29, Jan. 1940, p. 25. See the thirty-page supplement to *New Republic,* v. 10,

journal then occupied perhaps the most positive and concretely constructive position of its history.

"A war patronized by the *New Republic* could not but turn out to be a better war than any one had hoped," remarked Floyd Dell ironically.[60] A martial alliance between the shy and thoughtful Croly and the scholarly, professorial Wilson did appear, on the surface, to be incongruous. But the historian Wilson knew about the necessities of war, and Croly had made his apprehension of such an eventuality clear in a macabre sentence in his *Promise:* "Indeed, the probabilities are that in America as in Europe the road to any permanent international settlement will be piled mountain high with dead bodies, . . ." [61] By the spring of 1917 there was a kind of holy enthusiasm about the war in the pages of the *New Republic*. Democracy seemed to the editors to be globally infectious: "It is now as certain as anything human can be that the war . . . will dissolve into democratic revolution the world over." [62]

These were the times in which the *New Republic* was looked upon by many as a White House spokesman, and stock market operators rushed to the newsstands to get early copies.[63] Circulation doubled. Oswald Garrison Villard, then editor of the rival *Nation,* later wrote in his autobiography: "For a time during the war and immediately afterwards the *New Republic* was regarded by many as the mouthpiece of Woodrow Wilson; it was considered bad form in some official circles to be seen without it and its circulation climbed to about 45,000. It was believed that Walter Lippmann and the *New Republic* had won the President to our participation in the war in order to shape the peace and that Lippmann had written the fourteen peace points." [64] This last idea was false, as Lippmann himself

---

March 10, 1917, entitled "The Evolution of a National Policy in Relation to The Great War," a series of reprints from the paper. For a comprehensive study of the paper's attitudes toward Wilson, see Attwood, "Story of the *New Republic,*" pp. 35–103. Straight's article supporting Hughes against Wilson for the presidency was printed in the *New Republic,* v. 8, Oct. 28, 1916, pp. 313–14.

60 Quoted in Granville Hicks, *John Reed: The Making of a Revolutionary* (New York, 1936), p. 231.

61 Croly, *Promise,* p. 307.

62 *New Republic,* v. 10, April 7, 1917, p. 280.

63 Lippmann, "Notes," p. 251.

64 Oswald Garrison Villard, *Fighting Years* (New York, 1939), p. 361.

pointed out; but Wilson did take over, as he admitted in a letter to Croly, the slogan "Peace Without Victory." [65]

But even in these years of affirmation, the *New Republic* did not go along evenly with American popular opinion or public policy. It was severely critical of war hysteria and international hatreds. Long before the entry of the United States into the war, it had planned a League of Neutrals which might some day negotiate a League of All Nations to end all wars.[66] It was firmly committed to the doctrine that peace was possible only if a world view was taken, Germany was not humiliated in defeat, and general disarmament was realized. Now it began to lose faith in the aims of our British allies toward such an ideal. Laski was exasperated. "They give us sage advice," he wrote to Justice Holmes, "with the air of people who have private information about the constitution of the universe—and their moral hyperbolas grow at times nauseating." [67] All this led to the cry of Anglophobia being raised against the journal, and to wild accusations of disloyalty.[68] It seems at this distance, however, that Norman Hapgood was right when he described the *New Republic's* course in the war years as pulling a strong oar for victory, but, it "has the courage to reflect a world point of view in the midst of national chauvinism." [69]

The Treaty of Versailles fulfilled the worst fears of the *New Republic*. "A Punic peace of annihilation!" cried the editors.[70] Moreover, they were convinced that the League of Nations would perpetuate rather than correct the evils of the treaty. In short, the debacle of Versailles and the League brought a heart-breaking collapse of their hopes to Croly and his fellow editors. In an astute analysis of the early years of the *New Republic*,

65 Lippmann, "Notes," p. 252; Weingast, *Lippmann*, pp. 14–17; Forcey, "Intellectuals," pp. 352–58. Col. E. M. House's diary shows confidential relations with both Lippmann and Croly (Jan. 15, 22, 30; Feb. 5, 27; March 9, 26, 1917), but with many other journalists as well. As to the Wilson use of the "Peace Without Victory" phrase, see Ray Stannard Baker, *Woodrow Wilson*, v. 6 (New York, 1939), p. 425.

66 *New Republic*, v. 1, Jan. 2, 1915, pp. 7–9.

67 *Holmes-Laski Letters*, v. 1, p. 43. Laski to Holmes, Dec. 16, 1916.

68 The *Outlook* was the chief spokesman of this attack on the *New Republic*. See, for example, *Outlook*, v. 116, Aug. 29, 1917, p. 645; v. 117, Oct. 3, 1917, pp. 164–65.

69 *New Republic*, v. 13, Jan. 26, 1918, p. 380.

70 *New Republic*, v. 19, May 17, 1919, pp. 71–74.

David W. Noble thus sums up the abortion of the editors' plans for a brave new world: ". . . these war years undermined their vision of a better America by destroying the intellectual and emotional assumptions on which they had based their faith in progress. Herbert Croly, Walter Weyl, and Walter Lippmann, who were instrumental in the establishment of the *New Republic* in 1914 as the harbinger of an actual new republic, could leave no dynamic legacy of liberalism to the next generation because the heart of their philosophy—the culmination of progress in an evolutionary, middle-class Utopia, created by rational and good men—was shattered." [71]

And it was more than ideological failure that confronted the *New Republic* at the beginning of the 1920's. Straight had died in 1918, having been stricken with the "flu" while in military service in France. Weyl had resigned from the editorial board to enter government service shortly before the United States entered the war. Lippmann left it in 1921 to write editorials for the New York *World,* exchanging the more philosophic attitudes of the weekly for daily commentary on the hurly-burly of public affairs. Charles Merz, an associate editor, transferred to the *World* about the same time. The next year Hackett, of whom Justice Holmes (a faithful reader of the *New Republic*) once said that "in literary matters he has more power to utter the unutterable than anyone I can think of," resigned to travel in his native Ireland and his wife's native Denmark.[72] Laski and Angell, staff contributors, returned to England after the war.

The circulation of the *New Republic* began a slow decline in the early twenties. It was a decade of inflation, and a reform journal flourishes best in hard times. The price was raised to fifteen cents in 1919, or five dollars a year, and the size was decreased again to twenty-six pages. A paper stock of mechanical woodpulp was adopted; twenty-five years later, the pages of the *New Republic* printed in the twenties were cracking and falling apart when the bound volumes were used in libraries. But despite retrenchments, there were probably few years in the

[71] David W. Noble, "The *New Republic* and the Idea of Progress, 1914–1920," *Mississippi Valley Historical Review,* v. 38, Dec. 1951, p. 388.

[72] Mark DeWolfe Howe, ed., *Holmes-Pollock Letters,* v. 2 (Cambridge, Mass., 1941), p. 96; Hackett, *Denmark, passim.*

decade when the journal's deficit was less than $75,000.[73] Nevertheless, liberal salaries and payments were continued, the staff's dining room still dispensed hospitality, and Dorothy Straight footed the bills without complaint.

And Croly still held his banner high, though chastened in spirit and emphasizing more and more the religious side of his philosophy. Vacancies in the staff were filled by new editors who maintained the journal's reputation for good writing —George Soule, economist and sociologist who had really been associated with the paper almost from its beginning; Robert Morss Lovett, University of Chicago professor of English; Stark Young, playwright and critic; Bruce Bliven, journalist, and others. Johnson stayed on until 1926, although he had become director of the New School for Social Research in 1923. Daniel Mebane, a young instructor on the faculty of Indiana University, having tried to use the *New Republic* as supplementary reading for his classes, encountered objection from his superiors to the use of such incendiary material; he packed up in 1920 and came to New York to become for many years a business manager for the journal.[74]

Some change took place in the nature of the *New Republic's* materials. There was rather less of political theory and more about books, music, the theater, and contemporary customs and trends. There was more poetry—by Conrad Aiken, Amy Lowell, Edwin Arlington Robinson, Edgar Lee Masters, Elinor Wylie, Vachel Lindsay, Archibald MacLeish. From the first, there had been occasional supplements, such as those on "Sweated Labor" (March 27, 1915) and "Labor and the New Social Order, A Report on Reconstruction by the Sub-Committee of the British Labor Party" (February 16, 1918), and the seasonal book review sections.[75] These continued in the twenties, and there were also some articles in series, such as Bliven's muckraking "The Ohio Gang" (May 1924) and Waldo Frank's biting "Re-Discovery of America" (1927–1928).

[73] See the article by Beulah Amidon, a *New Republic* contributor, in *Survey Graphic,* v. 29, Jan. 1940, p. 24; also the circular soliciting subscriptions quoted by Forcey, "Intellectuals," p. 357.

[74] *New Republic,* v. 116, March 3, 1947, p. 44.

[75] The seasonal book sections were later incorporated into the regular numbers.

There was also a Washington column of the "Merry-Go-Round" type, signed by the cryptic initials T.R.B.[76]

The *New Republic* had published some English writers, such as Henry N. Brailsford, extensively in early numbers. During the war H. G. Wells and Rebecca West, as well as Laski and Angell, were prominent. But in the twenties about a fourth of the journal's contributors were English. Two chapters of Lytton Strachey's *Queen Victoria* were published in June 1921, and sixteen of his short biographical studies appeared in the *New Republic*. Virginia Woolf contributed many literary essays and reviews in the twenties. Bertrand Russell's 1920 series on Bolshevism began his connection with the journal; this was followed by essays on various topics. John Maynard Keynes was a frequent contributor on fiscal matters.

Among American writers, John Dewey kept a certain prominence that he had held in the pages of the *New Republic* from its first months. Then he had been an advocate of vocational education; later he had written much about China, Russia, the Near East, and Mexico. It is easy to forget the contributors whose work was somewhat less philosophical, and more in the nature of brilliant reporting—like William Hard, who wrote on strikes and other matters; and Frank H. Simonds, who wrote the military articles during the First World War. American contributors who were appearing more and more frequently in the twenties were Lewis Mumford, Gilbert Seldes, Edmund Wilson, Jane Addams, Eduard C. Lindeman, Leo Wolman, Van Wyck Brooks, Robert Herrick, and Rexford G. Tugwell.

Though diversity characterized the *New Republic* of the twenties more markedly than during its beginning years, the chief subjects remained politics, economics, and social problems. But so far as party adherence was concerned, Croly gee'd and haw'd a good deal. He was against the American party system anyway; he believed primarily in "executive leadership, administrative independence, and direct legislation." [77] In the presidential campaign of 1920, he abandoned middle-class progres-

[76] *New Republic Anthology,* p. 551.

[77] See his editorial "The Future of the Two-Party System," *New Republic,* v. 1, Nov. 14, 1914, pp. 10–11.

sivism for the labor movement as a better instrument for his nationalism and declared for the Farmer-Labor nominee. Four years later, however, he was enthusiastic in the support of La Follette, who in the end disappointed him by failing to make much impression in the entrenched Republican and Democratic positions. He had helped start a boom for Hoover back in 1919, thinking he had found a leader of liberal social outlook; but by 1928 he had lost faith in his hero and gave his support to Smith.

The years immediately following the peace offered plenty of editorial fuel—strikes, the I.W.W., the great "Red Scare," the renewed activity of the Ku Klux Klan, and the Volstead Act. The *New Republic* was constant in its testimony for organized labor and against oppressive movements, whether popular or governmental. It attacked Attorney General A. Mitchell Palmer with vigor and persistence as he tried to suppress strikes, Communist activities, and free speech in the years 1919–1920. The paper stated its position in regard to Russia clearly:

> Its ideals are not ours; its objectives do not inspire us with confidence; its methods cannot be approved. . . . That the Soviet Republic, by its example or by propaganda, can actually menace our own institutions appears to us absurd. . . . Let Soviet Russia alone. Let her failure as far as she must fail be upon her own head, not upon ours.[78]

The *New Republic* was always a severe critic of the American daily press, and at this juncture it attacked the *New York Times* especially for its mishandling of the Russian story. These attacks were summarized in a supplement to the number for August 4, 1920, edited by Lippmann and Merz, then both on the *New Republic's* editorial board, but later to be editors respectively of the *World* and the *Times* itself. That this criticism was effective is indicated by the fact that in 1921 the *Times* sent Walter Duranty to Russia to write with "complete freedom" [79] a series of articles that undoubtedly helped to bring about a better understanding in America of the Soviet experiment. The *New Republic* itself, throughout this decade and

[78] *New Republic,* v. 19, July 2, 1919, p. 267.

[79] *Duranty Reports Russia,* compiled by Gustavus Tuckerman (New York, 1934), p. ix.

later, watched the adventure of Soviet communism with sympathetic interest, followed the Five Year Plan closely, and set the Russian system against capitalism as comparative ideologies.

The *New Republic* was much concerned about the Sacco-Vanzetti case throughout its long progress.[80] Shortly before the execution, *New Republic* editors paid out of their own pockets for a full-page advertisement in the *New York Times* reviewing details of the defense.[81]

Worst of the Harding administration scandals was the one involving the Teapot Dome oil lease. The *New Republic* gave this breakdown of good government many columns, but it could scarcely have been surprised by the event. It had commented months before that the Dougherty and Fall cabinet appointments were "unspeakably bad"; these men, it had averred, "are full blown specimens of the manipulating politician who serves private and predatory interests . . . they are to operate the two departments of government—Justice and the Interior, that are the most rich in spoils." [82]

In the fall of 1928, Croly suffered a paralytic stroke, and he died on May 17, 1930. His friends and associates contributed to a memorial supplement (July 16, 1930) of the paper he had edited with so much fervor and sincerity. Bruce Bliven, who had come to the *New Republic* in 1923, took over the chief editorship on Croly's death. He had been trained in the newspaper school and was a more incisive writer than his predecessor.

The circulation of the *New Republic* had declined by the late twenties to an all-time low of ten thousand; but in keeping with the aforementioned principle that radical reform journals flourish better in hard times than good, it more than doubled in 1930 and seems to have been maintained at about 25,000 throughout the following decade.[83] When Dorothy Straight

[80] See Attwood, "Story of the *New Republic*," pp. 124–27.

[81] *New Republic*, v. 131, Nov. 22, 1954, p. 8.

[82] *Ibid.*, v. 26, March 2, 1921, p. 3.

[83] Attwood, who had special information from Mebane, says it dropped to 10,000 in 1925 ("Story of the *New Republic*," p. 11). Ayer gives an estimated circulation for 1929 (*Directory*, 1930) as 12,000, and a sworn circulation the next year at 25,000.

married the young English student of sociology, Leonard Elmhirst, in 1935 (Willard Straight having died in 1918),[84] she renounced her American citizenship; but she set up a trust for the support of the four magazines in which she was interested—the *New Republic, Asia, Theatre Arts,* and *Antiques.* Under this arrangement the *New Republic* subsidies, though steady, were not quite as liberal as before.[85] The journal derived, however, some income from the sale of its dollar books on social and economic problems, issued in paper covers; these numbered thirty-eight titles by 1935 and had sold some 250,000 copies.[86] New typography and make-up changed the appearance of the paper somewhat, and the trend toward variety of content was a little more marked in the thirties. Heywood Broun came over from the *Nation* to edit an outspoken column called "Shoot the Works," John T. Flynn wrote regularly on "Other People's Money," and "The Bandwagon" related absurdities from public speeches and newspapers.

Under Bliven and Soule the journal was less philosophical and more practical in its politics: as one acute observer said, it "plumped more and more for specific liberal reforms, and hammered less and less at the old Croly vision of liberalism as a basic, unifying, cultural belief." [87] Also it meandered again and again into the camp of the avowed anticapitalists, most notably in an article by Associate Editor Edmund Wilson. In the midst of the economic confusion following the great crash of 1929 Wilson wrote the famous indictment of a capitalistic society that was later so strongly attacked both within and without the pages of the *New Republic.*[88] A headnote declared that this article and some others to follow were "the outcome of conversations among the editors of the *New Republic* which have been occurring for several months, and the gist of which may be of interest as raw material for thought and discussion." The arti-

84 Villard, *Fighting Years,* p. 361, n. 4, tells of having introduced Elmhirst to Mrs. Straight when the former was "an impecunious English student at Cornell."

85 Amidon, *Survey Graphic,* v. 29, Jan. 1940, p. 25.

86 *Publishers' Weekly,* v. 128, Sept. 28, 1935, pp. 1175–76.

87 *Time,* v. 34, Nov. 13, 1939, p. 22.

88 Wilson, "An Appeal to Progressives," *New Republic,* v. 65, Jan. 14, 1931, pp. 234–38.

cle began with some analysis of the Croly political philosophy, but its thesis is that this has all been superseded and that the country is at the end of an era. Capitalism has collapsed. "Who in the United States really loves our meaningless life?" Wilson asked. "We liberals have professed not to love it"; but he admitted, "we have tried to believe in it none the less." Now that is all over; we "must openly confess that the Declaration of Independence and the Constitution are due to be supplanted by some new manifesto and some new bill of rights." Soule's reply in the next number did indeed find in this "raw material" many points for discussion and for disagreement as well. Soule and others who followed him in subsequent numbers [89] were not ready to scrap the American system, much as they might criticize it. Wilson resigned from the staff later that year.

But throughout most of the thirties the *New Republic* maintained its testimony against capitalism with much constancy. Early in 1935 it published an editorial called "Liberalism Twenty Years After" in which it looked back at Crolyology with nostalgic fondness, but again insisted firmly that capitalism had reached the end of the road: "The *New Republic* when it was founded twenty years ago was, like the American nation itself, the inheritor of a liberal tradition. But nothing is more obvious than that the economic and social order to which a liberal philosophy gave birth and in which it flourished is rapidly disintegrating and must in the course of time give way to some other." Even in the realignment which they foresaw, the editors preferred not to take sides. "Our general direction, our main policies are clear enough," they wrote, "but as to the rest we should rather present the varied points of view of those who are in the same large procession; we should rather exercise the privilege of criticism, favorable or the reverse; we prefer to mediate, as well as possible, among the many schools of radical thought and between them and the people who have not yet made up their minds. . . . We hope to participate, within the ranks of those who believe as we do that capitalism has outlived

[89] Soule, "Hard-Boiled Radicalism," *New Republic,* v. 65, Jan. 21, 1931, pp. 261–65. Robert Hallowell and Kenneth Burke wrote articles in the series, v. 65, Feb. 4, 1931, pp. 324–29; Matthew Josephson and Benjamin Ginzburg, v. 66, Feb. 18, 1931, pp. 13–17.

its usefulness, in the difficult search for objective truth."[90]

Realistically, however, the editors were willing to work within the capitalistic framework, not only in receiving the Straight largesse, but in supporting the effort to shore up the crumbling national structure by economic planning. "Nearly all the members of the Roosevelt Brain Trust had been collaborators of the *N.R.* before they began to work with President Roosevelt," wrote Bliven many years later, "and most of the ideas of the New Deal first saw the light in its pages."[91] There is much truth in this claim, and there is some reason for thinking that the watchword "New Deal" was suggested by an article in the *New Republic*.[92]

But the paper was at first no ally of the Roosevelt administration. It declared for Norman Thomas in the presidential canvass of 1932, though with reservations. Four years later it came out for Roosevelt, but characteristically it advised its readers who lived in the Democratic strongholds to give a testimonial vote for Thomas or Browder. In the midst of that campaign it issued a supplement (June 10, 1936) entitled "The Balance Sheet of the New Deal" in which it found some actions to palliate and somewhat even to praise. In 1940 it was for Roosevelt and Wallace. By that time such factors as the apparent success of the New Deal and the further development of the dictatorship in Russia had drawn the magazine away from the "extreme" left and about as near a conformist policy as it could ever allow itself to come. It was almost as close to the Roosevelt course by the end of the thirties as it had been to that of Wilson fifteen years earlier.

Important in the thirties was the journal's planned economy program. Soule's "Chaos or Control" appeared in March and April 1932; it was later enlarged in his book, *A Planned Society*. Elements in the *New Republic*'s blueprint for recovery were unemployment insurance, a public works program, and higher income, inheritance, and surplus profits taxes. But the editors were careful to specify that "the agitation for national

[90] *New Republic*, v. 81, Jan. 23, 1935, pp. 290–92.

[91] *Ibid.*, v. 131, Nov. 22, 1954, p. 9.

[92] See Arthur M. Schlesinger, Jr., *The Crisis of the Old Order, 1919–1933*, v. 1 of *The Age of Roosevelt* (Boston, 1957), pp. 403, 532.

economic planning is, of course, not agitation for the preservation of capitalism, but a movement toward an eventually socialized society, no matter what terminology may be used in describing it."[93] However, as the depression decade drew to a close and the Second World War seemed imminent, the paper's editorial emphasis seemed to change. It would be wrong to say that its campaign against capitalism had fizzled, because it had never really conducted such a campaign, and it had never renounced its antipathy; but what it did, almost inevitably, was to turn to the more workable reforms of the day and to the approaching storm of war.

Like most American magazines, the *New Republic* was slow to advocate intervention in the Second World War. On August 25, 1941, however, it placarded its cover: "For a Declaration of War." In its lead editorial it reminded its readers that "for a long time" it had assumed that the United States could do what was necessary without "a shooting war," but now that time was past. Armed intervention in Europe was now imperative, and the editors warned against waiting to be "precipitated into the fighting by a trick or an accident."[94]

As in the First World War, the *New Republic* was concerned early in the conflict with plans for the peace and for postwar reforms. The keynote of a series of articles on the war written by young Michael Straight in 1942, was that "a rising structure of world unity, worked for the purposes of democracy . . . must be the war aim of the United States."[95] But the editors were skeptical, and on the cover of the issue that contained Straight's statement they displayed the ominous query, "Will We Lose the Peace Again?" They followed the Dumbarton Oaks conference with distrustful eyes. They seemed to echo the admonitions of the editors in the other war when they demanded that the peace settlement should "open a channel for German energies which may benefit themselves and the world."[96] But their vision in 1944 was more truly worldwide; they urged the Dumbarton Oaks delegates not to forget that "wise economic policies" have more to do with halting aggres-

[93] *New Republic,* v. 69, Feb. 10, 1932, p. 337.

[94] *Ibid.,* v. 105, Aug. 25, 1941, p. 238.

[95] *Ibid.,* v. 107, Nov. 23, 1942, p. 666.

[96] *Ibid.,* v. 111, Oct. 30, 1944, p. 552.

sion than anything else, and they feared the expansion of international cartels after the war.[97]

The *New Republic's* chief commentary on the wartime race riots was embodied in a constructive and comprehensive "special section" for October 18, 1943, entitled "The Negro: His Future in America." One of its leading contributions to the great debate on postwar economics in the United States was its continuing argument to the effect that government should retain wartime controls, especially in industrial operations.[98]

Russia, its problems, policies, and actions were treated sympathetically in these years. *Time,* no *New Republic* fan, said that its left-wing contemporary was "firmly on a 'my ally, right or wrong' policy toward Russia." [99] "The basic aim of Soviet foreign policy," said Heinz H. F. Eulau, who often wrote on Soviet matters for the *New Republic,* was the "maintenance of peace." This primary aim had never changed "and is unlikely to be changed in the future." [100] Week after week the defense of Russia continued.

In the forties "special sections" and supplements became more frequent. They were mostly devoted to politics, social and economic questions, and new books. The seasonal literary numbers were attractive. Book reviewing in the *New Republic* was frequently brilliant and acute; also it was often governed by the "liberal" point of view. "Voters' Handbooks," giving the records of congressmen and senators, became a feature of the journal's service to its readers. Special supplements on candidates Willkie (September 2, 1940) and Dewey (September 25, 1945) were issued; and a memorial number on Franklin D. Roosevelt appeared on April 15, 1946.

Newcomers to the lists of "contributing editors" in the forties were Van Wyck Brooks, Julian Huxley, Max Lerner, Thomas Sancton, Alfred Kazin, Harold L. Ickes, Joseph P. Lash, Gus Tyler, and John Farrally. Ten installments from Arthur M. Schlesinger, Jr.'s *The Age of Jackson* appeared in 1946.

[97] *Ibid.,* v. 111, Sept. 4, 1944, p. 264; and v. 109, Oct. 11, 1943, pp. 476–78.

[98] See especially H. S. Person, "Postwar Control of Monopolies," *Ibid.,* Dec. 27, 1943, pp. 907–9.

[99] *Time,* v. 45, June 11, 1945, p. 49.

[100] *New Republic,* v. 109, Oct. 18, 1943, p. 509.

About a year after the end of World War II, Michael Whitney Straight took over as publisher of the *New Republic*. "Mike" was the son of the founders of the journal, had been educated in England, had served as a U.S. State Department economist, and had done a stint with the U.S. Air Force. He had been a contributor to the paper which was still supported by his family since the beginning of the war, and now, at twenty-nine, he was ready to throw himself into the task of remaking it along the lines that would bring it more circulation, influence, and prestige.

Cartoons appeared on the covers for a while, some color was used, and the paper, if not more attractive, was at least more striking on the newsstands. An occasional cartoon had been printed in the early years of the *New Republic*, and in the forties portraits and political caricatures had become somewhat more frequent. Now they were used systematically.

George Soule and Stark Young retired as associate editors; William Harlan Hale and Helen Fuller came in. Content became more diversified, with departments and columns. Radio commercials called attention to each new issue.[101] Average paid circulation went over forty thousand for 1946. One of the paper's chief features that year was a series of six articles about Russia by Earl Browder, recently returned from a visit to Moscow. "Needless to say," said an advertisement, "the *New Republic*, which stands for liberal democracy, does not share Mr. Browder's communist philosophy." [102]

Then in October 1946 began one of the most exciting episodes in the history of the *New Republic*.[103] Henry Agard Wallace was appointed editor. Wallace had been Vice-President during Roosevelt's third term, and had later served as Secretary of Commerce. President Truman had asked for his resignation because of his public utterances criticizing American foreign policy, especially regarding Russia. There was talk of a new party to be headed by Wallace in the 1948 presidential campaign.

[101] *Time*, v. 47, April 22, 1946, pp. 71–72.

[102] *New Republic*, v. 115, July 29, 1946, p. 112.

[103] Announcement was made in *New Republic*, v. 115, Oct. 21, 1946, pp. 499–501; Wallace took over office duties in mid-November; his first number as editor was that of Dec. 16.

"Today, we pick up our soapbox and move over to another corner," wrote Bliven the week before the new editor came in. "The old pitch was a good one," he added. "But the traffic has changed. . . . We still can't help feeling some twinges of nostalgia." [104] The tone of Wallace's first editorial was different. It was plain he did not regard the *New Republic* as a mere soapbox; he took the man-of-destiny approach. "My field is the world," he wrote. "My friends are all who believe in true democracy. . . . My master is the common man." Regarding Russia, the new editor was in step with the old paper: "I prefer to accept the willingness of the Soviet leaders to think more and more in democratic terms." [105]

For a few months Wallace was a fairly industrious editor, writing not only on international policy, but on living costs in the United States, labor disputes, and so on. But after a short time his attention seemed more and more diverted by his political activities, he was absent from the editorial conferences that were the very tradition of *New Republic* editing, and he took little part in the daily work that belonged to his job. Then he went on a tour of Europe, and on his return "was rarely seen around the *New Republic* offices." [106]

During the Wallace regime, however, the paper boomed. It was not merely that Wallace followers were supporting their leader: the magazine was larger and more varied than ever before. Straight filled forty-eight pages with sketches, cartoons (some with dabs of color), a United Nations column, labor and farm departments, theater and art criticism, and so on. He even advertised a short story contest, but that came to naught. Publisher Mebane's campaigns brought the circulation to nearly a hundred thousand by the end of 1947—an all-time high for the *N.R.*

But when Wallace decided in December 1947 to run for the presidency, Straight objected to making his paper a political organ and suggested that Wallace exchange the editorial chair for a contributing editorship, he himself becoming editor. That

104 *New Republic,* v. 115, Dec. 9, 1946, p. 774.

105 *Ibid.,* Dec. 16, 1946, pp. 787–89.

106 William Harlan Hale, in "What Makes Wallace Run," *Harper's Magazine,* v. 196, March 1948, pp. 243–44.

did not work much better and after another six months the *New Republic* cut loose from Wallace entirely. Straight declared for Justice William O. Douglas for President six weeks before he dropped Wallace's name from the paper's masthead.[107]

Doubtless its adherence to its old principle of critical detachment in this case cost the *New Republic* dearly, but the management crisis that ensued was not altogether the result of the parting with Wallace. The journal had embarked on a program of expansion that was not supported either by new advertising or by the development of a national circulation. It was reported that it had lost half a million dollars during its Wallace year. Then its circulation had dropped off sharply when Wallace retired as editor, and even more precipitously after he wrote his long thirteen-column farewell to his *New Republic* readers for the July 19, 1948, number. The decline did not stop until, by the end of the decade, circulation was only a fourth of what it was in the palmy Wallace months. Retrenchment was, of course, necessary. Amid confusion and bitterness, the staff was severely reduced to match a cut in the number of pages. Presswork declined in quality, many features were abandoned, morale suffered.[108] The price was raised to twenty cents a number, $6.50 a year, in 1949.

Editorially, the *New Republic* leaned toward the Fair Deal after the 1948 election. Immediately after that event, it had rejoiced that "we have in the White House a man with the most radical platform in presidential history." [109] But it eventually lost what faith it had seemed to have in Truman, and early in 1952 it was urging him to withdraw his name from consideration for a third term.[110] It urged the nomination of Eisenhower upon the Republican party, but eventually declared for Stevenson in the ensuing campaign.

As early as October 1950 the magazine's publication office had been transferred from New York to Washington, D.C., and

[107] *New Republic,* v. 118, June 14, 1948, p. 10.

[108] For circulation and staff reductions and losses, see *Time,* v. 51, Feb. 23, 1948, pp. 62, 64. See also *Ayer's Directory,* and *Standard Rate and Data Service.*

[109] *New Republic,* v. 119, Nov. 15, 1948, p. 3.

[110] *Ibid.,* v. 126, Feb. 4, 1952, p. 5.

two years later it moved its editorial base to the capital. Helen Fuller, who had been in charge of the Washington bureau since 1946, now became managing editor. But these changes did not mean that there was more emphasis on politics; the new shift in content was toward the proportions that had brought it a certain *éclat* in the twenties—more criticism of the arts, the cultural scene, the new mass culture. Listed as "contributing editors" were Malcolm Cowley for literary criticism, Robert Evett for music, and Eric Bentley for drama. Classified as "contributing critics" were many others, including W. H. Auden, Bruce Bliven, Gerald W. Johnson, Max Lerner, John Crowe Ransom, and Allen Tate. On the whole, the magazine's content was more attractive; but its format made obvious sacrifices to economy, and its circulation advanced only a few thousand.

Then in March 1953 came a rude shock. The trustees of the Straight fund announced that "in the interest of beneficiaries who are minors" they would no longer advance the money to meet the *New Republic's* deficits.[111] But Mike Straight scurried around among "businessmen, bankers, and lawyers" [112] and raised funds to keep publication going for another year. Best of all, he found a new publisher with hope and enthusiasm. Gilbert Harrison, of about the same age as Straight, had been associated with him in the leadership of the American Veterans Committee and shared his interest in liberal causes. A year later the funds raised from "businessmen, bankers, and lawyers" were gone, the weekly deficit was $1,600, and the *New Republic* was again on the brink. Just then the publisher's wife, Anne Blaine Harrison, not unexpectedly fell heir to well over ten million dollars of International Harvester money.[113]

And thus the paper was saved. It was not only saved, but it was improved in appearance and its quality maintained. A modest twenty-four page journal, it divided its main interests between the domestic politico-economic scene and international affairs. Book reviews were still important, there were glances at

[111] *Time,* v. 61, March 16, 1953, p. 95.

[112] It was later revealed that two of these backers were political leaders (Adlai E. Stevenson, Paul Douglas), one the president of the Studebaker Corporation (Paul G. Hoffman), and another the owner of a newspaper group (John S. Knight). See *New Republic,* v. 131, Nov. 22, 1954, p. 10.

[113] *Time,* v. 63, March 1, 1954, p. 44.

the theater and the new movies, and a concern with social problems was pervasive. The old special pleading for the Soviets was gone, but not the old urgent call for a liberal foreign policy.

Eisenhower was under a fairly steady fire during his administrations. In the "Voters' Guide" of 1954, in which the *New Republic,* honoring its long custom, summed up political records, it offered "friendly criticism" of the President on broad grounds, but chiefly because "with few exceptions the President's domestic program records concessions made to the predominant business group. . . . It was the abdication by President Eisenhower of his responsibilities that was a principal inducement to McCarthy to set himself up, in effect, as a second President on Capitol Hill." [114]

Frank Gorrel was a leading European correspondent of the paper in the fifties, Gerald Johnson was a leading commentator on domestic matters, and Malcolm Cowley continued to be a leading literary critic. In 1956, Michael Straight, who had been a hard-working editor and contributor, resigned in favor of Gilbert Harrison, who then became both editor and publisher.

It was a blow to the management when the American News Company refused at the beginning of 1957 to handle the *New Republic* any longer, declaring that its newsstand sales had fallen to an unprofitable two thousand.[115] Its net paid circulation through the fifties was somewhat under thirty thousand. An unkind commentator of 1958 called it "that faint voice of the left." [116]

The history of the *New Republic* cannot be summarized in a sentence or in a paragraph. It has traveled an uneven road. Never a worshiper of consistency, perhaps its only well-observed rule has been the one enunciated by Croly when he declared its purpose to be "to start little insurrections" in its readers' established convictions. But it is one of the most difficult things in the world to maintain for a long time the rebel's attitude without being taken for a chronic scold. Moreover, the crusading spirit does not always make for the best reporting or the best criticism. For example, there have been periods in the

[114] *New Republic,* v. 131, Oct. 11, 1954, Part 2, pp. 3–4.

[115] *Time,* v. 69, Jan. 14, 1957, p. 61.

[116] Raymond Moley, in a column syndicated by Associated Newspapers, Sept. 27, 1958.

journal's history when it seemed, on the whole, more doctrinaire than constructively helpful; and in respect to books that have not squared with its current concept of liberalism, its reviewers have at times been supercilious or summary, or both. On the other hand, it has printed some of the soundest and most brilliant criticism produced in America during its period.

The *New Republic* has doubtless tended to "overemphasize the interests (and the prejudices) of urban intellectuals" [117] at the expense of national appeal; but its insistence on hard thinking has made it important in our intellectual history for half a century. Early in its career, its editors wrote:

> At this period of wreck and ruin, the one power that can save, can heal, can fortify, is clear and intelligent thought. Opinion is no longer a parlor game, a matter of dinner-table conversation; it is a relentless necessity if we are to keep flying the flag of sanity above a tortured world.[118]

These words seem even more applicable today than when they were written. Less eloquent, but apt and rather pleasantly unassuming is the characterization in a remark of Bruce Bliven's (1954): "A paper like the *N.R.* is badly needed, if only to be the egg-heads' Committee of Correspondence." [119] *

[117] Amidon, *Survey Graphic,* v. 29, Jan. 1940, p. 26.

[118] From a promotion sheet included in the number for Nov. 13, 1915.

[119] *New Republic,* v. 131, Nov. 22, 1954, p. 10.

* This historical sketch was written in the late 1950's. Since that time, another resurgence in the fortunes of the *New Republic* has occurred, correlating with Robert Luce's term as publisher, and stimulated by a lively editorial staff. A circulation of over 100,000 in the mid-1960's has resulted. The magazine is, of course, currently sold at newsstands. Editorial changes that have taken place since this history was written are listed in n. 1.

16

POETRY [1]

HARRIET MONROE, the Chicago poet, returned early in 1911 from a trip around the world. She found the "Chicago Plan" humming, with its emphasis on boulevards, parks, architecture, the Art Institute, the Symphony Orchestra—on everything but poetry. Miss Monroe was not only a poet, but a devotee of poetry, and she was continually irked by the contemporary neglect of the muse in America.

Miss Monroe belonged to a respected Chicago family; it was not wealthy, but it was prominent in the arts and was accepted in the city's best society. Twenty years earlier, as a young woman of thirty, Miss Monroe had raised her voice in protest against the neglect of the Committee on Ceremonies of the Columbian Exposition in failing to make a place on its opening program for a commemoration ode. Indeed, she had suggested herself as the poet, had been accepted, and had written for the occasion her "Columbian Ode." Thereafter she had written an art column for the *Chicago Tribune,* contributed some verse to magazines, had found a volume or two of her poems well enough received, and had lectured and traveled. But all the time she had dreamed of a magazine to be devoted to "the Cinderella of the arts." [2]

[1] TITLE: *Poetry, A Magazine of Verse.*

FIRST ISSUE: Oct. 1912. Current.

PERIODICITY: Monthly (except Oct.–Nov., 1963; April–May, 1965). Regular semiannual volumes.

PUBLISHERS: Harriet Monroe, 1912–36 (Ralph Fletcher Seymour was printer for several years and his name sometimes appears as "publisher"); Harriet Monroe Estate, 1936–45; Modern Poetry Association, 1945–current.

EDITORS: Harriet Monroe, 1912–36; Morton Dauwen Zabel, 1936–37; George Dillon, 1938–42, 1946–49; Peter De Vries, 1942–46; Jessica Nelson North, 1942–43; Marion Strobel, 1943–49; Margedant Peters, 1946–47; John Frederick Nims, 1946–48; Hayden Carruth, 1949–50; Karl Shapiro, 1950–55; Henry Rago, 1955–current.

INDEXES: *Fifty Years of Poetry: A Magazine of Verse—Index* to vols. 1–100 (Oct. 1912–1962), compiled by Elizabeth Wright (New York, 1963); *Readers' Guide.*

[2] Harriet Monroe, *A Poet's Life* (New York, 1938), p. 247. The epithet is one that Miss Monroe often used. The volume here cited is useful for all of its author's life, with chaps. xxiv–xxxvi for the story of *Poetry.*

In the summer of 1911, Miss Monroe discussed the idea with several friends, of whom she found Hobart C. Chatfield-Taylor, novelist and patron of the arts, quite the most enthusiastic and helpful. The plan evolved was to ask for "an audacious advance vote of confidence" [3]—a subsidy of $5,000 a year for five years. This amount was to be obtained from one hundred donors of fifty dollars each. Miss Monroe made the solicitation herself. Some of those on whom she called thought the idea of a magazine of poetry funny, and she laughed with them, but finally got their names on the dotted line; some were genuinely interested, and others were irritated by the request. The first third of the required number of guarantors came easily, the next third was more difficult, but the last came with a rush; and the campaign ended by an over-subscription of about $1,000.[4] What had happened at the last was that it had become fashionable to be one of Miss Monroe's guarantors, along with Mrs. Potter Palmer, Cyrus H. McCormick, Rufus G. Dawes, and so on.

The next step was to write to the poets and win their interest, for Miss Monroe had no thought of publishing merely a fashionable journal for a Chicago coterie. She wrote to friends in England, and to respected writers East, South, and West. Best of all, she offered to pay for contributions by checks that could be cashed at a bank. What the magazine paid, and what it continued to pay for many years, was about fifty cents a line, or ten dollars a small page.[5]

The first number was hurried a little, in order to anticipate the publication of a Boston periodical, which threatened to take the name Miss Monroe had chosen, and which later appeared as the *Poetry Journal*. The first number of Miss Monroe's *Poetry* was dated October 1912. As a later editor observed, the magazine "found, by some miracle of anticipation, the exact psychological moment for its appearance on the scene." [6] There was a

[3] *Poetry*, v. 4, May 1914, p. 61.

[4] *Ibid.*, v. 40, April 1932, p. 30. An account of the solicitation campaign is in Monroe, *Poet's Life*, pp. 243–48.

[5] Frederick J. Hoffman, Charles Allen, Carolyn F. Ulrich, *The Little Magazine: A History and a Bibliography* (Princeton, N.J., 1946), p. 43. This information was received from Morton Zabel, a later editor. See also *Time*, v. 50, Oct. 27, 1947, pp. 74–75. The Hoffman volume cited contains a good short history of *Poetry*, pp. 34–44.

[6] *Poetry*, v. 51, Oct. 1937, p. 31.

HARRIET MONROE, 1860–1936

Miss Monroe was the founder of *Poetry* in 1912 and its editor and publisher for 24 years, until her death at age 75. Photograph by John Young.

ferment of poetry in new forms and with new ideas that seemed to be awaiting a catalyst.

That first number contained thirty-two small pages of verse and prose, with a pleasant typographical design by Ralph Fletcher Seymour. The price was $1.50 a year, or 15 cents a monthly number; the subscription rate was to be raised to $2.00 (with forty-eight pages) by 1917, and to $3.00 (with sixty pages) in 1920. The print order for the first number was one thousand; but forms fortunately were held, and another thousand was called for later.[7]

In her introduction for the new magazine Miss Monroe wrote: "The present venture is a modest effort to give to poetry her own place, her own voice. The popular magazines can afford her but scant courtesy—a Cinderella corner in the ashes—because they seek a large public which is not hers. . . . We believe that there is a public for poetry. . . ." [8] The poets represented in this historic first number were William Vaughan Moody (posthumously), Ezra Pound, Arthur Davison Ficke, Helen Dudley, Grace Hazard Conkling, and Emilia Stuart Lorimer. As in later issues, there were a dozen or more pages of editorial articles, criticism, book reviews, and news—always crisp, acute, informed.

The chief poets of *Poetry's* first four exciting years were W. B. Yeats, Rabindranath Tagore, Ezra Pound, Vachel Lindsay, Carl Sandburg, Robert Frost, Edwin Arlington Robinson, T. S. Eliot, Amy Lowell, and Edgar Lee Masters. Yeats, with his established reputation, encouraged the new project from its beginning and was a contributor to the third number. Tagore was introduced to the English-speaking world by *Poetry*. Pound became the magazine's "foreign correspondent" for a few years, and his letters enlivened its critical pages. Lindsay marched into the magazine's pages with General William Booth's big bass drum in January 1913, and Miss Lowell's first *Poetry* contribution soon followed. Sandburg's group of Chicago poems startled readers in March 1914. Frost and Robinson also appeared in 1914, as did the first *Poetry* contributions of Masters. In the next year came Eliot's "Prufrock." Here

[7] Monroe, *Poet's Life,* p. 286.
[8] *Poetry,* v. 1, Oct. 1912, p. 27.

were the leaders of what came to be called the "poetry renaissance"; here were the "new poets."

In 1914 Yeats visited America, and *Poetry's* guarantors gave a dinner for him on March 1 at the Cliff Dwellers' Club in Chicago. It was a distinguished social and literary occasion. After dinner, there were brief talks by the editor and others and a poetical greeting to the guest of honor by Ficke. Then, when Yeats rose, he began by saying that he was going to address his remarks "especially to a fellow craftsman." He continued: "For since coming to Chicago I have read several times a poem by Mr. Lindsay, one which will be in the anthologies, 'General Booth Enters Into Heaven.' This poem is stripped bare of ornament; it has an earnest simplicity, a strange beauty. . . ."[9] As Yeats proceeded in his address, however, he read some simple but definitely unoriginal verse by Mary E. Coleridge and Walter de la Mare, and he had much to say about Paris as the center of "all the great influences in art and literature."

After Yeats had finished, Lindsay was called upon to read "a new poem, which will soon appear in the *Metropolitan Magazine*"—a popular magazine, forsooth! Lindsay read "The Congo," and it made a sensation. As an encore, the Springfield poet read the "Booth." Writing about the occasion some months later, Alice Corbin Henderson, assistant editor of *Poetry,* exulted in Lindsay's success. "Nothing could have afforded greater contrast at the recent dinner given in Chicago than the reading by Mr. Yeats and Mr. Nicholas Vachel Lindsay of their poems," wrote Mrs. Henderson. Yeats had dwelt on "poetic fixities," so it was a great shock when Lindsay "broke the spell" with the primitive noise and vigor of "his newly quarried 'Congo.' " And Mrs. Henderson slyly mentioned the fact that these poems were produced as far away from Paris as Springfield, Illinois.[10]

Poetry was a kind of sponsor for Illinois-born Lindsay and Sandburg, whose first important poems it published. Its unswerving support of Frost and Robinson was somewhat different: they were less boisterous, they were eastern, and they had

[9] *Poetry,* v. 4, April 1914, pp. 25–29; Monroe, *Poet's Life,* chap. xxix, pp. 329–39. Citations cover the entire account of the Yeats dinner.

[10] *Ibid.,* June 1914, pp. 109–10.

their other outlets. But there was another group welcomed by *Poetry* that did much to save it from provincialism and give color to its early volumes; this was the small poetic fellowship that adopted the name "imagistes," later usually anglicized as "imagists."

Let Miss Monroe describe in brief the imagist episode:

> During *Poetry's* first years . . . the imagists and other *vers librists* were "stripping the art bare" of rhetoric, eloquence, grandiloquence, poetic diction—of all the frills and furbelows which had over-draped, over-ornamented its beauty. They brought it closer to life, to modern subjects, people and interests; they rebelled against its traditional prosody; they made it sing in new rhythms, and in the English of modern speech.[11]

It was Ezra Pound, then living in London, who brought the imagists into *Poetry*. Besides Pound, the original group consisted of T. E. Hulme, F. S. Flint, Richard Aldington, and Hilda Doolittle (H.D.). These were later joined by Amy Lowell, John Gould Fletcher, and D. H. Lawrence. Most of them contributed many poems over many years to Miss Monroe's magazine. It cannot be said that imagism, as a movement, produced any great poems; but it exerted a real influence on the current of verse, which was already moving in the direction of abandonment of the older poetic diction and the adoption of the language of everyday speech, the use of newer and freer rhythms, and an emphasis on clear images (ideas). The group of English-American imagists broke up after publishing a few anthologies, and a reaction set in during the late twenties; but a certain liberating effect continued.

That creature of enthusiasms and antagonisms, Ezra Pound, skilled in poetics but lost in the hallucinations of the modern world scene, quarreled bitterly at times with Miss Monroe; but he remained as "foreign correspondent" for the magazine's first six years, and many years later the editor testified that he had been "the most dynamic and stimulating of our early correspondents."[12] Even after he deserted the imagists for the "vorticists" and other strange gods, Pound kept coming back to

[11] *Poetry,* v. 33, Oct. 1928, p. 34.

[12] Monroe, *Poet's Life,* p. 258. See also Miss Monroe's tribute to Pound in *Poetry,* v. 26, May 1925, pp. 90–97.

Poetry at intervals with letters and some of his "Cantos." It was in a review of the latter that Allen Tate wrote of him: "We know that what Mr. Pound understands, as no other living man, is the craftsmanship of verse . . ."; but Tate complains of the "logical confusion of his intellect" when discussing both poetry and life.[13] Later another *Poetry* critic admitted the great influence of Pound, despite "the ineffable jargon of his public epistles." [14] "Why not laugh at Ezra Pound and all the other exiles and their rages?" Harriet Monroe once asked,[15] but after Pound's pro-Fascist broadcasts from Italy during the Second World War, there was no more laughing at him. Eunice Tietjens, associate editor of *Poetry,* issued a kind of formal anathema in 1942. "The time has come," she wrote, "to put a formal end to the countenancing of Ezra Pound. . . . In the name of American poetry, and of all who practise the art, let us hope that this is the end of Ezra Pound." [16]

[It was not quite the end, however.* In February 1949, Pound—then in prison under accusation of treason for his broadcasts—was given the Bollingen Prize for Poetry ($1,000) by the Fellows of American Letters of the Library of Congress, for his *Pisan Cantos.* The award immediately aroused controversy and drew vigorous editorial comment in newspapers. In the issue of *Poetry* for April of that year, the "News Notes" department included a brief unsigned comment noting the award and the controversy. It praised Pound for his influence on other poets, including Yeats, and—essentially endorsing the award—remarked: ". . . nothing is more understandable than that he should have adopted a rather cross attitude towards America. This has proved itself, however, to be in his case the creative and therefore the right attitude, and one

[13] *Poetry,* v. 41, Nov. 1932, p. 108.
[14] *Ibid.,* v. 51, March 1938, p. 325.
[15] *Ibid.,* v. 33, Jan. 1929, p. 207.
[16] *Ibid.,* v. 60, April 1942, pp. 38–40.
* This section enclosed in brackets was written by John T. Frederick to carry out the intention of the author as indicated in a note to himself appended to the *Poetry* sketch. Dr. Mott wanted to add material that related to the controversy resulting from the presentation of the Bollingen Award to Ezra Pound. The bracketed section ends on p. 235. Concerning Frederick see asterisk footnote on pp. 172–73.

NOTICE TO READERS

When you finish reading this magazine, place a one-cent stamp on this notice, mail the magazine, and it will be placed in the hands of our soldiers or sailors. No wrapper. No add[illegible]

Vol. XIII No. VI

A Magazine of Verse

Edited by Harriet Monroe

March 1919

Poems from Propertius
by Ezra Pound

Broken Windows, by
William Carlos Williams

Flying, by R. M. McAlmon

543 Cass Street, Chicago

$2.00 per Year Single Numbers 20¢

CONTROVERSIAL POETRY WITHIN A DIGNIFIED COVER

Harriet Monroe, always interested in new movements, did not hesitate to publish Ezra Pound's poetry—for example, in this issue of March 1919. Thirty years later, in 1949, *Poetry* was embroiled in a hot dispute over the award to Pound of the Bollingen Prize for Poetry.

VOLUME 109 NUMBER 6 MARCH 1967 ONE DOLLAR

DENISE LEVERTOV *A Vision*
JOHN LOGAN *Carmel: Point Lobos*
TOM CLARK *Three Poems*
JOHN WOODS *Trying To Keep Out of Trouble*
THOMAS McGRATH *All the Dead Soldiers*
EDWARD DORN *The Sundering U.P. Tracks*

BARRY SPACKS · ETTA BLUM · JAMES L. WEIL
JOHN INGWERSEN · LOUISE GLUCK · FRANK SAMPERI

LAURENCE LIEBERMAN *Poetry Chronicle*
HAYDEN CARRUTH *Booth and Wagoner*
DONALD W. BAKER *Five Poets*
ROBERT SWARD *Landscape and Language*
PHILIP LEGLER *Three Poets*

MODERN VERSION OF PEGASUS

Pegasus, the winged horse of the Muses, has always been a distinctive symbol on the cover of *Poetry*. It has appeared in several forms, none handsomer than this one in March 1967, outlined in white on a bright blue cover.

can only hope that the Bollingen Prize, with its official connotation, will not have an even slightly chastening effect. An uncantankerous Pound is unthinkable." [17]

In the June 1949 issue of *Poetry*—in which he was first named as editor—Hayden Carruth published a signed editorial offering a reasoned and reasonable defense of the award, in which he summarized the opposing views and distinguished between "the poem as object" and "the poem as communication." He wrote: "I think that the judges were honoring the whole work of the poet whom nearly all of us would have to nominate as the single living person who has done the most to explore and develop the technical capacities of poetry in English." He held, however, that "the terms of the award must be made more definite." [18]

In the same month, the *Saturday Review of Literature,* in the issue for June 11, published a six-column editorial signed by Norman Cousins, editor, and Harrison Smith, president, vigorously denouncing the award to Pound and taking full responsibility for two articles on the matter by Robert Hillyer, president of the Poetry Society of America.[19] The first of these articles appeared in the same number, under the title: "Treason's Strange Fruit: The Case of Ezra Pound and the Bollingen Award." [20] It is a violent attack on Pound, the Fellows of the Library of Congress who made the award, and the "new poetry" in general. In his second article, titled "Poetry's New Priesthood," Hillyer extended his attack to *Poetry* specifically:

> "Poetry: A Magazine of Verse" seems to be falling into the hands of the new aesthetes. In their April number the editors comment on what a hard time poor Ezra Pound must have had from lack of appreciation and add that "nothing is more understandable than that he should have adopted a rather cross attitude towards America." Some day someone is going to adopt a rather cross attitude towards the editors of *Poetry*. Maybe America. I will ask the reader to consider the childish frivolousness of such comment on the Bollingen Award at a time when the clouds of the New Fascism and the new aestheticism have perceptibly met in that award.[21]

[17] *Poetry,* v. 74, April 1949, p. 59.

[18] *Ibid.,* June 1949, pp. 154–56.

[19] *Saturday Review of Literature,* v. 32, June 11, 1949, pp. 20–21.

[20] *Ibid.,* pp. 9–11.

[21] *Ibid.,* June 18, 1949, p. 8.

Poetry's rebuttal appeared first in a brief letter in the *Saturday Review of Literature,* almost lost among the seven columns of "Letters to the Editor" commenting on Hillyer's first article:

Sir: "Treason's Strange Fruit" is undoubtedly a violence to good manners; it is also, I believe, an evil and dangerous corruption to the critical office. As an essay in unreason, it is a disservice to American letters and a demagogic threat to a number of innocent people.

Hayden Carruth
Editor, *Poetry* [22]

Then in his August number of *Poetry,* Carruth published "An Editorial: The Anti-Poet All Told," beginning:

The two recent essays concerning the award of the Bollingen Prize for Poetry to Ezra Pound, written by Robert Hillyer and published in *The Saturday Review of Literature,* contain so many errors, so many grievous misjudgments that I cannot unriddle them all in an editorial as condensed as this must be."

And he ended:

Whatever is the outcome of the Ezra Pound case, and certainly it is difficult to defend him on any but the narrow grounds of service to his craft, the enemies of poetry must not be allowed to damage the process of our art through untoward wrath.[23]

To the editorial Carruth appended "A Few Notes on the Recent Essays of Mr. Robert Hillyer," [24] devoted to identification and correction of some of the "errors" and "blurring of judgment" he had mentioned, including three mistakes in a two-line quotation from Pound.

Echoes of this controversy—perhaps the most colorful in *Poetry's* generally rather stormy history—continued to appear.]*

[22] *Ibid.,* July 2, 1949, p. 25.

[23] *Poetry,* v. 74, Aug. 1949, pp. 274, 280.

[24] *Ibid.,* v. 74, Aug. 1949, pp. 283–85. In November 1949, Carruth published a separate pamphlet of eighty pages containing "A Statement of the Committee of the Fellows of the Library of Congress," reprinting his article "The Anti-Poet All Told" and articles from the *New Republic, New York Times,* and the *Hudson Review,* and adding previously unpublished letters from prominent writers.

* Here ends the insertion by John T. Frederick.

A later editor, Karl Shapiro, an ardent admirer of the *Cantos,* contended in 1952 that Pound's poetry was inseparable from the crimes of which he was accused: "Whether Pound committed treason and advocated racism will remain a question vital to his poetry." [25] For good or ill, the Pound record, with all its complexities, remains an important part of *Poetry's* early history.

With its *vers libre,* imagism, and primitive singing, *Poetry* in its first few years made itself vulnerable to the attacks of all the conservatives. Chief among these was the *Dial,*[26] Chicago's own semimonthly literary review. "One must regret," wrote Wallace Rice in that periodical, "that *Poetry* is being turned into a thing for laughter"; and he claimed that "the practical identification of *Poetry* and Mr. Pound . . . involves not only a lowering of standards, but a defense of the thesis . . . that poor prose must be good poetry." [27] *Poetry* made reply, and the running controversy enlivened the pages of both magazines for a time.

It was Sandburg's group of Chicago poems, the first one beginning, "Hog butcher for the world," that really set the *Dial* spinning on its ear. *Poetry* was now described as "a futile little periodical," and the poems as "nothing less than an impudent affront to the poetry-loving public." The critic goes on: "The typographical arrangement of this jargon creates a suspicion that it is intended to be taken as some form of poetry. . . . It is not even doggerel." [28] Other critics contributed to the merry war.

But the innovators did not have it all their own way in *Poetry*. On two successive pages in the issue for August 1913 appeared two of the most anthologized poems that the magazine ever printed—Joyce Kilmer's "Trees" and Helen Hoyt's "Ellis Park." And such poets as Margaret Widdemer, Babette Deutsch, Grace Hazard Conkling, Clement Wood, William Rose Benét, Elinor Wylie, and Louise Bogan were often in its

25 *Poetry,* v. 80, June 1952, p. 183.

26 See F. L. Mott, *A History of American Magazines,* v. 3 (Cambridge, Mass., 1938), pp. 539–43.

27 *Dial,* v. 54, May 1, 1913, p. 370.

28 *Ibid.,* v. 56, March 16, 1914, pp. 231–32.

pages. Edna St. Vincent Millay's "Figs From Thistles" appeared in June 1918.

How many of the poets represented in the half-century of this magazine's publication should be mentioned in a brief history such as this? It seems a pity to neglect any of them, but most poets' tapers are blown out early, of course. Anyone running down the average table of contents, even if he is fairly well read in the books and magazines of the times, will recognize little more than half the names.

Wallace Stevens' stage-poem "Carlos Among the Candles" was printed in December 1917, following by a few months "Three Travelers Watch a Sunrise" (July 1916). Partly because of his preoccupation with the nature of art, Stevens exerted for many years a strong influence on other contributors to *Poetry*. Hart Crane's poems appeared until his career was cut short by his death in 1932. Robinson Jeffers long continued to be a valued but sombre contributor. Countee Cullen's lyric gift and Langston Hughes' more original and playful muse were well represented in the twenties. In that decade poems by Archibald MacLeish, Lew Sarett, and Marya Zaturenska also appeared. William Carlos Williams was an important contributor from the first, turning from imagism to a warm interest in common life. Dr. Williams and Marianne Moore, another important contributor, were sometimes styled "objectivists."

Poetry's scope was international. A long list of English poets could be compiled from its tables of contents; an "English Number" edited by W. H. Auden and Michael Roberts was published in January 1937. Twice *Poetry* has devoted entire issues to young French poets (October 1945, September 1952). Tagore has been mentioned. There was a special Chinese number in April 1935. "Of course *Poetry* from its beginning has emphasized the oriental influence, . . ." wrote the editor in 1918.[29] Pound, Ficke, Miss Tietjens, and Arthur Waley were among imitators and translators of Chinese verse. The Japanese Yone Noguchi was a contributor of *hokku* in November 1919. Special Canadian and Spanish-American numbers were issued in April 1941 and June 1925 respectively.

The scope of Miss Monroe's interest in literary movements,

[29] *Poetry,* v. 11, Feb. 1918, p. 271.

the catholicity of her taste, and the breadth of her sympathy with poetic endeavor are among the chief characteristics of her editorship. "Eclecticism was the very life of her magazine,"[30] wrote Horace Gregory after Miss Monroe's death. This meant, of course, printing many poems that did not look as well in print as they had in manuscript. It meant the acceptance of the work of unknowns, some of whom were to remain unknowns. "Fears have been expressed by a number of friendly critics," Miss Monroe once wrote, "that *Poetry* might become a house of refuge for minor poets." But she protested that the word "minor" was "presumptuous, since no contemporary can utter the final verdict." A sophistical defense, no doubt; but one can only applaud the principle which the editor stated with firm resolution: "The Open Door will be the policy of this magazine—may the great poet we are looking for never find it shut, or half-shut, against his ample genius!"[31]

Moreover, Miss Monroe's freshness of interest in new movements and new talent was maintained to the day of her death. "She alone," wrote Allen Tate in 1932, "has come from the beginning of the late renascence to the present, with all the vigor of a new start."[32] The motto of the magazine was a line from Whitman: "To have great poets we must have great audiences too." Writing a profile of Miss Monroe, Harry Hansen paraphrased this: "To have great poets there must be great editors too."[33] Harriet Monroe was indeed such an editor.

In the fall of 1936, Miss Monroe, now seventy-five years old, made a trip through South America. While crossing the Andes, she had a cerebral hemorrhage, and died in the mountain village of Arequipa, Peru. In a memorial number (December 1936) *Poetry* published six of her lyrics, the first of which began:

> If all the tents are falling,
> Arise, my soul!
> Under these you were crawling
> Blind as a mole.
> Seek out a new appalling
> Unmerciful goal.[34]

[30] *American Scholar,* v. 6, Spring 1937, p. 199.
[31] *Poetry,* v. 1, Nov. 1912, pp. 62–64; quotation on p. 64.
[32] *Ibid.,* v. 40, May 1932, p. 94.
[33] Harry Hansen, *Midwest Portraits* (New York, 1923), p. 253.
[34] *Poetry,* v. 49, Dec. 1936, p. 131.

Alice Corbin Henderson had been the first associate editor of *Poetry*. When ill health forced her retirement, she was followed by a procession of poets who kept that position for short terms —Eunice Tietjens, Helen Hoyt, Emanuel Carnevali, Marion Strobel, George Dillon, Peter De Vries, Jessica Nelson North, and Morton Dauwen Zabel. Longest in the associate editorship was Zabel, who had served seven years at the time of Miss Monroe's death and who succeeded her as editor. Four others among the associate editors named served later as editors-in-chief; Dillon succeeded Zabel and served two terms totaling over ten years, and he, and Miss Strobel, Peter De Vries, and Mrs. North, alone or in various associations, performed the editorial duties in the forties.

The financial history of *Poetry* under Miss Monroe was full of dangers and near-disasters; but always when bankruptcy threatened, money came from somewhere to keep the little magazine alive. After the first five-year guarantee ran out, it was possible to renew the subscriptions for another lustrum, and so on in 1922 and 1927; though the list of guarantors slowly diminished in these years, the magazine subscription list increased despite a rise in price to $3.00 a year. The budget in 1932, when a crisis was brought on by the widespread depression, was $12,000 a year.[35] Miss Monroe had at the first received no compensation, and had paid her associate editor only forty dollars a month; later salaries were a little better, and before her death the editor was receiving $100 a month.[36] But the editing of *Poetry* was a labor of love, after all, and the salaries it paid were never expected to be sufficient for anyone's sole support.

Long before Miss Monroe's death, imagism had waned, and other forms and schools had developed. The *Dial,* which had undergone a sea-and-land change in its removal to New York, was now criticizing *Poetry* for its emphasis on esthetic rather than social criticism, and Miss Monroe replied: "An artist *may* find his special beauty in the social movements of our time—in strikes, or war, or pacifism, or settlements, or the Bolsheviki; but has the critic any right to complain if he finds it, like Whistler, in the fall of a rocket or the turn of a girl's figure, or, like

35 *Ibid.,* v. 40, April 1932, p. 31.
36 Monroe, *Poet's Life,* pp. 284, 363.

Inness, in a sunset drift of autumnal colors?"[37]

The first notable reaction to the imagists was the work of a group that Miss Monroe called the "intellectualists" or the "aristocrats," rejecting the *profanum vulgus* for expression "unintelligible to all but specialists," essentially esoteric, and indulging sometimes in "typographical gymnastics." "*Poetry* has printed many of these poets, but not with the wide-open hospitality which complete sympathy might have demanded," wrote the editor in 1928, and added: "And even if now and then we miss a trick—as when we could not see Mr. E. E. Cummings for his *i's* that shone out of his page like an undimmed automobile headlight—I still feel that progress in the art lies along the good curve of the solid earth rather than along the euphuistic tangent, and that *Poetry* has followed this grander curve throughout its sixteen years."[38]

These words of Miss Monroe's constitute a kind of credo for the magazine that has been followed throughout its career. And yet, the things that attract the eye and catch the attention in its successive numbers are, perhaps, the more tangential poems. For example, this second stanza of "Calligrammes," by Philip Blair Rice, then a professor of philosophy at Kenyon College:

•
t-
he
he-g-
oat's horn
is a perf-
ect logarithm-
ic spiral with sine
and cosine bearing the e-
ternal relationship decreed
for inanimate matter for im-
material essences in the mind
of god the he-goat's horns have a magical
mathematical aphrodisiacal lure for the nan-
ny and furthermore arch in an exquisite sweep envied by artists[39]

[37] *Poetry,* v. 13, Oct. 1918, p. 40. See also the article by Randolph Bourne and Van Wyck Brooks in *Dial,* v. 64, April 25, 1918, pp. 410–11.

[38] *Poetry,* v. 33, Oct. 1928, p. 36.

[39] *Ibid.,* v. 65, Oct. 1944, p. 7. Reprinted with permission of *Poetry* and Mrs. Philip Blair Rice.

And so *Poetry* adhered to its policy of eclecticism. Another magazine, the experimentally minded *Little Review,* accused Miss Monroe's magazine in 1929 of being "Sound, sane, safe, and subsidized." [40] But as a matter of fact it continued year after year to print about the same proportions of the conservative and the unconventional styles of verse.

Poetry's "grander curve," though little affected by eccentricities of typography, has been determined to a considerable extent by the poets Miss Monroe called "intellectualists" and "aristocrats"—Tate, Crane, Williams, MacLeish, Laura Riding, Yvor Winters, Malcolm Cowley. Always critical, *Poetry's* reviewers were sometimes severe on these writers. "Allen Tate's poetry," wrote one of these commentators in 1929, "shares many of the perversities and stylistic mannerisms of what was called, a few years ago, the cerebral school." [41] After Miss Monroe's death, her successors were wise enough to know that they could not continue the magazine always along the old lines. They knew that the founder would have changed policy with changing times. In 1937 Editor Zabel wrote: ". . . *Poetry's* task today is far different from that of twenty-five years ago. . . . The impulse of that hour was still one of discovery. . . . Today the temper of literature, no less than of politics and society, is more critical, more hardened in skepticism and doubt. . . ." And Jessica Nelson North added: "Meanwhile the newest poets move about with assurance in their rare medium of symbolism, surrealism, and associational technique. . . . They may have first felt the inclination to write when they read Joyce, Wallace Stevens, or Eliot. . . . They embarked lightheartedly on a sea of that sort of poetry whose very cloudiness of import seems its chief charm. And where did these experimentalists first find attention and publication?" [42] The answer was, in many cases, "In *Poetry*"; just as that magazine had probably brought to the attention of these young poets the older "masters" mentioned. The Pound-Eliot-Tate succession of influence seems clear.

Without attempting to fit them into any schools or movements, it may be said that among poets yet unmentioned in this

[40] *Little Review,* v. 12, May 1929, p. 60.
[41] *Ibid.,* v. 33, Feb. 1929, p. 281.
[42] *Ibid.,* v. 51, Oct. 1937, pp. 32, 36.

brief history, the following were prominent in the 1930's: Conrad Aiken, Robert P. T. Coffin, Robert Penn Warren, Paul Engle, and Stephen Spender.

Poetry made its own distinctive contribution to the literature of two world wars. Its War Number of November 1914 attracted much attention, as it deserved to do. Louise Driscoll's "The Metal Checks" won the prize offered for the best poem on war or peace. Rupert Brooke's "War Sonnets" were published in April 1915. In the Second World War, a special number (August 1943) was devoted to the work of men serving in the armed forces.

About a third of each issue of *Poetry* has been, from the first, devoted to prose—editorial comment, book reviews, and news. Horace Gregory once declared that in these prose pages of *Poetry*, ". . . some of the finest critical prose ever written in America" has appeared.[43] At any rate, the editorial articles and the reviews have displayed a critical acumen superior to that found in most contemporary writing of this kind. This criticism has usually been keen and surgical, but constructive; magisterial, it has been informed and thoughtful. The chief writers of prose for the early volumes were Harriet Monroe, Alice Corbin Henderson, Ezra Pound and Amy Lowell. But there were many others; and to list the leading critics throughout the file of the magazine would be to repeat the names of the editors and many of the chief poets.

The finances of the magazine continued to be precarious throughout the thirties and the early forties. Three successive grants from the Carnegie Foundation kept it going through the worst years of the depression.[44] But in 1942, with the guarantees of the fifth lustrum running out, prospects were dark again; in both May and June of that summer, *Poetry* spoke gloomily of the probability of the next number being its last. But groups rallied in California (where *Poetry* stock was always high), in Chicago and Washington and other centers; and with the help of many small gifts and a few large ones, the crisis was passed.[45]

[43] *American Scholar,* v. 6, Spring 1937, p. 200.
[44] Monroe, *Poet's Life,* p. 443.
[45] *Poetry,* v. 60, May 1942, p. 111; June 1942, p. 173; and July 1942, p. 231.

In these war years, and in those immediately following, the magazine was edited by George Dillon, Miss Strobel, Mrs. North, Peter De Vries, John Frederick Nims, and Margedant Peters, in various combinations of two or three. The circulation increased in the 1940's from two thousand to double that figure.[46] For a few years in the middle of the decade the magazine inserted portraits of some of its contributors in its pages. For a decade, its typography was modernized, with blackface headings; but it later returned to a page of more classic style.

It seems apparent that after the Second World War, the magazine *Poetry* was inclined to follow American poetry itself into the cloisters of those devotees who were themselves poets, critics, or connoisseurs of the arts, thus separating itself more than ever from the more popular literary forms. Prominent in the magazine in the forties were Gertrude Stein, Dylan Thomas, Robert Lowell, Karl Shapiro, Muriel Rukeyser, John Ciardi, David Cornel DeJong and James Merrill.

Following a short but distinguished term of editorship by the young poet, Hayden Carruth, Karl Shapiro took over the management of the magazine in 1950. The verse that grew out of Shapiro's war experience, and his critical perceptions in the field of poetry, made him a good editor. Among outstanding contributors of the fifties, not mentioned earlier, were Juan Ramon Jiménez, Stanley Kunitz, Delmore Schwartz, and Thom Gunn.

Henry Rago followed Shapiro as editor in 1955. While still a boy, the new editor had been encouraged in poetical effort by Miss Monroe, and he was only fifteen when his first work was accepted by *Poetry*. Since then he had appeared there occasionally, in other magazines, and in published volumes. He holds a doctorate in philosophy and taught at the University of Chicago for seven years.

Under Rago's editorship were organized Chicago's famous "Poetry Days," which have done so much for the magazine. These grew out of the ideas of J. Patrick Lannan, Chicago industrialist and promoter; but they represent an extraordinary group effort. These Days, proclaimed by the mayor as dedicated to poetry and welcomed by hundreds on various levels of

[46] *Ibid.,* v. 75, Oct. 1949, p. 58; *Time,* v. 50, Oct. 27, 1947, pp. 74–75.

education, have resulted in untold good for the magazine and for poetry in general. Publishers, dealers, and other donors turn over rare editions, manuscripts, and association items to be offered by sale at a big auction—proceeds to go, of course, to *Poetry*. Then there is a big subscription dinner, after which a famous poet speaks; Frost and Sandburg were the first, in 1955 and 1956 respectively.[47] Tied in with this dinner is an expansion of the plan of diversified gifts begun in the forties. That is, all donors become members of the Modern Poetry Association. These are divided into six classifications, ranging from the "subscribing member" at $7.50 to the "benefactor" at $500 a year.* All members receive the magazine without further cost. The association is the owner and publisher, and in the late fifties there were more than five hundred members.

This new financing was a life-saver, for in spite of an increase to a record-breaking 5,500 circulation in the late fifties, costs had also increased greatly. It would be interesting to know how many of the magazine's subscribers are hopeful of being also contributors to its pages—how many even submit an occasional poem. It is said that *Poetry* receives fifty thousand manuscripts a year, of which it publishes about three hundred.[48]

Under the Rago suzerainty the magazine has continued to be alert and perceptive. Notable numbers were the one devoted to Dylan Thomas (November 1956) and the Japanese issue of May 1956. Attention has been given certain of the Lallans poets, such as Tom Scott and Sydney Goodsir Smith; to selections from the late Paul Claudel and current work of René Char; and to such newcomers as Charles Tomlinson, Ted Hughes, Kenneth Koch, Marie Ponsot, Jay Macpherson, Ned O'Gorman, and Robert Duncan.

The history and the file of *Poetry* is well worth study for three reasons. First, the magazine exemplifies and illustrates the course of American poetry over a long period, having "discovered" many of our leading modern poets and published virtually all of them at one time or another. Second, though the

[47] *Poetry,* v. 87, March 1956, pp. 360–61; v. 89, March 1957, pp. 393–94.
* A year's subscription in 1966 was $10.00.
[48] *Newsweek,* v. 40, Oct. 13, 1952, p. 104.

organ of a high art, and unvaryingly true to its mission, it has been kept alive in an era of materialism and of mass culture suffused with *kitsch*. And third, it is simply and unarguably a great pleasure to read through a magazine file which, though it has its low and soggy places, generally has kept to the high and stimulating road.*

* This historical sketch was written in the late 1950's. It may be noted that circulation has continued to increase and in 1966 was over 6,000.

17

THE SMART SET [1]

IN 1900 the fabulous Colonel William D'Alton Mann was banking big profits from several operations. Among them were his weekly *Town Topics,* a periodical of society news, gossip, criticism of the arts, and literary miscellany; his quarterly *Tales from Town Topics,* later to be transformed into *Transatlantic Tales;* his Town Topics Financial Bureau, a tipster service; and the publication of books, chiefly

[1] Titles: (1) *The Smart Set,* March 1900—March 1930; (2) *The New Smart Set,* April–July 1930. Subtitles: *A Magazine of Cleverness,* 1900–1913; *The Aristocrat Among Magazines,* 1914–24; *True Stories From Real Life,* 1924–28; *The Young Woman's Magazine,* 1928–30; and various other subtitles and slogans on cover, contents page, or half-title.

First issue: March 1900. Last issue: July 1930.

Periodicity: Monthly. Vol. 1, March–June 1900; 2, July–Dec. 1900 (Oct.–Nov. combined); 3–74, Jan. 1901—Aug. 1924, 4 nos. per vol. (56–57 have irregular numbering: Sept. 1918 called v. 56, no. 1; Oct.–Dec. called v. 57, nos. 2–4); 75–85, Sept. 1924—Feb. 1930, 6 nos. per vol.; 86, March–July 1930.

Publishers: Ess Ess Publishing Company (William D'Alton Mann, owner), 1900–1911; John Adams Thayer Corporation, 1911–14; Smart Set Company (Eugene F. Crowe, Eltinge Fowler Warner, George Jean Nathan, Henry Louis Mencken, owners), 1914–24; Magus Magazine Corporation (William Randolph Hearst, owner; George d'Utassy, pres.), 1924–25; Magus Magazine Corporation (W. R. Hearst, owner; Richard E. Berlin, pres.), 1925–28; Magus Magazine Corporation (James Robert Quirk, pres.), 1928–30.

Editors: Arthur Grissom, 1900–1901; Marvin Dana, 1902–4; Charles Hanson Towne, 1904–7; Fred C. Splint, 1907–8; Norman Boyer, 1909–11; Mark Lee Luther, 1911–12; Willard Huntington Wright, 1913–14; M. L. Luther, 1914; George Jean Nathan and Henry Louis Mencken, 1914–23; Morris Gilbert, 1924; F. Orlin Tremaine, 1924–25; William Charles Lengel, 1925–28; T. Howard Kelly, 1928–29; Margaret Elizabeth Sangster, 1929–30.

References: Carl Richard Dolmetsch, "A History of the *Smart Set* Magazine," unpub. diss., University of Chicago, 1957; [See also Dolmetsch, *The Smart Set* (New York, 1966)]; Charles Hanson Towne, *Adventures in Editing* (New York, 1926), chap. ii; C. H. Towne, *So Far So Good* (New York, 1945), chaps. xiii–xiv (mainly a reprint of the *Adventures*); William Manchester, *Disturber of the Peace: The Life of H. L. Mencken* (New York, 1950), chaps. iii–v; Isaac Goldberg, *The Man Mencken* (New York, 1925), chap. vii; Burton Rascoe, " 'Smart Set' History," in *The Smart Set Anthology* (New York, 1934), ed. by Rascoe and Groff Conklin (reprinted separately in a limited edition); Charles Angoff, ed., *The World of George Jean Nathan* (New York, 1952); [Andy Logan, *The Man Who Robbed the Robber Barons* (New York, 1965), a life of Col. W. D'A. Mann; and William H. Nolte, *H. L. Mencken, Literary Critic* (Middletown, Conn., 1966)].

the annual *Representative Americans,* often accused of being a blackmailing operation.[2] A commentator with a flair for the picturesque wrote that Mann's "offices were heavily carpeted in red; footfalls were to be deadened; the stealthy atmosphere was dense with cigarette smoke and in and out stole society reporters with shifty eyes, correct clothes, and heavy perfumes. In the innermost office sat a bulky old man with magnificent white hair and patriarchal beard, a pasha of the Gilded Age, who thunderously grudged the contributors to his periodicals their penny a word.[3]

As a companion to his society weekly, Colonel Mann in March 1900 launched the *Smart Set,* a monthly magazine of general literature with much the same kind of "snob appeal" that characterized *Town Topics.* In an early number, the publisher declared: "The *Smart Set's* writers are not only those famous in the literary field, but many are from the ranks of the best society in Europe and America."[4] To prime the pump for contributions, Colonel Mann relaxed his cent-a-word rule to offer generous prizes for novels, novelettes, short stories, poems, sketches, and witticisms.[5]

Accordingly, the first number of the new monthly led off with a thousand-dollar prize novelette of New York society entitled "The Idle Born," an amusing, Wilde-like satire by H. C. Chatfield-Taylor and Reginald DeKoven. The former of the collaborators was a wealthy Chicago writer who had spent much of his life abroad, and the latter was famous as a composer and musical critic; both were themselves social lions. This ideal opener was followed by such pieces as a satirical "true story" of a scandal about a former Duke of Portland by Edgar Saltus, sophisticate, esthete, familar figure in both American and English fashionable coteries; a one-act play about lords and ladies by "Julian Gordon" (Mrs. S. Van Rensselaer Cruger); and a story of the English nobility by Carolyn K. Duer. The three Duers—Carolyn, her sister Alice Duer Miller, and her

[2] See F. L. Mott, *A History of American Magazines,* v. 4 (Cambridge, Mass., 1957), pp. 459–60, 753–55.

[3] Ludwig Lewisohn, *Expression in America* (New York, 1932), pp. 314–15.

[4] *Smart Set,* v. 5, Nov. 1901; advertising section, p. 10.

[5] Prizes seem to have been continued for over a year. See *Smart Set,* v. 3, Feb. 1901, verso of title page.

mother Elizabeth Duer—were to become frequent contributors.

In this first number, which may be said to have set the pattern for the early *Smart Set,* the only nonfiction prose was a travel article by Mrs. Burton Harrison. The wits were well represented by R. K. Munkittrick, Gelett Burgess, Sewell Ford, and Oliver Herford. Among the poets were the young Theodosia Garrison, the established Bliss Carman and Clinton Scollard, and Ella Wheeler Wilcox, whose name still carried an aura of the shameless avowal that a former generation had found in her *Poems of Passion.*

There were 160 pages of text and 20 pages of advertising, the whole enclosed in a striking bluish-grey cover. The cover design by Kay Womrath depicted a dancing couple in evening dress controlled by strings held by a grinning Pan; the slashing S's of the title were in vermilion. The price was twenty-five cents. Altogether, it was an exciting Volume I, Number 1, intended, as the *New York Tribune* rather stuffily observed, "to entertain and amuse rather than instruct or edify." [6] Evidently many thousands of Americans were willing to forego instruction for amusement—100,000, indeed, if Mann's claim of the sale of his first number is to be trusted.[7]

The editor of the new magazine was a young poet named Arthur Grissom, a New York free-lance writer who had once collaborated with George Creel in publishing a weekly miscellany in Kansas City; [8] the business manager was Sam Ragland, Grissom's cousin. Death took the young editor in December 1901, and Marvin Dana succeeded him. Dana was a poet and novelist, and had edited the gay *Judy* in London before coming to the *Smart Set* as an assistant editor. Associated with him as he took over the reins were Charles Hanson Towne and Henry Collins Walsh. Towne was a poet in his mid-twenties, and had come to the *Smart Set* from *Cosmopolitan Magazine.* Walsh was an older man, a traveler, newspaper correspondent, and magazine editor of experience. The three made a good team, but it was broken when Dana left in 1904; then Towne became editor, with Walsh and Norman Boyer as associates.

6 *New York Tribune,* March 10, 1900, p. 7, col. 6.

7 *Smart Set,* v. 1, April 1900, advertising section, p. 5.

8 Mott, *American Magazines,* v. 4, pp. 97–98.

Throughout its first nine years, during which the *Smart Set's* circulation appears to have increased consistently, though by no means sensationally, it kept to much the same content formula. It sometimes relaxed its accent on high society for variety's sake; but the *bon ton,* the light satirical touch, social intrigue, love without benefit of clergy, and irony at the expense of conventions were of the essence of the magazine. Each number began with a novelette; continued with ten or a dozen stories, one of them in French; found a place two-thirds of the way through for an essay on literature, the stage, travel, or society; filled in odd pages or half pages with verse; and tucked in epigrams and jokes and little satires in chinks here and there.

Many well-known names are found in the by-lines of the fictional offerings—Jack London, Ambrose Bierce, Robert Herrick, Ludwig Lewisohn, James Branch Cabell, Theodore Dreiser, Barry Pain, Max Pemberton, Eden Phillpotts ("In the King's Chamber," May 1900), Mary Austin ("At Tio Juan," June 1906), Kate Masterson, Justus Miles Forman, Henry Sydnor Harrison. Among the authors of the novelettes were the Baroness von Hutten, Ralph Henry Barbour, "Christian Reid," and Cyrus Townsend Brady. Few serials were published; there was a short one by Gertrude Atherton in 1908 and one by E. Phillips Oppenheim in 1911. But by far the larger proportion of the *Smart Set's* story writers were unpublished amateurs, anxious to break into print even at a cent a word.

One such was William Sydney Porter, besieging editors in the first years of the new century with stories signed "O. Henry." The *Smart Set* was not the first magazine to publish "O. Henry,"[9] but as early as January 1902, it printed "The Lotos and the Bottle." This was a 6,000-word manuscript, but Porter offered it at the bargain rate of fifty dollars quick cash; he wanted to raise money so he could leave his newspaper job in Pittsburgh and come to the great city that he was to celebrate as "Bagdad on the Subway." Grissom sent him his full sixty dollars and suggested that he call when he arrived in New York—an invitation Porter apparently forgot in the rush of his new life.[10]

[9] Robert H. Davis and Arthur B. Maurice, *The Caliph of Bagdad* (New York, 1931), chap. xii.

[10] Towne, *Adventures,* pp. 63–64, recounts a colorful tale of the excitement

Ainslee's Magazine got more O. Henry stories than did the *Smart Set*. *Ainslee's,* which had experienced many vicissitudes in its five years' life,[11] changed policy in 1902 and became an out-and-out imitator of the successful *Smart Set*. For more than a decade thereafter, it looked much like that magazine, followed the same policy, used almost the same subtitles, and attracted many of the same contributors; and, selling for only fifteen cents, it soon attained double its rival's circulation. This competition brought about some increase in the rates paid by the *Smart Set* to its better known writers, although, as a compensatory measure, more material from obscure scribblers was used.[12]

Short stories, poems, and one-act plays in the French language appeared in the *Smart Set* for many years—one piece in French in nearly every number for over two decades, 1901–1923. The magazine had a contract with a literary agency in Paris, the *Société des Gens de Lettres,* to furnish such pieces at the incredibly low price of twenty-five dollars a year. Most of these were by obscure penny-a-liners and had already been published; a few were by writers already dead and gone.[13] Eventually short plays in either French or English became a regular feature of the magazine.

Poetry was by no means unimportant in the *Smart Set*. The early editors were all poets themselves, and they published much verse that was charming and amusing, and some that was very good. The going rate to poets was twenty-five cents a line, which led to the epigram current in the office, "Poets are born, not paid."[14] It seems doubtful if "Momus, Junior," who contributed a Juvenalian satire running to twenty pages in the May 1900 number, received as much as

caused upon receiving a story called "By Proxy," from "O. Henry." However, the order of publication of O. Henry stories in the *Smart Set* does not bear out the order of events detailed. The story Towne called "By Proxy" was evidently the one published as "His Courier," in May 1902, and later called "By Courier."

11 Mott, *American Magazines,* v. 4, pp. 48–49.

12 Towne, *Adventures,* pp. 89–90.

13 Dolmetsch, "A History of the *Smart Set* Magazine," pp. 12–13, based on statements of both Mencken and Nathan to the author. [Dolmetsch, *The Smart Set,* pp. 10–11.]

14 Towne, *Adventures,* p. 76.

the regular rate. Besides those named as contributors to the first number, the following poets, among others, apparently were satisfied with the modest payment rate of the *Smart Set:* Richard Le Gallienne, Arthur Stringer, Charles G. D. Roberts, John G. Neihardt, S. E. Benét and later William Rose Benét, and Zona Gale. Some of these contributed both verse and prose. Among the essayists were Arthur Symonds, James Huneker, Agnes Repplier, and William J. Lampton. The wits were numerous; to those already named may be added John Kendrick Bangs, Tom Masson, and Carolyn Wells.

The *Smart Set* had already established a reputation for "its sunny way of clever dialogue and incident in prose and out" [15] well before the coming of the pair of critics who were to stamp their names and personalities upon it in its second decade—Henry L. Mencken and George Jean Nathan. It is an exaggeration to say, as did one of Mencken's biographers in an oft-quoted phrase, that during Mann's ownership the magazine had "come to be associated with a sort of perfumed pornography." [16] Carl Van Doren observed more justly that it "was to the older magazines about what a circus is to a library"; and added that naturally the moralists objected to it, most of the love being "on the lawless side," passionate or professional rather than sentimental.[17]

In 1907 Fred Splint, who had been working under Dreiser on the Butterick publications, traded places with Towne and became editor of the *Smart Set*. Splint kept Boyer as associate editor. Boyer had been a Baltimore reporter and was much impressed with Mencken's work on the papers of that city, and he persuaded Splint to propose to the young critic (he was twenty-seven) to contribute a book article for each number of the *Smart Set*.[18] Channing Pollock had left *Ains-*

[15] Zona Gale in the *Critic,* v. 44, April 1904, p. 323.

[16] Goldberg, *Man Mencken,* p. 193.

[17] *Nation,* v. 139, Dec. 12, 1934, p. 680.

[18] Goldberg printed a communication from Dreiser claiming that the latter suggested Mencken for this work (*Man Mencken,* pp. 380–81); but Mencken himself heatedly denied this. See William Manchester, "A Critical Study of the Work of H. L. Mencken as Literary Critic for the *Smart Set* Magazine, 1908–14," master's thesis, University of Missouri, 1947. Manchester cites Mencken in both an interview and a letter to the effect that Boyer made the suggestion (pp. 11–12).

THE PRE-MENCKEN *SMART SET*

The date: July 1908. This cover by Kay Womrath, showing an elegant couple against a gray background, was used from 1900 to 1911. Then James Montgomery Flagg modernized the couple's dress, and soon the cover varied with each issue. The initial letters were always enlarged, as here, and were in color.

HENRY LOUIS MENCKEN (TAKEN IN 1906)

In November 1908, two years after this portrait was taken, H. L. Mencken began his column of literary reviews in the *Smart Set.* From 1914 to 1923 he was co-editor with George Jean Nathan. Mencken then edited the *American Mercury* for nine years (see page 3 above). Photograph by Meredith Janvier.

lee's to begin a monthly theatrical review in the *Smart Set* a year earlier, and now Mencken followed Pollock in the back of the book, his first article appearing in the issue for November 1908. It was entitled "The Good, the Bad, and the Best Sellers"; in it he attacked Upton Sinclair for taking himself too seriously in *The Moneychangers,* praised Mary Roberts Rinehart's *The Circular Staircase,* and called Marie Corelli's *Holy Orders* "a decidedly capable performance." [19]

Oracular, pungent, and racy, Mencken's book articles excited attention immediately; they were to continue for fifteen years, and upon them and the series of selections drawn mainly from them and entitled *Prejudices* was founded the Mencken cult of the second and third decades of the century. Mencken once wrote an article for the *Atlantic Monthly* in which he cited approvingly the advice tendered him when he entered upon the business of criticism by "an ancient" in the craft: " 'The main idea,' he told me frankly, 'is to be interesting, to write a good story. . . . Of course, I am not against accuracy, fairness, information, learning. . . . But unless you can make your people *read* your criticisms, you may as well shut up your shop.' " [20] Mencken was nearly always interesting. Often he was satirical or bitterly ironical. He sometimes clowned his way through a review; occasionally he made outlandish suggestions, as when he urged publishers of novels to perfume their books—the odor of new-mown hay for Gene Stratton Porter, that of frankincense for Hall Caine, and carnation for Richard Harding Davis.[21]

Just a year after Mencken became a regular contributor to the *Smart Set,* George Jean Nathan began his monthly theatrical reviews for that magazine, Pollock having resigned to join the *Green Book.* Nathan had been dramatic critic for *Outing* and *Harper's Weekly.* He matched Mencken in his defiance of conventional mores, his saucy style, his magisterial attitude. Together, these two critics were to bring the *Smart Set* increasingly to the attention of the intelligentsia and espe-

19 *Smart Set,* v. 26, Nov. 1908, pp. 155–59.

20 *Atlantic Monthly,* v. 113, March 1914, p. 289.

21 *Smart Set,* v. 42, Jan. 1914, p. 153.

cially to that of the younger groups that developed after the First World War.

Meanwhile, the magazine was not prospering. It had done well for its first few years, and a later owner declared that Colonel Mann had made $100,000 a year out of it.[22] It had a London edition for a few years, beginning in May 1901. The circulation of the American edition reached 161,000 in 1908, but gradually declined thereafter.[23] Advertising, never plentiful, also declined; at its height it had consisted chiefly of announcements of the *Town Topics* enterprises, patent medicines, cosmetics, clothing, books, insurance companies, railroads, automobiles, breakfast foods, and liquors. A by-product of the *Smart Set* was the publication of novelettes from that magazine in paper covers.

In the spring of 1911 Mann sold the *Smart Set* to John Adams Thayer, a well-known advertising man who had recently made a resounding success as one of the publishers of *Everybody's Magazine.* He immediately began to build up the advertising section, doubling or tripling the amount carried in the latter years of the Mann regime. The back cover sold for $500.[24] Thayer revived the London edition of the magazine, creating an independent English publishing company which was to continue operations long after Thayer had sold the American magazine. He also revived a department called "The Shops of the Smart Set," designed to stimulate advertising, and instituted another entitled "Café Guide." Following his custom on *Everybody's,* he wrote a monthly publisher's department that he called "Something Personal."

Thayer hired James Montgomery Flagg to redraw the *Smart Set's* cover design in a more modern style; soon the cover varied from month to month, but still a grinning Pan

[22] John Adams Thayer in "Something Personal," *Ibid.,* v. 35, Nov. 1911, p. 168.

[23] Figures for the *Smart Set* in *N. W. Ayer & Son's Directory* are not sworn to in this period, but may be taken as approximately correct. The issue for 1909 quotes the *Smart Set* at 161,000 for the preceding year; for the next two years no figures are given for it, and for 1911 the questionable round sum of 100,000 is quoted. Subsequently there is a steady decline.

[24] See *Smart Set,* v. 34, June 1911, advertising section; v. 37, June 1912, p. 160.

usually held the strings on a cavorting couple, now in modish costumes. For a couple of years Thayer used illustrations of scenes from classical literature as frontispieces in the magazine; they were by Garth Jones, André Castaigne, and others.

Splint had resigned to study medicine in 1909, and Boyer had succeeded him. Thayer, who considered himself editor-in-chief, kept Boyer on until that unfortunate took his own life; [25] thereupon he appointed Mark Lee Luther, a writer of mystery stories who had been one of Boyer's two associate editors. The other associate was Louise Closser Hale, actress and author, who conducted an essay department, entitled "The Trunk in the Attic," for several months. A far more tart and spicy department was one which was begun in the spring of 1912, called "Pertinent and Impertinent." This first brought into the *Smart Set's* table of contents the by-line of "Owen Hatteras," later written "Major Owen Hatteras, D.S.O." as a satire on war-time "brass." The name stood for a collaboration of Mencken and Nathan (and W. H. Wright, 1912–14). This first Hatteras department consisted of pungent commentaries on this and that—frequently on contemporary American life and ideas. That Thayer did not always approve of the work of staff contributors Mencken and Nathan is indicated by a statement in his own department at the beginning of 1912 to the effect that those worthies had resolved "even on the cloudiest, rainiest days in their respective fields they will carry optimism instead of a sharp-pointed umbrella." [26] But it was absurd to try to convert the critical team to sweetness and light; in the very next issue, Mencken opened his article with a tirade against the prohibitionists.[27]

For thirteen years now the *Smart Set* had been edited by a succession of six young men, most of them poets and fictioneers, and none of them lasting more than two or three years. Now came out of the West not a young Lochinvar, to be sure, but a youth of aggressive personality, to take over, for one

[25] Albert Payson Terhune, *To the Best of My Memory* (New York, 1930), pp. 196–98.

[26] *Smart Set,* v. 36, Jan. 1912, p. 167.

[27] *Ibid.,* v. 36, Feb. 1912, p. 151.

memorable year, the fortunes of the magazine. Save a ready typewriter he weapons had none; but he had a virile literary talent and ambitious ideas.

Willard Huntington Wright had been under twenty years of age when he had begun a three-year term as literary critic of the *Los Angeles Times*. From there he came to New York to become literary editor of Colonel Mann's *Town Topics*. In those days he wore a fierce, Kaiser-like mustache that was probably intended to support the image of the domineering personality that he cultivated. Moreover, he was an ardent admirer of Mencken, if not actually a disciple. He became an associate editor of the *Smart Set* in 1912; and the next year he "buffaloed" Thayer into making him editor of the *Smart Set* for a twelve-month term at double the salary of his predecessor and with an increased editorial budget, together with an agreement that the publisher would not interfere with the editorial conduct of the magazine.[28] After a few weeks he wrote his friend Dreiser that the fight he was making with the magazine was a difficult one and that the outcome was largely speculative.[29]

The new editor's fight was directed mainly to obtaining first-rate contributions which would reflect modern life frankly and with some power and cleverness. For his writers, he turned to England and the Continent and to the new group of brilliant Americans who, in the pre-war years, were flouting middle-class prejudices with realistic pictures of city life or more romantic pieces with a strong sex emphasis.

[28] The date of his promotion to the editorial chair is fixed by a letter from Wright to Dreiser, Jan. 18, 1913, in which he said he was now editor of the *Smart Set;* Dreiser MSS, University of Pennsylvania Library. The term "buffaloed" is that of Malcolm Cowley, *New Republic,* v. 81, Jan. 16, 1935, p. 281. Burton Rascoe says Wright "frightened" Thayer into the contract; Rascoe, "*Smart Set* History," p. xix. On the agreement with Thayer regarding the editorial conduct of the magazine, see Manchester, *Disturber of the Peace,* p. 70; Dolmetsch, "A History of the *Smart Set* Magazine," p. 26. [Dolmetsch, *The Smart Set,* p. 34.] Rascoe and the others following him say "an ample budget"; it probably allowed for authors' rates two or three times those of the niggardly Mann regime; but Terhune testifies that though Wright thought highly of his "Raegan" stories he paid only $75 apiece for them; Terhune, *Best of My Memory,* pp. 196–98.

[29] Letter dated March 14, 1913; Dreiser MSS, University of Pennsylvania Library.

Prominent among Wright's English contributors were D. H. Lawrence, Frank Harris, George Moore, Leonard Merrick, and W. L. George—and the Irishman W. B. Yeats. One-act plays and occasional stories and poems in French were continued; the *Société des Gens de Lettres* still collaborated with the *Smart Set,* and it may be presumed that the Continental tour made by Wright, Nathan, and Mencken in 1912 brought some results in the way of contributions. Such German writers as Schnitzler and Wedekind were prominent in the magazine in 1913, as was the Swedish playwright, August Strindberg. Among other European writers were D'Annunzio, "Maartens," and Artzybashev. Foreign writers already mentioned as contributors to earlier numbers were retained. On the whole Wright's period of editorship brought more contributions from abroad into the *Smart Set* than did any other single year.

American writers of distinction abounded. Theodore Dreiser, Floyd Dell, Ludwig Lewisohn, and Achmed Abdullah became familiar by-lines. Albert Payson Terhune, with his "Aloysius Raegan" stories of New York street life, and Barry Benefield, with realistic stories of the people of the cities, made distinguished contributions. Among the poets were Robinson Jeffers, Sara Teasdale, Richard Le Gallienne, John Hall Wheelock, and many other notables; in one number (January 1914) appeared George Sterling, Joyce Kilmer, Harriet Monroe, Witter Bynner, and Louis Untermeyer. Wrote William Stanley Braithwaite in the introduction to his first annual *Anthology of Magazine Verse* (1913, p. viii): "This year I have included the *Smart Set,* which under the new editorship of Mr. Willard Huntington Wright, himself a poet of considerable attainment, has been the means of offering the public a high and consistent standard of excellence in the verse it printed." And in his next year's volume Braithwaite credited the *Smart Set* with more "distinctive poems" than any other 1914 magazine.

The twelve numbers of the *Smart Set* edited by Wright (March 1913—February 1914) constitute a notable contribution to the magazine history of the times. One enthusiastic critic has written that the *Smart Set* under Wright was "the most memorable, the most audacious, the best edited, and the best remembered of any magazine ever published on this continent." [30] At any rate, it was exciting and, on the whole, well written.

But Thayer was by no means pleased with the image of the *Smart Set* that the general reader had formed, and his displeasure rose as the magazine's circulation fell. About the time Wright first joined the staff, an anonymous author made the following sprightly observations: "I'm most tickled to death at times, when I take *The Smart Set* on the cars to read it, and watch the eyes and mouths of the suburban population making round O's at it and me. I believe half of them regard it as a handbook to Hades, and the other half would like to read it in secret, and are disappointed and baffled when they discover that, in place of being suggestive, it is just plain clever and cultured and artistic." [31]

Thayer, however, was not "tickled," and as soon as Wright's year was over, let him go and made Luther managing editor again. In the number for March 1914 the publisher quoted a compliment from the *Boston Transcript* as follows: "During the past year *The Smart Set* has been gathering laurels unto itself as a unique magazine for those who desire to keep abreast and ahead of modern literary currents," and followed the quotation with the realistic verdict: "To gather laurels is one thing; to publish a successful magazine is quite another thing." [32] Thayer then recounted the *Smart Set's* triumphs in publishing famous authors and quality material. "*But*," he went on, "we have received stout protests . . . some of the stories . . . have struck them [the protesters] as too sombre; the frankness of certain others has displeased them." He concluded his little lecture by promising thenceforth "a good round measure of romantic and humorous relief." [33] In the next issue he was more specific. He declared

30 Rascoe, "*Smart Set* History," pp. xxii–xxiii. Rascoe's feud with Mencken leads him to eulogize Wright and underrate Mencken. He claims that neither Mencken nor Nathan "began to show the qualities as writers that later distinguished them" until Wright took editorial charge of the *Smart Set*: see "*Smart Set* History," p. xxiv.

31 *Smart Set*, v. 36, Feb. 1912, p. 167.

32 W. S. Braithwaite in *Boston Transcript*, Jan. 17, 1914.

33 *Smart Set*, v. 42, March 1914, pp. 159–60.

that the current number (April 1914) was "designed primarily to amuse and entertain. . . . In all of its pages will be found nothing that is depressing or sordid. . . . *The Smart Set* has abandoned the sort of fiction which . . . many readers last year criticized as sordid and pessimistic and unnecessarily realistic and plain-spoken. . . . But we do not intend to be goody-goody. . . . We shall publish stories that represent life in all its phases. . . . though we believe that there is more of joy than gloom in life after all, if people will only make it so." [34]

All this made Mencken unhappy, of course, and he wrote Dreiser that the old *Smart Set* had become "as righteous as a decrepit and converted madame." [35] But he knew that he and Nathan would not have to put up with their boss much longer. Thayer had been hit by the stock market slump of 1914, his magazine's circulation was down to 50,000 or less, and he was tired of trying to cope with its problems. That fall he turned the property over to his chief creditor, who agreed to assume all debts.[36] The number for September 1914 was Thayer's last; and next month the cover bore the slogan: "One Civilized Reader Is Worth a Thousand Boneheads," and an announcement in the advertising section exulted in the promise that from then on the *Smart Set* would be edited "without any other 'policy' in the world than to give its readers a moderately intelligent and awfully good time."

The new owner was a paper manufacturer, Eugene F. Crowe, who had acquired other magazines in the same way and made a success of them. Crowe's associate in the magazine part of his business was Eltinge F. Warner, who now appeared as publisher of the *Smart Set*. Warner happened to be a fellow passenger on the "Europa" with Nathan when both were returning from short trips abroad; they became acquainted when they mutually recognized that they were

[34] *Ibid.*, v. 42, April 1914, p. 160.

[35] Letter dated March 18, 1914; Dreiser MSS, University of Pennsylvania Library, quoted with permission of the library. The letter is included in *Letters of H. L. Mencken,* ed. Guy J. Forgue (New York: Alfred A. Knopf, 1961), pp. 42–43, and quoted with permission of the publisher.

[36] Dolmetsch, "A History of the *Smart Set* Magazine," p. 33; based on an interview with E. F. Warner. [Dolmetsch, *The Smart Set,* p. 44.]

wearing topcoats of the same cut and fabric, and, comparing notes, found that they had patronized the same London tailor. This not very extraordinary circumstance served to initiate a ship-comradeship in the course of which Nathan learned that Warner was the new manager of the *Smart Set* and Warner learned that Nathan had written a department for it during the preceding five years. Before they landed Warner had offered his new acquaintance the editorship of the magazine; and Nathan had accepted, with the proviso that Mencken should be co-editor with him.[37]

In the arrangement that ensued, Nathan and Mencken each took a one-sixth interest in the publishing company in lieu of salary, the owners took one-third, and the other third went to pay off debts.[38] Since there was a deficit of $24,000, increasing at the rate of $2,000 a month, the two editor-partners actually received no salary for several months.[39]

Various means of getting the publishing company out of the red were tried. Cheaper paper was used, and the number of text pages was cut for a while from 160 to 144. Back issues were bound up two together and sold under the cover title *Clever Stories* at fifteen cents on trains and newsstands outside *Smart Set's* metropolitan markets. This was a success, and it suggested other ventures. The war had stimulated interest in things French, and the *Parisienne* was begun in 1915 "in a satirical vein"; it was cheap in every sense, and was attacked in the courts, but it was soon making more money than the *Smart Set* itself.[40] The partners had been irked by Colonel Mann's *Snappy Stories,* on the cover title of which the big S's seemed to imitate those of the *Smart Set;* and early in 1916 they began a *Saucy Stories* of their own. This naughty magazine was also successful financially. The Smart Set Company was now making a profit; and that fall Nathan

[37] This anecdote is retold by all writers on *Smart Set* history and by biographers of Mencken and Nathan. It is told by Nathan in his article, "The Happiest Days of H. L. Mencken," *Esquire,* v. 48, Oct. 1957, p. 146—an article notable more for its nostalgic impressionism than for factual data.

[38] Dolmetsch, "A History of the *Smart Set* Magazine," p. 35; based on an interview with Warner. [Dolmetsch, *The Smart Set,* pp. 46–47.]

[39] Letter of Mencken to Dreiser, April 20, 1915 (on microfilm, Princeton University Library).

[40] Goldberg, *Man Mencken,* p. 197.

and Mencken sold their shares in the "louse magazines," as Mencken called them, to the Warner-Crowe concern. A few years later the partners started the *Black Mask,* a mystery magazine, also regarded as "boob bait"; it was an immediate money-maker, and again Mencken and Nathan sold out their shares very profitably after six months.[41]

Whatever shame they may have felt for their anonymous part in such more or less disreputable undertakings, that was not the only reason they always sold out their shares in them so promptly. The "louse magazines" had put the company on its feet financially; they were now drawing modest editorial salaries, and they had realized handsomely on the sale of their shares to Warner-Crowe. Besides, they were very busy. Both were engaged in varied activities aside from their editorship of the *Smart Set.* Mencken was still on the staff of the Baltimore *Sun* and Nathan on that of *Judge;* both were turning out books. But both worked hard on "the old *S.S.*" Nathan was office editor in New York, while Mencken continued to live in Baltimore, coming up to "Sodom and Gomorrah" twice a month. Mencken was first reader of manuscripts. When he found one that was amusing and made "as few compromises to public taste as possible," he sent it on to Nathan, who, if he agreed, sent a check at once, and if he disagreed, wrote a gracious rejection letter. Mencken carried on a voluminous correspondence with his authors and with would-be contributors.[42] The magazine's limited editorial budget required such methods, but both editors got a lot of fun out of it. There was always a liberal measure of the play-spirit in Mencken and Nathan's work on the *Smart Set.*

But it was hard at first, under the deficit-financing of the magazine. The two editors themselves wrote at least half of their first number.[43] The First World War added to the magazine's difficulties. Germany had declared war on France and

[41] Manchester, *Disturber of the Peace,* p. 108; Goldberg, *Man Mencken,* pp. 197–98.

[42] See pamphlets: "Owen Hatteras," "Pistols for Two" (New York, 1917); H. L. Mencken, "A Personal Word" (New York, 1922).

[43] Dolmetsch, "A History of the *Smart Set* Magazine," p. 45. [Dolmetsch, *The Smart Set,* p. 48.]

invaded Belgium the month that Thayer was going to press with his last issue. Mencken was pro-German and Nathan but little interested in the war during the two and a half years of their editorship that preceded America's formal entrance into the conflict. Neither before nor after that event did any martial echoes resound through the pages of the *Smart Set;* this was not a popular policy, and circulation declined slowly but unmistakably. At times the profits were nil, and the editors had no salaries; but when the price was raised to thirty-five cents a copy late in 1918, modest editorial stipends were restored. Modest, indeed; it is said that neither Mencken nor Nathan ever received more than fifty dollars a week from the *Smart Set* for editorial work. They did continue to get their hundred dollars apiece for their critical articles each month, and for a time they wrote many of the short stories themselves (sometimes half the magazine) under pen-names. Mencken's favorite pseudonym was "Duchess de Boileau." [44]

"Its tone is that of enlightened skepticism," declared a manifesto in the advertising pages of the *Smart Set* for October 1921. Its aims were to "discover new American authors as they emerge, and to give them their first chance to reach an intelligent and sophisticated audience. . . . To present the point of view of the civilized minority. . . . To introduce the best foreign authors to America. . . . To leaven American literature with wit and humor. . . . To encourage sound poetry." This discovery of new writers was a specialty of the *Smart Set,* and well suited to its slender budget. Thyra Samter Winslow's first short story appeared in Mencken and Nathan's first number; and, next to the editors themselves, she was the most frequent contributor during their control of the magazine. Ruth Suckow was another Mencken discovery, and many of her best stories were printed in the *Smart Set.* F. Scott Fitzgerald's "Babes in the Woods" (September 1919) was his first published story. Eugene O'Neill's *The Long Voyage Home* (October 1917) was his first published play; later

[44] Manchester, *Disturber of the Peace,* p. 76. For the statement "sometimes half the magazine," see *The Intimate Notebooks of George Jean Nathan* (New York, 1932), p. 118.

came *Ile* (May 1918) and *The Moon of the Caribees* (August 1918). Maxwell Anderson was another *Smart Set* discovery. There were many more.[45]

But, of course, most of the magazine's newcomers never reached the heights. Few issues contained contributions signed by more than eight or nine writers well known to the ordinary reader, or even recognizable by him; and that included the editors. Since each issue contained some thirty-six pieces (about twenty short stories, ten poems, four articles, one novelette, and one play), fully three-fourths were by unknowns.[46] Most of these were newcomers who proved to be "duds"; many of them did not deserve publication in the first place, and the editors took their work because they could find nothing better that they could afford. Mencken once confessed, with characteristic candor, that sometimes "only a small proportion of the contents" of the magazine had been "really fit to set before the readers we have in mind." [47]

But the contributors to the Mencken-Nathan *Smart Set* who had established reputations or who were just beginning to be recognized make up an impressive catalog. Among short story writers not already named as frequently found in the earlier numbers of the magazine were the following, here listed with the title of a notable *Smart Set* story: Stephen Vincent Benét ("Summer Thunder," September 1920), Willa Cather ("Coming, Eden Bower," August 1920, later called "Coming, Aphrodite"), James Branch Cabell ("Some Ladies and Jurgen," July 1918, embryo of the novel *Jurgen*), Sinclair Lewis ("I'm a Stranger Here Myself," August 1916), Howard Mumford Jones ("Mrs. Drainger's Veil," December 1918), Ben Hecht ("The Unlovely Sin," July 1917), Reginald Wright Kauffman ("The Lonely House," February 1917), and Charles Caldwell Dobie ("The Yellow Shawl," June 1915). Somerset Maugham consigned a story of his entitled

45 Dolmetsch counted forty-two writers whom he believes to have been first "introduced to the American reading public" by the *Smart Set* and later to have "attained a large measure of distinction in the world of letters"; "A History of the *Smart Set* Magazine," p. 133.

46 Dolmetsch counted 1,337 different contributors to the 110 numbers of the magazine edited by Mencken and Nathan; *ibid.*

47 Mencken, "A Personal Word," p. 3.

"Miss Thompson" to his American agent, who sent it to most of the leading magazines without success; finally it came to Nathan marked down to $200. This was more than the *Smart Set* had ever paid for a story, but only a fraction of Maugham's going rate. Warner authorized the extravagance, and the issue in which it was published (April 1921) was one of the few numbers of the *Smart Set* ever to sell out on the newsstands. "Miss Thompson" was later famous in a dramatic version with the title "Rain."[48]

Other story writers who brightened the pages of the *Smart Set* in the early twenties, when it probably shone most brilliantly in that department, were Hugh Walpole, Sara Haardt, Jeannette Marks, L. M. Hussey, Nancy Hoyt, and Leonard Cline. Edward J. O'Brien, who set himself up as a kind of arbiter of the American short story beginning with those of 1915, placed the *Smart Set* first among the magazines in the number of "distinctive" short stories published in 1920, and again in 1922 and 1923.[49]

Much of the nonfiction during the first years of the Mencken-Nathan regime was sensational hackwork. Series such as "The Sins of the Four Hundred" (1917–1918) and "Enchantresses of Men" (1918–1919) were anonymous or signed by pen-names; Nathan may have been responsible. But some of the nonfiction was more important; for example, articles on great cities appeared occasionally. The forerunner of such severe critical appraisals, and perhaps the best of them, was one published early in Wright's editorship and written by Wright himself—"Los Angeles, the Chemically Pure" (March 1913). In the same tone were John Macy's "Blue Boston," the anon-

[48] Dolmetsch, "A History of the *Smart Set* Magazine," p. 15; based on an interview with Warner. [Dolmetsch, *The Smart Set,* pp. 80–81.] Rascoe says Nathan showed him the manuscript and told him the story of its acquisition; "*Smart Set* History," pp. xi–xli.

[49] See the series entitled *The Best Short Stories . . . and the Yearbook of the American Short Story,* edited by O'Brien. Of course, the *Smart Set* published many more stories than *Harper's, Scribner's,* and the *Atlantic.* In 1920, when it was placed first in number of "distinctive" stories, only 40 percent of its total of published stories were said to be "distinctive." Before 1920 it was always credited with 20 percent or less; in 1921, 25 percent; in 1922, 35 percent; in 1923, 45 percent. In 1924 it was very properly dropped from consideration. One has the feeling that O'Brien did not discover the *Smart Set* until 1920.

ymous "Morals of Pittsburgh," and Lewis Sherwin's "The Morals of the Mormons," all published in 1917. American universities were taken apart in 1921; Hendrik Van Loon wrote on Cornell, John Peale Bishop on Princeton, and so on. These articles were not muckraking in the sense of exposés based on research, such as *McClure's Magazine* had once practiced; they were impressionistic and literary. And then there were some important articles of literary and dramatic criticism in addition to the regular contributions of the editors; for example, Thomas Beer's "Mauve Decade" (February 1922) was the germ of his later book of that title, and James Huneker made notable contributions.

Though the editors were against the "extravagances of the free verse movement," they published about a thousand poems in their nine years. In their galaxy of poets appeared, besides some already mentioned as *Smart Set* contributors, John McClure, Margaret Widdemer, Glenn Ward Dresbach, Harry Kemp, David Morton, Muna Lee, Orrick Johns, Zoë Akins, Leonora Speyer, Lizette Woodworth Reese, and Maxwell Bodenheim.

Notable among playwrights who contributed the short pieces that were a unique feature of each number were Eugene O'Neill, Lord Dunsany, Djuna Barnes, and George M. Cohan. Cohan's farces (for example "The Farrell Case," October 1920) were very amusing.

Dunsany was only one of a considerable list of foreign contributors. In this category, the Mencken-Nathan *Smart Set* lagged somewhat behind that of Wright, especially in its latter years; but in 1914–1920 there were often three or four pieces by writers from overseas. For a time Ezra Pound, Ernest Boyd, and Frank Harris acted as scouts for the magazine in England.[50] James Joyce was virtually unknown in England when the *Smart Set* published two stories from his pen in May 1915. The magazine continued its relations with the French syndicate until 1922, using material that was mostly second-rate—some detective stories, some scandalous bits, some short stories of character and setting. From Russia came stories by Leonid Andreyev and Count Alexey Tolstoy.

[50] Dolmetsch, "A History of the *Smart Set* Magazine," p. 109.

Mencken and Nathan discontinued the magazine's "Pertinent and Impertinent" department when they took over the editorship, consigning items such as it had formerly thrived upon to use as fillers. In 1919 they began the "Répétition Générale," a satirical review of the contemporary human comedy. One of its chief features was the award of a custard pie to some public figure for the most asinine utterance or action of the month. In it appeared in 1923 the announcement of Mencken and Nathan as candidates for the respective (if not respected) offices of President and Vice-President of the United States. In a burlesque platform they promised, if elected, to suppress the Y.M.C.A., to keep plenty of liquor in the White House, to write public papers "in language that their constituents can understand," to turn the Philippines over to Japan, and so on.[51] "The Nietzschean Follies" series lasted only ten months in 1922; it led off with an article by Thomas Beer attacking the prevalent idea of rural virtue. In July of that year a series of cartoons began, starting with William Gropper's "Portraits of American Ecclesiastics"; it lasted well into the next year. In May 1923 began the department entitled "Americana," under the Hatteras pen-name. Here were gathered together bits of news from all over the Union, demonstrating in what variety Americans were making fools of themselves; this department eventually became a leading feature of the *American Mercury*.

But of course, of all the contents of the *Smart Set,* year in and year out, the monthly critical articles of the two editors were paramount. They never failed to be readable, lively, challenging. Mencken and Nathan were a well-matched team; they drew well together in editorial harness, and they agreed generally in their critical principles.

Nathan, carrying on the sensitive esthetic tradition of Huneker, and employing also his friend's tools of learning and sharp attack, never failed in his opposition to sentimentality and to the worship of bourgeois morals. His wit, his love of shocking his readers out of their old ruts of judgment and thinking, and his amazing erudition in things theatrical were applied to the consideration of play after play and to trends as

[51] *Smart Set,* v. 71, June 1923, pp. 31–33; July 1923, pp. 41–44.

they appeared to develop. Though sometimes reckless and immoderate, he probably exerted a strong influence on the American theater. His *Smart Set* work, of course, extended much beyond dramatic criticisms.[52]

To Mencken, even more than to Nathan, criticism was a battle; and above the noise of clashing critical lances echoed ever and sometimes even anon his raucous and derisive laughter. His love of unusual words—occasionally invented, often rude, sometimes effective by mere piling on of insulting terms—was characteristic; it resulted in what came to be known as "Menckenese." Not a philosopher in any strict sense, he fought for certain basic ideas, chief of which was freedom of expression on the part of imaginative writers. He was a hater of cant, hypocrisy, and pretentiousness. An enemy of the romance of his period, he stood for the realism which meant honest facing of life. In the criticism of poetry, his attitudes seem, on the whole, undiscriminating and sometimes contradictory: here, he was far weaker than in prose. Over all, he was a dogmatist, never trying to understand "the other side." His leadership among critics of the twenties was founded mainly upon his championship of the advancing realism of the times and his ability as a striking and original writer.[53]

In the twenties the *Smart Set* stepped up its attack on the "booboisie," on the stupidity of the popular mores, on racism, patriotism, and reformers. It still held hard to the antimonogamy line, especially in its fiction; it fell in with the current assault on the small town; it multiplied its quips against Rotary Clubs and such organizations; it turned more and more to digs at politicians and political movements.

Of course, all this invited retaliation. Stuart P. Sherman began his famous crusade against Mencken as early as 1917, stressing what he conceived to be the latter's lack of loyalty to his country.[54]

Percy H. Boynton wrote his "American Literature and the

52 See Charles Angoff, ed., *The World of George Jean Nathan* (New York, 1952).

53 See William Manchester, "A Critical Study," *passim.*

54 The first blast was a review of *A Book of Prefaces* in the *Nation,* v. 105, Nov. 29, 1917, pp. 593–94.

Tart Set" for the *Freeman.*[55] *Time,* in its second number, predicted: "If Mr. Mencken carries on his abuse against Rotary much longer, Public Opinion may proclaim him a bully —or, to use his language—a cad, a double-barreled ass, a poltroon." In later numbers *Time* continued its attack.[56] Berton Braley wrote his parody on Eugene Field's "Wynken, Blynken, and Nod," which appeared in The Sun Dial column of the New York *Sun:*

There were three that sailed away one night
Far from the madding throng;
And two of the three were always right
And everyone else was wrong.
But they took another along, these two,
To bear them company,
For he was the only One ever knew
Why the other two should Be.
And so they sailed away, these three—
    Mencken,
    Nathan,
    And God.

And the two they talked of the aims of Art,
Which they alone understood;
And they quite agreed from the very start
That nothing was any good
Except some novels that Dreiser wrote
And some plays from Germany.
When God objected—they rocked the boat
And dropped him into the sea,
"For you have no critical facultee,"
    Said Mencken
    And Nathan
    To God.

The two came cheerfully sailing home
Over the surging tide
And trod once more their native loam
Wholly self-satisfied.

55 *Freeman,* v. 1, April 7, 1920, pp. 88–89.

56 *Time,* v. 1, March 10, 1923, p. 22; and, for example, July 30, 1923, p. 23; Aug. 27, 1923, p. 21.

And the little group that calls them great
Welcomed them fawningly,
Though why the rest of us tolerate
This precious pair must be
Something nobody else can see
  But Mencken,
  Nathan,
  And God![57]

Doubtless Mencken and Nathan chuckled over this effusion: how the third of the trio took it, only He knows—doubtless with divine tolerance.

By 1923 Mencken and Nathan had decided they deserved a more dignified forum than was afforded by a magazine handicapped by a rather silly title and overloaded with cheap stories. The *Smart Set* had brightened its covers by color in 1915 and used pretty girl pictures by John Held and Archie Gunn the next year; it screamed from its covers, "Startling! Daring! Unmasking!"; it increased its number of pages again. But it was playing the schizophrene in order to pursue two audiences, the intelligentsia and the low-IQ "smuthound"—and capturing neither of them. By 1923 it had dropped below the 25,000 mark in circulation.[58] Mencken and Warner quarreled over the publication of a proposed piece on the death of President Harding in the fall of 1923; as a result, the magazine was offered for sale to Alfred A. Knopf, with whom the editors had already been discussing the founding of a new monthly review. Knopf would not pay as much as Warner wanted. His mind was fixed on a brand new magazine anyway.[59]

Mencken and Nathan resigned with the number for December 1923. In his farewell, Mencken wrote, with a certain compunction that stopped well short of remorse: ". . . I have composed and printed no less than 182 book articles—in all, more than 900,000 words of criticism. An appalling dose, certainly! How many books have I reviewed, noticed, praised,

57 Berton Braley, "Three—Minus One," in New York *Sun,* Dec. 6, 1920, p. 16, col. 4. Reprinted with permission of Ian Braley.

58 Sworn statement in 1924 edition of *Ayer* was 22,127. Circulations given in later paragraphs are also based on sworn statements in *Ayer.*

59 Dolmetsch, "A History of the *Smart Set* Magazine," pp. 72–73; based on an interview with Warner. [Dolmetsch, *The Smart Set,* pp. 86–87.]

mocked, dismissed with lofty sneers? I don't know precisely, but probably fully 2,000." Then he went on to express his belief that the situation of the imaginative writer in America had improved greatly in his decade and a half of reviewing, especially in the matter of freedom. The gist of his valedictory seemed to be that he felt he had won his battle.[60]

And so Mencken and Nathan went on to found the *American Mercury,* and the *Smart Set* became a twenty-cent all-fiction monthly. Morris Gilbert, who had been a contributor, now became editor. He announced that he would fill the magazine with "fiction of a much wider appeal than that which it has offered in the last decade." [61] But after a few months it was sold to the Hearst interests for $60,000.[62]

In October 1924, the *Smart Set* was made a quarto with a flashy cover and the subtitle, "True Stories from Real Life." It now consisted largely of pictures, printed by offset; sex and sensation fiction, mainly of the "true story" type; sentiment by Edgar Guest and Dr. Frank Crane; and a little cheap advertising. "Look at the trollop! Why couldn't she have died before she lost her good name?" exclaimed a former reader as he passed a newsstand.[63]

But circulation, at a cover price of twenty-five cents, jumped to over 250,000 in 1925, and in the next few years to about 385,000. F. Orlin Tremaine was editor for a year or so, to be succeeded by William Charles Lengel. In 1928 James R. Quirk bought from Hearst both the *Smart Set* and the *New McClure's Magazine,* both of them now wallowing in a vulgarity unworthy of past achievements, and put T. Howard Kelly, a fellow newspaper man, to editing them. But the next

[60] *Smart Set,* v. 72, Dec. 1923, p. 138. This claim that the fight to free American literature had been won was also expressed in a broadside issued when the resignation was announced; Oct. 10, 1923.

[61] *Ibid.,* v. 72, Dec. 1923, pp. 11–12.

[62] Dolmetsch, "A History of the *Smart Set* Magazine," p. 145; based on an interview with Warner. [Dolmetsch, *The Smart Set,* p. 89.] According to Edgar Kemler in *The Irreverent Mr. Mencken* (Boston, 1950), p. 165, Mencken and Nathan each received from Hearst one-fourth of $60,000, the sale price of *Smart Set,* in addition to $40 per share for their stock.

[63] Exclamation of Terry Ramsaye, quoted by Randolph Bartlett in his review of *The Smart Set Anthology,* in *Saturday Review of Literature,* v. 11, Dec. 1, 1934, pp. 320, 326.

year a marked decline in circulation was noted, and advertising was still sickly. A change was determined upon.

It was a radical change indeed. The *Smart Set* and *New McClure's* were merged in May 1929, under the name of the former, and a new magazine, with the subtitle "The Young Woman's Magazine," was the result. Margaret E. Sangster, former contributing editor to the *Christian Herald* and author of novels and poems of pious and motherly kind, became editor. There were some good writers in this novel *Smart Set,* but the name and history of the magazine were handicaps to a journal for nice young ladies, and the number for July 1930 was the last. The title was taken over to appear as the heading for a column of society gossip in the Hearst papers signed by "Cholly Knickerbocker."

18

THE SOUTH ATLANTIC QUARTERLY [1]

IN launching the *South Atlantic Quarterly* in January 1902, Editor John Spencer Bassett wrote a little salutatory in which he asserted his belief in "liberty to think." He expected to present "the problems of today on all of their sides." He closed this initial statement by declaring that the editor's "ambition is that men shall say that he has sought truth without prejudice and with no more than a modest confidence in his own conclusions. To find truth absolutely might be a good thing, but it does not seem likely to be done. The next best thing is to have many people seeking it in the spirit of honest tolerance. It is this search which develops mind and brings culture; and it is with a reverent hope of attaining it among a large number of Southern men that the present enterprise is placed before the public." [2] Did Professor Bassett, as he put these words on paper, have any presentiment of the crisis that would soon be precipitated by the on-all-sides freedom of discussion he invited?

The *South Atlantic* was at first sponsored at Trinity Col-

[1] TITLE: *The South Atlantic Quarterly.*

FIRST ISSUE: Jan. 1902. Current.

PERIODICITY: Quarterly. Regular annual volume.

PUBLISHERS: 9019 Scholarship Society, 1902–7; South Atlantic Publishing Company, 1907–24; Duke University Press, 1925–current. All at Durham, N.C.

EDITORS: John Spencer Bassett, 1902–5; Edwin Mims and William Henry Glasson, 1905–9; William Preston Few and W. H. Glasson, 1909–19; William Kenneth Boyd and William Hane Wannamaker, 1919–30; Henry Rudolph Dwire (managing editor), 1930–44; William T. Laprade, 1944–57; William Baskerville Hamilton (associate managing editor), 1956–57; (managing editor), 1958–current. Joseph Francis Bivins, assistant editor, 1902–4. Oliver W. Ferguson, (associate editor), 1961–current. Editorial Board: W. H. Wannamaker, 1930–56; W. T. Laprade, 1930–44; Newman Ivey White, 1930–42; Calvin Bryce Hoover, 1930–57; Harvey Branscomb, 1944–47; R. Taylor Cole, 1944–59; Charles Sackett Sydnor, 1947–54; W. B. Hamilton, 1954–56; Lionel Stevenson, 1956–current; Herman Salinger, 1956–current; Arlin Turner, 1956–current; B. U. Ratchford, 1958–60; Ralph Braibanti, 1959–60; J. Harris Proctor, 1961–current; Robert F. Durden, 1961–65; Robert S. Smith, 1961–current; I. B. Holley, Jr., 1966–current; Aubrey W. Naylor, 1967–current.

INDEXES: *Poole's Index, Readers' Guide Supplement, International.*

[2] *South Atlantic Quarterly,* v. 1, Jan. 1902, p. 3.

lege, Durham, North Carolina, by a student organization known as "The 9019." This was a scholastic society founded by Bassett when he had first come to Trinity as an instructor; its cabalistic figures denoted that it was born in the ninetieth year of the nineteenth century.[3] Honorary members of the society from the faculty were soon meeting the deficits, however; and in its second year the journal had the somewhat more assured support of the South Atlantic Publishing Company, composed of members of the faculties of Trinity College and Trinity Park School.[4] Stock certificates, valueless except as badges of honor, were issued to contributors. In 1907 the company was officially chartered, and some business and professional men of Durham joined the devoted band; in all, twenty stockholders put in $1,225 and received the decorative certificates as mementoes.[5] It appears that after this money was spent (and most of it probably went to pay debts to printers) the college and its supporters made fairly regular subventions to the journal. The college and the town could be proud of their modest *Quarterly,* which was a presentable publication of about one hundred pages, including a little section of advertising, all bound in a neat olive-green cover.

It was a Negro question that furnished the major test of Bassett's doctrine of freedom of utterance for all sides. The first number of his magazine opened with "An Inquiry Regarding Lynching," by President John Carlisle Kilgo, of Trinity, in which the author blamed the frequent recurrence of this crime in the South upon "sensitiveness in social dispositions," and pleaded for an emphasis in southern education upon calmer, saner attitudes and abandonment of appeals to passion. This seems to have won a degree of acceptance, for Volume I, Number I of the journal was well received.

In the third number, Robert Watson Winston, president of the Durham Chamber of Commerce, was given a few pages for the presentation of "An Unconsidered Aspect of the Negro Question," which turned out to be an attack on the Negro

[3] John Cline, "Thirty-Eight Years of the *South Atlantic Quarterly,*" unpub. diss., Duke University, 1940, p. 2.

[4] *South Atlantic Quarterly,* v. 4, April 1905, p. 105.

[5] Cline, "Thirty-Eight Years," pp. 7–8.

worker, who "thinks idleness, vice, and impudence stand for manhood and freedom." Winston predicted: "Unless a marked change for the better soon occurs, not only will there be increased violence towards the average negro, but upon hatred of him will grow up a political party that will sweep away his schools, his orphan homes and his hospitals, and will expatriate him or make a chattel of him." [6] On the other hand, an editorial article appeared in the fourth number in which Bassett asserted that the Democratic party, then in the midst of a state campaign, had continuously used an appeal to passion against the Negro in order to gain votes: "Consciously or unconsciously it has bred race hatred and then fattened on it." [7]

This was provocative enough, but in the eighth number Bassett published an article entitled "Stirring Up the Fires of Race Antipathy" that certainly stirred up a tremendous flame of wrath throughout the South against the author, his journal, and his college. In this editorial, Bassett elaborated upon his theme of the political abuse of the Negro question, and then went on to make a startling prediction: "The only solution reserved for us is the adoption of these children of Africa into our American life. In spite of our race feeling, of which the writer has his share, they will win equality at some time." But perhaps even more incendiary was an *obiter dictum* that Booker T. Washington was "the greatest man, save General Lee, born in the South in a hundred years." [8]

As soon as this article came to the attention of Josephus Daniels, editor of the Raleigh *News and Observer,* he reprinted it in full in the editorial section of his Sunday edition, together with a three-column piece of his own in reply to it.[9] He used screamer headlines—"SAYS NEGRO WILL WIN EQUALITY," "SOUTHERN LEADERS SLANDERED"—over the Bassett article; and in his own editorial he called "bASSett" a freak and suggested that he always prayed with his face turned to-

[6] *South Atlantic Quarterly,* v. 1, July 1902, p. 267.

[7] *Ibid.,* v. 1, Oct. 1902, p. 307.

[8] *Ibid.,* v. 2, Oct. 1903, pp. 304, 299.

[9] Raleigh *News and Observer,* Nov. 1, 1903, p. 9. Daniels' own account of the entire episode is found in his *Editor in Politics* (Chapel Hill, N.C., 1941), "I Am Hung in Effigy," pp. 427–38.

ward Tuskegee. Thereafter, day after day, this newspaper reprinted editorials from its contemporaries replying indignantly to the Bassett article; there were floods of them, and the reaction seemed unanimous.

The involvement of the *News and Observer* in this matter must be made clear.[10] Daniels, later Secretary of the Navy and ambassador to Mexico, had made his paper a leader in southern journalism. For several years he had been engaged in a crusade against the Tobacco Trust, which he regarded as the oppressor of the planter, as well as a strong supporter of the Republican party in the South, which was the most heinous offense of all. When the Dukes, chief operators of the Trust, began to give liberal donations to Trinity College, the *News and Observer* included that institution within the circle of its criticism and objurgation and represented President Kilgo as the spokesman of the Trust and of the opposition party. And so, when the *South Atlantic Quarterly* was founded (including a full-page announcement of the virtues of Duke's Mixture in its very slender advertising section), the *News and Observer* looked upon it, not as an organ of the Trust, perhaps, but as belonging to the evil pattern. Still another reason for Daniels' anti-Trinity position was President Kilgo's bitter fight against state-supported higher education, which the editor, loyal to his alma mater, the University of North Carolina, strongly resented.[11]

Within ten days after the appearance of Bassett's article, such a fire of abusive and scurrilous criticism had been directed against the author that he wrote a statement for the local Durham newspaper in which he attempted to soften the terms of the original article. "I had no thought of social equality in my mind," he wrote; and he gave also a special definition of "greatness" to apply to Booker Washington.[12] This did nothing to put out the fire. Newspapers, church bodies (Trinity was a Methodist college), and educational and polit-

[10] Daniels, *Editor in Politics;* also his *Tar Heel Editor* (Chapel Hill, N.C., 1939) —both passim.

[11] See Paul N. Garber, *John Carlisle Kilgo* (Durham, N.C., 1937), chap ii, for this campaign of Kilgo's. Note also the account therein of the episode of the Bassett editorial, and particularly of the board of trustees meeting.

[12] Durham *Herald,* Nov. 10, 1903.

ical leaders were almost unanimous in adding their particular torches to the conflagration that rolled upon the review and its editor, and the college and its president.

Another ten days, and Bassett resigned his professorship. It was obviously done to save the college, but the entire faculty stood by Bassett by placing in the hands of President Kilgo sealed envelopes containing their own resignations, to be opened if Bassett's resignation was accepted. This action, though supposed to be secret, was undoubtedly a powerful club held over the board of trustees when it met in special conclave to consider the Bassett resignation; indeed, both faculty and students, though they disagreed more or less with some of the things their colleague and teacher had said, supported him faithfully on the ground of his right to say them. It is interesting to note that Walter Hines Page, then a kind of unofficial national spokesman for the South, wrote to Benjamin N. Duke repeatedly suggesting that he bring his influence to bear on the board to retain Bassett.[13]

The board meeting began the evening of December 1, 1903, and lasted into the early hours of the next day. Weary students kept their watch at the door of the board room; and when, at nearly three o'clock in the morning, the news came out that the trustees had voted 18 to 7 to reject Bassett's resignation, the college bell was rung, and immediately the campus was crowded with cheering students. A huge bonfire was kindled to enliven the celebration, and in its lurid light was seen an effigy of Josephus Daniels hanging from a persimmon tree, and even a second one on a telegraph pole. The student monthly was very apologetic, when it told about the hanging in its next issue; [14] but the reader seems to detect a certain satisfaction in this reply to the varied and long continued attacks of the *News and Observer* on their college.

And so Trinity and the *South Atlantic Quarterly* went on, and the fire of criticism died down. Bassett resigned his editorship about eighteen months later. He may have been influ-

[13] Cline, "Thirty-Eight Years," pp. 93–97. Later Page wrote an article about the whole episode for *World's Work,* v. 7, Jan. 1904, pp. 4284–87.

[14] *Trinity Archive,* Dec. 1903; reprinted in *South Atlantic Quarterly,* v. 3, Jan. 1904, pp. 68–72; and William Baskerville Hamilton, ed., *Fifty Years of the South Atlantic Quarterly* (Durham, N.C., 1952), pp. 68–72.

enced by the loss of his assistant editor, Joseph Bivins, who was killed in a railway accident in the fall of 1904. In 1906 Bassett left Trinity for Smith College, where he continued a long career as teacher and author. The incident of his "Race Antipathy" article remains an almost classic case of freedom of the press, since the real test in such an issue is not whether those in control believe in the statements that have been made, but whether they believe in the right of a responsible and sincere author to make them.[15]

Bassett was succeeded in his editorship of the *South Atlantic* by William H. Glasson and Edwin Mims, who shared the work for four years. Glasson was an economist and Mims a professor of English who had just published a distinguished life of Sidney Lanier. When Mims went to the University of North Carolina, William P. Few took his place as joint editor of the *Quarterly;* but Few became president of Trinity the next year, and Glasson was the journal's mainstay until 1919.

Contents for the first decade of the *South Atlantic* were nearly all southern, either by authorship or topic. "The fact that every article in the present number is by a native Southerner is a matter of gratification to the editor," wrote Bassett of one of his issues.[16] The magazine was saved from monotony by the fact that southern writers frequently held forth on topics—literary, historical, or philosophical—which were by no means regional; and there were, as time went on, articles by non-southern writers on wholly non-southern topics.

The perennial debate over Negro rights and Negro character continued. A symposium on lynching was printed in the number for October 1906; and an article on that subject by Robert Russa Moton, who had succeeded Washington as principal of Tuskegee Institute, appeared in July 1919. James W. Garner, Mississippi born but now a professor of political science at Illinois, wrote about the savage Negrophobia of Gov-

[15] A short account of the episode is found in William B. Hamilton's "Fifty Years of Liberalism and Learning," *South Atlantic Quarterly,* v. 51, Jan. 1952, pp. 7–32; reprinted as the first article in Hamilton, ed., *Fifty Years,* an anthology which contains also Kilgo's article on lynching, Bassett's famous editorial, and the statement embodying the decision of the trustees. The fullest account is in Cline, "Thirty-Eight Years," chap. ii.

[16] *South Atlantic Quarterly,* v. 4. Jan. 1905, p. 91.

Volume IV. Number 2.

The

SOUTH ATLANTIC QUARTERLY

EDITORS { EDWIN MIMS, WILLIAM H. GLASSON.

APRIL, 1905.

CONTENTS.

EDITORS' ANNOUNCEMENT - - - - - - - - - - - 105

THE NEW NORTH - - - - - - - - - - - - - 109
HAMILTON WRIGHT MABIE.

SIDNEY LANIER: REMINISCENCES AND LETTERS - - - 115
DANIEL COIT GILMAN.

THE HAGUE COURT - - - - - - - - - - - - - - 123
JOHN H. LATANE, Ph. D.

RUSKIN'S LETTERS TO CHARLES ELIOT NORTON - - - 138
HENRY NELSON SNYDER.

THE OVERPRODUCTION OF COTTON AND A POSSIBLE REMEDY 148
ULRICH BONNELL PHILLIPS.

MATTHEW WHITAKER RANSOM: A SENATOR OF THE OLD REGIME - - - - - - - - - - - - - - 159
ROBERT LEE FLOWERS.

THE PEABODY EDUCATION FUND - - - - - - - - 169
R. D. W. CONNOR.

SOME CONTEMPORARY AMERICAN ESSAYISTS - - - - 182
WILLIAM P. FEW.

BOOK REVIEWS - - - - - - - - - - - - - - 189

LITERARY NOTES - - - - - - - - - - - - - - 200

DURHAM, N. C.

$2.00 a YEAR. 50 CENTS A COPY.

Founded by the "9019"
Trinity College

Entered May 3, 1902, as second class matter, Postoffice at Durham, N. C., Act of Congress of March 3, 1879.

THE *SOUTH ATLANTIC QUARTERLY* IN ITS FOURTH YEAR

John Spencer Bassett had just retired as editor, and in this April 1905 issue the new editors, Edwin Mims and William H. Glasson, introduced themselves. Nowadays brighter colors have replaced the gray and olive-green of earlier years.

ernor Vardaman, of his native state, in January 1908. Gilbert T. Stephenson, a Winston-Salem judge, discussed urban segregation in January 1914; and in the following two numbers he debated rural segregation with Clarence Poe, editor of the *Progressive Farmer,* of Raleigh.

Historical studies, which have been important throughout the whole of the *South Atlantic* file, were especially prominent in the first two or three decades. Its first editor was a historian; and he and his colleagues and followers were committed to the new Johns Hopkins idea of a more "scientific" history, drawn from sources and less diluted with sentiment and preconceived ideas. Bassett, William E. Dodd, James G. Randall, and Gamaliel Bradford, Jr., were conspicuous contributors. Bradford's Robert E. Lee studies (1911–1912) were his first contributions to the *Quarterly;* but his later articles, and many by other historians and biographers, were non-southern.

In the early volumes, as in the later ones, there were many studies in literary history and criticism. The chief student of the *South Atlantic* file concludes that "The outstanding emphasis of the magazine has been on literature and literary criticism."[17] These were frequently academic in tone, and even dull sometimes; but often they were valuable. Daniel Coit Gilman's reminiscences of Sidney Lanier (April 1905), James Routh's "Essay on the Poetry of Henry Timrod" (July 1910), and Albert Edmund Trombly's studies of Rossetti (1919–1920) were notable studies of poets and their work.

There was not much about contemporary southern letters. Here was illustrated the recurrent dilemma of the journal; it wanted to be loyal to the South, but it resented regional separations and distinctions. It wanted to be at once southern and national. "That really pathetic phrase, Southern Literature, we are never allowed to forget," wrote President Henry N. Snyder, of Wofford College, in the second number; yet "one never hears the books written by Longfellow, by Lowell, by Emerson, spoken of as *Northern* Literature." Then Snyder goes on, in a fashion typical of commentators on southern literature, to call the roll of the romantic period of southern fic-

[17] Cline, "Thirty-Eight Years," p. 160.

tion then drawing to an end; finally he saw, or hoped he saw, that the South offered the seed-bed of a rich literary growth in the future.[18] Professor Carl Holliday, a frequent and always interesting contributor, worked a similar vein in the issue for January 1910, offering a catalog of southern writers. But John Raper Ormond, reviewing three new southern novels in 1904, said that the formula of romantic southern fiction had been exhausted, and that it never represented southern society anyway. He had praise only for Ellen Glasgow, who had "a grasp on actual life." [19] Aside from such rare articles, there was little about twentieth-century belles-lettres—northern or southern—in the first few decades of the *South Atlantic.* At first there were occasional notices of contemporary fiction and poetry in the extensive book-review section, but even these were abandoned after the fourth volume. The journal never printed original verse or short stories.

A leading theme in the first two decades of the review was the backwardness of the South in education on all levels. Kilgo set the pattern in the second volume, when he declared that the South lacked "an educational conscience": it had "as much education as it wants." [20] The next year Professor (soon to be President) Few wrote a definitive article about southern educational needs (July 1904) in which he declared that "the most ruinous waste of our civilization" had been a "gross neglect of the lower classes of the whites." Later came other articles on these and many other phases of American education. Usually they were by professors—often by presidents—of southern colleges, and very often they got back to the basic matter of the needs of the South in this field.

Religion and philosophy also occupied some space in the earlier volumes of the journal. Notable was a series of papers by President William Louis Poteat of Wake Forest College, in 1907, on religion and science, which angered many readers in the author's own Baptist denomination by its acceptance of the evolutionary theory.[21]

[18] *South Atlantic Quarterly,* v. 1, April 1902, pp. 146, 155.
[19] *Ibid.,* v. 3, July 1904, p. 288.
[20] *Ibid.,* v. 2, April 1903, p. 137.
[21] *Ibid.,* v. 51, Jan. 1952, p. 18; Hamilton, *Fifty Years,* p. 14.

Articles on economics and industry were not uncommon. Thomas F. Parker, president of the Monaghan Mills, of Greenville, South Carolina, presented in 1909–1910 a survey of the mills and their management that showed some feeling for reform. Contributions in this field were usually liberal in tone, as Lyman Abbott's "Significance of the Present Moral Awakening in the Nation" (July 1908). Trinity's Laprade a decade later (October 1919) advocated new democratic practices in labor-management relations. However, the official (but candid) historian of the *South Atlantic* admits that "by and large" the journal's discussion of southern industrialism "has been inadequate"—though it was better in earlier volumes than in the later ones.[22]

Although political theory was occasionally discussed in one phase or another, contemporary politics was eschewed; thus the *South Atlantic* has never made a practice of reviewing the issues even at the time of the national presidential elections.

Contributors to the journal were, first of all, members of the Trinity faculty; the editors themselves were leading writers for it. Bassett in history and sociology, Mims in literary history and criticism, Kilgo in education, and Few in theology carried much weight in the early years of the journal. Mims was outstanding; not only were his own articles on American literature readable and scholarly, but he became an industrious and ingenious editor. Was Charles W. Eliot about to make the key address at some conference or other? Mims wrote him and begged the manuscript. Did a northern editor ask Mims for a contribution? Mims sent him one promptly, and asked Hamilton W. Mabie or Bliss Perry for a piece for his own journal. It was somewhat ironical that Mims got paid and Mabie and Perry did not, but the scheme often worked; and it was all for the good of the *South Atlantic Quarterly*.[23] Probably the tables of contents of the journal during Mim's editorship contained more nationally known names than they did in any other period.

[22] *South Atlantic Quarterly,* v. 51, Jan. 1952, p. 20; Hamilton, *Fifty Years,* p. 16.

[23] See Edwin Mims, "Early Years of the *South Atlantic Quarterly,*" *South Atlantic Quarterly,* v. 51, Jan. 1952, pp. 33–63.

In 1924 the Duke Foundation was organized, with its liberal provision for Trinity College, which now became Duke University. This generosity apparently extended to the *South Atlantic Quarterly,* which had, for a number of years, been receiving some financial help from the college and now was able to increase its size to 120 pages or more. The new Duke University Press took over, and by 1927 the *Quarterly* was even paying its contributors, at the rate of two dollars a page.[24] Size shrank a little during the early years of the depression, but from the later thirties through the early fifties there were at least 150 noble, well-designed pages in each issue. It retained its good pages, though commonly fewer of them, and these a little less lavish in margins, at the end of the fifties. The *South Atlantic Quarterly* has never circulated as many as a thousand copies an issue. For a long time it printed only four or five hundred; later somewhat more.[25] Many copies go to libraries and thus multiply readership.

When Glasson and Few retired from the editorship, their places were taken by William K. Boyd and William H. Wannamaker, professors respectively of history and German, who served until 1930. When they completed their term of a little more than a decade, a managing editor was chosen to conduct the *Quarterly* with the aid of an editorial board. The lot fell upon a journalist and public relations director, Henry R. Dwire. A leading member of his board was historian William T. Laprade, who succeeded him as managing editor in 1944. William B. Hamilton, who had served as associate managing editor for a year, succeeded Laprade in 1958.

As the *South Atlantic Quarterly* approached its semicentennial, it became less regional, less controversial, and more definitely literary. By the late fifties, it published an occasional number without a single distinctively southern article, and many with only one or two of regional interest. It fell in with the revival of interest in the Civil War, and it was always friendly to the history of the southern colonies; but it also printed many historical and critical studies the subject matter

24 Cline, "Thirty-Eight Years," p. 10.

25 *Ibid.*, p. 6; also Rowell's *American Newspaper Directory* and *N. W. Ayer & Son's Directory of Newspapers and Periodicals.* [The circulation in 1966 was over eight hundred.]

of which was far removed from the Southland. Ever since the late thirties, it had given somewhat more attention to contemporary movements in literature. In the forties and fifties it attracted such contributors as Jay B. Hubbell, Charles I. Glicksberg, Eudora Welty, and Julian Huxley for articles on such themes. But there was no reaching for big names, and most writers for the journal were comparatively obscure (though competent and often effective) academicians.

Many articles bearing on war and peace, and the social and economic concomitants of the war years, appeared during both great world conflicts. Occasionally half the articles of a single number during World War II dealt with war matters.

In political and economic theory the *South Atlantic* has followed the liberal side in more recent years as in the past. Two articles approving the National Recovery Administration were published in the successive numbers for October 1933 and January 1934, and one favoring unemployment insurance appeared in April 1933. Clearly, the journal was New Dealish. But the tendency to make peace with the conservatives was common, in the fifties at least. Kathleen Thayer's "Socialism is Irrelevant" is an example; we already have enough of it in the United States, Britain, and Sweden, she says, and internationally it is "for the present out of the question." [26]

The Negro question has received some attention in the latter half of the *South Atlantic* file. In the thirties and forties there were several sentimental pieces by Archibald Rutledge, South Carolina poet laureate, about the old plantation Negro —"charming but antediluvian writings," a later editor calls them.[27] There were occasional articles on Negro literature: a notable one by Harold P. Marley in 1928 repeated a statement made in the *Journal of Social Forces* to the effect that "a considerable number of white strains in this country would be greatly elevated by the infusion of some of the better blood of the Negro race." [28] This point of view, cited to illustrate the attitudes of some intellectuals, might have brought the author a visit from the Ku Klux Klan in an earlier day.

[26] *South Atlantic Quarterly,* v. 51, July 1952, p. 354.

[27] Hamilton, *Fifty Years,* p. 11; *South Atlantic Quarterly,* v. 51, Jan. 1952, p. 16.

[28] *South Atlantic Quarterly,* v. 27, Jan. 1928, p. 31.

School segregation was sometimes criticized; the outstanding example was an article by Elizabeth Stevenson, of Atlanta, in the number for October 1949. And the epochal Supreme Court decision on segregation was greeted with joy by James McBride Dabbs in the number for January 1956. In the bitter debate which followed, however, the *South Atlantic* took little part.

It has become, indeed, mainly a journal given to the criticism of literature and culture in general; to history, including that of recent times; and to philosophy and allied matters. It is rather less a regional journal than one with worldwide horizons, for every number has some articles dealing with foreign or international questions or conditions. The book review section remains, as it has always been, an extensive and important part of the magazine—almost never scintillating, but always solidly reliable. The reviews are written (as probably most of the articles are) by scholars to be read by scholars.

The quality that lifts the *South Atlantic* to a position of importance in the history of our periodical literature is not merely the unflagging effort over many years to present important ideas to thinking people, but also its ebbing and flowing liberalism, best illustrated in the famous Bassett episode of its early years.*

* This chapter was written in the late 1950's and has not been updated, except for footnotes 1 and 25.

19

SUCCESS [1]

ORISON SWETT MARDEN, having won an education and a fortune against great odds, lost the latter in the hard times of the early nineties; but in 1894 he started a new career which was to make him the prophet of the will-to-success philosophy which had suddenly become a cult.[2] He started this new career with a very successful book entitled *Pushing to the Front,* and in 1897 he succeeded, after an extended campaign, in inducing Louis Klopsch to finance a magazine to spread his gospel of getting ahead.

Klopsch was publisher of the *Christian Herald,* of New York, and was genuinely interested in the self-help ideas which Marden had derived from reading Samuel Smiles' books and from his own experiences. There were two preliminary numbers of the new magazine—one issued October 1896 and the other just a year later—but the regular Volume I, Number 1 was dated December 1897.

Success was a large quarto of forty pages and cover, and sold for ten cents a number or one dollar a year. It contained a great variety of nonfiction material about techniques of success, illustrated by case studies of men and women who had won prominence and power. It was at once evident that Marden's concept of success was a broad one, and that his ideal of a successful man, though wealthy and powerful, was also

[1] TITLES: (1) *Success,* 1897–1904; (2) *Success Magazine,* 1905—July 1911; (3) *Success Magazine and the National Post,* Aug.–Dec. 1911.

FIRST ISSUE: Dec. 1897. LAST ISSUE: Dec. 1911.

PERIODICITY: Monthly, Dec. 1897—Nov. 1898, Jan. 1900—Dec. 1911; weekly, Dec. 1898—Dec. 1899. Vol. 1, Dec. 1897—Nov. 1898; 2, Dec. 1898—Nov. 1899; 3, Dec. 1899—Dec. 1900; 4–14, 1901–11.

PUBLISHERS: Success Company, New York and Boston, 1897–1900; McGraw-Marden Company, New York, 1900–1911; National Post Company, New York, 1911.

EDITORS: Orison Swett Marden (with Robert Mackay, 1906–8; Samuel Merwin, 1909–10; Howard Brubaker, 1910–11).

INDEXES: Vols. 12–14 in *Dramatic Index.*

[2] See F. L. Mott, *A History of American Magazines,* v. 4 (Cambridge, Mass., 1957), pp. 167–69.

healthy, well-educated, benevolent, and religious. There were departments of books, health, science, and "The Young Man in Business," as well as one for the juniors.

In the second number Theodore Dreiser began a series on successful men, with an article on Joseph H. Choate, entitled "A Talk With America's Leading Lawyer." Dreiser soon became a regular contributor, at twenty-five to fifty dollars an article; he sometimes had two pieces in a single issue, using a pen-name for the second one.[3] The magazine was full and overflowing with biographical material about famous personages. Many of the articles were by unknowns, but there was a good sprinkling of famous names in the *Success* tables of contents. George W. Cable, Mary A. Livermore, Julia Ward Howe, Frances E. Willard, Edward Everett Hale, and Booker T. Washington were among the magazine's early contributors. If New England names seem conspicuous, it must be remembered that for over two years the main editorial office was in Boston, though publication was in New York. Arthur W. Brown, of Providence, was an assistant editor for a time, and Margaret Connolly became the associate editor in New York.

Though there had been considerable fiction in the trial numbers, there was none whatever in the first two regular issues, and a short story by "Octave Thanet" in the third number was the first of that kind; after a year or two, however, there was usually a fiction story in each issue. Illustration was fairly copious and attractive, chiefly halftones from photographs. During the Spanish-American War there were many pictures and sketches from Cuba and the military camps. The cover usually carried a big portrait of a famous contemporary figure, or some picture suggesting the road to success.

After a year of publication, the magazine had a circulation of less than fifty thousand. It was then changed to a five-cent weekly, with sixteen pages and cover, for a year. At the beginning of 1900 the editorial offices were moved to New York, ending the divided management, and the magazine resumed monthly publication. Circulation began a slow increase.

[3] Dreiser MSS, University of Pennsylvania Library. See also John F. Huth, Jr., "Dreiser the Successmonger," *Colophon,* N.S., v. 3, Winter 1938, pp. 120–33; Summer 1938, pp. 406–10.

In these turn-of-the-century years, *Success* printed much about the English war with the Boers in South Africa and other events of wide interest. There were short pieces by Joseph Chamberlain, Ballington Booth, Admiral George Dewey, General Nelson A. Miles, Arthur T. Hadley, David Starr Jordan, and so on. Some short fiction appeared, most memorable of which, perhaps, was Frederick Van Rensselaer Dey's "The Magic Story," with its formula for success, which was later very widely circulated in cheap editions.

In 1900, Klopsch was supplanted as financial "angel" of the magazine by James H. McGraw, well-known publisher of technological periodicals. Two years later the McGraw-Marden Company was incorporated for $1,000,000,[4] and from that time onward *Success* began to live up to its name. Marden wrote to Dreiser in October 1902 that they were then carrying $30,000 a month advertising.[5] Four years later *Success* had reached 300,000 circulation, and a good advertising patronage at $800 per page; and soon thereafter it had its own building on East Twenty-second Street, near Broadway, with its own printing plant. Robert Mackay was co-editor 1906–1908.

But its prosperity in 1910 could not match that which had suddenly come to *Hampton's* and *Everybody's* as the result of their incursions into the muckraking field. And so in that year, blind to the fact that the surfeit of exposés had destroyed the public's appetite for them and that the muckraking cycle was almost complete, *Success* plunged into the reformatory fray with vigor. For years, it had represented success as a virtue in itself, and the successful man as a paragon. When *McClure's* was attacking Standard Oil, it had published its "Impartial Study of John D. Rockefeller" (July 8, 1899). Now its chief writers were the belligerent Judson C. Welliver and the socialist Charles Edward Russell. This made a great shift in the mood and tempo of the magazine; and the transformation was further emphasized by the introduction of fiction by big-name writers, under the associate editorship of Samuel Merwin.

[4] *New York Tribune,* April 22, 1902, p. 2, col. 6.

[5] Dreiser MSS, University of Pennsylvania Library; letter dated Oct. 24, 1902.

DID HE SUCCEED IN WINNING HER?

This bright cover of *Success Magazine* for July 1906, drawn by J. C. Leyendecker, was probably intended to illustrate one of the roads to success.

Samuel Hopkins Adams, Zane Grey, Henry Kitchell Webster, John Luther Long, James Oppenheim, and other popular magazinists, their work copiously illustrated, completed the change-over of *Success* into a general monthly of wide appeal. The single-copy price was raised to fifteen cents.

In making this change, however, *Success* lost its specialized audience and became a competitor in the class which was now aiming at million circulations. Within less than a year, it became evident that *Success* would not make the goal it had set itself. Marden's biographer says the trouble was that big business did not like the muckraking policy and forced the bankers to call back their loans to the publishing company.[6] However that may be, *Success* was purchased in the summer of 1911 by the National Post Company.

The *National Post* was a fortnightly which had been founded by E. E. Garrison and Samuel Merwin three months earlier. It specialized in current news and comment, but contained articles, fiction, and verse. After the merger, and during the five months which ended with its suspension in December 1911, *Success Magazine and the National Post* published a serial by James Oliver Curwood, some household departments, a generous offering of news and comment of a prevailingly liberal cast, and a quantity of miscellany. But it belied its name; as a general illustrated monthly at 300,000 circulation, it was a failure.

Marden had been so long preaching the doctrine of never-say-die, however, that he believed in it himself; and he kept on the lookout for another financial "angel." Frederick C. Lowrey, a Chicago manufacturer and a long-time admirer of Marden's books and of his magazine, offered in 1917 to finance a new series of *Success*. The United States was already in the midst of a world war, and some established magazines were having trouble with the high labor and paper costs of the time; but it seemed to Marden and Lowrey that America needed *Success* now more than ever before. Accordingly, *The*

[6] Margaret Connolly, *The Life Story of Orison Swett Marden* (New York, 1925), pp. 227–28. This work throws some light on other phases of the history of the magazine *Success*.

New Success: Marden's Magazine[7] appeared in January 1918.

The *New Success* was much like the old one in its first phase; even the title was shortened to *Success* before long. It was subtitled "A Magazine of Optimism, Self-Help, and Encouragement." It was a small quarto of some fifty pages, selling at fifteen cents and containing much of Marden but little of the well-known writers of the day. Robert Mackay was back as associate editor. Personality sketches, success stories, war material, some fiction, and editorials about Americanism and ambition and the will to succeed furnished most of the contents. It was a handsome and interesting magazine, though its persistent optimism was eventually a little galling; and at the close of the war its circulation was about one hundred thousand.

Marden, his willpower unimpaired but his financial resources dwindling, kept at his desk until a few months before his death in March 1924. He was succeeded for two years by Walter Hoff Seely, who had been a newspaper man, writer, and lecturer. The new editor was apparently allowed funds to buy the work of some of the better magazine writers of the twenties; and names like E. Phillips Oppenheim, Charles G. Norris, and Irvin S. Cobb began to appear in the contents of the new *Success*. Circulation passed the 150,000 mark in 1925, but in the competition of the twenties that was not enough. After Seely left, Francis Trevelyan Miller, who had been managing editor under Marden and Seely, steered the magazine until relieved by David Arnold Balch in 1926.

Lowrey remained as president of the publishing company

[7] Titles: (1) *The New Success: Marden's Magazine*, 1918–20; (2) *The New Success*, Jan.–Sept. 1921; (3) *Success*, Oct. 1921—Aug. 1926; (4) *Success Magazine*, Sept. 1926—Oct. 1927; (5) *New Age Illustrated*, Nov. 1927—April 1928.

First issue: Jan. 1918. Last issue: April 1928.

Periodicity: Monthly. Vols. 1–2, semiannual, 1918; 3–12 (no. 4), annual, 1919—April 1928.

Publishers: Lowrey-Marden Company, New York, 1918–21; Success Magazine Corporation, New York, 1921–27; Central Magazine Company, Chicago, 1927–28.

Editors: Orison Swett Marden, 1918–24; Walter Hoff Seely, 1924–25; Francis Trevelyan Miller (managing editor), 1923–26; David Arnold Balch (managing editor), 1926–28.

until 1927, when the magazine was sold to A. C. G. Hammesfahr, of Chicago. Its name was now changed to *The New Age Illustrated,* and it was printed in Chicago and mailed from that city, though the editorial office was still in New York. It was diversified and attractive, but it was still not a success, and with the issue for April 1928 it was abandoned.

The significance of the magazine *Success* lies chiefly in its embodiment of the cult of the will to win, which was so prominent an element of the national spirit at the beginning of the twentieth century, but it is also important as a popular general magazine of its period, and as a participant in the last phase of the muckraking movement.

20

TIME [1]

MEDIOCRE nor commonplace was never *Time*. Lucelanted, now and then prejudiced, unfair was The Newsmagazine, but Timediting was always a smart art. Headman Henry Robinson Luce hired helpers of

[1] TITLE: *Time: The Weekly Newsmagazine*. (*News-Magazine*, with the hyphen, was used 1923–26. *The Weekly News-Paper* was given as a subtitle on p. 23 of the first number, but was soon discarded.)

FIRST ISSUE: March 3, 1923. Current.

PERIODICITY: Weekly. Vol. 1, March–Aug. 1923; 2, Sept.–Dec. 1923; thereafter regular semiannual volumes, except for 9, Jan.–July, 1927; 10, Aug.–Dec. 1927.

PUBLISHER: Time Inc. (New York, 1923–25, 1927–current; Cleveland, Ohio, 1925–27; chief office of printing and U.S. distribution 1928–current, Chicago, with branches in Philadelphia, 1940–1962; Old Saybrook, Conn., 1962–current; Washington, 1957–current; Albany, 1959–current; and Los Angeles, 1944–current.) President, Briton Hadden, 1923–25; Henry Robinson Luce, 1925–39; Roy Edward Larsen, 1939–60 (Chairman, Executive Committee, 1960–current); James Alexander Linen III, 1960–current. Business manager, H. R. Luce, 1923–27; B. Hadden, 1928–29. Publisher, Ralph McAllister Ingersoll, 1937–40; Pierrepont Isham Prentice, 1941–45; J. A. Linen, 1945–60; Bernhard Machold Auer, 1960–66; James R. Shepley, 1966–current.

EDITORS: B. Hadden, 1923–27; H. R. Luce, 1928–43, 1947–49; H. R. Luce and Manfred Gottfried, 1943–46; Thomas Stanley Matthews, 1950–53; Eben Roy Alexander, 1960–66. Editor-in-chief, H. R. Luce, 1945–64; Hedley Donovan, 1964–current. Editorial chairman, H. R. Luce, 1964–67. Managing editors (for some terms two or even three shared this title): John Stuart Martin, 1929–37; John Shaw Billings, 1933–37; M. Gottfried, 1937–43; Frank Norris, 1937–40; T. S. Matthews, 1938–42, 1943–49; Roy Alexander, 1950–60; Otto Fuerbringer, 1960–current. Executive editors: T. S. Matthews, 1942–43; E. R. Alexander, 1947–49; Dana Tasker, 1952–53. Editorial director, J. S. Billings, 1945–54; Hedley Donovan, 1959–64.

INDEXES: *Readers' Guide*, July 1935–current; full indexes for each semi-annual volume.

REFERENCES: Noel F. Busch, *Briton Hadden: A Biography of the Co-Founder of Time* (New York, 1949); T. S. Matthews, *Name and Address: An Autobiography* (New York, 1960), pp. 215–74; Thomas Griffith, *The Waist-High Culture* (New York, 1959), chap. vii; Theodore Peterson, *Magazines in the Twentieth Century* (Urbana, Ill., 1956), pp. 219–24, 298–301 [see also rev. ed.; Urbana, Ill., 1964, pp. 234–44]; *What Makes Time Tick* (New York, 1956), a portfolio of folders issued by Time Inc.; Eric Hodgins, *The Span of Time* (New York, 1946), 14 pp. unbound, issued by Time Inc.; *The Story of an Experiment* (New York, 1946), 12 pp. *Time* size, issued by Time Inc.; Ellsworth Chunn, "History of News Magazines," unpub. diss., University of Missouri, 1950; "Time at 40," *Time*, v. 81, May 10, 1963, pp. 10–11; Robert Heady, "Now 40, 'Time' Notes Own Growth, Mushrooming Brother Enterprises," *Advertising Age*, v. 34, March 25, 1963, pp. 35–36.

many talents, built amazing circulation, accumulated advertising, made millions. No piker he.

Having made our own strained effort to parody what was once known as "Timestyle" (as many before us have done), let us abandon such perversities of syntax and vocabulary (as *Time* itself laid many of them aside after the 1930's) and try to tell the story of this important periodical as straightforwardly as possible.

Briton Hadden was born in Brooklyn in 1898. The twin hobbies of his boyhood were amateur journalism and baseball. His family was comfortably well-to-do, and when he arrived at prep-school age he was sent to the Hotchkiss School in Lakeville, Connecticut. There he met Henry Luce, a boy of his own age, whose twin hobbies were journalism and books. Luce had been born in Tengchow, China, the son of Presbyterian missionaries. Hadden became editor of the school newspaper, the *Hotchkiss Record;* and Luce edited the *Hotchkiss Literary Monthly,* for which he wrote essays and poetry.

From Hotchkiss, both boys went to Yale University, where Hadden became chairman of the *Yale News* and Luce its managing editor. They interrupted their college work in 1918 to enlist in the Student Army Training Corps at Camp Jackson, South Carolina, where they found time for long talks about the possibility of founding a new national weekly devoted to a concise and orderly presentation of the news. They were back at Yale in time to be graduated with the class of 1920.

Following graduation, Luce went to Oxford for a year, then worked for a few months as a reporter on the *Chicago Daily News.* Hadden joined the New York *World* staff. Late in 1921, both men were offered jobs on the *Baltimore News* through the influence of Walter Millis, a Yale classmate. Both accepted, less for their modest salaries than for the opportunity to be together again for discussions of their magazine dream. After a few months they made a decision, resigned from the *News* staff, and set about organizing and financing their own publishing venture.

The name first chosen for the new periodical was *Facts,* but this was soon discarded in favor of *Time.* The original prospectus, "for private circulation," is interesting not only because it shows what was in the minds of the founders at the beginning but also because it points up changes in policy that took place later. It began:

Although daily journalism has been more highly developed in the United States than in any other country of the world—

Although foreigners marvel at the excellence of our periodicals, *World's Work, Century, Literary Digest, Outlook,* and the rest—

People in America are, for the most part, poorly informed.

This is not the fault of the daily newspapers; they print all the news.

It is not the fault of the weekly "reviews"; they adequately develop and comment on the news.

To say with the facile cynic that it is the fault of the people themselves is to beg the question.

People are uninformed BECAUSE NO PUBLICATION HAS ADAPTED ITSELF TO THE TIME WHICH BUSY MEN ARE ABLE TO SPEND ON SIMPLY KEEPING INFORMED.

TIME is a weekly news-magazine, aimed to serve the modern necessity of keeping people informed, created on a new principle of COMPLETE ORGANIZATION.

TIME is interested—not in how much it includes between its covers—but in HOW MUCH IT GETS OFF ITS PAGES INTO THE MINDS OF ITS READERS.

Later in the prospectus, under the subtitle "The Process," we are told:

From virtually every magazine and newspaper of note in the world, TIME collects all available information on all subjects of importance and general interest. The essence of all this information is reduced to approximately 100 short articles, none of which are over 400 words in length (seven inches of type). Each of these articles will be found in its logical place in the magazine, according to a FIXED METHOD OF ARRANGEMENT which constitutes a complete ORGANIZATION of all the news.

One other section of the long prospectus must be quoted; it is headed "Editorial Bias":

There will be no editorial page in TIME.

No article will be written to prove any special case.

But the editors recognize that complete neutrality on public questions and important news is probably as undesirable as it is impossible, and are therefore willing to acknowledge certain prejudices which may in varying measure predetermine their opinions on the news.

A catalogue of these prejudices would include such phrases as:

1. A belief that the world is round and an admiration of the statesman's "view of all the world."
2. A distrust of the present tendency toward increasing interference by government.
3. A prejudice against the rising cost of government.
4. Faith in the things which money cannot buy.
5. A respect for the old, particularly in manners.
6. An interest in the new, particularly in ideas.

But this magazine is not founded to promulgate prejudices, liberal or conservative. "To keep men well informed"—that, first and last, is the only axe this magazine has to grind. The magazine is one of news, not argument, and verges on the controversial only where it is necessary to point out what the news *means*.[2]

The writers of the prospectus were at pains to explain that *Time* was not to be modeled upon the *Literary Digest*, then at the height of its success as a news weekly. The *Digest* presented its news chiefly through the editorial commentary of newspapers, while *Time* proposed to set forth the news more directly, as well as to cover more topics "in a brief, organized manner."

Now our two twenty-four-year-old adventurers in the magazine field set out to sell $100,000 worth of stock to get their project going. They actually sold $86,000 worth, mostly to Yale acquaintances and their families. The largest purchase was made by the wealthy mother of a Yale admirer of Hadden and Luce. To her the two made their best "sales pitch," after which, without asking any questions, the kind lady wrote out a check for $20,000. The young men congratulated themselves on their increasing skill as salesmen, only to learn later that their new stockholder's hearing-aid had not been working well that afternoon and her purchase had been motivated by their own very apparent enthusiasm and her son's recommendations of his friends. The stock the old lady

[2] Quotations are from mimeographed copy furnished by Time Inc., but most of the prospectus is found in Busch, *Briton Hadden,* pp. 60–64. Many of the data given here concerning the early lives of the founders are also derived from the Busch biography

bought, however, was worth a million dollars long before she died.[3]

Though stock sales had fallen short of the sum they had set for the capitalization of their venture, Hadden and Luce, depending on a promise of further help, if needed, from Grandfather Crowell Hadden, a banker, and assisted by a small editorial and management staff, brought out Volume I, Number 1 of *Time* under the date of March 3, 1923. It consisted of thirty-two pages, including the self-cover. Pages measured about eight by eleven inches and each was divided, in the editorial sections, into three columns—a format that became permanent.

The portrait on the first cover was made from a charcoal sketch of Joseph Gurney Cannon; and the "cover story," less than a column long, celebrated the retirement of "Uncle Joe," who was called "the grand old man of Congress." The red margins of the cover, which were to become a distinguishing mark of *Time,* did not appear until 1927. Cover portraits in color began the next year, with one of the Japanese Emperor Hirohito;[4] but they did not become the rule until the latter 1930's. The *portraits chargées,* to which backgrounds indicating the activities of the subjects brought an added interest, began to appear in 1941; paintings made especially for these covers became common in later years, and in the 1960's came the "gate-fold" covers. But at the beginning all was black and white, including the dozen or so pages of advertising in each of the early numbers.

Eleven single-column portraits of dubious quality were found in the first issue, and this inadequate illustration was continued through *Time's* early years. Pictures already used were repeated sometimes in connection with later stories. By 1928, however, the editors had become aware of the importance of their portraits; they were using more, and they were making a studied effort to avoid the stodgy conventionality of most news portraits by emphasizing the subject's special characteristics and peculiarities. Mme. Schumann-Heink, for ex-

[3] This story may be more or less apocryphal; but it is told in Busch, *Briton Hadden,* pp. 76–78; in a mimeographed biography of Luce distributed by *Time;* and in other places. Busch is also the source for facts given regarding other phases of the sales of stock.

[4] *Time,* v. 12, Nov. 19, 1928.

ample, was pictured singing, with her mouth very widely open.[5] Such illustrations, stopping just this side of caricature, were in harmony with the personal descriptions that had come to characterize the magazine's news stories.

The appearance of *Time's* first number was greeted, says Hadden's biographer, with "a burst of total apathy on the part of the U. S. press and public." [6] The two young editors personally took a copy to Albert D. Lasker, head of the great advertising firm of Lord and Thomas, and asked his opinion of it. He looked it over and then advised them to let the first number be the last. "You haven't a chance against the *Literary Digest,*" he said.[7] A further discouragement came from an extraordinary muddle in mailing out the first issues. Most of the original nine thousand subscribers [8] had been secured by a mail campaign on a three-weeks trial basis; but the young ladies hired to prepare the copies for the post office managed, as they worked "in a spirit of good-humored sorority fun," to mix the labels so that some trial subscribers received no copies at all, others received two, and still others three. Later distribution, as well as the entire business and editorial operation, ran more smoothly. Renewals were gratifyingly large, so that by the end of 1925 circulation had reached a hundred thousand, about three-fourths of which consisted of mail subscriptions. Basic rates were five dollars a year, and fifteen cents an issue at the newsstands.

Gross advertising revenue for *Time's* ten months in 1923 was only $14,635, but in 1924 it was $52,827 and the next year $129,074. It virtually doubled annually for the next three years. At the end of 1927, the magazine was clearly a success, with a circulation of about 175,000, gross receipts of nearly half a million from advertising,[9] and a small net profit.

5 *Time,* v. 5, April 27, 1925, p. 13.

6 Busch, *Briton Hadden,* p. 87.

7 Roy Quinlan in *Magazine Industry Newsletter,* March 4, 1958. Quinlan says he was present at the interview.

8 James A. Linen, in an address to the Poor Richard Club, Philadelphia, Feb. 25, 1958, p. 5 of mimeographed copy; and Busch, *Briton Hadden,* p. 87.

9 The source of these figures is the Magazine Publishers Information Bureau, as quoted in *Business Week,* no. 966, March 6, 1948, p. 94. They do not agree with those given by Busch, *Briton Hadden,* p. 186, which may represent net revenue.

JOHN L. LEWIS IN BLACK AND WHITE

Time was three months old when this issue of June 4, 1923, came out. The covers of *Time* have usually been portraits. For the first few years they were black and white only, and the decorative borders shown here were used until 1938. Red margins outside this border motif began in 1927.

MAY 7, 1945—HITLER IS CROSSED OFF

The first issue of *Time* after Hitler's disappearance carried this cover by Boris Artzybasheff. The dripping X is dark red.

JANUARY 13, 1967—MAO AND THE DRAGON

Portraits chargées—that is, with backgrounds indicating the activities of the subjects—brought additional interest. They began in 1941.

Hadden and Luce had begun by paying themselves salaries of thirty-five dollars a week, raised after a year or two to fifty dollars; [10] but now they found themselves wealthy, mainly through their comparatively small holdings of stock in Time Inc. When Hadden died in 1929, he left stock worth over a million dollars to his mother.

The founding partners complemented one another by their differing abilities and personalities. It may seem remarkable that extrovert Hadden, with his little mustache and trim figure, original, prankish, active, could work well in double harness with the serious, shaggy-browed Luce, solid, pragmatic, self-contained; but mutual respect made them a successful team. The original plan was for them to alternate, in short terms, as editor and business manager, but Hadden did the main editorial job for the first four years (except during a vacation of a few months in Europe in 1925) before trading with his partner and becoming general manager. Business was not Hadden's forte, however; the upward curve of advertising revenue, for example, was halted in 1928, the first year of his business control.[11] A week before the sixth anniversary of *Time's* founding, and not long after his own thirty-first birthday, Hadden died of a streptococcus infection. In a boxed announcement on the first page of its next issue, *Time* said, "Creation of his genius and heir to his qualities, *Time* attempts neither biography nor eulogy of Briton Hadden." [12]

Luce had become president of Time Inc. when Hadden left for his European tour and continued in that position until 1939. He was listed also as editor from 1928 to 1949, though he shared that title with Manfred Gottfried for a few years in the mid-forties. He was called editor-in-chief from 1945 to 1964 when he became editorial chairman, but whatever his title or titles, Luce was *Time*'s suzerain after the death of his founding partner, and eventually he became chief stockholder in Time Inc.

The use of many title variants for members of *Time's* staff,

[10] Hodgins, *Span of Time,* p. 3; Busch, *Briton Hadden,* p. 164.

[11] *Business Week,* no. 966, March 6, 1948, p. 94.

[12] *Time,* v. 13, March 11, 1929, p. 9. However a brief biography occupies about a column in the "Milestones" department of this number, and p. 64 is devoted to eulogistic tributes from various persons of distinction.

frequent shifts of personnel, discontinuances and later revivals of some titles, and lack of clear definition of the duties appertaining to each [13] combine to make it difficult to indicate the development of the magazine's staff pattern. A few personalities in the group, however, stand out as significant in the early years.

John Stuart Martin was a cousin of Hadden. A sportsman, he had lost his left arm in a shooting accident, but was still good at golf and soccer. He was graduated from Princeton shortly before Hadden and Luce set out to sell stock in Time Inc., and he joined them in that enterprise with zeal, carrying the campaign into the country club sets in and around Chicago, his home city. Enterprising and genial, Martin helped to develop various Time Inc. ventures; and he was managing editor of *Time* itself for eight years after his cousin's death.

Manfred Gottfried was also a Chicagoan. He was graduated from Yale in 1922 and immediately joined the *Time* organization. A hard worker, he handled the "National Affairs" department for several years, was managing editor (often in collaboration with others) from 1937 to 1943, then co-editor with Luce for three years, and later chief of *Time* and *Life's* staff of foreign correspondents.

John Shaw Billings came to *Time* from the *Brooklyn Eagle*'s Washington bureau in 1929, edited the "National Affairs" department, and was later managing editor for a few years. He was then moved over to *Life,* and eventually became editorial director of all Time Inc. publications for some ten years.

T. S. Matthews, educated at Princeton and Oxford, also joined the *Time* staff in 1929. He was an intellectual, with a sharply critical mind. He had served four years on the *New Republic,* and later he wrote: "The contrast I felt between the *New Republic* and *Time* was a contrast between scholarly, distinguished men and smart, ignorant boys. . . . In any case, I didn't like *Time.* On every piece of copy I typed I could have written with truth, 'I do not like my work.' " [14] Yet he remained on *Time*'s staff (including a few leaves of ab-

[13] See Matthews, *Name and Address,* pp. 261, 270.
[14] *Ibid.,* p. 222.

sence) for some twenty-four years. He served first as book reviewer and editor of the "Religion" and "Press" departments, and later as managing editor, executive editor, and editor. He had his quarrels with Luce, who seems nevertheless to have valued him highly, and with his friend Martin, who once accused him of looking down his nose at *Time*[15]—justly enough, it would appear.

Roy Alexander came to *Time* from the *St. Louis Post-Dispatch* in 1939, serving first as a departmental editor and then for a comparatively long term, 1950–1960, as managing editor. The title of "editor" was revived for him in 1960.

Roy E. Larsen, a Harvard graduate of 1921, joined the *Time* group during its planning period and became its first circulation manager. He succeeded Luce as president of Time Inc., serving in that capacity from 1939 to 1960, after which he was made chairman of the executive committee of that top organization. Robert L. Johnson, Yale '18, was the first advertising manager. He was an employe of E. R. Crowe and Company, advertising agents, but devoted himself wholly to the *Time* account. Crowe himself, Yale '08, was a stockholder in the new venture.[16]

The slogan of *Time* for many years was "Curt, Concise, Complete." The first of these epithets had an unfortunate connotation of rudeness. The magazine was indeed occasionally rude, but the word as used in the slogan was clearly intended to emphasize the brevity of its stories. In the twenty-four editorial pages of the first issue appeared more than two hundred "items" (as Hadden liked to call its separate pieces), ranging in length from three to a hundred lines; and even the leading articles of the "National Affairs" department ran only to two or three hundred words. As to conciseness, in the early years *Time* generally cultivated a terse condensation in its reporting, except perhaps for its "cover stories" and critical articles; later, descriptive settings, dramatic narrative, and editorial commentary tended to change *Time* policy in this respect. If "complete" be taken to mean "comprehensive" (though the words are by no means synonymous), it is meaningful as a

[15] *Ibid.*, p. 231.
[16] Busch, *Briton Hadden,* pp. 81–82.

statement of the magazine's performance. Comprehensive *Time* was from the start, and comprehensive it remained.

This breadth of coverage, together with the fact that its orderly arrangement of content was from the beginning one of the chief virtues of *Time,* calls for a brief examination of the several departments and how they developed. The leader, nearly always in front-of-the-book position, was "National Affairs," its title later shortened to "The Nation." Usually the first section under this heading was "The Presidency," followed often by "The Cabinet," "Congress," "The Supreme Court," "Politics," "Labor," "The States," and other sections suggested by leading topics in the week's domestic news budget. In later years the order of these sections was likely to vary according to the editorial evaluation of the news. The second department was "Foreign News," later called "The World"; it was divided into sections headed by the names of various nations and regions.

In *Time*'s first number "Books" was the third department, rather than the back-of-the-magazine division that it later became. And it is not strange that it was thus honored in the early volumes, for its reviewers were such distinguished writers as Stephen Vincent Benét, John Farrar, and Archibald MacLeish. For the first year or two the book reviews were expected to keep to rather definite patterns; thus the notice of a novel considered first "The Story," then "The Significance," "The Critics," and "The Author." Through the years, as the "Books" department was gradually shuffled backward in the magazine, it lost this rather admirable design and showed much unevenness in quality. When John S. Martin was its editor, books were picked up by various members of the staff, who did notices of them, as Matthews says, "with their left hands." [17] When Matthews took over the department in 1929, he made it a more consistently planned and executed performance. *Time's* book reviews, over the years, gave importance to long summaries of content and trenchant, positive evaluations. They were readable and informative; and they were often severe, making far more use of the hatchet than the honey-jar. Louis Bromfield had been a member of the

[17] Matthews, *Name and Address,* p. 219.

staff in its early months, but his somewhat inferior , *A Good Woman,* was not spared when it appeared in The review began: "This book were better left unpub- . . . . Florid, artificial, repetitious, it is incredibly dull oppy work."[18] On the other hand, no *Time* writer ever rode off on over-enthusiasm in a runaway review.

Other critical departments were "Art," "The Theatre," "Cinema," and "Music." "Art," which began with a single column of items rewritten from the newspapers, varied from year to year under several editors but generally improved as a chronicle of developments in painting, sculpture, and architecture; it became more arresting and valuable in 1945, when full-color illustration was introduced. "Cinema" was a brilliant department at various times, and especially under the editorship from 1941 to 1955 of the poet and fiction writer James Agee. Here was a critic who was tart, witty, and knowledgeable in *Time,* for which he wrote his pieces anonymously, as did all the members of the editorial staff, and much more bitter and blistering in the *Nation,* for which he wrote at the same time, signing his name. After Agee's death, his successors seemed to try to carry on the pattern he had set. "Theatre" was at first largely a guide to current New York plays; later it carried more ambitious reviews of dramatic and musical productions. Louis Kronenberger, drama critic for *Time* from 1938 to 1961, was a distinguished reporter of Broadway. In 1958 "Show Business," devoted to both television and the theater, reduced the importance of the older department. In the same year began a page of "Time Listings" (a revival of an older "Time Table") which catalogued current productions in the theater, the cinema, television, and books, with brief annotations.

Other departments that appeared in the first number of *Time* and became fixtures were "Education," "Religion," "Medicine," "Law," "Science," "Finance" (later divided into "U.S. Business" and "World Business"), "Sport," "The Press" (newspapers and magazines), and "Milestones." This last was a column of paragraphs recording deaths, marriages, divorces, and births of prominent persons. Other departments

[18] *Time,* v. 10, Aug. 1, 1927, p. 32.

were dropped after a year or two, such as the rather pointless "Imaginary Interviews," "View with Alarm," and "Point with Pride." "Aeronautics" eventually became a part of "Transport" and then the "Aviation" section of "U.S. Business." "Crime" became an occasional section of "National Affairs." A department devoted to "Animals" was carried in the 1930's.

When a European war threatened in 1939, *Time* published an excellent special section entitled "Background for War,"[19] later reissued separately. The conflict that began four months later was christened by *Time* "World War II," and a new department was headed "World War," to become eventually "U.S. at War."

The department called "Letters," in the front of the magazine, began in the second year and, stimulated by editorially planted communications,[20] became one of *Time's* most interesting features for many readers; indeed, it attracted so much attention that for a few years (1934–1937) it was made a separate periodical. *Letters* was a fortnightly of twenty pages selling at fifty cents a year and attained a circulation of 21,000. Its motto: "Its writers are its readers are its writers."

How did *Time* get the news reports that filled most of its pages? At first, it simply rewrote newspaper stories, using especially those of the *New York Times*. This was a process already made respectable by the *Literary Digest,* and the courts had made it clear that news itself had no protection under the copyright laws. But by the end of its first decade, *Time* had begun to feel a need for its own services; and besides, it could now afford the cost of such help. It became a member of the Associated Press in 1936, but by that time it had already begun to build its own network of bureaus and stringers.

Of course, a weekly publication must accept the handicap of seeming slow to the readers of the dailies, and moreover *Time* emphasized its tardiness by predating its issues for distribution reasons. For example, the Lindbergh baby was kidnaped the night of March 1, 1932; but the event was not mentioned in *Time* until its issue of March 14, and then it was

19 *Ibid.,* v. 33, May 1, 1939, pp. 30–34.
20 Busch, *Briton Hadden,* pp. 122–23.

said to have happened "one evening last week."[21] The "last week" device, with the actual time not mentioned, was used continually; but the magazine's chief (and proper) method of making up for its lack of timeliness was to emphasize the colorful, supplementary, and often interpretive happenings and situations associated with the main event.

Coverage was enlarged gradually in later years until, by the early 1960's, *Time* had a full-time staff of 17 in its Washington bureau (and this did not include *Life* and *Fortune* men), and 11 bureaus in other United States news centers (averaging four workers to each), besides 113 stringers scattered about the country. In Canada it had 4 bureaus and 34 scattered stringers; and in other countries it maintained 14 bureaus, with 40 staffers and a total of 145 stringers.*

Although it had begun by using newspaper stories as sources, *Time* made a studied effort from the first to avoid the stereotyped style of the dailies. It rejected the "lead" pattern in favor of an expository or narrative form. This was part of its effort to compensate for its lack of timeliness; it had to attract readers by fresh devices. Other techniques were used to this end. Early in *Time's* career, Hadden wrote: "If a President dies, don't run his picture—run the picture of the man who wrote the magazine article which drew from the President his last approving words." Do not feature Edison's birthday when it occurs; wait until the week of the Democratic national convention, "when readers will turn with relief to items on any subject other than politics."[22] Also making up for the new magazine's time-lag was its pungent style of writing—its use of word coinages, blends, puns, inverted syntax, esoteric words, and tropes and epithets of various kinds in nearly every paragraph.

These eccentricities of vocabulary and syntax came to be called "*Time* style." They perhaps owed something to H. L. Mencken, and possibly something to journalists like Walter Winchell and Sime Silverman. Some of *Time's* esoteric

[21] *Time,* v. 19, March 14, 1932, p. 16.

* As of March 1967, there were 18 bureaus abroad and 133 stringers. There were 43 *Time* magazine correspondents outside the United States.

[22] Doris Ulmann, *A Portrait Gallery of American Editors* (New York, 1925), p. 64.

words have found familiar places in the American language—tycoon, a Japanese word not unknown in English before *Time's* advent but given currency by that magazine; pundit, a Hindu word of which the same may be said; and kudos, a Greek term used by *Time* mainly to refer rather sarcastically to honorary degrees. In listing some such degrees of the 1933 crop, *Time* declared, with much truth, under its heading "Kudos": "U.S. colleges give honorary degrees 1) to honor the great and the near-great, 2) to get good commencement speakers, 3) to get benefactions." [23] Fifteen honorary degrees had Headman Luce at last count.

Time's chief word coinages have been blends—scores of combinations of cinema, for example, with other words such as cinemactor and cinemagazine. Some blends were puns, such as politricks and sexational.[24] Others in the early volumes were far-fetched but funny—Menckinsults, Wodehumor, improperganda, Hindenburglary, and tobacconalia.[25] Some seem to need a glossary—Parkavian, cinemanimator, and radiorating—but the context helps out.[26] Compound adjectives in the Homeric pattern were common; bald-domed, moonfaced, and white-maned were favorite Timepithets.[27] Famed, able, potent, nimble, and late great became trademark words of *Time* stories. *Time* also followed occasionally the Mencken style of multiplying epithets. Here is the first paragraph of its review of Sinclair Lewis' *Elmer Gantry:*

BIBLE BOAR

Author Sinclair Lewis, whose position as National Champion Castigator is challenged only by his fellow idealist, Critic Henry Louis

[23] *Time,* v. 21, June 12, 1933, p. 31.

[24] *Ibid.,* v. 12, Oct. 22, 1928, p. 12; *sexational* was used frequently in the 1930's and 1940's.

[25] *Ibid.,* v. 4, Oct. 6, 1924, p. 24; v. 7, April 19, 1926, p. 39; v. 1, July 30, 1923, p. 24; v. 31, Feb. 14, 1938, p. 18; v. 1, Aug. 13, 1923, p. 18. Tobacconalia was used in connection with statistics of tobacco consumption.

[26] Parkavian, *ibid.,* v. 23, Jan. 8, 1934, p. 34, related to Park Avenue, New York City; cinemanimator, v. 23, Jan. 1, 1934, p. 34, applied to Walt Disney; radiorating, v. 28, Sept. 7, 1936, p. 54, applied to speaking over the radio.

[27] For a competent study of *Time's* use of esoteric words, blends, and compounds, see Joseph J. Firebaugh, "The Vocabulary of *Time* Magazine," *American Speech,* v. 15, Oct. 1940, pp. 232–42. See also Busch, *Briton Hadden,* pp. 109–18; and Gerald Frederick Handte, "Some Aspects of Prose Style in *Time* Magazine," unpub. diss., University of Missouri, 1949.

HENRY ROBINSON LUCE, 1898–1967

Luce, with Briton Hadden, conceived the idea of *Time* and made Time Inc. into the greatest magazine publishing success in history. Photograph by Philippe Halsman.

Mencken, has made another large round-up of grunting, whining, roaring, mewing, driveling, snouting creatures—of fiction—which, like an infuriated swineherd, he can beat, goad, tweak, tail-twist, eye-jab, belly-thwack, spatter with sty-filth and consign to perdition. The new collation closely resembles the herd obtained on the Castigator's last foray, against the medical profession (*Arrowsmith,* 1925) and a parallel course is run, from upcreek tabernacles, through a hayseed college and seminary to a big-city edifice with a revolving electric cross. But the *Arrowsmith* plot is altered. This time the Castigator, instead of exerting his greatest efforts in harrying a fine-mettled creature to refuge in the wilderness, singles out the biggest boar in sight and hounds him into a gratifyingly slimy slough. The tale has an obscure hero, another Lewisian lie-hunter who, to purge the last bitter dregs of pity and fear, gets his gentle eyes and mouth whipped to a black pulp by the K.K.K. before he is released. But the boar is the chief sacrifice and its name has the inimitable Lewis smack, Elmer Gantry.[28]

Word caricatures were by no means limited to the critical departments of *Time,* but frequently made their appearance in political commentary:

A paunchy, bald-headed double-chinned man, whose trousers seem never to have been pressed, smiled the smile of vindication. He, Roy Asa Haynes, bright morning star of the Anti-Saloon League from Hillsboro, Ohio, had suffered two years of nearly total eclipse. Last week President Coolidge had him appointed Acting Prohibition Commissioner. . . .[29]

But *Time* style was not based on vocabulary alone; it had other eccentricities. Chief of these was the up-ended sentence, which has been satirized and parodied often.[30] Usually this was an inoffensive device, and it sometimes commanded special interest. President Coolidge's visit to Pine Ridge, South Dakota, to announce the signing of the Indian Citizenship Act, began, with overtones from *Hiawatha:*

To his haughty redskin brothers, to the haughty strong Sioux nation, with his wife and son beside him, with big medicine in his

[28] *Time,* v. 9, March 14, 1927, p. 38.

[29] *Ibid.,* v. 9, April 4, 1927, p. 12.

[30] The most famous of them, and justly so, is the Wolcott Gibbs profile, "Time . . . Life . . . Fortune . . . Luce," in the *New Yorker,* Nov. 28, 1936, pp. 20–25.

pocket, came the pale Wamblee-Tokaha, New White Chief and High Protector—otherwise Calvin Coolidge, 29th U. S. President, but first President ever to visit any Amerindians on one of the reservations set aside for them by their Caucasian conquerors.[31]

Most famous of its preliminary phrases was the one *Time* used with death notices, "As it must to all men, death came last week to . . ." A variation of this locution was sometimes used for birthdays: "As it does to many men, a 42d birthday came to Benito Mussolini, Premier of Italy."[32] When this phrase had become a too familiar *Time* cliché, it was laid aside, as was the inverted sentence. "But nowadays *Time* editors do not think highly of backward syntax," wrote Publisher Prentice in 1945, "except as an occasional way of emphasizing a point."[33] Probably Matthews had much to do with reducing eccentricities of style in *Time*.[34]

Not that the magazine failed in later years to maintain a notable individuality in its use of language. Latter-day *Time* style was sharp and shiny; it had the great virtue of fresh readability. It retained some old devices, such as using a descriptive word as a man's title (Reformer Jones, Beatnik Smith, Frozen-Pie Tycoon Brown); inserting initial possessives (G.O.P.'s Fred Seaton, Iowa's Bourke Hickenlooper, Harvard's Arthur Meier Schlesinger, Jr.); the use of the ampersand for "and" (latterly found mainly in heads); and omission of articles and conjunctions (less frequent by the 1960's). The insertion of bits of information to emphasize *Time's* "research" was notable, such as always giving the middle name of anyone mentioned in the news; telling his age (Pope John XXIII, 80); dropping an identifying word or phrase parenthetically into the middle of his name, as Henry Morton ("Dr. Livingstone, I presume?") Stanley; often supplying a paragraph of historical background in connection with a story; and introducing an occasional footnote.

Nor did *Time* lose its fondness for puns, usually clever but often too studied. A few from 1961 issues are reprinted here.

31 *Time,* v. 10, Aug. 29, 1927, p. 6.

32 *Ibid.,* v. 6, Aug. 10, 1925, p. 13.

33 *Ibid.,* v. 46, July 16, 1945, p. 9.

34 See Griffith, *Waist-High Culture,* p. 82; Matthews, *Name and Address,* p. 218.

In a review of two books of selections from the works of H. L. Mencken, always a *Time* target, we read: "His aim was to high-browbeat 'the populace' with a club: to fight American Gothic, Mencken became the great American Goth."[35] Another book reviewer, or perhaps the same one, wrote: "Disciples are the undoing of holy men, and so it is with Richard Condon, a talented and satirical fantast whose fiercely proselytizing followers regard him as the fifth hoarse man of the Apocalypse."[36] Walter Winchell is criticized for serving the purposes of "pufflicity seekers."[37] In a notice of the motion picture "Breakfast at Tiffany's," based on Truman Capote's "peekaresque short story," we are told that the heroine comes home from work "in the whee hours of the morning" and is eventually induced "to give up mattress money for matrimony. . . . Holly isn't the sort of girl who wears her rue with a diffidence. Holly is the sort of girl who thinks that guilt is less valuable than gold."[38] And we must not omit the parenthetical exclamation in the story summarized from a recent novel: the versatile hero tries a little week-end sketching "and (here we Gauguin!) is startled to find that he is an artist of astonishing power."[39]

Almost from the first, pedant-purists have faulted *Time* more or less seriously for the aberrations of its prose, but the severest criticisms levied against the magazine have been based upon its opinionated reporting of the news. In 1922, when *Time's* prospectus was written, newspaper spokesmen generally were talking about the "objectivity" in their news columns and the limitation of "opinion" to editorial pages. "Objectivity" as thus used was not a scientific word, however; it took little psychology to realize that the news report could never be completely objective, passing, as it must, through the minds and hands of a group of human beings each with his own conscious or unconscious prepossessions. But what the word meant to newspapermen was the quality resulting from an honest effort to see things clearly and report them without

[35] *Time,* v. 78, Sept. 29, 1961, p. 89.
[36] *Ibid.,* v. 78, July 21, 1961, p. 70.
[37] *Ibid.,* v. 77, April 14, 1961, p. 81.
[38] *Ibid.,* v. 78, Oct. 20, 1961, p. 95.
[39] *Ibid.,* v. 74, July 20, 1959, p. 104.

conscious bias and with as little comment as possible. However, by the mid-century editors realized that the world had become so complicated in its politics, economics, and ideologies that more commentary was necessary in order to present the news clearly; and so they swung toward what they called "interpretive reporting." [40] Now, this was very like the policy *Time's* founders had set out in their 1922 prospectus, in which, while renouncing an editorial page and at the same time scoffing at "complete neutrality" in reporting "important news," they went on to promise that theirs would be a magazine of "news, not argument" and would "verge on the controversial only where it is necessary to point out what the news *means*." [41]

But it was not long before *Time* had gone far beyond its stated policy of merely "verging on the controversial in its comment." By the 1930's it had clearly gone quite over the "verge." Much of its "slanted" reporting in that decade and the next one or two consisted of the use of emotion-laden adjectives and epithets—"lean, spidery Léon Blum, whose double hate of the Nazis is that of a Socialist who is also a Jew," "Demagogue McCarthy: does he deserve well of the republic?" and "roly-poly George E. Allen bobbed around Washington like a pneumatic rubber horse." [42] As Bernard DeVoto once observed, in discussing *Time* techniques, "there can be no appeal, by protest or rebuttal, to an adjective." [43]

Then by the mid-forties, while keeping up its adjectival attacks, *Time* launched more and more frequently into full-scale editorializing. In the fall of 1936 it said: "The Spanish Government, a regime of Socialists, Communists and rattle-brained Liberals had emptied the jails of cutthroats to defend itself. . . ." [44] Ten years later: "In the eyes of most U.S. citizens Harry Truman's Administration had bogged down in

[40] For full discussion of this point, see F. L. Mott, *The News in America* (Cambridge, Mass., 1954), chap. viii.

[41] For a fuller statement of the prospectus, see above, pp. 295–96.

[42] *Time,* v. 28 (Aug. 3, 1936), p. 15; v. 58, Oct. 22, 1951, "cut line" for cover portrait of McCarthy; v. 56, Oct. 16, 1950, p. 20, in cover story about Truman's friends of the White House group. Later, when George E. Allen was a golfing companion of Eisenhower, he was referred to in more flattering terms.

[43] *Harper's,* v. 174, March 1937, p. 447.

[44] *Time,* v. 28, Aug. 3, 1936, p. 18.

ludicrous futility."[45] And in between and afterward, judgments were expressed with equal vigor in *Time's* news reports. Secretary of State Dean Acheson was attacked, his successor John Foster Dulles was highly praised, and so on.[46] In the early 1960's *Time* carried a eulogistic "cover story" on Senator Barry Goldwater,[47] and consistently disparaged the Kennedy administration.

Time's attitude of omniscience, strengthened by its rule of anonymity among its writers, irritated many critics. "Each week the world is created absolute and dogmatic," wrote one of them, "the good guys on one side, the bad guys on the other, with *Time* holding the only scorecard."[48] And Norman Cousins, commenting on *Time's* advertising campaign based on the idea of the people's "need to know," observed: "It is important to know. Especially is it important to know the difference between hard facts and sly innuendoes, between information and defamation."[49] A little fable was going the rounds in New York in the 1940's; here is the *New Yorker's* version of it:

> There is a man working for Time, Inc., who has a very dangerous idea. We met this renegade in a saloon the other night and listened to him for a long while as he talked of life in Luce's clean, appalling tower. Looking nervously over his shoulder, he told us of an atmosphere as brisk and antiseptic and charged with muted suffering as a dental clinic, of a queer, lost race of men who have come to speak only upside down and backward, of vast and by no means impossible projects to remake the world beautifully in the image of Yale, of new schemes everyday to put the lonely, desperate art of communication on a business basis, with Timen on the top. Most of all, however, he was troubled by a terrible air of omniscience that seemed to him to mark every man, woman, and child on the payroll, from the tiniest Timan to the boss himself. His eyes were wide and wild as he told us this, draining the green stuff in his glass. "It's all right, though," he said at last. "I know how to fix them. One of these days I'm coming out of my office and I'm going to stand in the

45 *Ibid.*, v. 47, June 3, 1946, p. 20.

46 *Ibid.*, v. 57, Jan. 8, 1951, pp. 10–14, cover story entitled "The Fatal Flaw?" and v. 65, Jan. 3, 1955, "Man of the Year" cover story on Dulles.

47 *Ibid.*, v. 77, June 23, 1961.

48 Ben H. Bagdikian in *New Republic,* v. 140, Feb. 23, 1959, p. 9.

49 *Saturday Review,* v. 41, May 3, 1958, p. 48.

hall and, as loud as I can, I'm going to shout, 'I don't *know!*' " He looked at us blankly, lost in his furious dream. "The whole damn thing will just come tumbling down," he said.[50]

By the 1960's *Time* had become, in the main, a collection of editorial articles, filled with information about news events and situations, and emphasizing vivid narrative and description. Not all the "items" contained expressions of editorial opinion, but a large proportion of them did. Thus *Time* had become not only a newsmagazine but also definitely a journal of opinion.

Taking at random the number dated October 12, 1962, we find the lead story that of the mob violence attending the enrollment of a Negro in the University of Mississippi. This is preceded by an epigraph quoting a few sentences from Lord Mansfield's famous opinion in the 1768 trial of John Wilkes, containing the Latin maxim, *Justitia fiat, ruat coelum.* Then the story begins, in the Victorian manner well established as *Time* style for introductions to major articles:

> Beneath the rich golden-toned sky that October brings to the Deep South, a pleasant morning coolness lingered on the University of Mississippi campus at Oxford. A bell signaled the end of 9 o'clock classes, and students poured from the stately, white-columned buildings. They merged into a sea of laughing, chattering youngsters, milling about on spacious green lawns.

This is soon followed by a statement of the crisis, and that by a vigorous narrative, with a tendency toward the melodramatic when occasion offers, and by picturesque descriptive phrases—the "stony-faced U.S. marshals," the reported "wild, dazed look" in the eyes of General Walker, the "frenzied mob [that] had fought a bloody, nightlong battle," leaving the campus "a nightmarish shambles." And before we have finished the article we find *Time* sitting in judgment and fixing responsibilities: Governor Barnett "was undoubtedly to blame, both for failing to help preserve order, and for bringing on the crisis in the first place." But President Kennedy should have handled the matter more as President Eisenhower had handled "the Little Rock crisis"; "his timing was terrible."

[50] *New Yorker,* v. 20, April 15, 1944, p. 19.

The next article is headed "The Cuba Debate," which *Time* thinks "might even lead to effective action some day." Then comes a report on "The 87th Congress: A Balky Beast"; it begins, "The 87th Congress tried desperately to die last week —and could not even make a success of that." The next "item" is about President Kennedy's speeches in the congressional campaign; at Cincinnati he is said to have "scowled angrily, and declared in a voice made husky by a cold" opinions that somehow do not sound angry in quotation. In the Ohio campaign, "tubby, quippy Mike Di Salle," who had "quarreled with everyone," had "come out of his sulk" and is challenging Republican James Allen Rhodes, 53, weight 193, whom the reporter interviews as he is "dribbling a basketball in the church gym." In California, Democratic Governor Pat Brown had discovered, when "lured reluctantly into a statewide TV debate" with Republican Richard Nixon, "That in a head-on clash he was a dub." But the campaigner after *Time's* heart was "Republican Horace Seely-Brown, Jr., 54, running for the Senate seat being vacated by retiring Republican Prescott Bush" in Connecticut. "Husky Horace" was campaigning by giving away pot-holders.

And so *Time* goes on in this typical number. The international news is just as good reading, just as information-filled, and just as opinion-loaded as that of the United States. In Great Britain, Hugh Gaitskell was "taking a shortsighted, narrowminded stand on the vital issue of British entry into the Common Market—a stand that ranges Gaitskell alongside the most abject left-wingers in his own party and the most bullheaded jingoists on the Tory side."

The "cover story" in this issue deals with advertising and the leaders of that great industry understandingly and comprehensively. *Time* likes advertising, of which it has sixty-seven pages in this number. This informative, typically *Time*-researched article is six pages long. It takes occasion to ridicule mildly the concern of the admen over the footless criticism of a group of economists, sociologists, and historians, whom it names. It decries the "fretting over the attacks of fashionable critics such as Arthur Vance (*The Hidden Persuaders*) Packard, one of the nation's most talented self-advertisers, who pipes the old tune that advertising twists truth and debases public taste."

To finish our leafing through this 112-page number of *Time* with our eyes peeled for editorialized opinion, we must note the consideration that in any periodical critical departments dealing with books and the arts have an inescapable function of opinion commentary, though they may be largely devoted to description and summary, as in *Time*. The department headed "People" often contains no little opinion, as witness the following from the issue we have been reviewing:

> Sharing the bill in the Broadway debut of Liz's estranged husband, Crooner Eddie Fisher, 34, was Frankie's ex-fiancée, South African Dancer Juliet Prowse, 26, who displayed vast areas of skin and even more gall. She pranced onstage as a barely garbed Joan of Arc and slithered her way through a song that pictured the saint as a call girl; then she turned up in some Egyptian gauze and launched into *Cleo, the Nympho of the Nile,* ending with a belly dance that would have fazed Farouk. Snorted one of the critics giving the show a universal pan: "Aside from getting 'A' for anatomy and 'E' for effrontery, Miss Prowse should do herself a favor: forget her career and take Frank Sinatra up on his marriage proposal."

A brief recapitulation of *Time's* positions during ten presidential elections may be interesting. In 1924 it seemed to give Coolidge an advantage, though an effort to be fair was evident. Four years later the same desire for fairness was apparent, though Hoover received more and better space than Smith. In 1932 partisanship, if any, was reversed, and Roosevelt had the advantage in the "play" given to his campaign. F.D.R. was *Time's* "Man of the Year" for 1932, 1934, and 1941. Clearly he had *Time's* support against opposing candidates in 1932 and 1936; but his Supreme Court "packing project" alienated Luce, and Wilkie became *Time's* favorite by October 1940. "For the first time in U. S. history," said the magazine in that campaign, in a characteristically loose historical generalization, "citizens are being asked to judge between the State's rights and the people's."[51] In 1944 *Time* was mildly pro-Dewey in "one of the queerest, bitterest—and closest—of all

[51] *Time,* v. 36, Oct. 21, 1940, p. 36.

the Presidential races in U. S. history."[52] Four years later the magazine was anti-Truman rather than pro-Dewey; it never could warm up to the New York governor. It later observed that it "was just as wrong as everybody else" in its certainty of a Truman defeat.[53] In 1952 it had "cover stories" during the campaign on both Stevenson and Eisenhower; but the latter was clearly its favorite, and it gave prominence to Nixon's attempt to connect Stevenson with Alger Hiss. In the 1956 campaign, *Time* attacked Stevenson severely, saying, for example, that he "promised the farmers everything but the moon," and it ridiculed his running-mate, "Estes-lestes" Kefauver.[54] Meanwhile Eisenhower was the "happy traveler" in his campaigning.[55] Its reputation as a partisan Republican journal, gained in 1956,[56] clung to *Time* between campaigns and in succeeding years. In 1960 there were "cover stories" for both candidates, with fairly even treatment; criticisms of both were pointed out as well as their elements of strength, but the magazine was quick to show anti-administration bias following the election.

The question of *Time's* factual accuracy is not easy to discuss. Probably no issue of any periodical was ever wholly without error. Weekly publication instead of daily issue gives little if any advantage in this respect when coverage is comprehensive. Only the small and highly specialized journals can expect to be comparatively free from error. *Time,* in its early years, made a point of its claim of presenting events "accurately chronicled,"[57] and this made it particularly vulnerable to fault-finders. By the mid-fifties *Time* was employing no less than seventeen full-time staff members to take care of the letters written by readers to the editors, a preponderant number of which were "discussion" letters, arguing points of opinion, and "critical," letters, putting fingers on alleged errors.[58] All these letters were answered, in polite and sometimes even flat-

[52] *Ibid.,* v. 44, Oct. 30, 1944, p. 11.

[53] *Ibid.,* v. 52, Nov. 15, 1948, p. 19.

[54] *Ibid.,* v. 68, Oct. 1, 1956, p. 19; Oct. 29, 1956, p. 17.

[55] *Ibid.,* v. 68, Oct. 29, 1956, p. 18.

[56] See the analysis of partisanship in *UAW Ammunition,* v. 14, Dec. 1956, *passim.*

[57] *Time,* v. 5, June 29, 1925, p. 21.

[58] See *What Makes Time Tick,* folio 4.

tering terms, but by no means always satisfactorily to their writers. As for all men, it has been hard for *Time* editors to admit errors, but they have done so not infrequently. In the letters carried weekly in the front of the magazine, occasionally one appears with such a note as an apology to Admiral Nimitz for saying that his fingers were "gnarled," or the statement: "Misled by a correspondent, *Time* regrets implying that Mrs. Wing . . . hurt her knee at Dr. Shaw's school. where he has substituted square dancing for football. . . ."[59] James A. Linen once acknowledged occasional slips, telling us in his weekly "Letter from the Publisher" that *Time* kept a black book in which its errors were entered, with the proper corrections.[60] He did not tell us how large the black book was. It can scarcely be forgotten that the President of the United States once announced to an audience of many millions in a televised news conference that *Time's* account of the abortive attack on Cuba's Bay of Pigs beachhead in April 1961 was the most inaccurate story of the event he had seen.[61]

By the 1960's *Time* was listing on its "Contents" page more than seventy "Editorial Researchers." "Research" is a word much abused; in contemporary usage, it may stand for looking up a word in a dictionary or gazetteer, or it may mean critical, discriminating, and exhaustive investigation, based on a knowledge of backgrounds and of the most authoritative sources. Certainly the senior editors, the associate editors, and the contributing editors, placed above the editorial researchers in the *Time* staff hierarchy, have dug and delved for much of their material, as true researchers must; and doubtless some of the seventy-odd young ladies have looked up statements in books and even used the long-distance telephone to obtain offhand information from specialists. But in the main, the "research" staffers have been checkers rather than researchers. "Charged with verifying every word, they put a dot over each one to signify that they have." More importantly, we are told,

[59] *Time,* v. 45, April 2, 1945, p. 9; v. 38, Sept. 29, 1941, p. 2.

[60] *Ibid.,* v. 46, Dec. 10, 1945, p. 15.

[61] *Ibid.,* v. 78, Sept. 1, 1961, pp. 14–15. This was an "excerpt" from a forthcoming article in *Fortune.* The President did not point out specific errors, nor were the details of the government's part in the operation ever fully revealed officially.

"their job is to make sure that the story as a whole adds up." [62]

There is a certain fascination about the long lists of staffers that *Time* carried in its "flag" after the 1940's. This is exploited in William Saroyan's play, "Love's Old Sweet Song," in which a subscription salesman for *Time* visits a middle-class home (a term that would offend Saroyan) and in the course of his sales talk begins to name some of the editors. Cabot, the man of the house, insists on repeating each name after him, rolling it on his tongue, and asking if he is "a college man"; but Leona, his wife, interrupts him and says, "Cabot, let the man talk!" So the salesman repeats some fifty names and then goes on, "The Editorial Assistants of *Time* Magazine are—" and Leona encourages him, "Yes, tell us who *they* are!" The salesman, getting the swing of it, then names some thirty more; and when he stops, Leona says wistfully, "No more names?" The salesman, whose own name is Windmore, replies, "No, that just about winds up the editorial department." But Leona begs him, "What were some of those nice names again?" and Windmore obliges. Of course, the family takes a subscription.[63] If Leona still existed in the 1960's, she would be pleased to know that the list consisted of 235 names.

In 1960 came some shifts among *Time's* top names and positions, with younger men moving up. James Alexander Linen III, who had been publisher since 1945, became president of Time Inc. A graduate of Hotchkiss School and Williams College, he had begun as an advertising salesman for *Time* in 1934 and had been advertising manager of *Life* before becoming *Time's* publisher. Succeeding him as publisher of *Time* was Bernhard Machold Auer, former promotion and circulation director of the magazine. Otto Fuerbringer, a member of *Time's* editorial staff for the preceding eighteen years, suc-

[62] For a description of *Time's* editorial processes, see *The Story of an Experiment,* pp. 10–11. Busch, *Briton Hadden,* pp. 136–39, presents a favorable treatment of *Time*'s research and checking system in its early years. For a detailed account of the black and red system of dots used by the checkers, see J. Wendell Sether, "News Magazines Go to Press," *Quill,* April 1959, p. 24.

[63] William Saroyan, "Love's Old Sweet Song," pp. 72–75, in *Three Plays* (New York, 1940).

ceeded Alexander as managing editor in 1960, when Alexander became editor. Hedley Donovan, editorial director of Time Inc. from 1959, became editor-in-chief of Time Inc. when Luce took the title editorial chairman in 1964.*

Time Inc. management was always active, enterprising, ready for new ventures, whether it was purchasing a television station or building a paper manufacturing plant. New magazines were begun: *Fortune,* 1930; *Life,* 1936; *Sports Illustrated,* 1954. These were uniformly successful; the only stumble was an advertising journal called *Tide,* begun in 1927 and sold three years later, when *Fortune* was started. *Architectural Forum* was purchased in 1932, and twenty years later *House and Home* became heir to a part of successful *Forum's* content.† In 1961 Time Inc. established a book publishing division, and soon thereafter Time-Life International set up a Books Department for selling translations of Time-Life books abroad.

Another adventure—this one based on the magazine *Time* itself and promoted largely by Roy E. Larsen—was "The March of Time," which began March 6, 1931, as a weekly CBS radio news program paid for as promotion by Time Inc. It had been preceded by a New York area quiz show called "The Pop Question Game" on WJZ, begun when *Time* was only a yearling; but the network show drew a large national audience. After about a year on CBS, Time Inc. refused to pay the network for air-time and the program was dropped for about six months, during which CBS received so many complaints about its lapse that it was resumed on the basis of free time and free use of the network facilities. The motion picture series "March of Time" was produced by Twentieth Century-

* See footnote 1 for post-1964 changes in editorial personnel.

† In the summer of 1964 *House and Home* was sold by Time Inc. to the McGraw-Hill Publishing Co. In September 1964, Time Inc. ceased its publication of *Architectural Forum.* Time Inc. gave the publishing rights "as a gift" to the American Planning and Civic Association, now called Urban America, Inc., a non-profit educational organization, and publication was resumed with the April 1965 issue, under the same general manager and managing editor.

Time-Life International had begun *Life en Español* in 1953, its only foreign language magazine. In 1962, as a joint project with a local publisher in Japan, the magazine, *President,* modeled on *Fortune,* was begun. The same year, in collaboration with Editorial Abril of Buenos Aires, the general monthly, *Panorama,* began publication.

Fox in 1935, and at the peak of their success these shows were presented thirteen times a year at over nine thousand theaters (some in foreign countries) to an estimated audience of thirty million for each showing. But when the motion picture business declined about 1950, "The March of Time" was transferred to television; it marched out in 1954.

An important factor in *Time's* history throughout these years was the increasing use of color—a development shared by many leading periodicals but not by other newsmagazines. Though occasional full-color covers began as early as 1928, and advertisers began using such illustration more frequently in the thirties, it was not until 1945 that *Time* first placed color pages in its editorial sections. The art department was the earliest beneficiary of this development, but in the next decade full color was extended to other sections—"Theater," "Travel," "Science," "Modern Living," and so on. In the 1960's a total of eight four-color editorial pages in one issue was not uncommon, and at least a third of the advertising was so illustrated.[64]

Time's "Man of the Year" feature, including a full-color portrait of the great man on the cover (painted in latter years by such artists as Boris Artzybasheff, Peter Hurd, and Andrew Wyeth) to accompany a long "profile" sketch in the body of the magazine, became a feature of much interest to readers, many of whom proffered suggestions as to the selection of a subject each December. The list of men so honored began in 1927 with Charles A. Lindbergh; his picture and that of Franklin D. Roosevelt (1934) were the only "Man of the Year" portraits in black and white.[65]

[64] See Bernhard M. Auer, "Letter from the Publisher," *Time,* v. 78, Nov. 3, 1961, p. 7. A large part of this color development has been made possible through research on color-printing techniques carried out by Time Inc.'s subsidiary, Printing Developments, Inc.

[65] Following is a list of those honored by *Time*'s "Man of the Year" recognition: 1927, Charles A. Lindbergh; 1928, Walter P. Chrysler; 1929, Owen D. Young; 1930, Mohandas K. Gandhi; 1931, Pierre Laval; 1932, Franklin D. Roosevelt; 1933, Hugh S. Johnson; 1934, Franklin D. Roosevelt; 1935, Haile Selassie; 1936, Wallace Warfield Simpson; 1937, Gen. and Mme. Chiang Kaishek; 1938, Adolf Hitler (on May 7, 1945, *Time* gave Hitler another cover portrait, with a great "X" scrawled across it); 1939, Joseph Stalin; 1940, Winston Churchill; 1941, Franklin D. Roosevelt; 1942, Joseph Stalin; 1943, George C. Marshall; 1944, Dwight D. Eisenhower; 1945, Harry S. Truman

Time could well afford luxuries in illustration in the years following the depression of the 1930's because it was increasingly prosperous; and the more it expended to make an attractive and informative magazine, the more its prosperity grew. It sold more than nine-tenths of its copies through mail subscriptions, and its renewal rate was high. It reached a half-million circulation in 1934, in the midst of the depression. When it absorbed the *Literary Digest* in May 1938, it gained thereby only a small accession to its list; but it attained the million mark in July 1942. By 1950 it had a million and a half, ten years later two million and a half, and by 1964 almost three million in the United States. It raised its subscription price in 1946 from $5.00 to $6.50 (from 15 to 20 cents at the newsstands) and in 1957 to $7.00 (25 cents at the stands); in 1964 it was $9.00 (35 cents a single copy).*

Multimillion circulations were proving disastrous to many magazines shortly after the mid-century, partly because management of these periodicals thought it necessary to direct their appeal to the mass audience on all levels, as television did. But *Time* aimed at the mass level of college graduates.[66] To use the lingo of some sociologists, *Time* did not expect the "upper highbrow" (or the self-styled "intellectual") to like it; but the "middle highbrow" and the "lower highbrow" were expected to compose its audience, with the addition of some am-

---

(with a rather derogatory "cover story"); 1946, James F. Byrnes; 1947, George C. Marshall; 1948, Harry S. Truman; 1949, Winston Churchill ("Man of the Half-Century"); 1950, "The American Fighting Man"; 1951, Mohammed Mossadegh; 1952, Queen Elizabeth II; 1953, Konrad Adenauer; 1954, John Foster Dulles; 1955, Harlow Curtice; 1956, "Hungarian Freedom Fighter"; 1957, Nikita Khrushchev; 1958, Charles de Gaulle; 1959, Dwight D. Eisenhower; 1960, "16 U.S. Scientists"; 1961, John F. Kennedy; 1962, Pope John XXIII; 1963, Martin Luther King; 1964, Lyndon B. Johnson; 1965, General William Childs Westmoreland; 1966, "Today's Youth."

* *Time's* circulation in the United States in 1966 was over 3,100,000. Its annual subscription price was ten dollars; a single copy was fifty cents.

[66] This aim has been repeatedly stated, notably in Publisher James A. Linen's address to the Poor Richard Club, Philadelphia, Feb. 25, 1958, mimeographed copy, p. 3. The advertisement, "Reaches 2,450,000 well educated, higher income families" (Standard Rate and Data Service, Consumer Magazine Section, Feb. 27, 1960, p. 203) repeats a familiar claim.

bitious "upper lowbrows". With the colleges and universities turning out some half-million graduates a year, here was a large field from which to reap. Of course, this was by no means a specialized audience, but neither was it the general mass audience.

In 1941 *Time* initiated its Latin-American edition, the first magazine ever to be delivered by air express. Editorial content was identical with that of the New York edition, though advertising was not; later four pages of regional news were added. All was in English. Beginning with twenty thousand copies (yearly subscription $10.00), the edition had over eighty thousand by 1964. In 1943 a Canadian edition was begun; it has long been the largest of *Time's* foreign editions, reaching over 250,000 in the early sixties. This also had four additional pages of regional news, eventually edited at Montreal, where the Canadian edition had been printed from airborne film. The Atlantic Overseas edition began in 1944—before the end of the war—"in Stockholm—inside the German blockade and right under Adolf Hitler's nose!"[67] After the war, Time-Life International's Atlantic edition of *Time* was printed in Paris from film flown in from New York and distributed by air to various points in Europe, the Middle East, and Africa. The total circulation of this edition had reached over 200,000 by 1964. *Time* Pacific was established in 1946 for similar distribution from Honolulu, Manila, Sydney, and Tokyo; in 1960 this was separated into two editions—one for Asia and one for the South Pacific. Four years later these had circulations of about 80,000 each.

It will be noted from the above dates that *Time's* growth as an international magazine was correlated with the global outlook growing out of World War II. *Time* was a leader in supplying magazines to U.S. troops abroad. It was the first to offer a miniature "pony" edition for fast transportation overseas (November 1942) and the first to print a "fly-weight" edition for distributions to the armed forces in South Pacific installations—produced in Honolulu and sent by V-mail March 27, 1944—and it claimed many other "firsts."[68] Be-

[67] *Time,* v. 43, Jan. 24, 1944, p. 9.
[68] *Time,* v. 43, April 10, 1944, p. 15.

fore the end of that war it was printed in twenty editions, on every continent except Antarctica.[69] *

Time had trouble, as was to be expected, with foreign governments because of its free-spoken ways. In 1936 it was in difficulties in England because of its treatment of Edward VIII's abdication. In 1939 it was banned from newsstand sales in England, Germany, and Italy for various reasons and for various terms; in Germany it did not return until after the war. Luce, visiting in Paris in that year, found himself sued for five million francs by the Paris Press Association for libeling its members. He got off by saying he was sorry for a "too general indictment of the Parisian press,"[70] but later the venality of many of these papers was disclosed as one of the main causes of the French national catastrophe. Later *Time* had trouble with foreign governments growing out of stories in its various international editions. It drew Peron's wrath in Argentina, and in Bolivia a 1959 article on that country's sad economic condition caused an "international incident" and mob demonstrations against the U.S. embassy at La Paz.[71] The magazine has long been barred from the U.S.S.R. and its satellites.†

Though the circulation of *Time's* five international editions totaled only 621,000 in 1960, the magazine undoubtedly found its way into the hands of many influential leaders and was important in the arena of world thinking. Moreover, it was, on the whole, a good interpreter of its own country to

[69] *Time,* v. 44, Sept. 18, 1944, p. 17.

* In 1966 Time International still has the five basic editions: *Time* Canada, *Time* Latin America, *Time* Atlantic, *Time* Asia, *Time* South Pacific, but there has been great expansion in the number of regional editions within the five areas. Altogether there are now thirty-two regional editions, and in addition, four military editions. These international editions, excluding the military, have over 800,000 circulation. They are printed in Montreal, Atlanta, Ga. (for the Latin American editions), Paris, Tokyo, Melbourne, and Auckland.

[70] *Time,* v. 34, Aug. 28, 1939, p. 45.

[71] *Ibid.,* v. 73, March 2, 1959, p. 25. The sentence that most offended Bolivia did not appear in U.S. editions. It quoted a diplomatic official at La Paz as saying that Bolivia might as well divide its territory and its problems among its neighbors.

† As of March, 1967, no newsstands distribute *Time* in the U.S.S.R., but *Time* reaches 157 subscribers, probably almost all, if not all, officials of the government. The satellite countries of the U.S.S.R. each have some subscribers. Thirty-seven copies go into Red China. Poland has actually allowed some limited newsstand sale.

readers abroad. Publisher Linen, reviewing the story of these editions, once wrote:

The Latin American experiment also demonstrated a basic journalistic principle: most men and women the world over want to read honestly reported news, not propaganda.

Many have disagreed with this belief. Within a year after the air edition began in 1941 . . . a few well meaning people in the U. S. took us to task for publishing in South America the same news stories we distributed at home. They felt that in the interest of hemispheric unity *Time Air Express* should sugar-coat its stories about the U. S. and print only "diplomatic" (*i.e.,* bland and friendly) news about the republics to the south. We would have dropped the whole export project rather than hoodwink readers in any such fashion, but we passed the complaint along to more than 400 business and political leaders in this hemisphere. Ninety percent of them came back with firm support for our decision.[72]

Meantime, the advertising revenue of *Time* outpaced its circulation in growth. Through the 1950's it maintained a third-place position among American magazines in annual advertising revenue, and in 1960 it "became the fourth magazine in history in which advertisers invested more than $50,000,000 for advertising."[73] Advertising rates then ranged from $11,650 for a black-and-white page when used every week in the year to $23,815 for a single full-color advertisement occupying the fourth cover page.

Time Inc. enjoyed a net income in 1936, when the country was recovering from the worst of the great economic depression of that decade, of $2,700,000. In 1960, in which a limited "recession" occurred, it was $9,303,000.[74]

Time's editorial and management staff occupied various headquarters in its early years. At one time it shared, not very happily, a suite of offices with the *Saturday Review of Literature*. In the fall of 1925 it moved to Cleveland, a more central distribution point; but it returned to New York two years later, shortly thereafter contracting with R. R. Donnelly and

[72] *Time,* v. 57, May 7, 1951, p. 18; see also seven of these letters in v. 38, July 28, 1941, pp. 4–6.

[73] *Magazine Industry Newsletter,* March 25, 1958, p. 3; *Annual Report to Stockholders,* 1960, p. 14. [In 1965 Time was in second place in advertising revenue with $80,691,000; see Annual Report to Stockholders, 1965, p. 11.]

[74] *Annual Report to Stockholders,* 1936, p. 6; 1960, pp. 6, 9. [By 1966 Time Inc.'s net income was $37,253,000.]

Sons, of Chicago, for its printing and distribution. In 1940 it began a similar operation in Philadelphia for its eastern circulation; this was transferred to Old Saybrook, Conn., in 1962. In 1944 it set up a printing operation in Los Angeles for western readers, using offset printing from cellophane transparencies flown from Chicago. Later, printing plants in Washington, D.C., and Albany, N.Y., also turned out *Time*.[75]

Time Inc. moved its editorial and management offices to the Chrysler Building in 1932, and soon thereafter began the erection of the great Time and Life Building at Rockefeller Center. In 1960 it moved into a new Time and Life Building at the corner of the Avenue of the Americas and Fiftieth Street. This structure, erected at a cost of $83,000,000, was owned jointly by Time Inc. and Rockefeller Center. It was *Time's* tenth corporate home. Sixteen floors of the building were occupied by 2,200 Time Inc. employees; and five more, sublet at first, would doubtless be filled eventually with more workers for the Time Inc. family of magazines.

This magnificent building, "the tallest and most modern magazine office building in the world," was topped by a ninety-foot sign which flashed alternately upon awed night-time pedestrians forty-eight stories below the blazing words *Time* and *Life*.[76] The structure stood as a monument to the greatest magazine publishing success in history.*

[75] *Time,* v. 43, Jan. 31, 1944, p. 15. [Printing of domestic editions began in Atlanta, Ga., in 1966.]

[76] See the four-page color insert in *Annual Report to Stockholders,* 1960.

* This historical sketch was written in 1962, with some updating in 1964. Because *Time* magazine and Time Inc. have expanded extensively in the past five years, this growth has been noted in starred footnotes. The information in these footnotes was furnished by Frank R. Shea, assistant to the managing editor of *Time,* or was taken from *So We Went Abroad—20 Years of World-wide Publishing by Time-Life International* (New York: Time Inc., 1965).

In 1966 *Time*'s world-wide circulation was nearly 4,500,000. Time-Life Books became one of the ten top book publishers in the world on the basis of its sale of sixteen million books.

Since 1962 Time Inc. has bought its fifth television station (1963), has branched out into the record business with Capital Records (1965), has bought the New York Graphic Society publishing house (1966); and has entered, with General Electric, into a project to create and market educational materials in the United States and abroad (1966). As would be expected, the number of Time Inc. employees has leaped since this original sketch was written. There are now over nine thousand.

On March 3, 1967, Henry R. Luce died. See *Time,* v. 89, March 10, 1967, pp. 26–33.

21

THE YALE REVIEW [1]

YALE'S *New Englander,*[2] grand old quarterly that it was, was much too heavy with theology to compete in the forum of the 1890's. An attempt to popularize it had been made in 1885, when it had been changed to a monthly, and had added a regular discussion of "University Topics" to its table of contents, as well as the words *and Yale Review* to its title. But the new devices had not brightened its fortunes; and when its long-time editor, the Rev. William L. Kingsley, fell ill early in 1892,[3] he decided to discontinue his periodical to make room for another of different character.

The newcomer was the quarterly *Yale Review,* a journal of

[1] TITLES: (1) *The Yale Review,* 1892–1911, 1915–current; (2) *Yale Review,* 1911–15. Subtitles: *A Journal of History and Political Science,* 1892–96; *A Quarterly Journal for the Scientific Discussion of Economic, Political and Social Questions,* 1896–1911.

FIRST ISSUE: May 1892. Current.

PERIODICITY: Quarterly. First Series, May 1892—Feb. 1911 (vols. 1–19; each vol., May, Aug., Nov., Feb.); New Series, Oct. 1911–current (v. 1–current; each vol., Oct., Jan., April, July, until 1928 when they changed to Sept., Dec., March, June, and covers bore names of seasons, *i.e.,* Autumn, Winter, Spring, Summer).

PUBLISHERS: Ginn & Company, Boston, 1892–93; Tuttle, Morehouse & Taylor, New Haven, 1893–1907; Yale Publishing Association, New Haven, 1907–26; Yale University Press, New Haven, 1926–current.

EDITORS: Henry Walcott Farnam, 1892–1911; George Park Fisher, 1892–96; George Burton Adams, 1892–96; Arthur Twining Hadley, 1892–1900; John Christopher Schwab (managing editor), 1892–94; William Fremont Blackman, 1896–1902; Edward Gaylord Bourne, 1896–1908; Irving Fisher, 1896–1911; Clive Day, 1902–11; Albert Calloway Keller, 1902–11; Henry Crosby Emery, 1908–11; Wilbur Lucius Cross, 1911–40 (editor emeritus, 1940–48); Helen MacAfee, managing editor, 1925–49 (editor emeritus, 1950–56); William Clyde DeVane, Edgar S. Furniss, Arnold Wolfers, associate editors, 1940–54; David Morris Potter, associate editor, 1949–54; Paul Pickrel, managing editor, 1949–66; John James Ellis Palmer, 1954–current.

INDEXES: *Yale Review Index, 1892–1911* (New Haven, 1911); *Poole's Index, Readers' Guide, International, Dramatic, Jones, Cumulative.*

[2] See F. L. Mott, *A History of American Magazines,* v. 2 (Cambridge, Mass., 1938), pp. 312–15.

[3] Wilbur L. Cross, *Connecticut Yankee: An Autobiography* (New Haven, 1943), p. 187; also Cross, "Our Historical Antecedents," *Yale Review,* N.S., v. 31 (Spring 1942), pp. 645–48.

116 pages in light green cover, devoted to the discussion of national and international politics, economics, history, and literature. It was edited by Kingsley's son-in-law, Henry Walcott Farnam, professor of economics at Yale.

From the first the *Review* contained many articles about foreign affairs. The lead-off article in the first number was an analysis of "German Tariff Policy, Past and Present" by Henry Villard and Farnam. Edward Porritt, an English journalist and student of politics and economics who had settled in Connecticut, wrote many articles for the journal.

Contributors were drawn chiefly from the home university. William G. Sumner contributed a notable article, "The Mores of the Present and the Future" to the number for November 1909; this was just before his death, and after that event the *Yale Review* carried a symposium on his career and his contribution to American ideas (May 1910). Theodore S. Woolsey was an occasional contributor; and so were Farnam's coeditors, George P. Fisher, Arthur T. Hadley, George B. Adams, Edward G. Bourne, and Irving Fisher. Francis A. Walker (ex-Yale-man) had a strong article advocating the restriction of immigration in the second number. But there were also many from outside the charmed circle. E.R.A. Seligman, of Columbia, was a frequent contributor; and so was H. T. Newcomb, famous railroad lawyer and editor.

The *Yale Review's* own political and economic position may be described as conservative. In an editorial opposing government in industry, printed in its fourth number, it nailed down one plank of its platform with an epigram: "Our strongest means of keeping money out of politics is to keep politics out of money."[4] It opposed government regulation of railroad rates; but its editors were by no means blind to the trends in the relation of government to business, and it gave both sides in the two articles in its issue for November 1905, following this the next year with an editorial advocating putting our house in order by a constitutional amendment "acknowledging" the phases of government control that had grown up.[5]

The *Review* consistently opposed American imperialism. At

[4] *Yale Review,* v. 1, Feb. 1893, p. 341.
[5] *Ibid.,* v. 15, Nov. 1906, pp. 227–29.

the very beginning of the war with Spain, it observed that one way to prove the English critics of our attitude to be wrong was to abstain from any annexation of territory following the war.[6]

The journal's positions on these matters were made plain in a section called "Comment" in the fore part of each number. With Volume V, it began a department of "Notes," in which current events were interpreted, with much emphasis on foreign affairs. Book reviews were important in the journal; they occasionally ran to three or four pages in length, and they occupied from a sixth to a third of the total space.

On the whole, the First Series of the *Yale Review* was pretty dull. There were too many long articles, occasionally running to thirty or forty pages, and the day of the comprehensive dissertation for magazine fare was past. Moreover, specialized learned journals were closing in on its field, and the *Review* felt the pressure. When the *American Historical Review* began in 1896, the *Yale Review* withdrew from the field of history, and Professors George P. Fisher and George B. Adams, specialists in religious and European history respectively, withdrew from the editorial board. This made Farnam's *Review* mainly a politico-economic journal; and when the American Economic Association announced its intention to found a journal in 1911 which, as Farnam wrote, "will cover practically the field hitherto covered by the *Yale Review*,"[7] the end of the road seemed to have been reached.

There was a disinclination to give up, however, and much faculty discussion ensued, with confusion of opinion about what ought to be done under the circumstances. About the only unanimous decision that emerged was that a New Series should be edited by Wilbur Lucius Cross. It is not strange that this choice should have fallen upon Cross. He was an English professor of widely ranging interests in history, politics, economics, society, and the arts, and a strong personality. His brilliant life of Laurence Sterne had recently been published amid general applause. He was in his mid-forties, at the height of his powers. Later he was to become dean of the

[6] *Ibid.*, v. 7, May 1898, p. 3.
[7] *Ibid.*, v. 19, Feb. 1911, pp. 337–38.

graduate school, was to be elected governor of Connecticut four times, running on the Democratic ticket in a Republican state, and was to be honored as chancellor of the American Academy of Arts and Letters.

The decision on an editor was, in fact, enough to start the new magazine. Cross tells how he outlined the policy which was to create a greater *Yale Review* one rainy day under President Hadley's large umbrella. The two met by accident when the president, despite the weather, was on his way to his tailor's to be measured for a suit of clothes; and the meeting afforded Cross the opportunity to submit his ideas for the new journal and obtain Hadley's hearty approval.[8]

It was a new journal indeed. Its attractive blue cover enclosed 224 pages of varied content and wide appeal. The articles were of reasonable length, and there was usually a light essay or sketch and some verse, as well as a section devoted to independent, signed book reviews. Though Yale contributors were prominent (the first article in the New Series, Vol. I, No. 1, October 1911, was an essay entitled "War" by Sumner, published posthumously), the table of contents was spangled with names of writers of nationwide and worldwide reputation. Cross had stipulated that he should pay for contributions. Compared to its forerunners, the New Series of the *Yale Review* was sprightly; it was certainly stimulating and often challenging. Cross once observed that "generous intellectual hospitality promoted liveliness." [9]

There was no comparable publication in America at the time, unless it was the *South Atlantic Quarterly,* which was more regional; the *Sewanee Review* was mainly literary and historical. The new Yale journal was more like the monthly *North American Review* and *Forum.*

If the *Yale Review* under Farnam had been prevailingly conservative, under Cross it showed liberal inclinations. However, it never enlisted under the banner of any cause, firing fusillades in its favor quarter after quarter. Cross was always wary of the special pleading of propaganda. He once wrote: "One of the most important services an editor can render to

[8] Cross, *Connecticut Yankee,* pp. 189–90.
[9] *Yale Review,* N.S., v. 31, Autumn 1941, p. 3.

his readers is to keep the road open for candid statements of different standpoints from writers of exceptional ability and equipment, and to let these writers present their material as their own consciences and minds may direct." [10] Yet, it seems clear that Cross particularly liked such castigators of old-fogeyism as Walter Lippmann, H. L. Mencken, Norman Hapgood, Alvin Johnson, William Allen White, A. A. Berle, Jr., and so on.

It is interesting to note the articles about candidates in the Presidential campaign years. The *Review* was for Yale-man Taft in 1912, and it fired a big shot for him in an article in May of that year; but in the fall it carried pieces about the other candidates as well. Taft himself wrote articles in the campaign years of 1916 and 1920 endorsing Hughes and Harding respectively, while Norman Hapgood wrote for Wilson and Cox. In 1924 and 1928 there were likewise pairs of campaign articles; but in 1932 and 1936 there were nonpartisan reviews of all candidates by Walter Millis, a well-known journalist and Yale alumnus. In 1940 there was a series of fairly nonpartisan articles on the issues from various hands, introduced by Cross; and thereafter comprehensive discussion of the issues appeared in the fall number of each campaign year.

It was almost inevitable that an editor so deeply involved in Democratic politics should have made the *Yale Review* somewhat more than fair to the New Deal. There were certainly "balancing" articles, but they by no means brought the scales even against those in support of Franklin D. Roosevelt and his policies. For example, Alvin Johnson's "The Issues of the Coming Election" in the Summer 1944 number had an unpartisan sound, but it did not, in the end, leave much ground for Republicans to stand upon. It was followed, however, by a plea for the postwar encouragement of private enterprise by James J. O'Leary, Wesleyan University economics professor.

Foreign affairs received much attention in Cross's *Review,*

[10] For general statements of Cross's editorial policy, see Cross, *Connecticut Yankee,* chap. xv; *Yale Review,* v. 19, Feb. 1911, pp. 337–38; *Yale Review,* N.S., v. 31, Autumn 1941, p. 1; Doris Ulmann, *A Portrait Gallery of American Editors* (New York, 1925), pp. 34–37. The quotation from Cross given above is in Ulmann, p. 34.

THE

YALE REVIEW

Edited by WILBUR CROSS

APRIL 

1918

The Strategy that Will Win the War . . .	*Emile Mayer*
The Connaught Rangers. *A Poem*	*W. M. Letts*
The Submarine	*William O. Stevens*
Scandinavian Neutrality	*Maurice Francis Egan*
The New Chemical Warfare	*Julius Stieglitz*
Good Temper in the Present Crisis	*L. P. Jacks*
A New Heaven. *A Poem*	*John Gould Fletcher*
Labor and Reconstruction	*Ordway Tead*
Two Poems	*Louis Untermeyer*
Is the English Language Decadent? . . .	*Brander Matthews*
Dr. Holmes, the Friend and Neighbor .	*M. A. DeWolfe Howe*
Retrospection. *A Poem*	*John Jay Chapman*
Robert Browning and Alfred Austin .	*William Lyon Phelps*
Art, Caviar, and the General	*A. Kingsley Porter*
A Litany in the Desert	*Alice Corbin*
German Intrigues in Persia	*A. C. Edwards*
Book Reviews	

Published Quarterly by the

YALE PUBLISHING ASSOCIATION, Inc.

PUBLICATION OFFICE: 10 DEPOT STREET, CONCORD, N. H.

EDITORIAL OFFICE: 120–125 HIGH STREET, NEW HAVEN, CONN.

Copyright, 1918, by The Yale Publishing Association, Inc.

$2.50 a year 75 cents a copy

Application pending for entry as second-class matter at the Post Office at Concord, N. H.

Notice to reader: When you finish reading this magazine place a one-cent stamp on this notice, hand same to any postal employee and it will be placed in the hands of our soldiers and sailors at the front. No wrapping—no address—
A. S. Burleson, *Postmaster General.*

AFTER A QUARTER OF A CENTURY—

The *Yale Review* for April 1918. The quarterly had been founded in 1892. Wilbur Cross, whose name appears beneath the title here, was the editor from 1911 to 1940.

THE

YALE REVIEW

A National Quarterly

SPRING 1967

Latin American Left Wings . . . . *John J. Johnson*

Wallace Stevens: The Ironic Eye . . . *Frank Lentricchia, Jr.*

Ballistic Missile Defense . . . . . *Bruce M. Russett*

The Tragedy of Justice in *Billy Budd* . . . *Charles A. Reich*

Moscow's New Look in Western Europe . . *John H. Hedley*

HCE's Chaste Ecstasy . . . . . . *J. Mitchell Morse*

Four Summers. *A Story* . . . . *Joyce Carol Oates*

Verse . . . . *Ramona Weeks, Jay Wright, Myron Turner, Jean Valentine, John Unterecker, Cynthia D. Logan*

New Books in Review . . . . . *Laurence B. Holland, Marie Borroff, C. Vann Woodward, Angus Fletcher, A. Dwight Culler, Georges May, Daniel X. Freedman*

New Records in Review . . . . . . *B. H. Haggin*

Letters and Comment:
Notes from a Flood Journal . . . . . *Peter W. Denzer*

Reader's Guide . . . . Contributors

YALE UNIVERSITY PRESS

—AND AFTER THREE QUARTERS OF A CENTURY

The *Yale Review* for Spring 1967, not greatly changed in outward appearance. The subtitle "A National Quarterly" began to appear on the cover in January 1920.

especially during the periods of the two world wars. During and after the first of the great conflicts, much appeared about life and attitudes and problems in Europe. There was some notable discussion of the literature produced by the war. In the thirties domestic problems seemed to predominate, though Cross turned more than ever to foreign writers for his contributions. From England he brought in John Galsworthy, H. G. Wells, W. R. Inge, John Maynard Keynes, Virginia Woolf, Julian and Aldous Huxley, Harold J. Laski, and others. Edith Wharton acted as literary scout for the *Yale Review* in France, and wrote much about French matters herself. Perhaps André Maurois was the journal's most faithful French contributor, and Thomas Mann the most assiduous of the Germans. Then when another world war threatened, the *Review* became concerned more and more with affairs overseas. Out of nine nonfiction pieces in the number for Winter 1940, seven dealt with foreign matters. The journal continued during the war and for a number of years thereafter to give more than half its space to the consideration of the problems of foreign states and our relations with them. "Are We Doing Our Home Work in Foreign Affairs?" asked an article by John W. Gardner in the number for Spring 1948; the author urges readers and schools to study such matters, and he also admonishes government to find men educated in this field for the state department.

The *Yale Review* had an important influence on contemporary verse. Many of Robert Frost's poems appeared in its pages, including "The Hill Wife" (April 1916). The number for January 1917 contained work by Frost, Amy Lowell, Edgar Lee Masters, and Louis Untermeyer—a good quartet. Stephen Vincent Benét's "American Names" was in the number for October 1927. Edwin Arlington Robinson, John Gould Fletcher, Sara Teasdale, Conrad Aiken, John Crowe Ransom, Robert P. Tristram Coffin, Witter Bynner, and Leonard Bacon were among the better known poets who contributed to the *Review*. From England came work by John Masefield, John Drinkwater, Walter de la Mare, and Alfred Noyes. Two or three poems usually appeared in each issue.

From the beginning, the New Series was accustomed to

tuck into each number, just ahead of the book review section, a light essay, or a scene from American folklore, or a bit of interesting reminiscence. Essayists often seen in its pages were Arthur Colton, Charles S. Brooks, and Agnes Repplier. Though some of these sketches were virtually short stories, it was not until about 1930 that the *Review* began the practice of printing a piece of short fiction in that position each quarter. These stories were commonly of high quality. Two that Cross picked out as masterpieces he had been proud to publish were de la Mare's "Broomsticks" (October 1925) and Ivan Bunin's "On the Great Road" (Summer 1934). Kay Boyle, Dorothy Canfield, Evelyn Scott, William Saroyan, Paul Horgan, and Walter Van Tilburg Clark were among leading American contributors of short stories; while from England came work by Hugh Walpole, John Galsworthy, and L. A. G. Strong.

Book reviews continued to be important; there were usually some fifty pages of them. One can almost never generalize about any set of reviews by separate hands; but on the whole, those that Cross got together for his quarterly were keen, astute, and often authoritative. Though often about half of the reviewers were drawn from the Yale faculty, many other institutions and diverse walks of life were represented. Literary criticism was found outside this department, of course. Thomas Mann wrote on "Goethe" for the Summer 1932 number; and from time to time William Lyon Phelps, Henry Seidel Canby, Henry A. Beers, Chauncey B. Tinker, Robert Herrick, and John Erskine wrote literary articles. For some years Robert Littell wrote a quarterly review of "Outstanding Novels" that was published in the front advertising section.

From the foregoing informal analysis of content, it will be noted that the *Yale Review* has not lacked for famous names. Perhaps it may be instructive if, Jack Horner-like, we stick in a thumb and pick out a plum here and there from the numbers of the early thirties. Thornton Wilder's *Queens of France* (Autumn 1931) was the only play the *Review* ever published. In Leon Trotsky's "Hitler's National Socialism" (Winter 1934) the author prophesied war in a few years. Carl L. Becker's "When Democratic Virtues Disintegrate" (Summer

1939) was a brilliant article by a favorite contributor. A notable trio were John Dewey's "The Liberation of Modern Religion" (Summer 1934), H. L. Mencken's "American Language" (Spring 1936), and Robert M. Hutchins' "University Education" (Summer 1936).

Most of the tables of contents in the twenties and thirties were studded with famous names. Let us take one number (January 1921) at random. Here we have, among those already mentioned, Frost, Inge, Drinkwater, Low, Repplier, and Cross; and besides them, Israel Zangwill, Brander Matthews, Archibald MacLeish, and Franz Boas. Among the book reviewers in this number were James Harvey Robinson, Vida D. Scudder, Dallas Lore Sharp, and John Gould Fletcher.[11]

When Cross took over the management of the *Yale Review,* its ownership was transferred from Farnam (who had employed Tuttle, Morehouse & Taylor, of New Haven, as publishers) to the Yale Publishing Association. This organization, of which Edwin Oviatt was president, was already issuing the *Yale Alumni Weekly.* Oviatt became business manager of the *Review.* Farnam donated "a generous subvention to the business management for a period of three years,"[12] which enabled the new publication to get off to a flying start.

The New Series was greeted with plaudits from many readers, and the editors were heartened by such remarks as the one by a great newspaper that a star of the first magnitude had "swum into the constellation of our magazines."[13] The circulation, which long had been quoted at eight hundred, quadrupled in the first year of the New Series, and went on steadily to ten thousand at the end of World War I, and then to eighteen thousand shortly before the 1929 crash. This cir-

[11] The following ought also to be mentioned as frequent contributors to the *Review:* Marquis Childs, who began with articles based on his research in the life and economics of Sweden, and later wrote political articles; H. A. De Weerd, who wrote on military operations; James Truslow Adams, a Yale-man who wrote much on American society and history; Gamaliel Bradford, who did biographical studies; Sir Arthur Salter, who wrote on economic questions; William Henry Chamberlin, who contributed discussions of foreign trade and politics; William Ernest Hocking, who discussed philosophy, society, and the universe.

[12] Cross, *Connecticut Yankee,* p. 188.

[13] *Ibid.,* p. 191.

culation growth was aided by the reduction in price during the war years from the old $3.00 to $2.50 a year. The price was raised again to $3.00 in 1920 and to $4.00 in 1921 without injury to circulation growth; but when circulation dropped in the depression thirties, lowering the price once again to $3.00 apparently did little good. It was set at $3.50 in 1949.[14] The size declined in the forties to 190 pages, and in the fifties to 160. Moderate prices—a few hundred dollars per article—were paid to contributors. In 1928 "a friend of the University Press" established a yearly award of $2,000 for the best article in the *Review* on national or international affairs.

At the crest of its prosperity, the journal was taken over by the Yale University Press, which was then (1926) in its own eighteenth year. It was a suitable union. President Hadley had observed, upon his retirement several years earlier: "The thing on which I look back with most satisfaction in my whole administration is the developing of the publishing work of the University and the recognition it has obtained throughout the world. I regard the *Yale Review* and the Yale University Press as our best products in the last twenty years."[15]

Cross continued as editor-in-chief throughout his incumbency as governor of Connecticut. Henry Seidel Canby and Edward Bliss Reed were helpful assistants in the early years of his editorship; but the former went to New York in 1920 to edit the *Saturday Review of Literature,* and the latter resigned a few years later to become educational director of the Commonwealth Fund. Miss Helen MacAfee had joined the staff in 1914; she had then just returned from teaching in the American College for Girls in Constantinople, and her wide interests and literary sense made her an able managing assistant, and from 1935 until 1949 she was *de facto* editor-in-chief;[16] in the latter year she retired, with the title of editor emeritus. She was followed in the editorial chair by David

[14] The above figures are derived from the reports in *N. W. Ayer & Son's* annual *Directory of Newspapers and Periodicals.* [The price was $5.00 a year in 1966; circulation was around 7,000.]

[15] Quoted in an eight-page brochure issued by Yale University Press in 1929, entitled "A University Press Comes of Age." The quotation is found in slightly different form in Cross, *Connecticut Yankee,* p. 199.

[16] See obituary note, *Yale Review,* N.S., v. 45, Summer 1956, pp. 496–97.

Morris Potter, professor of American history, who had the assistance of an able advisory board and of Paul Pickrel, of the English department, as managing editor. In 1954 J. E. Palmer brought to the editorship of the *Yale Review* a rich experience as a teacher of English in southern universities and editor of the *Southern Review* through 1940–1942, and the *Sewanee Review* through 1946–1950.[17]

The *Yale Review* at its best realized with adequacy the dream of its editor, which he once expressed thus:

> I thought of it . . . as a quarterly addressed to the "general reader," and devoted to all the many-sided interests of the mature mind—public affairs and social questions, literature and art, science and philosophy. That is, it would be cultural and educative in the broadest meaning of these words, and yet good reading. Keeping abreast of the times, this quarterly review of my imagination would show behind its material a rich background of knowledge of the past. Above all, it would give scope and leeway for the free play of the creative intelligence over the whole configuration of the contemporary scene.[18]

The table of contents in the fifties was not so bright with illustrious names as it had once been, but there was still that "free play of the creative intelligence" which has long distinguished the *Yale Review*.*

[17] See Mott, *American Magazines,* v. 4 (1957), pp. 739–40.

[18] Ulmann, *Portrait Gallery,* p. 34.

* This historical sketch was written about 1960. Footnotes 1 and 14 have been updated.

Here is Frank Luther Mott's own account of his *History of American Magazines.* He wrote it at a time when he was partway through volume V and still hoped to complete the projected six-volume work. "Unfinished Story" was a chapter in his *Time Enough: Essays in Autobiography,* which was published in 1962, approximately two years before his death. The University of North Carolina Press, publisher of that book, has permitted the reprinting of "Unfinished Story" here.

UNFINISHED STORY; OR, THE MAN IN THE CARREL

THIS is the story of a project. It is the unfinished story of something that began in a boyish enthusiasm, developed over a term of years into what may be fairly called "a large undertaking," and eventually became a lifetime work. This is how it all came about.

Country editors in the 1890's could receive all the magazines they wanted free, provided they inserted in their weekly papers little excerpts from the current issues, usually with taglines telling about how interesting *Harper's* or *McClure's* was that month. These were attractive "fillers" and also good advertising for the magazines.

Throughout his long career as editor of weekly papers, my father took advantage of this exchange arrangement with many good magazines. Since we never threw any of them away, they accumulated in piles and dusty heaps. Thus the roomy closet of the upstairs room assigned to my brother and me came to be filled with old copies of *Harper's, Scribner's, Century, Atlantic, Review of Reviews, McClure's, Cosmopolitan, Chautauquan, St. Nicholas,* and so on. These old magazines were a source of endless pleasure to me on Sunday afternoons, rainy days, and many long evenings. Am I wrong in thinking that the stories, essays, and poems in those old pages were really ambrosial fare? Or have they been transformed from something very ordinary by the magic of my fond recollection? No; as I have thumbed through them in recent years, looking at pictures by the "high society" Charles Dana Gibson, the romantic Howard Pyle, the humorous A. B. Frost, and others, including the matchless engravings of old masters by Timothy Cole, and rereading Kipling and Hardy, Howells and Garland, and T. R. and Carnegie and Tarbell—I still find that the nineties seem to me a golden age in our periodical literature.

Certainly those magazines were precious to me when I pored over them in my boyhood. Moreover, it seemed shameful to allow them to lie in their sterile stacks there in our closet. So I arranged them in proper files and then set out to index them. I had never heard of *Poole's Index,* or of the newer *Readers' Guide to Periodical Literature;* I was thinking only of making the treasures I had at hand more accessible for a rather indeterminate use in a vague future. My father had discarded a big ledger after brief use of it in one of his less successful side-ventures in business, and its empty pages were just what I needed. Mine was an author-title index. I worked on it pretty faithfully in my spare hours for the better part of a year, as I recall—until other activities diverted my attention. Occasionally thereafter I came back to it to index a few numbers of the beautiful and superior *Scribner's* of the nineties, or the old John Brisben Walker *Cosmopolitan,* with the broad red band up and down the left side of its cover.

My parents did not quite approve of this too sedentary, inkhorn occupation of mine, but they did not forbid it. I stuck to it through a kind of compulsion that I am not psychologist enough to explain. Boyhood is always subject to brief zealotries and manias, which sometimes have important effects on later life. My indexing experience tended to systematize my liking for old magazines—to put it on paper, as it were, and give it a kind of permanence. The names of the great magazinists were like a chime of bells in my memory—Brownell, Boyesen, Garland, Hardy, Howells, Kipling, Stevenson, Stockton. . . .

And so, years later, when Professor Trent, at Columbia University, asked me what topic I wished to explore in a doctoral dissertation, I suggested a historical essay on the *Galaxy,* and he warmly approved. The *Galaxy* was a New York magazine distinguished by the contributions of Henry James, Mark Twain, and Walt Whitman. Begun in 1866, it was merged twelve years later with the *Atlantic Monthly*. But I soon found that the story of the *Galaxy* and its editors and contributors was only part of the closely-woven pattern of the history of American periodicals in the decade or two following the Civil War; and before I realized it, my plan had broadened and I was writing about the whole output of magazines and journals and their various trends and phases during that active and yeasty post-bellum period.

Long before this study was finished, however, I had become disturbingly conscious of the fact that the roots of the publishing and editorial movements of the period I was examining were deep in the preceding years, and also what I saw developing in the seventies was to continue with greater momentum and clearer meaning in the eighties and nineties. In the concluding paragraph of my dissertation, I declared that the years I had been studying comprised a transition period; but I have since learned that all historical "periods" are transitional, each of them not only displaying the effects of causes discernible in times that have gone before but also containing the seeds of things that may flower in times to come. As an idea, this may seem obvious and unexciting; but as a practical, working situation, based on an array of facts, it was dynamic and revolutionary in my own plans for study and writing.

What I then resolved to do was to write a comprehensive history of American magazines from the beginnings by Franklin and Bradford down to the present—and to include in the term "magazines" the journals, reviews, periodicals, and all the salmagundi of serials that were not actually newspapers. I have often thought that a more suitable title for my work would be "A History of American Periodicals." But when I took the project to academic advisers and publishers, it was "A History of American Magazines," and the title stuck, and so it is, for better or worse.

I must say that not all of those academic advisers looked with favor on my project. One very great scholar shook his grey head gravely and told me that two lifetimes would not be enough to do what I contemplated. Others here and there (and I canvassed opinions widely) were also skeptical. But when I took these discouraging verdicts to Thomas A. Knott, himself as great a scholar as any of them, he removed the corncob pipe from between his teeth and asked, "You really want to do this, don't you?"

"That I do," I replied.

Knott took one of those big kitchen matches that he carried about with him from his pocket and lit his pipe; and when he had taken a puff or two, took the pipe out of his mouth, blew out a cloud of smoke, grinned, and said: "Go ahead!"

With men like Craig and Knott at Iowa and Trent and Van Doren at Columbia believing in me, it was easier to buckle down to work. And support soon came from another quarter. Francis G. Wickware was a Canadian-born mining engineer who had early turned to academic and literary pursuits and was, when I knew him, the suave and scholarly editor for D. Appleton and Company. He became interested in my project, and in due time I had a contract for the publication of the first volume of my history.

Perhaps the very great scholar who was once my adviser had a clearer understanding of the difficulties of the task I had set myself than I did. I have sometimes thought he was right about his "two lifetimes." I had a full academic load of teaching and administration, and my writing and research had to be done at night and on week ends and holidays. The "I Led Three Lives" chap on television had nothing on me: I led one life in classroom and office, one in libraries and at my typewriter, and a third as a family man and a social being of sorts. I am not complaining; I loved it.

My family never failed in sympathy and helpfulness. When the time came to make an index for the first volume, my wife and our daughter Mildred and I locked the doors of our house, answered no telephone calls, and lived on canned soup, sandwiches, and coffee until the job was done. My wife and daughter accompanied me on visits to great libraries: we once made a family junket of a tour of eastern repositories, moving into a Worcester apartment while I was at work in the American Antiquarian Society collection, and living for a while in Concord while I commuted to Boston to dig in the Boston Public Library and that of the Massachusetts Historical Society. Later, when Mildred was a graduate student in archeology at the University of Chicago, we made trips to the Newberry and Crerar occasions for family reunions.

When the second volume was ready for the press, I had publisher trouble. Appleton had been impatient for it; but it was not finished until the years of the great depression were upon us, bringing with them embarrassments for that publishing house. The first volume had done well enough in sales; but quick-moving titles were now considered imperative by the bankers of the D. Appleton-Century Company, which was soon to become D. Appleton-Century-Crofts. They might be able to take my book in a year or two, but if I did not want to wait . . . I did not, and soon had the manuscript back on my hands. I queried other publishers; but I was now in the position of trying to place the second volume of a series that the publishers of the first volume had rejected, and all were wary. They were more than wary; they were unanimously uninterested. Eventually the Modern Language Association set up a committee to read my manuscript and report on its acceptability for issue by means of the organization's Revolving Book Publication Fund. But when the three scholars had waded through the two thousand typed pages and had agreed to recommend publication, it was discovered that the Revolving Fund had no funds in it to set it revolving any more—or at least not for some time. Then it was that the incisive, ever-helpful Howard Mumford Jones, who had just joined the Harvard faculty and who had been a member of the M.L.A. committee that had read my manuscript, wrote me that this thing must be published and that he was taking the matter up with Dumas Malone, the new director of a rejuvenated Harvard University Press. This made the beginning of a happy connection with a publishing house that has been as tolerant and forbearing as any author could wish. In 1938 it brought out under its own imprint the first three hefty volumes of my history.

There were some protests (rather amused and mild ones, I think) over the publication of a work carrying some very rude and raucous material by this decorous press. They were apparently called forth largely by Malone's impish insertion in the fall announcement of the press of an illustration from my second volume showing a scandalous cover page from the *Police Gazette.* Out in St. Louis the *Post-Dispatch* carried an editorial entitled "An Eyebrow-Raiser," which I have since learned was written by Irving Dilliard, and which is amusing enough to reprint here:

> Things must be in a pretty way in old Cambridge as the brown leaves float down through these October afternoons from the arching elms in Harvard Yard. It is the "Autumn Announcement" of the Harvard University Press, 38 Quincy St., hard by President Conant's house, which gives cause for the alarm.
>
> For the Harvard University Press is a dignified adjunct of our oldest institution of learning, presided over by the scholarly Dr. Dumas Malone, lately editor of the monumental "Dictionary of American Biography." Its publications are sizable tomes on such things as prehistoric remains, Indo-Iranian languages, early Greek elegists, boundary conflicts in South America, Chinese historiography, time budgets of human behavior, the physiocratic doctrine of judicial control, and the old Frisian Skeltana-Riucht.
>
> And yet the first illustration in the current catalogue to fall beneath our eye was of deepest saffron. Two buxom dames of the hourglass school of feminine charms are presented as entertaining two heavily-mustached, silk-hatted gentlemen in a lavish chamber. The blonde is reclining on a royal couch, while the brunette perches on the knee of the other guest, an endearing arm about his neck. Champagne bottles are in evidence and tell-tale goblets in air. The caption: "A masher mashed—How a Chicago youth of the 'too awfully sweet for anything' variety, while essaying the role of a lady killer, was taken in and done for, like the veriest countryman, by a brace of sharp damsels and their male accomplice. See page 7."
>
> And then we found that we were looking at the cover of the *Police Gazette* for July 26, 1876, reproduced as an illustration from Frank Luther Mott's three-volume "History of American Magazines," which the Harvard Press is issuing this fall!
>
> Let the editor and his cohorts defend their illustration on the score of historical scholarship if they will. Just wait until they hear from the teacups that tinkle across the blue Charles in prim and proper Back Bay!

The *Harvard Alumni Bulletin* further reported that some private letters to the press had commented on the fact that "this reprehensible illustration from the naughty Seventies" appeared on the verso of a reproduction of a portrait of Oliver Wendell Holmes which was being used as the frontispiece of Felix Frankfurter's *Mr. Justice Holmes and the Supreme Court,* also announced for publication that fall. "To pained protestors against the indignity to the revered Justice," observed the editor of the *Bulletin,* "the reply has been made that he himself would undoubtedly be tickled to find the *Police Gazette* on his august back."

Such publicity, I assume, did not injure the sale of the books. Deeply aware of the faults and shortcomings of my work, I awaited the reviews with trepidation. I have always envied those authors who say they never read reviews of their books, and have wondered why, when they do not read the criticisms, they rail so fiercely at the critics. But the reviewers—both those who have really read the books and those who have only thumbed through them—have nearly always been more than kind to me. Thus publishing troubles, crowded schedules, the expense of travel to distant repositories, and the occasional laborious searching, enumerating, and recording of the contents of the great directories and catalogs—all of this at last began to seem like a tale of harrowing adventure turning out well in the end. Then came the satisfaction of a Pulitzer Prize for the second and third volumes, and later a Bancroft Prize, even more rewarding both in sentimental value and in cash, awarded by Columbia University to the fourth volume. Nor was I unappreciative of recognition by Sigma Delta Chi and Kappa Tau Alpha. And so I have been heartened to go on in my later years with the fifth and sixth volumes.

I do not wish to imply that I have found my labor on these big books generally irksome. Quite the contrary. A great deal of it has been tedious and tiresome, indeed; but on the whole, the essential fascination of the task has remained fresh and strong enough throughout the years to make the work continuously enjoyable.

A great library has always been to me a kind of minor heaven, and its librarians angels in disguise. Sometimes a very dusty, ill-ventilated and ill-lighted heaven, to be sure, with its angels carefully concealing their wings. There may seem to be no end of monkey-like climbing of winding iron stairs, ramps, and runways in the great bookstacks; of lifting heavy volumes from high shelves and blowing the dust off them; of hunting comfortable, lighted desks and table on which to work—but there is nevertheless a feeling of romantic adventure about it all and, more than that, a kind of satisfaction and contentment in the midst of such rich treasures.

Yet I see a certain irony in the figure of a lone researcher working in the stacks of a great library. I remember one of those "fillers" with which Mencken and Nathan used to stop up chinks in pages of the old *Smart Set.* I cannot find it now, but it ran somewhat like this:

> A man sits at a small desk in a carrel in the midst of the bookstacks of a great library. All about him tower the high shelves—mountains of books with little iron paths running high up along their sides. Thousands, millions of books, bound in cracked calfskin, faded cloth, stout buckram. Serried row on row of books in battalions and armies—ancient, medieval, modern—fat and thin, tall and short. Multitudes of dusty books towering above and about the man in the carrel. What is the man doing? He is writing a book.

They may laugh at the men in the carrels, and we may laugh at ourselves; but we continue to dig away, and to enjoy it, and to hope that the results may, in some strange way, justify our activities. I have spent many happy hours among the treasures that lie behind the small green door of the library of the American Antiquarian Society in Worcester, Massachusetts. For months and years I had a passing acquaintance with the stone lions that guard the great edifice at Fifth Avenue and Forty-second Street in New York. I have invaded many of the cloistered repositories of books held by the older historical societies in the East, as well as less formally guarded collections in the Midwest. The AP-2 stacks of the Library of Congress have been a second home to me through sweltering summer months as well as weeks of winter cold. I knew the L.C. when its Rare Book Room was a littered, airless attic, and when many magazine files were shelved along dark corridors; now the Rare Book Room is a place of light and joy, with controlled temperature and humidity, and the class periodicals are also to be found in the great air-conditioned annex.

I have spent long days and evenings in Chicago's Newberry Library, where I found the shelves richly laden and the staff helpful; and when its doors closed at night I would hurry down North Clark Street's "skid row," illuminated mainly by bursts of light from cheap nightclubs, on the half-hour walk to my hotel. In the John Crerar Library, then in the Chicago Loop but now soon to be moved, I found exciting files of rare technical journals. The Iowa State Library in Des Moines formerly possessed a surprising abundance of files of old magazines, and the officials there would allow me to work in its stacks all alone at nights and on Sundays when I would run away from Iowa City over week ends and holidays. Perhaps I owe most of all to the great university libraries at Iowa, Missouri, Wisconsin, Columbia, Pennsylvania, Western Reserve, Northwestern, and Harper Memorial at Chicago. I have worked, too, from time to time in some of the great city libraries; New York's I have mentioned, but I have vivid memories too of those in Boston, Chicago, and St. Louis. All these I list out of sheer gratitude and could name many more. Few libraries have seemed to me unfriendly; few librarians have seemed reluctant to afford all the help that could reasonably be asked by the man in the carrel.

Long ago I set up a time-and-work program that called for finishing my magazine project in 1950. What has chiefly prevented such a consummation has been the interruption of my schedule by other writing tasks that have forced themselves (or so it seemed) upon me from time to time—a history of American newspapers, a history of best sellers in the United States, an expository and descriptive book on news and how it is handled in the United States for the "Library of Congress Series in American Civilization," a study of Jefferson and his relations with the press, annual collections of best news stories in the thirties, and other books I have wanted to write or, in some cases, to edit. Then there were extensive contributions to the *Britannica* and some to several other encyclopedias, many book reviews, some work for USIS, occasional more or less scholarly papers, and even some short stories. Many of these books and articles have been rather closely connected with my magazine undertaking; but, after all, they were diversionary. A more single-minded dedication to a fixed goal would have brought my chief work to completion on schedule. Yet I have always returned faithfully—after other "pursuits and excursions"—to the magazine study, as I shall return to it again after this little book is finished. As the errant lover in Ernest Dowson's poem protested, "I have been faithful to thee, Cynara! in my fashion."

I should be unhappy if, by devoting as much space as I have here given to one man's experience in a big research-and-writing project, I should leave any reader with the thought that I consider these books of mine to be history on the grand scale. There are many kinds of historical writing. There is, for example, what I am wont to think of as "grand history," which deals with epic movements of peoples or elucidates the meaning of a series of great events. But, among the various types, there is also a humble kind of history that Moses Hadas recently called "ancilla," and Justin Winsor once referred to (in describing his own work) as "shreds-and-patches history." This is the category in which my work belongs—though I am encouraged to think that I have, here and there, helped to define patterns of thought (and sometimes lack of thought) in the American past.

And I do hope yet to see all six fat volumes of my *History of American Magazines,* in their handsome Belknap Press bindings, on my shelves. If not, however, I shall never complain that I have not found time enough but I shall confess frankly that my dereliction has been due to finding, through the years of my life, too many allurements in too many projects, all of them tempting me from the straiter path.

BIBLIOGRAPHY OF FRANK LUTHER MOTT'S WRITINGS ON AMERICAN MAGAZINES

1928 *American Magazines, 1865–1880.* Submitted in partial fulfillment of the requirements for the Ph. D., Faculty of Philosophy, Columbia University. Iowa City: The Midland Press.

1928 "*The Galaxy:* An Important American Magazine," *Sewanee Review,* v. 36 (Jan.–March), pp. 86–103.

1928 "A Brief History of *Graham's Magazine,*" *Studies in Philology,* v. 25 (July), pp. 362–74.

1928 "The *Christian Disciple* and the *Christian Examiner,*" *New England Quarterly,* v. 1 (April), pp. 197–207.

1930 *A History of American Magazines,* vol. I, 1741–1850. New York: D. Appleton and Co.
 2nd printing, Cambridge, Mass.: Harvard University Press, 1939.
 3rd printing, Belknap Press of Harvard University Press, 1957.
 4th printing, 1966.

1935 "One Hundred and Twenty Years," *North American Review,* v. 240 (June), pp. 144–74.

1938 *A History of American Magazines,* vol. II, 1850–1865. Cambridge, Mass.: Harvard University Press.
 2nd printing, Belknap Press of Harvard University Press, 1957.
 3rd printing, 1967.

1938 *A History of American Magazines,* vol. III, 1865–1885. Cambridge, Mass.: Harvard University Press.
 2nd printing, Belknap Press of Harvard University Press, 1957.
 3rd printing, 1967.

1944 "Evidences of Reliability in Newspapers and Periodicals in Historical Studies," *Journalism Quarterly,* v. 21 (December), pp. 304–10

1948 "Fifty Years of *Life:* The Story of a Satirical Weekly," *Journalism Quarterly,* v. 25 (September), pp. 224–32.

1951 "Periodicals," *Collier's Encyclopedia.*

1954 "The Magazine Revolution and Popular Ideas in the Nineties," *Proceedings of the American Antiquarian Society,* v. 64, Part 1 (April), pp. 195–214.

1955 "Magazines and Books, 1975: A Merging of Two Fields," *Journalism Quarterly,* v. 32 (Winter), pp. 21–26.

1957 "The Magazine Called 'Success,'" *Journalism Quarterly,* v. 34 (Winter), pp. 46–50.

1957 *A History of American Magazines,* vol. IV, 1885–1905. Cambridge, Mass.: Belknap Press of Harvard University Press.

1960 "A Twentieth Century Monster: The Mass Audience," *Saturday Review,* v. 43 (Oct. 8), pp. 59–60.

1962 "The Midland," *Palimpsest,* v. 43 (March), pp. 133–44.

1962 "Unfinished Story; or, The Man in the Carrel," in *Time Enough: Essays in Autobiography* (Chapel Hill: University of North Carolina Press), pp. 169–180.

1963 "Iowa Magazines—Series 1," *Palimpsest,* v. 44 (July), pp. 285–316.

1963 "Iowa Magazines—Series 2," *Palimpsest,* v. 44 (August), pp. 317–80.

1967 "The American Mercury," *Menckeniana,* no. 22, Summer, pp. 9–10.

1968 *A History of American Magazines,* vol. V: Sketches of 21 magazines, 1905–1930. Cambridge, Mass.: Belknap Press of Harvard University Press.

INDEX TO THE FIVE VOLUMES

BY ROBERT J. PALMER

AE (George William Russell), IV:425
A. M. E. Church Review, III:71
Abbey, Edwin Austin, II:397, 401, 477; III:188; IV:151, 544
Abbot's Monthly, III:53
Abbott, Edward, III:233, 454*n,* 455–56; IV:124
Abbott, Eleanor Hallowell, IV:550; V:83
Abbott, Elenore Plaisted, IV:724
Abbott, Ernest Hamlin, III:422*n,* 433–34
Abbott, Francis Ellingwood, III:78
Abbott, Jacob, I:367, 745; II:387, 395
Abbott, John Stephens Cabot, I:353, 745; II:58, 176, 302, 362, 389, 429; III:76*n,* 258, 263, 377; IV:293
Abbott, Lawrence Fraser, III:422*n,* 428, 431, 434
Abbott, Lyman, II:253, 273; III:76*n,* 86, 304, 423*n;* IV:59, 295, 398, 546, 547, 776; V:282
  as editor, III:422*n,* 426–33
Abbott, Willis John, IV:362, 617
Abbott, Willys S., III:53
Abdullah, Achmed, III:490; IV:114*n,* 422; V:86, 119, 258
Aberdeen, Dakota Territory, III:158
Abolition, *see* Slavery debate
Abolition Intelligencer, I:164, 797
Abolitionist periodicals
  in nationalist era (1794–1825), I:164
  in expansionist era (1825–50), I:797; II:275–90
    circulation, II:281, 283
    financing, II:283–85
    format, II:278
    restrictions, II:279
  in Civil War era (1850–65), II:290–96
    trends, II:140–42
Abolitionists
  in expansionist era (1825–50), I:456–63, 597
    antislavery agitation and, I:456–57
    persecutions, I:457–58, 460–61
    satires, I:781
  in Civil War era (1850–65), II:38
    Emancipation Proclamation and. II:294
    John Brown's raid, II:292
    restrictions against, II:108
    sentiment for, II:140
  antipolitical position of, II:290–91
  clergy and, I:286, 290
  political views of, II:290
  Thirteenth Amendment and, II:295
  women's rights and, II:291
Academician, I:148, 796
Academy, IV:268
Acanthus, III:177
Accident Assurance, IV:351*n*
Acetylene Journal, IV:184*n*
Acheson, Dean, V:315
Ackermann, Jessie, IV:765
Acme Haversack of Patriotism and Song, IV:254*n*
Acta Columbiana, III:166, 269; IV:560
"Ada Clare," *see* McElheney, Jane
Adam, III:69*n*
Adam, G. Mercer, IV:54*n*
Adamic, Louis, V:12
Adams, Brooks, IV:225
Adams, Charles, I:115
Adams, Charles Francis, I:697; II:236, 237; IV:721, 777
Adams, Charles Francis, Jr., II:244; III:123, 289, 337, 439
Adams, Charles Kendall, II:248; IV:517
Adams, Cyrus Cornelius, II:414, 415; IV:458
Adams, F. B. ("Yank"), III:210
Adams, Frank Ramsay, IV:618
Adams, Franklin P., III:487, 531; IV:566; V:84
Adams, Frederick Upham, IV:204
Adams, George Burton, V:329*n,* 330–31
Adams, Henry, II:220*n,* 247–48, 260; III:21, 23, 31, 263, 282; IV:136; V:121
Adams, Herbert Baxter, III:545; IV:181, 263, 264
Adams, J. Q. (religious editor), II:63
Adams, James Alonzo, III:77*n*

Adams, James Truslow, II:404; IV:522, 730; V:57, 338*n*
Adams, John, I:116; II:227
Adams, John Coleman, IV:194
Adams, John Quincy, I:123, 155, 176, 226, 255, 409, 748, 778; II:41
Adams, John T., I:345
Adams, John Taylor, IV:520
Adams, Joseph Alexander, I:322, 522, 612
Adams, Phineas, I:124, 253
Adams, Robert, II:467
Adams, Samuel Hopkins, III:487; IV:458–59, 460, 465, 466, 471, 595, 604, 744; V:85, 290
Adams, William Taylor ("Oliver Optic"), I:493; II:101; III:174, 175*n*, 176, 178, 210; IV:274, 420
Adams' Magazine, I:139
Addams, Jane, III:514; IV:192, 195, 546, 547, 603, 744, 745, 746, 747; V:211
Addisonian essay, I:41, 89
Ade, George, IV:196, 458, 497; V:121, 134
Adee, David Graham, III:533
Adeler, Max, I:592; III:558
Adenauer, Konrad, V:323*n*
Adjuster, IV:351*n*
Adler, Elmer, V:4
Adler, Felix, II:252; IV:200, 278, 279
Adult education, IV:264–66, 357
Adulteration of food, IV:460; V:137–38
Advance (Chicago), II:374*n*; III:76, 86, 297; IV:292–93
Advance (New Orleans), IV:93
Advance (San Francisco), IV:175
Advance Advocate, IV:221*n*
Advent Harbinger, II:74
Advent Review, II:74
Adventist magazines, II:74
Adventure, V:84
Advertising
  in early magazines (1741–94), I:116
    first, I:34–35
    Massachusetts tax, I:92
  in nationalist era magazines (1794–1825), I:200
  in expansionist era magazines (1825–50), I:466, 516–17, 754, 766; II:266
    agricultural magazines, I:720
    eclectic magazines, IV:674
    literary magazines, IV:674
    patent medicine, I:426
    "puffing," I:478–79
    scientific periodicals, II:319
  in Civil War era magazines (1850–65)
    business magazines, II:342
    contraceptive advertising, II:37
    eclectic magazines, II:450; IV:679
    expenditures, II:16
    family magazines, II:417, 471; IV:679
    literary magazines, II:383–84; IV:679
    military magazines, II:549
    police gazettes, II:328
    rates, II:14
    religious magazines, II:368, 372
    taxes on, II:7
    trends, II:13–16
    women's magazines, II:437
  in post-Civil War magazines (1865–85)
    abuses, III: 11–12
    agricultural periodicals, III:11
    booksellers' magazines, III:492
    comic magazines, III:553–54
    decorative design, III:12
    family magazines, III:10–11, 423, 425
    illustrated weeklies, III:10
    juvenile magazines, III:11
    literary magazines, II:399; III:9–10, 322, 378, 399, 405
    mail-order, III:37–39, 99
    music journals, III:196
    police gazettes, III:11
    political magazines, III:12
    rates, III:10–11
    reading notices, III–11
    religious magazines, II:375
    trends, III:9–12
    women's magazines, III:11
    women's rights magazines, III:391, 394, 447
  in Gilded Age magazines (1885–1905)
    abuses, IV:31–32, 245, 460–61
    agricutural magazines, IV:337
    charity magazines, IV:743
    circulation-building, IV:17
    comic magazines, IV:565, 667
    family magazines, IV:484, 492
    general magazines, IV:596–97, 611, 614, 681
    growth, IV:245
    illustrated periodicals, IV:460, 464, 565
    improved artistry, IV:28–29
    jingles, IV:30–31, 133

literary magazines, IV:126, 245–46, 674–75, 681
major advertisers, IV:22–28
market-advertising patterns, IV:21–22
medical journals, IV:526–27
national advertising, IV:22–28
pets, IV:382
rates, IV:21, 484, 492, 539
reform campaigns, IV:460–61
revenues, IV:21, 586, 597, 611
review periodicals, IV:66, 662
salacious advertising, IV:32
satirical magazines, IV:646, 667, 669
threat of trusts, IV:33
trade-marks and, IV:33–34
urban weeklies, IV:654
women's magazines, IV:362, 537, 539, 766
in modern magazines (1905–)
agricultural magazines, II:435; V:37–38
art magazines, V:167–68
booksellers' magazines, V:62–63, 66, 69
current events magazines, IV:574; V:298, 322, 327
family magazines, IV:497, 504
fashion magazines, IV:760, 762
gardening magazines, V:37–38, 44, 48
general periodicals, IV:606, 692, 694, 696, 698–99, 711, 715, 723; V:32
geographic magazines, IV:631
homes magazines, V:37–38, 44, 155, 158
illustrations, V:34–35
literary magazines, V:122–23, 167–68
publishers' magazines, V:62–63, 66, 69
rates, IV:423
revenues, IV:473, 699–700, 715
review magazines, IV:787–88
society magazines, IV:760, 762
women's magazines, IV:549, 554, 586, 768, 771
abuses of, V:138
newspaper, III:272–73; IV:538
rate directories for, V:69
techniques of, II:17–18, 358–59; III:12
Advertising Age, IV:247*n*
Advertising agencies, III:12
Advertising codes, IV:549
Advertising directories, V:68–69
Advertising journals, II:17; III:98, 109, 155, 195, 273–74; IV:246–47
Advocate of Christian Holiness, III:81
Advocate and Family Guardian, II:211*n*
Advocate of Moral Reform, II:211
Advocate of Peace, II:211; III:312
Aegis, III:94
Aeronautical World, IV:335
Aesculapian, IV:143*n*
Aetna, III:146
Afric-American Presbyterian, III:75*n*
African Repository, I:457, 798; II:141; IV:238
Afro-American Press Association, IV:214
Agassiz, Louis, I:304; II:78, 138, 504*n;* III:106, 503
Age, II:113
Age of Jackson (Schlesinger, Jr.), V:218
Age of Steel, II:92
Agee, James, V:306
Aggressive Methodism, IV:305
Agitator, III:94
Agnew, John Holmes, I:306*n*, 307*n*, 398, 397*n*, 606*n*, 613
Agnosticism, II:257; III:88; IV:277–78
Agnostic periodicals, III:89; IV: 277–78
Agora, IV:97
Agrarian discontent, III:124, 148–51
See also Populist movement; Populist periodicals
"Agrarians," V:116
Agricultural Advertising, IV:337
Agricultural college magazines, IV:341*n*
Agricultural machinery magazines, III:151; IV:188
Agricultural magazines
before 1865, I:152–54, 194, 317–19, 441–45, 494, 524, 728–32; II:11, 14, 34, 88–91, 432–34, 435–36
in post-Civil War era (1865–85), II:376, 434; III:128, 151–62, 465
in Gilded Age (1885–1905), II:434; IV:186*n*, 336–45
modern (1905–), I:732; II:434–35; V:36–38
See also Agriculture; *names of specific agricultural magazines*
Agricultural Museum, I:152–53, 794
Agricultural Review, II:348
Agricultural Student, IV:341*n*
Agriculture
discussed in magazines
before 1850, I:61, 82, 93, 96, 106, 112, 115, 221, 538, 563

Agriculture—*Continued*
Civil War era, II:91, 222, 319, 343, 471
after Civil War, III:99, 424; IV:336, 779
economic depressions and, IV:157–58
technological advances in, III:151
See also Agrarian discontent; Prices, agricultural; *and names of specific agricultural magazines*
Agriculturist and Legal Tender, III:155
Aguinaldo, Emilio, V:73
Ahern, Mary Eileen, IV:143
Aiken, Albert W., III:43
Aiken, C. A., I:534*n*
Aiken, Charles Sedgwick, IV:105
Aiken, Conrad, II:260; III:541; IV:440, 729; V:210, 242, 336
Aikman, Duncan, V:12
Ainslee's Magazine, IV:49; V:250–54
Ainslee's Smart Love Stories, IV:49*n*
Airplane magazines, IV:335
Airplanes, *see* Aviation
Aitken, J. F., III:186
Aitken, Robert, I:26–27, 36–37, 87–91
Aked, Charles F., V:32
Akeley, Carl Ethan, IV:785
Akerly, Dr. Samuel, I:215*n,* 267
Akers, Mrs., *see* Allen, Elizabeth Akers
Akins, Zoë, IV:654; V:266
Akron, Ohio, information periodical in, IV:54
Alabama Baptist, II:65*n;* III:73*n*
Alabama Historical Reporter, III:262
Alabama Medical Journal, IV:313*n*
Alabama School Journal, IV:270*n*
Alarçon, Pedro de, V:117
Alarm, III:302; IV:172–73
Alaska-Yukon-Pacific Exposition (1909), IV:782
Alaskan Herald, III:57*n*
Alaskan Magazine, IV:109
Alaskan periodicals, III:57; IV:108–9
Albany, N.Y.
magazines in, before 1865, I:154, 347, 442*n,* 443, 445, 491; II:88–90, 432*n*
post-Civil War magazines in (1865–85)
agricultural magazines, II:90, 432*n*
educational periodical, III:170
legal journal, III:144
medical journal, III:140*n*
music periodical, III:197*n*
nondenominational magazine, III:83
sports magazine, III:210*n*
magazines after 1885
agricultural magazines, II:432*n,* IV:340
astronomical journal, II:79*n*
eclectic magazine, IV:56
historical periodical, IV:140*n*
legal journal, IV:347*n*
medical journal, III:140*n*
music periodical, III:197*n*
nondenominational periodical, III:83
outdoor magazine, IV:633
Albany Law Journal, III:144, IV:347*n*
Albany Medical Annals, III:140*n*
Albee, Ernest, IV:303*n*
Alberti, L. B., I:295
Albion, I:131, 358, 397, 427, 513, 797; II:128, 129, 198: III:256
Albion, N.Y., III:111
Alboni, Marie Emma Lajeunesse, II:195
Albrand, Martha, IV:713
Albrecht, Heinrich, IV:58*n*
Album, I:354, 400, 798; IV:674
Alcoholism, I:57, 440
See also Prohibition movement; Temperance; Temperance magazines
Alcott, Amos Bronson, I:487, 687, 691*n,* 703, 704, 705, 707; II:239; III:78, 163, 386
Alcott, Louisa May, I:713*n,* 714–15; II:20–21, 270, 551; III:99*n,* 175, 247, 327, 423, 501; IV:538
Alcott, William Alexander, I:541*n,* 543
Alden, Henry Mills, I:1; II:469*n,* 484, 487, 504*n;* III:23, 32; IV:35, 36–37, 43, 114, 190
as editor, II:383*n,* 396–97, 401, 403
Alden, Isabella (Mrs. G. R.), III:177
Alden, Joseph, I:669; II:265
Alden, William Livingston, IV:559
Aldine, III:184, 191, 199
sketch of, III: 410–12
Aldington, Richard, V:173, 230
Aldrich, Bess Streeter, III:389; IV:552, 709
Aldrich, Mrs. E. A., II:52
Aldrich, James, I:361
Aldrich, Mildred, IV:389
Aldrich, Nelson Wilmarth, IV:462, 494
Aldrich, Thomas Bailey, I:613, 651; III:28, 175*n,* 228, 229, 237, 238, 240, 257, 321, 549; IV:35, 451, 680
as contributor, II:26, 39, 174, 271, 377, 400, 497, 504*n,* 507, 523, 524
as editor, II:45, 353, 493*n,* 510; II:357

Alethian Critic, I:206*n,* 792
Alexander, Archibald, I:530, 533, 767
Alexander, Caleb, I:134*n*
Alexander, Charles, I:343, 355, 425, 427, 544, 674; IV:671*n,* 672–75, 683–84
Alexander, Eben Roy, V:293*n,* 304, 321
Alexander, Hartley Burr, IV:390*n;* V:179*n,* 180, 184
Alexander, Jack, IV:709, 712
Alexander, James Waddel, I:530, 533
Alexander, John White, II:397, IV:151, 720
Alexander, Joseph Addison, I:530, 533
Alexander's Messenger, see: Weekly Messenger
Alexandria, Va., II:70
Alfred Center, N.Y., III:85*n*
Alfriend, Frank H., I:629*n,* 656
Alger, Horatio, Jr., II:35, 101, 410; III:175*n,* 178, 511; IV:274, 417–18, 609, 610
Alger, William Rounseville, I:284*n,* 286, 290
Alkahest, IV:92*n,* 390*n*
"All God's Chillun Got Wings" (O'-Neill), V:13
All the Year Round, II:509*n*
"Alleghan," I:465
Allen, A. B., I:444, 728
Allen, Charles A., V:179*n*
Allen, Devere, III:355
Allen, E. C., III:37–38; IV:246, 365
Allen, Edward Frank, III:396*n,* 401
Allen, Mrs. Eliza C., II:57
Allen, Elizabeth Akers (Mrs. Akers), II:504*n;* III:229, 231, 374, 463
Allen, Fred W., IV:466
Allen, Frederick Lewis, II:493*n*
Allen, George E., V:314
Allen, Grant, II:255; IV:51, 514, 685
Allen, Hervey, IV:503
Allen, J. S., I:448–49
Allen, James Lane, II:398*n;* III:400, 465, 549; IV:93, 113–14, 389–90, 490
Allen, Joseph Henry, I:284*n,* 285*n,* 286, 289–91; II:72; III:506*n,* 597
Allen, Nathan, I:447
Allen, Paul, I:204, 239, 293–94
Allen, Richard L., I:444, 728
"Allen, Samantha," *see* Holley, Marietta
Allen, Stephen T., I:713
Allen, T. Ernest, IV:304, 407–8
Allen, Thomas, I:364*n*
Allen, William Francis, III:336, 347
Allen, William Henry, I:669; III:267*n*
All-fiction magazines, IV:417–23
Alliance, III:53, 83, 539
Alliance-Populist movement, *see* Populist movement
Allibone, Samuel Austin, II:551
Alligator, II:186
Allingham, Margery, IV:475
Allinson, William J., I:773*n,* 774
Allison, Edward P., II:93
Allison, William O., II:92*n;* III:133; IV:188
Allison, Young E., IV:351*n*
Allston, Washington, I: 173, 255, 409, 436, 546*n,* 723
All-Story Weekly, IV:421, 618
Allyn, Dwight, IV:115
Allyn, Lewis B., IV:360*n,* 465
Almoner, I:206*n,* 794
Along the Way, IV:184*n*
Alphabet reform, II:212
Alsop, Joseph Wright, Jr., IV:713
Alsop, Stewart, IV:713
Alston, R. A., III:154
Alt, Adolph, III:142
Altemus, Henry, IV:141
Altgeld, John Peter, IV:115*n,* 172, 181
Altruist, III:300
Altruist Community, III:300
Altruistic Review, IV:52, 284
Altsheler, Joseph Alexander, III:400*n*
Aluminum World, IV:183*n*
Alumni quarterlies, IV:74–75
Amalgamated Copper, V:75
Amalgamated Journal, IV:221*n*
Amateur Gardener, V:131
Amateur magazines, II:100; IV:386–91
Amateur photography, IV:149, 634, 636
Ambler, R. P., II:210*n*
America (Chicago), III:54*n,* IV:60–61
America (Jesuit magazine), III:68*n*
American (Omaha), IV:300
American (Philadelphia), III:41; IV:60, 178
American Academy of Arts and Letters, V:332
American Advertiser Reporter, IV:247*n*
American Advocate of Peace, II:211*n*
American Agency Bulletin, IV:351*n*
American Agriculturist, I:444; II:11, 88, 435–36; III:7, 99*n,* 152; IV:337
  sketch of, I:728–32
American Amateur Photographer, IV:149
American Analyst, IV:363
American Ancestry, IV:140*n*
American Angler, III:210
American Annals of the Deaf, IV:194

American Annals of Education
founding of, I:491
on *Ladies' Magazine*, I:350
sketch of, I:531–43
American Anthropologist, IV:308
American Antiquarian (Chicago), III:112*n*
American Antiquarian (New York), III:113*n*
American Antiquarian and Oriental Journal, III:112
American Antiquarian Society, V:344, 348
American Anti-Slavery Reporter, I:457, 802
American Anti-Slavery Society, I:457–58, II:140, 283; III:333
American Apiculturist, III:161
American Apollo, I:31*n*, 789
American Architect, III:129
American Art in Bronze and Iron, IV:148*n*
American Art Journal, III:185, 191, 196*n*
American Art News, IV:147
American Art Printer, IV:248*n*
American Art Review, III:185, 191
American Art Union, I:437; II:190
American Artisan, III:136
American Artisan and Patent Record, II:80; III:115
American Athlete, IV:379
American Author, 142, IV:142
American authors and themes, neglect of, II:229, 387, 393
American Banker, II:94; IV:349
American Baptist, II:65*n*; III:73*n*
American Baptist Magazine
founding of, I:134
sketch of, I:251–52
American Baptist Reflector, III:73*n*; 292*n*
American Bar Association, Code of Professional Ethics, IV:346
American Bee Journal, II:91; III:161; IV:345
American Berkshire Record, III:160
American Biblical Repository, I:308, 371
American Bibliopolist, III:235
American Bicycling Journal, III:213
American Bimetallist, IV:163*n*
American Blacksmith, IV:183
American Bookseller, III:235; IV:127
American Booksellers' Guide, III:235
American Botanist, IV:310
American Boy, II:274; IV:273, 393
American Brewer, III:135
American Brewers' Gazette, III:135
American Brewers' Review, IV:186*n*
American Builder, III:130
American Building Association News, III:130
American Cabinet Maker and Upholsterer, III:136
American Canoeist, III:211
American Catalogue, III:493
American Catholic Historical Researches, III:261; IV:137*n*
American Catholic Quarterly Review, III:68
American Catholic Review, IV:298
American Celt, II:77
American Chatterbox, III:175*n*
American Checker Review, IV:382
American Cheesemaker, IV:186*n*
American Chemical Journal, III:109
American Chemical Review, III:110
American Chess Bulletin, IV:382
American Christian Review, II:74
American Church Monthly, II:69
American Church Review, II:364; III:75
American Churchman, II:70*n*
American Citizen, I:160*n*
American Civil Liberties Union, V:14, 21, 22
American Clubman, IV:116
American Colonization Society, II:141
American Contractor, III:130
American Cookery, IV:364
American Cotton Planter, II:89
American Counting Room, III:147*n*
American Creamery, IV:186*n*
American Cricketer, III:220; IV:377
American Cultivator, I:444*n*, 804; III:151
American Cyclist, III:213*n*; IV:379
American Dairyman, III:160
American Dental Journal, IV:317
"American Destiny," II:151
American Druggist, III:133; IV:318
American Druggists' Circular and Chemical Gazette, II:92
American Ecclesiastical Review, IV:298
American Eclectic, I:307*n*, 397–8, 805
American Economic Association, V:331
American Economist, IV:166
American Educational Digest, III:169*n*
American Educational Monthly, II:99*n*; III:167
American Electrician, IV:321
American Elevator and Grain Trade, III:135

American Engineer, III:113
American Engineer: the Railway Mechanical Monthly, II:297*n*
American Engineer, Car Builder and Railroad Journal, II:297*n*
American Engineering and Railroad Journal, II:297*n*; IV:332–33
American Equal Rights Association, III:393
American Exchange and Review, II:94*n*
American Exporter, III:147
American Fabian, IV:203–4
American Farmer, I:153; II:88, 436; III:154, 215
American Farmer, Livestock and Poultry Raiser, III:161*n*
American Fashion Review, III:134
American Federationist, IV:220
American Field, III:210*n*
American Florist, IV:342*n*
American Forestry, IV:343*n*
American Forests, IV:342–43
American Forget-Me-Not, IV:3*n*
American Freedman, III:283
American Freeman, IV:206*n*
American Freemason, II:215; III:314
American Free Trader, III:292
American Friend, I:774; IV:296
American Fruit Grower, IV:341
American Funeral Director, III:133
American Furniture Gazette, III:136*n*
American Furrier, IV:187*n*
American Garden, III:161; IV:341
American Gardening, III:161
American Gas Journal, II:92
American Gas-Light Journal, IV:184
American Gas-Light Journal and Mining Reporter, II:92
American Gentleman, IV:187*n*
American Geologist, IV:309
American Glass Review, III:129*n*
American Glass Worker, III:129*n*
American Gleaner and Virginia Magazine, I:205*n*, 793
American Globe, IV:186*n*
American Golf, IV:376
American Grange Bulletin, III:149*n*, 180
American Grange Bulletin and Scientific Farmer, IV:176–77
American Grocer, III:134; IV:187
American Gynecological and Obstetrical Journal, IV:315*n*
American Hairdresser and Perfumer, III:132
American Hatter, III:134
American Hebrew, III:80; IV:300
American Historical Magazine, IV:139
American Historical Record, III:35, 260
American Historical Register and Monthly Journal, IV:140*n*
American Historical Review, IV:158; V:331
American Home, IV:363*n*
American Home Journal, IV:253*n*, 363*n*
American Home Missionary, IV: 196*n*
American Homes, IV:324
American Homes Congress, V:38
American Homes and Gardens, II:321*n*
American Homoeopathic Observer, II:85*n*
American Homoeopathic Review, II:85*n*
American Homoeopathist, III:143
American Horological Journal, III:113*n*
American Horse Breeder, III:215
American Illustrated Magazine, III:510*n*
American Illustrated Methodist Magazine, IV:291
American Industries, IV:183
American Insurance Digest and Insurance Monitor, II:94*n*
American Insurance Journal, IV:351*n*
American Insurer, III:146*n*
American Inventor, III:116; IV:320
American Israelite, II:77; IV:300
American Jeweler, III:136; IV:188*n*
American Journal of Anatomy, IV:314
American Journal and Annals of Education, I:541*n*, 542
American Journal of Archaeology, IV:140
American Journal of Art, III:130
American Journal of Conchology, III:111
American Journal of Dental Science, II:91
American Journal of Education
founding of, I:491
on physical education for women, I:143
sketch of, I:541–43; II:442–47
other mentions, II:98; III:167; IV:270
American Journal of Education (St. Louis), III:168–69
American Journal of Education and College Review, II:442*n*
American Journal of Eugenics, III:302*n*
American Journal of Fabrics and Dry Goods Bulletin, III:134*n*
American Journal of Homeopathia, I:440*n*, 802

American Journal of Homeopathy, I:440*n*, 804; II:85*n*
American Journal of Insanity, II:85
American Journal of Mathematics, III:110
American Journal of Mathematics Pure and Applied, III:110*n*
American Journal of the Medical Sciences
founding of, I:151
payment to contributors, I:505
sketch of, I:566–68
other mentions, II:84; III:139; IV:313
American Journal of Miscroscopy and Popular Science, III:111
American Journal of Mining, III:114
American Journal of Numismatics, III:113*n;* IV: 391
American Journal of Nursing, IV:315
American Journal of Obstetrics and Diseases of Women and Children, III:141
American Journal of Ophthalmology, II:85; III:142
American Journal of Otology, III:142*n*
American Journal of Pharmacy
founding of, I:439
sketch of, I:539–40
other mentions, II:92; III:133; IV:317
American Journal of Philately, III:113*n;* IV:391
American Journal of Philology, III:236; IV:127–28
sketch of, III:535–38
American Journal of Photography, III:186
American Journal of Photography and the Allied Arts and Sciences, II:194*n*
American Journal of Physiology, IV:315
American Journal of Politics, IV:181
American Journal of Psychology, IV:303
American Journal of Public Hygiene, IV:316
American Journal of Railway Appliances, III:126*n*
American Journal of Religious Psychology and Education, IV:303
American Journal of Science, II:78–79
founding of, I:151–52
payment to contributors, I:505
on phrenology, I:448
sketch of, I:302–5
American Journal of Surgery, IV:315
American Journal of Syphilography and Dermatology, III:142*n*
American Journal of Theology, IV:302
American Journal of Urology and Sexology, IV:315*n*
American Journalist (Philadelphia), III:273
American Journalist (St. Louis), III:274
American Jubilee, II:141
American Jurist and Law Magazine, I:154, 451, 800
American Kennel Gazette, IV:382
American Kindergarten Magazine, III:163
American Kitchen Magazine, IV:364*n*
American Knit Goods Review, IV:185*n*
American Labor Reform League, III:301
American Labor World, IV:220
American Laboratory, III:110
American Ladies' Magazine, I:349*n*
American Laundry Journal, III:132
American Law Journal, I:154, 451, 793, 797; II:93
American Law Magazine, I:451, 806
American Law Record, III:145*n*
American Law Register, IV:346, 348
American Law Register and Review, II:93; III:144
American Law Review, III:144, 336; IV:346
American Law School Review, IV:348
American Lawn Tennis, IV:377
American Lawyer, IV:347
American Legal News, IV:347
American Legion, magazine comment on, V:9
American Library Journal, III:517*n*, 518
American Life Assurance Magazine and Journal of Actuaries, II:94*n*
American Literary Churchman, III:75
American Literary Gazette and Publishers' Circular, III:491, 492
American Literary Gazette and Weekly Mirror, II:40
American Literary Magazine, I:347–48, 477, 808
American literature, *see* Literary criticism
American Lumberman, IV:325*n*
American Lyceum, I:489
American Machinist, III:115
American Magazine (Bush's), IV:15, 39, 45
American Magazine (business women's periodical), IV:354*n*
American Magazine (*Frank Leslie's Popular Monthly*), II:130, 441, 513; III:36, 37, 191; IV:20, 44, 109, 473, 600; V:88, 204

advertising in, III:10, 11
circulation of, III:7
end of, IV:479
sketch of, III:510–16
American Magazine (Hearst's), IV:47
American Magazine (Webster's), I:13, 34, 37, 40, 58, 62, 64
founding of, I:29–30
sketch of, I:104–7
American Magazine, or General Repository, I:26*n*, 33, 36, 788
American Magazine, or A Monthly View of the Political State of British Colonies
founding of, I:24
sketch of, I:71–72
American Magazine of Civics, IV:181
American Magazine and Historical Chronicle, I:33*n*, 40, 47
founding of, I:25
sketch of, I:78–79
American Magazine and Monthly Chronicle, I:22, 33*n*, 35–36, 41, 45, 47, 54, 57, 66
founding of, I:25
sketch of, I:80–82
American Magazine of Useful and Entertaining Knowledge, I:364, 523, 696, 802
American Mail, I:362, 808
American Manufacturer and Iron World, II:92*n;* IV:183*n*
American Mathematical Monthly, IV:310
American Meat Institute, IV:186*n*
American Meat Trade and Retail Butchers' Journal, IV:187*n*
American Mechanic, II:317
American Mechanics' Magazine, I:445, 556–57
American Medical Compend, III:141*n*
American Medical Gazette, II:84*n*
American Medical Intelligencer, I:438–39, 804
American Medical Journal, III:143
American Medical Library and Intelligencer, I:439*n*, 804
American Medical Monthly, II:84*n*
American Medical Recorder, I:151*n*, 795
American Medical Times, II:84*n*, 456
American Medical Weekly, III:141*n*
American Medicine, IV:314
American Merchant, III:147
American Mercury, V:267, 271
sketch of, V:3–26
American Mercury Books, V:22
American Merino, III:160
American Messenger, II:10, 75; III:8*n*
American Metal Market, III:128; IV:183*n*
American Meteorological Journal, III:112
American Meteorologist, III:112
American Methodist, III:71*n*
American Miller, III:128; IV:185
American Mineralogical Journal
founding of, I:152
sketch of, I:266–67
American Minerva, I:156, 329, 789
American Mining Gazette and Geological Magazine, III:81
American Mining Index, II:80
American Miscellany, II:42; III:39*n*
American Missionary, II:71; IV:237
American Model Printer, III:121
American Modiste, IV:188*n*
American Monitor, I:29*n*, 788
American Monthly (New York, 1860), II:59*n*
American Monthly Jewish Review, IV:300
American Monthly Knickerbocker, see Knickerbocker Magazine
American Monthly Magazine (Boston)
founding of, I:344
sketch of, I:577–79
American Monthly Magazine (D.A.R.), IV:140
American Monthly Magazine (New York, 1833–38)
absorbed by *New-England Magazine,* I:602
founding of, I:345
sketch of, I:618–21
American Monthly Magazine (Philadelphia), I:129, 274
American Monthly Magazine and Critical Review, I:167, 177, 179, 187, 192
founding of, I:126
sketch of, I:297–98
American Monthly Review, I:122*n*, 789
American Monthly Review, or Literary Chronicle
founding of, I:344
quarrel with *American Quarterly,* I:274
sketch of, I:604–5
American Moral and Sentimental Magazine, I:790
founding of, I:132
purpose of, I:43
quoted, I:57, 65, 140
American Motherhood, IV:364
American Municipalities, IV:198

American Museum, I:14, 15, 18*n,* 19–20, 34, 35, 39–40, 41, 43–44, 45
founding of, I:30
quoted, I:32, 49, 51–52, 57–58, 59–60, 63, 65, 66, 67
sketch of, I:100–3
American Museum Journal, IV:309
American Museum of Natural History, scientific periodical of, IV:309
American Museum of Science, Literature and the Arts, I:345, 804
American Music Journal, IV:254*n*
American Musical Journal, I:434, 802
American Musical Magazine (Hartford), I:29, 172*n,* 788
American Musical Magazine (Northampton), I:791
American Musician, III:196
American Musician and Art Journal, III:196*n*
American National Preacher, I:308
American Naturalist, III:108
American News Company, II:13; III:8; IV:18, 66, 84, 584, 610–11; V:82, 223
American Newspaper Directory (Rowell's), III:7*n*
American Newspaper Publishers' Association, V:66
American Newspaper Reporter and Printers' Gazette, III:273*n*
American Notes and Queries, IV:64
American Nurseryman, IV:343*n*
American Odd Fellow, II:215; III:37*n*
American Paper Trade and Wood Pulp News, IV:188*n*
American Peace Society, II:211
American Penman, III:170
American Penny Magazine, I:364–65, 807
American People's Journal, II:210
American Philatelic Magazine, IV:391*n*
American Philatelist, IV:391
American Photographer, IV:14*n*
American Phrenological Journal, II:87
American Physical Education Review, IV:272*n*
American Physician, III:143; IV:314*n*
American Pigeon Keeper, IV:345
American Pioneer, I:422, 805
American Planning and Civic Association, V:322*n*
American Polytechnic Journal, II:80*n*
American Potter's Journal, IV:184
American Poultry Advocate, IV:345
American Poultry Journal, III:161
American Poultryman, III:161*n*
American Practitioner, IV:314*n*
American Presbyterian, I:373
American Presbyterian Review, I:533–34; II:62*n;* III:32*n,* 73
sketch of, II:516–17
American Presbyterian and Theological Review, II:62*n,* 516*n,* 517
American Press, III:274; IV:243
American Pressman, IV:221*n*
American Primary Teacher, IV:272
American Produce Review, IV:186*n*
American Progress, III:109*n*
American Protestant, IV:299
American Publishers' Circular and Literary Gazette, II:159; III:492
American Punch, III:267
American Quarterly, V:xi
American Quarterly Church Review and Ecclesiastical Register, II:364*n*
American Quarterly Microscopical Journal, III:111, 112
American Quarterly Observer, I:367, 802
American Quarterly Register, I:491, 520, 799; II:28
American Quarterly Register and Magazine (Stryker's), I:368, 809
American Quarterly Review, I:367
founding of, I:129
sketch of, I:272–76
American Quarterly Review of Freemasonry, II:215
American Queen, IV:751*n,* 752
American Railroad Journal, I:446, 801; II:81; III:113*n,* 123–24
sketch of, II:297–300
American Railroad Journal and Advocate of Internal Improvements, II:297*n*
American Railroad Magazine and Mechanics' Magazine, II:297*n*
American Railway Review, II:81
American Railway Times, II:81
American Register, III:42
edited by Walsh, I:272
founding of, I:124
sketch of, I:221–22
American Register and International Journal, II:42
American Review (educational journal), III:169*n*
American Review: A Whig Journal, see American Whig Review
American Review of History and Politics (Walsh's), I:161, 178, 179, 192
founding of, I:129
sketch of, I:271–72

American Review and Literary Journal
founding of, I:124
sketch of, I:219–20
American Review of Reviews, IV:657*n*, 661
See also: Review of Reviews
American Review of Shoes and Leather, IV:185*n*
American Revolution, *see* Revolutionary War
American Rifleman, IV:381*n*
American Rural Home, III:153
American School Board Journal, IV:272
American Scrap-Book and Magazine of United States Literature, II:130
American Sentinel, IV:296
American Sheep Breeder, IV:344
American Sheep Breeder and Wool Grower, III:160
American Shoemaking, IV:185
American Silk Journal, III:134
American Soap Journal, IV:184*n*
American Socialist, II:207*n*; III:300
American Society of Civil Engineering, Proceedings of, III:113
American Sociological Review, IV:192*n*
American Spectator, IV:90
American Spirit and Wine Trade Review, III:135
American Sportsman (New York), III:210*n*
American Sportsman (West Meriden, Conn.), III:210*n*
American Standard, IV:107
American Stationer, III:135
American Stock Journal, II:91; III:159*n*
American Stockman, III:160
American Suburbs, V:159
American Sunday-School Magazine, I:144, 797
American Swineherd, IV:344
American System, I:463
American Tailor and Cutter, III:134*n*; IV:187
American Telegraph Magazine, II:92
American Theological Review, II:62, 516, 518
American Tract Society, II:75
American Trade, IV:183
American Turf Register, I:479, 800
American Tyler, IV:222*n*
American Undertaker, IV:189
American Underwriter, IV:351*n*
American Union, II:35, 151, 411*n*
American Universal Magazine, I:53, 122, 790
American Vegetarian and Health Journal, II:87
American Veterans Committee, V:222
American Veterinary Review, III:143
American Whig Review, II:13, 15, 29, 420
founding of, I:346
payments to contributors, I:505
sketch of, I:750–54
American Wine Press, IV:189*n*
American Woman's Journal, IV:354*n*
American Woman's Review, IV:361; V:151*n*
American Woodworker and Mechanical Journal, III:130*n*
American Wool and Cotton Reporter, IV:185*n*
American Woman Suffrage Association, III:94, 393
American Yachtsman, IV:373
American Yorkshire Weekly, IV:344
American Youth, IV:275
Ames, Eleanor Kirk, IV:356*n*
Ames, Fisher, I:184
Ames, James Barr, IV:348
Ames, Mary Clemmer, II:429; III:358, 393
Amphion, III:198*n*
Amundsen, Roald, II:402
Anaesthesia, early uses of, III:138
Analectic Magazine, I:145, 152, 173, 175, 177, 189, 191, 207, 210
founding of, I:125
sketch of, I:279–83
Analyst, III:110; IV:363
Anarchism, II:482; IV: 171–73
anarchist periodicals, III:301–2; IV:172–73, 176
financial periodicals and, IV:182
Haymarket bombing and, IV:172–73, 217–18, 561
press opposition to, II:530; IV:171, 561
press support for, V:92, 169
political science journals and, IV:180–81
Anatomy journals, IV:314
Anchor and Shield, III:315
Andersen, Hans Christian, III:255, 461
Anderson, Alexander, I:210, 522
Anderson, Carl, IV:714
Anderson, Henry James, I:335
Anderson, Margaret, V:166–78
Anderson, Mary, III:204; IV:257
Anderson, Maxwell, V:264
Anderson, Melville Best, III:541

Anderson, Sherwood, III:543; IV:518, 729, 769; V:25, 119, 168, 173, 176–78
Andover, Maine, I:371–72, 491; II:70; IV:395
Andover doctrine, IV:399–400
Andover Review, III:76, 164, 314, 317; IV:293
sketch of, IV:395–400
Andrée, Salomon August, IV:596
Andrew, G. T., IV:719
Andrew, John, II:43, 390, 410, 523; IV:308
Andrew, John Albion, I:660*n*
Andrew, W. R., III:102
Andrews, Ebenezer T., I:108*n*
Andrews, Elisha Benjamin, III:72*n;* IV:74*n,* 398, 486, 662, 721
Andrews, J. C. B., IV:385
Andrews, John, I:138; II:63*n*
Andrews, Joseph, I:736
Andrews, Kenneth, IV:439
Andrews, Mary Raymond Shipman, IV:724
Andrews, Stephen Pearl, II:212; III:444, 446, 450–52
Andrews, W. R., IV:751–52
Andrews, William E., II:76
Andrews, William W., I:644
Andrew's American Queen, III:102; IV:751–52
Andrew's Bazar, III:98*n*
Andrew's Fashion Bazar, IV:751
Andreyev, Leonid, V:266
Angell, George T., III:312
Angell, Norman, III:542; V:23, 51, 206, 209, 211
Angel's Food, IV:390
Anglican Prayer Book, V:ix
Anglo-African Magazine, II:141
Anglo-American Magazine, IV:228
Anglo-American periodicals, IV:227–29
Anglo-Japanese-American Treaty (1922), V:5
Anglo-Saxon, II:212
Angoff, Charles, III:331*n;* V:3*n,* 8, 15, 17, 19, 23–24
Animal-feed trade magazines, IV:189
Animals, magazines on prevention of cruelty to, III:311–12
See also Wildlife
Ann Arbor, Mich., III:112, 141*n,* 143; IV:294, 364
Annals of the American Academy of Political and Social Science, IV:180, 192–93
Annals of Gynaecology and Pediatry, IV:315*n*
Annals of Hygiene, III:139
Annals of Iowa, II:176*n;* III:259; IV:139
Annals of Mathematics, III:110
Annals of Ophthalmology and Otology, IV:315
Annals of Otology and Laryngology, IV:315
Annals of Surgery, IV:314–15
Annan, Mrs. A. M. F., I:546*n;* II:308
Annuals, I:9, 273, 353, 420–21, 672, 746; II:192
Annular World, IV:285*n*
Anonymity in magazines, I:40, 196, 503–4; II:25–26, 420, 496*n,* 532; III:19, 321
Ansley, Clarke Fisher, V:179*n,* 180
Ansonia, Ohio, III:169
Anthology of Magazine Verse (Braithwaite), V:258
Anthology Society (Club), I:124, 130, 194, 254–59
Anthon, Charles, I:669–70
Anthony, Andrew Varick Stout, II:43
Anthony, Edward, IV:447–78, 770
Anthony, Joseph, III:479
Anthony, Norman, III:552*n,* 555; IV:556*n,* 567–68
Anthony, Susan Brownell, III:91, 93, 94, 172, 391*n,* 392–94, 445–46; IV:72
Anthony's Photographic Bulletin, III:186
Anthropology articles, IV:622
Anthropology periodicals, IV:308
Anti-Catholicism, *see* Catholicism
Anti-evolution trial, Dayton (1925), V:116
Anti-Imperialist, IV:165*n*
Anti-Imperialist Broadside, IV:165*n*
Anti-Masonic Magazine, I:297
Anti-Masonic Review and Magazine, I:799
Anti-Philistine, IV:389, 647
Anti-Polygamy Standard, III:313
Antiquarian Papers, III:259
Antiques, V:214
Anti-Semitism in magazines, IV:565
Antislavery, *see* Slavery debate
Anti-Slavery Bugle, I:458
Anti-Slavery Examiner, I:457, 803
Anti-Slavery Record, I:457, 802
Anti-Slavery Reporter, I:457, 802
Anti-Slavery Standard, see National Anti-Slavery Standard
Anti-Tobacco Journal, III:311
Antitrust issue, *see* Trusts
Apollo Association, founding of, I:437

Apostolic Guide, III:80
Appalachia, III:210
Appeal to Reason, III:514; IV:204–5
Apple, Theodore, 380*n*
Apple, Thomas Gilmore, II:380*n*, 381
Apples of Gold, III:174
Appleton-Century Company, V:345
Appleton-Century-Crofts, V:47, 345
Appleton, Daniel, I:375
Appleton, (Miss) E. P., II:173
Appleton's Booklovers' Magazine, IV:393
sketch of, V:27–33
Appleton's Journal, II:462; III:41, 90, 105, 139, 184, 187, 199, 231, 253, 279, 290, 307; V:29
sketch of, III:417–21
Appleton's Literary Bulletin, III:236
Appleton's Magazine, V:30
Appleton's Popular Science Monthly, *see: Popular Science Monthly*
Applied physics, II:319
Apthorp, William Foster, II:197*n*, 507*n*; III:192, 194*n*; IV:722
Aquarium, IV:309
Aquarium periodicals, IV:309
Aquatic Monthly and Sporting Gazeteer, III:211
Aquatic sports, *see* Water sports
Aquatints, I:209, 210, 296
Arabian Nights, V:123
Arcadian, III:184, 233
Archaeology, II:402, 449; III:112; IV:140, 397, 629
Archer, Frederick, III:197
Archer, William, III:350, 551
Archery articles, III:219–20; IV:634
Archery and Tennis News, III:220
Archibald, James F. J., IV:458, 726
Archipenko, Alexander, V:178
Architects' and Builders' Magazine, III:129*n*
Architectural Forum, IV:323; V:322
Architectural Record, IV:323; V:193
Architectural Review, III:129*n*; IV:323
Architecture, IV:323
Architecture, II:189, 425, 445; V:158
architectural periodicals, II:321–22; III:129; IV:145, 197, 323
Architecture and Building, III:129*n*
Archives of Dermatology, III:142*n*
Archives of Gynaecology, Obstetrics and Pediatrics, IV:315*n*
Archives of Laryngology, III:142*n*
Archives of Ophthalmology, III:142
Archives of Ophthalmology and Otology, III:141
Archives of Otology, III:142
Archives of Pediatrics, III:142
Arcturus
founding of, I:346
sketch of, 1:711–12
Arena, IV:3, 10, 35, 51–52, 79, 207, 216
sketch of, IV:401–16
Arena Quarterly, IV:414
Arey, Harriet Ellen Grannis, II:100, 466, 467
Argonaut, III:56–57; IV:106
Argosy, II:311, 509*n*; III:317; IV:6, 608–9, 614, 618
sketch of, IV:417–23
Argus, III:146*n*
Argus (Baltimore), IV:90
Argus (insurance journal), IV:351*n*
Argus (Seattle), IV:108
Argyll, Duke of, *see* Campbell, George John Douglas
Arid America, IV:339
Arid Region, I:339
Aristidean, I:347, 807
"Aristocrat" poetry, V:240–41
"Arizona Kicker," IV:384
Ark, III:312
Arkansas Baptist, IV:292*n*
Arkansas Farmer, III:155; IV:341
Arkansas Magazine, II:110*n*
Arkansas Methodist, III:71*n*
Arkansas School Journal, IV:271*n*
Arkansas Tom Cat, IV:386
Arkansas Traveler, III:270; IV:383
Arkell, William J., II:452*n*, 463; III:553, 554; IV:386
Arlen, Michael, IV:436, 498; V:86
Armenia, IV:233
Armfield, Eugene, III:491*n*
Arminian Magazine, I:29, 789
Armour, Philip, III:74; IV:293, 775
Arms, H. Phelps, IV:82
Arms and the Man, IV:381*n*
Armstrong, A. C., & Son, I:529*n*, 535
Armstrong, Samuel T., I:247*n*, 249, 262*n*
Armstrong, Thomas A., III:299
Army, United States
literary sketches on, I:643
medical services in, II:86
See also specific wars
Army and Navy Chronicle, I:456, 803
Army and Navy Chronicle and Scientific Repository, I:456, 806
Army and Navy Gazette, II:150, 549
Army and Navy Journal, II:551; III:362, 363
sketch of, II:547–49

Army and Navy Life, III:533*n*
Army and Navy Official Gazette, II:150
Army periodicals, *see* Military periodicals
Arnold, Edwin, III:35*n,* IV:132, 226, 489, 722
Arnold, George, II:39, 182, 520, 521, 525–26; III:322
Arnold, Henry Harley, IV:626, 631
Arnold, James Newell, III:260
Arnold, Matthew, III:250; IV:131, 281; V:x, 92
Around the World, IV:224
"Arp, Bill," *see* Smith, Charles Henry
Arp, Jean (Hans), V:178
Arrowsmith (Lewis), V:311
Art
in magazines before 1885, I:303, 436–38, 522, 548, 592; II:188–94; III:180–83
popularization, II:190
in Gilded Age magazines (1885–1905), III:472–73; IV:144–45
advertising improvements, IV:28–29
comic periodicals, IV:561, 564
eclectic periodicals, IV:590–91, 594–95, 603, 611, 685
literary periodicals, IV:685
urban periodicals, IV:87
in modern magazines (1905–), IV:575
general magazines, IV:616, 725–26; V:28
literary magazines, III:542
social welfare magazines, IV:746
women's magazines, III:489; IV:549
See also Art criticism and comment
Art Age, III:185
Art Amateur, III:185, 191; IV:146
Art criticism and comment
in nationalist era magazines (1794–1825), I:173, 321, 324, 329
in expansionist era magazines (1825–50), I:435–38
general periodicals, I:610, 623
literary magazines, I:712, 757–58, 766, 769–72
women's magazines, I:589, 701
in Civil War era magazines (1850–65), II:532
illustrated weeklies, II:453
quality, II:188–92
women's magazines, II:437
in post-Civil War magazines (1865–85), II:253; III:35, 233
current-events magazines, III:335–36
family magazines, III:428
general magazines, III:358, 418, 465, 511
literary magazines, II:398, 495; III:40, 320, 323–24, 369–70, 398, 403, 416, 548, 550
quality and type, III:183–84
religious magazines, II:376
in Gilded Age magazines (1885–1905)
Chautauqua magazines, III:546
general magazines, III:472, IV:719, 721, 727, 731
home magazines, V:158
literary magazines, II:401
trends, IV:144–45
women's magazines, II:311; IV:768
in modern magazines (1905–)
family magazines, III:430
general magazines, V:6, 75
literary magazines, II:431
review periodicals, IV:520
Art Education, IV:147
Art education periodicals, IV:147–48
Art Folio, III:186
Art Interchange, III:185; IV:146
Art Journal, III:186
Art journals, II:193–94; III:184–86, 191, 410–12; IV:146–48; V:166–78
Art News, IV:147*n*
Art Review, III:186
Art Review of Pictures and Frames, IV:148*n*
Art Student, III:185; IV:148*n*
Art trade magazines, III:136
Art Union, III:185
Art unions, I:437–38, 769; II:190–91
Art work, *see* Engravings; Format and size; Illustrations; Photography
Arthur, Chester Alan, III:287, 345; IV:155
Arthur, Timothy Shay, I:204, 378; II:36, 57, 171, 308, 362, 394, 410; III:24, 176, 224, 256; IV:679
as contributor, I:499, 585, 672, 743, 745, 770
as editor, I:353, 381, 381*n,* 734; II:416, 418
Arthur McEwen's Letter, V:107
Arthurs, Stanley M., IV:498
Arthur's Home Gazette, II:57, 416
Arthur's Home Magazine, II:58, 59, 303; III:98, 224, 311
sketch of, II:416–18
Arthur's Ladies Magazine, see: Ladies Magazine (Philadelphia)
Arthur's Magazine, IV:87, 359

Artificial gas periodicals, III:131
Artisan, III:116
Artist, II:308; IV:147
Artist and Lady's World, II:306*n*
Artistic Japan, IV:233
Arts for America, IV:148*n*
Artsman, IV:148
Artzybasheff, Boris, V:123, 258, 323
Arvin, Newton, V:96
Asa Gray Bulletin, IV:309
Asbury, Francis, I:29
Asbury, Herbert, IV:476, 607; V:13
Asepsis, development of, IV:310–11
Ashby, N. B., III:157*n*
Ashland, Ohio, III:81
Ashmore, Ruth, *see* Mallon, Isabel A.
Asia
American interest in, III:280; IV:232–33
See also specific Asian countries
Asia, IV:233; V:214
Asiatic Journal of Commerce, IV:233
Asquith, Margot, IV:584
Assembly Herald, III:544; IV:293*n*
Associated Labor Press, III:299
Associated Press, V:66, 156, 307
Associated Sunday Magazines, IV:70
Associate Teacher, IV:270*n*
Association of American Advertisers, V:68
Association Boys, IV:275
Association of Friends to Evangelical Truth, I:263
Association Men, III:85; IV:287
Association News, III:85
Association Notes, IV:287
Assurance, IV:351*n*
Astor, John Jacob, IV:488
Astor, Lady (Nancy Langhorn), IV:519, 584
Astor, Mrs. Vincent, IV:760
Astrological guides, III:113
Astrological Journal, III:113*n*
Astronomical Journal, II:79
Astronomy, magazines on, II:79, 113*n*, 319
Astronomy and Astro-Physics, III:111*n*
Astrophysical Journal, III:111*n*; IV:308
Astrophysical periodicals, III:111*n;* IV:308–9
Atchison, Kan., IV:340
Athenæum gallery (Boston), I:437
Atheneum, or Spirit of the English Magazines, I:130, 795
Athens, Ga., II:88*n*, 110*n*; III:154
Athens, Ohio, IV:269*n*
Athens, Tenn., II:67*n*
Atherton, Gertrude, I:592; II:311; III:400, 408; IV:105, 228, 482; V:249
Athletic clubs, III:220–21
Atkeson, Ray, IV:630
Atkinson, Samuel Coate, I:343, 440, 544*n*; IV:671*n*, 672–76, 683–84
Atkinson, Wilmer, III:23, 153
Atkinson's Saturday Evening Post, IV:671*n*, 675
Atlanta, Ga.
agricultural periodicals, I:444*n;* III:149*n*, 154; IV:341
magazines before 1885, I:444*n;* II:67*n*, 84*n;* III:45–46, 82*n*, 136, 143*n*, 146*n*
magazines after 1885
amateur periodical, IV:390*n*
dental journal, III:143*n*
education periodical, IV:270*n*
engineering periodical, IV:321
financial periodical, IV:349*n*
historical journal, IV:139
home weekly, IV:92
illustrated magazine, IV:92
insurance periodicals, III:146*n;* IV:351*n*
manufacturing periodicals, IV:184*n*, 185*n*
medical journals, II:84*n;* III:141*n;* IV:313*n*, 351*n*
Negro periodical, IV:214*n*
Populist periodical, IV:178
promotional magazine, IV:92
railroad journal, IV:333*n*
religious periodical, IV:291
trade journal, III:136
women's periodical, IV:363*n*
Atlanta Christian Advocate, II:67*n*
Atlanta Journal-Record of Medicine, IV:313*n*
Atlanta Medical and Surgical Journal, II:84*n*
Atlantic cable, II:126
Atlantic City, N.J., IV:265
Atlantic Journal, I:312*n*
Atlantic Magazine, I:185–86, 189–90, 197
founding of, I:128
sketch of, I:334–35
Atlantic Monthly, II:106, 107, 156, 173, 245; III:13, 17, 18, 20–21, 29, 32, 48, 49, 90, 91, 105, 151, 166, 184, 189, 192, 223, 224, 227, 228, 229, 231, 232, 237, 254, 255, 263, 279, 281, 284, 298, 307, 308, 311, 357, 361–62, 381, 399, 403; IV:8–9, 13, 21, 35, 44, 78, 112, 120, 207, 717,

Atlantic Monthly—Continued
773; V:30, 159, 188, 354, 341, 343
advertising in, II:13, 15; III:10, 11
contributors' payments by, III:12, 13, 17, 18, 20–21, 29, 48, 58, 59, 90, 91, 105, 151, 166, 184, 189, 192, 223, 224, 227, 228, 229, 231, 232, 237, 254, 255, 263, 279, 281, 284, 298, 307, 308, 311, 357, 361–62, 381, 399, 403
criticism in, II:158
editorial salaries of, II:24
founding of, II:32–33, 428
politics in, II:134, 140, 148, 149, 416
regionalism of, II:102–3
relationship to other magazines
Blackwood's, II:130
North American Review, II:243
Putnam's, II:431
Atlantic Monthly Company, V:159
Atlas, II:37, 39
Attica, Ohio, III:141
Attwood, Francis G., III:268, 466; IV:484, 559
Atwater, Layman Hotchkiss, I:533, 539*n*, 624, 741; III:23
Atwell, George C., IV:82
Atwood, Albert William, IV:604, 662, 709
Auburn, Ind., IV:162
Auden, Wyston Hugh, IV:739; V:222, 237
Audit Bureau of Circulations, V:68
Audubon, John James, III:106
Audubon Magazine, IV:310*n*
Auer, Bernhard Machold, V:321
Auerback, Berthold, II:164, III:255
Augusta, Ga., II:89, 110*n;* III:73
Augusta, Maine, I:444*n;* III:37–39, 152; IV:417
Auk, III:111
Aumonier, Stacy, V:119
Aurévilly, Jules Barbey d', V:123
Aurora, Ill., III:71
Aurora, Mo., IV:416
Auslander, Joseph, IV:440, 714; V:13, 113
Austen, Jane, II:160
Austin, Alfred, IV:132
Austin, Frank B., III:315
Austin, Henry Willard, IV:203
Austin, James Trecothic, II:228
Austin, Jane G., II:309, 394, 429; III:13*n*, 22, 256, 372, 373, 511
Austin, Mary, IV:105, 117*n*, 439, 748; V:9, 249
Austin, Samuel, I:134*n*
Austin, Tex., magazines in, III:269–70; IV:139, 303*n*, 313*n*, 442–43, 665–70
Austin, William, I:127, 197, 600
Author, IV:142
Authors, American
leading, IV:128–31
magazine, *see* Contributors
popularity of, III:237–46
See also names of specific authors
Authors, European
American criticisms of, IV:135
as lecturers, III:249–51
popularity of, III:248–56; IV:131–36
See also names of specific authors
Author's Magazine, IV:117*n*
Auto Review, IV:331
Autobiography
in magazines before 1905, II:253, 257; III:430, 514; IV:721
in modern magazines, III:432, 514; IV:500, 553, 602, 605, 607, 725, 728; V:83
See also Reminiscences
Automobile, IV:330–31
Automobile Magazine, IV:331
Automobile Topics, IV:331
Automobile Trade Journal, IV:331
Automobiles
Gilded Age magazines on (1885–1905)
advertising, IV:28, 327–30, 464, 565
articles on, IV:33, 488, 593
specialized periodicals, IV:330–31
modern magazines on (1905–), II:322; IV:725
advertising, IV:694, 696, 725
anticipations of, IV:327
invention of, IV:319
Automotive accessories periodicals, IV:183
Automotive Industries, IV:331
Automotive Manufacturer, II:92
Autumn Leaves, IV:296
Ave Maria, III:68; IV:298
Averchenko, Arkadi, V:119
Averill, E. A., II:298
Avery, B. F., III:156
Avery, Benjamin P., III:184, 402*n*, 406
Avery, Claire, IV:760
Avery, Samuel Putnam, II:410
Aviation
early comment in magazines, I:467–

68; II:319–20, 322, 334–35; III:126
prize essays, IV:487–88
modern magazines on (1905–), II:320; IV:494, 626; V:152
Axford, C. B., II:95*n*
Ayer, Adams, III:436
Ayer, Francis Wayland, IV:539
Ayer, N. W. & Son, IV:16
Ayer (*N. W.*) *& Son's Newspaper Annual,* III:5*n,* 7*n*
Aylward, W. J., IV:725
Azarias, Brother, III:69*n*

Babbitt, Irving, III:349; IV:441, 520
Baby Book, V:44, 47
Babyhood, IV:364
Babyland, III:177
Bache, Alexander Dallas, II:413
Bacheler, Origen, I:363*n,* 364
Bacheller, Irving, III:471; IV:115, 485; V:85
Bachelor of Arts, IV:271
Bachmann, Max, II:464
Back, Jacques, V:100*n,* 112
Backus, J. S., III:64
Bacon, Edwin Munroe, IV:390*n*
Bacon, George Andrew, IV:268
Bacon, Leonard, II:312*n,* 313, 367*n,* 368, 369; V:336
Bacon, Leonard Wolsey, IV:210
Bacon, William Thompson, II:312*n,* 313, 315
Badger, Richard G., IV:121, 125
Baer, George Frederick, IV:219
Bagby, George William, I:629*n,* 642, 651–52; II:24–25, 30, 112; III:46*n,* 397
Bailey, C. P., II:65*n*
Bailey, Gamaliel, I:457, II:22, 140
Bailey, J. M., III:271*n*
Bailey, Jackson, III:115*n*
Bailey, John, IV:712*n*
Bailey, Liberty Hyde, IV:338
Bailey, Milton, III:544
Bailey, Philip James, II:162
Bailey, Temple, IV:585
Bailie, Charles, II:112*n*
Bailsford, Henry N., V:211
Baird, Robert, I:532
Baird, Spencer Fullerton, II:395
Bakeless, John, IV:578
Baker, George Barr, III:481*n,* 487
Baker, Lawrence H., III:538
Baker, Marcus, IV:620*n*
Baker, Norman, IV:531
Baker, Ray Stannard, III:510*n,* 512; IV:167, 465, 595–600, 778
Baker, S. F., II:454
Baker, Sir Samuel, II:477
Baker, Thomas F., IV:68
Baker, William, I:522, 714
Baker, William Mumford ("George F. Harrington"), II:393, 477, 504, 506*n;* III:224, 397, 502, 558
Baker, William T., IV:68
Baker & Scribner, I:375
Baker's Helper, IV:185*n*–186*n*
Baking magazines, III:135; IV:185*n*–86*n*
Balance and Columbia Repository, I:127, 792
Balbi, Adrian, I:342*n*
Balch, David Arnold, V:291
Balch Edwin Swift, II:415
Balch, Frank O., IV:367
Balch, Vistus, I:322
Balch, William R., III:35*n,* 41
Balche, Alexander Dallas, I:556*n,* 558
Balden, John, III:256*n*
Baldwin, Charles Sears, IV:74
Baldwin, E. C., III:100
Baldwin, Elbert Francis, III:429
Baldwin, Faith (Mrs. Hugh Cuthrell), IV:475, 503, 585, 771
Baldwin, Hanson Weightman, IV:478
Baldwin, James, IV:94
Baldwin, James Mark, IV:303
Baldwin, Joseph G., I:651
Baldwin, O. C., III:35*n*
Baldwin, Oliver R., II:110*n,* 112n
Baldwin, Thomas, I:251–52
Baldwin, Thomas Tilestone, IV:347*n*
Baldwin's Monthly, III:35
Baldwin's Musical Review, III:197*n*
Balfour, Arthur James, II:255
Ball Player's Chronicle, III:217
Ballantyne, W. H., I:730*n*
Ballinger, Richard Achilles, IV:462; V:150
Ballooning articles, IV:634
Balestier, Wolcott, III:268*n*
Ballot Box, III:94
Ballou, Hosea, I:138, 372; II:72, 409
Ballou's Magazine, IV:79*n*
Ballou, Maturin Murray, II:31, 35*n,* 43, 409–11; III:102*n*
Ballou's Dollar Monthly, III:39*n;* IV:3*n*
Ballou's Dollar Monthly Magazine, II:31
Ballou's Pictorial Drawing-Room Companion, see: Gleason's Pictorial Drawing-Room Companion

Ballyhoo, IV:568
Balmer, Edwin, IV:457; V:148
Balmer, Thomas, IV:545
Baltimore, Md.
  early magazines in (1793–94), I:19, 31*n*, 32
    postal regulations (1792), I:19
  nationalist era magazines in (1794–1825)
    comic and satiric magazines, I:170, 172
    general magazines, I:122, 125, 128, 152, 163, 268
    literary clubs, I:194
    literary and theatrical magazines, I:167, 204, 293–96
    magazine center, I:204
    religious magazine, I:204
  expansionist era magazines in (1825–50)
    agricultural journal, I:442
    general and literary magazines, I:268*n*, 269, 362, 380–81
    magazine center, I:380–82
    mammoth magazines, I:362
    medical journals, I:439
    religious magazines, I:371, 716–17
    sports magazine, I:47–80
    women's magazine, I:381
  Civil War era magazines in (1850–65)
    agricultural magazine, II:90
    religious periodicals, II:67*n*, 68, 69, 77
  Post-Civil War magazines in (1865–85)
    agricultural magazines, II:90; III:154
    general magazines, III:46, 47, 256
    insurance periodical, III:146*n*
    legal journal, III:144
    manufacturers' journal, III:127
    medical journal, III:140*n*
    religious magazines, II:68, 77; III:71*n*, 73*n*, 382*n*
    society notes, III:102
    trade magazine, III:134
    women's rights magazine, III:96
  Gilded Age magazines in (1885–1905)
    agricultural periodicals, II:90; III:154
    insurance periodical, III:146*n*
    leading periodicals, IV:90
    literary magazine, IV:90, 92
    manufacturers' journals, III:127; IV:183
    medical journals, III:140*n*; IV:314
    religious magazines, II:68, 77; III:71*n*
    society notes, III:102
    success magazine, IV:169
    trade journals, III:134; IV:189*n*
    urban weeklies, IV:90
    woodworkers' journal, III:130*n*
  modern magazines in (1905–)
    insurance periodical, III:146*n*
    Jewish periodical, IV:300
    manufacturers' journals, III:127; IV:183
    medical journals, III:140*n*; IV:314
    photography periodical, IV:149
    religious magazine, II:68
    trade journals, III:134; IV:189*n*
Baltimore Christian Advocate, II:68*n*
Baltimore Herald, IV:90
Baltimore Life, IV:90
Baltimore Literary Monument, I:381*n*
Baltimore Literary and Religious Magazine, I:381, 802
Baltimore Medical and Surgical Journal and Review, I:439*n*, 802
Baltimore Methodist, II:67*n*
Baltimore Minerva, I:380, 800
Baltimore Monthly Journal of Medicine and Surgery, I:439*n*, 800
Baltimore Monument, I:381, 803
Baltimore News, V:294
Baltimore & Ohio Railroad, I:340, 466
Baltimore and Richmond Christian Advocate, I:382, 801
Baltimore Sun, V:10, 262
Baltimore Underwriter and National Agent, III:146*n*
Baltimore Weekly Magazine, I:122, 791
Baltimorean, IV:90
Balzac, Honoré de, II:162, 163, 532, 535; IV:122, 434–35; V:119, 123
Bancroft, George, I:129, 138, 192, 275–76, 335, 454, 535, 687; II:156, 175, 232, 234, 361, 413; III:238
Bancroft, Mark, I:545; IV:675
Bancroft Prize, V:xv, 347
Bancroft, Wilder Dwight, IV:309
Bangor, Maine, III:149*n*; IV:138, 285*n*, 381*n*
Bangor Historical Magazine, IV:138
Bangs, Francis Hyde, IV:550
Bangs, John Kendrick, II:399, 400, 469, 482, 484: III:165*n*, 166, 389–90, 504, 520*n*, 530; IV:49*n*, 66, 543–44, 556*n*, 559–63, 608*n*, 609, 616, 768; V:121, 251
Bangs, Nathan, I:299*n*; II:66*n*
Bank and Quotation Record, III:147*n*

Banker and Business, IV:349*n*
Banker and Financier, II:96
Banker and Tradesman, III:147*n;* IV:349
Bankers' Encyclopedia, IV:349
Bankers' Magazine, I:808; II:94; III:146; IV:349
Bankers' Monthly, III:147*n*
Banking and Insurance Chronicle, III:147
Banking Law Journal, IV:348
Banking and Mercantile World, IV:349*n*
Banking periodicals, *see* Financial journals
Banner of Light, II:209; III:81
Banner Weekly, III:43; IV:117
Banning, Margaret Culkin, IV:504, 585, 586
Baptist, II:64*n,* 65*n*
Baptist Advance, IV:292*n*
Baptist Argus, IV:292*n*
Baptist Banner, II:65*n;* IV:292*n*
Baptist Banner and Western Pioneer, II:64*n,* 65*n*
Baptist Beacon, III:72
Baptist Chronicle, IV:292*n*
Baptist Commonwealth, III:73*n;* IV:291
Baptist controversies, I:369
Baptist Courier, III:73*n*
Baptist Exponent, III:73*n*
Baptist Flag, III:73*n*
Baptist and Herald, III:73*n*
Baptist Home Mission Monthly, I:252; III:72
Baptist Messenger, III:73*n*
Baptist Missionary Magazine, I:134, 251–52; II:63; IV:237, 305
Baptist News, IV:292
Baptist Observer, IV:292*n*
Baptist Outlook, III:73*n*
Baptist periodicals
  before 1885, I:138, 251–52, 370, 371, 666–68; II:63–65; III:67, 72–73, 180, 422
  in Gilded Age (1885–1905), IV:274, 275, 291–92, 305
Baptist Quarterly, III:72
Baptist Quarterly Review, III:72*n;* IV:292
Baptist Record, III:73*n*
Baptist Reflector, II:65*n;* III:73
Baptist and Reflector, IV:292*n*
Baptist Review, III:72
Baptist Standard, IV:292
Baptist Teacher, III:67, 72
Baptist Union, IV:275
Baptist Visitor, III:73*n*
Baptist Weekly, II:65*n;* IV:291
Baptist Weekly Journal of the Mississippi Valley, II:65*n*
Baptist World, IV:292*n*
Barber, George F., IV:324
Barber, Henry Hervey, III:506*n,* 507
Barber, Joseph, Jr., II:493*n*
Barber's Journal (Cleveland), IV:221*n*
Barber's Journal (New York), IV:189*n*
Barbers' magazines, III:132; IV:189*n*
Barbers' National Journal, III:132
Barbour, Ralph Henry, III:504; IV:116*n,* 637; V:249
Bardeen, Charles William, II:443*n;* III:168
Bardstown, Ky., II:63*n*
Barker, George Frederick, I:556*n,* 558
Barker, James Nelson, I:170
Barker, Joseph, I:134*n*
Barker, Wharton, III:34*n,* 35, 41*n;* IV:60
Barkley, Alben William, IV:476
Barlow, Joel, I:106, 153, 176, 186, 232, 257
Barnard, Charles, III:460; IV:308
Barnard, Daniel Dewey, I:455, 697, 751, 752
Barnard, Frederick Augustus Porter, IV:514
Barnard, Mrs. Helen, III:94
Barnard, Henry, I:491, 492, 694–95; II:98; III:167
  as editor, II:443–47
Barnard's American Journal of Education, see: American Journal of Education
Barnay, Ludwig, III:205
Barnes, Albert, II:62*n,* 517*n*
Barnes, Charlotte M. S., I:641
Barnes, Djuna, V:266
Barnes, Harry Elmer, V:5
Barnes, John K., IV:785
Barnett, B. G., III:402*n*
Barnett, Ross R., V:316
Barnouw, Adrian Jacob, III:350
Barns, Charles Edward, IV:84*n;* V:145*n*
Barnum, H. L., I:444*n*
Barnum, P. T., II:43, 44, 185*n,* 194, 213–214, 412, 452, 541; IV:266, 421, 543
Barnwell, R. Grant, II:338*n,* 341*n,* 348; III:261*n*
Barr, Amelia Edith Huddleston, I:593; III:41*n,* 328, 400, 471, 485, 504, 511; IV:122; V:28
Barr, Robert, III:400; IV:48*n,* 115*n,* 592, 691, V:29
Barrel and Box, IV:184*n*
Barrett, George C., I:317*n,* 318

Barrett, George Hooker, I:248
Barrett, J. C., III:82*n*
Barrett, John, IV:233
Barrett, Lawrence, III:199, 203; IV:256
Barrie, James Matthew, II:482; IV:44, 226, 720
Barring, Maurice, V:121
Barritt, Mrs. Frances Fuller, II:466
Barron, Alfred, II:207*n*
Barron, C. W., V:79
Barrow, H. C., II:112*n*
Barrows, Anna, IV:364
Barrows, Samuel June, IV:294, 744, 745
Barrows, Willard, II:518
Barry, David Sheldon, IV:63*n*
Barry, Patrick, II:90*n*
Barrymore, Ethel, III:489
Barrymore, Georgiana, III:204
Barrymore, Lionel, IV:713
Barrymore, Maurice, III:204
Bartine, H. F., IV:163*n*
Bartlett, Frederick Orin, III:504; IV:79*n*
Bartlett, John Sherren, I:131
Bartlett, Samuel Colcord, II:115*n*, 315, 374, 518*n*, 519
Bartlett, W. C., III:402–03, 406
Bartlett's *Familiar Quotations,* V:ix
Barton, Benjamin S., I:267
Barton, Bruce, IV:472
Barton, Ralph, III:489, 531; IV:567
Barton, William E., II:262*n*, 273
Bartram, William, I:201
Baruch, Bernard Mannes, IV:549; V:56
Bascom, Henry Bidleman, II:66*n*
Bascom, John, II:517
Baseball
  in Civil War era (1850–65), II:202–3
  in post-Civil War era (1865–85), III:209
    amateur, III:217
    college baseball, III:222
    popularity, III:216–17
    salaries of ballplayers, III:217
    specialized periodicals, III:218
  in Gilded Age (1885–1905), IV:634, 636; V:374
Basford, George M., II:298*n*, 299
Bashford, Herbert, III:402*n*; IV:126
Basis, IV:171
Baskervill, William Malone, IV:91
Bass, John Foster, II:483
Basset, Abbot, III:213
Bassett, Allen Lee, III:33
Bassett, George B., II:364*n*
Bassett, John Spencer, IV:73, 213; V:273–80, 282, 285
Bassett, William, II:275*n*, 285
Bateman, Alan M., I:302*n*
Bateman, M. B., I:443
Bates, Arlo, IV:122, 480, 634, 719
Bates, Elisha, I:162
Bates, Ernest Sutherland, IV:730
Bates, Harry Wakefield, I:580*n*
Bates, Herbert, IV:389
Bates, Katharine Lee, IV:724
Bates, Mary E., IV:143*n*
Bath, N.C., II:89
Bathing, comment on, I:475–76
Bathing beauty illustrations, IV:152
Battle Creek, Mich., III:139, 210*n*; IV:238, 314*n*, 345*n*, 382
Bauble, IV:48, 390*n*
Baum, Henry Mason, II:364*n*, 365, 366; IV:140
Baum, Vickie, IV:475
Baumes, J. R., III:72
Baxter, Katherine, IV:98
Baxter, Sylvester, IV:633*n*, 635
Baxter Springs, Kan., III:81
Bay State Monthly, IV:79*n*
Bay View Magazine, IV:54, 223, 265
Bayard, James Asheton, II:545
Bayles, James C., III:128*n*
Baynes, Ernest Harold, IV:627
Bayonet, IV:178*n*
Bazar, Der, III:388, 389
Beach, Alfred Ely, II:40, 316*n*, 317, 320, 322
Beach, Mrs. C. Y., III:161
Beach, Charles F., III:74
Beach, Frederick Converse, II:316*n*, 321, 322; IV:149
Beach, H. D., II:22
Beach, James S., I:389*n*
Beach, Moses Yale, I:781
Beach, Rex, IV:116*n*, 367*n*, 457, 497, 501, 602, 692; V:30, 32, 80, 83, 148,
Beach, Stewart, IV:261*n*
Beadle, Erastus Flavel, II:100, 466; III:43; IV:117
Beadle, Irwin, III:43, 179, 210
Beadle & Adams, III:223
Beadle magazines, II:466–68
Beadle's Dime Library, IV:118
Beadle's Home Monthly, II:466
Beadle's Monthly, II:396, 467; III:33
Beadle's Weekly, III:43
Beane, Charles Everett, IV:79*n*
Beard, Charles Austin, II:404; III:542; IV:180, 521, 730; V:54, 93, 95–96, 200
Beard, Daniel Carter, III:178*n*; IV:602, 633, 636

Beard, Frank, II:184, 185*n*, 481; III: 504, 552; IV:103, 301
Beard, Mary, V:93
Beards, magazine comment on, I:477–78, 643; II:214
Beardsley, Aubrey, IV:450
Bearings, IV:379
Beaton, Kenneth Carrol, III:532
Beatrice, Neb., III:95
Beatty, A. P., IV:69*n*
Beatty, Bessie, IV:580*n*, 584
Beatty, George, I:268*n*, 269
Beaumont, Tex., IV:184*n*
Beauregard, Pierre Gustave Toutant, II:253; III:469
Beauty and Health, IV:316
Beauty hints, V:139, 143
Beaverbrook, 1st Baron (William Maxwell Aitken), IV:787
Bechdolt, Frederick Ritchie, IV:116*n*
Bechdolt, Jack, IV:618
Beck, George, I:312
Beck, Thomas Hambly, IV:468–78, 763*n*
Becker, Carl L., V:337
Becker, Joseph, II:460, 462
Becker, May Lamberton, III:500*n*, 505; IV:439
Becker, Thomas A., III:69*n*
Beckett, Harry, IV:258
Beckley, Zoe, IV:366*n*
Beckwith, George, II:211*n*
Bedford-Jones, Henry James O'Brien, IV:114*n*, 422
Bee (Philadelphia), IV:672
Bee Keepers' Guide, III:161
Bee Keepers' Magazine, III:161
Beebe, M. A., IV:764
Beebe, William, III:349; IV:439, 637
Beebee, William, I:488*n*
Beecher, Catherine Esther, III:92
Beecher, Edward, I:532; II:374; III: 423
Beecher, Henry Ward, I:443–44; III:23, 76, 87, 92, 171, 172, 211, 526; IV:16, 32, 44, 543
  as contributor, II:270, 361, 369, 371
  as editor, II:24, 71, 367*n*, 371–74; III:422–26
  on French literature, II:164
  scandal, II:328
  on theaters, II:200
Beecher, J. A., III:39*n*
Beecher, Luther, II:116*n*
Beecher, Lyman, I:286, 569–71, 659, 745
Beecher, Thomas Kinnicut, III:423
Beecher-Tilton scandal, III:76, 87, 426, 447–51, 526
Beecher's Illustrated Magazine, III:39*n*
Beekeepers' Magazine, IV:345
Bee-Keeper's Review, IV:345
Bee-keeping journals
  in post-Civil War era (1865–85), III:161
  in Gilded Age (1885–1905), IV:345
Beer, Thomas, IV:440, 696, 730; V:266–67
Beerbohm, Max, IV:451, 452; V:121
Beers, Henry Augustin, IV:263, 560; V:337
Beeville, Tex., IV:363*n*
Belasco, David, IV:500
Belcher, Joshua, I:247*n*, 249
Belcher, Robert W., 296*n*
Belden, Henry Marvin, IV:726
Belford, Robert J., IV:45*n*
Belford's Monthly, IV:39, 45
Belgium, independence of, I:339
Belknap, Jeremy, I:96, 106
Belknap, Joseph, I:31*n*
Bell, Alexander Graham, III:108, 121; IV:307, 582, 620–23, 626
Bell, Clark, III:142
Bell, Edward Price, IV:577
Bell, Edwin, Q., II:338*n*, 348
Bell, Horace, IV:107
Bell, J. D., III:107
Bell, L. H., II:77*n*
Bell, Lillian, IV:766–67
Bellah, James Warner, IV:606, 697, 709
Bellaire, Robert, IV:476
Bellamy, Edward, IV:110, 178, 300–3, 204, 205, 280, 406, 514
Bellamy, Francis, IV:58*n*
Bellamy, Francis Rufus, III:422*n*, 434; IV:732
Bellamy nationalism, IV:191, 202–3
Bellamy Review, IV:203*n*
Belles and Beaux, II:468; III:179
Belles-lettres
  in magazines before 1865, I:3, 72, 79, 102–3, 210, 276, 292, 368, 452, 620, 683; II:33, 43, 69, 423, 462, 503
  in magazines after Civil War, III:344, 358; IV:41, 521, 601, 666, 669
Bellew, Frank Henry Temple, I:426; II:179, 181, 182*n*, 184, 185, 390, 480, 521, 523; III:102, 265, 266, 441, 557
Bellew, Frank P. W., III:552; IV:564
Bellingham, Washington, V:6
Belloc, Hilaire, III:330; IV:326

Bellows, Albert F., III:187
Bellows, Henry Whitney, I:284*n*, 285*n*, 291, 374; III:23, 85, 87, 507
Belmont, August, III:214
Belmont, Oliver Hazard Perry, IV:386
Beloit, Wis., IV:285*n*
Beloit College Monthly, II:99
Belton, Tex., III:155
Bemis, Elizabeth P., IV:269
Benavente y Martinez, Jacinto, IV:121*n*
Benavides y Diez Canseco, Alfredo, IV:107
Benchley, Robert C., IV:439, 441, 566, 568
Benda, Wladyslaw Theodor, III:487; IV: 501, 602
Bender, Eric J., III:500*n*, 505
Benedict, Frank Lee, II:306*n*, 310; III:511; IV:48*n*
Benedict, S. W., II:312*n*, 313
Benedict's Fashion Journal, III:98*n*
Benefield, Barry, V:258
Benét, Stephen Vincent, IV:439, 471, 701, 709; V:251, 264, 336
Benét, William Rose, V:236, 251
Benezet, Anthony, I:102
Benham, P. D., III:270*n*
Benham's Musical Review, III:197*n*
Ben-hur, IV:141, 259–60
Benjamin, Charles Love, IV:246*n*
Benjamin, Park, II:35, 455
as contributor, I:546, 578, 587*n*, 608 627, 642, 651, 734, 743, 760, 770
as editor, I:344–45, 358–62, 499, 599*n* 601–02, 618*n*, 619–20
quoted, I:448, 495
Benjamin, Samuel Greene Wheeler, III: 186; IV:45*n*
Benjamin, Walter Romeyn, IV:391
Benjamin, William Evarts, IV:127
Benn, R. Davis, III:185*n*
Bennett, Arnold, III:390, 488, 489; IV:438, 439, 466, 472, 604, 618, 696, 769
Bennett, Emerson, II:362; IV:680
Bennett, Ira Elbert, IV:108*n*
Bennett, James Gordon, I:330; II:2–5, 361, 524, 525; III:441, 527
Bennett, John, III:504
Bennett, Orlando, 671*n*, 680
Bennett, Mrs. S. R. I., II:211*n*
Bennington, Vt., I:31*n*, 163; II:275
Benson, Arthur Christopher, II:431
"Benson, Carl," *see* Bristed, Charles Astor
Benson, Edward Frederick, II:463
Benson, Eugene, III:18, 184, 279, 369, 376, 377, 393, 418
Benson, Frances M., IV:580*n*, 581
Benson, Stuart, IV:465
Bent, George, IV:104*n*
Bent, Silas, III:479; IV:577
Bentley, Eric, V:222
Bentley, Max, IV:605
Bentley's Book Buyer, III:456*n*
Bentley's Miscellany, II:384, 424
Benton, Caroline French, IV:769
Benton, Joel, III:37*n*, 427, 483; IV:271, 482, 616
Benton, Myron, II:535
Benton Harbor, Mich., III:112*n*
Benyon, John Foster, IV:50
Benziger's Magazine, IV:298–99
Bercovici, Konrad, III:479, 490; IV:607
Berea, Ohio, III:197
Beresford, J. D., V:96
Berg, Albert Ellery, IV:261
Berg, Susie, V:24
Bergh, Henry, III:311–12
Berghaus, Albert, II:458–459, 460
Bergson, Henry, V:168
Bergstresser, J. C., III:146
Beringer, George M., I:539*n*, 540
Berkeley, Cal., IV:310
Berkeley Club (University of California), IV:74
Berks, Bucks, and Oxon Archaeological Journal, IV:140*n*
Berkshire Archaeological Record, IV:140*n*
Berkshire Courier, V:125
Berle, A. A. Jr., IV:730, 749; V:333
Berlin, Congress of (1878), III:275
Berlin, Irving, IV:697
Berlin, Richard E., V:140, 162
Bernard, John, I:248
Bernard, Peter D., I:644
Bernhardt, Sarah, III:205; IV:122, 257
Berwick, Edward, IV:779
Besant, Walter, II:463, 482; IV:12, 226, 489, 490, 592
Bess, Demaree, IV:709, 712
Bessom, Harold E., IV:428*n*, 431
Best, James B., IV:55*n*
Best in Print from Book and Journal, IV:56
Best sellers, II:171–72; III:246–48; IV: 110–11, 131, 141–42, 435, 439
Best Short Stories, V:182–83
Best Things, IV:71
Best's Insurance News, IV:351*n*
Bethany, Va., II:74
Bethlehem, Pa., II:74

Bethune, George Washington, II:424
Better Farming, III:156*n*
Better Homes and Gardens, V:142
sketch of, V:36–48
Bettleheim, Edward S., III:198*n*
Betts, Lillian W., III:429
Beverage Journal, III:135
Beveridge, Albert Jeremiah, IV:46*n,* 164, 500, 689, 690, 692, 703, 706, 754*n;* V:32
Bibelot, sketch of, IV:424–27, 388
Bibelot magazines, IV:386–91, 639–48
Bibesco, George (Prince), IV:519
Bible
early magazines on (1741–94), I:63–64
Civil War era magazines on (1850–65)
illustrated version, II:192
proslavery arguments, II:138–39
post-Civil War magazines on (1865–85), III:526
specialized journals, III:84
Gilded Age magazines on (1885–1905), IV:140, 404
revision of, III:88, 248
Bible Convention (1853), II:286
Bible Review, IV:304*n*
Bible stories, I:623
Biblia, IV:140
Biblical Recorder, II:65*n*
Biblical Repertory, II:62; *see also: Princeton Review*
Biblical Repository, I:367, 371, 800
Biblical World, III:84; IV:301
Bibliotheca Platonica, III:89
Bibliotheca Sacra, II:70, 130; III:76; IV:276, 293, 395
debate with *Princeton Review,* I:532–33
founding of, I:371–72
sketch of, I:729–42
Bickford, Clarence A., IV:72*n*
Bickley, G. W. L., II:115*n*
Bicknell, Thomas Williams, III:168
Bicycle advertising, IV:24, 29
Bicycle clubs, IV:378
Bicycle fashions, IV:379
Bicycle magazines, III:211, 213; IV:379–80, 632
Bicycles
in post-Civil War era (1865–85), III:211–13, 550
in Gilded Age (1885–1905)
magazine accounts, IV:379, 634, 636
pneumatic tires, IV:377
popularity, IV:326, 377–78
sales, IV:377–78
women and, IV:370, 378
Bicycling World, II:213; IV:379
Bicycling World and the Archery Field, III:213*n,* 220
Bicycling World and Motorcycle Review, III:213*n*
Biddle, Margaret Thompson, IV:772
Biddle, Nicholas, I:223*n,* 239
Bidwell, Walter Hilliard, I:306*n,* 308
Bierce, Ambrose, III:56–57, 406; IV:77, 106, 492, 656; V:119, 249
Bigelow, David, II:448
Bigelow, Frederic Southgate, IV:708
Bigelow, John, I:671; II:448; III:465*n*
Bigelow, Poultney, IV:231, 495, 633*n,* 634–35
Bigelow, William, I:108, 109, 111, 127*n,* 177–78
Bigelow, William Frederick, V:125*n,* 133–37
Biggers, Earl Derr, IV:469, 695, 697
Biglow, H., I:126, 297
Bikle, Philip Melancthon, II:73; IV:295
Biles, J. H., IV:326
Bilioustine, IV:647
Billboard, IV:261
Billheimer, Thomas C., II:73*n*
Billiard Cue, II:203; III:220
Billiard playing, II:203, 455; III:220
Billings, John Shaw, V;293*n,* 303
"Billings, Josh," *see* Shaw, Henry Wheeler
Bimonthlies, *see names of specific bimonthlies*
Binney, Horace, II:155, 244
Biographical Magazine, III:263
Biography
in early magazines (1741–94)
general magazines, I:90, 94, 97
popularity, I:39
in nationalist era magazines (1794–1825)
literary magazines, I:295, 312–13, 321; II:230, 233
missionary magazines, I:262
popularity, I:175–76
religious magazines, I:299, 315
women's magazines, II:311
in expansionist era magazines (1825-50), I:753
literary magazines, II:236
popularity, I:421
religious magazines, I:563
women's magazines, I:547, 553, 589

Biography—*Continued*
in Civil War era magazines (1850–65) II:30
education magazines, II:44
family magazines, III:471
general magazines, II:384, 389–90, 449, 491
literary magazines, II:407, 425, 429
popularity, II:176
in post-Civil War magazines (1865–85)
Chautauqua magazines, III:546
current events magazines, III:337, 347
general magazines, II:418, 470, 472
literary magazines, II:398; III:36, 263, 375–76
specialized journals, III:263
in Gilded Age magazines (1885–1905), IV:783
current events magazines, II:347
general magazines, III:472, 590–91, 675
popularity, IV:136–37
in modern magazines (1905–30)
booksellers' periodicals, IV:439
current events magazines, V:55
general periodicals, IV:602, 606, 721, 725, 727; V:85, 287
literary magazines, II:431
review periodicals, IV:521
Biological Bulletin, IV:309
Biology, *see* Botany; Darwinian theory; Natural history; Zoology magazines
Bioren, John, I:166
Birch, Reginald Bathurst, III:502
Birch, Thomas, I:436
Bird, Albert A., IV:263
Bird, E. B., IV:451–52
Bird, Frederic Mayer, III:396*n*
Bird, J., III:396*n*
Bird, J. Malcolm, II:323
Bird, Milton, II:62*n*
Bird, Robert Montgomery, I:378, 408, 409, 587*n*, 609, 638
Bird, Robert Montgomery, Jr., III:400*n*
Bird, William A., III:296*n*
Bird-Lore, IV:310*n*
illustrations of, I:243
magazines on, IV:627–28
"Birds, The" (Daphne du Maurier), V:136
Birge, Benjamin, I:312
Birkbeck, Morris, I:596
Birmingham, Ala., magazines in, III:73*n*; IV:126, 183, 270*n*, 313*n*, 341
Birmingham, Ernest F., IV:244, 751*n*, 752
Birney, James G., I:457
Birnie, William Alfred Hart, IV:763*n*, 771
Birrell, August, IV:722
Birth control
advertising of contraceptives, II:37
magazine comment on, IV:520; V:169
Bisbee, Frank A., IV:88
Bisbee, Frederick Adelbert, IV:296
Bisco, John, I:760–61
Bishop, John, IV:712
Bishop, John Peale, V:266
Bishop, Joseph Bucklin, III:346; IV:727
Bishop, William Henry, II:506*n*, 510; III:224
Bisland, Elizabeth, IV:482
Bismarck, Otto von, IV:231, 685
Bistoury, III:142
Bittner, A. H., IV:417*n*
Bivins, Joseph Francis, V:273*n*, 278
Bivouac, III:132
Biweeklies, *see names of specific biweeklies*
Bizarre, II:210*n*
Bjerrgaard, Carl Henry Andrew, IV:287
Björnson, Bjornstjerne, III:255; IV:121
Black, Jeremiah Sullivan, II:251, 252; III:88, 286, 376; IV:88
Black, William, II:393; III:224, 250, 358, 378, 389
Black, Winifred, IV:98
Black Cat, IV:48, 116
sketch of, IV:428–31
Black Diamond, IV:189*n*, 322*n*
Black Friday (1869), III:296
Black and White, IV:351*n*
Blackboard, IV:117*n*
Blackburn, William Maxwell, I:534*n*
Blackman, William Fremont, V:329*n*
Black Mask, V:262
Blackmore, Richard Doddridge, II:393; III:224, 529
Blackwell, Alice Stone, III:94*n*; IV:355–56
Blackwell, Henry Brown, III:94; IV:355
Blackwood, Algernon, III:479
Blackwood's Edinburgh Magazine, II:130, 420–421, 489
Blackwood's Magazine, III:279; IV:228
Blade and Ledger, III:53*n*
Bladworth, Mrs. George H. ("May Manton"), IV:360*n*, 580*n*, 581
Blaine, James Gillespie, II:254, 269, 376, 481; III:345, 524, 553; IV:51, 155, 165, 481
Blair, Emma Helen, IV:14

Blake, Alexander, I:669*n*, 670
Blake, E. V., III:255
Blake, George W., IV:170
Blake, T. C., II:62*n*
Blake, William, IV:425
Blakely, George E., III:54
Blanchard, C. Elton, IV:64*n*
Blanchard, Frank LeRoy, V:59*n*, 62–64
Blanchard, Joshua, I:78
Bland, Mrs. M. Cora, III:96
Bland, Richard Parks, IV:161
Blasco-Ibañez, Vincente, IV:498, 501, 605
Blashfield, Albert Dodd, IV:385, 564, 767
Blashfield, Edwin Howland, III:411; IV:144, 151, 719
Blast Furnace, II:92
Blavatsky, Helena Petrovna, IV:286–87, 304*n*
Bledsoe, Albert Taylor, I:669, 690; II:66*n*; III:23, 70, 382–84
Bleecker, Mrs. Ann Eliza, I:114–15
Bleecker, Anthony, I:115
Blind, Karl, II:532; III:35*n*
Blind-aid periodicals, IV:194
Bliss, Charles H., IV:162–63
Bliss, Edward Munsell, IV:571
Bliss, Harriet, III:457*n*
Bliss, William Dwight Porter, 203, 204, 282–83
Bliss' Quarterly, IV:162–63
Bliven, Bruce, V:55, 191*n*, 202, 210, 213, 219, 222–24
Block, Lewis J., III:51*n*
Blodgett, Thomas Harper, IV:633*n*, 638
Bloe, W. C., V:6
Blood, James H., III:443*n*, 444–46
Bloomer, Amelia Jenks, II:50; III:96
Bloomer, Harvey M., IV:86
Bloomer, William J., IV:86
Bloomer dress, II:51, 54, 55; III:307
Bloomfield, Maurice, III:535*n*, 536
Bloomfield, Robert, I:178
Bloomington, Ind., III:111, 169*n*
Bloomington, J. S., III:146
Blossom, Sumner Newton, III:495*n*, 499, 510*n*, 516
Blot, Pierre, III:279, 308, 376
Blouet, Paul ("Max O'Rell"), II:255
Blue, E. N., III:528
Blue Eagle, V:71
Blue Grass Blade, IV:277–78
Blue and Gray, 119*n*
Blue laws, II:34
Blue Sky, IV:389–90
Blum, Emil, IV:136
Blum, Léon, V:56, 314
Blum, Robert, IV:151
Blumenberg, Marc A., III:196
Blumer, Herbert, IV:192*n*
Blunden, Edmund, IV:441
Blythe, Samuel George, IV:484, 692, 693, 696, 707
Blythe, Stuart O., II:435
Board of Trade Journal, IV:186
Boarding schools, women's, II:46–47
Boardman, E. H., III:235*n*
Boas, Franz, IV:308, 489; V:338
Boat racing, II:203; *see also* Water sports; Yachting magazines
Bob Brooks Library, IV:119*n*
Bobbett & Hooper, II:390, 454, 523
Boccaccio, Giovanni, V:119
Bodenheim, Maxwell, IV:440; V:176, 266
Bodmer, C. H., I:548
Bodwell, J. C., II:518*n*
Boer War, II:256; IV:227, 486, 780
Bogan, Louise, V:236
Bogardus, A., IV:543
Bogart, Elizabeth, II:265
Bogert, J. A., III:187, 411, 420
Boggs, Edward B., II:364*n*, 365
Bohemian, II:112
Bohemian (Boston), IV:117*n*
Bohemian (Ft. Worth), IV:72
Bohémienne, IV:254*n*
Bohen, Fred, V:42
Bohm, Charles, IV:751*n*
Boiler Maker, IV:333*n*
Boilermakers' Journal, IV:221*n*
Boissevain, Natasha, V:25
Bojer, Johan, III:543; IV:501; V:119
Bok, Edward William, IV:15, 32, 35, 37, 45, 60, 168, 353, 355, 357, 359, 536*n*, 539–50, 641
Boker, George Henry, I:771; II:542, 551; III:361–62, 396, 397, 558; IV:87
Bolce, Harold, IV:496, 644
Bolitho, William, IV:748
Bolles, A. S., II:94*n*
Bolles, William E., IV:54
Bollingen Prize for Poetry, V:231–35
Bolton, Sarah Knowles, III:511
Bombast in magazines, I:194–95, 235, 449, 582, 724
Bonaparte, Charles Joseph, III:296*n*
Bonaparte, Napoleon, II:389, 390; IV:137, 230, 485, 590–91, 719
Bond, Thomas E., II:66*n*
Bond Buyer, IV:349*n*
Bonds and Mortgages, IV:349*n*
Bonesteel, Chesley, IV:478
Boneville Trumpet, III:268*n*

Bonfort's Wine and Spirit Circular, III:135; IV:251
Bonheur, Rosa, IV:544, 685
Bonner, John, II:469*n,* 470; IV:105, 239
Bonner, Robert, II:15–16, 23, 356–63; IV:65
Bonner, Robert E., II:356*n,* 363
Bonnet, Theodore Firmin, IV:106
Bonney, Mrs., P. P. II:267
Bonney, Therese, IV:761–62
Bonsal, Stephen, IV:465, 596, 730; V:54
Book Bulletin, III:236
Book Buyer, III:236; IV:126–27
Book Chat, IV:127
Book Culture, IV:126
Book Exchange Monthly, III:256
Book Keeper, III:147*n*
Book Lover, IV:127
Book and News Dealer, IV:127
Book News Monthly, III:235; IV:127
Book Notes, IV:127
Book Notes for the Week, III:234, 262*n;* IV:127
Book reviews, IV:127
  in nationalist era magazines (1794–1825), I:128, 174, 241, 323–24
    foreign books, I:191–92
    general magazines, I:253, 257–58
    literary magazines, I:241, 313, 329, 331–32
    political magazines, I:276
    religious magazines, I:263, 287
    women's magazines, I:329
  in expansionist era magazines (1825–50), I:359; II:240
    business magazines, II:340
    education periodicals, I:543
    general magazines, I:674, 755
    literary magazines, I:620, 635–36, 640–42, 652, 660, 726, 736, 770
    political magazines, I:777–78
    specialized periodicals, I:766–68
    women's magazines, I:547, 553–54; II:301
  in Civil War era magazines (1850–65), II:22, 534–35
    family magazines, II:417
    illustrated weeklies, II:453
    literary magazines, II:420, 507
    military magazines, II:551
    religious magazines, II:365
    women's magazines, II:308, 436, 466
  in post-Civil War magazines (1865–85), II:248–49, 259; III:430, 434
    current events periodicals, III:322, 334–35
    family magazines, III:424, 427
    fashion magazines, III:482
    literary periodicals, III:232, 399, 403, 540, 549
    religious magazines, III:439
    scientific magazines, III:496
  in Gilded Age magazines (1885–1905)
    booksellers' magazines, IV:433–34
    comic periodicals, IV:560
    digest periodicals, IV:571, 573
    family magazines, IV:482
    illustrated weeklies, II:464; IV:560
    literary magazines, III:540, 551
    women's periodicals, IV:768
  in modern magazines (1905–30), IV:410
    comic magazines, III:555
    current events magazines, III:354; V:55, 56, 305
    general magazines, III:555; V:7, 10–11, 21, 23, 95–96, 331, 337
    juvenile magazines, III:504
    literary magazines, III:542
    review periodicals, IV:521
  See also Literary criticism
Book of the Royal Blue, IV:333*n*
Book-Keeper, IV:351–52
Bookkeeping magazines, IV:351–52
Booklovers Bulletin, V:27*n*
Booklovers Libraries, V:27
Booklovers' Magazine, IV:393; V:27–29, 33
Booklovers Weekly, V:27*n*
Bookman, sketch of, IV:432–41, 112, 124, 141
Bookmart, III:235; IV:127
Books, III:235–36
  advertising of, IV:27
  magazine articles and, IV:41
  publishing of, I:375
  See also Book reviews
Bookseller (Chicago), IV:127
Bookseller, Newsdealer and Stationer, IV:127
Bookseller and Latest Literature, IV:127
Bookseller and Newsman, IV:127
Booksellers' magazines
  in post-Civil War era (1865–85), III:135, 235–36, 491–93
  in Gilded Age (1885–1905), III:493–94; IV:126–27, 432–36
  modern (1905–), III:494; IV:436–41
  See also Publishers' periodicals
Bookworm, IV:126
Boomerang, III:269
Boone, Daniel, I:102, 755–56

Boone, Richard Gause, III:168*n*
Boot and Shoe Recorder, III:127; IV:185
Booth, Ballington, V:288
Booth, Edwin, III:203, 416; IV:226, 256
Booth, Ernest, V:9
Booth, Mary Louise, III:388, 390
Booth, William, IV:201
Boots and Shoes, III:127*n*
Borah, Leo Arthur, IV:630, 632
Borah, William Edgar, III:486; IV:728
Borie, A. J., II:204*n*
Borrow, George, I:481*n*
Boss, Benjamin, II:79*n*
Boss, Lewis, II:79*n*
Bostelmann, Else, IV:628
Boston, Mass.
  as literary and cultural center, I:202–3, 376, 378–80; II:32–33; III:29–30; IV:78–79
  early magazines in (1741–94), I:19, 25–26, 29–32, 50
    general magazines, I:78–79, 83, 104
    literary magazine, I:92
    postal regulations (1792) and, I:19
  nationalist era magazines in (1794–1825)
    abolitionist magazine, I:164
    agricultural magazine, I:317–19
    comic magazine, I:170
    general magazines, I:121, 124–25, 127–30, 247–50
    literary clubs and, I:194
    literary magazines, I:253–59, 331–32
    religious magazines, I:138, 277–78
  expansionist era magazines in (1825–50)
    abolitionist periodicals, I:457, 460; II:276
    agricultural journal, I:317*n*, 442
    general periodicals, I:615–17, 622–23
    juvenile magazines, I:492–93; II:262*n*, 265
    "knowledge" magazine, I:364
    legal periodical, I:451
    literary magazines, I:343–44, 346–47, 355, 367, 577–79, 599*n*, 604*n*, 718, 735, 747*n*
    "mammoth" papers, I:361–62
    medical journal, I:438
    music magazines, I:435
    number of periodicals, I:375*n*
    pedagogical periodicals, I:491, 541*n*
    personal periodicals, I:685–91
    religious magazines, I:368–69, 371, 372, 666*n*
    temperance magazine, I:473; II:275
    theatrical criticism, I:427
    transcendentalist magazine, I:702–10
    vocational magazines, I:445
    women's magazine, I:349
  Civil War era magazines in (1850–65)
    agricultural magazine, II:88
    education journal, II:99*n*
    historical journals, II:175
    home magazines, II:59
    illustrated weeklies, II:45, 409*n*
    juvenile magazines, I:492–93; II:100, 101, 262*n*
    legal periodicals, I:451*n*; II:93
    literary and general magazines, I:747*n*; II:31, 32–33, 35, 43, 219*n*, 494
    magazine center, II:106–7
    Masonic journal, II:215
    music journals, I:435; II:197
    police gazette, II:187
    political magazine, II:540–43
    prison reform periodical, II:211–12
    religious periodicals, I:372; II:64, 65, 67, 69, 71–72, 74, 75, 76, 101, 516, 518
    spiritualist magazine, II:209
    Sunday papers, II:35–36
    temperance magazine, II:275
    theatrical periodical, II:198
    women's magazines, II:52, 57
  post-Civil War magazines in (1865–85)
    agricultural magazine, III:151–52
    art journals, III:185
    banking periodical, III:147
    booksellers' periodical, III:236
    chromolithographic journal, III:186
    comic, III:266–67, 268*n*–69*n*
    construction periodicals, III:129
    education journal, II:99*n*
    engineering periodical, III:114
    freedmen's journal, III:283
    freethinker journal, III:88–89
    gardening magazine, III:162
    general magazines, III:39*n*, 256, 357
    historical journals, II:175; III:259, 262*n*
    humane societies, III:312
    insurance periodicals, III:146*n*
    juvenile magazines, II:101, 262; III:175–80, 508*n*
    kindergarten magazines, III:163
    labor periodical, III:299
    legal journal, III:144

Boston, Mass.—*Continued*
literary magazines, I:747*n;* II:219*n,* 493*n;* III:34, 36*n,* 39*n,* 233, 454
manufacturers' journal, III:127
Masonic journal, II:215; III:315
military periodical, III:132
music journals, II:197; III:196–98
police gazette, II:187
religious magazines, I:372; II:65, 69, 74*n,* 75, 76, 101, 518*n;* III:34, 68, 70, 72, 75–76, 77*n,* 78, 84, 85*n,* 436, 506
scientific periodicals, III:108, 109*n,* 110, 111
society notes, III:101–2
spiritualist magazines, II:209; III:81, 82*n*
sports periodicals, III:209–10, 213, 215, 218
temperance periodical, III:310*n*
trade magazine, III:134
women's magazines, III:98, 100
women's rights magazine, III:94
Gilded Age magazines in (1885–1905)
advertising journal, IV:247
all-fiction magazines, IV:115, 117
amateur periodicals, IV:390*n*
anarchist periodical, IV:173
architectural periodicals, IV:323
art periodicals, IV:147
brick periodical, IV:325*n*
chess periodical, IV:382
country-life periodicals, IV:338
culinary periodicals, IV:364
education periodicals, IV:268–69, 272
family magazine, IV:67
financial periodicals, III:147; IV:349*n*
forestry periodical, IV:342
fruit-growers' periodical, IV:342
general magazines, IV:44, 46
historical periodical, III:259; IV:140*n*
hobby periodicals, IV:391
home periodicals, IV:82, 363*n*
illustrated periodical, IV:80
insurance journal, III:146*n*
juvenile magazines, II:101, 262*n;* III:508*n*; IV:16, 273, 275
library periodical, IV:143
literary sheets, I:747*n;* II:493*n;* III:454*n;* IV:80, 124–25
local topics, IV:80–82
mail-order periodicals, IV:366
manufacturing periodicals, III:127; IV:183*n,* 185
missionary periodical, III:70; IV:305
music periodical, III:196–98; IV:254
Negro periodical, IV:214
pharmacy periodical, IV:318
philology journal, IV:128
philosophy journals, IV:302–3
photography periodical, IV:149
physical culture periodicals, IV:316
poetry magazine, IV:121
police gazette, II:187; IV:372
political science journal, IV:181
poultry periodical, IV:345
printers' periodical, IV:248*n*
regional periodicals, II:85*n;* IV:79–80
religious magazines, III:436*n,* 506*n;* IV:285, 291–92, 294–97
review periodicals, IV:52, 60, 62, 72*n*
scientific periodicals, III:108*n,* 112
settlement-house periodical, IV:195*n*
socialist periodicals, IV:204, 282–83
spelling reform periodical, IV:212
spiritualist periodicals, II:209; III:81; IV:81, 414*n*
sports periodicals, III:213, 215; IV:372, 381, 633
statistical periodical, IV:310*n*
Sunday periodicals, IV:69*n*
tariff periodicals, IV:166
temperance periodical, III:310*n*
theater periodicals, IV:261
trade periodicals, IV:186, 187*n,* 189*n*
urban periodicals, IV:81–82
women's club periodical, IV:356
women's periodicals, IV:361, 366
writers' magazine, IV:142
modern magazines in (1905–)
architectural periodicals, IV:323
banking periodical, III:147*n*
brick periodical, IV:325*n*
chess periodical, IV:382
country-life periodical, IV:338
culinary magazine, IV:364
education periodical, IV:268–69
general magazine, V:329*n*
horticultural magazine, IV:342
juvenile magazines, II:101, 262*n*
library periodical, IV:143
literary magazines, I:747*n;* II:493*n*
medical journal, II:84*n*
music periodical, IV:254*n*
pharmacy periodical, IV:318
philosophy journal, IV:303
photography periodical, IV:149

poultry periodical, IV:345
regional periodical, IV:79–80
religious magazines, II:367*n*; III:85*n*; IV:285, 294
spiritualist periodical, III:81
sports periodicals, III:213, 215; IV:381, 633*n*
tariff periodical, IV:166
temperance periodical, III:310*n*
textile magazines, IV:185*n*
trade journals, III:134; IV:187*n*, 189*n*
women's periodical, IV:361
writers' magazine, IV:142
economic decline of, III:30
music in, IV:249
newspapers in, III:270*n*
public bathing in, I:475–76
smoking restrictions in, I:474–75
theater in, I:169
Watch and Ward Society in, V:13–15
Boston Atheneum, I:397
Boston Beacon, III:42*n*, 102; IV:81
Boston Budget, III:42, 102*n*, 267*n*; IV:81
Boston Censor, I:48
Boston Commonwealth, II:141
Boston Congregationalist, *see: Congregationalist*
Boston Contributor, III:85*n*
Boston Cooking School Magazine, IV:364
Boston Courier, III:270*n*
Boston Cultivator, I:444*n*, 804
Boston fire (1872), III:118
Boston Home Journal, III:101; IV:81
Boston Ideas, IV:81
Boston Intelligencer, *see Saturday Evening Gazette*
Boston Journal of Chemistry, III:110
Boston Journal of Commerce, III:147; IV:186
Boston Journal of Philosophy and Arts, I:152, 797
Boston Magazine (1783–86), I:28–29, 37, 40, 166*n*, 167, 788
Boston Magazine (1805–06), *see: Boston Weekly Magazine*
Boston Mechanic, I:445, 801
Boston Medical Intelligencer, I:151*n*, 797
Boston Medical and Surgical Journal, I:151*n*, 800; II:84; III:139; IV:313
Boston Miscellany, I:346, 510, 712
sketch of, I:718–20
Boston Monthly Magazine, I:343, 798
Boston Museum, II:36
Boston Musical Herald, III:197
Boston Musical Review, I:435, 808
Boston Musical Times, II:198*n*
Boston Notion, II:45
Boston Pathfinder, II:181
Boston Pearl, I:356, 800
Boston Public Library, V:344
Boston Pulpit, III:84
Boston Quarterly Review
founding of, I:367–68
sketch of, I:685–91
Boston Recorder, I:138, 373, 795; II:71; III:76
Boston Review, II:71, 516; III:76
sketch of, II:518–519
Boston Spectator, I:160*n*, 794
Boston Transcript, V:184, 259
Boston Weekly Magazine (1743), I:25, 787
Boston Weekly Magazine (1803–6)
founding of, I:127
sketch of, 247–50
Bostonian, IV:80
Bostwick, Arthur Elmore, IV:515, 572
Bostwick, Helen Louise, II:417, 466
Botanical Bulletin, III:111*n*
Botanical Gazette, III:111
Botanical periodicals, III:111; IV:309–10
Botany, I:303, 311; II:228, 243
Both Sides, IV:210
Bothwick, J. D., II:118
Botta, Vincenzo, IV:83*n*
Bottome, Margaret, IV:542–43
Boucicault, Dion, II:199, 253; II:202–3; IV:245, 410
Bourget, Paul, IV:230, 489, 514, 612; V:28
Bourjaily, Monte, III:552*n*, 556
Bourke-White, Margaret, IV:761–62
Bourne, Edward Gaylord, V:329*n*, 330
Bourne, Henry Eldridge, IV:138*n*
Bourne, Randolph S., III:541; V:98, 206
Boutelle, De Witt Clinton, II:188
Boutwell, George Sewall, I:697; II:542
Bowden, H. L., IV:326
Bowditch, Nathaniel, II:228
Bowditch's American Florist and Farmer, III:162
Bowdoin Scientific Review, III:109*n*
Bowen, Abel, I:522
Bowen, Charles, II:218*n*
Bowen, Clarence W., II:367*n*, 377
Bowen, Francis, I:367, 414, 415; II:125, 134, 168, 218*n*, 220*n*, 238, 239–40, 242, 445

Bowen, Henry Chandler, II:367*n*, 368–77; III:6, 11, 23, 76; IV:7–8, 59
Bowen, T. P., I:122
Bowen, William H., II:64
Bowen & McNamee, II:367*n*, 371
Bower, Bertha Muzzy, IV:116*n*
Bowers, Claude Gernade, IV:503
Bowker, Richard Rogers, III:491*n*, 493, 494, 517*n*, 518, 519; IV:143, 166, 198
Bowlend, George B., III:441
Bowlers' Journal, IV:380
Bowles, Leonard C., II:72*n*; III:506
Bowles, Samuel, III:58, 458; V:126
Bowles, William Lisle, I:231
Bowling, III:220; IV:380
Bowman, George Ernest, IV:140
Bowman, Isaiah, II:415
Bowne, Borden Parker, II:315; III:455
Boxer Rebellion (1900), III:485; IV:233
Boxing, *see* Prize fighting
Box-Maker, IV:184*n*
Boyce, William D., III:53*n*, 54; IV:67–68
Boyd, Ernest, III:434; IV:439; V:5, 7–8, 11, 98–99, 266
Boyd, James, IV:709, 729
Boyd, John, I:209
Boyd, Thomas, IV:728
Boyd, William, IV:699
Boyd, William Kenneth, V:273*n*, 283
Boyden, Albert Augustus, III:513; IV:595, 600
Boyer, Norman, V:246*n*, 248, 251, 256
Boyesen, Hjalmar Hjorth, I:593; II:248, 271, 506*n*; III:41, 61, 224, 255, 372, 400, 461, 502, 545; IV:60, 238, 264, 267, 271, 480, 482, 484, 490, 513; V:342
Boyle, Harold V., IV:478
Boyle, Kay, IV:712, 771; V:337
Boynton, Henry Van Ness, III:289
Boynton, Henry Walcott, II:431; III:349; IV:438
Boynton, Percy, V:96, 268
Boys of America, III:174
Boys' and Girls' Magazine, I:492, 809
Boys' Library of Sport, Story and Adventure, III:179
Boys of New York, III:178
Boys' World, IV:275
Bozman, John Leeds, I:245
Brace, Charles Loring, II:28; III:28, 424
Brackenridge, Henry Marie, I:294
Brackenridge, Hugh Henry, I:27, 51
Brackett, Anna Callender, III:386
Bradbury, William Batchelder, II:197
Braddon, Mary Elizabeth, II:112*n*, 439, 462, 482; III:343, 389
Bradford, Amory Howe, III:429
Bradford, Andrew, I:24, 71–72, 73–74
Bradford, Gamaliel, III:347; IV:398, 439, 737
Bradford, Gamaliel, Jr., V:280, 338*n*
Bradford, Roark, II:404; IV:472, 473, 498, 521
Bradford, Thomas, I:26*n*
Bradford, William, I:25, 80–82; V:343
Bradford, Pa., III:131
Bradlaugh, Charles, III:249
Bradley, Alice, IV:769
Bradley, Horace, II:401
Bradley, La Verne, IV:630
Bradley, Will H., IV:100*n*, 389, 452, 456
Bradley, William Aspenwall, IV:126
Bradley, His Book, IV:389
Bradstreet's, III:147; IV:349
Brady, Albert, IV:594
Brady, Cyrus Townsend, III:400*n*, 485; IV:689, 724; V:249
Brady, Mathew B., II:191
Bragdon, Claude Fayette, IV:451–52
Brahms, Johannes, V:118
Braibanti, Ralph, V:273*n*
Brainard, John Gardiner Calkins, I:204
Brainard's Musical World, III:197*n*
Braine, Robert, III:197*n*
Brainerd, Thomas, II:62*n*, 517*n*
Braithwaite, William Stanley, IV:214; V:184, 258
Braley, Berton, IV:498, 606; V:269
Brancusi, Constantin, V:178
Brand, Max, *see* Faust, Frederick
Brandeis, Louis Dembitz, IV:462, 465, 500
Brandes, George, IV:225
Brandl, Alois, IV:225
Brandt, Albert, IV:401*n*, 415–16
Brandt, Erdmann Neumister, IV:708, 711
Brandt, Lillian, IV:744
Brann, William Cowper, IV:292, 372, 442–48, 656, 665
See also: Brann's Iconoclast
Brann's Iconoclast, IV:18, 94, 665; V:xiii
sketch of, IV:442–48
Branscomb, Harvey, V:273*n*
Bransom, Paul, IV:698
Braque, Georges, V:178

Brass Check, The (by Sinclair), V:151*n*
Brass Founder, IV:183*n*
Brattleboro, Vt., III:100; IV:339, 344*n*, 361
Braun, Will C., IV:527
Bray, Frank Chapin, III:544*n*, 546; IV:510
Bray, James M., IV:63*n*
Brayley, Arthur Willington, IV:80
Brayman, J. O., II:100
Breadnell, W. L., IV:50*n*
Breck, Joseph, I:317*n*, 319
Breck, Robert L., II:537*n*, 538
Breckenridge, John, II:155, 538
Breckinridge, Robert Jefferson, II:537, 538
Breed, Jack, IV:630
Breed, Joseph B., V:25
Breeder and Sportsman, III:215
Breeder's Gazette, III:159; IV:344
Breeze, III:269*n*
Brehm, George, IV:698; V:30
Bremer, Frederika, I:415
Brennam, Alfred, IV:564
Brennam, Frederick Hazlitt, IV:473
Brennan, J. F., III:314
Brentano's Monthly, III:211
Bresnahan, John F., V:82
Brethren Evangelist, III:81
Brewer, David Josiah, II:269
Brewers' magazines, III:135
Bribery, II:479; III:289
Brick, IV:325*n*
Brick and Clay Record, IV:325*n*
Brick, Tile and Metal Review, III:130
Brick-trade magazines, III:130; IV:325*n*
Brickbat, III:269*n*
Brickbuilder, IV:323
Bricklayer, Mason and Plasterer, IV:221*n*
Brickell, Herschel, II:259
Bridge, James Howard, III:402*n*, 408
Bridgeport, Conn., II:209; III:268*n*
Bridgman, Henry, II:92*n*
Bridgeman, L. H., I:435
Bridgeman's Magazine, IV:221*n*
Bridges, Robert, IV:458, 551, 560, 717*n*, 722, 726–29
Briffault, Robert, IV:730
Briggs, Charles Augustus, III:74, 196; IV:277, 288
Briggs, Charles Frederick ("Harry Franco"), II:160; III:231
  as contributor, I:341, 348, 362, 478, 499, 608
  as editor, I:366, 757–61; II:419–20, 426, 428–29
Briggs, Robert, I:556*n*
Brigham, Charles Henry, I:292*n*; III:507
Brigham, James H., III:39*n*
Brigham, Johnson, IV:96–97
Bright, Edward, II:64, 64*n*; III:72
Bright, James Wilson, III:236*n*
Brinkley, John R., IV:530–31
Brinton, Daniel Garrison, III:386, 557
Brisbane, Albert, I:366, 471, 687, 763; II:207
Brisbane, Arthur, IV:241–42, 490, 492, 495
Brissaud, Pierre, III:489
Bristed, Charles Astor ("Carl Benson"), I:399, 511–12, 753; II:551; III:13*n*, 18, 164, 231, 363, 376, 397, 398, 421
Bristed, John, I:205, 260*n*, 261
British Californian, IV:228
British magazines
  early American magazines and (1741–94)
    borrowings by American magazines, I:27, 39–40, 79, 105
    influence of British magazines, I:21–22, 36–37, 41*n*, 44–45, 54, 79
  nationalist era magazines and (1794–1825), I:188–89
  expansionist era magazines and (1825–50)
    influence, I:392–401
    paper war, I:394
    pirating, I:392–401
  Civil War era magazines (1850–65), II:128–29
  Gilded Age magazines and (1885–1905), IV:4, 150
  in America, III:83; IV:228–29, 301
  postal regulations of 1710 and, I:21
British Medical Journal, IV:529–30
British Weekly Pulpit, IV:229*n*
Britt, Albert, IV:633*n*, 638
Britt, George, IV:749
Britt, W. W., I:524
Brittan, S. B., II:209; III:82*n*
Brittan's Journal of Spiritual Science, Literature, Art, and Inspiration, III:82*n*
Britten, Clarence, II:542
Britten, Emma Hardinge, III:82*n*
Britton, Nathaniel Lord, IV:627
Broad-Axe, IV:163*n*
Broadway (New York City), III:26, 486
Broadway Journal, I:330, 366, 646; II:419; III:196
  sketch of, I:757–62

Broadway Magazine, IV:47, 152, 393; V:145–46, 150
Broadway Publishing Company, V:146
Broadway Quarterly, V:146
Broadway Weekly, IV:67; V:146
Brodney, Spencer, V:49*n,* 56–58
Brodovitch, Alexey, III:390
Brokmeyer, H. C., III:385
Bromfield, Louis, IV:439, 498, 503; V:305
Bromo-Seltzer, IV:133
Bronson, E., I:279*n*
Brook farm, publications of, I:763–65
Brooke, Rupert, V:242
Brooklyn Advance, III:99
Brooklyn Chess Chronicle, III:220
Brooklyn Eagle, V:303
Brooklyn Life, IV:87
Brooklyn Magazine, III:37, 317
  See also: American Magazine (Brooklyn)
Brooklyn Medical Journal, IV:313*n*
Brooks, Allen, IV:627, 628
Brooks, Charles A., V:337
Brooks, Charles Timothy, I:662, 767
Brooks, Edward, II:229
Brooks, Elbridge Streeter, III:502, 509
Brooks, James Gordon, I:128, 326, 409
Brooks, Mrs. Maria Gowen, I:203, 546*n;* II:161
Brooks, Nathan Covington, I:204, 345, 587*n*
Brooks, Noah, III:402–3, 407, 465*n,* 501, 549
Brooks, Phillips, II:99; III:87, 426
Brooks, Robert Clarkson, IV:198
Brooks, Sydney, II:483
Brooks, Van Wyck, III:541; IV:748
Brooks, William E., IV:749
Brooms, Brushes and Mops, IV:184*n*
Bross & Bogart, II:454
Brother Jonathan, I:359–61, 396, 513, 524, 804
Brotherhood of Locomotive Firemen's Magazine, III:126*n*
Brotherhood of Maintenance of Way Employees' Journal, IV:21*n*
Brotherhood Path, IV:287
Brougham, John, II:181
Broughton, Rhoda, III:558
Broughton's Monthly Planet Reader, III:113*n*
Broun, Heywood, III:354, 555; IV:439, 469, 585; V:214
Browder, Earl, V:216, 219
Brown, A. E., I:590*n*
Brown, Arthur W., V:287
Brown, Abbie Farwell, IV:765
Brown, Alice, II:398*n;* III:485; IV:360*n,* 451, 602, 724, 768
Brown, Andrew H., IV:630
Brown, Bernice, IV:471
Brown, Carleton, III:236*n*
Brown, Charles Brockden, I:174, 232
  as contributor, I:123, 174, 243
  editorial career, I:124, 218–22
  his essay series, I:41, 97, 115, 122, 193
  quoted, I:141, 146, 160–61, 188, 193
Brown, Charles Farrar, IV:105
Brown, Cowley Stapleton, IV:390
Brown, Cyril, V:50
Brown, E. C., IV:184
Brown, E. Francis, V:54
Brown, George P., III:169*n*
Brown, George W., II:135
Brown, Goold, I:543
Brown, H. T., III:115*n*
Brown, Helen E., II:211*n*
Brown, Herbert S., IV:742*n*
Brown, J. G. L., I:580*n*
Brown, James A., II:73*n*
Brown, James E. ("Mose Skinner"), III:441
Brown, James Wright, IV:244*n;* V:59*n,* 63–68
Brown, James Wright, Jr., V:70
Brown, John, II:133, 285, 472, 474, 534
  Civil War era magazines on (1859–65)
    abolitionist, II:292
    attacks, II:146, 459
    execution, II:156
    support, II:146–47
Brown, John George, IV:196
Brown, John Mason, IV:762
Brown, Joseph, I:123*n*
Brown, Katharine Holland, IV:729
Brown, Pat, V:317
Brown, Peter A., I:632
Brown, Raymond J., III:495*n,* 499
Brown, Robert U., V:59*n,* 70
Brown, Sevellon, IV:63*n*
Brown, T. Allston, II:204*n*
Brown, Theron, II:262*n,* 270, 272
Brown, Thomas, I:444; II:89
Brown, William Garrot, II:272
Brown, William Hill, IV:80
Brown, Zenith J., IV:709
Brown Book of Boston, IV:82
Brown Magazine, III:165*n*
Brown University, literary magazine of, III:165
Browne, Charles Farrar ("Artemus Ward"), II:37, 126, 178, 180,

184, 192, 520, 526–527; III:172, 264; IV:26, 247; V:121
Browne, Charles Francis, IV:147
Browne, Francis Fisher, III:53, 83, 184, 234; IV:12–13, 51, 99, 112, 124
as editor, III:413*n*, 414–16, 539–41
Browne, H. K., I:711
Browne, John Ross, II:477; III:58, 405
Browne, Junius Henri, III:18, 37*n*, 411, 420; IV:39, 45, 45*n*
Browne, Porter Emerson, V:30
Browne, Waldo Ralph, III:539*n*, 541
Browne, William Hand, III:46, 382–83; IV:736
Brownell, Agnes Mary, V:342
Brownell, Atherton, IV:81*n*
Brownell, F. C., II:433*n*
Brownell, Henry Howard, II:170, 392–93; III:237, 238, 344
Brownell, William Crary, III:184, 347, 375, 463; IV:719, 722, 727, 728
Browne's Phonographic Monthly, III:170
Brownies, in Gilded Age era (1885–1905), IV:151–52, 384
Browning, Elizabeth Barrett, I:720, 737; II:162, 373, 377
Browning, Robert, I:399–400; II:162, 509*n*; III:249, 252; IV:121, 131, 134, 770
Browning's Magazine (Browning, King & Co.), IV:50; V:xi
Browning's Magazine (women's fashions), IV:363*n*
Brownson, Orestes Augustus, I:292, 367–68, 372, 470, 538, 681, 685–91, 703, 716, 740; II:381; III:69*n*, 329, 384
Brownson's Quarterly Review, II:76, 130
founding of, I:372
sketch of, I:685–91
Brubaker, Howard, V:286
Bruce, Archibald, I:266–67
Bruce, B. G., III:215
Bruce, Edward C., III:293
Bruce, Henry Addington Bayley, IV:604, 651
Bruce, L. C., III:215*n*
Bruce, Philip Alexander, IV:73, 139
Bruce, S. D., III:215
Brundidge, Harry T., V:25
Brunetière, Ferdinand, IV:250
Brunonian, III:165
Bruns, John Dickson, II:488
Brunswick, Maine, III:109*n*; IV:149
Brush, George DeForest, III:475
Brush, Isabel, IV:695
Brush, Katharine, II:404; IV:472, 696, 700
Brush and Pencil, IV:147
Bruun, Laurids, III:390
Bryan, Charles Page, IV:61
Bryan, Charles Wayland, IV:162*n*
Bryan, Clark W., V:125–26, 130, 137
Bryan, Joseph, III, II:355
Bryan, Mary Edwards, IV:48*n*
Bryan, William Jennings, II:377, 484; III:300*n*, 346, 349, 530, 554; IV:46*n*, 161, 162, 163, 177, 227, 386, 411, 460, 520, 565, 655, 703; V:10, 32, 88
Bryan Democrat, IV:163*n*
Bryant, William Cullen, I:257, 274, 408, 409, 412; II:430*n*; III:35*n*, 237, 241, 374, 421; IV:680
as contributor, I:177, 326, 546, 547, 608, 679; II:193, 211*n*, 225, 230, 253, 361, 362*n*, 377, 424, 429, 497, 498, 504
as editor, I:128–29, 160, 199, 331–33
evaluation of, II:166
Bryant, William McKendree, III:51*n*, 99*n*, 184, 238
Bryce, C. A., III:140*n*
Bryce, James Lord, II:253, 255, 269; III:250, 337, 347; IV:227; V:84
Bryce, Lloyd, II:220*n*, 254–256; IV:51
Bryn Athyn, Pa., IV:296
Bryologist, IV:310
Bubble, II:185*n*
Bucaneer, I:357*n*
Buchanan, James, II:136, 361, 471, 472, 523
Buchanan, Joseph, III:300
Buchanan, Dr. Joseph R., II:85
Buchanan's Journal of Man, II:85
Buck, Mrs., A. Truchart, IV:92
Buck, E. A., II:204*n*
Buck, Pearl, IV:475, 503, 554, 769
Buckingham, Edwin, I:344, 599–601
Buckingham, James Silk, I:679
Buckingham, Joseph Tinker, I:125, 127, 160*n*, 169, 224–25, 344, 578, 599–601; II:494
Buckley, Edmund, IV:499*n*
Buckley, George D., IV:763*n*
Buckley, James Monroe, II:66*n*, 257; IV:290–91
Buckminster, Joseph S., I:255, 263–64, 277
Buddhist periodicals, IV:287
Buddhist Ray, IV:287
Budget, II:185*n*

Buel, Clarence Clough, III:457*n*, 468, 470, 477
Buel, Jesse, I:443
Buell, George P., II:116
Buffalo (animal), massacre of, III:60
Buffalo, N.Y.
Civil War era magazines in (1850–65)
home magazine, II:59
humor magazine, II:185*n*
juvenile magazine, II:100
religious magazines, II:75, 77
women's magazines, II:466*n*
post-Civil War magazines in (1865–85)
dental journal, III:143*n*
general magazine, III:39*n*
manufacturers' periodical, III:128
religious magazine, III:69*n*
science periodical, III:109*n*
Gilded Age magazines in (1885–1905)
current events periodicals, IV:72*n*
education periodical, IV:270
five-cent magazine, IV:48
horse-racing periodical, IV:343
information magazine, IV:55
manufacturing periodicals, IV:183, 184*n*
photography periodical, IV:150*n*
poetry magazine, IV:121
political magazine, IV:171
printers' periodical, IV:248*n*
temperance periodical, IV:210
modern magazines, in (1905–)
genealogical periodical, IV:140*n*
horse-racing periodical, IV:343
industrial periodicals, IV:183, 184*n*
secret societies, III:315
Buffalo Bill Stories, IV:120
Buffalo Christian Advocate, II:67*n*
Buffalo Express, III:364
Buffalo Medical Journal, II:84*n*
Buffum, Mrs. A., III:82*n*
Bugle-Horn of Liberty, II:185
Builder, Decorator and Woodworker, IV:364
Builders' Magazine, III:129*n*
Building, III:129
Building Age, III:129
Building magazines, *see* Construction magazines
Building Trades Journal, III:130
Building Witness, III:129
Bulger, Bozeman, IV:700
Bull, Charles Livingston, IV:637, 692
Bull, Ephraim Wales, II:433
Bull, Henry Adsit, II:349*n*
Bull, Jerome Case, IV:617
Bull, Louise, III:396*n*, 401
Bull, Ole Bornemann, I:434; II:195
Bullard, Arthur, III:433
Bullard, Laura Curtis, III:391*n*, 394
Bulletin (Philadelphia), IV:88
Bulletin (Springfield, Mass.), V:131*n*
Bulletin of the American Academy of Medicine, IV:313*n*
Bulletin of the American Art-Union, I:437; II:193
Bulletin of the American Bureau of Geography, IV:224
Bulletin of the American Geographical Society of New York, II:413*n*
Bulletin of the American Geographical and Statistical Society, II:79
sketch of, II:413–415
Bulletin of the American Iron and Steel Association, III:128
Bulletin of Bibliography, IV:143
Bulletin of the Commercial Law League, IV:348
Bulletin of International Meteorological Observations, III:112
Bulletin of the National Association of Credit Men, IV:349
Bulletin of the New York Mathematical Society, IV:310*n*
Bulletin of the Nuttall Ornithologica Club, III:111
Bulletin of Pharmacy, IV:317
Bulletin of the Spelling Reform Association, IV:212
Bullinger's Monitor Guide, III:147*n*
Bullion, III:147*n*
Bullitt, William S., V:98
Bullock, William H., I:728*n*
Bülow, Heinrich William von, I:235
Bulwer-Lytton, Edward George, I:359, 398, 417, 700; II:160, 385, 387, 406, 471; III:224, 251
Bunce, Oliver Bell, III:231, 417*n*, 418–20; IV:353
Bungay, George W., III:325
Bunin, Ivan, III:543; V:337
"Bunkum Flagstaff," I:610
Bunner, Henry Cuyler, III:37*n*, 41, 233, 267, 428; IV:719, 720; V:118
as editor, 520–23, 530
"Buntline, Ned," *see* Judson, Edward Z. C.
Burch, Charles Sumner, III:160
Burchard, R. B., IV:636
Burdette, Robert Jones, III:271, 408, 528; IV:538, 542, 685
Burdick, William, II:35*n*
Burg, Amos, IV:630

Burger, Max, IV:477
Burgess, Ernest W., IV:192*n*
Burgess, Gelett, II:431; III:503, 514, 551; IV:66, 106, 388–89, 768; V:248
Burgess, George, I:741
Burk, John Daly, I:168
Burke, Edward, IV:189*n*
Burke, J. W., III:176
Burke, John J., III:329*n*, 330
Burke, Kenneth, III:543
Burke, T. A., III:176
Burke, Thomas, IV:439
Burke's Weekly for Boys and Girls, III:176
Burkett, Charles William, I:728*n*
Burkhard, John P., IV:381
Burleigh, Charles, II:283
Burleigh, William Henry, I:390*n*, 543, 546*n*
Burleson, Albert Sidney, III:350–51
Burleson, Rufus Columbus, IV:447
Burlesque, II:331, 337; III:198, 206–8; IV:258–59
Burlingame, Edward Livermore, IV:35, 43, 717–26
Burlington, Iowa, newspaper in, III:271*n*
Burlington, Vt., IV:225, 313*n*
Burlington Hawkeye, III:271*n*
Burnet, Dana, III:531; IV:713
Burnett, Frances Hodgson (Fannie Hodgson), I:587; II:271, 309; III:202, 224, 261, 502; IV:141
Burney, Mrs., Mary Chase, I:381
Burns, Robert, I:178; V:118
Burns, William John, IV:604
Burr, C. Chauncey, II:154, 544, 546; III:281
Burr McIntosh Monthly, IV:390
Burroughs, Edgar Rice, IV:618
Burroughs, John, II:429, 498*n*, 504*n*; III:54, 231, 375, 421, 426, 463, 486, 503, 545; IV:35, 40, 121, 302*n*, 451, 728
Burroughs, W. B., Jr., II:93*n*
Burrows, Frederick M., IV:79*n*
Burrows, Jay, IV:176
Burruss, John C., II:73*n*
Burt, Albert L., IV:141
Burt, Charles, I:753
Burt, Henry M., III:152
Burt, (Maxwell) Struthers, II:260; IV: 439, 553, 724, 729
Burt, Thomas Gregory, IV:74*n*
Burton, Ernest DeWitt, III:84*n*
Burton, Harry Payne, IV:480*n*, 503–04, 580*n*, 583
Burton, Richard, III:540; IV:45*n*, 451
Burton, Sir Richard Francis, V:118
Burton, William Evans, I:343, 587*n*, 609, 673–76
Burton's *Gentleman's Magazine,* I:392, 508, 512, 520, 545
  founding of, I:343
  sketch of, I:673–76
Burwell, William MacCreary, II:113*n*, 338*n*, 348
Busbey, Hamilton, III:215*n*
Busche, J. F., IV:174
Bush, Charles G., II:477; III:92, 528
Bush, Prescott, V:317
Bush, Rufus T., IV:15
Bush, Sam Stone, IV:93
Bushnell, Horace, II:312*n*, 313, 315, 371; III:32*n*
Business, IV:351
Business
  Gilded Age magazines on (1885–1905), IV:688–89, 690, 721, 774, 776
  modern magazines on (1905–), IV:777, 787; V:32
  women in, IV:354
  See also Trusts; Wealth; *and specific branches of business*
Business and Finance, IV:349*n*–350*n*
Business magazines
  in expansionist era (1825–50), I:696–98; II:339–42
  in Civil War era (1850–65), II:342–46
  in post-Civil War era (1865–85), II:346–48; III:146–47
  in Gilded Age (1885–1905), IV:92–93, 186*n*
Business Woman's Journal, IV:354
Business Woman's Magazine, IV:354*n*
Business World, IV:351
Buss, Kate, V:182
Busy Bee, IV:88
Butcher's Advocate, IV:187*n*
Butchers' Advocate and Market Journal, III:135
Butchers' magazines, III:135; IV:187*n*
Butler, Benjamin Franklin, I:679; III: 340, 445, 525, 527; IV:562
Butler, Burridge Davinal, IV:340
Butler, Ellis Parker, III:512, 555; IV:49*n*, 80, 96, 366*n*, 421, 429, 493, 618; V:121, 133
Butler, Mann, I:660, 661
Butler, Merrill, I:170
Butler, Nicholas Murray, III:166, 432; IV:268, 730

Butler, William Allen, II:472
Butler, William Mill, IV:186
Butte, Mont., III:75*n;* IV:108, 117, 322*n*
Butter and Cheese Review, IV:186*n*
Butterfield, Consul Willshire, III:262*n*
Butterick, Ebenezer, III:97, 481, 484
Butterick Publishing Company, V:74, 81, 251
Butterworth, Hezekiah, II:262*n,* 267, 269, 270, 271; III:504, 509; IV:80, 390*n*
Buttre, John Chester, I:612; II:444
Butts, Asa K., III:107
Butzgy, Helen, IV:502
Buzz Saw, IV:390
By the Wayside, IV:310*n*
Byers, Samuel Hawkins Marshall, IV:96
Byles, Mather, I:103
Bynner, Witter, IV:518, 601–02, 654; V:96, 113, 119, 185, 258, 336
Byrd, Richard Evelyn, IV:625
Byrd, William, I:97
Byrne, Charles Alfred, III:198; IV:243*n*
Byrne, Donn, III:479; IV:697; V:119
Byrnes, James F., V:323*n*
Byrnes, Thomas, IV:195
Byron, Lord (George Noel Gordon), I:179, 399, 573; II:230, 505

Cabell, James Branch, II:402; III:479; IV:421, 439, 440, 605, 691; V:7, 30, 249, 264
Cable, George Washington, III:16, 48, 224, 227, 228, 238, 461, 471; 503; IV:265, 451, 506*n,* 507, 513, 720; IV:287; V:287
Cabot, Charles M., IV:745
Cabot, James Elliot, I:720, 775–76; II:494; III:386
Cade, J. J., I:309
Cadenza, IV:254
Cadwalader, Thomas, I:146
Cady, C. B., III:197*n*
Caffin, Charles Henry, IV:776, 791
Cahan, Abraham, IV:517
Cain, James M., V:13, 22
Caine, Hall, III:489; IV:49*n,* 226, 281, 456, 501, 612, 689; V:28, 30, 80, 254
Cajori, Florian, IV:302*n*
Caldwell, Charles, I:154, 223*n,* 239–40
Caldwell, Erskine, IV:729
Caldwell, Howard H., II:490
Caldwell, John E., I:135
Caldwell, Taylor, IV:554, 771
Caledonian, IV:227
Calendar, II:69
Calhoun, John Caldwell, I:184, 463, 752
California
  Chinese immigration to, III:276
  Gold Rush to (1848), I:464
  magazine comment on, II:119–20; III:58
  See also specific towns and cities
California, University of, III:407
  magazines published at, IV:74
California (periodical), III:402
California Architect, III:129
California Banker's Magazine, IV:349*n*
California Cackler, IV:345*n*
California Christian Advocate, II:67*n*
California Country Journal, III:159
California Farmer, II:90; III:158; IV:341
California Fruit Grower, IV:342
California Horticulturist, III:161
California Independent, IV:301
California Journal of Technology, IV:306*n*
California Mail-Bag, III:56
California Maverick, III:270
California Medical Journal, III:141*n*
California Medicine, IV:314
California Mining and Scientific Press, III:114
California Municipalities, IV:198*n*
California Nationalist, IV:203*n*
California Patron, III:149*n*
California Police Gazette, II:187
California Socialist, IV:176*n*
California Spirit of the Times, II:204
California Teacher, II:99*n*
Californian, II:118
Californian: a Western Monthly, III:56, 406
Californian Illustrated Magazine, IV:105
Calkins, Franklin Welles, IV:96
Calkins, Norman A., I:493; II:100*n,* 101
Callaghan, Morley, IV:728
Callender, A. M., IV:184
Callender, Joseph, I:36
Callitypy, IV:574
Calumet, II:211*n*
Calvé, Emma, IV:697
Calvert, George Henry, I:204; II:425, 429
Calverton, Vernon F., V:56
Calverton, Victor Francis, IV:730

Calvinist periodicals
in expansionist era (1825–50), I:530–35, 569–72, 739–42
in Civil War era (1850–65), I:740–41; II:516–19
in post-Civil War era (1865–85), I:741; II:517, 519; III:73–74
Camac, William, II:520*n*, 529
Cambridge, Mass.
chapbooks in, IV:450
kindergarten magazine in, III:163
literary magazine in, I:344
mathematics journal in, II:79
science periodicals in, II:79; III:108; IV:307
Cambridge, Ohio, III:169
Camden, New Jersey
Irish-American periodical in, IV:227
music periodical in, IV:254*n*
temperance magazine in, III:310*n*
Camera, IV:149
Camera Craft, IV:150*n*
Camera and Dark Room, IV:149*n*
Camera Notes, IV:150*n*
Cameron, Andrew C., III:132*n*, 299
Cameron, Ann, IV:697
Cameron, George C., IV:630
Camp, D. N., II:443*n*
Camp, Enos E., I:481; II:325, 327
Camp, Walter, III:503; IV:271, 457, 466, 469, 478, 634
Camp Kettle, II:151
Camp meetings, religious, I:134
Campaign papers, II:137
Campanini, Italo, III:193
Campbell, Alexander (nineteenth century), I:561; II:74
Campbell, Alexander (of *New Republic*), V:191*n*
Campbell, Andrew, III:117
Campbell, Bartley, III:202
Campbell, Charles, I:645
Campbell, Helen, III:313, 558; IV:45*n*, 203, 204, 360, 404; V:130
Campbell, Heyworth, IV:760
Campbell, J., I:389*n*
Campbell, James, IV:652*n*, 653
Campbell, James M., I:398
Campbell, Killis, IV:737
Campbell, Lewis, III:536
Campbell, Thomas, I:231
Campbell, William Alexander, IV:390*n*
Campbell, William Henry, I:491*n*
Campbellite sect, I:369
Campbell's Foreign Monthly Magazine, I:397–98, 806
Campbell's Illustrated Monthly, IV:99
Canada, imperialist designs on, II:127
Canajoharie, New York, trade magazine in, IV:189*n*
Canal building, I:207
Canby, Henry Seidel, III:479; IV:439; V:117*n*, 123, 337, 339
Candy, III:135
Candy and Ice Cream Retailer, IV:187*n*
Canfield, Dorothy, III:487, 488; IV:584, 616, 748, 769; V:80, 83, 337
Canfield, Henry S., IV:442*n*, 448
Canham, Erwin, IV:478
Cannan, Gilbert, V:97
Canner, IV:186
Canning Trade, III:134
Cannon, Frank J., V:83
Cannon, George Q., II:74, 75; III:180
Cannon, Joseph Gurney, IV:461; V:297
Canoeing magazines, III:211
See also Water sports
"Cantelman's Spring-mate," V:175
Canton, Maine, horse-breeding magazine in, III:215*n*
Canton, Ohio, workingmen's magazine in, IV:95
Cap and Gown, III:165
Capital (Los Angeles), IV:107
Capitol Records, V:328*n*
Capote, Truman, V:313
Capper, Arthur, II:260; IV:340, 362
Capper's Farmer, IV:340
Capper's Weekly, IV:340
Carew, Thomas, V:115
Carey, Henry C., I:393, 471; III:34*n*
Carey, John, I:44*n*
Carey, Mathew, I:159–60, 361, 601, 609, 638
as editor, I:30, 94–99, 100–3, 166
Carey, William, III:20, 457*n*, 474
Carl Pretzel's National Weekly, III:266
Carl Pretzel's Pook, III:266
Carleton, George W., III:265
Carleton, Henry Guy, III:202; IV:556*n*, 559
Carleton, S. B., IV:106
Carleton, Will, III:231; IV:45, 159, 538
Carleton College, III:111
Carlisle, Pa., IV:215*n*
Carlisle Arrow, IV:215
Carlisle, David, Jr., I:156*n*
Carlisle, W. B., II:489
Carlson, John Roy, V:23
Carlton & Smith, III:12*n*
Carlyle, Thomas, I:292, 398–99, 401, 402, 610, 616, 703–5, 776; II:159, 161, 236; III:253

Carman, Bliss, III:454*n*, 456; IV:46*n*, 66, 120, 124, 389, 450, 451, 457, 506*n*, 507, 612, 645, 654, 690; V:248
Carman, Elbert S., IV:340
Carmany, John H., III:402*n*, 405–6
"Carmen Sylvia," *see* Elizabeth, Queen of Roumania
Carnahan, James, I:530
Carnegie, Andrew, II:255; III:83*n*; IV: 157, 158, 163*n*, 164*n*, 218, 226, 495, 776; V:342
Carnegie Foundation, V:242
Carnevali, Emanuel, V:239
Carpenter, Frank George, I:732; IV:482, 689
Carpenter, George Rice, IV:398, 517
Carpenter, Stephen Cullen, I:194–95, 202
as editor, I:166, 205, 260–61
Carpenter, William Henry, IV:434
Carpenter, III:129*n*, 130*n*
Carpentry and Building, III:129
Carpentry magazines, III:129
Carpet-Bag, II:180–81
Carpet Trade, III:136*n*
Carpet trade magazines, III:136
Carpet Trade Review, III:136
Carpet and Upholstery Trade Review, III:136
Carpetbaggers, press comment on, III: 283–84
Carpets, Wall Paper and Curtains, III:136*n*
Carr, Edward Ellis, IV:283
Carriage Journal, III:216
Carriage Monthly, III:216; IV:327
Carriage trade magazines, III:216; IV:326–27
Carriell, Cruse, IV:107*n*
Carrier Dove, III:82; IV:304*n*
Carrington, John B., II:312*n*, 313
Carroll, Alfred L., III:265
Carroll, Bartholomew R., I:664*n*
Carroll, Charles, III:199*n*
Carroll, Gordon, V:19
Carroll, Lewis, V:121
Carruth, Hayden, V:225*n*, 234–35, 243
Carruthers, William A., I:700
Carryl, Charles Edward, III:502
Carryl, Guy Wetmore, IV:436, 612, 690
Carse, Matilda B., III:310
Carse, Robert, IV:422, 712
Carson, Joseph, I:539*n*
Carson, Norma Bright, III:235*n*
Carson, Will, IV:108
Carter, Henry, *see* Leslie, Frank
Carter, James Gordon, I:331–32, 541*n*, 542
Carter, Joseph, III:44
Carter, Matilda P., I:352*n*
Carter, Robert, I:735–38; II:240; III:417*n*, 418–19, 455
Carter, Robert, & Brothers, I:375
Carter, William Harding, IV:627
Carter's Monthly, IV:100
Cartoon comic books, IV:196
Cartoons, III:125, 192, 265–68, 287–88, 420, 441
in early magazines (1741–94), I:36, 48, 85–86
in expansionist-era magazines (1825–50), I:782
in Civil War era magazines (1850–65), II:144–45, 457, 475–76, 521, 523
in post-Civil War magazines (1865–85), II:477–82; III:56, 67, 91–92, 191, 265–67, 269*n*, 280–86, 521–30, 552–53
in Gilded Age magazines (1885–1905), II:483; III:522–26, 553–54, 667; IV:61, 387*n*, 415, 650–51, 775
Carus, Mary, IV:303
Carus, Paul, IV:302, 303
Carvalho, Solomon Solis, IV:331
Carver, George, V:179*n*
Cary, Alice, I:388, 499–500, 771; II:19, 36, 114, 115*n*, 170, 302, 303, 360, 377, 407, 410, 417, 466, 468, 504*n*; III:229, 374, 393; IV:680
Cary, F. G., II:89
Cary, Phoebe, I:388, 499–500, 771; II:36, 114, 170, 302, 377, 410, 466, 468; III:14*n*, 229, 374, 393, 394
Casamajor, George, IV:484
Case, Theodore S., III:109
Case and Comment, IV:347
Casey, Francis de Sales, IV:468, 566
Cash, W. J., V:10
Cash Grocer, III:135*n*
Cash-in-advance subscriptions, I:242
Casket, III:132; IV:674–77
founding of, I:343
illustrations in, I:520
prizes offered by, I:500
sketch of, I:544–55
Casket (undertaking periodical), III: 132; IV:189
Casket magazines, III:132–33; IV:189
Casket and Sunnyside, III:133
Cass, Lewis, I:409, 614, 781; II:232

Cassel, John, III:530; V:30
Cassell's Family Magazine, IV:228
Cassell's Monthly, III:278
Cassier, Louis, III:121*n*
Cassier's Magazine, IV:320–21
Cassino, Herman E., 428*n*, 431
Cassino, Samuel E., IV:428, 431
Casson, Herbert N., IV:616; V:149
Castaigne, André, III:473; V:256
Castle, William Richards, Jr., IV:75*n*
"Castlemon, Harry" (Charles Austin Fosdick), III:175*n*; IV:274, 420
Castleton, D. R., II:394
Cat Journal, IV:382
Cat Review, IV:382
Caterer and Hotel Proprietor's Gazette, IV:189*n*
Caterer and Household Magazine, III:100
Catering Industry Employee, IV:221*n*
Cates, J. Sidney, II:435
Cather, Willa Siebert, III:408; IV:79*n*, 89, 471, 521, 552, 601, 769; V:119, 264
Catherwood, Mary Hartwell, III:471, 485, 508; IV:100*n*
Catholic Almanac, I:716
Catholic Book News at Home and Abroad, III:70
Catholic Bulletin, III:69*n*
Catholic Central Advocate, II:77*n*
Catholic Champion, IV:294*n*
Catholic Charities Review, IV:194
Catholic Citizen, III:69*n*, 70*n*; IV:298
Catholic Guardian, II:77*n*
Catholic Herald, I:373, 801; II:77*n*; III:69*n*
Catholic Herald-Citizen, III:69*n*
Catholic Journal, I:373, 801
Catholic Journal of the New South, III:69*n*
Catholic Magazine, I:717
Catholic magazines
early (1741–94), I:56
in nationalist era (1794–1825), I:136
in expansionist era (1825–50), I:371–73, 381, 688–89, 716–17
in Civil War era (1850–65), II:76–77
in post-Civil War era (1865–85), III:67–70, 329–30
in Gilded Age (1885–1905), III:261, 330; IV:138, 275, 297–99
modern (1905–), III:330
Catholic Mirror, I:717; II:77
Catholic Miscellany, I:383
Catholic News, IV:298
Catholic Press, I:373
Catholic Reading Circle Review, IV:265
Catholic Religious Cabinet, I:371
Catholic Review, III:70; IV:298
Catholic School Journal, IV:272, 275
Catholic Standard, III:69; IV:298
Catholic Telegraph, I:389, 801; II:77
Catholic Times, III:69; IV:298
Catholic Total Abstinence Union, III:310–11
Catholic Transcript, III:69*n*
Catholic Union, III:69*n*
Catholic Union and Times, IV:298
Catholic Universe, III:69*n*
Catholic University Bulletin, IV:299*n*
Catholic Vindicator, III:69*n*
Catholic World, III:68, 69*n*; IV:298
sketch of, III:329–30
Catholic Youth's Magazine, I:717; II:77
Catholicism and anti-Catholicism
in nationalist era (1794–1825), I:204
in expansionist era (1825–50), I:371, 597, 602
in post-Civil War era (1865–85), III:67–68, 266, 342, 526–27
in Gilded Age (1885–1905), IV:61, 272, 299–300
in modern era (1905), IV:416
Catlettsburg, Ky., III:71
Cat-owner magazines, IV:382
Cattell, James McKeen, III:108*n*, 495*n*, 498; IV:303, 307
Cattell, Josephine Owen, IV:308*n*
Cattle-raising, western, III:61–62
Caucasian, II:154
Cauldwell, William, II:37; III:209; IV:169
Cause, IV:279
Cavalier, IV:617*n*
Cave, Edward, IV:381*n*
Cawein, Madison, III:511; IV:48*n*, 690
Cedar Rapids, Iowa
post-Civil War magazines in (1865–85)
agricultural magazines, III:157, 161
penmanship magazine, III:170
railroad magazine, III:125*n*
Gilded Age magazines in (1885–1905)
Masonic journal, IV:221*n*
poultry periodical, IV:345*n*
Celtic Magazine, IV:227
Cement, IV:325
Cement Age, IV:325*n*
Cement and Engineering News, IV:325*n*
Cement Era, IV:325*n*
Cement periodicals, IV:325
Censor, I:26*n*, 788; IV:100
Censorship, problems of, V:174–75

Census, *see* Population
Centennial Exposition (1876), III:116, 181, 185, 398, 493; IV:144
Centennial Record, III:39*n*
Center, Alfred, III:85*n*
Central Baptist, III:73*n;* IV:292
Central Christian Advocate, II:67; III:70
Central Law Journal, III:144; IV:346
Central Magazine, III:95
Central Methodist, III:71
Central News Company, III:8
Central Presbyterian, II:63*n*
Central School Journal, III:169
Century Illustrated Monthly Magazine (*Scribner's Monthly* 1870–81), II:396–98, 430; III:19–20, 34, 47*n,* 48, 90, 103, 119, 176, 184, 192, 227, 228, 231, 234, 271, 278, 281, 290, 295, 304, 307, 312, 384, 399, 415, 439, 500, 502, 505; IV:2, 5, 9, 14, 17, 19, 20, 21, 35, 37, 40, 43, 211, 216, 229, 409, 521, 719; V:294, 341
  circulation of, III:6
  advertising in, III:9, 11
  illustrations in, III:187–90
  sketch of, III:457–80
Century Path, IV:287*n*
Century Quarterly, III:457*n,* 479
Ceramic Monthly, IV:184*n*
Cesnola, Luigi Palma di, III:185; IV:562
Cézanne, Paul, III:542
Chadbourne, John S., II:116*n*
Chadwick, H. A., IV:108
Chadwick, Henry, III:217; IV:635
Chadwick, John White, III:337, 424, 507; IV:178
Chagall, Marc, V:178
Chaille-Long, Charles, IV:136
Challenge, IV:206
Challis, Luther C., III:449–51
Chamberlain, Arthur, IV:391
Chamberlain, Arthur H., III:402*n,* 409
Chamberlain, George Agnew, IV:473
Chamberlain, George D., IV:131
Chamberlain, Jo Hubbard, IV:663
Chamberlain, John, IV:731; V:99*n,* 288
Chamberlain, Joseph Perkins, IV:750
Chamberlain, Mary, IV:746
Chamberlain, Samuel Selwyn, IV:480*n,* 492
Chamberlin, Joseph Edgar, II:262*n,* 272
Chamberlin, Thomas Chrowder, IV:309
Chamberlin, William Henry, V:20, 97
Chambers, C. E., II:402
Chambers, Joseph M., II:89
Chambers, Robert William, IV:49*n,* 367, 450, 496–97, 501, 584, 689, 691, 693; V:30, 85, 152
Chambers, Whittaker, IV:713
Chameleon, I:427, 803
Champagne, III:269*n*
Champion, IV:210
Champion of Fair Play, III:311
Champion of Freedom and Right, III:311
Champlain Educator, IV:265
Champlin, John Denison, II:267, 270
Champney, James Wells, II:477; III:185*n,* 464
Chandler, H. P., III:256
Chandler, Hannibal H., III:156
Chandler, Joseph Ripley, I:544*n,* 551, 587*n*
Chandler, Seth C., II:79*n*
Chandler, William Eaton, IV:615
Channing, Edward Bruce, IV:241
Channing, Edward Tyrrel, I:130, 180; II:220*n,* 224, 225, 238
Channing, Grace Ellery, IV:107; V:158
Channing, Walter, I:151, 187; II:212, 227
Channing, William Ellery, I:138, 263, 285, 287, 411, 471, 571, 659, 662, 777; III:347, 386
Channing, William Ellery, Jr., I:660*n,* 709, 723
Channing, William Henry, I:658*n,* 663, 704, 706, 764; II:207
Chantecler (Rostand), V:148
Chap-Book, IV:99, 125, 387, 388, 450–52, 640; V:156, 158
Chapbooks, IV:99, 125, 386–91, 450–52, 640; V:156, 158
Chaperone, IV:361; 151*n*
Chapin, Aaron Lucius, II:315, 374, 518*n,* 519
Chapin, Alonzo Bowen, I:669
Chapin, Edwin Hubbell, I:640; III:87, 172
Chapin, John, II:390
Chapin, S. A., III:503
Chapin, William Wisner, IV:626
Chapman, Alfred F., III:315
Chapman, Arthur, IV:108*n*
Chapman, Bertrand L., IV:79*n*
Chapman, Frank Michler, IV:627
Chapman, Frederick L., IV:52, 301
Chapman, Henry Grafton, III:296*n;* IV:775
Chapman, John Jay, II:512; IV:520, 737
Chapman, Nathaniel, I:244, 566

Chapple, Joseph Mitchell, IV:80–81, 338
Char, René, V:244
Character Builder, IV:275
Chariot, IV:222*n*
Charities, II:241; IV:193, 195, 743
  sketch of, IV:741
Charities Review, IV:193
  sketch of, IV:741–43
Charity magazines
  in Civil War era (1850–65), II:241
  in post-Civil War era (1865–85), III:313–14
  in Gilded Age (1885–1905), IV:193–94, 195, 741–44
  modern (1905–), IV:744–50
Charity Work, IV:744
Charles City, Iowa, IV:271
Charleston, S.C.
  nationalist-era magazines in (1794–1825), I:167
    literary center, I:204–5
    literary periodical, I:260
  expansionist-era magazines in (1825–50), I:382–83; II:112*n*
    eclectic periodicals, I:573, 722, 755
    literary magazines, I:646, 664, 700
    magazine center, I:379–80, 382–83
    religious magazine, I:136
    slavery issue, I:458
  Civil War era magazines in (1850–65), II:33
    general magazine, II:488–92
    literary magazines, II:110*n*
    magazine center, II:107, 488
    religious magazines, II:63*n*
  post-Civil War magazines in (1865–85)
    agricultural magazine, III:155
    religious magazine, III:73*n*
  Gilded Age magazines in (1885–1905)
    historical periodical, IV:139
    women's club periodical, IV:356*n*
  persecution of abolitionists in, I:460
  theater in, I:169
Charleston Medical Journal and Review, II:84*n*
Charlotte, N.C., II:63*n*, IV:185*n*, 314
Charlotte Medical Journal, IV:314
Charnay, Désiré, II:254
Chase, Edna Woolman, IV:756*n*, 760–62
Chase, Frank H., III:132
Chase, Ilka, IV:762
Chase, Jason Frank, V:13–14
Chase, Joseph Cummings, IV:577
Chase, Stuart, IV:478, 748, 749*n*
Chase, Thomas, II:161
Chase, William Merritt, IV:144–46, 484
Chatard, Francis Silas, III:69*n*
Chateaubriand, François René Auguste, Vicomte de, II:116*n*
Chatfield-Taylor, Hobart C., IV:49*n*, 61, 485; V:226, 247
Chattanooga, Tenn., III:71*n*, 73*n*; IV:271*n*, 291, 292*n*
Chatter, IV:66–67
Chaucer, Geoffrey, V:111
Chautauqua Farmer, III:153
Chautauqua Herald, III:173
Chautauqua magazines, III:153, 173, 177, 544–47; IV:95, 104, 264–65, 357
Chautauqua programs, III:173, 544, 547; IV:357
Chautauqua Young Folks' Journal, III:177
Chautauqua Young Folks' Reading Union, III:509
Chautauquan, II:378; III:173; IV:54, 95, 216, 223, 264; V:341
  sketch of, 544–57
Chawner, Mary Grove, V:179*n*
Cheap books, I:362, 362*n*, 418
Checker playing, III:220
Checker World, IV:382
Checkers' periodicals, IV:382
Cheer, III:100
Cheerful Moments, IV:367*n*
Cheese Reporter, IV:186*n*
Cheetham, James, I:160*n*
Cheever, George Barrell, I:409, 572; II:141
Chef and Steward, IV:189*n*
Chekhov, Anton, V:119–21
Chelsea, Mass., III:299
Chemical Engineer, IV:322*n*
Chemical Engineering, IV:322*n*
Chemistry, I:303; II:228, 319
Chemistry periodicals, III:109–10; IV:309, 323*n*
Chenery, William Ludlow, IV:453*n*, 469–75, 747
Cheney, John Vance, III:407; IV:104
Cheney, Warren, III:56*n*, 402*n*, 406
Cherniss, Harold, III:535*n*
Cherokee Gospel Tidings, IV:215*n*
Cherokee Rosebud, II:99
Cherub, III:39*n*
Cheseboro', Caroline, *see* Chesebrough, Caroline
Cheseborough, Essie, II:490
Chesebrough (Cheseboro'), Caroline, I:553; II:173, 387, 395, 429, 467, 504*n*, 543; III:13*n*, 224, 373, 411

Chess, II:437; III:220, 324
Chess Monthly, II:203
Chess periodicals, II:203; IV:382
Chessman, William O., IV:470, 477
Chester, George Randolph, IV:299*n*, 493, 497, 602, 691, 693; V:85, 134, 148
Chester, Stephen M., I:352, 743*n*, 744
Chesterfield, Ruth, II:270
Chesterton, Gilbert Keith, II:260; III:330; IV:501, 518, 520, 521, 604, 694, 697; V:84, 121
Chew, Samuel C., V:5
Chiang Kai-shek, V:323*n*
Chic, III:97, 267
Chicago, Ill.
expansionist-era magazines in (1825–50), I:389, 444*n*
Civil War era magazines in (1850–65)
agricultural magazines, I:444*n*; II:90
home magazine, II:59
law journal, II:93
Masonic periodical, II:215
medical journal, II:84
printers' magazine, II:93
railroad journal, II:81
religious magazines, II:66, 71*n*, 74
trade union periodical, II:212
post-Civil War magazines in (1865–85)
agriculture machinery magazines, III:151, 161
agricultural magazines, III:156–57
art journals, III:186
bee keepers' magazine, III:161
booksellers' periodical, III:235
comic magazines, III:266, 269*n*
construction periodicals, III:129, 130
drama periodical, III:199
educational periodical, III:168
engineering periodicals, III:114
free love periodical, III:301*n*
grange magazine, III:149
Greenback magazine, III:301
health magazine, III:139
home magazines, III:51, 101
humane societies, III:312
illustrated weeklies, III:53
insurance journal, III:146
journalist periodical, III:273
juvenile periodicals, III:175–76, 177
labor periodical, III:299
legal journal, III:144
library periodical, III:171
literary magazines, III:233–35, 413–16, 539*n*
magazine center, III:30, 51–54
mail-order periodicals, III:54
manufacturing periodicals, III:128
medical journals, III:141*n*, 142*n*, 143
music periodicals, III:198*n*
philology journal, III:236*n*
poultry magazine, III:161
printers' magazines, II:93; III:132
railroad magazines, III:125
religious magazines, II:519; III:7, 72, 74–78, 80–85
scientific magazines, III:109–12
secret societies, III:315
society notes, III:102
story papers, IIII:53–54
technical periodicals, III:116*n*, 117, 121–22
temperance periodicals, III:310, 311
trade magazines, III:132–36, 216
trade union periodicals, III:125*n*, 126*n*
women's magazines, III:94–95, 101
Gilded Age magazines in (1885–1905)
advertising journals, IV:247, 337
agnostic periodicals, IV:277
agricultural periodicals, I:444*n*; IV:337–39, 341, 343, 344–45
airplane conference, IV:335
all-fiction magazines, IV:115–16
amateur periodicals, IV:389, 390*n*, 391, 450
anarchist periodicals, IV:172
architectural periodical, IV:323
art periodicals, IV:147
automobile periodicals, IV:331
brick periodical, IV:325*n*
booksellers' magazine, IV:127
cement periodical, IV:325*n*
checkers' periodical, IV:382
comic periodicals, IV:385, 387*n*
construction periodicals, IV:325
current events magazines, IV:499
dental periodicals, IV:317
education periodicals, IV:264, 269
engineering periodicals, IV:321–22
family magazines, IV:67–68
financial periodicals, IV:349, 350*n*
five-cent magazines, IV:4
flower periodical, IV:342*n*
free-silver periodical, IV:163*n*
general magazine, IV:45
health magazine, III:139
home decorating magazine, IV:324
home-finding magazine, IV:200

home magazines, V:154*n*
horse-racing periodical, IV:343
humor periodicals, IV:385, 387*n*
illustrated magazines, IV:99–100, 153
information periodicals, IV:54–55
insurance periodical, IV:351*n*
Jewish periodicals, IV:300
juvenile periodical, IV:275
lecture magazine, IV:266
legal magazines, IV:346, 347*n*, 348
library magazine, IV:143
literary magazines, III:539*n;* IV:88, 124–25
lumber periodicals, IV:325*n*
magazine center, IV:98–100
mail-order periodicals, IV:367
manufacturing periodicals, IV:183–85, 186*n*
Masonic periodical, IV:222*n*
medical journals, IV:314–16, 524*n*
mining periodicals, IV:322*n*
missionary periodicals, IV:305
music periodicals, IV:253–54
Negro periodical, IV:214*n*
news periodicals, IV:64
office-practice periodicals, IV:352
philology journals, IV:128
philosophical journal, IV:302
photography periodical, IV:149
pigeon periodical, IV:345
political magazines, IV:170, 178
populist periodical, IV:176
poultry magazine, III:161*n*
printers' magazine, IV:247
railroad periodicals, IV:333*n*
reactionary periodicals, IV:448
religious periodicals, III:82; IV:284, 285*n*, 291
review periodicals, IV:52–53, 60–61, 65
Scandinavian-American periodical, IV:231
scientific periodical, IV:310*n*
socialist periodicals, IV:175, 176
social-work periodical, IV:194
sociology journal, IV:191
sports' periodicals, IV:385, 387*n*
stock-breeding periodicals, IV:344
"success" periodical, IV:169
tariff periodical, IV:167
telephone periodicals, IV:335
temperance periodical, IV:210
theater periodicals, IV:261, 269, 271–72
trade periodicals, IV:186*n*, 187–89
trade union periodical, IV:221*n*
travel periodicals, IV:224
urban weeklies, IV:100
women's periodicals, IV:367
YMCA periodical, IV:287*n*
modern magazines in (1905–)
agricultural machinery journal, IV:188*n*
dental journals, IV:317
literary center, V:156
literary magazines, III:539*n;* V:179*n*
manufacturing periodicals, IV:183–85, 186*n*
medical periodicals, IV:315, 525*n*
religious periodicals, III:82; IV:300
social welfare magazine, IV:743
women's periodicals, IV:367
anarchist movement in, II:482
anarchist periodicals, IV:172
Haymarket bombing, IV:172–73, 217–18, 561
press opposition, II:530; IV:561
Columbian Exposition (1893) in, *see* Columbian Exposition
corruption in, III:291–92
cultural movements in, V:166
growth of, III:51–52
economic, III:30; IV:98
as magazine publishing center, II:115
muckraking articles on, IV:600
music in, IV:249
newspapers in, III:270*n*
Chicago, University of, IV:74, 128
Chicago Apparel Gazette, IV:187*n*
Chicago Art Union, II:191
Chicago Banker, IV:349*n*
Chicago Chronicle, IV:70
Chicago Clinical Review, IV:314*n*
Chicago Commerce, IV:350*n*
Chicago Commercial Advertiser, III:127
Chicago Commons, IV:743*n*
Chicago Daily News, III:270*n;* IV:70; V:294
Chicago Dairy Produce, IV:344*n*
Chicago Evening Post, IV:168
Chicago Evening Post Literary Review, V:196
Chicago Field, III:210*n*
Chicago Figaro, IV:100, 385
Chicago fire, III:118, 145, 415
Chicago Fireside Friend, III:39
Chicago Grocer, III:135*n*
Chicago Herald, III:270*n*
Chicago Household Guest, IV:367*n*
Chicago Index, III:54

Chicago Journal of Commerce, II:92
Chicago Journal of Nervous and Mental Diseases, III:142
Chicago Ledger, III:39, 53–54; IV:4, 18, 68
Chicago Legal News, IV:346, 347*n*
Chicago Lumberman, IV:325*n*
Chicago Magazine, IV:53*n*
Chicago Magazine of Fashion, Music and Home Reading, III:95
Chicago Medical Journal, II:84*n*
Chicago Medical Recorder, IV:314
Chicago Medical Review, III:141*n*
Chicago Medical Times, III:141*n*
Chicago Mining Review, III:114
"Chicago Plan," V:225
Chicago Pulpit, III:84
Chicago Record, II:69, 97, 200
Chicago Saturday World, IV:68*n*
Chicago Socialist, IV:175*n*
Chicago Specimen, III:132*n*
Chicago Teacher, IV:271
Chicago Tribune, III:297; V:225
Chicago World, IV:68
Chicagoan, III:52
Chicopee, Mass., II:94*n*
Child, Francis Washburn, IV:465, 468
Child, Lydia Maria, I:350, 434, 634; II:141, 504*n*
Child, Richard Washburn, V:83
Child at Home, II:100
Child labor, IV:404, 462, 746, 767
Child of Pallas, I:791
Child Study Monthly, IV:272
Child-care magazines, IV:364
Children of the United States, IV:275
Children's Hour, III:176
Children's Magazine, I:29, 789; II:101; IV:275*n*
Children's magazines, *see* Juvenile magazines
Childs, Cephas G., I:208, 209
Childs, Francis James, IV:128
Childs, George William, I:365, 549, 554; II:158; III:492
Childs, Henry E., III:422
Childs, John Lewis, IV:342
Childs, Marquis W., V:12, 338*n*
Child's Friend, I:492–93, 807
Child's Paper, II:100; III:8*n*
Child's World, III:8*n*
Chillicothe, Ohio, II:63*n*
Chilocco Beacon, IV:215*n*
Chin, IV:88
China, III:280; IV:232–33, 239; V:192
  immigration from, III:276–77
  See also Boxer Rebellion
China, Glass and Lamps, IV:188*n*
China Decorator, IV:147
Chip Basket, III:269*n*
Chirico, Giorgio di, V:178
Chironian, III:143
Chisholm, Samuel S., III:128*n*
Chittenden, Simeon, II:367*n*, 370
Chivers, Thomas Holley, I:756; II:116
Choate, Joseph Hodges, IV:570; V:206, 287
Choate, Rufus, I:751
Choice Literature, III:256*n*
Choir, IV:254*n*
Choir Herald, IV:254*n*
Choir Journal, IV:254*n*
Choir Leader, IV:254
Choir music journals, IV:254
Cholera epidemics, III:137; IV:311–12
"Cholly Knickerbocker," V:272
Choral Advocate, II:197
Chosen People, IV:300*n*
Christendom, IV:198, 499
Christensen, Parley Parker, III:352
Christian, II:63; III:80
Christian Advocate (Nashville), II:68*n*; III:71; IV:291
Christian Advocate (New York), I:300, 373, 799; II:66, 67, 206; III:67, 70, 224; IV:288, 290–91
Christian Advocate (Philadelphia)
  founding of, I:136
  sketch of, I:315–16
Christian Banner, III:85; IV:292*n*
Christian Banner and Tract Journal, II:75
Christian Century, IV:295, 393; V:xvi
Christian City, IV:305
Christian Contributor and Free Missionary, II:65
Christian County School News, IV:271
Christian Cynosure, III:315
Christian Disciple, see: Christian Examiner
Christian Educator, IV:305
Christian Endeavor World, III:180; IV:275
Christian-Evangelist, III:80; IV:296
Christian Examiner, I:349, 569–72, 690; II:71; III:30, 34, 77, 436–37, 506, 597
  founding of, I:135
  sketch of, I:284–92
Christian Freeman, II:72*n*
Christian Gospel Banner, II:72
Christian Guide, III:80
Christian Hebrew, III:80*n*
Christian Herald, I:135, 795; II:63*n*; IV:391; V:272, 286
Christian Herald (Detroit), III:73*n*

Christian Herald (New York), III:28, 83
Christian Herald (Omaha), III:75*n*
Christian History, I:25, 78, 787
Christian Index, I:138, 796; II:64*n;* III:73; IV:291–92
Christian Inquirer, I:374, 808; II:72; III:77; IV:291
Christian Instructor, II:63
Christian Intelligencer, II:73
Christian Journal, I:135, 795
Christian Leader, II:72; III:79*n;* IV:296
Christian Life, IV:200
Christian Literature and Review of the Churches, IV:301
Christian Metaphysician, IV:286
Christian Mirror, II:71
Christian Missionary, IV:238*n*
Christian Nation, III:81
Christian Observer, I:137, 794; II:63, III:71; IV:293
Christian Oracle, IV:295
Christian Parlor Magazine, II:14
  founding of, I:372
    sketch of, I:745–46
Christian Quarterly, III:79–80; IV:296
Christian Quarterly Review, III:80
Christian Recorder, II:68*n;* III:71*n*
Christian Register (Boston), I:138, 290, 570, 797; II:72; III:77, 507; IV:294
Christian Register (Lexington), I:206*n*, 797
Christian Repository, II:72
Christian Review, II:63
  founding of, I:371
  sketch of, I:666–68
Christian Science, II:257; IV:285–86, 413, 493
Christian Science Journal, IV:285
Christian Science Sentinel, IV:285
Christian Science Thought, IV:286
Christian Science Weekly, IV:285
Christian Secretary, II:65*n*
Christian socialism, IV:176, 190–91, 280–83
Christian Socialist, IV:283
Christian Spectator, I:179, 197, 370
  founding of, I:135–36
  sketch of, I:310
Christian Spiritualist, II:210*n*
Christian Standard, III:80*n;* IV:295
Christian Standard and Home Journal, III:72
Christian Student, IV:291
Christian Sun, II:74
Christian Times (Chicago), II:65*n*
Christian Times (New York), II:70*n*
Christian Union, II:374, 375, 379; IV:59, 288, 292
  See also: Outlook
Christian Union Herald, IV:294
Christian Watchman, see: Watchman-Examiner
Christian Witness (Boston), II:70*n;* III:82
Christian Witness (Columbus), III:82
Christian Work, III:81; IV:301
Christian Worker, III:81; IV:296
Christian World (Cleveland), II:74
Christian World (New York), II:77
Christianity in Earnest, IV:305
Christian's Magazine, I:793
Christian's Monitor, I:791
Christian's Scholar and Farmer's Magazine
  on "female education," I:64
  sketch of, I:112
Christians at Work, III:82
Christie, Agatha, IV:475, 503, 700, 709, 713
Christman, Henry, IV:749*n*
Christmas Ideas, V:47
Christy, Howard Chandler, II:464; III:484; IV:151, 361*n*, 456, 501, 602, 726
Chromatic Art Magazine, III:186
Chromolithographic journals, III:186
Chromolithographs, III:29
  in post-Civil War magazines (1865–85), III:191, 528, 552
    comic magazines, III:268
    as premiums, III:7, 191, 411, 425, 437, 442
    quality, III:182
  in Gilded Age magazines (1885–1905)
    colored cartoons, IV:61
    comic magazines, III:554
    eclectic magazines, IV:720
    fashion periodicals, IV:363
    sentimental, IV:18
    urban periodicals, IV:84–85
  in modern magazines (1905–)
    eclectic magazines, IV:726
    women's magazines, IV:767
  See also Prang, Louis
Chronological relationship of magazines
  early (1741–94), I:70
  in nationalist era (1794–1825), I:214
  in expansionist era (1825–50), I:528
  in Civil War era (1850–65), II:218
  in post-Civil War era (1860–65), III:318
Chronotype, III:262*n*
Chrysler, Walter, V:323*n*

Chubbuck, Emily, III:229
Church, III:75*n*
Church, Benjamin, I:48
Church, C. A., III:53*n*
Church, declining interest in, III:86–87
See also specific denominations
Church, Francis Pharcellus, II:150, 547; III:21, 33, 361*n*, 362, 377
Church, Frederic Edwin, II:188; III:182
Church, Frederick Stuart, II:477; III: 20, 189; IV:484
Church, John Adams, III:363; IV:661
Church, Joseph M., II:210*n*
Church, Rev. Pharcellus, II:64*n*, 547
Church, William Conant, II:150, 547; III:21, 33, 361*n*, 362–77; IV:721
Church Advocate, II:70*n*, 74
Church Building Quarterly, III:76
Church Choir, IV:254*n*
Church Eclectic, III:75
Church Economist, IV:301*n*
Church of God, magazine of, II:74
Church at Home and Abroad, IV:293*n*
Church Journal, II:69
Church Kalendar, III:75*n*
Church Militant, IV:294*n*
Church Monthly, II:69; III:75
Church music periodicals, IV:254
Church News, III:75*n*
Church Progress, III:69*n*
Church Record, II:69
Church Review, I:372, 809; II:68
sketch of, II:364–66
Church School Magazine, III:71*n*
Church Standard, II:70*n*
Church Union (1867–69), III:82, 422–23
Church Union (1873–1899), III:82
Church Weekly, III:75
Churchill, Allen, V:23
Churchill, Mrs. C. M., III:95
Churchill, John Wesley, IV:395
Churchill, Winston (American novelist), IV:112, 141, 502; V:56, 97, 323*n*
Churchill, Sir Winston Spencer, IV:473–74, 661, 727, 780
Churchman (Hartford), II:69
Churchman (New York), II:70*n*; III:75; IV:294
Churchman's Magazine, I:204, 796
Churchman's Monthly Magazine, II:68, 70*n*
Church's Bizarre, II:210*n*; IV:3*n*
Church's Musical Visitor, III:197*n*
Ciardi, John, V:243
Cigar Maker's Official Journal, II:212*n*
Cigar and Tobacco, IV:189*n*
Cigarette advertising, IV:699
Cincinnati, Ohio
nationalist-era magazines in (1794–1825), I:126, 205–7
expansionist-era magazines in (1825–50), I:375, 386–89, 444*n*, 457, 491, 559, 596, 658*n*, 662, 693; II:92*n*, 301
Civil War era magazines in (1850–65), II:33, 52, 57, 59, 65*n*, 74, 77, 81, 85, 92*n*, 114, 212, 301–4, 534, 535
post-Civil War magazines in (1865–85), III:55
comic magazines, III:266, 267
construction periodical, III:129–30
dental periodical, II:92*n*
grange magazines, III:149*n*, 179–80
historical journal, III:262
juvenile magazine, III:179–80
legal journal, III:145*n*
music periodicals, III:197*n*
publishing center, III:55
religious magazines, III:71–72, 74, 80
scientific periodicals, III:109, 112
secret societies, III:314
technical periodicals, III:116
trade magazine, III:135*n*
trade union periodicals, III:126*n*, 127*n*
women's magazines, II:301, 304–5; III:55, 94
Gilded Age magazines in (1885–1905)
advertising journal, IV:247
agnostic periodical, IV:278
all-fiction magazine, IV:117
comic periodical, IV:387*n*
dental periodical, II:92*n*
engineering periodical, IV:321
fashion periodical, IV:751
five-cent magazine, IV:48
grange magazines, III:149*n*, 179–80
humor periodical, IV:387*n*
insurance periodical, IV:351*n*
Jewish periodical, IV:300
manufacturing periodicals, IV:183*n*, 184*n*, 186*n*
medical journals, III:197*n*; IV:316
missionary periodical, IV:305
music periodicals, IV:254*n*
religious periodicals, IV:292–93, 295, 298–9
settlement-house periodical, IV:196*n*
"success" magazine, IV:169
theater periodical, IV:261
trade periodical, IV:187*n*
trade union periodical, IV:221*n*
modern periodicals in (1905–)

advertising journal, IV:247
dental periodical, II:92*n*
medical journal, IV:315*n*
trade-union periodical, IV:221*n*
music in, IV:249
Cincinnati College of Music's Courier, III:197*n*
Cincinnati Enquirer, III:366–67
Cincinnati Grange Bulletin, III:149*n*
Cincinnati Literary Gazette, I:126, 207, 798
Cincinnati Medical Journal, IV:313*n*
Cincinnati Medical News, III:141*n*
Cincinnati Medical Repertory, III:141*n*
Cincinnati Mirror, I:398, 801
Cincinnati Pioneer, III:261
Cincinnati Quarterly Journal of Science, III:109
Cincinnati Times, III:55
Cincinnati Weekly Law Bulletin, III: 145*n*
Cincinnatus, II:89
Circuit Court of Appeals, V:14
Circular (Oneida periodical), II:78, 150, 207, 210*n;* III:300
Circular Staircase (Rinehart), V:254
Circulation
of early magazines (1741–94), I:13–14, 87, 101, 104
of nationalist-era magazines (1794–1825), I:199–200; II:231
eclectic magazines, I:326
juvenile magazines, I:144
religious magazines, I:144
scientific periodicals, I:304
of expansionist-era magazines (1825–50), I:359, 561, 768; II:231
abolitionist magazines, II:281, 283
agricultural magazines, I:729–30
by city and state, I:375*n*, 379, 386
children's magazines, I:713–14; II:264, 266
general magazines, IV:674, 678
literary magazines, I:607, 638, 702; IV:674, 678
"mammoth" papers, I:359, 361–62
political magazines, I:753
problems, I:513–16
scientific periodicals, II:317, 319
of Civil War era magazines (1850–65), II:35, 37–38, 535
agricultural magazines, I:730–31; II:102–3
business magazines, II:342
effects of war, II:6–7
exchange lists, II:11–12
family magazines, II:473, 475–76
general magazines, II:450
high-circulation periodicals, II:10–11
humor magazines, II:182*n*
illustrated weeklies, II:44–45, 410–11, 458, 460–61
literary magazines, II:36, 37, 42, 391, 393, 426
military periodicals, II:549
national magazines, I:102–3
religious magazines, II:370–71, 381
scientific periodicals, II:319
trends, II:9–13
women's magazines, II:51, 303, 441
of post-Civil War magazines (1865–85)
agricultural magazines, II:433–34
booksellers' magazines, III:492
business magazines, II:348
club system, III:8
current events periodicals, III:338–39, 350
family magazines, II:354, 359; III:7, 101, 425–26
fashion magazines, III:482
general magazines, III:467, 510–11, 558
illustrated weeklies, II:463
insurance journals, III:145–46
juvenile magazines, II:268; III:501
legal periodicals, III:144
literary magazines, II:430; III:6–7, 40, 323, 378, 405, 415, 551
medical journals, III:140
music journals, III:196
news companies, III:8
newspapers, III:6
penmanship periodicals, III:170
premium system, III:7–8
religious periodicals, II:315, 376; III:7, 67, 70, 76*n*, 422, 436, 507
scientific periodicals, II:322
trends, III:6–9
women's magazines, II:309, 441; III:6–7, 100, 388
women's rights magazines, III:450
of Gilded Age magazines (1885–1905), II:254–56
agricultural magazines, II:434
all-fiction magazines, IV:115–16, 420–21
booksellers' magazines, III:494; IV:436
charity magazines, IV:741
comic magazines, III:528–29, 554; IV:558, 561, 565
current events periodicals, IV:500

Circulation—*Continued*
digest periodicals, IV:571
dishonest reports of circulation, IV:15–16
education periodicals, IV:268–70, 271*n*
family magazines, II:480, 482; III: 429, 481–82, 484, 491–92; IV:68, 88; V:131–32
fashion magazines, III:482–83; IV: 363, 581–82
flower periodicals, IV:342
general magazines, III:475; IV:115–16, 507, 590, 596, 599, 611, 613–14, 680, 686, 689–91, 717–18, 723
geographic magazines, IV:622, 631
high circulation, IV:13, 16–17, 59
home periodicals, IV:764
illustrated weeklies, II:464; IV: 454, 457, 464, 558, 561, 565
juvenile magazines, I:273; IV:273
legal periodicals, IV:346–47
literary magazines, II:511; III:407, 540, 551; IV:430, 680, 686, 734, 736
mail-order periodicals, IV:365, 367
mail rates and, IV:20
medical journals, IV:525–26
military periodicals, II:549
news periodicals, IV:650
outdoor magazines, IV:635, 638
police gazettes, II:333, 335
populist periodicals, IV:162–63, 411, 414
poultry periodicals, IV:345
promotional magazines, IV:106*n*
reactionary periodicals, IV:443, 449
religious magazines, IV:293*n*
review periodicals, IV:52*n*, 65–67, 658
satiric magazines, IV:646, 670
scientific periodicals, II:322, 498; IV:308*n*
socialist periodicals, IV:205
spiritualist periodicals, IV:304
techniques for building, IV:17–18
urban periodicals, IV:84, 86
veterans' magazines, IV:69
of modern magazines (1905–), II:258
agricultural magazines, I:732; II:435
all-fiction magazines, IV:422, 430–31
art magazines, V:171
booksellers' magazines, III:494; IV:438, 440
charity magazines, IV:745–46, 749
comic periodicals, IV:565, 567
current events magazines, III:356
digest periodicals, IV:574, 578–79
family magazines, III:434; IV:497, 503, 505; V:133, 141, 143
fashion periodicals, IV:629
gardening magazines, V:38, 41–42, 44, 48
general magazines, III:479, 515, 555; IV:510, 604, 606–7, 617–18, 692, 694, 696, 699, 706, 710, 715, 730–31; V:4, 17, 22–23, 32, 41–42, 74, 81, 83, 85–86, 248–49, 255, 259–60, 263, 270–71, 338–39
geographic periodicals, IV:629
home magazines, V:38, 41–42, 44, 48, 133
illustrated weeklies, II:464; IV: 467, 473, 477, 565, 567
library periodicals, III:519; IV:736
literary magazines, II:431, 515; III:407–8, 542, 551; IV:422, 430–31, 502–3, 738; V:118, 123, 171, 186
military magazines, III:534
men's magazines, IV:423
newspaper-trade magazines, V:63, 66, 68, 70
poetry magazines, V:112–13, 123, 171
police gazettes, II:336
publishers' magazines, V:63, 66, 68, 70
reactionary periodicals, IV:449
religious magazines, II:378
review periodicals, IV:521–22, 661–63, 786–88
scientific periodicals, III:499
women's magazines, III:490; IV: 549, 551, 554, 583, 587, 729, 768, 770–71; V:133, 141, 143
delinquent subscriptions and, *see* Delinquent subscribers
of newspapers, *see* Newspapers
See also Subscriptions
Circuses, III:209
Cist, Charles, I:94, 94*n;* II:114*n*
Cist's Advertiser, II:114*n*, 176*n*
Cities
corruption in, *see* Municipal corruption
dirtiness of, I:475
Citizen, III:69*n*
Citizen (Boston), IV:181
Citizen (New York), IV:77, 85

Citizen (Philadelphia), IV:263
Citizen (Salt Lake City), IV:104*n*
City Budget, II:185*n*
City and Country, III:156
City Government, IV:198
City Hall, IV:198*n*
City Item, II:37
City and State, IV:60
Civil engineering periodicals, III:113
Civil rights, *see* Indians; Negroes
Civil Service Chronicle, IV:199
Civil Service Record, III:295
Civil service reform
post-Civil War magazine on (1865–85), III:295, 334, 341–42, 392, 463, 470, 525
Gilded Age magazines on (1885–1905), IV:211
Civil Service Reformer, III:295*n*
Civil War, I:612–13; II:59, 61, 77, 84, 87, 88, 245; V:283, 343
abolitionists and, II:292–94
antislavery magazines in, I:301
financial causes of, II:147
histories of, II:548; III:261–62, 468–70; IV:56, 490
magazines on, II:59, 61, 77, 84, 87, 88, 245; III:376; IV:679–80
engravings, II:460
freedmen, II:131
Northern magazines, II:6–7
patriotism, II:149
political issues, II:131
reportage, II:7, 149–56, 440, 459–60, 474–75, 503, 548
sectional hatreds, II:156
slavery, II:131
Southern magazines, II:8–9; III:111–13
memoirs of, II:253
religious magazines and, II:314
secession of South and, *see* Secession
songs of, II:196–97
theater and, II:199–200
Clack Book, IV:390
Claflin, Tennie C. (Tennessee), III:95, 443–44, 449–52
Clapp, E. B., 580*n,* 582
Clapp, Henry, II:38–40
Clapp, Henry Austin, III:200
Clapp, J. Milton, I:721*n,* 725
Clapp, Robert P., III:295*n*
Clapp, William Warland, II:35
Clapper, Raymond, IV:663; V:55
"Clara Augusta," II:417
"Clare, Ada," *see* McElheney, Jane
Clare, Israel Smith, IV:53*n,* 55
Clarendon, J. Hayden, IV:617
Claretie, Jules, II:255
Clark, Champ, IV:73, 165
Clark, Charles D., III:179
Clark, Davis Wasgatt, II:301*n,* 303
Clark, Edward B., V:81
Clark, Francis Edward, III:180
Clark, J. S., II:71
Clark, John Maurice, IV:180*n*
Clark, Kate Upson, IV:45, 366, 633
Clark, Lewis Gaylord, I:274–75, 345–46, 402, 606–14; II:388
Clark, T. Edward, IV:89*n*
Clark, Victor S., I:747*n,* 749
Clark W. G. C., II:111
Clark, Walter Van Tilburg, V:337
Clark, Willis Gaylord, I:274, 326, 546, 608
Clark, Z., II:504*n*
Clarke, Charles S., IV:88
Clarke, Dorus, I:745
Clarke, George Herbert, IV:733*n,* 737
Clarke, Helen Archibald, IV:121
Clarke, James Freeman, I:292*n,* 374, 658*n,* 659, 662–63, 703, 764; II:254; III:507
Clarke, Joseph Ignatius Constantine, IV:66
Clarke, Mary G., II:57*n*
Clarke, Rebecca Sophia ("Sophie May"), III:509; IV:680
Clarke, Thomas Cottrell, I:354; IV:671*n,* 673–74
Clarke, William Fayal, III:500, 502, 504
Clarke, William T., III:41*n,* 391*n,* 394–95
Clarke's School Visitor, II:101
Clary, C. C. Tennant, IV:97
Class periodicals, *see* Railroad journals; Scientific periodicals; Trade periodicals
Class Struggle, IV:175
Classmate, III:180; IV:274
Claudel, Paul, V:244
Clay, Henry, I:184, 620, 750, 781
Clay, Thomas Hart, II:262*n*
Clay Record, IV:325*n*
Clay-trade magazines, III:130
Clay Worker, III:130
Cleaning-materials' advertising, IV:25–26
Cleona, Pa., IV:301*n*
Clearing House Quarterly, IV:350*n*
Cleghorn, Sarah Norcliffe, IV:616, 724, 748
Clemenceau, Georges, IV:696

Clemens, Samuel Langhorne ("Mark Twain"), I:740; II:40, 118, 178, 255, 257, 400, 402, 506*n*; III:13, 56, 58, 172, 206, 228, 238, 247, 257, 261, 264, 271, 403, 469, 474, 503; IV:51, 105, 130, 141, 165, 255, 285, 383, 490, 491, 544, 642; V:119–21, 342
at *Atlantic Monthly* dinner, III:59–60
criticism of, III:243–44
in *Galaxy*, III:363–68
Clemens, Will M., III:234; IV:125
Clement, E. W., II:116*n*
Clement, Jesse, II:116
Clements, Edith Schwartz, IV:627
Clements, Frederic Edward, IV:627
Clements, John A., V:3*n*, 25–26
Clergy
early magazines and (1741–94), I:58
nationalist-era magazines and (1794–1825), I:334
expansionist-era magazines and (1825–50), I:493; II:302–3, 313–14
Civil War era magazines and (1850–65), II:44, 227, 544, 551
post-Civil War magazines and (1865–85), II:252; III:337, 425, 546
Gilded Age magazines and (1885–1905), IV:569
abolitionists and, II:286, 290
slavery and, II:314, 368
theater and, II:200
See also Christian socialism
Cleveland, Grover, II:251, 271, 376, 481, 512; III:288, 345, 475, 525, 529, 553; IV:156, 241, 516, 602, 655
as contributor, IV:547, 688, 706
as political leader, IV:62, 161, 165, 211, 219, 227, 386, 387*n*, 448, 561
Cleveland, H. L., IV:775
Cleveland, H. M., III:422*n*
Cleveland, Henry Russell, II:238
Cleveland, Ohio
Civil War era magazines in (1850–65), II:115
agricultural magazine, II:89
literary weekly, II:36*n*
religious magazines, II:68, 74
post-Civil War magazines in (1865–85)
agricultural magazine, III:152–53, 156
historical journal, III:262
literary magazine, III:234
manufacturers' periodical, III:128
music periodical, III:197*n*
printers' magazine, III:131
religious magazines, III:69*n*, 85
technical periodical, III:116
women's magazine, III:100
Gilded Age magazines in (1885–1905)
automobile periodical, IV:331
Chautauqua magazines, III:544*n*; IV:95, 264
financial periodicals, IV:349, 350*n*
historical periodical, IV:139
Jewish periodical, IV:300*n*
literary magazine, IV:125
magazine center, IV:95
manufacturing periodicals, III:128; IV:183*n*
marine periodical, IV:334
medical periodicals, IV:313*n*
music periodical, IV:254*n*
religious magazine, IV:301*n*
trade union periodicals, III:126*n*; IV:221*n*
women's magazines, IV:356, 763*n*
YMCA periodical, IV:287*n*
modern magazines in (1905–)
Chautauqua magazine, IV:264
financial periodical, IV:350*n*
manufacturing periodicals, III:128, IV:183*n*, 184*n*, 186*n*
news magazine, V:293*n*
Cleveland, Rose Elizabeth, III:234
Cleveland Medical Gazette, IV:313*n*
Cleveland Medical Journal, IV:313*n*
Cleveland Plain Dealer, II:526; III:266
Clever Stories, V:261
Clews, Henry, IV:216, 414*n*
Cliff Dwellers' Club, V:229
Clifford, John D., I:312
Clifford, Josephine, III:405, 406
Clift, William, I:731
Cline, Howard F., IV:404
Cline, Leonard, V:5, 184, 265
Clinedinst, B. West, II:464
Clinical Medicine and Surgery, IV:314*n*
Clinton, Miss., III:73*n*
Clinton, DeWitt, I:298
Clipper, IV:373, 384
Clips, IV:385
Clissold, H. R., IV:185*n*
Cloak and Suit Review, IV:187*n*
Close, Upton, IV:730
Closson, William Baxter Palmer, IV:719
Clothier and Furnisher, III:134; IV:187
Clothier and Hatter, III:134
Clothiers' and Haberdashers' Weekly, IV:187*n*
Clothing, *see* Fashions in dress
Clothing advertising, IV:22–24
Clothing Gazette, III:134*n*

Clothing-trade magazines, III:134; IV:187
Cloud, Charles F., I:380
Clough, Arthur Hugh, II:243, 424, 509*n*
Clough, John, I:139
Club Life, IV:356*n*
Club Woman, IV:356
Club Worker, IV:355
Clubs, literary, I:194; 254–57, 287; II:226–28; III:231, 233
see also Anthology Society; Delphian Club; Examiner Club; Friendly Club; Literary Club of Walpole; Transcendental Club; Tuesday Club
Clubs, sports, III:213, 219–22
Clubs, subscribers', I:516; II:11; III:8; IV:537, 691
Clubs, women's, IV:356
Clute, Willard Nelson, IV:309–10
Clutz, Jacob A., II:73*n*
Clymer, Ernest F., IV:603
Coaching articles, IV:634
Coach-Makers' International Journal, III:216*n*
Coach-maker's Magazine, II:92
Coal and Coke, IV:189*n*
Coal Dealer, IV:189*n*
Coal miners' strike (1869), III:303; IV:219
Coal retailers' magazines, IV:189
Coal Trade Bulletin, IV:189*n*
Coal Trade Journal, III:135; IV:189*n*
Coan, Titus Munson, II:376; III:18, 257
Coast, IV:108
Coast Review, III:146*n*
Coates, Foster, IV:249, 543
Coates, Grace Stone, V:13
Coates, Reynell, I:546*n*, 769*n*
Cobb, H., II:116*n*
Cobb, Irvin S., IV:498, 693, 695, 696, 697, 708; V:119, 134, 291
Cobb, Samuel T., IV:81*n*
Cobb, Sanford, III:491*n*
Cobb, Sylvanus, II:72*n;* III:46*n,* 224, 246
Cobb, Sylvanus, Jr., II:35, 38, 358, 360, 362, 410
Cobbett, William ("Peter Porcupine"), I:131, 150, 157, 158–59
Cobbett's American Political Register, I:131, 795
Cobden, Ill., IV:341
Cocoa, Fla., IV:270*n*
Cocran, G. C., III:54*n*
Cockerill, John A., IV:240, 490
Cockrill's Magazine, IV:93
Cocktails, III:266
Cocteau, Jean, IV:761
Cody, Sherwin, IV:94, 115
Coe, Charles Francis, IV:618
Coe, Francis, IV:700
Coe, Franklin, II:355, 547*n,* 549
Coffee, A. B., III:408
Coffee and Tea Industries, IV:187*n*
Coffin, C. D., 452*n*
Coffin, Charles Carleton, III:178*n*
Coffin, R. F., IV:634–35
Coffin, Robert Barry ("Barry Gray"), II:352
Coffin, Robert Peter Tristram, IV:730, 748; V:242, 336
Coffin, Robert S., IV:671–72
Coggeshall, William Turner, II:114, 303, 445, 466
Coghlan, Joseph Bullock, III:534
Coghlan, Rose, IV:256
Cogswell, Joseph Green, I:367, 669*n,* 670; II:228, 229, 232
Cogswell, William, I:491*n;* II:175*n*
Cohan, George M., V:266
Cohen, Alfred J., IV:60, 492, 496, 560
Cohen, Octavus Roy, IV:421, 429, 472, 585, 618, 695
Cohn, Adolph, IV:434
Coin Collector, III:113*n*
Coin-collectors' magazines, IV:391
Coin's Financial School, IV:111, 162
Coit, Stanton, IV:279
Coke, Thomas, I:29
Colby, Clara Bewick, III:95
Colby, Frank Moore, IV:432*n,* 437
Colcord, Lincoln, III:355, 514
Cold Storage, IV:183*n*
Cole, Ashley, W., III:265*n*
Cole, G. D. H., V:97
Cole, R. Taylor, V:273*n*
Cole, Thomas, I:436
Cole, Timothy, III:85, 188, 191, 411, 466, 472; IV:5, 146
Colebaugh, Charles Henry, IV:453*n,* 470, 475
Coleman, Oliver, V:156, 158
Coleman, William, IV:166
Coleridge, Mary E., V:229
Coleridge, Samuel Taylor, I:180, 231, 257
Coles, Edward, I:596
Coles, G., 299*n*
Colesworthy, Daniel Clement, II:265
Collector (art periodical), IV:147
Collector (autographs periodical), IV:391
College Courant, III:168*n*

College Journal of Medical Science, II:85
College magazines, I:172, 427; II:99–100; III:165–66; IV:272–73
quality and variety of, I:488–89
See also names of specific colleges and universities
College sports, II:203; III:221–22; IV:634
Colleges and universities
alumni quarterlies of, IV:74–75
curriculum of, IV:263
debates, III:164
enrollment in, I:488; II:97
expansion of, IV:262
extension programs of, IV:263–64, 357
magazine comment on, I:472, 488
number of, II:97
women in, IV:357
See also specific colleges and universities; specific periodicals
Collegian, I:488, 800
Collens, T. Wharton, III:299
Collier, Ezra, I:434
Collier, Peter Fenelon, IV:453
Collier, Price, IV:636, 726
Collier, Robert Joseph, IV:59, 453*n,* 454–67, 754
Collier, William, I:165*n,* 473
Collier's, IV:10, 21, 31, 37, 58–59, 208–209, 235–36, 245, 528, 686, 754
sketch of, IV:453–79
Colliery Engineer, III:115*n*
Collin, W. E., IV:738
Collingwood, Herbert Winslow, IV:340
Collins, Alan C., IV:773*n,* 787–88
Collins, Frederick Lewis, IV:360*n,* 589*n,* 602–03, 763*n,* 768
Collins, James H., IV:604, 607
Collins, Paul Valorous, IV:361
Collins, Seward, IV:432*n,* 440–41
Collins, Wilkie, II:393, 406, 439, 463, 471, 476, 482; III:223, 224, 249, 251, 389
Collitz, Hermann, III:535*n*
Collyer, Robert, III:52, 78, 83, 101, 416
Colman, Henry, I:317*n,* 318, 443
Colman, Norman J., I:444
Colman's Rural World, III:157
Colonization, Negro, II:281
Colonization Herald, II:141
Colonization Society, II:281
Colonizationist, I:802
Color photography, IV:149, 626, 630
Colorado Engineer, IV:321*n*
Colorado Medicine, IV:314*n*
Colorado School Journal, IV:270*n*
Colorado Springs, Colo., IV:104
Colorado University, IV:321*n*
Colorado Workman, IV:204
Coloradoan, IV:104*n*
Colored American Magazine, IV:214
Colored cartoons, III:56, 525; IV:61
Colored comic strips, IV:366
Colored illustrations
in expansionist era magazines (1835–50), I:442, 493, 519–21, 545, 548, 591–92, 719, 744, 771
in Civil War era magazines (1850–65), II:18, 192, 416–17, 437–39, 441
in post-Civil War magazines (1865–85), II:309; III:325, 528
in Gilded Age magazines (1885–1905), II:311, 402; III:475, 483; IV: 456, 545, 602, 689; V:144
in modern magazines (1905–), III:475, 484–85, 531; IV:496, 550, 588, 626–31, 786; V:120, 122–23, 128, 161, 270, 289, 297, 300–1, 323
in newspapers, V:70
See also Chromolithographs
Colored maps, IV:574
Colson, Ethel, V:157
Colton, Arthur Willis, IV:724, 737; V:337
Colton, Asa L., II:543
Colton, Delia M., II:542
Colton, F. Barrows, IV:632
Colton, George Hooker, I:376, 488, 546*n,* 750*n,* 751–52
Colton, Walker, I:546*n*
Colton, Wendell P., IV:30–31
Colum, Mary M. (Mrs. Padraic Colum), IV:522; V:23, 96
Colum, Padraic, III:330, 541; IV:436, 438
"Columbia," I:464
Columbia, Mo., III:80
Columbia, S.C.
Civil War era magazines in (1850–65), II:68*n,* 89, 110*n;* III:8, 63*n*
post-Civil War magazines in (1865–85), III:73*n*
Gilded Age magazines in (1885–1905), IV:295*n,* 296
Columbia Churchman, III:75*n*
Columbia Jurist, IV:347
Columbia Law Review, IV:348
Columbia Law Times, IV:348
Columbia and Oregon Timberman, IV: 325*n*

Columbia-Sterling Company, V:152
Columbia University, IV:83; V:347
magazines published at, III:115, 165–66
Acta Columbiana, III:166, 269; IV:560
legal periodicals, IV:348
political science quarterly, IV:180
school news, IV:75
Columbia University Quarterly, IV:74
Columbian, II:114*n;* IV:366; V:151*n,* 152
Columbian Agricultural Society, I:153
Columbian Exposition (1893), II:255, 483; III:428, 530; IV:144, 320; V:487, 508
Columbian and Great West, II:114*n*
Columbian Lady's and Gentleman's Magazine, I:352, 743–44, 807
Columbian Magazine, I:18, 34, 37, 41, 42*n,* 52, 54, 57–58, 63, 100
founding of, I:30
sketch of, I:94–99
Columbian Museum, I:31*n,* 789
Columbian Phenix, I:145, 203, 203*n,* 791
Columbian Star, see: Christian Index
Columbus, Ga., II:89
Columbus, Kan., IV:285*n*
Columbus, Miss., III:149*n*
Columbus, Ohio
expansionist era magazines in (1825–50), I:389
agricultural magazine, I:444
literary magazine, I:692–93
medical journal, I:439
pedagogical periodical, I:490
Civil War era magazines in (1850–65), II:73
education magazine, II:99*n*
post-Civil War magazines in (1865–85)
agricultural magazine, III:156
educational periodical, III:169
secret societies, III:315
Gilded Age magazines in (1885–1905)
advertising journal, IV:247
amateur periodical, IV:390*n*
comic periodical, IV:387*n*
genealogical periodical, IV:140*n*
insurance periodicals, IV:351*n*
Irish-Amercan periodical, IV:227
medical periodicals, IV:316
pharmacy periodical, IV:318*n*
scientific periodical, IV:310
sports periodical, IV:381
modern magazines in (1905–)
advertising journal, IV:247
art periodical, IV:148
insurance periodical, IV:351*n*
Irish-American periodical, IV:227
juvenile magazine, III:500*n*
Columbus, Tenn., IV:382
Columbus Medical Journal, III:141*n*
Column Review, IV:522
Colver, Frederick L., III:511; IV:44, 45
Colver, Henry Clay, IV:109*n*
Colvin, John B., I:122
Colvin, Sidney, IV:720
Comfort, IV:16, 17, 365–66
Comfort, Will Levington, III:400*n*
Comic books, IV:196
Comic Bouquet, II:56, 185*n*
Comic Library, IV:119*n,* 385
Comic magazines
in nationalist era (1794–1825), I:139, 170–72
in expansionist era (1825–50), I:425–27, 610, 730–83
in Civil War era (1850–65), II:123, 136, 199
engravings, II:193
longevity, II:179
monthlies, II:529
quality and type, II:179–85
Southern, II:112–13, 155, 185
weeklies, II:34, 520–29
in post-Civil War era (1865–85)
quality and type, III:263–71
weeklies, III:440–42, 520–22, 524, 552–53
in Gilded Age (1885–1905), IV:387*n,* 557–6, 664–70
characters, IV:383–84
college periodicals, IV:383
leading periodicals, IV:385–86
slang and, IV:384–85
weeklies, III:522–31, 533–54
modern (1905–)
fortnightlies, III:532
monthlies, III:552*n,* 568
weeklies, III:531–32, 555–56; IV:64–68
Comic Monthly, II:184
Comic News, III:268*n*
Comic opera, III:194–95
Comic strips, IV:366, 472, 498
Comic Ventilator, III:269*n*
Comic Weekly, III:269*n*
Comic World, II:183; III:267
Coming Age, IV:413–14
Coming Crisis, IV:204
Coming Light, IV:413

Coming Nation, IV:204
Cominskey, Charles, IV:374
Commager, Henry Steele, IV:750; V:55
Commentator, IV:731–32
Commerce Monthly, IV:350*n*
Commercial Advertiser, I:637; II:282
Commercial America, IV:350*n*
Commercial and Financial Chronicle, I:697–98; III:146; IV:349
Commercial Law Journal, IV:348
Commercial magazines, *see* Business magazines
Commercial Record, III:147*n*
Commercial Review, IV:350*n*
Commercial Review of the South and West, II:338, 339
  See also: DeBow's Review
Commercial Telegrapher's Journal, IV:221*n*
Commercial Traveler's Home Magazine, IV:186
Commercial Traveler's Magazine, IV:187
Commodore Rollingpin's Illustrated Humorous Almanac, IV:385
Commoner, III:129*n*; IV:162, 460
Common Market, European, V:317
Common School, IV:270*n*
Common School Advocate, I:491, 803
Common School Assistant, I:491, 803
Common School Journal, I:491, 804; II:98–9
Commons, IV:743–44
Commons, John Rodgers, IV:178, 662, 744
Common Sense, V:24
Common-Sense (advertising journal), IV:247*n*
Common Sense (Populist), IV:176*n*
Commonwealth (Boston), IV:60
Commonwealth (Concord), II:536
Commonwealth (Denver), IV:104
Commonwealth (New York), IV:204
Commonwealth (St. Louis), IV:101
Commonwealth Fund, V:339
Communism
  magazine opposition to, V:20–23
  See also Fourierism; Russia; Russian Revolution; Socialism
Communist, III:300
Communist magazines, II:207; III:300
Communist Party, V:20, 22–26, 212–13, 218–20, 314
Community periodicals, III:101
Companion and Weekly Miscellany, I:204*n*, 792
Company K (a novel), V:182
Company of Newspaper Makers of London, V:64
Compiler (Richmond), I:636–37
Compressed Air Machine, IV:184*n*
Compromise of 1850, II:3, 133–34
  abolitionists and, II:290
Comrade, IV:176
Comstock, Alzada, V:58
Comstock, Anthony, II:335; III:308, 449, 553; IV:52*n*, 199, 210, 267, 562, 565
Comstock, William T., III:129
Comte, Auguste, V:193
Conan Doyle, *see* Doyle, Sir Arthur Conan
Conant, Lawrence M., IV:787
Conant, Samuel Stillman, II:428, 430, 469*n*, 484; III:184, 363
Conant, William Cowper, IV:300*n*
Concert-Goer, IV:254*n*
Conchology magazines, III:109
Concord, N.H., I:31*n*; II:71*n*; III:77*n*; IV:82
Concord Observer, II:71*n*
Concord School of Philosophy, III:386
Concordia Magazine, IV:48, 295
Concrete, IV:325*n*
Condensations, IV:560, 570, 658; V:136
Condie, Thomas, I:46
Condie, Thomas G., Jr. I:144
Condit, J. B., II:517*n*
Condon, Frank, IV:421, 470
Condon, Richard, V:313
Condor, IV:310*n*
Cone, Helen Gray, II:511*n*
Cone, Orello, IV:295
Cone, Spencer, W., I:687*n*
Confectioner and Baker, III:135
Confectioners' Gazette, III:135
Confectioners' Journal, III:135; IV:187
Confectioners' magazines, III:135; IV:187*n*
Confectioners' Review, IV:187*n*
Confederate Annals, III:262*n*
Confederate States of America
  Civil War magazines on, II:147–49, 154–56, 292, 473–74
  effects of war on, II:8–9, 155
  theater in, II:200
  See also South—in Civil War era; Southern magazines—in Civil War era
Confederate States Medical and Surgical Journal, II:87
Conference News, III:71*n*
Confessions (Rousseau), V:123
Confessions, personal, IV:493

Congdon, Charles Tabor, III:273
Congregational Church, Presbyterian Church and, II:367–68
Congregational Herald (Chicago), II: 71*n*
Congregational Herald (Lawrence, Kan.), II:71*n*
Congregational Iowa, III:77*n*
Congregational Journal, II:71
Congregational Quarterly, II:71; III:76
Congregational Review, II:518*n*, 519; III:76
Congregationalist, I:138; II:22, 71; III:76 IV:292
Congregationalist magazines
 in expansionist era (1825–50), I:371, 374, 458, 569–72, 624–25; II:312–15; III:76–77
 in Civil War era (1850–65), II:70–71, 368–73
 in post-Civil War era (1865–85), II: 373–77, 519; III:76–77
 in Gilded Age (1885–1905), II:377–78; IV:292–93
 modern (1905–), II:378–79
Congress, I:340
 in early magazines (1789–94), 52, 93, 109
 in expansionist era magazines (1825–50), I:423, 517–18
 in Civil War era magazines (1850–65), II:148
 in post-Civil War magazines (1865–85), II:255; III:441
 Gilded Age magazines on (1885–1905), IV:461–62, 666
Congress of Industrial Organizations, IV:20*n*
Congressional elections, *see* Election campaigns
Congress Register, II:41
Conkey's Home Journal, IV:253
Conkling, Grace Hazard, V:228, 236
Connecticut Catholic, III:69*n*
Connecticut Churchman, II:69 70*n*
Connecticut Common School Journal, II:98, 443; III:168*n*
 founding of, I:491
 sketch of, I:694–95
Connecticut Courant Supplement, II:36
Connecticut Evangelical Magazine, I:133, 791
Connecticut Farmer, III:152
Connecticut Magazine, IV:82
Connecticut Quarterly, IV:82
Connecticut School Journal, III:168*n*; IV:270*n*
Connecticut War Record, II:150
Connecticut Wits, *see* Hartford Wits
Connell, Richard, IV:472
Connery, T. B., IV:453*n*, 454
Connolly, Christopher Powell, IV:458, 600–1; V:83
Connolly, James Brendon, IV:465, 471, 724, 726, 786
Connolly, Margaret, V:287
Conqueror, IV:288*n*
Conrad, Joseph, IV:436, 518, 618, 691, 787; V:28, 119, 148
Conrad, Robert Taylor, I:544*n*, 546*n*, 551, 587*n*
Conscription, military, in Civil War, II:8
Conservation, IV:62, 343*n*, 548, 705, 779; V:32
Conservative, IV:178–79
Conservative Review, IV:73
Conservator, IV:129, 279–80
Considine, Robert, IV:476, 504
Constellation, I:425; II:45
Constitutional convention (1787), reportage of, I:50–52, 93, 96
Construction magazines, 11:321; III:129–30; IV:324–25
Construction News, IV:325
Consumer information, V:137–43
Consumer Services division (N.I.R.A.), V:139
Consumers Information Service, V:139
Contemporary Review, III:278
Continent, sketch of, III:557–59, 42, 74*n* 281, 284
Continental Magazine, III:47
Continental Monthly, II:33, 149, 151–52 165, 172, 524*n*
 sketch of, II:540–43
Contemporary Review, IV:228
Continental Illustrated Magazine, IV:3*n*
Continental Monthly, I:613
Contraception, *see* Birth control
Contractor, IV:325
Contributors
 to early magazines (1741–94)
  anonymous, I:40
  character of, I:14–16
  literary, I:42–44, 63, 103
  payment, I:15
  shortage of, 1:14–15
  women, I:15, 66, 109
 to nationalist era magazines (1794–1825)
  literary clubs, I:194
  payment, I:327, 197–99; II:232
  quality, I:194

Contributors—*Continued*
shortage, I:192–94
women, I:244
to expansionist era magazines (1825–50), I:345–48
authors' rights, I:502–4
by cities, I:376, 378, 381
growing number, I:494
low literary quality, I:194–96
most famous contributors, I:344
payments, I:494–95, 504–12, 633–34, 725, 738, 771–72
shortage, I:192–93
shortcomings, I:500–502
style, I:495, 500–502
variety, I:498–500
women, I:388, 400–1, 409, 412–13, 482, 499–500, 583–89, 743; II:308
to Civil War era magazines (1850–65)
new trends, II:3–4
payment, II:19–24, 182*n*, 232, 244–45, 368, 385–86, 411, 427
women, II:21–22, 46–49, 170–71, 173–74, 352–53, 357, 462, 467–68, 551; IV:679, 680
to post-Civil War magazines
forgotten, III:18
payment, II:509; III:12–17, 358, 364, 368, 371, 372*n*, 377–78, 469, 470, 515
popularity, III:237–46
women, II:357–58, 546; III:90–101, 224–27, 231, 246, 327, 368, 371, 374, 377, 389, 397–400, 403, 423–24, 439, 483, 501–3, 508–12, 549–50
to Gilded Age magazines (1885–1905)
complaints against editors, IV:35–37
leading writers, IV:128–31
payment, IV:39, 40, 41, 458, 543, 725
women, III:503–4, 546; IV:120, 141, 204, 242, 354, 360–63, 366, 397, 404, 409, 490, 537–38, 542, 612, 616, 654, 765–66
to modern magazines (1905–)
payment, III:408, 515, IV:698, 705
women, III:354–55, 479, 489, 504, 514, 543; IV:466, 470–71, 475–76, 503, 584–85, 601–2, 604, 616, 655, 693 697, 700, 708, 709, 712*n*, 713, 727, 729, 761–62, 768–71; V:20, 23, 25, 28, 73–74, 96, 110, 122–23, 133–34
Converse, Florence, II:483*n*
Converse, Frank H., IV:420, 609
Converted Catholic, IV:299
Conway, Katherine Eleanor, IV:297
Conway, Moncure Daniel, II:33, 141, 302, 497, 505*n*, 534–36; III:78, 322, 507; IV:302*n*, 410
Conybeare, Fred C., III:537
Cook, Albert Stanburrough, III:407, 536; IV:128
Cook, Charles Emerson, III:42*n*
Cook, Clarence, II:425, 426, 429, 430; III:184, 463
Cook, David, IV:274
Cook, Frederick, IV:593, 625
Cook, Howard Norton, IV:747
Cook, Joseph, III:426; IV:52, 242
Cook, Martha Elizabeth Duncan Walker, II:540*n*, 542
Cook, William I., IV:90*n*
Cook, William Wallace, IV:115
Cook County School News, IV:271
Cooke, Douglas H., III:55*n*, 555
Cooke, Edmund Vance, III:485
Cooke, George Willis, I:709; III:78, 107; IV:80
Cooke, Grace Macgowan, IV:93, 361*n*, 362, 612
Cooke, James Francis, III:197*n*
Cooke, Jay, III:3–4, 61
Cooke, John Esten, I:439, 650; II:112, 161, 163, 398, 462, 545; III:13*n*, 46, 47, 48, 362, 397, 418, 420, 421; IV:482
Cooke, Philip Pendleton, I:633, 646, 650
Cooke, Rose Terry, II:26, 173, 395, 398, 495, 501, 505*n*; III:99*n*, 100, 227, 372, 397, 424; IV:80, 292, 538; V:131
Cooke, St. George, I:643
Cookery articles, V:46
See also Recipes
Cooking Club, IV:365*n*
Cooking magazines, IV:363–64
Cooksley, Sidney Bert, III:402*n*
Coolbrith, Ina, II:118; III:403, 404; IV:105, 107
Coolidge, Calvin, III:354, 489, 515; IV:471, 472, 502, 552, 576, 626, 698, 707, 769; V:311–12, 318
Coolidge, Emelyn L., IV:548
Coolidge, Grace, III:515
Coolidge, Susan, III:58; 175*n*, 465*n*, 502; IV:722, 765
Cooper, Alfred Duff, V:57
Cooper, Courtney Riley, II:435; IV:421, 471

Cooper, Edward, I:419*n*
Cooper, Frederic Tabor, III:487; IV: 437, 511*n*, 518
Cooper, Jacob, II:537*n*
Cooper, James, II:539
Cooper, James Fenimore, I:174, 185, 392, 408, 409, 411, 507, 546, 547, 608; II:423, 424
Cooper, Thomas, I:151*n*, 245, 446, 574
Cooper, Thomas Abthorpe, I:248
Co-Operation, IV:194
Cope, Edward Drinker, III:108*n*
Copley, John Singleton, I:436
Coppard, A. E., III:543
Coppée, Henry, II:550, 551; III:34*n*
"Copperhead" magazines, II:154, 544–46
Copper-plate illustrations, I:86, 110, 115, 282, 519, 521, 547, 592, 628; II:192, 309; III:186
Copperud, Roy H., V:68
Copyright
  Clay on, I:620
  drama and, I:429
  early problem of, I:356, 502–4
  international, *see* International copyright
  magazines and, I:503
  See also Pirating
Corbett, James J., IV:371, 697
Corbin, John, II:483, IV:636
Corbyn, Wardell, II:180
Corcoran, James A., III:68
Corcoran, William, V:72*n*
Corelli, Marie, IV:111, 141, 501, 685; V:254
Corey, N. J., III:197*n*
Corey, Paul F., V:184
Corinth, Miss., III:155
Cornelius, Elias, I:419*n*
Cornell Civil Engineer, IV:321
Cornell Countryman, IV:341*n*
Cornell Review, III:166
Cornell University, III:166; IV:309, 321
Cornhill Booklet, IV:390*n*
Cornhill Magazine, III:279
Cornwallis, Kinahan, I:606*n*, 613
Corporate wealth, *see* Wealth
Correct English, IV:272*n*
Corrector, I:170, 792
Correspondence, in magazines, I:76, 80, 85; II:221–22; III:460, 542; IV: 434, 548
Correspondence schools, IV:28, 320
Correspondence University Journal, IV: 55*n*
Corrigan, Michael A., IV:179
Corruption, *see* Bribery; Municipal corruption; Scandals
Corry, Pa., IV:304*n*
Corsair, I:356–58, 804; IV:382
Corsets, I:477
Cort, Howard, IV:66
Cortesi, Salvatore, IV:73, 225
Cortissoz, Royal, IV:154, 727
Cosgrave, John O'Hara, IV:100; V:72*n*, 73–74, 76, 84
Cosmopolitan Art Association, II:19, 193
Cosmopolitan Art Journal, II:157, 193
Cosmopolitan Magazine, IV:4, 5, 6, 15, 17, 18, 21, 35, 37, 39, 41, 46, 209, 216, 234, 328, 596; V:85, 133, 248, 341–42
  sketch of, IV:480–505
Cosmopolite, IV:321*n*
Cost of living, I:60; III:342; IV:494
Costain, Thomas B., IV:708
Coster, Morris, III:260
Costs of publication, II:18
  See also Editors; Payments to contributors
Cottage Hearth, III:100; IV:366
Cotton, III:147; IV:185*n*
Cotton-crop periodicals, IV:339
Cotton economy, II:134, 343
Cotton Gin, IV:185*n*
Cotton and Oil Press, IV:339
Cotton Plant, III:155
Cotton Trade Journal, IV:185*n*
Coues, Elliott, III:337
Coulter, John Merle, III:111
Council Fire, III:314
Counting-House Monitor, III:147*n*
Country Gentleman, I:443; III:153; IV:340, 698, 715; II:10, 89
  sketch of, II:432–35
Country Home, IV:473
Country Life in America, IV:338; V:73*n*
Country-life magazines, IV:338
Countryman, II:111–12
Countryside, II:378
Country Superintendents' Monthly, IV: 272*n*
Courant (Minneapolis), IV:96, 356*n*
Courant (Washington), IV:69*n*
Courier (Boston), I:578, 509, 713
Courier (Charleston, S.C.), I:260
Courier (New York), II:38
Courier and Enquirer, I:329, II:205, 282, 392
Courier of Medicine, III:141*n*
Courtney, William Basil, IV:470, 476

Cousins, Norman, V:18, 56–57, 234
Covarrubias, Miguel, III:489
Coverly, Nathaniel, I:31*n*
Cowen, Louise, V:102
Cowles, Henry Chandler, III:111*n*
Cowles, Merrick, III:113
Cowley, Malcolm, IV:730; V:191*n*, 222–23, 241
Cowper, William, I:178, 231, 293
Cox, Jacob Dolson, III:337, 340, 343, 347
Cox, James M., III:352, 503; V:333
Cox, Kenyon, III:557; IV:145, 484
Cox, Palmer, III:269*n*; IV:151–52, 384, 561
Cox, William, 324, 326
Coxe, Arthur Cleveland, I:620, 712; II:364; IV:226, 514
Coxe, John Redman, I:151
Coxe, Tench, I:40, 51
Coxey, Jacob Sechler, III:530; IV:158–59, 666
Coxey's Army, IV:1, 158–59
Coyne, Vertie A., III:500*n*, 505
Cozens, Frederick S., I:609; II:183, 211, 424
Cozzens' Wine Press, II:183
"Craddock, Charles Egbert," *see* Murfree, Mary Noailles
Cradle of Liberty, II:287
Craftsman (art periodical), IV:148
Craftsman (labor organ), III:300
Craig, A. H., III:160
Craig, F. D., III:160
Craig, Hardin, V:344
Craig, Neville B., I:422
Craig, Thomas, III:110
Craik, Dinah Maria Mulock, II:385, 393, 454; III:224; IV:679
Cram, George F., IV:55
Cram, Mildred, III:390
Cram, Ralph Adams, V:20
Cram's Magazine, IV:55
Cranbrook Papers, IV:389
Cranch, Christopher Pearce, I:659, 663, 680, 692, 704, 705*n*, 764; III:507
Crandall, Lee, IV:163
Crandall, Prudence, II:282
Crane, Anne Moncure, III:229
Crane, Charles R., II:486
Crane, Frank, IV:493, 500, 506*n*, 510; V:271
Crane, Hart, V:113, 173, 176, 237, 241
Crane, Stephen, II:398*n*; III:400, 512, 541; IV:49, 72, 196, 252, 451, 645, 646, 689, 721: V:119
Crapsey, Edward, III:28
Craven, Thomas, IV:730, 731
Crawford, Francis Marion, II:510; III:242, 248, 471, 486, 514; IV:49*n*, 457, 513, 544, 612, 616
Crawford, John W. (Jack), IV:104
Crawford, Nelson Antrim, V:12, 179*n*, 180
Crawford, Will, III:531
Crawfordsville, Ind., III:111, 169*n*
Crayon, II:158, 193
"Crayon, Porte,'" *see* Strother, David Hunter
Creamer, Joseph, III:126*n*
Creamer, Thomas J., IV:77, 84, 85
Creamery Journal, IV:186*n*
Credit and Financial Management, IV:349*n*
Crédit Mobilier scandal, III:289
Credit Monthly, IV:349*n*
Creel, George, III:478, IV:77, 97–98, 207, 409, 472, 496; V:248
Creelman, James, IV:485, 490, 491, 596, 661
Creighton, James Edwin, IV:303
Crèvecoeur, J. H. St. John de, I:58
Cricket, III:220; IV:377, 636
Cricket Library, IV:120*n*
Crime, III:27–28
  See also Crime stories and reports; Municipal corruption; Prostitution
Crime magazines, I:481–82; II:187, 328, 458; III:43–45; IV:199
  See also Detective stories
Crime stories and reports, II:37, 326–29, 458; IV:199–200, 477
  See also Lurid magazines; Police gazettes: Sensational magazines
Crimean War, II:122
Criminal Law Magazine and Reporter, III:145*n*
"Crinkle, Nym," *see* Wheeler, Andrew Carpenter
Crisler, Herbert Orin (Fritz), IV:700
Crissey, Forrest, IV:367*n*, 690, 768
Crist, Arthur H., IV:364
Criswell, R. W., IV:86
Criterion, II:158, 159, 165, 168; III:492; IV:65–66, 100*n*
Criterion of Fashion, III:98
Critic (Baltimore), III:221*n*
Critic (New York, 1828), I:355, 427–29, 800
Critic (New York, 1881–1906), II:430; III:184, 199, 231, 232, 234, 254, 255, 456; IV:124, 649
  sketch of, III:548–51
Critic (Philadelphia), I:796

Critic (St. Louis), IV:100
Criticism, *see* Art criticism and comment; Drama criticism and comment; Literary criticism; Music comment and criticism
Croasland, William T., IV:179
Crocker, S. R., III:454–55
Crockery and Glass Journal, III:128; IV:184
Crockery periodicals, III:128
Crockett, Samuel R., IV:612; V:73
Croker, Richard, III:530
Croly, David Goodman, III:322; V:193
Croly, Herbert David, IV:46*n*; V:191*n*, 192–215, 223
Croly, Mrs. Jane Cunningham ("Jenny June"), I:580*n*, 593, 683; II:45; III:97, 325–27; IV:356; V:193
Cronin, Archibald Joseph, IV:477, 503
Cronin, Patrick, IV:298
Cronyn, Thoreau, IV:469
Crookes, William, IV:308, 514
Crooks, George R., II:67
Croome, William, I:521, 592
Cropsey, Jasper, Francis, II:188
Croquet, I:590
Croqueting, articles on, IV:636
Crosby, Ernest Howard, IV:136*n*, 390*n*
Crosby, Margaret, IV:719
Crosby, Nichols & Co., II:242
Crosby, Percy Lee, IV:567, 568
Cross, Mary Ann Evans ("George Eliot"), II:161, 385, 509*n*; III:223, 224, 251–52
Cross, Sidney, IV:636
Cross, Wilbur L., IV:410; V:329*n*, 331–39
Crossman, John C., I.:522
Crossword puzzles, III:555; IV:567
Crow, Carl, IV:783
Crowe, E. R., V:304
Crowe, Eugene F., V:260, 262
Crowe, John Finley, I:164
Crowell, Chester T., IV:471; V:12
Crowell, John S., IV:337, 763*n*, 764, 768
Crowell, Merle, III:510*n*, 515, 516
Crowninshield, Frank, III:475; IV:436, 617, 760–61
Crowther, Samuel, IV:605, 784, 786, 787
Croy, Homer, III:487, 555; IV:618
Crucible, III:82*n*
Cruger, F. R., IV:692
Cruger, Mrs. S. Van Rensselaer, V:247
Cruse, Peter Hoffman, I:172, 204; II:233
Crystal Fountain, II:210
Cuba, I:465, 597; II:122; III:280; IV:234–35
  American interest in, IV:236
  magazine comment on, I:465, 725; II:485; III:280
  schemes for annexing, II:139
  See also Spanish-American War
Cuba: Political Weekly, IV:236
Cuba Review, IV:236
Cuddihy, Robert Joseph, IV:509*n*, 573–74
Culbertson, James Coe, IV:312, 524*n*
Culinary magazines, IV:363–64
Cullen, Countee, V:12, 237
Cullom, Shelby Moore, IV:494, 514, 516*n*
Cultivator (Albany), I:443, 802; II:88, 432, 434, 435; III:153; IV:340
Cultivator (Boston), II:88
Cultivator and Country Gentleman, III: 153
Cumberland Presbyterian Quarterly, II: 62
Cumberland Presbyterian Review, I:372, 807; II:62; III:74
Cummings, Amos J., IV:689
Cummings, Charles R., IV:82
Cummings, Edward Estlin, III:543; IV: 440, 739; V:176, 240
Cummins, Maria S., II:171
Cunniff, Michael Glen, IV:778
Cuppy, Hazlitt Alva, IV:52, 284, 649*n*, 650–51
Curie, Marie, III:489
Curiosity Shop, II:185*n*
Current, III:54; IV:65
Current Education, IV:271
Current Encyclopaedia, IV:55, 499
Current events
  in early magazines (1741–94), I:34, 72, 75, 77–78, 81, 84, 90, 93, 102, 109, 113
  in nationalist era magazines (1794–1825), I:219, 243, 247, 268, 331
  in expansionist era magazines (1825–50), I:563, 781; IV:674
  in Civil War era magazines (1850–65), I:656; II:122–23, 272, 429, 439–40, 454, 470
  in post-Civil War era magazines (1865–85), III:40, 545
  in Gilded Age magazines (1885–1905), III:430; IV:8–10, 346–49; 454–56, 458, 561, 596, 613, 666, 673; IV:62–64, 71, 499
  in modern magazines (1905–), III: 347; IV:63*n*

Current events—*Continued*
See also International affairs; Political writing
Current Events, IV:63–64
Current events magazines, III:331–56; IV:62–64, 649–51; V:49–58, 191–224, 293–328
Current History, IV:219, 223, 508, 522
sketch of, V:49–58
Current History and Forum, V:57
Current Literature, IV:10, 21, 56, 120, 573
sketch of, 506–10
Current Opinion, IV:506*n*, 509–10, 570; V:50, 55
Current Topics, IV:53, 94*n*
Current Topics for Leisure Hours, IV:93
Currie, Barton W., II:432*n;* IV:536*n*, 550–51, 773*n*, 787
Currie, Gilbert E., II:94*n*
Currier & Ives, III:182
Curry, Daniel, I:299*n*, 301; II:301*n*, 304
Curry, Otway, I:597, 661, 692; II:302
Curry, Walter Clyde, V:110*n*, 101, 111
Curti, Merle, IV:738
Curtice, Harlow, V:323*n*
Curtis, Cyrus H. K., III:100; IV:34, 59, 536–39, 681–701
Curtis, F. G. B., IV:171
Curtis, George William, I:535, 608, 764; II:45, 173, 244, 376, 389, 402, 407, 505*n;* III:22, 40, 172, 231, 238, 281, 295, 308, 332*n*, 389; IV:57
as editor, II:419–20, 422, 425, 427, 469*n*, 471, 474
Curtis, Hugh Everette, Jr., V:36*n*, 44–45
Curtis, Louisa Knapp ("Mrs. Louisa Knapp"), III:100; IV:536*n*, 536–39
Curtis, Theodore, IV:406
Curtis, William Eleroy, IV:224, 482, 622, 625
Curtiss, Glenn Hammond, IV:334
Curwen, M. E., I:425*n*
Curwood, James Oliver, III:408; IV:125, 389, 498, 584, 616; V:134, 290
Curzon, George Nathaniel, IV:780
Cusacha, Philip G., II:335
Cushing, Caleb, I:155, 276, 335, 490; II:228, 229, 232; IV:784
Cushing, Christopher, II:71*n*
Cushing, Luther Stearns, I:451
Cushing, Otho, IV:566
Cushman, Charlotte, III:204
Cushman, Elisha, II:65*n*
Custer, George Armstrong, III:58, 376
Customs, social, *see* Social customs and manners
Cuthrell, Mrs. Hugh (Faith Baldwin), IV:475, 503, 585, 771
Cutler, E., II:518*n*
Cutter, Charles Ammi, III:517*n*, 518, 519
Cutting, Elizabeth B., II:259
Cutting, Mary Stewart, III:487; IV:360*n*, 601; V:133
Cutting, Sewall Sylvester, I:666*n;* II:64
Cuyler, Theodore Ledyard, II:376; IV:685
Cycle Age, IV:331
Cycle Age and Trade Review, IV:379
Cycle Trade Journal, IV:331
Cycling, *see* Bicycle clubs; Bicycle magazines; Bicycles
Cycling Life, IV:379
Cyclopedic Review of Current History, IV:71
Cytherean Miscellany, II:186

Dabbs, James McBride, V:285
Dabney, Richard, I:205
Dacey, C. Joseph, IV:88
Daft, Leo, III:126
Daggett, Nella I., IV:366
Daggett, Rollin M., II:117
Daguerreian Journal, II:194*n*
Daguerreotypes, II:191, 194
Dailies, I:159, 329, 466; II:183, 212*n;* III:66
See also Newspapers
Daily Advertiser (Boston), I:706, 718
Daily Press, II:212*n*
Daintrey, Laura, IV:123
Dairy and Creamery, IV:343
Dairy journals, IV:343–44
Dairy Record, IV:344*n*
Dairy World, III:160
Dakin, Roger, IV:453*n*, 478, 771
Dakota Farmer, III:158
Dale, Alan, III:532
See also Cohen, Alfred J.
Dallas, Texas
post-Civil War magazines in (1865–85), III:73*n*, 143*n*
Gilded Age magazines in (1885–1905), III:155; IV:94, 185*n*, 188*n*, 339, 270*n*, 292, 363*n*
modern magazines in (1905–), III:155; IV:339
Dallas, Alexander James, I:94*n*, 96

Dallas, Jacob A., I:521, 592; II:454
Dallenbach, Karl M., IV:303*n*
Dalrymple, Louis, III:528, 530
Daly, Augustin, II:509
Daly, Charles Augustus, I:467
Daly, Charles Patrick, II:414, 415
Daly, John J., IV:127
Dalziel, Davison, IV:84
Dam, Henry Jackson Wells, IV:429, 592–93, 595
Damrosch, Leopold, IV:249
Damrosch, Walter, IV:249, 550
Dana, Charles Anderson, I:129, 341, 349, 764; II:207, 270, 420, 425, 426, 524; III:221, 441, 527; IV:544, 562, 593
Dana, Edward Salisbury, I:302*n*, 304; IV:306
Dana, J. Cotton, V:117*n*, 118
Dana, James Dwight, I:302*n*, 304; II:314; III:108; IV:306
Dana, Marvin, V:246*n*, 248
Dana, Richard Henry, I:172, 174, 203; II:224, 226, 230; III:295*n*
  comment on, I:408, 409, 412
  as contributor, I:331, 335, 367, 512, 546, 760
Dana, Richard Henry, Jr., II:243
Dana, William B., I:696*n*; III:146*n*
Danbury, Conn., III:140*n*, 271*n*
Danbury News, III:271*n*
Dancing, magazine comment on, I:479
Dancing Master, IV:254*n*
Dandy, John M., III:101; IV:100
"Dangerous Classes of New York, The," III:28
Daniels, Dixie, IV:667
Daniels, George Henry, IV:224
Daniels, Josephus, V:275–77
Daniel's Texas Medical Journal, IV:313*n*
Danielson, Richard Ely, II:367*n*, 379
Dannenhower, W. W., II:115
D'Annunzio, Gabriele, II:257; IV:121, 501; V:258
Dansville, N.Y., II:53
Danville, Ill., IV:271*n*
Danville, Ky., II:537
Danville Quarterly Review, II:62, 155
  sketch of, II:537–39
Da Ponte, Lorenzo, I:335, 608
Darby, Rufus H., IV:89*n*
Dare, H. Craig, IV:244*n*
Darien, Conn., IV:269*n*
Dark Flower, The (Galsworthy), V:168
Darley, Felix Octavius Carr, I:592, 680, 771, 782; II:37, 41, 390, 397; III:187, 359, 420
Darley, Mr. and Mrs. John, I:168*n*, 248
Darling, Jay Norwood, IV:469
Darrow, Clarence, IV:283, 390, 703, 730
Darrow, L. B., III:213
Darwin, Charles, II:243; III:496
  Darwinian theory, II:78–79, 243, 248, 252, 253; III:107, 497; IV:785; V:116
Darwin, Erasmus, I:178
Dashiell, Alfred Sheppard, IV:717*n*, 729–30
Daskam, Josephine Dodge, III:485; IV:601
Dater, John Grant, IV:616
Daudet, Alphonse, V:119
Daughters of the American Revolution, IV:140; V:9
Daugherty, Harry, V:213
d'Aurévilly, Jules Barbey, V:123
Davenport, Iowa, II:99*n*; III:75*n*
Davenport, Benjamin Rush, IV:653
Davenport, Frederick Morgan, III:432; IV:618
Davenport, Russell, V:23
Davenport, Walter, IV:453*n*, 470, 475, 477
Daves, Jessica, IV:756*n*, 762
David, E. W., I:451*n*
Davidson, Donald Grady, V:100*n*, 101–7, 110–11, 114–16
Davidson, Frank C., 511*n*
Davidson, Mrs. Grace L., IV:65–6, 100*n*
Davidson, Henry P., IV:747
Davidson, J. Wood, II:490
Davidson, Thomas, III:51, 386
Davies, Mary Carolyn, V:185
Davis, A. E., III:54*n*
Davis, Andrew Jackson, II:210
Davis, Bancroft C., II:295*n*
Davis, Charles Belmont, IV:457, 465*n*
Davis, Charles Palmer, IV:64
Davis, Cornelius, I:131*n*, 133*n*
Davis, Edward P., I:566*n*; IV:313
Davis, Elmer, IV:473, 606
Davis, Forrest, IV:712
Davis, George Royal, IV:267
Davis, Harry Orville, IV:536*n*, 550
Davis, Jefferson, I:654; III:382
Davis, John (Massachusetts senator), I:752
Davis, John M., III:116, 299
Davis, John Parker, III:379, 411
Davis, John S., III:411
Davis, John William, IV:177, 407
Davis, Lemuel Clarke, III:397; IV:87
Davis, Nathan Smith, IV:524–26

Davis, Oscar King, II:483
Davis, Paulina Wright, II:52; III:393
Davis, Preston, IV:63*n*
Davis, Rebecca Harding, II:26, 173, 270, 309, 398*n*, 501, 505; III:21, 99*n*, 224, 361, 372, 373, 377, 397, 421, 461, 501, 558; IV:87
Davis, Richard Harding, II:398*n*, 400, 469, 482, 483, 484; IV:87, 154, 261, 458, 465, 720, 721, 722, 725, 726; V:118–19, 254
Davis, Robert Hobart, IV:36, 608*n*, 616–18
Davis, Robert S., III:557, 558
Davis, Samuel Harrison, IV:350
Davis, Shelby Cullom, IV:523
Davis, Singleton Waters, IV:277
Davis, T. E., IV:447
Davis, Theodore R., II:475
Davis, Thomas, II:113
Davis, Watson, V:55
Davis, William H., IV:749
Davis & Berlett, II:454
Davison, Lucretia and Margaret, I:409, 409*n*
"Daw, Marjorie," III:228
Dawes, Charles Gates, II:260
Dawes, Henry Laurens, IV:214
Dawes, Rufus, I:128, 204, 326, 331, 578
Dawes, Rufus G., V:226
Dawn, IV:282–83
Dawson, Benjamin Franklin, III:141
Dawson, Coningsby, V:84, 134
Dawson, G. F., III:114*n*
Dawson, Henry Barton, II:175; III:259
Day, Ben, II:462
Day, Clive, V:329*n*
Day, Mrs. F. H., II:59
Day, Frank Miles, IV:324*n*
Day, George Edward, I:739*n*, 740, 741; II:517*n*
Day, George T., II:64
Day, Henry Noble, II:315
Day, Holman, IV:429
Day Book, II:154
Day's Doings, II:44, 218, 309
Dayton, Katherine, IV:700
Dayton, Ohio, I:137; II:74; III:80, 81, 156; IV:254, 295–96, 382
Dayton, Tenn., anti-evolution trial, V:116
Deacon, Edmund, II:36; IV:671*n*, 678
Dead Souls (Gogol), V:95
Deaf Mutes' Journal, IV:194
Deaf-aid periodicals, IV:194
Dean, Harriet, V:172
Dean, John Ward, II:175*n*, 176*n*
Dean, Teresa, II:464
Dean, Thomas, I:247
Dearborn, George, I:669*n*, 670
De Bow, Benjamin Franklin, II:342
De Bow, James Dunwoody Brownson, I:384, 464, 575–76, 722, 723–25, 808, II:148, 149, 338–48
De Bow's Review, II:14, 18, 30, 96, 97, 110, 133, 134, 138, 140, 148, 149, 192, 423; III:45, 147, 281, 283
  sketch of, II:338–48
Debs, Eugene Victor, III:352, 300*n;* IV:175, 181, 205, 218, 283, 509
De Bury, Countess, II:243
deCasseres, Benjamin, V:12
Declaration of Independence, I:49, 90, 227, 524; V:215
Decorative Furnisher, IV:188*n*
Decorator and Furnisher, III:136*n*
De Costa, Benjamin Franklin, III:260*n*
Dedham, Mass., IV:138
Dedham Historical Register, IV:138
Deemer, Samuel, IV:185*n*
Deems, Charles Force, III:83*n*
Deeping, Warwick, IV:606
Deer Lodge, Mont., III:75*n*
Defectives, education of, II:445
  periodicals for, IV:194
Defender, III:310*n*
De Forest, John William, II:395, 505*n;* III:13*n*, 58, 224, 244, 284, 372, 377
De Forest, Robert Weeks, IV:741–47
Degan, Henry V., I:493
De Garmo, Charles, III:169
Degas, Hilaire Germain Edgar, IV:145
De Gaulle, Charles, V:323*n*
DeGraw, John L., I:769
Deist magazines, I:56, 132–33
DeJong, David Cornel, V:243
De Kay, Charles, III:549; IV:66, 154
De Kock, Paul, II:240
De Koven, Reginald, III:268; IV:61, 250, 544; V:247
De Koven, Mrs. Reginald, IV:376, 378
De Kruif, Paul, II:435; IV:553
De la Mare, Walter, V:119, 229, 336–37
Deland, Fla., III:155
De Land, Fred, IV:335
Deland, Margaret, II:273, 363, 398, 402; IV:281, 390*n*, 457, 769; V:133
Delaplaine, Joseph, I:151*n*

De la Ramée, Marie Louise ("Ouida"), II:255, 439; III:91, 252, 397; IV:51, 514, 679
De la Salle Monthly, III:68
Delaware, public education, I:145
De Leon, Daniel, IV:174–75
De Leon, Edward, I:418
Delineator, IV:16, 17, 21, 360, 597*n;* V:74
sketch of, III:481
Delinquent subscribers
to early magazines (1741–94), I:13, 19–20, 82, 101, 103
to nationalist era magazines (1794–1825), I:200, 237–38, 242, 326, 359
to expansionist era magazines (1825–50), I:514–15, 561, 595, 628, 644–45, 647–48, 700, 722, 724
to Civil War era magazines (1850–65), II:11–12
Dell, Ethel M., III:488; IV:584; V:72
Dell, Floyd, V:95, 207, 258
Delmar, Vina, IV:503
Delphian Club, I:194, 293–96
De Menil, Alexander Nicolas, IV:72, 101, 112
De Meza, Wilson, IV:564
Deming, E. D., IV:185
Deming, Henry Champion, I:361
Deming, Philip, II:506*n*
Democracy, I:1–2; IV:171, 510
Democratic party
donkey as symbol of, II:480
See also Election campaigns
Democratic-party periodicals, IV:170–71
Democratic Review, I:348, 505, 510*n,* 520, 687, 750; II:5, 143, 165, 192, 532–33
founded, I:346
sketch of, I:677–84
De Monvel, Bernard, III:489
Demorest, Ellen Louise, III:325
Demorest, Henry C., III:325, 327
Demorest, William C., III:325*n,* 327
Demorest, William Jennings, II:45; III:97, 176, 265, 325, 327
Demorest's Family Magazine, III:327
Demorest's Illustrated Monthly, I:593; III:325
Demorest's Magazine, IV:152, 359
Demorest's Monthly Magazine, III:97, 98
sketch of, III:325–28
Demorest's New York Illustrated News, II:45
Demorest's Young America, III:175
Dempsey, William Harrison (Jack), IV:700
Demuth, Charles, V:178
Denby, Charles, IV:230
Denison, E., I:294
Denison, Grace E., IV:630
Denison, Mary A., II:172, 270; III:175*n;* IV:360, 366, 680
Dennett, John Richard, II:507*n;* III:47, 227, 334, 344
Dennett, Roger Herbert, IV:769
Dennie, Joseph, I:109, 147–48, 156, 190, 191, 198–99
as editor, I:121, 123, 223–46
sketches of, I:171, 223–24
Dennis, Charles Henry, IV:499
Denny, George V., V:56
DeNormandie, James, III:506*n,* 507
Denslow, V. B., II:429
Denslow, William Wallace, IV:260
Denson, John, IV:477
Dental Advertiser, III:143*n*
Dental Brief, IV:317
Dental Cosmos, II:91; III:143; IV:317
Dental Digest, IV:317
Dental Headlight, III:143*n*
Dental Items of Interest, III:143*n;* IV:317
Dental Luminary, III:143*n*
Dental journals, II:91; III:143; IV:317
Dental News-Letter, II:91
Dental Office and Laboratory, II:92*n:* III:143
Dental Practitioner and Advertiser, III:143*n*
Dental Quarterly, II:92*n,* III:143
Dental Register, II:92*n*
Dental Register of the West, II:92*n*
Dental Review, IV:317
Dental Summary, III:143*n*
Dentifrice advertising, IV:26
Denver, Colo.
post-Civil War magazines in (1865–85)
engineering periodicals, III:114
labor periodical, III:300
medical journal, III:141*n*
religious magazine, III:75*n*
women's rights magazine, III:95
Gilded Age magazines in (1885–1905)
agricultural periodicals, IV:341
education periodical, IV:270*n*
financial periodical, IV:350*n*
insurance periodical, IV:351*n*
Masonic periodical, IV:222*n*

Denver, Colo.—*Continued*
medical periodicals, IV:314*n*
mining periodicals, IV:322*n*
pharmacy periodical, IV:318*n*
regional magazine, IV:103–4
religious periodical, IV:291*n*
sports periodical, IV:381
women's rights magazine, III:95
modern magazines in (1905–)
agricultural periodicals, IV:341
education periodical, IV:270*n*
insurance periodicals, IV:351*n*
medical journal, III:141*n*
mining periodical, IV:322*n*
pharmacy periodical, IV:318*n*
Depew, Chauncey Mitchell, IV:50, 84, 233, 488, 494, 612, 727
De Peyster, General John Watts, III:533
Depressions, economic
early, I:453–54
Panic of 1857, II:5–6, 144–45; III:123
Panic of 1869, III:286
Panic of 1873, III:4, 10, 149, 296–98
Panic of 1893, IV:1, 157–60
Panic of 1907, IV:691
Panic of 1929, IV:699, 701, 770
magazine longevity and, IV:4–5, 15, 159–60; V:17, 42, 55, 123–24, 188, 214
"DeQuille, Dan," *see* Wright, William
Derby, Indiana, pet periodical in, IV:382
Derby, George Horatio ("John Phoenix"), II:117, 178, 180
Derby, James Cephas, I:375
Derleth, August W., IV:729; V:184
Dernburg, Bernhard, IV:696
Derrickson, Marione Reinhard, IV:709, 712
Deseret News, II:75
De Seversky, Maj. Alexander P., V:23
Design, IV:148
Designer, III:486, 490; IV:303
Des Moines, Iowa
early magazines in, II:89; III:145*n*, 157
Gilded Age magazines in (1885–1905)
agricultural periodicals, IV:340
education periodical, IV:270*n*
financial periodical, IV:349*n*
illustrated magazine, IV:97*n*
insurance periodicals, IV:351*n*
literary magazine, IV:96–97
mail-order periodicals, IV:367
stock-breeders' periodicals, IV:344
women's periodical, IV:367
modern magazines in (1905–)
education periodical, IV:270*n*
financial periodical, IV:349*n*
gardening magazines, V:36*n*
home magazines, V:36*n*
insurance periodicals, IV:351*n*
women's periodical, 367*n*
Desmond, Henry W., IV:323
Dessert to the True American, I:791
Detective, IV:198*n*
Detective Fiction Weekly, IV:422
Detective stories, III:400–1; IV:465, 697, 701, 728; V:83
De Toledano, Ralph, V:25
Detroit, Mich.
early magazines in, I:444*n*, 490; II:58, 85*n*
post-Civil War magazines in (1865–85)
insurance periodical, III:146*n*
medical journals, II:85*n*, III:141*n*
music periodical, III:198*n*
religious magazine, III:71
temperance periodical, III:311
trade periodical, III:216
Gilded Age magazines in (1885–1905), IV:96
agricultural periodicals, IV:339, 340
all-fiction magazine, IV:115
financial periodicals, IV:349*n*, 350*n*
insurance periodicals, III:146*n*; IV:351*n*
juvenile periodical, IV:273
legal periodicals, IV:347, 347*n*, 348*n*
manufacturing periodicals, IV:183
medical journals, IV:313*n*, 314*n*
pharmacy periodical, IV:317
religious periodicals, III:71, IV:284, 293*n*, 294*n*
review periodical, IV:54
temperance periodical, III:311
modern magazines in (1905–)
cement periodical, IV:325*n*
financial periodicals, IV:349*n*, 350*n*
insurance periodical, III:146*n*, IV:351*n*
legal periodicals, IV:347, 347*n*, 348*n*
medical journals, IV:313*n*, 314*n*
religious periodicals, III:71, IV:294*n*
trade periodical, IV:188*n*
newspapers in, III:271*n*
Detroit Churchman, IV:294*n*
Detroit Free Press, III:271*n*

Detroit Legal News, IV:341
Detroit Medical Journal, IV:313*n*
Detroit Monthly, IV:115
Deutsch, Babette, IV:654; V:236
DeVane, William Clyde, V:329*n*
De Vere, Aubrey, III:330
De Vere, Schele, III:397, 418, 465*n*
Devereaux, Thomas, III:270*n*
Devereux, Mrs. C. A. R., IV:95
Devereux, George Thomas, II:409
Devine, Edward Thomas, IV:192, 195, 741–47
DeVinne, Theodore Low, III:189, 466–67; IV:248
Devoe, Alan, V:21, 23, 25
De Vore, Robert, IV:476
De Voto, Bernard, II:402; IV:75*n*, 701; V:314
Devoy, John, IV:227*n*
De Vries, Peter, V:225*n*, 239, 243
Dew, Thomas Roderick, I:634, 637
Dewar, James, IV:308
Dewart, William Thompson, IV:417*n*, 422, 608*n*, 618
De Weerd, H. A., V:338*n*
Dewees, William Potts, I:566
Dewey, Adm. George, IV:235, 236, 661; V:288
Dewey, George W., I:771
Dewey, John, III:542; IV:74, 269, 303, 398, 520, 730, 746; V:200, 211, 338
Dewey, Melville, III:170, 517*n*, 518; IV:143
Dewey, Orville, I:287, 490
Dewey, Stoddard, III:350
Dewey, T. E., IV:97
Dewey, Thomas E., V:218, 318–19
Dewey, William, III:386
DeWitt, R. M., II:182*n*
De Wolf, Townsend, IV:88*n*
Dexter, Franklin, II:227, 233
Dexter, George, I:426
Dexter, George T., II:208, 209
Dexter, Henry Martyn, II:71
Dexter Smith's Musical, Literary, Dramatic and Art Paper, III:197*n*
Dey, Frederick Van Rensselaer, IV:421; V:288
Dial (Boston), II:535
  comment on, I:723
  founding of, I:368
  sketch of, I:702–10
Dial (Chicago and New York), III:171, 194, 232, 234, 254, 456; IV:99, 124, 452; V:90, 93, 156, 167, 236, 239
  sketch of, III:539–43
Dial (Cincinnati), II:33, 165, 239, 314
  sketch of, II:534–36
Dialect Notes, IV:128
Dialogues, dramatic, V:13
Diamond Dick, IV:120, 274
Diaz, Mrs. Abby Morton, II:505*n*
Dicey, Albert Venn, III:337, 347
Dicey, Edward, III:336
Dick, Archibald L., I:322, 328, 521, 522, 548, 592, 620, 744; II:69
Dickens, Charles, II:24, 159, 160, 352, 361, 384–87, 393, 454, 471, 476, 482, 506*n*, 509; III:223, 224, 249–251, 358, 359; IV:434–35, 543, 679; V:119
  criticism of, I:641–42
  his popularity in U.S., I:398
  and copyright laws, I:393
Dickerson, J. A. Spencer, IV:100*n*
Dickey, Carl C., IV:773*n*, 786, 787
Dickins, Asbury, I:223*n*
Dickins, Elizabeth, I:223*n*
Dickins, John, I:132
Dickinson, Anna Elizabeth, II:64*n*; III:91, 93, 171, 172, 393
Dickinson, Emily, II:377; V:118
Dickinson, J. J., IV:652*n*, 656
Dickinson, John, I:102
Dickinson, Richard William, II:75*n*
Dickinson Law Review, IV:348*n*
Dickinson, Samuel Henry, I:575; II:488, 491
Dictionaries, I:263; II:177
Didier, Eugene Lemoine, IV:90, 142, 169
Didier, John L., IV:101
Diet Book, V:47
Dieter, Berthold, V:36*n*, 45, 48*n*
Dietetic and Hygienic Gazette, IV:315*n*
Digest, IV:569*n*, 578–79
Digests, *see* Condensations
Dike, Samuel Warren, IV:397
Dilg, John, IV:61
Dilke, Sir Charles, II:255
Dilliard, Irving, V:346
Dillingham, John H., I:562*n*, 565
Dillon, George, V:225*n*, 239, 243
Dillon, John B., I:660
Dillon, John Irving, IV:88
Dillon, Philip R., V:59*n*, 62
Dime Library, III:43*n*
Dime novels, II:38, 172, 467; III:43–44; IV:117–20
Dimitry, Charles P. J., II:112*n*

Dimnet, Ernest, V:57
Dingle, A. E., IV:421
Dinners, literary, II:509–10
Dinnies, Anna Peyre, I:412
Diogenes hys Lanterne, II:179, 181–82, 188
Dio Lewis's Monthly, III:221, 311
Diorama (art form), II:191–92
Direct Legislation Record, IV:178
Dirigo Rural, II:149*n*
Di Salle, Michael V., V:317
Disciples of Christ, magazines of, II:74; III:79–80; IV:295–96
Discovery of America, IV:136*n*
Diseases, *see* Cholera epidemics; Medical information; Smallpox epidemics; Yellow fever epidemics
Dishware trade magazines, IV:188
Dispatch (New York), IV:69
Dispatch (Philadelphia), II:37
Disraeli, Benjamin, III:252
Distribution of magazines, I:13, 16–20; IV:610–11; V:82
See also Circulation: Delinquent subscribers; Newsstand sales; Postal regulations; Subscriptions
District School Journal, I:491, 805
Dithmar, Edward Augustus, IV:126, 261*n*
Ditson, Oliver, II:197
Divorce, II:255; III:312, 486; IV:200, 513
See also Free Love
Dix, John Ross, II:42
Dix, William Frederick, II:349*n*
Dix & Edwards, II:427
Dixie, IV:92, 184*n*
Dixie Farmer, I:444*n*, 806; III:154
Dixie Game Fowl, IV:382
Dixie Manufacturer, IV:183
Dixie Miller, III:128*n*, IV:185*n*
Dixie Wood-Worker, IV:184*n*
Dixieland (Dallas), IV:94
Dixon, Ill., IV:254*n*
Dixon, Charles A., IV:44, 88
Doane, Augustus Sidney, I:364*n*
Doane, George W., II:365; IV:355
Doane, William Croswell, IV:52*n*
Dobbs Ferry, N.Y., IV:142
Dobie, Charles Caldwell, V:264
Dobson, Austin, I:535; II:377; III:428; IV:719
Doctor, IV:316
Dr. Foote's Health Monthly, III:139
Doctors
early magazines and (1741–94), I:58–59, 62
nationalist era magazines and (1794–1825), I:139, 150, 154–55, 243, 334
expansionist era magazines and (1825–50), I:438, 494, 589–90
education of, II:86; III:138
medical writing by, *see* Medical information: Medical journals
Dod, Albert Baldwin, I:530, 533
Dodd, Frank Howard, IV:432–37
Dodd, Moses S., I:375
Dodd, William E., V:12, 280
Dodge, Louis, IV:729
Dodge, Mary Abigail ("Gail Hamilton"), I:2; II:22, 25, 255; III:91, 99, 175, 389, 424; IV:51, 292
Dodge, Mary B., III:381*n*, 424
Dodge, Mary Mapes, III:99, 177, 500–1, 503–4; IV:273
Dodge, Ossian E., II:36
Dodge Idea, IV:321
Dodge's Literary Museum, see: Boston Museum
Dodson, Richard W., I:520, 684
Doerflinger, William, V:23
"Doesticks, Philander," *see* Thomson, Mortimer
Dog Fancier, IV:382
Dog-owners' magazines, IV:382
Dog shows, articles on, IV:636
Dogdom, IV:382
Doggett, Daniel Seth, II:66*n*
Dole, Nathan Haskell, IV:72*n*, 126, 410
Dolge, Alfred, IV:166
Dollar Magazine, II:57*n*
Dollar Magazine (monthly *Brother Jonathan*), I:360, 805
Dollar Magazine (New York), *see: Holden's Dollar Magazine*
Dollar Magazine (Philadelphia), I:365
Dollar Rural Messenger, III:55*n*
Dollar Weekly Mirror, II:90*n*
Domestic Engineering, IV:323*n*
Domestic magazines, *see* Family periodicals; Home magazines
Domestic Monthly, III:99
Dominant, IV:254
Donahoe, Patrick, II:76; III:36*n*
Donahoe's Magazine, III:36, 69; IV:298
Doney, Thomas, I:684, 744, 753
Donlin, George Bernard, III:539*n*, 541, 542
Donne, John, V:115
Donnelly, Ignatius, II:253; IV:132, 178
Donnelly, R. R., and Sons, V:327–28
Donner, Mrs. S. A., II:117
Donohoe, Denis, IV:651; V:79

Donovan, Hedley, V:*293n*, 321
Doolittle, Hilda, IV:440; V:230
Doré, Paul Gustave, II:477; III:410; V:122
Dorr, Julia Caroline Ripley, I:553, 771, II:303, 417, 511*n*; III:374, 411, 427; IV:722
Dorr, Rheta Childe, IV:362; V:149, 152
Dorsey, George Amos, IV:502
Dosch-Fleurot, Arno, IV:783, 785
Dos Passos, John, V:98
Dostoevski, Fëdor M., IV:135
Doty, Douglas Zabriskie, III:457*n*, 478; IV:480
Doty, W. L., IV:105*n*
Double Cross and Medical Missionary Record, IV:238
Doubleday, Frank Nelson, IV:723, 775, 787
Doubleday, Russell, IV:773*n*, 787
Doubleday and Page, V:73, 118
Dougal, W. H., I:328
Dougall, John, III:83
Doughty, Thomas, I:436
Douglas, Wyo., IV:387*n*
Douglas, George W., II:262*n*, 273
Douglas, Lloyd Cassel, IV:503
Douglas, Malcolm, IV:419
Douglas, Paul, V:222*n*
Douglas, Stephen Arnold, II:523
Douglas, William O., V:221
Douglass, Frederick, I:458; II:503; III: 172, 283
Douglass' Monthly, II:141
Doumic, René, IV:230
Dove, Leonard, III:489
Dover, N.H., IV:140*n*
Dow, Moses, II:42
Dowie, Alexander, IV:286
Downes, William Howe, II:510*n*
Downey, Henry T., IV:440
Downing, A. J., II:90*n*
"Downing, Major Jack," *see* Smith, Seba
Down-Town Topics, IV:150*n*
Dowson, Ernest, V:350
Doxey, William, IV:388
Doyle, Alexander P., III:329*n*; IV:298
Doyle, Sir Arthur Conan, II:463, 482; III:400, 486; IV:7, 49*n*, 66, 134, 141, 199, 226, 433, 457, 465, 501, 544, 590, 592, 612
Drake, Alexander Wilson, III:187, 466
Drake, Charles, I:215*n*, 216, 660
Drake, Daniel, 439, 439*n*
Drake, J. G., 660
Drake, John N., III:39*n*
Drake, Samuel Gardner, II:175*n*, 176
Drake University, V:37, 45
Drake's Magazine, III:39*n*, IV:3, 39, 44–45
Drama, *see* Plays; Theaters
Drama criticism and comment
  before 1825, I:54–56, 114, 165–66, 167–70, 227, 275, 321, 324, 328–29, 348–49
  in expansionist era magazines (1825–50), I:359, 427–31, 610, 620, 627, 719, 751–52, 757, 766
  in Civil War era magazines (1850–65), II:198–200, 437, 450, 453
  in post-Civil War magazines (1865–85), II:253, 401, 416; III:198–200, 418, 421, 441, 528, 548
  in Gilded Age magazines (1885–1905), II:311; IV:255–60, 410
    comic magazines, IV:564–65
    current events magazines, III:347
    family magazines, II:483
    illustrated periodicals, II:464, IV: 564–65
    literary magazines, III:540; IV:673
    urban periodicals, IV:87
  since 1905, III:351, 354, 489, 555
Dramatic Journal, IV:261
Dramatic Magazine, IV:261
Dramatic Mercury, I:427
Dramatic Mirror, III:198*n*
Dramatic Mirror *and Literary Companion,* I:427, 805
Dramatic News, III:220*n*
Dramatic Review, IV:261
Dramatic Times, III:198*n*, 199; IV:260
Draper, Arthur S., IV:569*n*, 577–78
Draper, E. D., III:96*n*
Draper, John Christopher, III:460
Draper, John William, I:640
Draper, William F., IV:631
Drayton, J., I:210
Dred Scott case, II:133,242
Dreiser, Theodore, III:349, 481*n*, 485–86, 487; IV:38, 40*n*, 46, 49*n*, 124, 125, 252–53, 436, 439, 440, 485, 496, 520, 612, 643; V:5, 28, 72, 119, 145*n*, 146–48, 173, 176, 249, 251, 257–58, 260, 287–88
Dresbach, Glenn Ward, V:184, 266
Dress, *see* Fashion in dress
Dresser, Horatio W., IV:413
Dresser, Paul, IV:252
Drew, Daniel, III:4
Drew, Edwin C., IV:82*n*
Drew, John, III:204
Drew, Mrs. John, IV:721

Drew, Louisa Lane, III:204
Dreyfus, Alfred, IV:230
Drinking, I:51
See also Prohibition movement; Temperance magazines
Drinkwater, John, V:336, 338
Driscoll, Louise, V:242
Droll Stories, (Balzac), V:123
Dromgoole, (Miss) Will Allen, III:46*n*; IV:409, 415, 765
Drover's Journal, III:159
Drug Bulletin, III:133
Drug, Oil, and Paint Reporter, IV:188*n*
Drug Topics, III:133
Druggists' Circular, III:133; IV:188, 318
Druggists' magazines, *see* Pharmacy journals
Drugs, Oils, and Paints, IV:318*n*
Drumbeat, II:87
Drummond, Henry, IV:226, 397, 590
Dry Goods, IV:188*n*
Dry Goods Economist, II:92–93; IV: 187–88
Dry Goods Guide, IV:188*n*
Dry goods periodicals, III:134; IV:187–88
Dry Goods Reporter, III:134
Dry Goods Reporter and Commerical Glance, II:93
Dryden, Helen, III:489; IV:760
Dryden, Hugh Latimer, IV:626
Drygoodsman and Southwestern Merchant, IV:188*n*
Duane, William, I:228
Dublin University Magazine, II:384
Du Bois, James T., IV:320*n*
Du Bois, W. E.B., IV:520, 723, 780
DuBose, Horace M., II:66*n*
Du Bose, William P., IV:735
Dubuque, Iowa, II:89; III:147*n*, 169
Dubuque Trade Journal, III:147*n*
Du Chaillu, Paul Belloni, III:172
"Dudes" as comic characters, IV:384
Dudevant, Armandine Lucille Aurore Dupin, III:254
Dudley, Helen, V;228
Duell, Sloan & Pearce, V:47
Duelling, I:57, 165, 244*n*; II:214
Duer, Carolyn, V:247
Duer, Elizabeth, V:248
Duffield, George, I:741; II:75*n*
Duffield, Samuel Willoughby, III:463
Duffus, Robert L., V:12
Duffy, Richard, IV:49, 617
Duganne, Augustine Joseph Hickey, I:504, 592, 734; II:410; IV:679
Dugmore, Arthur Radclyffe, IV:458, 775
Duke, Basil W., III:47; IV:93
Duke, Benjamin N., V:277
Duke Foundation, V:283
Duke University (Trinity College), magazines published by, IV:73; V:274, 276–78, 282–83
Duke University Press, V:283
Dulles, John Foster, V:315, 323*n*
Dumas, Alexandre, *fils*, III:254
Dumas, Alexandre, *père*, I:404; II:162, 163, 240; III:249, 254; V:117, 119
Du Maurier, Daphne, IV:554; V:136
Du Maurier, George Louis Palmella Busson, II:400; III:550; IV:43, 133, 141, 230
Dumay, Henri, IV:65–66
Du Mond, F. V., II:397
Dumont, Julia Louisa, II:302
Dun, Robert Graham, IV:349
Dunbar, Charles Franklin, IV:182
Dunbar, Paul Laurence, III:400; IV: 451, 690
Duncan, John, III:156
Duncan, Norman, IV:601, 781
Duncan, Robert, V:244
Duncan, Dr. T. C., 85*n*
Duncan, Thomas W., V:184
Dunglison's College and Clinical Record, III:140*n*
Dunham, Curtis, IV:454
Duniway, Abigail Scott, IV:108
Dunkirk, N.Y., III:153
Dunlap, William, 55, 56, 109, 114, 170, 232, 609
Dunlop's Stage News, IV:260
Dunmore, 8th Earl of (Alexander Edward), IV:493
Dunn, A. M., IV:107
Dunn, Charles, Jr., IV:82
Dunn, Harvey, IV:695
Dunn, Samuel Orace, III:125*n*, IV:466
Dunne, Peter Finley, III:510*n*, 512, 513; IV:209, 453*n*, 457, 458, 465, 500, 600
Dunning, Abigail Scott, III:9
Dunning, Albert Elijah, IV:292
Dunning, William Archibald, IV:180*n*
Dunraven, 4th Earl of, II:414; IV:373
Dun's Review, III:147*n*, IV:349
Dunsany, Lord Edward, V:121, 266
Dunster, Edward Swift, III:140*n*
Dunton's Spirit of the Turf, III:215*n*
Du Ponceau, Peter Stephen, I:155, 276
Dupont, Henry Algernon, I:749

Durand, Asher Brown, II:188; III:182
Durand, E. L., IV:609
Durand, John, II:193
Duranty, Walter, IV:748; V:212
Durboraw, Raymond H., V:179*n*, 180, 186
Durden, Robert F., V:273n
Durham, Howard, II:114*n*
Durham, N.C., II:110*n*; V:273*n*
Durivage, Francis Alexander, II:362, 410, 411
Duroc, III:160
Duroc Bulletin, IV:344
Duse, Eleanora, IV:256, 257
Du Solle, John S., IV:671*n*, 676–77
d'Utassy, George, IV:331, 494, 497
Dutton, Samuel William Southmayd, II:312*n*, 313, 314, 315
Duyckinck, Evert Augustus, I:346, 362, 610; II:158, 429; III:511
  as contributor, I:669, 720, 756, 760
  as editor, I:346, 711–12, 766–68
Duyckinck, George Long, I:610, 766–67; II:158
Dwight, Francis, I:491*n*
Dwight, Harrison Griswold, IV:726
Dwight, James H., III:425
Dwight, John Sullivan, I:403, 411, 432, 659, 662, 680, 703, 704, 736, 737, 764, 771; II:197; III:13*n*, 507
Dwight, Theodore, I:364–65, 409
Dwight, Timothy, I:58, 102, 106, 186, 232; II:269, 312*n*, 315; IV:513
Dwight's American Magazine, I:365*n*, 807; II:30
Dwight's Journal of Music, II:196, 197; III:196
Dwire, Henry Rudolph, V:273*n*, 283
Dwyer, Charles, III:481*n*, 482, 483; IV:360, 367*n*
Dwyer, James Francis, IV:114*n*
Dyer, George C., IV:100
Dyer, George Leland, IV:621
Dyer, Heman, II:68*n*
Dyer, Louis, III:350
Dyer, Theresa E., IV:431
Dyer, Walter Alden, IV:783
Dye's Government Counterfeit Detector, II:96
Dyestuffs, IV:185
Dynamo, invention of, III:121

Eads, James Buchanan, II:318; III:469
Eagle, Edward E., II:325*n*
Eakins, Thomas, IV:144
Eames, Charles, I:361
Eames, Mrs. Jane Anthony, I:353, 644, 651
Earle, L. H., III:85*n*
Earnings, II:254, 463; IV:614, 698; V:136
Earth, IV:333*n*
East, Edward Murray, IV:728
East Aurora, N.Y., IV:390*n*
East Canterbury, N.H., III:81
East and West, IV:126
Eastburn, Manton, I:334
Eastern Magazine, I:352*n*, 803
Eastern Philatelist, IV:391*n*
Eastern Star, IV:222*n*
Eastern Underwriter, IV:351*n*
Eastman, E. R., I:728*n*, 732
Eastman, George, IV:148
Eastman, Lucius Root, IV:747
Eastman, Max, IV:730; V:203, 206
Eastman Kodak, V:81
Easton, Pa., III:310*n*; IV:184*n*, 309
Eaton, Lucien, III:144
Eaton, Mary, IV:627
Eaton, Seymour, V:27–29
Eaton, Walter Prichard, III:555; IV:438, 638, 728; V:96
Eaton, William O., II:36*n*
Eaton, Wyatt, IV:151
Eatonton, Ga., II:111
Eberhart, Mignon Good, IV:473
Echo, III:198*n*
Echo (chapbook), IV:390*n*
Echo (insurance periodical), IV:351*n*
Echo (music periodical), IV:251
Echo (Scripps), IV:70
Eckels, James Herron, IV:158
Eckener, Hugo, IV:626
Eckstein, Louis, IV:116
Eclaireur, II:150; III:533
Eclectic and general magazines
  early (1741–94)
    bimonthlies, I:112–13
    monthlies, I:101–2
    trends, I:39–41
  in nationalist era (1794–1825)
    monthlies, I:279–83, 306–9
    trends, I:122, 125–26, 128, 130–31
    weeklies, I:233–46, 320–30
  of expanionist era (1825–50)
    biweeklies, I:622–23
    monthlies, I:692–93, 699–701, 743–44
    trends, I:365–66, 442
    weeklies, IV:672–78
  in Civil War era (1850–65), II:264, 383
    monthlies, II:448–51, 488–92
    quarterlies, II:531–32

Eclectic and general magazines—*Cont.*
trends, II:129
weeklies, IV:678–80
in post-Civil War era (1865-85)
monthlies, III:457–66, 510–11
quarterlies, II:530–33
trends, III:39, 46–47, 256
weeklies, III:357–60, 417–21, 557–59; IV:680–81
in Gilded Age (1885–1905)
monthlies, IV:43–56, 82, 97, 507–9, 589–607 717–23; V:72–80, 145–48, 246–51, 286–88
quarterlies, V:273–78, 329–30
weeklies, IV:65–67, 453–58, 672–91
modern (1905), V:238
monthlies, III:475–80, 512–16; IV: 509–10, 723–32; V:27–29, 51, 80–87, 145–53, 251–72, 289–92
quarterlies, V:278–85, 330–40
weeklies, III:555–56, IV:458–79, 616–19, 691–716; V:88–99
Eclectic Magazine, II:129, 192; III:32*n*, 186, 256; IV:56
founding of, I:131
sketch of, I:306–9
Eclectic Medical Gleaner, IV:316
Eclectic Medical Journal, II:85
Eclectic Medical Journal of Pennsylvania, II:85
Eclectic medical journals, III:143; IV:316
Eclectic Museum, I:308, 308*n*
Eclectic Repertory, I:151, 94
Economic controls, press attitudes toward, IV:705–6
Economic issues
before 1850, I:59–62, 75–76, 268, 318, 453–54, 463, 470, 471, 642, 696–98, 722
in Civil War era magazines (1850–65), II:5–7, 134, 144–45, 531
in post-Civil War magazines (1865–85), III:40
corporate wealth, III:293
female employment, III:92–93
Henry George, III:293–94
monopoly, III:292–93
railroad speculation, III:122–23
silver question, III:294–95
tariffs, III:292
in Gilded Age magazines (1885–1905), II:254–55
silver issue, IV:161–62
tariff issue, IV:165–67
trusts, IV:33, 156–57, 165–66, 706, 775
in modern magazines (1905–), II:259; III:432–34; V:216
See also Depressions, economic
Economic journals, IV:181–82
Economic World, III:147
Economist, III:147*n;* IV:350*n*
Economy Advertising Company, V:185
Eddy, James, I:322
Eddy, Mary Baker, IV:285
Eddy, Richard, II:72*n*
Eddy, Sherwood, IV:53*n*
Eddy, Dr. Walter H., V:138
Edenton, N.C., II:65*n*
Edes, Benjamin, I:380
Edgar, Day, IV:712
Edholm, Charles Lawrence, IV:107*n*
Edinboro, Pa., IV:271*n*
Edinburgh Review, II:129, 130, 221; IV:228
Edison, Thomas Alva, II:318, 324; III:118–21; IV:28, 226, 307, 320, 592, 593
Editor, IV:14
Editor & Publisher, IV:244, 393
sketch of, V:59–71
Editor & Publisher's Market Guide, V:69, 71
Editorial comment
before 1885, II:389, 471, 475–76; III:231, 286, 368
in Gilded Age magazines (1885–1905)
comic periodicals, IV:560
digests, IV:573
general magazines, IV:615
literary magazines, II:258, 399–400; III:231
satiric periodicals, IV:668
women's magazines, II:311
in modern magazines (1905–)
booksellers' magazines, V:67
current events magazines, V:56, 200, 217, 314
general magazines, IV:714; V:27–28, 94–95, 152
poetry magazines, V:105–6, 144, 242
publishers' magazines, V:67
urban weeklies, IV:655
Editorial control, I:196, 256, 503–4
Editors
of early magazines (1741–94) I:71, 73, 80, 94–95, 104, 108, 112, 114
lawyers, I:71, 78
radicals, I:83, 88–89, 92
salaries of, I:87
of nationalist era magazines (1794–1825), I:304, 307–8, 313, 317, 320–21, 324–27, 331, 334–35

clergymen, I:155, 198, 315
clubs, I:256
doctors, I:154–55
lawyers, I:154, 282, 297
salaries, I:198–99, 239, 272*n*, 279
teachers, I:155, 198, 288
women, I:121, 244, 295
of expansionist era magazines (1825–50)
lawyers, I:551, 601–2, 664
salaries, I:512–13, 549*n*, 612, 627, 634, 635, 707, 725, 764
women, I:350, 356, 484–85, 537, 583-85; II:307
of Civil War era magazines (1850–65)
censorship, II:26
clergymen, II:44, 544
lawyers, II:224
salaries, II:24–25
women, II:50
of post-Civil War magazines (1865–85), III:10–20, 377, 474
authority over writers, III:20–22
clergymen, III:425
great editors, III:22–24
salaries, III:12, 332, 339, 405
techniques, III:19–22
women, II:463; III:94–96, 177, 390, 404–5, 407, 428–29, 500–1, 508
of Gilded Age magazines (1885–1905)
authors' complaints, IV:35–37
great editors, IV:35
salaries, IV:35, 687; V:146
women, IV:142-43, 273, 360–64, 413, 539, 581
of modern magazines (1905–)
salaries, III:431; IV:469, 497, 549, 768; V:302
women, III:354–55, 489, 504, 543; IV:470, 584, 700, 708, 712*n*, 768–71; V:25, 122–23
Edmonds, John Worth, II:208, 209
Edmonds, Walter Dumaux, IV:701, 709
Edmunds, George Franklin, III:477
Edmunds, Richard Hathaway, III:127
Edmunds Act (1882), III:313
Edson, Clement M., I:607
Education, IV:268
Education
in early magazines (1741–94), I:102, 104
curriculum, I:62–64, 105
poetry on, I:63–64
religion and, I:63–64, 105
women's education, I:63–64
in nationalist-era magazines (1794–1825), I:300, 145
classical education, I:146
colleges, I:146
discipline, I:147
specialized periodicals, I:144, 148
women's education, I:143, 145
in expansionist-era magazines (1825–50), I:624, 723
colleges, I:488
criticisms, I:472, 490
free schools, I:487
lyceums, I:489–90
physical culture, I:440–41
public schools, I:487
specialized periodicals, I:491–92
women's education, I:349–50, 484–85, 583, 672
in Civil War magazines (1850–65)
defectives, II:445
medical education, II:86
public education, II:96
religious periodicals, II:97
women's education, II:46–47
in post-Civil War magazines (1865–85), II:253
college magazines, III:165–66
educational journals, III:167–70, 408
general magazines, II:418, 465
kindergarten journals, III:163–64
medical education, III:138
quarterlies, II:445–47
public schools, III:163–64
religious magazines, II:376; III:439
scientific education, III:105–6
trends, III:4
women's education, III:102–3, 483
in Gilded Age magazines (1885–1905), IV:267–73
adult, IV:264–66, 357
expansion, IV:262–63
expositions and fairs, IV:266–67
university extension, IV:263–64
women's education, IV:357–58
modern magazines on (1905–), IV:781
current events magazines, III:354
public schools, III:163–64
review periodicals, IV:517
of Negroes, I:537
in South, V:281
Education magazines
in expansionist era (1825–50)
irregular, I:694–95
monthlies, I:541–43
trends, I:491–92

Education magazines—*Continued*
in Civil War era (1850–65)
number, II:98
quarterlies, II:442–45
trends, II:98–99
weeklies, II:34
in post-Civil War era (1865–85)
college curriculum, III:164
kindergarten magazines, III:163
pedagogical journals, III:167–70
public school magazines, III:163–64
in Gilded Age (1885–1905)
general, IV:267–69
regional periodicals, IV:270–71
teachers' trade papers, IV:269–70
Educational Digest, III:169*n*
Educational Exchange, IV:270*n*
Educational Foundations, IV:270
Educational Gazette, IV:269*n*
Educational Independent, IV:271*n*
Educational Journal of Virginia, III:168
Educational Monthly, II:59
Educational News, IV:55*n,* 269*n*
Educational Review, IV:268
Educator, IV:270
Educator-Journal, IV:270*n*
Edward VIII (Duke of Windsor), V:326
Edwards, A. S., IV:175*n*
Edwards, Mrs. Annie, II:439; III:371–72
Edwards, Arthur, IV:217, 291
Edwards, Bela Bates, I:367, 372, 491, 739*n*
Edwards, George Wharton, IV:719
Edwards, Harry Stillwell, III:465; IV:429
Edwards, James L., I:170
Edwards, Walter M., IV:628
Edwin, David, I:208, 209
Egan, Maurice Francis, III:69*n;* IV:297–98, 299, 438
Egan, Pierce, II:454; IV:680
Egg journals, IV:345
Egg and Poultry Review, IV:186*n*
Egg Reporter, IV:345
Eggleston, Edward, II:374; III:99, 175*n,* 224, 244, 247, 264, 347, 423, 461, 471, 502; IV:513
Eggleston, George Cary, II:506*n;* III:13*n,* 48, 99, 421
Eggleston George T., IV:556*n,* 568
Ehmann, John, IV:184*n*
Ehrhart, J., III:530
Ehrlich, Henry, IV:587
Ehrick's Fashion Quarterly, III:98*n*
Eight-hour-day movement, IV:219–20
Eisenhower, Dwight David, IV:478, 715; V:25, 221, 223, 316, 319, 323*n*
Elam, W. C., I:653
Elder, A. P. T. III:234
Elder, John A., II:113
Elder, Paul, IV:126
Elderkin, John, IV:65*n*
Eleanor Kirk's Idea, IV:356*n*
Election campaigns, I:452–54
campaigns of 1850's, II:135–37
campaign of 1860, II:135–37
1868, II:476
1872, III:286, 341
1876, III:286, 341
1880, III:287
1884, III:345, 553; IV:561
1888, III:529, 554
1892, III:529, 554: IV:94
1896, III:346; IV:411, 660
1900, IV:660, 782
1904, II:257; III:349; IV:782
1908, II:258; III:531; IV:782
1912, II:258; III:349; IV:660, 782–83; V:333
1916, II:258; IV:575; V:333
1920, II:259, 378-79; III:352; IV:576; V:333
1924, II:259; III:352; IV:576, 785; V:333
1932, III:352; IV:576, 707; V:318, 333
1934 (California), IV:578
1936, IV:577; V:318, 333
1940, V:318, 333
1944, V:318–19, 333
1948, V:319
1952, IV:478; V:319
1956 and 1960, V:319
Election polls by *Literary Digest,* IV:575–77
Electoral reform, campaigns for, IV:407, 462
Electric Age, III:121*n*
Electric dynamo, development of, III:121
Electric Journal, IV:322
Electric light, invention of, III:119; IV:319–20, 592
Electric Power, IV:322
Electric Railway Gazette, IV:333
Electric Railway Journal, III:126; IV:333
Electric railway magazines, III:126
Electric Railway Review, IV:333
Electrical Engineer, III:122
Electrical Industries, IV:321
Electrical inventions, III:118–21

Electrical periodicals, III:121–22; IV: 321–22
Electrical Review, III:122
Electrical World, III:121, 122; IV:321
Electrician and Mechanic, IV:321–22
Electricity, IV:322
Electro-Chemical Industry, IV:322*n*
Electrotyper, III:132*n*
Electrotyping, III:186–87
Elementary School Journal, IV:272
Elephant, I:780, 809
Eliot, Charles William, I:535; II:376; III:164, 337, 558; IV:73*n*, 75, 262, 514, 547, 776, 779, 785; V:282
"Eliot, George," *see* Cross, Mary Ann Evans
Eliot, George Fielding, V:25, 54
Eliot, John, I:28
Eliot, Samuel, I:78
Eliot, Samuel Atkins, I:287; II:233
Eliot, Thomas Stearns, III:542, 543; IV:441, 738, 739, 740; V:94, 106, 173, 178, 228, 241
Eliot, William, II:402
Eliot, William G., I:662
Elite, IV:93
Elizabeth, N.J., IV:221*n*
Elizabeth, Queen of Belgium, IV:549
Elizabeth, Queen of Roumania ("Carmen Sylvia"), IV:768
Elizabeth II, Queen of England, IV:555; V:323*n*
Elizabethtown, N.J., I:122–13
Elkhart, Ind., III:81
Elks-Antler, IV:222*n*
Ellard, Roscoe, V:67
Ellet, Mrs. Elizabeth Fries, I:276, 401, 412, 499, 546, 584, 620, 637, 641, 665, 680, 723, 734, 743, 751, 756, 770; II:308, 352; IV:679
Elliot, Sydney Barrinton, IV:405
Elliott, Aaron Marshall, III:236*n*; IV:128
Elliott, Ashbel R., III:133*n*
Elliott, Charles, II:67*n*
Elliott, Charles Wyllys ("Thom White"), II:429; III:151
Elliott, Francis Perry, IV:361
Elliott, George, I:299*n*, 301
Elliott, Sarah Barnwell, IV:720
Elliott, Stephen, I:382, 573–76
Elliott, William Yandell, V:100*n*, 108, 110
Elliott's Magazine, IV:379*n*
Ellis, Benjamin, I:539
Ellis, Edward Sylvester, II:171, 462, III:43, 178, 502; IV:116*n*, 274, 418
Ellis, G. B., I:521
Ellis, George Edward, I:284*n*, 288*n*; II:128, 241; III:507
Ellis, George H., IV:294
Ellis, Havelock, V:21
Ellis, Robinson, III:536
Ellis, Rufus, II:72*n*; III:507
Elmendorf, Dwight Lathrop, IV:725
Elmer Gantry (Lewis), V:309–11
Elmhirst, Leonard, V:214
Elmira, N.Y., III:125*n*, 142, 149*n*; IV:68
Elmira Telegram, IV:68
Elting, Mary Letha, V:117*n*, 123
Elton, Robert H., I:425
Elverson, James, III:42, 178; IV:117
Elwell, E. H., II:36
Ely, Richard T., III:407, 558; IV:52*n*
Emancipation Proclamation, II:294, 542
Emancipator, I:162, 373, 457, 802; II:369
Emanu-El, IV:300*n*
Embalmers' magazines, IV:189
Embalmers' Monthly, IV:189
Embree, Elijah, I:162
Embury, Mrs. Emma, I:326, 412, 499, 544*n*, 546, 626*n*, 627, 770
Emerald
  dramatic department of, I:167, 168, 169
  founding of, I:127
  sketch of, I:247–50
Emerald and Baltimore Literary Gazette, I:380, 799
Emerson, Edwin, II:464, IV:458
Emerson, G. H., I:691*n*; II:57, 72
Emerson, J. M, II:32
Emerson, Oliver Farrar, III:540
Emerson, Ralph Waldo, I:289–90, 410–11, 534, 723, 777; II:147, 169, 494, 510; III:59, 172, 237, 238, 548; IV:680; V:286
  criticism of, II:166–67; III:455
  as contributor, I:504, 586, 659, 661–62, 702–10, 764; II:20, 33, 175, 238, 244 253, 387, 495, 502–4, 535
  as editor, I:368, 402, 775–77
Emerson, William, I:124, 253–55
Emerson's United States Magazine, see: United States Magazine (New York)
Emery, Henry Crosby, V:329*n*

Emlen, S., Jr., I:151*n*
Emmons, Nathaniel, I:134*n*
Emory, Frederick, IV:782
Emory, John, I:299*n*
Emory, Percy McCarthy, IV:87
Empire State Agriculturist, III:153
Empire State Workman, III:315
Employee magazines, IV:335
Employment, II:92–93; IV:354–55
Emporia, Kan., IV:270*n*
Emporium of Arts and Sciences, I:151*n*, 362, 794
Encyclopedias, I:263
Ende, Alice Ankeney von, III:350
Enfant Terrible (1898), IV:389
Engel, Conrad, Jr., IV:88
Engel, Louis, III:233
Engelhard, G. P., IV:99
Engels, Friedrich, IV:206
Engineer, III:166*n*
Engineer of the Pacific, III:114*n*
Engineer and Surveyor, III:113*n*
Engineering, magazine comment on, I:303
Engineering Magazine, IV:321
Engineering-Mechanics, III:116
Engineering and Mining Journal, III:114, 363
Engineering News, III:113
Engineering News-Record, III:113*n*
Engineering periodicals, II:80–81; III:113–14, 116; IV:320–22
Engineering Record, III:113*n*
Engineering Review, IV:322*n*
Engineers and Engineering, III:113*n*
Engineers' Club of Philadelphia, Proceedings of, III:113
England, *see* British magazines; English authors; English literature; Great Britain
England, Isaac W., II:452*n;* III:510–11
England, Bishop John, I:136, 383; II:76
Engle, Paul, V:242
Englehardt, George W., II:95*n*
English, Thomas Dunn, I:330, 347, 426, 651, 675, 760, 771, 780–83; II: 181, 544*n*, 546; III:465*n*
English authors
  criticism of, II:159–62
  as lecturers, III:249–51
  popularity of, III:248–52; IV:131–34
English Church Review, IV:229*n*
English Illustrated Magazine, IV:228
English Leaflet, IV:272*n*
English literature
  and magazines before 1865, I:178–80, 231, 295, 309, 399–401, 415, 617; II:129, 159–62, 172, 230–31, 236, 383, 386–87, 393, 406, 421, 508
  and post-Civil War magazines (1865–85), III:456, 549
    mutual influence, III:278–79
    popularity, III:248–49, 251–53, 278
  serial fiction, III:224–25, 358
  and Gilded Age magazines (1885–1905), popularity, IV:131–34
Engraver and Electrotyper, IV:248*n*
Engraver and Printer, IV:248*n*
Engravings
  in early magazines (1741–94), I:36–38, 94–95
  in nationalist-era magazines (1794–1825), I:309
    quality and uses, I:239, 243, 296, 300, 307, 309
  in expansionist-era magazines (1825–50), I:343–44, 347–48, 365, 417–18, 620, 622–23, 626, 753; II:302, 307
    agricultural, I:731
    artistic, I:437
    colored, I:442, 545
    famous engravers, I:520–23, 684
    fashion, I:519, 545, 548, 591–92, 656, 719, 744
    growing use, I:521–24, 683–84
    humorous, I:425
    medical, I:567
    obscene, I:475
    quality, I:519–20
    technical, I:557
  in Civil War era magazines (1850–65), I:656
    fashion, II:437–41
    illustrated periodicals, III:325
    news, II:454
    quality, II:192–93, 397
  in post-Civil War era (1865–85)
    artistic, III:187, 191, 410–11
    family magazines, II:477–78
    fashion, II:309, 325; III:389
    prominent engravers, III:187–88
    trends, III:187–91
  in Gilded Age magazines (1885–1905), fashion, II:311, IV:85, 363
  See also Aquatints; Chromolithographs; Copper-plate illustrations; Half-tone pictures; Illustrated periodicals; Lithographs; Steel-plate engravings; Stipple engravings; Woodcuts
Enright, Walter Joseph, III:531

Enterprise, II:461*n*
Entomology magazines, III:111
"Ephemeral bibelots," IV:386–91
Epidemics, disease, *see* Cholera epidemics; Smallpox epidemics; Yellow fever epidemics
Epilark (1895), IV:388
Episcopal Methodist, III:71*n*
Episcopal Recorder, I:138, 797; II:70; III:75
Episcopal Watchman, I:799
Episcopalian, II:70*n*
Episcopalian magazines
  before 1865, I:56, 135, 372; II:68–70, 364–65
  after 1865, II:365–66; IV:294
Epoch, IV:60, 610
Epstein, Jacob, III:542
Epworth Era, IV:275
Epworth Herald, IV:275
Equitable Record, III:146
Equity, III:299; IV:178
Era, IV:125
Ericsson, John, II:318
Erie, Pa., IV:178
Erie Canal, I:340
Erie War, III:289
Erlanger, Abraham Lincoln, IV:255
Ernst, Max, V:178
Ernst, William E., IV:55, 499
Errett, Isaac, III:80
Erskine, John, II:260; III:479, 489; IV:126, 439, 471; V:337
Erwin, Ray, V:67
Erythea, IV:310
Esenwein, Joseph Berg, III:396*n*, 400–1
Eshleman, G. R., III:144*n*
Esoteric, IV:304*n*
Esperanto, II:257
Esquimaux, III:57*n*
Esquire, IV:422, 568, 731
Essays
  in early magazines (1741–94)
    general magazines, I:82, 93, 97, 103, 109
    trends, I:41
  in nationalist-era magazines (1794–1825)
    decline, I:175
    general periodicals, I:233–34, 257
    literary magazines, I:219, 260
    religious periodicals, I:262, 290, 315
    trends, I:122, 124
    women's magazines, I:321
  in expansionist-era magazines (1825–50)
    general magazines, I:577; IV:674–75
    literary magazines, I:563, 601; IV:674–75
    religious magazines, I:563
    women's magazines, I:547, 589; II:301
  in Civil War era magazines (1850-65), literary magazines, II:420, 424, 495
  in post-Civil War magazines (1865–85
    family magazines, III:423–24, 428
    general magazines, III:419, 459, 463
    literary magazines, III:231–32, 548–49
  nature, III:54
  in Gilded Age magazines (1885–1905)
    family magazines, IV:491
    literary magazines, IV:425
    urban weeklies, IV:654
  in modern magazines (1905–), IV:728
    family magazines, III:431; IV:498
    general magazines, IV:728; V:28, 95
    illustrated magazines, IV:472
    literary magazines, IV:425
    urban weeklies, IV:654
    women's magazines, IV:553
Essex Antiquarian, IV:138
Essex Institute Bulletin, III:259
Essex Institute Historical Collections, II:176*n;* III:259
"Estelle," *see* Bogart, Elizabeth
Estes, Dana, IV:41
Etchings, I:437
Eternal Progress, IV:169
Ethical Addresses, IV:279
Ethical Culture movement, III:82; IV:278–80
Ethical Record, IV:279
Ethnology, III:112; IV:140, 622
Etiquette, III:308, 482
Étude, III:197; IV:251, 253
Eude, Louis-Marie, II:355
Eugenics, III:452
Eulau, Heinz H. F., V:218
Euripides, V:121
European Architecture, IV:323
Eustis, James B., IV:230
Evan, Adm. Robley D., V:148
Evangel, III:81
Evangelical and Literary Magazine, I:205
Evangelical Lutheran magazines, II:73

Evangelical Magazine and Gospel Advocate, I:799
Evangelical Messenger, II:68
Evangelical Record, I:794
Evangelical Repository, II:62*n*
Evangelical Review, II:73; III:79
Evangelist (Chicago), III:80
Evangelist (New York), I:308, 373, 457, 800; II:18, 63, 140, 369; III:64, 74, 224, 291; IV:288, 293
Evans, Augusta Jane, I:653; II:171; III:246
Evans, B. R., I:343
Evans, Bergen, V:23, 25
Evans, Charles, I:562*n*, 564
Evans, Edward Payson, II:510*n*
Evans, Hugh Davey, II:69
Evans, Marie, IV:93
Evans, Robley Dunglison, III:512, 534
Evanston, Ind., IV:128
Evarts, Jeremiah, I:262*n*, 263–65, 572; II:233
Evarts, William Maxwell, I:488
Evelyn, William, III:45
Evening Bulletin (Philadelphia), I:552
Evening Fireside, I:127, 792
Evening Lamp, III:53
Evening Mirror, I:329
Evening and the Morning Star, IV:296
Evening Post (New York), I:160, 356
Events (St. Louis), IV:101
Events (Scotch Plains, N.J.), IV:522; V:57
Everest, Charles William, I:641
Everett, Alexander Hill, I:155, 490; II:218*n*, 227, 229, 232, 234
as contributor, I:176, 255, 258, 587*n*, 680, 687, 719
as editor, I:253*n*, 367
quoted, I:394, 409, 458–59
Everett, Charles Carroll, II:243; IV:295
Everett, Edward, II:23–24, 149, 232, 238, 360, 361, 445
as contributor, I:138, 155, 189, 192, 227, 600, 718, 753
as editor, I:130, 172; II:220*n*, 226–32
estimate of, I:409
Everett, Oliver, II:227
Everett, P. Y., III:118*n*
Evergreen, II:69
Everitt, S. A., IV:775
Every Bodie's Album, I:425, 803
Every Other Saturday, III:256
Every Saturday, I:749; II:386, 462, 510; III:13, 131, 189, 256, 279; IV:90
sketch of, III:357–60
Every Saturday Journal, IV:92
Every Where, IV:45
Everybody's, II:511
Everybody's Combined with Romance, V:86
Everybody's Magazine, III:484, 487; IV: 47, 208, 393, 614; V:150, 152, 255, 288
sketch of, V:72–87
Everybody's Own, II:185*n*
Everybody's Poultry Magazine, IV:345*n*
Evett, Robert, V:191*n*; 222
Evolution, III:107
Evolution, theory of, II:78–79, 243, 248, 252, 253, 381; III:107, 497; IV:785
anti-evolution trial, V:116
Ev'ry Month, IV:252–53
Ewer, Ferdinand Cartwright, II:117; III:406
Ewing, Samuel, I:155, 240, 244, 279*n*
Ewing, Thomas, IV:506*n*
Examiner, III:89
Examiner (New York), IV:288, 291
Examiner (Omaha), IV:97
Examiner (Pittsburgh), I:508*n*
Examiner and Chronicle, III:72
Examiner Club, I:287
Examiner and Hesperian, see: Literary Examiner
Exchanges, magazine, I:515–16; II:11–12; V:341
Exodus, IV:285*n*
Expenses
before 1885, II:6–7, 18, 411, 427, 430, 446
of Gilded Age magazines (1885–1905), IV:5, 15, 412, 429, 484, 617; V:156
Experienced Christian's Magazine, I:131–32, 790
Experiment Station, V:137–38
Exploration, II:402, 413–14
Exponent, IV:183
Export, IV:186*n*
Export Implement Age, IV:186*n*
Export-trade magazines, IV:186*n*
Exporters' and Importers' Journal, IV:186*n*
Expositions, IV:266–67, 621, 629, 782
Expositor, III:146*n*
Expositor and Current Anecdotes, IV:301*n*
Extension programs, university, IV:263–64
Eyre, Wilson, Jr., IV:324*n*
Eytinge, Sol, Jr., II:397, 477; III:359, 379, 504, 509

Fabian Socialism, IV:191, 203, 204
Fabrics, Fancy Goods and Notions, III:134*n*
Factory Management and Maintenance, III:122*n*
Factory system, early, I:471
Facts, III:82*n;* V:294
Facts About the Filipines, IV:236
Fad, IV:290
Fadazines, *see* Chapbooks
Fadiman, Clifton, V:99*n*
Fairbanks, C. M., IV:50*n*
Fairchild, David G., IV:625
Fairchild, Henry Pratt, IV:749
Fairchild, Lee, IV:108
Fairfield, Jane, I:345
Fairfield, Sumner Lincoln, I:345
Fairman, Gideon, I:209
Fairman, Henry Clay, III:46*n*
Fairs, IV:266–67
Falkner, Roland Post, IV:193
Fall, Albert, V:213
Fallows, Samuel, IV:55, 499*n*
Family Library Monthly, I:228*n*
Family Lyceum, I:489, 801
Family Magazine, Weekly Abstract of General Knowledge, I:363–64, 448, 522, 802
Family Newspaper, II:58
Family periodicals
  in expansionist era (1825–50), I:377
    illustrations, I:522
    quality, I:448
    weeklies, II:349–50
  in Civil War era (1850–65), II:303, 470–71
    monthlies, II:416–17
    trends, II:56–59
    weeklies, II:350–54, 356–62, 470–76
  in post-Civil War era (1865–85), III:46
    monthlies, II:417
    religious, III:82–83
    trends, III:98–101
    weeklies, II:269–70, 354, 357, 476–82; III:423–27
  in Gilded Age (1885–1905), V:158
    biweeklies, V:125–31
    mail-order, IV:365–67
    monthlies, II:362–63, 417–18; III:327; IV:92, 480–92; V:131–32, 154–57
    weeklies, II:354–55, 362–63, 482–85; III:427–31; IV:67–69, 92
  modern (1905)
    monthlies, IV:492–505; V:36–48, 132–43, 157–65
    weeklies, II:273–74, 355, 431–35, 485–87
Family Treasure, II:59
Family Visitor, II:15, 115
Famous Stories Book, V:124
Fanciers' Gazette, III:161*n*
Fancy Goods Graphic, III:134*n*
Fanning, Michael A., IV:652*n*, 653
Fanning, Neville O., IV:401*n*, 414
Fanshaw, Daniel, I:327
Far and Near, IV:354–55
Far West Magazine, IV:49*n*
Faribault, Minn., IV:178, 315*n*
Fargo, N.D., III:158
Faris, Ellsworth, IV:192*n*
Farjeon, Benjamin Leopold, II:482
Farm, Field and Fireside, III:156
Farm, Field and Stockman, III:156*n*
Farm, Stock and Home, III:157
Farm and Dairy, III:157; IV:340
Farm Equipment Retailing, IV:188*n*
Farm and Fireside, III:7, 100, 152*n*, 156, 515; IV:337, 468
Farm and Garden, III:153
Farm and Hearth, III:152
Farm and Home, III:152; IV:337
Farm Implement News, III:151; IV:188*n*
Farm Implements, IV:188*n*
Farm implements trade magazines, IV:188
Farm and gardening magazines, *see* Agricultural magazines; Gardening magzines
Farm Journal, III:11–12, 153; IV:17, 63*n*, 337, 597*n*
Farm Journal and Live Stock Review, III:157
Farm Life, III:153; IV:338
Farm Machinery, IV:188*n*
Farm–Poultry, IV:345
Farm Progress, IV:338
Farm and Ranch, III:155
Farm Stock and Home, IV:341
Farm Stock Success, III:161*n*
Farman, Ella, III:177, 508
Farmer, Henry Tudor, I:177
Farmer, I:731
Farmer and Breeder, III:158*n*
Farmer and Farm, Stock and Home, III:158*n*
Farmer and Mechanic, III:155
Farmer and Planter Monthly, II:89
Farmer and Stockman, III:159
Farmers
  contributors, I:494
  conflict with railroads, III:124, 148–50

Farmers—*Continued*
See also Agriculture; Agricultural magazines
Farmers' Alliance, IV:176
Farmers' Alliance magazines, III:149–50
Farmer's Cabinet, I:444*n,* 729, 803
Farmers' Call, III:156
Farmers' Friend and Grange Advocate, III:149*n*
Farmer's Guide, I:444; IV:340–41
Farmer's Home, III:156
Farmer's Home Journal, III:155
Farmer's Journal, II:89
Farmer's Museum, I:156*n,* 198, 225, 789
Farmer's and Planter's Guide, II:90
Farmers' and Planters' Guide, III:154
Farmer's Register, I:801
Farmer's Reporter, I:444*n,* 801
Farmer's Review, III:156
Farmers' Tribune, III:149*n*
Farmers' Union, III:149*n*
Farmer's Voice, IV:340
Farmer's Wife, IV:341
Farming, IV:341
Farmington, Maine, III:168*n*
Farnham, Henry Walcott, V:329*n,* 330–32, 338
Farnol, Jeffery, IV:115*n,* 435, 604
Farnum, A. M., III:53*n*
Farragut, Admiral David Glasgow, II:548
Farrally, John, V:218
Farrar, Frederick William, II:253; IV:45*n,* 226, 274, 513
Farrar, John, II:227
Farrar, John Chipman, IV:432*n,* 438–40; V:305
Farrar, Timothy, II:176*n,* 242
Farrell, James T., V:184
Fashion Bazar, III:98
Fashion Book, IV:694*n*
Fashion magazines, III:97–98, 481–83; IV:363, 580–88, 756–70
See also Fashions in dress
Fashion plates, III:325, 389, 484, 485
Fashions, IV:363*n*
Fashions in dress
before 1825, I:57, 66–67, 140–41, 219, 227, 234–35, 248, 321–22, 324, 328
in expansionist era magazines (1825–50), I:476–77, 589, 628; II:45
engravings, I:519, 545, 548, 591–92, 656, 719, 744
in Civil War era magazines (1850–65), I:656; II:53–56, 222, 306, 351, 384, 390, 416, 449, 453, 477
engravings, II:437–41
in post-Civil War magazines (1865–85), III:97–98
critical comment, III:96–97
engravings, II:309, 325; III:389
in Gilded Age magazines (1885–1905), IV:358–59, 363, 378, 537
engravings, II:311; IV:85, 363
reform campaigns, IV:406
in modern magazines (1905–30), V:135
juvenile, II:274
reform campaigns, IV:547–48
See also Patterns
Fat Contributor's Saturday Night, III:266
Father Abraham, II:137
Fatherland, IV:510
Faulkner, H. C., III:99
Faulkner, William, III:504; IV:701, 729; V:12, 201
Faust, Frederick, IV:421, 473, 618
Fawcett, Edgar, II:310, 429, 506*n;* III:37*n,* 51*n,* 54, 229, 244, 374, 400*n,* 416, 420, 508; IV:45, 58*n,* 83*n,* 84, 135, 186, 408, 765
Faxon, Charles, Jr., II:116*n*
Faxon, Frederick Winthrop, IV:143, 386–88, 452
Fay, Gaston, III:187, 379, 420
Fay, Sidney B., V:58
Fay, Theodore Sedgwick, I:320*n,* 324–25, 546, 587*n,* 608, 635
Fayetteville, N.C., II:63*n*
Fearnley, John, IV:735
Feather, A. G., III:261*n*
Featherstone, Joseph, V:191*n*
Featherstonehaugh, George William, I:446
Federal Gazette (Baltimore), I:294
Federal Trade Commission, V:140–41
Federation Bulletin, IV:356
Feedingstuffs, IV:189*n*
Feigl, Fred, IV:170
Felch, W. Farrand, IV:82
Fellows, John, I:122*n*
Fellows of American Letters of the Library of Congress, V:231–35
Fellowship, IV:221*n*
Fels, Joseph, IV:62
Fels, Samuel S., IV:749
Felt, Joseph Barlow, II:176*n*
Felter, J. D., I:522, 714
Felton, Cornelius Conway, I:289, 367, 394, 409, 416; II:236, 237, 240
Female Advocate, I:484
Female Student, II:46

Feminism, *see* Women; Women's rights; Women's suffrage
Fencing articles, IV:634
Fenderich, Charles, I:520
Fenn, Edward P., III:101
Fenn, George Manville, IV:117
Fenn, Harry, III:187, 420; IV:484
Fenner, A. E., IV:609
Fenno, Harriet, I:244
Fenollosa, Ernest, V:175
Fenwick, Benedict Joseph, I:373
Ferber, Edna, III:488, 514; IV:498, 503, 552, 605
Ferguson, Oliver W., V:273*n*
Fergusson, John W., I:629*n*, 640*n*, 647
Ferman, Joseph W., V:24
"Fern, Fanny," *see* Parton, Sara Payson Willis
Fern Bulletin, IV:310
Fernald, Chester Bailey, V:119
Fernow, Richard Eduard, IV:622
Ferrero, Guglielmo, II:431; IV:500
Ferrin, Wesley W., II:367*n*, 379
Ferris, Charles D., II:116*n*
Ferris, Mary Lanman Douw, IV:142
Fess, Simeon D., IV:53*n*
Fessenden, Thomas Green, I:154, 156, 194, 232, 317–18, 442
Fessenden's Silk Manual, I:442, 803
Fetter, George Griffith, IV:93
Fetter's Southern Magazine, IV:93
Feuchtwanger, Lion, IV:475
Few, William Preston, V:273*n*, 278, 281–82
Fewkes, Jesse Walter, IV:140
Fibre and Fabric, IV:185*n*
Fichte, Johann Gottlieb, III:386
Ficke, Arthur Davison, IV:724; V:168, 176, 184, 228–29, 237
Ficken, Dorothy, IV:30
Fiction, III:43
Fiction, III:344; IV:111–20
  defense of, I:175
  devotional, I:716
  formula-written, IV:703–4
  prejudices against, I:174
  trends in, IV:110
  See also All-fiction magazines; Literary criticism; Literary magazines; Novels; Serial fiction; Short stories
Fiction Parade, V:124
Fiction Parade and Golden Book, V:124
Field, III:210
Field, Charles K., IV:105*n*
Field, David Dudley, II:251; III:294; IV:200
Field, Eugene, III:270*n*; IV:61, 66, 390, 451, 541, 543, 646, 765; V:269
Field, Frederica Pisek, V:117*n*, 123
Field, Henry, IV:629–30
Field, Henry Martyn, II:63*n*, 252; III:88; IV:293
Field, James Alfred, IV:181*n*
Field, Kate, III:37*n*, 172, 271, 322, 358, 398, 557; IV:40, 45, 61–62, 160, 218, 371
Field, Marshall, III:53; IV:147*n*
Field, Roswell Martin, II:262*n*, 273
Field and Fancy, IV:382
Field and Farm, IV:341
Field and River, III:210*n*
Field Sports, IV:381*n*
Field and Stream, III:210*n*; IV:381, 393
Fielding, Henry, II:160
Fields, Mrs. Annie Adams, II:505*n*
Fields, James Thomas, I:326, 587; II:33, 493*n*, 503, 504, 505, 507; III:20, 32, 465*n*
Fields, Mrs. James Thomas, IV:722
Fiery Cross, IV:227
Fife, George Buchanan, II:485
Fifth Avenue Journal, III:102
Figaro (New Orleans), III:45
Figaro! or Corbyn's Chronicle of Amusements, II:180, 198
Fighting cocks, IV:382
Filatelic Facts and Fallacies, IV:391
Filene, Edward A., IV:730
Fillmore, Charles, IV:285–86
Film Fun, III:554*n*
Filmer, John, II:523; III:187, 191
Finance, IV:349
Finance and Trade, III:147*n*
Financial Age, IV:349
Financial Bulletin, IV:350*n*
Financial issues, I:59, 75; II:147; III:294–95; V:75–78
  See also Depressions, economic; National-bank controversy; Silver issue
Financial journals, II:94–96, 255; III:146–47; IV:182, 349–50
Financial Review, IV:350*n*
Financial scandals, III:3
Financial World, IV:349
Financier, II:96
Fincher, J. C., II:212
Fincher's Trades Review, II:212
Finck, Henry Theophilus, III:197*n*, 336, 347; IV:60, 73*n*, 225, 261*n*
Fin de siècle, IV:167–69
Fine Arts Journal, IV:147
Finger, Charles Joseph, III:504; IV:656
Finkel, Benjamin Franklin, IV:310

Finlay, J. W., II:128
Finley, John Huston, IV:595, 742
Finn, Francis James, IV:299
Fire Engineering, III:118*n;* IV:323*n*
Fire Service, III:118*n*
Fire and Water, III:118*n*
Fire and Water Engineering, IV–323*n*
Firelands Pioneer, II:176; IV:137*n*
Fireman, Peter, V:99*n*
Fireman's Herald, III:118
Fireman's Journal, II:204*n;* III:118*n*
Fires, major, III:118
Fireside Companion, III:7*n,* 16, 39, 43; IV:17, 117
Fireside at Home, III:99; IV:360
Fireside Monthly, II:59
Firkins, Oscar W., III:349
First, Jean, IV:659*n*
First Aid Book, V:48
"First Locomotive, The," I:468
Fischer, Anton Otto, IV:692, 710
Fischer, Carl, IV:254
Fish, Hamilton, I:751
Fish, Mrs. Stuyvesant, IV:756, 759–60
Fish, Williston, III:528
Fishbein, Morris, IV:524*n,* 529–35
Fisher, Alvan, I:436
Fisher, C. J. B., I:480
Fisher, Dorothy Canfield, *see* Canfield, Dorothy
Fisher, E. B., I:390*n*
Fisher, Franklin L., IV:628
Fisher, George Park, II:252, 312*n,* 315; III:322, 337, 424, 546; IV:52*n;* V:329*n,* 330–31
Fisher, Harrison, IV:49*n,* 151, 360*n,* 502, 565, 685, 689, 698
Fisher, Irving, V:329*n,* 330
Fisher, Sydney George, II:139, 242
Fisher, Vardis, IV:729
Fisher, Walt M., III:402*n,* 406
Fishing articles, V:122
Fishing Gazette, III:135
Fishing magazines, III:210; IV:380–81, 634
Fishing trade magazines, III:135; IV:186*n*
Fisk, James, Jr., III:4, 440–42
Fiske, Daniel Willard, II:414*n*
Fiske, Harrison Grey, III:198*n,* 199; IV:255, 261*n*
Fiske, John, II:248, 272, 506*n,* 507*n,* 510*n;* III:35*n,* 301, 337, 421, 518
Fiske, Lyman O., III:199*n*
Fiske, Mary H., III:199*n*
Fiske, Stephen, III:185*n*
Fiske, Willard, III:336
Fitch, Asa, I:596
Fitch, Clyde, IV:257
Fitch, E. H., III:109
Fitch, George, III:514; IV:458, 693
Fitch, John, I:96
Fitch, John Andrews, IV:745, 747
Fitten, J. H., II:110*n*
Fitts, James Franklin, II:468; III:13*n,* 376
Fitzgerald, Edward, IV:133–34
Fitzgerald, F. Scott, V:263
Fitzgerald, Francis Scott Key, IV:585, 729
Fitzgerald, O. P., II:68*n*
Fitzhugh, George, II:165, 345, 346
Fitzsimmons, Robert, IV:371–72
Five Little Peppers (Sidney), V:126
Five-cent magazines, IV:4, 6, 47–51, 88–89, 93, 107, 115, 117, 428–31
Five Year Plan, V:213
Flag of Our Union, I:508*n,* 808; II:10, 35, 409, 411
Flagg, James Montgomery, II:483; III: 554; IV:151, 456, 501, 502, 565, 584; V:84, 134, 255
Flagg, Willard Cutting, III:99*n*
Flagg, Wilson, II:243
Flammarion, Camille, II:270
Flanders, Mrs. C. W., II:270
Flandrau, Charles Macomb, II:262*n*
Flandrau, Grace, IV:729
Flash, II:186
Flashner, Amy, IV:440
Fleay, F. G., III:237*n*
Fleeson, Doris, IV:771
Fleet, Samuel, I:442*n*
Fleming, Maybury, IV:719
Fleming, Thomas, IV:86
Flemington, N.J., IV:138
Fletcher, Jefferson Butler, IV:128
Fletcher, John Gould, IV:436, 441, 739; V:96, 98, 113, 116, 230, 336, 338
Fletcher, William Isaac, III:518, 549
Flinders-Petrie, William Matthew, II:402
Flint, Mich., IV:54, 265, 345
Flint, F. Cudworth, IV:739
Flint, F. S., V:230
Flint, Timothy, I:409, 607
as editor, I:559–61, 606*n,* 638
quoted, I:146, 332, 419–20, 432, 478, 514–15
Floerscheim, Otto, III:196; IV:252
Flohri, E., III:554
Flood, Theodore L., III:544–46; IV:264
Floral Life, IV:342
Floral Park, N.Y., IV:342

Florance, Howard, IV:663
Florence, Mass., IV:363
Florence, Thomas B., II:28*n*
Florence Crittenton Magazine, IV:200
Florida Agriculturist, III:155
Florida Baptist, III:73*n*
Florida Baptist Witness, III:73*n;* IV:292*n*
Florida Christian Advocate, IV:291
Florida Dispatch, III:155
Florida Magazine, IV:92
Florida School Journal, IV:270*n*
Florists' Exchange, IV:342*n*
Florists' Review, IV:342*n*
Flour and Feed, IV:189*n*
Flour Trade News, IV:189*n*
Flower, Benjamin Orange, IV:35, 51–52, 201, 204, 256, 276, 304, 353, 376, 401–16
Flower, Elliott C., III:268
Flower, Richard G., IV:402
Flower, Sydney, IV:284
Flower Garden, III:161
Flower illustrations, I:521–22, 545, 745, 771; IV:627
Flower magazines, III:161–62; IV:342
Floy, James, II:31*n*
Floyd, J. G., II:49*n*
Fly Leaf, IV:389, 646
Flynn, John Thomas, IV:470; V:25, 214
Flynn, Lucinda, IV:556*n*
Flynn, Maurice D., IV:83–84
Foard, J. MacDonough, II:117
Foederal American Monthly, I:606*n*, 613–14
Foerster, Friedrich Wilhelm, III:355
Foerster, Norman, III:349; IV:441, 730, 737, 738
Folding plates, II:192
Folio, III:197*n*
Folk, V:26*n*
Folk, Joseph Wingate, IV:100, 598–99
Folk-Lorist, IV:128
Folks, Homer, IV:742, 744
Folsom, Charles, I:129, 333, 615–17; II:234
Folsom, George, II:175*n*
Folwell, Arthur Hamilton, III:520*n*, 531
Fonetic Propagandist, II:212
Fonetic Techer, III:312
Food, Drug and Cosmetics Act of 1938, V:139–40
Food adulteration, IV:460; V:137–38
Food advertising, IV:23, 25–27, 29
Food magazines, III:134–35; IV:185, 186*n*, 363–64
Foolish Book, IV:386
Foord, John, II:469*n*, 484; IV:60
Football, III:222; IV:374–76, 478, 634, 636
Foote, A. E., III:109*n*
Foote, Allen Ripley, IV:181
Foote, Henry Wilder, III:506*n*, 507
Foote, John P., I:207
Foote, John Taintor, IV:695
Foote, Mary Hallock, III:465*n*, 504
Foraker, Joseph Benson, IV:494, 514, 777
Forbes, A. Holland, IV:323
Forbes, Archibald, III:250
Forbes, Charles Spooner, IV:82
Forbes, Edwin, III:187, 420
Forbes, Leonard, IV:108
Forbes-Roberson, Johnston, IV:256–57
Force, Peter, II:175*n*
Forcey, Charles B., V:196, 202
Ford, Corey, IV:472, 566, 709
Ford, Daniel Sharp, II:262*n*, 266–72; IV:273
Ford, Edward Lloyd, III:425–26
Ford, Ford Madox, V:20, 173–74
Ford, Henry, IV:605
Ford, Isaac Nelson, II:262*n*
Ford, J. B., & Company, III:422–26
Ford, James Lauren, III:474–75, 528; IV:37, 66, 117*n*, 256, 383, 612; V:147
Ford, Leslie, *see* Brown, Zenith J.
Ford, Patrick, IV:298
Ford, Paul Leicester, III:400, 472, 517*n*, 519; IV:141, 435, 684, 742n
Ford, Samuel Howard, II:63
Ford, Sewell, III:512; IV:46*n*, 429; V:248
Ford, Worthington C., III:292; IV:225
Ford's Christian Repository, II:63
Foreign affairs, *see* International affairs
Foreign-language publications, I:730; III:521; IV:175, 231
Foreign literature, *see* Authors, European; *and specific countries*
Foreign Missionary, II:63
Foreign Missionary Journal, II:64*n*
Forest, Forge, and Farm, III:210*n*
Forest and Stream, III:210
Forester, IV:343*n*
Forester, Cecil Scott, IV:422, 476, 503, 713
"Forester, Frank," *see* Herbert, Henry William
Forestry and Irrigation, IV:343*n*
Forestry periodicals, IV:342–43
Forestry Quarterly, IV:34*n*
Form, IV:85

Forman, Allan, IV:230, 243
Forman, Ezekiel, I:122
Forman, Justus Miles, IV:754; V:73, 249
Format and size
of early magazines (1741–94), I:35–36, 104
attractiveness, I:99
first magazines, I:72, 75, 77, 79, 81
newspaper format, I:92–93
of nationalist era magazines (1794–1825)
agricultural magazines, I:318
attractiveness, I:126, 321
general magazines, I:238, 247, 249; II:221
literary magazines, I:283, 296, 321, 332
political magazines, I:270
of expansionist era magazines (1825–50)
abolitionist magazines, II:278
attractiveness, I:343
business magazines, II:339
comic periodicals, I:782
general magazines, I:676; IV:674, 676
juvenile magazines, II:265–66
literary magazines, I:736, 769; IV:674, 676
"mammoth" papers, I:359–60
police gazettes, II:325
women's magazines, II:308
of Civil War era magazines (1850–65), II:242, 368
agricultural magazines, II:433
comic magazines, II:184, 521
family magazines, II:471
illustrated magazines, II:409
literary magazines, II:384, 406, 420
scientific periodicals, III:319
weeklies, II:33, 35, 36*n*, 45
of post-Civil War magazines (1865–85), II:270
advertising, III:12
comic magazines, III:553
current events magazines, III:333
family magazines, III:423
fashion magazines, III:482
general magazines, III:358, 467, 511, 557
humor magazines, III:441
illustrated magazines, III:327
juvenile magazines, III:501
literary magazines, II:398; III: 319, 321, 377–78, 454, 539–40
military magazines, III:533*n*
religious magazines, II:375
women's magazine, III:388–89
women's rights magazines, III:391
of Gilded Age magazines (1885–1905)
amateur periodicals, IV:451
booksellers' periodicals, IV:433
charity magazines, IV:741
digest periodicals, IV:570, 574
family magazines, IV:484; V:126, 155
general periodicals, IV:453, 490, 597, 608, 619, 680, 717; V:286–87
geographic magazines, IV:621
illustrated periodicals, IV:453
juvenile periodicals, IV:764
literary magazines, IV:424–25, 734
medical journals, IV:527
news periodicals, IV:649–50
outdoor magazines, IV:634
satiric periodicals, IV:667, 669
women's periodicals, IV:537, 543, 550, 582, 765, 771; V:126
of modern magazines (1905–)
art magazine, V:168
booksellers' magazines, V:62
charity periodicals, IV:749
current events magazines, V:58, 200, 209, 297
gardening magazines, IV:37
general periodicals, IV:605, 695, 698–99, 700, 710; V:4, 20, 30, 97–98, 270–71, 291
home magazines, V:37, 159
illustrated periodicals, IV:475
literary magazines, III:409, 542; IV:502; V:117–18, 123, 168, 185
poetry magazines, V:104, 228, 243
publishers' magazines, V:62
review periodicals, IV:63
women's magazines, IV:554, 584–85
Formulas, literary, IV:703–4
Fornaro, C. D., IV:66
Forney, John Weiss, III:41
Forney, Mathias N., II:297*n*, 299; IV:333, 335
Forney's Progress, III:41, 281
Forney's Sunday Chronicle, IV:69*n*
Forrest, Edwin, I:428; II:199, 353; III:204
"Forrester, Fanny," *see* Chubbuck, Emily
Forrester, Francis, I:493
Forrester's Boys and Girls, II:100
Forrester's Boys' and Girls' Companion, I:493
Forrester's Playmate, II:100

Forshey, Calib Goldsmith, I:469; II:345
Forstall, E. J., II:340
Forsyth, Ga., II:85
Forsyth, John, I:533, 534*n*
Forsythe, Davis H., I:562*n*, 565
Fort Atkinson, Wis., IV:344
Fort Scott, Kan., III:141*n*
Fort Wayne Journal of the Medical Sciences, III:141*n*
Fort Worth, Texas, III:141*n*; IV:72
Fortieth Street Station Leisure Hours, IV:88
Fortnightly Index, IV:55*n*
Fortnightly Journal of Information and Discussion, II:367*n*
Fortnightly Review, IV:228
Fortune, V:308, 322
Fortune, Timothy Thomas, IV:214
Fortune, William, IV:322*n*
Forum, II:512; III:317, 479; IV:3, 10, 13, 21, 35, 51, 207, 216, 403, 773; V:19, 332
  sketch of, IV:511–13
Forum and Century, V:57
Forward, III:180; IV:274
Fosdick, Charles Austin ("Harry Castlemon"), III:175*n*; IV:274, 420
Fosdick, Harry Emerson, II:404; IV:550; V:121
Fosdick, William Whiteman, II:535
Foss, Sam Walter, IV:80, 390*n*
Foster, Alan, IV:475
Foster, Charles James, III:215*n*
Foster, Francis A., II:176*n*
Foster, Frank H., I:739*n*
Foster, Frank Pierce, III:140; IV:313
Foster, Freeling, IV:472
Foster, George Burman, V:168
Foster, George G., I:425, 426, 780–83; II:181, 186; III:28*n*
Foster, John Watson, IV:625
Foster, Judith Ellen Horton, IV:355
Foster, Paul P., II:262*n*, 272
Foster, Stephen, II:278
Foster, Stephen Collins, II:196
Foster, Theodore A., I:678*n*, 68–83
Fouillée, Alfred, IV:279
Foundry, IV:183*n*
Fountain-pen advertising, IV:32
400, The, IV:224
Four O'Clock, IV:389
Fourier, François Marie Charles, II:207
Fourierism, I:366; II:48
  magazines based on, I:763–65; II:207
  satires on, I:781
  slavery controversy and, I:458
  working class and, I:470
Fournier, Henry, IV:326
Fourth Estate, V:62–66
Four-Track News, IV:224
Fowle, William Bentley, I:143, 491
Fowler, C. H., II:66*n*
Fowler, J. A., II:94*n*
Fowler, Lorenzo Niles, I:441, 447
Fowler, Orson Squire, I:441, 447
Fox, Charles James, II:325*n*, 336
Fox, Dorus M., III:82
Fox, Ed (Moduc), IV:752
Fox, John, Jr., II:483; III:465; IV:93, 723
Fox, Richard Kyle, I:481*n*; II:325*n*, 328–36; III:44, 218
Fox, Thomas Bailey, I:284*n*, 285*n*, 289–90
Fox's Illustrated Week's Doings, III:44
Foxcroft, Frank, I:747*n*, 749
Fra, IV:648
France, I:103*n*
  American interest in, III:279–80; IV:230, 397
  attacks on, I:47, 81, 158–59, 190–91
  Commune of 1871 in, IV:718
  feeling against, I:47, 81, 103, 158–59
  literature of, *see* French literature
  Napoleonic politics, I:129, 271–72
  political reports on, I:129, 271–72
  revolution of 1830 in, I:339
  socialist ideas from, I:471
  visitors from, IV:230
France: A Monthly Magazine, IV:231*n*
France, Anatole, III:355, 543; IV:490; V:117, 119, 122
Francis, Frederick, IV:567
Francis, Susan M., II:493*n*
Franck, Harry Alverson, III:479
"Franco, Harry," *see* Briggs, Charles Frederick
Franco-Prussian War, II:477; III:275, 279–80
Frank, Glenn, III:457*n*, 478
Frank, James Marshall, V:100, 102–4, 107, 109–11
Frank, Stanley, IV:713
Frank, Tenney, III:535*n*, 538
Frank, Waldo, III:543; IV:730; V:95, 210
Frank Leslie's Boys of America, II:100
Frank Leslie's Boys' and Girls' Weekly, III:174
Frank Leslie's Budget, III:39*n*
Frank Leslie's Budget of Fun, II:184, 455; III:267
Frank Leslie's Budget of Wit, II:184*n*
Frank Leslie's Chatterbox, III:175
Frank Leslie's Chimney Corner, III:42
Frank Leslie's Christmas Book, III:175*n*

Frank Leslie's Fact and Fiction for the Chimney Corner, III:42
Frank Leslie's Gazette of Fashion, see Frank Leslie's Ladies' Gazette of Fashion
Frank Leslie's Illustrated Newspaper, see: Leslie's Weekly
Frank Leslie's Illustrated Weekly, III:218
Frank Leslie's Ladies' Gazette, III:97
Frank Leslie's Ladies' Gazette of Fashion, II:58, 192, 453
sketch of, II:437–39
Frank Leslie's Ladies' Journal, II:441; III:98
Frank Leslie's Lady's Magazine, II:47, 58, 439*n*, 440–441; III:98
Frank Leslie's Magazine, V:73*n*
Frank Leslie's Monthly, II:149, 439*n*, 440, 513
Frank Leslie's New Family Magazine, II:439, 455
Frank Leslie's New Monthly, III:36*n*
Frank Leslie's New York Journal of Romance, General Literature, Science and Art, II:31, 453
Frank Leslie's Pleasant Hours, III:36*n*, 39*n*
Frank Leslie's Popular Monthly, II:441
See also American Magazine
Frank Leslie's Sunday Magazine, III:83
Frank Leslie's Ten-Cent Monthly, III:36*n*; IV:3*n*
Frank Reade Library, IV:119
Frankel, Lee K., IV:744
Frankfort, Ky., III:144*n*
Frankfurter, Felix, II:514; IV:749; V:200, 204, 347
Franking privileges, I:17
See also Mails; Postal regulations
Franklin, Benjamin, I:17, 58, 71, 81 186; IV:682–85; V:343
as contributor, I:40, 49, 102, 103
as editor, I:24, 73–77
Franklin, Edgar, IV:695
Franklin, Fabian, II:367*n*, 379; III:347, 349; IV:73*n*
Franklin, Jay, IV:522
Franklin Journal, I:556*n*, 557
Franks, L. P., I:171
Frantz, Harry W., V:97
Fraser, James K., IV:26
Fraser, John, III:233
Fraser, William Lewis, III:46
Fraternal Friend, IV:351*n*
Fraternal journals, III:314–15; IV:221–22
Fraternal Monitor, IV:351*n*
Fraternal societies, *see* Secret societies
Frazer, John Fries, I:556*n*, 558
Frazier, James H., IV:89
Frazier, Julius Leroy, III:132*n*
Freak, IV:390
Frederic, Harold, IV:490, 685, 719, 720
Frederick, Esther Paulus, V:179*n*, 180, 185*n*, 186, 188
Frederick, John T., V:172, 179*n*, 180–90, 231*n*, 235*n*
Frederick Douglass' Paper, II:133, 135, 140, 141
Fredericks, Alfred, II:471
"Fredonia," I:150–51, 464
Free Baptist, III:73*n*
Free Christian Commonwealth, I:137
Free Church Circular, II:207*n*
Free love, III:83*n*, 301, 445–52
Free Man, IV:285*n*
Free Methodist, III:71
Free Press, II:275; IV:90
Free Religious Association, III:78
Free Russia, IV:232
Free schools, *see* Public schools
Free silver issue, II:255; IV:160–63, 411
Free silver periodicals, IV:162–63
Free Soil party, II:134–35, 292, 369
Free-Soiler, III:294; IV:179
Free Thought Magazine, IV:277
Free-Trade Broadside, IV:166*n*
Free trade, I:722
Free Universal Magazine, 1:31*n*, 32, 489
Freedman's Friend, III:283
Freedmen, I:774; II:131, 245, 347; III:283, 333–34, 341
Freedmen's Aid Association, III:333
Freedmen's Record, III:283
Freedom and periodical literature, I:1
Freeman (Whitman's journal), II:168*n*
Freeman, The, V:202–3, 269
sketch of, V:88–99
Freeman Book, The, V:95
Freeman, Douglas Southhall, IV:727
Freeman, Edward Augustus, I:535; II:272; III:35*n*, 250, 546
Freeman, J. B., I:165
Freeman, James, I:28
Freeman, Mary Eleanor Wilkins, *see* Wilkins, Mary Eleanor
Freeman's Journal, II:77; IV:297–98
Freemason periodicals, *see* Masonic journals
Freemason's Monthly Magazine, II:215; III:314
Freene, F. V., IV:719
Freeport, Ill., IV:345*n*

Free-soilers, *see* Free Soil party; *Free-Soiler*
Freeston, Charles Lincoln, IV:726
Freethinkers, II:78, 252, 534–36; III:88–89
Freeville, N.Y., IV:275
Freewill Baptist Quarterly, II:64, 130
Freiberger, Edward, IV:100
Freight, IV:333*n*
Frelinghuysen, Theodore, I:624
French, Alice ("Octave Thanet"), II:311, 398*n*, 506*n*; III:51*n*, 397, 398, 483; IV:46*n*, 96, 482, 490, 685, 720–21, 767; V:287
French, Alvah P., III:260*n*
French, George, V:79
French, James S., I:637
French literature
  influence of, I:191, 232, 260, 404, 415; III:254
  nationalist-era magazines and (1794–1825), I:190–91, 232, 260, 282, 304
    romantic movement, I:339
  Civil War era magazines and (1850–65), II:162–64, 172, 240, 243, 450, 490
  after 1865, III:254, 357, 375, 418, 421, 460; IV:134–35; V:119
French periodicals, IV:230–31
Freneau, Philip, I:40, 45, 121, 176–77
Frentz, Edward Williston, II:262*n*
Freudeneau, William, IV:100
Freund, Harry E., III:197
Freund, John C., III:196*n*, 197; IV:214, 251–52
Freund, Mrs. John C., III:197
Freund's Music and Drama, III:197, 199
Freund's Musical Weekly, IV:251
Freund's Weekly, III:197
Frey, Albert R., III:235*n*
Friend, I:562–65; II:74, 140; IV:296
Friend of Peace, I:285
Friend of Virtue, II:211*n*
Friendly Club, I:114–15, 194, 215, 218
Friend's Intelligencer, II:74; IV:296
Friend's Review, I:773–74; II:74, 140
Friends' Missionary Advocate, IV:238*n*, 305
Friendship Community, III:300
Frierson, William, V:100*n*, 108–9, 111
Frobel, B. W., III:45*n*
Frohman, Charles, IV:255, 260
Frontier, significance of, III:49
Frontier, The, IV:104; V:188
Frontier Monthly, IV:104
Frost, A. B., V:118, 341
Frost, Andrew, II:327
Frost, Arthur Burdett, I:592; II:397; III:473, 528, 557; IV:151, 456, 602, 637, 719, 720, 726
Frost, Charles W., I:580*n*
Frost, George Henry, III:113
Frost, Robert, III:479; IV:654; V:121, 201, 228–29, 244, 336, 338
Frost, S. Annie, *see* Shields, Mrs. S. A.
Frothingham, Arthur Lincoln, IV:140
Frothingham, David, I:122*n*
Frothingham, Nathaniel Langdon, I:292, 600, 658; II:542
Frothingham, Octavius Brooks, II:534; III:78, 85, 336
Frothingham, Robert, V:82
Froude, James Anthony, II:252, 253; III:35*n*, 172, 249; IV:490
Fruit, Garden and Home, V:37, 42
Fruit-Growers' Journal, IV:341
Fruit-growers' magazines, IV:341–42
Fruit Trade Journal, IV:342*n*
Fruitman and Gardener, IV:343*n*
Fry, Joseph Reese, I:595*n*, 597
Fuel Magazine, IV:322*n*
Fuerbringer, Otto, V:293*n*, 321
Fuertes, Louis Agassiz, IV:627
Fugitive, V:xiv
  sketch of, V:100–16
Fugitive slave law, II:290, 369
Fulbright, James William, IV:761
Fuller, Andrew S., I:731; III:99*n*
Fuller, H. S., IV:270
Fuller, Harold deWolf, II:367*n*, 379; III:331*n*, 348–49
Fuller, Helen, V:191n, 219, 222
Fuller, Henry Blake, II:482
Fuller, Hiram, I:320*n*, 329–30
Fuller, Horace B., I:714–15
Fuller, Horace W., IV:347*n*
Fuller, Margaret, I:368, 496, 659, 661, 682, 687, 702–09, 760; II:239
Fuller, Melvin Weston, III:540
Fuller, Metta Victoria, *see* Victor, Metta Victoria Fuller
Fuller, R. B., IV:567
Fuller, Richard, I:461
Fuller, Walter Deane, IV:536*n*, 552, 671*n*, 708, 711; V:140
Fuller, Walter G., V:88*n*, 90–91
Fulton, Ky., III:73*n*
Fun Quarterly, IV:386
Funk, Isaac Kauffman, IV:569–73
Funk, Wilfred John, IV:569*n*, 578
Funston, General Frederick, IV:725; V:73
Fuoss, Robert, IV:711, 712

Fur, Fin, and Feather, III:210*n*
Fur Trade Review, III:134
Furlong, Charles Wellington, IV:783
Furness, H. W., III:34*n*
Furness, Horace Howard, IV:121
Furnishing Gazette, III:134
Furniss, Edgar S., V:329*n*
Furniture Buyer and Decorator, III:136; IV:188*n*
Furniture Index, IV:188*n*
Furniture Journal, IV:188*n*
Furniture magazines, III:136; IV:188
Furniture Trade Review, III:136
Furniture Workers' Journal, III:130*n*
Furniture World, IV:188
Furnivall, Frederick James, IV:410
Furr, La Vonne Doden, V:3*n*
Furrier, III:134
Futrelle, Jacques, IV:697
Future, I:366

Gable, D. H., III:169
Gabo, Naum, V:178
Gaboriau, Émile, V:117
Gaelic American, IV:227*n*
Gaffney, Fannie Humphreys, IV:84*n*
Gage, Frances Dana, III:51, 114, 303
Gage, George M., III:168*n*
Gage, Lyman Judson, IV:617
Gage, Matilda Joslyn, III:94
Gaillard, Edwin Samuel, III:140*n*
Gaillard, M. E., III:141*n*
Gaillard's Southern Medicine, III:141*n*
Gailor, Thomas F., IV:735
Gaitskell, Hugh, V:317
Galaxy, II:396, 508, 547; III:17, 18, 20–21, 33, 58, 90, 105, 125, 151, 184, 199, 206, 222, 223–24, 227, 228, 231, 249, 254, 271, 272, 279, 281, 307, 308, 309, 311, 399, 495; V:342–43
  advertising in, III:9–10
  payments to contributors III:13–14
  sketch of, III:361–81
Gale, Zona, III:485, 487, 489; IV:360*n*, 361*n*, 389, 471, 472, 583, 637, 691, 748; V:30, 80, 83, 251
Gallagher, William Davis, I:387, 389, 595*n*, 597, 660, 661, 662, 692–93; II:114
Gallaudet, Thomas Hopkins, I:543
Gallico, Paul, IV:701, 709, 713
Gallison, John, II:224
Galop, III:198
Galsworthy, John, III:489; IV:501, 518, 521, 552, 723–24, 726, 727, 728, 730, 769; V:134, 168, 336–37
Galton, Lawrence, IV:504
Galveston, Tex., II:59
Gambier Observer, II:70*n*
Gambling, III:4
Game Bird, IV:382
Game Fanciers' Journal, III:210*n*
Gameland, IV:381*n*
Gandhi, Mohandas K., IV:748; V:323*n*
Gannett, Ezra Stiles, I:284*n*, 288
Gannett, Frank Ernest, IV:88*n*
Gannett, Henry, III:35*n*; IV:620, 621, 622*n*
Gannett, Lewis Stiles, III:354–55; IV:749*n*
Gannett, William Howard, IV:365*n*
Garden and Forest, IV:342
Garden of the Gods Magazine, IV:104
Garden Ideas, V:47
Garden Magazine, V:73*n*
Garden Street Methodist Church (Bellingham, Wash.), V:6
Gardener's Monthly, II:90; III:161; IV:342
Gardener's Monthly and Horticultural Advertiser, II:90
Gardening, IV:342
Gardening hints, IV:537
Gardening magazines, II:376; III:161–62; IV:34, 324, 341–42; V:36–48
Gardening and Outdoor Living, V:163
Gardette, Charles D., II:551
Gardiner, Maine, II:36*n*
Gardiner, J. B. W., IV:783, 785; V:50
Gardiner, John Sylvester John, I:244, 255
Gardiner, William Howard, II:229, 233, IV:786
Gardner, Charles K., I:130, 313
Gardner, Dorsey, III:319*n*, 323, 425
Gardner, E. C., V:131
Gardner, Erle Stanley, IV:422, 713
Gardner, Helen H., IV:412
Gardner, John W., V:336
Garfield, James Abram, II:463; III:287, 524
Garfield, James Rudolph, IV:549
Garland, Hamlin, II:273, 398, 482; III:485; IV:45, 50, 61, 73*n*, 96, 109, 112, 179, 256, 304, 441, 451, 483, 514, 544, 593, 641, 643, 689, 691, 767; V:80, 342
  in *Arena,* IV:406–9
Garland, James A., IV:79*n*
Garment Buyer and Manufacturer, IV:188*n*
Garment Worker, IV:221*n*
Garner, James W., V:278
Garnett, James Mercer, I:638

Garnett, Porter, IV:388
Garnett, Richard, IV:225, 248
Garno, Benjamin, II:204*n*
Garretson, Carleton G., III:552*n*, 555
Garrett, Edward Peter, IV:459, 696, 707, 709, 711
Garrett, Garet, *see* Garrett, Edward Peter
Garrigues, J. C., II:75
Garrison, J. H., IV:296
Garrison, Theodosia, III:485; IV:38, 120, 737; V:248
Garrison, W. H., IV:64
Garrison, Wendell Phillips, III:232, 331*n*, 332–34, 344, 347–49; IV:60, 75, 398
Garrison, William Lloyd, I:138, 163, 165*n*, 456, 457, 473, 781; II:140, 146, 373; III:94, 332–33
  as editor, II:275–96
Garvan, Francis Patrick, IV:467
Garvey, Andrew J., II:478
Garvice, Charles, IV:134, 366
Gary, Joseph Easton, IV:172, 466, 606
Gas Age, III:131*n*; IV:184
Gas Engine, IV:321
Gas Industry, IV:184*n*
Gas industry periodicals, IV:184
Gas lighting, I:152
Gas Power, IV:188*n*
Gas Record, III:131*n*
Gaskell, Elizabeth Cleghorn, II:471
Gaskell's Literary Review, IV:100
Gatcomb's Musical Gazette, IV:254
Gates, Moody B., IV:605
Gates, Thomas A., IV:283
Gateway, IV:96
Gathman, Henry, IV:184*n*
Gatlin, Dana, IV:604
Gatling, Richard Jordan, II:318
Gaudier-Breska, Henri, V:178
Gavit, John Palmer, IV:743, 747*n*, 748
Gayarré, Charles, II:251, 345
Gayler, Charles, II:183
Gayley, Charles Mills, III:540; V:117*n*, 118
Gazette (Philadelphia), I:608, 705
Gazette du Bon Genre, IV:760
Gazette of the Union, II:215
Gazlay's Pacific Monthly, III:58
Geike, Archibald, IV:225
Gem Library, IV:120*n*
Gem of the Prairie, I:389, 807; II:115
Gem of the West and Soldiers' Friend, III:52*n*
Genealogical Exchange, IV:140*n*
Genealogical journals, III:262; IV:137, 140
Genealogical Quarterly Magazine, IV:140
General Building Contractor, III:130
General and eclectic magazines, *see* Eclectic and general magazines; Family magazines
General Electric, V:328*n*
General Electric Company Review, IV:322
General Federation of Women's Clubs, V:38, 158
General Magazine, I:24, 33, 34–45, 47, 56
  sketch of, I:76–77
General Magazine and Impartial Review, I:791
General Repository and Review, I:124, 180; II:220
  sketch of, I:277–78
General science magazines, III:34*n*, 107–9
General strikes, III:303; V:93
General Woodworkers' Journal, III:130*n*
General Working-Men's League, II:207
Genesee Farmer, I:442–43, 801; II:88*n*, 90*n*, 435–36
Genius of Liberty, II:52
Genius of Temperance, I:473
Genius of Universal Emancipation, I:162–64, 796; II:275
Genius of the West, II:114
Gentleman's Magazine, II:221
  See also: Burton's Gentleman's Magazine
Gentleman's Vade-Mecum, I:427, 803
Gentlemen and Ladies Town and Country Magazine, I:31*n*, 789
Gentlemen and Lady's Town and Country Magazine, I:29, 788
Genung, C. H., III:347
Genung, John Franklin, III:72*n*
Geographical Review, II:415
Geography, I:623, 714
  Geographic periodicals, II:413–15; IV:224–25, 621–32
Geography of magazines
  before 1865, I:31–33, 200–208, 375–90; II:102–30
  after 1865, III:25–62; IV:76–109
Geology
  in magazines, I:266–67, 303, 446, 611, 632; II:78, 228
  geology periodicals, I:266–67; III:112; IV:309

George, Henry, II:251; III:293, 498; IV:110–11, 179, 406; V:88, 93
George, Herbert, IV:103
George, Milton, III:149; IV:176
George, W. L., V:258
George, Walter Lionel, III:390, 489
George P. Rowell & Company's American Newspaper Reporter and Advertiser's Gazette, III:273
George's Weekly, IV:103–04
Georgetown, Colo., III:114
Georgetown (D.C.), I:153
Georgia Analytical Repository, I:205*n*, 792
Georgia Baptist, III:73
Georgia Medical Companion, III:141*n*
Georgia Teacher, IV:270*n*
Gerald, G. B., IV:446–48
Gerard, James Watson, IV:549
Gerhart, Emanuel Vogel, II:380*n*
German Correspondent, I:191–92
German drama in United States, I:168
German-language magazines, III:521; IV:175
German literature
  before 1865, I:191–92, 227, 232, 401–3, 415, 616, 620, 680, 778; II:164–65, 231
  after 1865, III:254–55, 375, 385–87, 417–21, 456; IV:136; V:95–96
  influence of, I:168, 191–92, 227, 232; II:255; III:255
German music in U.S., I:403
Germantown, Pa., IV:296
Germany, I:339
  American interest in, IV:231
  Der Bazar, III:388
  influence on scientific study, III:106
  Kaiser's interview in *Century,* III:476–77
  liberalism in, I:339
  literature of, *see* German literature
  Nazi regime in, *see* Naziism
  romantic movement in, I:339
  woodcuts from, III:411
Gerould, Gordon Hall, IV:728
Gerould, James Thayer, V:54
Gerould, Katherine Fullerton, IV:724, 727; V:20
Gervasi, Frank, IV:476
Gessner, Frank M., IV:184*n*
Gessner, Solomon, I:191
Gettysburg, Pa., II:73
Geyer's Stationer, III:135
Ghourki, IV:390*n*
Gibbon, Perceval, IV:604, 605; V:50
Gibbons, Herbert Adams, III:479
Gibbons, James Cardinal, II:376; III:69*n*; IV:44*n*, 299, 685
Gibbs, George, I:267, 302; IV:689
Gibbs, Hamilton, IV:521
Gibbs, Philip, III:489; IV:498; V:50
Gibbs, Wolcott, I:304
Gibney, Albert J., IV:417
Gibson, Charles Dana, II:400, 483; III:473; IV:19, 90, 151, 456, 484, 496–97, 501, 502, 545, 556*n*, 563–64, 566–67, 591, 602, 720; V:136, 341
Gibson, W. T., III:75
"Gibson girl" illustrations, IV:151, 563–64
Gibson's Monthly Review, III:134*n*
Giddings, Franklin Henry, II:379; IV:180, 182*n*, 192
Giddings, Joshua R., II:302
Gidley, Will S., IV:49*n*
Gifford, John Clayton, IV:342
Gifford, Sandford Robinson, II:188
Gift trade magazines, III:136
Gilbert, E. W., II:62*n*
Gilbert, Grove Karl, IV:622*n*
Gilbert, Grove Sheridan, I:545
Gilbert, John, III:204; IV:256
Gilbert, Morris, V:246*n*, 271
Gilbert, Samuel, I:247–49
Gilbert, Simeon, III:77*n*
Gilbert, Sir William Schwenck, III:195; V:121
Gilder, Jeannette Leonard, II:419*n*, 430; III:234, 548, 551; IV:604, 769
Gilder, Joseph B., II:419*n*, 430; III:234, 548
Gilder, Richard Watson, II:377; III:20, 22, 32*n*, 33*n*, 234, 428, 549; IV:9, 35, 43, 83, 154, 195, 409, 641
  as editor, III:457*n*, 458–63, 470, 472–74, 477
Gildersleeve, Basil Lanneau, I:535; II:488; III:46, 236, 337, 535–38; IV:127–28
Gildersleeve, Mrs. C. H., II:466
Giles, Henry, II:505*n*, 532
Giles, Howard, II:402
Gilhooley's Etchings, III:269*n*
Gillam, Bernard, II:464, 481; III:288, 524, 525–26, 527*n*, 528, 553, 554
Gillam, F. Victor, III:554
Gillen, Daniel F., III:70
Gillett, Alfred S., II:94*n*
Gillette, Edward Hooker, III:157
Gillette, William, IV:257

Gillis, James Martin, III:329*n*
Gilman, Arthur, III:455, 545
Gilman, Caroline, I:412
Gilman, Charles, I:352*n,* 452*n*
Gilman, Charlotte Perkins (Charlotte Perkins Stetson), IV:45*n,* 61, 80, 107, 204
Gilman, Daniel Coit, II:269, 376, 414, 445; III:72*n,* 108, 322, 336, 406, 535; IV:307, 398, 744; V:280
Gilman, Lawrence, II:259
Gilman, Nicholas Paine, III:454*n,* 456; IV:124, 202, 404
Gilman, Samuel, II:227, 233
Gilmore, James Roberts ("Edmund Kirke"), II:33, 171, 540, 542
Gilmore, Thomas J., IV:101
Gilmour, Richard, III:69*n*
Gimber, Stephen H., I:620, 744
Gimbrede, Joseph Napoleon, I:210, 322, 522; II:69
Ginner and Miller, IV:339
Girard, Kan., IV:204–5
Girl covers on magazines, IV:602; V:128, 144, 270
Girlie magazines, *see* Sex magazines
Girls, IV:200
Girls' Companion, IV:275
Girls of Today, II:468; III:179
Gizycky, G. von, IV:279
Glackens, L. M., III:531
Gladden, Washington, II:375; III:39*n,* 427, 470; IV:177, 282, 397
Gladstone, William Ewart, II:252–253, 254, 269, 376; III:88; IV:41, 51, 165, 274, 280
Glasgow, Ellen, IV:769; V:134, 281
Glaspell, Susan Keating, IV:421, 429; V:29
Glass, Montague, IV:498, 566, 616, 693, 695; V:148
Glass industry periodicals, III:127–28; IV:184
Glass and Pottery World, IV:184*n*
Glasson, William Henry, V:273*n,* 278, 283
Glassworker, III:129*n*
Gleanings in Bee Culture, III:161; IV:345
Gleason, Arthur Huntington, III:355; IV:464; V:98
Gleason, Frederick, II:35, 44; IV:79*n*
  as editor, II:409–12
Gleason, Herbert W., IV:283
Gleason's Line-of-Battle Ship, II:45
Gleason's Literary Companion, II:43*n*
Gleason's Monthly Companion, II:411; III:39*n*
Gleason's Pictorial Drawing-Room Companion, II:10, 14, 18, 43, 44, 193, 196, 198, 358, 453
  sketch of, II:409–12
Glennie, Mich., V:179*n*
Glenville, Ohio, IV:335
Glicksburg, Charles I., IV:738; V:284
Globe (New York), IV:62
Globe Quarterly Review, IV:72
Globe Trotter, IV:224
Glover, Lyman Beecher, III:101
Glover, Thaddeus, II:180*n*
Glovers' Journal, III:134*n*
Glyn, Eleanor, IV:497, 501
"Glyndon, Howard," *see* Searing, Laura Catherine Redding
Godbe, William S., III:57*n*
Goddard, Anson N., IV:365*n*
Goddard, William, I:17*n*
Godden, Rumer, IV:554
Godey, Louis Antoine, I:350–51, 354, 496, 580–94; II:306; III:24; IV:675, 677
Godey's Lady's Book, I:350–51, 503, 509–10, 514, 515–16, 521–23; II:11, 14, 18, 21, 56, 57, 102, 192, 301, 309; III:98, 186, 224, 309
  advertising rate, III:11
  circulation of, III:6
  founding of, I:350–51
  sketch of, I:580–94
Godey's Magazine, IV:5, 87, 359, 361
Godfrey, Thomas, Jr., I:45, 81
Godkin, Edwin Lawrence, I:535; II:86*n,* 244, 249, 270, 512; III:19, 22, 40, 64–65 527; IV:60, 198, 201, 570
  as editor, III:331–32, 334–35, 338–41, 344–46
Godman, John D., I:566–67
Godwin, Frank, IV:471
Godwin, Harold, IV:506*n,* 507
Godwin, J. S., III:528
Godwin, Parke, I:764; II:140, 407, 419*n,* 420, 430, 495, 500; III:281
  as editor, II:422–23
Goebel, Julius, IV:128
Goebel, William, IV:206*n*
Goethals, George Washington, IV:626, 725
Goethe, Johann Wolfgang von, I:191, 192, 401–2, 616; II:164, 165, 231; III:255, 386

Goetz, Philip Becker, IV:645
Gogol, Nikolai Vasilievitch, IV:135; V:95
Gold rush
  California, I:464, 753
  Klondike, IV:1, 108–9, 322
Goldberg, Isaac, V:7
Golden Age, III:41, 394, 448
Golden Argosy, III:178; IV:114, 273, 417–20
Golden Book Magazine, sketch of, V:117–24
Golden Days, IV:87, 273
Golden Days for Boys and Girls, III:178
Golden Era, II:117; III:56; IV:105–6
Golden Hours, III:55; IV:118, 273–74
Golden Library, IV:120*n*
Golden Moments, IV:365
Golden Rule, III:180; IV:275
Golden Rule and Odd Fellows' Family Companion, II:215
Golden Weekly, IV:274
Goldsmith, J. C., II:452*n*
Goldthwaite, William M., IV:391
Goldthwaite's Geographical Magazine, IV:225
Goldwater, Barry, V:315
Golf, IV:376
Golfer, IV:376
Golfer's Magazine, IV:376
Golfing, IV:376
Golfing magazines, IV:376
Golsan, H. Logan, IV:88*n*
Gompers, Samuel, III:350; IV:183, 219
Gontier, A. J., III:270*n*
Good Cheer, III:152*n*; IV:390*n*
Good Company, III:39*n*
Good Government, III:295*n*; IV:211
Good Health, III:139
Good Housekeeping, IV:360, 393; V:xiv, 44, 163
  sketch of, V:125–43
  Institute, V:137–39
  Seal of Approval, V:137–42
Good Literature, III:551; IV:366
Good News (juvenile), IV:274
Good News (New Thought periodical), IV:285*n*
Good Roads, IV:379–80
Good Times, III:177
Good Woman, A (Bromfield), V:306
Good Words, II:509*n*; III:278
Good Work, I:252
Goodale, George Lincoln, III:337
Goodall's Farmer, III:159
Goodell, William, II:141
Goodman, Charles, I:208, 210
Goodman, John D., I:207
Goodman, Joseph, IV:379
Goodman, Jules Eckert, IV:506*n*, 508
Goodrich, Charles A., I:347; II:58
Goodrich, F. E., IV:60
Goodrich, Samuel Griswold ("Peter Parley"), I:492, 602, 622–23, 713–14
Goodsell, B. G., II:35
Goodspeed, Edgar Johnson, III:537
Goodwin, H. M., II:315
Goodwin, William H., III:159
Goodwin's Weekly, IV:104
Goose-Quill, IV:390
Gordon, Armistead C., IV:729
Gordon, Arthur, IV:480*n*
Gordon, Caroline, IV:739
Gordon, Elizabeth, V:154*n*, 163, 165*n*
Gordon, J. G., I:522
Gordon, Margaret, IV:142
Gore, Mrs. Catherine, I:359
Gorky, Maxim, V:30, 97
Gorman, Mrs. Henrie Clay Ligon, IV:72
Gorman, Herman, III:479
Gorrel, Frank, V:223
Gorton, David A., II:530*n*, 532–533; III:31
Goshen, Ind., IV:364*n*
Gospel Advocate, III:80
Gospel Advocate and Magazine, II:72
Gospel Age, IV:291
Gospel Banner, III:79; IV:296
Gospel Herald, III:80
Gospel Messenger (Baptist), III:73
Gospel Messenger (Episcopal), II:70*n*
Gospel Messenger (United Brethren), III:81
Gospel Trumpet, III:81
Goss, Joe, II:331
Gosse, Edmund William, I:535; II:255, 377; IV:124, 410, 433, 451, 490, 513
Gossip, II:462; IV:567, 609
Gotham Monthly Magazine, IV:139
Gottfried, Manfred, V:293*n*, 302–3
Gottschalk, Laura Riding, V:100*n*, 110, 113
Gottschalk, Louis Moreau, II:195
Gotwald, F. G., II:73*n*
Goudge, Elizabeth, IV:554
Goudy, Frederic William, IV:451
Gough, John Bartholomew, III:171, 172
Gould, Beatrice Blackmar, IV:536*n*, 552–55
Gould, Benjamin Apthorpe, II:79*n*
Gould, Bruce, IV:536*n*, 552–55, 708
Gould, Curtis, IV:185

Gould, Edward Sherman, I:398, 405–6, 408, 624
Gould, Hannah Flagg, II:303
as contributor, I:350, 499, 585, 597, 601, 623, 770
evaluation of, 408, 412, 413
Gould, Jay, III:4, 273, 293, 296, 440, 525, 527
Gould, S. C., III:259
Gourmont, Rémy de, III:543
Governmental magazines, IV:90
Grade Teacher, IV:269*n*
Grady, Henry Woodfin, IV:91; V:105
Graetz, F., III:525, 526, 527*n*, 528
Graeve, Oscar, III:481*n*, 489; V:72*n*
Grafton, Grace, I:620
Grafton, Mass., IV:304
Grafton, N.D., IV:270*n*
Graham, Albert W., I:322, 675
Graham, Billy, V:26
Graham, George Edward, II:464
Graham, George Rex, I:343–44, 496, 544–55; II:30, 37, 306; IV:671*n*, 676–78
buys *Gentleman's,* I:673*n*, 676
Graham, Stephen, IV:465
Graham, Sylvester, I:478–79
Graham Journal of Health and Longevity, I:479, 804
Graham's American Monthly Magazine, I:544*n*
Graham's Illustrated Magazine, I:544*n*
Graham's Lady's and Gentleman's Magazine, I:544*n*
Graham's Magazine, I:344, 503, 506–09, 512, 521; II:5, 21, 24, 30, 132, 306, 351, 396, 426, 495*n*, 541; IV:677
sketch of, I:544–55
Graham's Monthly Magazine, III:15
Grain Cleaner, III:128
Grain Dealers' Journal, IV:189*n*
Grain and Feed Journals Consolidated, IV:189*n*
Grain feed trade magazines, III:128; IV:189
Grain and Provision Review, III:135
Gram, Hans, I:110
Grand, Sarah, II:255; IV:51, 255
Grand Army Gazette, III:132
Grand Man, Notes and Queries, III:259*n*
Grand Rapids, Mich., III:109*n*, 133, 310; IV:186*n*, 188*n*
Grand Rapids Furniture Record, IV:188*n*
Grandgent, Charles Hall, III:236*n*
Grange movement, III:148–50
Granger, Alfred, V:158
Granger, James, IV:12
Granite, Marble and Bronze, IV:325*n*
Granite Monthly, III:36, 259; IV:82
Grant, E. P., I:764
Grant, Gordon, III:531
Grant, James, III:327
Grant, Jesse R., II:361
Grant, Percy Stickney, IV:195
Grant, Robert, IV:60, 390*n*, 489, 560, 721, 722, 767
Grant, Ulysses Simpson, II:253, 476, 480, 532, 548; III:214, 281, 285–86, 340, 341–42, 441, 524, 527, 557, 559; IV:44*n*; V:126
as author, III:16, 469
Grant, Ulysses Simpson, Jr., IV:481
Graphic (Chicago), IV:99–100
Graphic (London), III:279
Graphic (Los Angeles), IV:107
Graphic (New York), 191
Grasty, Charles H., V:54
Grattan, Clinton Hartley, IV:738; V:12
Grattan, Thomas Coley, I:546*n*
Graves, C. D., IV:58*n*
Graves, George S., IV:337*n*
Graves, J. R., II:63, 65
Graves, John Temple, IV:496
Graves, Ralph A., IV:632
Graves, Robert, V:113
Graves, William E., II:35*n*
Gray, Asa, I:304, 732; II:78, 243; III:337, 456; IV:398
"Gray, Barry," *see* Coffin, Robert Barry
Gray, David, IV:695
Gray, F. T., II:218*n*, 231
Gray, Francis C., II:224, 227, 228, 229, 234
Gray, George L., I:245
Gray, John Chipman, I:172
Gray, Mrs. M. A. Browne, II:309
Gray, William C., III:74*n*; IV:293
Gray Goose, IV:117
Gray-Parker, C., IV:561, 751–52
Graydon, William Murray, IV:610
Grayson, A. J., II:118
Grayson, William J., I:726; II:490, 491
Great Awakening (1734–c. 1765), I:25
Great Britain
attacks, I:188–90, 269, 313
Dennie's defence of, I:228–30
paper war, I:188–90, 269, 313, 394–97; II:222
Civil War era, II:126–28
magazines on (1865–1905), III:277–79; IV:225–30
American magazines in, II:130, 322, 399; IV:229

Great Britain—*Continued*
antislavery activities of, II:282, 284, 289
lecturers from, IV:226
literature of, *see* English authors; English literature
magazines of, *see* British magazines
Oregon Territory issue and, I:463
Reform Bill of 1832 in, I:339
romantic movement in, I:339
socialist ideas from, I:471
Great Catherine (George Bernard Shaw), V:85
Great Divide, IV:103
Great Falls, Mont., III:158
Great Game of Politics (Kent), V:10
Great Northern Bulletin, IV:333*n*
Great Pictures, IV:153
Great Republic Monthly, II:450
Great Round World, IV:64
Great West, II:114*n*
"Great Western," arrival of, I:306
Greatorex, Eliza, III:411
Greatorex, Elizabeth Eleanor, I:593
Greece, independence of, I:339
Greeley, Horace, I:471, 472, 480, 761–62, 781; II:39, 205, 208, 361, 373, 386*n,* 406, 420, 426, 480, 523, 542; III:172, 340, 441
as contributor, I:587*n,* 620, 697, 753, 764
as editor, I:358–59
Greely, Adolphus Washington, IV:49*n,* 593, 620, 621, 685
Green, Anna Katherine, IV:114*n*
Green, Annie Douglas, II:505*n*
Green, Ashbel, I:136, 315–16
Green, Elizabeth Shippen, II:402
Green, Joseph, I:103
Green, William Henry, I:533, 534*n*
Green Bag, IV:347
Green Book, V:254
Green Springs, Ohio, III:146*n*
Greenaway, Kate, IV:544
Greenback periodicals, III:301
Greene, Anna Katharine, III:400
Greene, Asa, I:425
Greene, Charles Samuel, III:408
Greene, Colonel, V:79
Greene, George Washington, II:238, 420
Greene, Hiram Moe, IV:367*n*
Greene, William Batchelder, II:95*n*
Greenfield, Ind., III:169
Greenfield, Mass., III:152; IV:366
Greenhow, Robert, I:632
Greenleaf, Joseph, I:26, 83*n,* 85–86
Greenleaf, Oliver C., I:247*n*
Greenough, B. F., I:523
Greenough, J. J., I:523
Greenough, James Bradstreet, II:99
Greenough, Richard, II:189
Greenough, William, I:108*n,* 111
Greensburg, Ind., IV:204
Greenslet, Ferris, II:493*n,* 513
Greenville, Tenn., I:163; III:73*n*
Greenwood, Francis William Pitt, I:204*n,* 284*n,* 286–87; II:232–33
"Greenwood, Grace," *see* Lippincott, Sara Janc Clarke
Gréfe, Will, IV:49*n*
Gregg, Thomas, III:55
Gregg Writer, IV:352
Gregg's Dollar Monthly and Old Settlers' Memorial, III:55
Gregory, Alyse, III:543
Gregory, Horace, V:238, 242
Gregory, Isaac M., III:552*n,* 553
Gregory, Jackson, IV:607
Gregory, Lady Augusta, V:121, 173
Greusel, Joseph, IV:96*n*
Grey, Zane, II:435; IV:421, 471, 550, 584, 605; V:290
Gribayédoff, Valerian, IV:58*n*
Gridley, Jeremy, I:25, 78, 78*n*
Grierson's Underwriter's Weekly Circular, II:94*n*
Griffin, Martin Ignatius Joseph, III:261
Griffin's Journal, III:261
Griffith, Ivor, I:539*n*
Griffith, R. Egglesfield, I:539*n*
Griffith, William, IV:510, 580*n,* 582
Griggs, Robert Fiske, IV:629
Grigorieff, Boris, IV:747
Grimké, Thomas Smith, I:205, 543, 575
Grimm, Baron F. M. von, II:222
Grinnell, Charles Edward, III:144
Grinnell, Iowa, III:77*n*
Gris, Juan, V:178
Grissom, Arthur, IV:46, 97–98, 389; V:246*n,* 248–49
Grisson, Arthur C., II:463
Griswold, A. Miner, III:266, 270*n*
Griswold, Rufus Wilmot, I:761–62, 767; II:31, 44, 163, 166, 406*n,* 407; IV:677
as contributor, I:505, 644, 771
as editor, I:358, 359, 512, 544*n,* 550–52
Grit, IV:18, 68–69
Grocer (Cincinnati), III:135*n*
Grocer (Philadelphia), III:135*n*
Grocer and Canner, III:134
Grocer and General Merchant, IV:187
Grocer's Criterion, III:135*n;* IV:187
Grocer's Journal, III:135*n*

Grocer's Magazine, IV:187*n*
Grocers' magazines, III:134–35; IV:187
Grocers' Price Current, III:135*n*
Grocers' Review, IV:187*n*
Grocery World, IV:187*n*
Grönlund, Laurence, IV:205
Gropper, William, III:555; IV:438; V:267
Gross, Milt, III:555; IV:568
Grosvenor, Cyrus P., II:65
Grosvenor, Edwin Augustus, IV:623, 629
Grosvenor, Edwin Prescott, IV:623
Grosvenor, Elsie Graham Bell, IV:623, 630, 632
Grosvenor, Gilbert Hovey, IV:224, 620*n*, 622*n*, 623–32
Grosvenor, Gilbert Melville, IV:628
Grosvenor, Melville Bell, IV:620*n*, 628, 632
Grosz, George, V:178
Growoll, Adolphus, III:494
Gruening, Ernest, III:354–55; IV:520
Grunwald, Charles, III:484
Gryzanowski, E., III:337
Guardian Angel, III:70
Guenther, Otto, IV:349
Guérin, Jules, III:475, 484
Guernsey, Alfred Hudson, II:383*n*, 392, 396; III:32, 511
Guernsey, Clara F., I:592; IV:480
Guernsey County Teacher, III:169
Guest, Edgar Albert, IV:498; V:271
Guild, Curtis, Jr., IV:560
Guild, Frank S., IV:361
Guild socialism, V:93
Guiney, Louise Imogen, III:330, 508; IV:73*n*, 297
Guiterman, Arthur, III:531; IV:66, 713
Gulf Messenger, IV:357*n*
Gulick, Luther H., IV:781
Gulliver, John P., II:374; IV:395
Gummere, Francis Barton, III:236*n*, 537
Gun, Robert, II:179
Gundell, Glenn, IV:712
Gunn, Archie, IV:47*n*, 84; V:270
Gunn, Thom, V:243
Gunn, Thomas Butler, I:426; II:180
Gunsaulus, Frank Wakeley, I:741; IV:389
Gunter, Archibald Clavering, IV:131, 141
Gunther, John, IV:476, 554
Gunton, George, IV:171*n*
Gunton's Magazine, IV:171
Gurney, Ephraim W., II:220*n*, 246; III:31, 336
Gurney, Joseph John, I:563
Guthrie, William Norman, IV:735
Guyer's Stationer, IV:188*n*
Gwynn, William, I:294

H. D., *see* Doolittle, Hilda
"H. H.," *see* Jackson, Helen Hunt
Haardt, Sara Powell, IV:606, 729; V:265
Habberton, John, I:593; III:248, 400, 422; IV:464, 765
Haberdasher, III:134; IV:187
Haberdashery magazines, IV:187
Hach, H. Theodor, I:435
Hackett, Alice P., III:491*n*
Hackett, Francis, V:191*n*, 196–200, 209
Hackett, James Henry, I:429
Hackett, John T., IV:578; V:49*n*, 57
Hadas, Moses, V:350
Hadden, Briton, V:293*n*, 294–305, 308
Hadden, Crowell, V:297
Haddon, William, II:94*n*
Hadley, Arthur Twining, II:402; IV:174, 180, 398, 514, 662; V:288, 329*n*, 330, 332, 339
Hadley, James, II:269
Hagen, Theodore, III:196
Hagenback, Karl, IV:593
Haggard, Henry Rider, IV:117, 141, 226, 612; V:119
Haggard, Sewell, IV:480*n*, 500–1, 601; V:72*n*, 86
Hahnemannian Monthly, III:142
Haight, Rufus James, IV:189
Hailmann, William Nicholas, II:163
Haines, E. M., III:93
Haines, Helen Elizabeth, III:519; IV:142
Haines, Oakley P., II:112*n*
Hairdressers' magazines, III:132
Haiti, press comment on, III:352
Halbert, Mrs. Caroline A., II:466
Halbert, N. A., II:75
Haldane, John Burdon Sanderson, IV:519
Haldeman-Julius, Emanuel, IV:206*n*
Haldeman-Julius Weekly, IV:206*n*
Hale, Charles, II:159
Hale, Edward Everett, I:138, 284*n*, 289, 291; II:168, 173, 241, 242, 249, 272, 398, 494, 504, 505*n*; III:13*n*, 34, 99, 100, 224, 231, 232, 377, 424, 429, 430, 508, 545, 549, 558; IV:7, 50, 60, 79, 181, 202, 203, 281, 398, 404, 410, 482, 513, 742, 768; V:287
  as editor, III:436–39

Hale, Enoch, I:438; II:227, 232
Hale, George Ellery, III:111*n;* IV:308, 728
Hale, Louise Closser, IV:435; V:256
Hale, Lucretia Peabody, II:505*n;* III:501
Hale, Nathan, I:718; II:224, 232, 238
Hale, Nathan, Jr., I:346, 718–20
Hale, Ruth, III:555; IV:439
Hale, Mrs. Sarah Josepha, I:326, 412, 488; II:46; III:309
as editor, I:349–50, 580*n,* 583–92
Hale, Mrs. Sarah Preston Everett, I:718, 719
Hale, W. H., III:139
Hale, William Bayard, III:476–77; IV:490, 506*n,* 508, 777, 783
Hale, William Harlan, V:191*n,* 219
Halévy, Jacques Fromental Élie, IV:114*n*
Half-Dime Library, III:43*n*
Half Hour, IV:48
Half-tone pictures, I:252, 593; III:328; IV:7, 617
in Gilded Age magazines (1885–1905)
all-fiction magazines, IV:610
declining costs of, IV:5
general magazines, IV:685, 719–20
home magazines, V:155
illustrated magazines, IV:454
police gazette, II:335
review magazines, IV:775, 786
women's magazines, II:311; IV:767
in modern magazines (1905–)
police gazette, II:335
scientific periodicals, II:322
women's magazines, III:484
development of, IV:719–20
impact of, IV:153–54
technical development of, IV:5
Hall, A. Oakey, II:541; III:4, 266, 441
Hall, A. Wilford, III:89
Hall, Blakely, IV:46, 47*n,* 84
Hall David, IV:683–84
Hall Edward Brooks, I:288
Hall, Edwin, I:534*n*
Hall, Elial F., II:414
Hall, Fitzedward, III:369, 309, 536
Hall, Gerald Stanley, IV:79*n,* 192, 268, 303, 398
Hall, Gertrude, V:148
Hall, Gilman, IV:49*n;* V:84
Hall, Granville Stanley, III:286
Hall, Harrison, I:223*n,* 240–42
Hall, Hazel, V:184
Hall, Helen, IV:749*n*
Hall, Holworth, IV:466
Hall, J. Basil, IV:532
Hall, James, I:459, 467 660–61
as contributor, I:240, 560, 609
as editor, I:387, 595–98
Hall, James Norman, IV:701, 709
Hall, John, I:533
Hall, John Elihu, I:123, 154, 155, 223*n,* 240–42
Hall, John M., IV:54
Hall, Samuel Carter, II:477
Hall, Mrs. Samuel Carter, I:623, 734
Hall, Mrs. Sarah Ewing, I:240, 244
Hall, Thomas, I:240
Hall, Tom, IV:84*n*
Hall, William W., II:87
Hall's Fireside Monthly, II:59
Hall's Journal of Health, II:87; III:139
Halle, Ernest von, IV:225
Halle, R. J., III:311
Halleck, Fitz-Greene, II:166, 352, 498
as contributor, I:129, 313, 326, 335, 608, 627, 637
evaluation of, I:408, 409, 412
Hallett, Richard Matthews, IV:694
Hallgren, Mauritz A., III:355
Halliburton, Maurine, V:3*n,* 26
Halligan's Illustrated World's Fair, IV:99
Hallo, IV:387*n*
Hallock, Charles, III:210
Hallock, Joseph Newton, III:83*n,* 394; IV:480*n,* 481–82
Hallock, W. W., III:83*n*
Hallowell, Robert, V:200
Halper, Albert, V:184
Halpin, J., I:322
Halpine, Charles Graham ("Miles O'Reilly"), I:683; II:37, 180, 181
Halsey, Abraham, I:363
Halsey, Ashley, IV:712*n*
Halsey, Francis Whiting, IV:126
Halsey, William Frederick, IV:713
Halstead, Murat, IV:482, 489, 662
Halsted, Byron David, I:731
Halsted, Sara D., III:407
Hambidge, Jay, III:473; IV:84; V:84
Hamblen, Herbert, IV:331, 593
Hamersley, G. W., III:199
Hamersley, Lewis R., III:533
Hamersley, Lewis R., Jr., III:533*n,* 534
Hamersley, T. H. S., III:533*n,* 534
Hamerton, Philip Gilbert, I:534; III:35*n;* IV:719

Hames, Edward H., III:454*n,* 455
Hamilton, Ill., III:55
Hamilton, N.Y., IV:268
Hamilton, R.I., III:260
Hamilton, Alexander, I:244*n;* V:195–97, 202
Hamilton, Clayton, IV:437, 517, 737; V:84
Hamilton, Cosmo, IV:606
Hamilton, Earl Jefferson, IV:181*n*
Hamilton, Edith, IV:631
"Hamilton, Gail," *see* Dodge, Mary Abigail
Hamilton, Grant E., III:531, 552, 553, 554
Hamilton Jean, IV:355
Hamilton, John Brown, IV:524*n,* 527
Hamilton, Philip, I:244
Hamilton, Robert, I:626–27
Hamilton, Thomas, II:141
Hamilton, Williams Baskerville, V:273*n,* 283
Hamline, Leonidas Leut, II:301
Hammer and Pen, IV:221*n*
Hammerstein, Oscar, III:486; IV:189*n*
Hammesfahr, A. C. G., IV:464; V:292
Hammett, Dashiell, IV:473
Hammit, Charles K., III:147
Hammond, Marcus Claudius Marcellus, I:725
Hammond, William A., III:91
Hampton, Va., IV:186*n*
Hampton, B. B., V:145*n,* 147–53
Hampton, Jesse D., V:151
Hampton, Wade, IV:199
Hampton-Columbian Magazine, V:152
Hampton's Broadway Magazine, sketch of, V:145–53
Hampton's Magazine, IV:47, 210, 393; V:150, 152, 288
Hancock, John, I:84; II:42
Hancock, Silas D., II:181*n*
Handicrafts, I:60
Handy, Robert Gillis, IV:64*n*
Handyman's Book, V:47
Hanemann, H. W., IV:441
Haney, J. C., II:184
Haney, Jesse, II:180*n,* 184, 185*n*
Hanff, Minnie Maud, IV:30
Hangman, II:212
Hankins, Marie Louise, II:58
Hannay, James, II:495
Hanover, Pa., IV:345*n*
Hanses, Harry, V:238
Hanson, Charles H., II:421
Hanson, John Wesley, II:73*n*
Hanway, Patrick J., IV:350
Hapgood, Hutchins, IV:779
Hapgood, Isabelle, III:347
Hapgood, Norman, II:379, 469*n,* 486; IV:73*n,* 121, 208–9, 271 453*n,* 457–64, 499*n,* 500, 643; V:28, 79, 195, 208, 333
Happy Days, IV:119*n*
Happy Thought, IV:81
Harbaugh, Henry, II:380*n*
Harbaugh, Thomas Chalmers, III:179
Harben, William Nathaniel, II:262*n,* 272; III:400, 485; IV:361, 429, 685, 767
Harbinger, I:366, 763–65; II:207
Harbinger of Peace, II:211*n*
Harbor Lights, IV:288*n*
Harbour, Jefferson Lee, II:262*n,* 270; IV:765
Hard, William, III:487; IV:461, 663, 749; V:55, 72*n,* 81, 84–85, 211
"Hard times" of 1890's, IV:157–60
Harden, Percival L., IV:89*n*
Harding, Warren Gamaliel, II:378, 379; III:352; IV:707, 785; V:213, 270, 333
Hardy, Thomas, II:269, 393, 401, 482; III:224, 242, 327, 358, 549; IV:66, 134, 433, 451, 490, 592; V:342
Hare, James Henry, IV:455, 458, 465
Hargis, James, V:26
Hargrove, Charles R., V:97
Harkness, John C., III:31*n*
Harkness' Magazine, III:31*n*
"Harland, Marion," *see* Terhune, Mary Virginia
Harlem Life, IV:86
Harlequin, IV:93
Harley, J., III:187, 191
Harmon, Moses, III:301; IV:277
Harmon's Journal, IV:187*n*
Harmony (music), IV:254
Harmony (theosophy), IV:287
Harned, Virginia, IV:133
Harness and Carriage Journal, II:92; III:216
Harness Gazette, III:216
Harness trade magazine, IV:188, 189*n*
Harness World, IV:189
Harper, Fletcher, II:383, 388, 391–92, 393, 396, 398; III:23, 32, 388
  as editor, III:469–70, 476, 478–79, 485
Harper, J. Henry, II:398, 485
Harper, Joseph Wesley, II:385, 485
Harper, Robert Francis, III:237*n*
Harper, Samuel Northrup, IV:785

Harper, William Rainey, III:84, 236; IV:74, 301, 499, 690
Harper & Brothers, I:202*n*, 360, 375
  bankruptcy of, II:401, 484
  reprinting of English books by, II:128–30
Harper Memorial Library, V:349
Harper's Bazaar, III:97, 98, 308; IV:360; V:162, 165*n*
Harper's Family Library, II:383
Harper's Ferry raid, II:146–47, 292
Harper's Magazine, V:200, 341
Harper's Monthly, III:32, 48, 90, 92, 105, 184, 223, 227, 231, 271, 278, 280, 311, 314, 362, 369, 378, 399; V:29, 188
  advertising in, III:10, 11
  circulation of, III:6
  illustration of, III:188
  payments to contributors, III:16
Harper's New Monthly Magazine, I:548, 553, 648, 655, 726; II:30, 107–8, 110, 121, 132, 149, 176, 406–7, 424, 449, 467, 476, 495*n;* IV:5, 9, 14, 19, 20, 21, 35, 41, 43, 229, 717
  advertising in, II:14
  circulation of, II:11, 102, 121
  humor in, II:177
  illustration of, II:193
  payment to contributors, II:20, 21
  sketch of, II:383–405
Harper's Round Table, III:178*n*
Harper's Weekly, II:44–45, 54, 121, 130, 136, 146, 256, 378, 386, 393, 396, 428; III:6, 10, 40, 86, 92, 125, 139, 188, 222, 276–77, 358, 359, 363, 389; IV:10, 39, 57, 292; V:195, 254
  advertising in, II:14
  circulation of, II:10
  relationship to *Frank Leslie's Illustrated Newspaper,* II:454, 460, 462
  reporting of war by, II:150, 156
Harper's Young People, III:178, 191
Harraden, Beatrice, III:328; IV:125, 490
Harrell, Eugene, III:168
Harrigan, Edward, IV:259
Harriman, Karl Edwin, IV:362
"Harrington, George F.," *see* Baker, William Mumford
Harrington, Henry F., I:127*n*, 626
Harrington, John, I:426; II:179
Harrington, John J., III:57*n*
Harris, Ben Jorj, IV:475
Harris, C. H., III:266
Harris, Carrie Jenkins, III:47
Harris, Chapin A., II:92*n*
Harris, Corra, II:435; IV:550, 693, 696, 697, 703
Harris, Frank, IV:390; V:258, 266
Harris, George, IV:395–96
Harris, J. W., IV:446
Harris, Joel Chandler, II:111; III:228, 347, 465, 548, 558; IV:451, 544, 592, 689, 721, 774; V:73
Harris, Joseph, I:443, 731; II:432*n*, 433
Harris, S. D., I:444
Harris, Samuel, I:208; II:314
Harris, Samuel R., IV:64
Harris, Thaddeus Mason, I:108*n*, 111
Harris, Thomas Lake, II:207, 209, 210
Harris, William Charles, III:210; IV:637
Harris, William Torrey, I:402; II:175*n;* IV:303, 513
Harrisburg, Pa., magazines in, II:99*n;* III:71*n*, 262*n;* IV:214, 269*n*, 313*n*, 338*n*
Harrison, Anne Blaine, V:222
Harrison, Benjamin, IV:543; V:72
Harrison, Mrs. Burton, II:546; III:471, 486; IV:725, 767; V:248
Harrison, E. L. T., III:57*n*
Harrison, Frederic, IV:513, 516
Harrison, Gilbert A., V:191*n*, 222–23
Harrison, H. S., III:77*n*
Harrison, Henry Sydnor, V:249
Harrison, James Albert, III:536, 549; IV:73
Harrison, Jonathan Baxter, II:510*n*
Harrison, Marie, IV:756*n*, 759
Harrison, Mark W., III:112
Harrison, Russell B., II:452*n*, 463
Harrison, Selig S., V:191*n*
Harrison, W. P., II:66*n*
Harrison, William Beverley, IV:64
Harrison, William Henry, I:453, 751
Harry Hazel's Yankee Blade, see Yankee Blade
Harryman, A. H., III:54*n*
Hart, Albert Bushnell, II:401; III:347; IV:138, 140*n*, 499, 593, 662; V:51, 54
Hart, Charles, III:186
Hart, E. Stanley, II:418
Hart, Edward, III:110*n;* IV:309
Hart, Frances Noyes, IV:697
Hart, H., I:132
Hart, H. D., IV:88*n*
Hart, Harry, III:553
Hart, J. C., IV:442*n*, 448

Hart, J. Wilson, IV:484
Hart, Jerome Alfred, III:57*n*
Hart, John Seely, I:769*n*, 770; II:75*n*; III:397
Hart, R. D., III:402*n*
Hart, Tony, IV:259
Harte, Francis Bret, II:117, 118, 377, 506*n*; III:23, 56, 58, 203, 224, 227, 228, 229, 238, 242–43, 264, 358, 374, 400*n*, 461, 503, 511, 521; V:118–19
Harte, Walter Blackburn, IV:80, 98*n*, 125, 389, 390*n*, 404, 408, 412, 645, 646
Hartford, Conn.
  magazines in, before 1850, I:20, 133, 204, 347–48, 491, 694*n*; II:312*n*
  Civil War era magazines (1850–65)
    education periodical, II:443*n*
    religious periodicals, II:65*n*, 71*n*, 74
    "Sunday" periodical, II:36
  post-Civil War magazines in (1865–85)
    education periodical, II:443*n*
    insurance periodical, III:146
    poultry periodicals, III:161
    railroad periodical, III:126*n*
    religious magazine, III:69*n*
    university periodical, II:312*n*
  Gilded Age magazines in (1885–1905)
    Indian rights' periodical, IV:215*n*
    regional periodical, IV:82
    sporting periodical, IV:379
    university periodical, II:312*n*
Hartford Wits (Connecticut Wits), I:102–3, 176, 204
  See also Barlow, Joel; Dwight, Timothy; Humphreys, David; Trumbull, John
Hartman, Lee Foster, II:383*n*, 404
Hartmann, Karl Robert Eduard von, III:497
Hartshorne, Henry, I:773*n*, 774
Hartt, Rollin Lynde, IV:784, 786
Hartwell, Alonzo, I:522
Hartwick, Harry, V:184, 187
Harvard Advocate, III:165
Harvard Alumni Bulletin, V:346
Harvard Crimson, III:165
Harvard Engineering Journal, IV:321*n*
Harvard Graduates' Magazine, IV:74–75
Harvard Lampoon, III:269; IV:383, 557–60
Harvard Law Review, IV:347–48
Harvard Lyceum, I:172, 794
Harvard Magazine, II:99
Harvard Monthly, IV:273
Harvard Register, I:488, 799
Harvard University, I:76, 110, 130, 152, 192, 262, 264, 287, 488, 570; II:223, 260, 499
  enrollment in, I:278
  as literary center, I:124–25, 203, 277–78, 604–5
  magazines published at, I:172, 488
    alumni periodicals, IV:75
    comic magazines, III:269; IV:383
    economic journals, IV:182
    engineering periodicals, IV:321*n*
    legal periodicals, IV:347–48
    literary magazines, III:165–66
    mathematics journals, III:110*n*
    religious magazines, I:277, 370
    satiric magazines, III:268
    student periodicals, IV:273
  sporting activities at, IV:375–76
Harvard University Press, V:345–46
Harvardiana, I:488, 803
Harvey, Alexander, IV:509, 737; V:95
Harvey, Charles Mitchell, IV:781
Harvey, E. B., IV:763*n*, 764
Harvey, George Brinton McClellan, II:220*n*, 256, 261, 401, 469*n*, 485, 486; IV:51, 57, 566
Harvey, George M., IV:111
Harvey, H. B., V:154*n*, 155
Harvey, William Hope, IV:162
Harvey's Weekly, II:259
Harvier, Ernest, III:198
Hasbrouck, John W., II:52
Haseltine, William Stanley, III:187
Haskell, Burnette G., III:302
Haskell, Mrs. Mehitable, II:49
Hassard, John Rose Greene, III:329
Haste, Gwendolen, V:13
Hastings, Thomas, I:434
Haswell, A., I:31*n*
Hatboro, Pa., IV:343*n*
Hatch, George W., I:548
Hatcher, John Bell, IV:622
"Hatrack" (by Asbury), V:13–15
Hatter and Furrier, III:134
Hat-trade magazines, *see* Millinery magazines
Haulenbeek, J. H., I:580*n*, 593
Haupt, Paul, III:537
Hauptmann, Gerhart, III:543; IV:121, 136, 196, 256; V:95–96
Hauser, Carl, III:524*n*; IV:387*n*
Hauser, Ernest O., IV:712
Havell, George F., IV:578–79
Haven, Alice Bradley Neal, II:410
Haversack, II:87
Haviland, C. Augustus, III:52

Hawaii
annexation of, II:255
magazines published in, IV:109
Hawkins, Anthony Hope (Anthony Hope), III:485; IV:49*n*, 141, 226, 230, 437, 544, 591, 612, 616
Hawkins, Joseph, I:203*n*
Hawks, Francis Lister, I:367, 669–70, 711; II:364, 413, 420, 425
Hawthorne, Hildegarde, III:504
Hawthorne, Julian, I:593, 678; II:310, 393; III:37*n*, 224, 235*n*, 400, 411, 420, 461, 558; IV:37, 38, 39, 45, 60, 154, 480, 485, 489, 634
Hawthorne, Nathaniel, II:167, 387, 407, 503, 504; III:224; V:ix, 119
as contributor, I:326, 344, 365, 586, 602, 609, 620, 678, 679, 680, 711, 719, 737
as editor, I:364, 364*n*
evaluation of, I:412
Hay, John, II:306*n*; III:14*n*, 242–43, 248, 257, 264, 358, 465*n*, 470, 471, 503; IV:40, 43, 137, 483
Hay Trade Journal, IV:189*n*
Haycox, Ernest, IV:473
Hayden, Horace H., I:294
Hayes, Isaac Israel, II:414
Hayes, John W., III:300*n*
Hayes, Rutherford B., III:342, 524; IV:45*n*
Hayes, William Morris, IV:324*n*
Hayman, Al, IV:255
Haymarket bombing (1886), IV:172–73, 217–18, 561
Hayne, Paul Hamilton, I:651; II:33, 110*n*, 112, 343, 496, 497*n*, 498, 506*n*; III:35*n*, 41, 46, 46*n*, 47, 48, 54, 229, 238, 358, 374, 384, 397, 418, 424, 463; IV:398
as editor, II:488–91
Hayne, Robert Young, I:205, 469, 575
Haynes, D. O., IV:188*n*
Haynes, Roy Asa, V:311
Haynes, William, IV:637
Hays, Arthur Garfield, V:14, 21
Hays, Isaac, I:566*n*, 567; II:84; III:139
Hays, Isaac Minis, I:566*n*
Hayward, T. B., I:435
Haywood, William Dudley, IV:206*n*, 458
Hazard, Caroline, IV:397–98
Hazard, Ebenezer, I:106
Hazeltine, Mayo Williamson, II:258, 356*n*; IV:453*n*, 454
Hazen, George B., IV:763*n*
Hazenplug, Frank, IV:451–52
Hazewell, Charles Creighton, II:495, 503, 542
Hazlewood, W. M., III:47
Hazlitt, Henry, III:331*n*, 354–55, 479; IV:730; V:3*n*, 19, 99*n*
Headley, Joel Tyler, I:553, 745
Headley's Magazine, I:745
Health, I:441*n*; III:139; IV:316
Health Culture, IV:316
Health foods, I:479
Health hints, II:417; IV:472, 504
See also Medical information
Health and Home, III:8*n*, 139
Health magazines, I:440–41; II:87; III:138–39; IV:316–17
Healy, Fred Albert, IV:699, 711
Heap, Jane, V:166*n*, 171–75
Heard, John, IV:121*n*
Hearn, Lafcadio, II:397, 398*n*, 482; III:47, 267, 400
Hearst, James, V:184
Hearst, William Randolph, III:390; IV:241, 331, 461, 491–505, 606, 777; V:25, 62, 162
Hearst Corporation, V:139
Hearst Magazines, V:133, 136, 163, 271–72
Hearst's International Magazine, IV:55, 461
sketch of, IV:499–502
Hearst's Magazine, see: Hearst's International Magazine
Heart of the Home, II:90*n*
Hearth and Home, I:731; III:99, 152, 224, 500
Hearthstone, IV:17, 367
Heath, E. Addie, III:177*n*
Heath, James E., I:409*n*, 497, 629*n*, 631–34, 651
Heathen Woman's Friend, III:70; IV:305
Heating periodicals, IV:322*n*–23*n*
Heating and Ventilating, IV:323*n*
Heating and Ventilation, IV:322*n*
Hebraica, III:236
Hebrew Leader, II:77
Hebrew Observer, II:78; III:81; IV:300*n*
Hebrew Standard, III:80*n*
Hebrew Student, III:84
Hecht, Ben, IV:701; V:173, 176, 264
Hecker, Isaac Thomas, III:68, 329; IV:298
Hedge, Egbert, II:297*n*
Hedge, Frederick Henry, I:284*n*, 289–90, 374, 410, 601, 659, 702, 764;

II:71*n;* III:164*n,* 386, 506; IV: 78
Heenan, John C., II:202, 458, 525
Hegel, Georg Wilhelm Friedrich, III:385, 386
Hegeler, Edward Carl, IV:302–03
Heilman, Robert B., IV:739
Heilprin, Angelo, II:415; IV:109, 224, 308
Heilprin, Michael, III:336, 347
Heine, Heinrich, II:165; V:117
Held, John, Jr., III:531, 555; IV:502, 567, 606; V:270
Helena, Mont., III:71*n,* 75*n;* IV:108
Hell, theological debates on, III:85
Helmbold, Henry K., I:170–71
Helmuth, Dr. William Tod, II:85*n*
Helper, Hinton Rowan, II:114
Helpful Thought, IV:300
Helping Hand, II:64
Hemans, Mrs. Felicia Dorothea Browne, I:400, 615
Heming, Arthur, IV:637
Hemingway, Ernest, IV:476, 504, 729; V:11, 173
Hemment, J. C., IV:613
Hemstreet, Charles, III:551
Hemyng, Bracebridge, II:330
Henderson, Alice Corbin, V:229, 239, 242
Henderson, Archibald, IV:409
Henderson, Charles Richmond, IV:191, 415
Henderson, Joseph Franklin, IV:763*n,* 766
Henderson, Josephine, IV:355
Henderson, Samuel, II:65*n*
Henderson, William James, III:197*n,* 528; IV:251, 261*n,* 560
Hendrick, Burton Jesse, III:512; IV:600–1, 777, 783–84, 786
Hendricks, J. E., III:110
Henkle, Rev. M. M., II:57
Henley, William Ernest, II:256; IV:451
Henneman, John Bell, IV:733*n,* 735–36
Hennessey, Roland Burke, IV:47, 58*n,* 67, 261; V:145
Hennessey, William J., II:471; III:359, 379
Henrotin, Ellen M., V:158
Henry, Albert, III:235*n*
Henry, Caleb Sprague, I:367, 669–70; II:542
"Henry, O.," *see* Porter, William Sydney
Henry, R. Norris, I:306
Henry, Robert, I:574
Henshaw, Henry Wetherbee, IV:627
Henshaw, John Prentiss Kewley, II:365
Henty, George Alfred, III:503; IV:420
Hentz, Mrs. Caroline Lee, I:584, 597, 756
Herald (New York), I:329
Herald of Freedom, II:135
Herald of Gospel Liberty, I:137, 793; II:74; III:80; IV:295
Herald of Health, I:441*n;* II:87; III:139
Herald of Life, II:74
Herald of Light, II:210
Herald of Mission News, IV:238*n*
Herald and Presbyter, II:63*n;* IV:293
Herald of Progress, II:210
Herald of Truth, I:388, 808; III:81
Heraldic Journal, III:262*n*
Herbert, B. B., III:274*n*
Herbert, Henry William ("Frank Forester"), I:480, 481, 546, 618–19, 680; II:424, 453
Herbert, Hilary Abner, IV:232
Herbert, Victor, IV:252
Herbert S. Stone & Company, V:156
Herbst, Josephine, IV:729
Herder, Johann G. von, I:192
Herford, Oliver, II:400; III:487, 504, 514; IV:134, 389, 458, 564, 602, 604, 722; V:84, 248
Hergesheimer, Joseph, III:479; IV:438, 503, 518, 584, 695; V:85
Herget, H. M., IV:629, 631
Hering, Constantine, II:85
Herman, Theodore F., II:380*n*
Hermann, Karl Stephen, IV:125
Herndon, E. W., III:80
Herne, James A., III:202; IV:256, 410
Herold, Don, III:555; IV:568, 731
Heron-Allen, Edward, IV:123, 134
Herrick, Anson, II:38
Herrick, Clarence Luther, IV:314
Herrick, Robert, III:355; IV:441, 689, 721, 724; V:211, 249, 337
Herrick, Sophia Bledsoe, III:382*n,* 384, 457*n,* 465
Herriot, Edouard, IV:519
Herron, George Davis, IV:283
Hersey, Heloise E., 262*n,* 273
Hersey, John, IV:504
Hersey, Mrs. Merle Williams, II:325*n,* 337
Herter, Christian Archibald, 367*n,* 379; III:434
Herts, Benjamin Russell, IV:511*n,* 518
Herzberg, Oscar, IV:246*n*
Herzog, A. W., III:142

Hesperian, I:388, 692–93; II:58, 118*n;* IV:72
Hewit, Nathaniel Augustus (Augustine Francis), III:329
Hewitt, Emma C., IV:538
Hewitt, John H., I:381*n*
Hewitt, Mary Elizabeth, I:760
Hewitt, Peter Cooper, II:318
Hewlett, Maurice, III:400*n;* IV:435, 518, 723
Hexamer, F. M., I:728*n;* III:161
Heyliger, William, IV:115
Heyward, DuBose, IV:439
Heywood, Ezra H., III:301
Hibbs, Ben, IV:671*n,* 711–16
Hibernarian, IV:227
Hichens, Robert, III:390, 477, 487; IV:498
Hickey, Patrick Vincent, III:70; IV:298
Hicks, Elias, I:562
Hicks, Irl, IV:309
Hicks, Mrs. R. B., II:59, 420, 425
Hicksite controversy (c. 1827), I:562
Hide and Leather, IV:189*n*
Hiestand, Eleanor Moore, I:580*n*
Higbee, Elnathan Elisha, 380*n*
Higginson, Thomas Wentworth, I:764; II:26, 243, 252, 496, 501, 503, 504; III:35*n,* 78, 90, 91, 94, 107, 172, 175*n,* 195, 231, 261, 327, 337, 347, 389, 427, 455, 463; IV:131, 202, 203, 483, 513
Higginsville, Mo., IV:345
High, Stanley, IV:709
Hildebrand, Hans, IV:630
Hildebrand, Jesse Richardson, IV:632
Hilder, John Chapman, III:388*n*
Hildreth, Richard, I:578, 778; II:175
Hill, Daniel Harvey, III:46*n,* 469
Hill, David Bennett, IV:565; V:73
Hill, David Jayne, II:259, 403; III:72*n*
Hill, E. Trevor, V:49*n,* 57
Hill, Ebenezer, IV:625
Hill, Edwin Conger, IV:731
Hill, Frederick Trevor, IV:437
Hill, George, 546*n*
Hill, H. H., 132*n*
Hill, James J., IV:494, 690, 778, 784
Hill, John Alexander, III:115*n;* IV:333
Hill, Marion, IV:604
Hill, Ruth, IV:121*n*
Hill, Samuel, I:37, 110, 111
Hill, Thomas, I:292*n;* III:507
Hill, Thomas Edie, IV:325
Hill, W. E., III:531, 555
Hillard, George Stillman, I:451, 600; II:236; III:322
Hillebrand, Karl, II:248; III:337
Hillhouse, James Abraham, I:204
Hillis, Newell Dwight, I:741; IV:520, 641–42
Hillman, George Sidney, IV:126
Hillman, Harry, III:132*n*
Hillman, William, IV:476
Hillquit, Morris, V:84
Hills, William Henry, IV:142
Hillyer, Robert, V:234–35
Hilson, Thomas, I:167*n*
Hilton, James, IV:473; V:134
Hinchman, Walter Swain, IV:521
Hinckley, C. A., I:782
Hincks, Edward Young, IV:395
Hine, C. C., II:94*n;* III:146*n*
Hine, Lewis W., IV:748
Hine, Lucius A., I:388; II:212
Hinshelwood, R., I:522; II:303; III:187
Hint, II:183
Hinton, C. H., IV:263
Hinton, Henry L., III:233
Hinton, J. W., II:66*n*
Hinton, Richard Josiah, III:298; IV:65
Hirohito, Emperor, V:297
Hirsch, Emil Gustav, IV:300
Hirsch, Nat, V:101
Hirsch, Sidney Mttron, V:100–3, 110, 115
Hirschfield, Al, V:23
Hirst, Henry Beck, I:553
Hirth, Frank, III:301
Hiscox, Mrs. Caroline O., II:57*n*
Hiss, Alger, V:319
Historic Magazine and Notes and Queries, III:259*n*
Historical journals, II:175–76; III:47, 258–63; IV:137–40
Historical Magazine, II:175; III:259
Historical novels, I:416
Historical Record of Wyoming Valley, IV:139
Historical Register, III:262*n*
Historical societies in expansionist era (1825–50), I:422
Historical Studies and Records, IV:138
History
  in early magazines (1741–94), I:3–4, 53, 77, 85, 93, 97–98, 102–3, 106, 112
  in nationalist era magazines (1794–1825), I:176, 276; II:230–33
  in expansionist era magazines (1825–50), I:421–22, 597, 645, 648, 666, 723; II:236–37, 301
  in Civil War era magazines (1850–65), II:71*n,* 175–76, 225, 230, 248,

272, 314, 343, 387, 395, 398, 429, 444
in post-Civil War magazines (1865–85), III:35–36, 347, 375–76, 533
in Gilded Age magazines (1885–1905), III:347, 546; IV:136–40, 574, 721
in modern magazines (1905–), II:402; IV:520, 550, 725; V:5, 8, 75, 280
See also Current events; *and specific historic events*
History of American Journalism (Lee), V:67
Hitchcock, De Witte C., II:471
Hitchcock, J. Irvine, I:153*n,* 154*n*
Hitchcock, Romyn, III:111
Hitchcock, Roswell Dwight, II:517*n*
Hite-Smith, Charles, IV:324*n*
Hitler, Adolf, V:300, 323*n,* 325
Hittell, John S., III:405
Hoadley, George A., I:556*n*
Hoag, Clarence Gilbert, IV:178
Hoar, Ebenezer Rockwood, II:503; IV:399
Hoar, George Frisbie, II:271; IV:171, 514, 516, 721
Hoar, Samuel, III:144
Hoard, William Dempster, IV:344
Hoard's Dairyman, IV:344
Hobart, Arthur, III:295*n*
Hobart, George Vere, IV:90
Hobart, John Henry, I:135
Hobby magazines, IV:391
Hobson, John A., III:355
Hobson, Richmond Pearson, III:475; IV:235, 494
Hocking, William Ernest, V:338*n*
Hodge, Archibald Alexander, III:74
Hodge, Charles, I:136, 370, 530–33; II:155, 517, 537; III:73
Hodge, Frederick Webb, IV:308
Hodge, Moses D., III:46
Hodges, Charles A., V:56
Hodges, Nathaniel Dana Carlile, IV:307
Hodgkinson, John, I:168
Hodgson, Fannie, *see* Burnett, Frances Hodgson
Hodgson, Richard, IV:407
Hodgson, Telfair, IV:733
Hoeber, Arthur, IV:435, 781
Hoffman, Allan C., II:323
Hoffman, Arthur Sullivant, III:486; IV:589*n,* 606–7
Hoffman, Charles Fenno
as contributor, I:323, 499, 546, 608, 627, 642, 720, 743, 770
as editor, I:320*n,* 326, 345, 606, 606*n,* 618*n,* 619–20, 766–67
Hoffman, Josiah Ogden, I:115
Hoffman, Paul G., V:222*n*
Hofman, Josef, IV:544
Hogan, David, I:127*n*
Hogan, John F., IV:96
Hogan, Thomas, III:187
Hogeboom, Amy, V:122
Hogg, James Stephen, IV:667
Hoke, Travis, III:541
Holbrook, Josiah, I:446, 489
Holbrook, Silas Pinckney, I:127*n*
Holbrook, Stewart H., V:21, 25
Holbrook, Weare, V:179*n*
Holbrook, Z. Swift, I:739*n*
Holcombe, William Henry, I:651
Holden, Charles W., I:348
Holden's Dollar Magazine, I:347–48, 809; II:30, 42, 53, 419
Holder, Charles Frederick, IV:105, 108*n,* 415
Holding, Elisabeth Sanxay, IV:504, 618
Holiday, IV:715
Holiday Magazine, IV:275*n*
Holland, Edward Clifford, I:280
Holland, F. P., III:155
Holland, F. R., I:436
Holland, George, III:206
Holland, Josiah Gilbert, I:2; III:19–20, 23, 32–33*n,* 34, 172, 224, 231, 233, 247, 281, 457–68, 473, 497, 501; V:126
Holland, Lewis, IV:292
Hollander, Jacob H., IV:182*n*
Holley, C. I., I:126
Holley, Horace, I:164, 311–12
Holley, I. B., Jr., V:273*n*
Holley, Marietta ("Samantha Allen"), II:310; III:512; IV:538, 685, 767; V:133
Holley, Orville Luther, I:297
Holliday, Carl, IV:629, 737; V:281
Holliday, Robert Cortes, IV:432*n,* 438, 439
Hollister, John Hamilcar, IV:524*n*
Holloway, J. Starr, II:417
Holloway, William, I:178
Holly, D. W., I:678*n,* 682
"Holm, Saxe," III:461. *See also* Jackson, Helen Hunt
Holman, Alfred, III:57*n*
Holman, F. Day, V:75
Holme, George, IV:612
Holme, John, IV:168
Holmes, Abiel, I:134*n,* 263, 277, 572
Holmes, E., I:444*n*

Holmes, George Frederick, I:724, 726; II:345
Holmes, John Haynes, III:79*n;* IV:405
Holmes, Mary Jane, II:171, 466; III:16, 223, 224, 246, 400*n;* IV:366, 538, 767
Holmes, Oliver Wendell, I:412, 488, 497*n,* 546, 586, 600–01, 609; II:168, 170, 175, 197*n,* 211, 243, 254, 377, 494, 495, 499, 504, 510; III:35*n,* 59, 99*n,* 172, 224, 231, 237, 238, 240, 264, 362, 541; IV:61, 129–30, 593; V:121
Holmes, Oliver Wendell, Jr., III:144; V:121, 208, 209, 347
Holst, Hermann Eduard von, III:336
Holstein-Friesian World, IV:344*n*
Holt, Hamilton, II:367*n,* 378
Holt, Henry, II:249, 431; IV:557
Holy Cross Magazine, IV:294*n*
Holy Orders (by Corelli), V:254
Holyoke, Mass., III:128; IV:360; V:126
Holzapfel, Gustav, IV:301*n*
Homans, Benjamin, I:456; II:94*n*
Homans, Isaac Smith, I:696*n;* II:94
Homans, Isaac Smith, Jr., II:94*n*
Hombre, II:185*n*
Home (Boston), IV:366
Home (Buffalo and New York), II:58
  sketch of, II:466–67
Home (Cleveland), IV:763
Home, Farm and Factory, III:157
Home, Orff's Farm Review, V:151*n*
Home Advocate, IV:367*n*
Home Building Ideas, V:47
Home Circle, II:58; IV:79*n*
Home Companion, III:100; IV:763*n,* 764
Home and Country, IV:154
Home economics, V:158
Home Education, IV:53
Home and Farm, III:7, 46, 152*n,* 156; IV:337–38
Home and Field, V:162
Home and Flowers, IV:342*n*
Home Furnishings Ideas, V:47
Home Guard, IV:366
Home Guardian, II:211*n*
Home Guest, IV:366
Home Improvement Ideas, V:47
Home Journal, I:330, 366, 808; II:57, 150, 198; III:101
  sketch of, II:349–55
Home Journal (New York), IV:83, 212, 359–60
Home Library Magazine, IV:55*n*
Home Life, IV:367
Home Magazine, see Arthur's Home Magazine
Home Magazine (Commercial Travelers Home Association periodical), IV:362
Home Magazine (Washington, D.C.), IV:361
Home magazines
  in expansionist era (1825–50), I:377
    illustrations, I:522
    quality, I:448
    weeklies, II:349–50
  in Civil War era (1850–65), II:303, 470–71
    monthlies, II:416–17
    trends, II:56–59
    weeklies, II:350–54, 356–62, 470–76
  in post-Civil War era (1865–85), III:46
    monthlies, II:417
    religious, III:82–83
    trends, III:98–101
    weeklies, II:269–70, 354–357, 476–82; III:423–27
  in Gilded Age (1885–1905), V:158
    biweeklies, V:125–31
    mail-order, IV:365–67
    monthlies, II:362–63, 417–18; III:327; IV:92, 480–92; V:131–32, 154–57
    weeklies, II:354–55, 362–63, 482–85; III:427–31; IV:67–69, 92
  modern (1905–)
    monthlies, IV:492–305; V:36–48, 132–43, 157–65
    weeklies, II:273–74, 355, 431–35, 485–87
Home Market Bulletin, IV:166*n*
Home Mission Echo, IV:195*n*
Home Mission Herald, II:64*n*
Home Mission Monthly, IV:195*n*–196*n*
Home Missionary, II:71; IV:196*n*
Home Monthly (Boston), II:59*n;* IV:366*n*
Home Monthly (Buffalo), II:59
Home Monthly (Pittsburgh), IV:89
Home Music Journal, IV:254*n*
Home Needlework Magazine, IV:363
Home plans, IV:545
Home Queen, IV:367*n*
Home Remodeling, V:163
Home and School Visitor, III:169
Home Science Magazine, IV:364*n*
Home Study, IV:320*n*
Home Topics, IV:367*n*
Home Visitor, IV:367*n*
Home Weekly and Household Newspaper, I:365; II:57*n*

Home World, III:100
Home-Builder, IV:324
Home-decorating magazines, IV:324, 364
Home-decoration articles, V:157
Homefolks, IV:367*n*
Homeless children, IV:200
Home-Maker, IV:356
Homeopathic journals, IV:315–16
Homer, Louise, 489
Homer, Winslow, II:397, 471; III:182, 187, 211, 359, 379, 420; IV:144
"Homespun, Henry," *see* Southwick, Solomon
Homestead Act, II:121; III:61
Homestead strike (1892), IV:218
Homesteading, III:61
Home-study magazines, III:153, 173, 177, 544–47; IV:51–54
Homiletic Monthly, IV:298
Homiletic and Pastoral Review, III:84
Homiletic Review, IV:569
Homiletical periodicals, III:83–84
Homing Exchange, IV:345
Homoeopathic Eye, Ear and Throat Journal, IV:316
Homoeopathic Journal of Obstetrics, III:143
Homoeopathic medicine, II:84–85; III:138, 142–43
Homoeopathic Recorder, IV:315
Honey Grove, Tex., IV:292
Honey Jar, IV:390*n*
Hooey, IV:568
Hoogs, Frank L., IV:109
Hooker, Isabelle Beecher, III:91, 393
Hooker, Joseph D., II:78
Hooper, Edward James, I:443*n*
Hooper, Lucy Hamilton, II:310, 551; III:54, 398, 420, 511
Hooper, W. W., I:322
Hooper, William De Matoos, IV:351*n*
Hoops, dress, II:54, 56
Hoover, Calvin Bryce, V:273*n*
Hoover, Herbert Clark, III:353, 489; IV:549, 576, 606, 626, 629, 660, 698, 707, 769, 785; V:43, 71, 212, 318
Hope, Anthony, *see* Hawkins, Anthony Hope
Hope, James Barron, I:651
Hopkins, Albert A., II:323
Hopkins, Daniel, I:134*n*
Hopkins, Emma Curtis, IV:286
Hopkins, Harry Lloyd, IV:476
Hopkins, Henry Clayton, IV:92
Hopkins, John Henry, II:69, 365
Hopkins, Livingston, II:504, 552
Hopkins, Mark, IV:398
Hopkins, Pauline F., IV:214
Hopkinsian, I:136, 798
Hopkinson, D. H., III:199
Hopkinson, Francis, I:40, 46, 52, 63, 81, 94*n*, 95–96, 102
Hopkinson, Joseph, I:123, 140, 155, 230, 244, 273, 276, 638
Hopper, James, III:408; IV:465, 466, 473, 601, 607; V:80, 148
Hoppin, Augustus J., II:183, 390, 397, 471, 472; III:265*n*, 266, 441
Hoppin, William Jones, I:437
Horace, V:119
Horgan, Paul, V:337
Horn, T. N., III:533*n*, 534
Hornaday, William Temple, III:503; IV:380, 481, 725
Hornblow, Arthur, II:311, 463; IV:260, 612
Hornung, E. W., V:83
Horse racing, II:201, 453; III:214–16; IV:373
  horse magazines, I:479–80; III:215; IV:343, 373
Horse Review, IV:343
Horse Shoers' Journal, III:216
Horse Show Monthly, IV:343, 373*n*
Horse World, IV:343
Horseless Age, IV:327
Horseman, I:48*n;* II:204*n;* III:215; IV:317
Horseman and Fair World, III:315*n*
Horticultural magazines, *see* Agricultural magazines; Gardening magazines
Horticultural Register and Gardener's Magazine, I:442, 803
Horticulture, IV:342
Horticulturist, I:319, 808; III:161
Horticulturist and Journal of Rural Art and Rural Taste, II:90, 432
Horton, George M. S., IV:84*n*
Horton Act (New York State). IV:372
Hoskin, Robert, III:188
Hosmer, George Washington, I:659
Hosmer, Harriet, III:82
Hosmer, James Kendall, III:51*n;* IV:80
Hosmer, William (Methodist editor) II:67
Hosmer, William Henry Cuyler, I:767
Hoss, Elijah Embree, IV:291
Hot Corn, III:28*n*
Hot Solder, IV:387*n*
Hot Springs, Ark., IV:386
Hotchkiss, J. Elizabeth, IV:287*n*
Hotchkiss, Velona Roundy, I:666*n*
Hotchkiss Literary Monthly, V:294
Hotchkiss Record, V:294
Hotel Bulletin, IV:189*n*

Hotel Gazette, III:136
Hotel Mail, III:136
Hotel Monthly, IV:189*n*
Hotel Register, III:136
Hotel trade magazines, III:136; IV:189*n*
Hotel World, III:136
Hough, Emerson, III:512; IV:46*n,* 96, 495, 584, 685, 692, 693, 695, 696; V:30, 148
Houghton, George W. W., IV:121
Houghton, Henry Oscar, II:493*n,* 505; III:360, 436–37
Houghton, Louise Seymour, IV:293
Houghton, William Norris, III:555; IV:577
Hours at Home, III:32–33, 457, 458, 464
House Beautiful, IV:342, 393
sketch of, V:154–65
"House Beautiful, The" (Stevenson), V:154–55
House Beautiful Building Manual, V:163
House Beautiful's Vacation Homes, V:163*n*
House and Garden, I:321*n;* IV:324
House and Home, IV:364; V:322
Household, IV:362–63
Household Companion, IV:363*n*
Household goods advertising, IV:24
Household Guest, IV:53
Household hints, IV:537, 545
Household Journal, II:59; IV:367*n*
Household Magazine, II:59; V:180
Household Monthly, II:59; IV:366
Household News, IV:363
Household Words, II:384
Housekeeper, III:101; IV:367
Houses and Plan Book, V:163
Housewife, III:99; IV:366
Housh, Esther T., III:100
Housh, Frank E., III:100
Housing problems, III:313; V:95–97
Housman, Alfred Edward, IV:602
Housman, Laurence, V:96
Houston, David Franklin, IV:787
Houston, George, I:128
Houston, Herbert Sherman, IV:775
Houston, Tex., III:168; IV:186*n,* 357*n;* V:3*n*
Hovey, Charles F., II:141*n*
Hovey, Richard, II:377; IV:49*n,* 66, 645, 722; V:119
How Diplomats Make War (Neilson), V:89
How to Grow Flowers, IV:342*n*
Howard, Bronson, III:202; IV:256
Howard, Charles H., III:77, 156
Howard, John R., III:422*n,* 425
Howard, Justin H., II:182, 523
Howard, Oliver Otis, III:76*n,* 407
Howard, Philip E., II:75*n*
Howard, Roy W., V:66
Howard, S. M., III:269*n*
Howard, Sidney, IV:439
Howard, T. C., III:154
Howard, William Guild, III:236*n*
Howard's Negro American Monthly, IV:214*n*
Howe, Elias, II:318
Howe, Ernest, III:108*n*
Howe, Fredric Clemson, III:432
Howe, Henry, I:662
Howe, Irving, V:25
Howe, Julia Ward, II:164, 174–75, 197*n,* 252, 504; III:14*n,* 37*n,* 90, 91, 94, 172, 327, 439, 486, 549; IV:280, 493, 542; V:287
Howe, Mark Antony DeWolfe, II:262*n,* 272, 274, 493*n;* IV:75*n*
Howe, Samuel Gridley, I:599*n,* 601, 775, 778; II:212
Howell, Robert Boyte Crawford, II:64*n*
Howells, William Dean, I:3, 613; II:40, 248, 255, 257, 270, 398, 399, 429, 482, 493*n,* 535; III:13*n,* 16, 20–21, 23, 32, 58, 166*n,* 203, 207, 223, 224, 231, 232, 237, 238, 257, 266, 312, 335–36, 358, 377, 389, 471, 503; V:342
as contributor, IV:35–36, 44*n,* 543, 593, 612, 720
criticism of, III:244–45
as editor, II:505–10; IV:43, 83, 480*n,* 483
quoted, IV:39*n,* 41, 111–12, 132, 201, 370
standing of, IV:130, 409, 641
Howison, George H., II:385
Howitt, Mary, I:623
Howitt, Richard, I:623
Howland, Edward, II:38
Howland, Harold Jacobs, III:432
Howland, Hewitt Hanson, III:457*n,* 479; IV:390*n*
Howland, Howard J., II:378
Howland, Karl V. S., II:367*n,* 378
Howland, W. B., III:210
Howland, William Bailey, II:355; IV:633–34
Hows, John William Stanhope, II:180
Hoyt, Albert Harrison, II:176*n;* III:259
Hoyt, Helen, V:184, 236, 239
Hoyt, Nancy, V:265
Hrdlicka, Ales, IV:308

Hub, II:92; III:216; IV:327
Hubbard, Elbert, III:486; IV:72, 125, 170, 206, 264, 389, 390*n,* 410, 493, 500, 639–48, 656
Hubbard, Gardner Greene, IV:307, 590, 620–22, 624
Hubbard, James Mascarene, IV:233
Hubbard, Leonidas, Jr., IV:636
Hubbard, M. F., I:541*n,* 543
Hubbard, Robert L., IV:104*n*
Hubbard, William, II:221
Hubbell, Jay B., V:284
Huckfield, Leland, V:184
Hudson, Henry Norman, II:69
Hudson, N.Y., I:127, 170; II:112*n*
Hudson, W. H., V:175
Hudson, William Henry, IV:74
Hudson, William W., IV:54*n, 72n*
Huebsch, B. W., V:89, 91, 95*n*
Hughes, Charles Evans, IV:478; V:333
Hughes, Dorothy, IV:714
Hughes, Jeremiah, I:268*n,* 269
Hughes, Archbishop John, II:77*n*
Hughes, John W., IV:104
Hughes, Langston, IV:729; V:237
Hughes, Llewellyn, IV:521
Hughes, Richard, IV:761
Hughes, Rupert, I:593; III:503, 551; IV:66, 429, 472, 501, 521, 607, 618; V:72
Hughes, Ted, V:244
Hughes, Thomas, III:249
Hugo, Victor Marie, I:404, 417; II:162–63; III:223, 249, 254, 418
Huie, William Bradford, V:3*n,* 24–25
Hulbert, William Davenport, IV:593
Huling, C. A., IV:127
Hull, Cordell, IV:520
Hull, Moses, III:82*n*
Hull House Bulletin, IV:195
Hulme, T. E., V:230
Humane societies, III:311–12
Humanitarian, III:452
Humanitarian Review, IV:277
Humble, Margaret, III:185*n*
Humbug's American Museum, II:185*n*
Hume, Robert W., III:451
Hummel, James H., III:45, 155,
Humming Bird, I:791
Humor and wit
  in nationalist-era magazines (1794–1825), I:123, 236–38, 295–96
  in expansionist-era magazines (1825–50), I:423–27, 481, 609–10
  in Civil War era magazines (1850–65), II:362, 388–89, 439–40, 471, 541
  in post-Civil War magazines (1865–85), III:58, 365–68, 405, 440–42, 460, 512
    criticisms, III:264
  in Gilded Age magazines (1885–1905), III:474; IV:507
  in modern magazines (1905–), II:431; III:514; IV:439, 472, 693, 709, V:121, 133, 185
Humor magazines
  in nationalist era (1794–1825), I:139, 170–72
  in expansionist era (1825–50), I:425–27, 610, 780–83
  in Civil War era (1850–65), II:123, 136, 199
    engravings, II:193
    longevity, II:179
    monthlies, II:529
    quality and type, II:179–85
    southern, II:112–13, 155, 185
    weeklies, II:34, 520–29
  in post-Civil War (1865–85)
    quality and type, III:263–71
    weeklies, III:440–42, 520–22, 524, 552–53
    women's suffrage, III:91
  in Gilded Age (1885–1905), IV:387*n,* 557–64, 664–70
    characters, IV:383–84
    college periodicals, IV:383
    slang and, IV:384–85
    weeklies, III:522–31, 553–54
  modern (1905–)
    fortnightlies, III:532
    monthlies, III:552*n,* 568
    weeklies, III:531–32, 555–56; IV:564–68
Humorist, III:269*n*
Humphrey, Edward Porter, II:537*n,* 539
Humphrey, Frances A., III:177*n*
Humphrey, S. D., II:194*n*
Humphreys, David, I:102, 232
Humphrey's Journal of Photography, II:194*n*
Huneker, James Gibbons, III:197*n,* 531; IV:86, 250, 251, 654, 724, 754; V:5, 251, 266–67
Hungary, II:123–25
Hungerford, Edward, II:483; IV:469
Hunt, Frazier, IV:503, 607
Hunt, Freeman, I:364*n,* 696–97
Hunt, Jonathan, II:367*n,* 370
Hunt, Leigh, I:231
Hunt, Percival, V:179*n*
Hunt, Samuel Valentine, I:522; III:187
Hunt, Seth B., II:367*n,* 370
Hunt, William Gibbes, I:207, 311–12
Hunt, William Morris, III:182

Hunt's Merchants' Magazine, II:14, 96, 110, 134; III:147
Hunter, James V., III:140*n*
Hunter, William, 17*n*
Hunter-Trader-Trapper, IV:381
Hunting and Fishing, IV:38*n;* V:22
Hunting, articles on, IV:634, 636, 781, 785
Hunting clubs, III:221
Hunting magazines, III:210; IV:380–81
Huntington, Ellsworth, II:415
Huntington, Emily C., II:303
Huntington, Frederick Dan, II:69, 72*n*
Huntington, F. P., II:445
Huntington, Ind., IV:163*n*, 340
Huntington, W.Va., IV:292*n*
Huntley, Lydia, *see* Sigourney, Lydia Huntley
Huntress, I:356, 803; II:40
See also: Merchant's Magazine
Hurd, Peter, V:323
Hurja, Emil, IV:63*n*
Hurlbert, William Henry, II:426
Hurlbut, George C., II:414, 489
Hurlbut, J. E., I:390
Hurlbut, Jesse Lyman, III:180
Hurley, Edward Nash, IV:617
Huron, S.D., III:158
Hurst, Fannie, IV:365, 498, 503, 521, 654, 709
Hurst, Vida, IV:606
Hurt, Walter S., IV:95
Husbandman, III:149*n*
Hussey, L. M., V:7, 265
Huston, L.D., II:58
Hutchings, James H., II:117
Hutchings, Richard B., II:179, 181, 183
Hutchings' Illustrated California Magazine, II:117
Hutchins, Robert M., V:338
Hutchinson, Arthur Stuart-Menteth, III:489; V:86
Hutchinson, Paul, IV:522, 730
Hutchinson, Woods, IV:209, 302, 616; V:134
Hutt, Henry, III:484; IV:49*n*, 151, 456, 602, 689
Hutton, Laurence, III:200
Huxley, Aldous, IV:436, 439, 441; V:121, 173, 336
Huxley, Julian, V:218, 284, 336
Huxley, Thomas Henry, II:270, 404; III:250, 496
Hyde, Edward Everett, IV:527–29
Hyde, George Merriam, IV:113
Hyde, James Clarence, IV:147
Hyde, John, II:462; IV:620*n*, 622
Hyde, William, II:265–66
Hyde, William Henry, IV:561
Hyde's Weekly Art News, IV:147
Hydropathy, *see* Water cure
Hygiene magazines, III:139
Hygienic Teacher, I:441*n*
Hyne, Cutcliffe, IV:117, 186, 692
Hypnotic Magazine, IV:284

Ibañez, Blasco, *see* Blasco-Ibañez, Vincente
Ibsen, Henrik, III:347,540; IV:121, 122, 124, 256, 409
Ice and Refrigeration, IV:183
Ice Trade Journal, III:135; IV:183*n*
Ichthyology magazines, III:109
Ickes, Harold L., IV:476; V:218
Ideal American, IV:285*n*
Ideal Review, IV:287*n*
Idle Man, I:172, 797
Ilion, N.Y., III:210*n*
Illini, III:166
Illinois, University of, philology periodical at, IV:128
Illinois Agriculturist, IV:341*n*
Illinois Farmer and Farmer's Call, III:156
Illinois Federation of Women's Clubs, V:x–xi
Illinois Medical Journal, IV:314*n*
Illinois Medical and Surgical Journal, II:84*n*
Illinois Monthly Magazine, I:387, 595–96
Illinois School Journal, III:169
Illinois Teacher, II:99*n*
Illustrated American, IV:36, 58
Illustrated American News, II:43
Illustrated Bee, IV:97
Illustrated Catholic American, III:70; IV:298
Illustrated Chicago News, III:53
Illustrated Christian Weekly, III:85, 191
Illustrated Companion, IV:367*n*
Illustrated Day's Doings, IV:372, 384
Illustrated Day's Doings and Sporting World, III:44
Illustrated Family Herald, IV:365
Illustrated Home Guest, III:39*n*
Illustrated Home Journal, IV:363*n*
Illustrated Indiana Weekly, IV:96
Illustrated Kentuckian, IV:94
Illustrated London News, III:279; IV:228
Illustrated Mercury, II:113

Illustrated Milliner, IV:188*n*
Illustrated Monthly Magazine of Art, II:194
Illustrated News, II:43, 412, 437, 453, 474, 541
Illustrated Outdoor News, IV:381*n*
Illustrated Outdoor World, IV:381*n*
Illustrated periodicals
  in Civil War era (1850–65), II:10, 43–45, 58, 108, 112–13, 409–12, 452–60
  in post-Civil War era (1865–85), II:460–63; III:40–41, 53, 99, 109, 118, 191, 258, 325–28, 552–53
  in Gilded Age (1885–1950), II:463–64; III:553–54; IV:57–59, 92, 95–100, 154, 372, 453–58, 557–64, 596
  modern (1905–), II:464–65; III:555–56; IV:558–79, 564–68
Illustrated Police News, II:187; IV:372
Illustrated Scientific News, III:109*n*
Illustrated World, IV:47
Illustrations, V:29–30, 84, 122–23
  cover, I:72, 75, 81; IV:689, 718
  early variety of, I:94–95
  fashion, *see* Fashions in dress
  nude, IV:46–47, 152–53, 611; V:145–46
  obscene, I:475
  photography and, IV:148–54
  popularity of, II:192–93
  portraits, *see* Portraits
  quality of, I:208–10, 344, 519–20, 547–48; II:192–93; III:186–87, 190–91; IV:12–13
  scenic, I:115
  of Western scenes, III:58
  See also Aquatints; Cartoons; Chromolithographs; Colored illustrations; Copper-plate illustrations; Engravings; Half-tone pictures; Illustrated periodicals; Lithographs; Steel-plate engravings; Stipple engravings; Woodcuts
Illustrator (Atlanta), IV:92
Illustrator and Process Review, IV:248*n*
Illustrators, leading, IV:150–51
Ilsley, Charles P., II:36
Imagist poetry, V:230, 239
Immigration, I:469; II:122–23; III:50, 275–277; IV:61, 238–39, 668, 743
Imperialism, II:127; IV:163–65; V:89, 330–31
Implement and Hardware Age, IV:188*n*
Implement Journal, IV:188*n*
Implement Review, IV:184*n*
Implement and Tractor (Cincinnati), IV:184*n*
Implement and Tractor (Kansas City), IV:188*n*
Implement and Tractor Age, IV:188*n*
Implement and Vehicle News, IV:183*n*
Implement anl Vehicle Record, IV:184*n*
Impressionist, IV:261
Impressions, IV:126
Improved Order of Red Men, periodical for, III:37*n*
Improvement Era, IV:272, 297
In Our Time (Hemingway), V:11
Income tax, IV:211, 462
Incorporated Society of New York Teachers, I:148
Independence, Mo., IV:296
Independence, Wis., IV:210
Independent (insurance periodical), IV:351*n*
Independent (Kansas City), IV:77, 97–98
Independent (New York and Boston), I:373, 374, 809; II:71, 135, 140, 149, 175, 206, 486, 516, 518; III:6, 11, 14*n*, 63–65, 67, 76, 91, 192, 231, 281, 283, 320, 369, 378, 434, 547; IV:10, 59, 211, 212, 288, 292, 301
  advertising, II:14
  circulation, II:11
  payment to contributors, II:21, 22,
  sketch of, II:367–79
Independent Balance, I:170–71, 795
Independent Order of Odd Fellows, periodicals of, II:215
Independent Practitioner, III:143*n*
Independent Reflector, I:25, 47–48, 787
Independent Thinker, IV:285*n*
Index (Pittsburgh), IV:88
Index (Toledo and Boston), III:78, 91, 146*n;* IV:302
India Rubber Review, IV:184
India Rubber World, IV:184
Indian Bulletin, IV:215*n*
Indian Citizenship Act (1927), V:311
Indian Helper, IV:215*n*
Indian Leader, IV:215*n*
Indian School Journal, IV:215*n*
Indian Sentinel, IV:215*n*
Indiana, University of, philology publication at, IV:128
Indiana Baptist, III:73*n*
Indiana Baptist Outlook, III:73*n*
Indiana Bulletin of Charities and Correction, IV:193

Indiana Farmer (1837), I:444*n*
Indiana Farmer (1845), I:444, 807
Indiana Farmer and Gardener, I:443–44, 807
Indiana magazines, IV:95–96
Indiana Medical Journal, III:141*n*
Indiana School Journal, II:99*n;* IV:270
Indiana Woman, IV:96
Indianapolis, Ind.
  magazine center, IV:95
  magazines before 1865, I:389, 443*n*–44*n;* II:89, 99*n*
  magazines after Civil War
    agricultural, III:161*n*
    amateur, IV:390*n*
    comic, III:268*n*
    dairy, IV:343
    educational, IV:270*n*
    engineering, IV:322*n*
    general, IV:36
    illustrated, IV:95–96
    insurance, III:146*n*
    journalists' periodical, III:274
    manufacturers' periodical, III:128*n*
    Masonic, IV:222*n*
    medical, III:141*n;* IV:313*n*
    music, III:197*n*
    religious, III:74, 80; IV:292*n*
    secret societies, III:315
    sports, III:215*n;* IV:379
    trade, III:216; IV:188*n*
    trade union, IV:220, 221*n*
    women's, IV:361
    women's rights, III:96
Indianapolis Medical Journal, IV:313*n*
Indianian, IV:95–96
Indians, I:774, 778; II:279
  civil rights of, III:314; IV:62, 214–15
  education of, I:563
  literary works on, I:280
  magazines devoted to, IV:214–15
  wars of, I:312; II:548; III:60, 407
Indian's Friend, IV:215
Indicator, III:146*n;* IV:351*n*
Indoors and Out, IV:367*n*
Indoors and Outdoors, V:159
Industrial Age, III:149
Industrial Arts Magazine, IV:272*n*
Industrial Engineering, III:122*n*
Industrial Journal, III:115*n*
Industrial magazines, *see specific industries*
Industrial Review, IV:321
Industrial Workers of the World, III:352; V:212
Industrial World, III:127
Industrial World and Iron Worker, IV:183*n*
Industry, I:340
  magazines on, I:60–61, 340; II:92–93, 251; IV:782
  See also Business; Labor
Information, IV:55*n,* 64
Information periodicals, IV:54–56, 62–64
Ingalls, John James, IV:84, 690
Ingalls' Home and Art Magazine, IV:366
Inge, William Ralph, II:260; IV:520; V:336, 338
Ingelow, Jean, II:377; III:253
Ingersoll, Charles Jared, I:123, 243, 409
Ingersoll, E. P., IV:327
Ingersoll, Ernest, III:54; IV:482
Ingersoll, Robert Green, II:252, 253; III:88; IV:277, 359, 404, 444
Ingersoll, W. H., III:410
Ingersoll Memorial Beacon, IV:177
Ingerson, Carl I., III:126*n*
Inglis, William, II:483
Ingraham, Joseph Holt, I:589*n,* 675, 679; II:37, 410
Ingraham, Prentiss, III:43
Ink, I:20, 85–86; II:8
Ink Fountain, II:93
Inland Architect and Builder, III:129
Inland Monthly Magazine, III:95
Inland Printer, III:132
Inlander, IV:273
Inman, Henry, I:352, 436
Inman, John (editor), I:320*n,* 323, 326, 352, 743–44
Inman, John Hamilton, II:398–99
Innes, George, III:182; IV:144; V:240
Innocent Weekly Owl, II:185*n*
Inquirer (Philadelphia), I:354
Institute Tie, IV:301
Instructor, I:25*n,* 787
Insurance, III:146*n;* IV:350
Insurance Advocate, IV:350*n*
Insurance Advocate and Journal, II:94*n*
Insurance Age, III:146*n*
Insurance companies, III:145; IV:27
Insurance Critic, III:145
Insurance Engineering, IV:322*n,* 351*n*
Insurance Field, IV:351*n*
Insurance Herald, IV:351*n*
Insurance Herald-Argus, III:146*n*
Insurance Index, III:146*n*
Insurance and the Insurance Critic, III:146*n*
Insurance Journal, III:146*n*
Insurance Law Journal, III:146*n;* IV:348
Insurance Magazine, IV:351*n*
Insurance Monitor, II:94*n;* IV:350

Insurance Monitor and Commercial Register, II:94*n*
Insurance Monitor and Wall Street Review, II:96*n*
Insurance News, III:146*n*
Insurance Observer, IV:351*n*
Insurance periodicals, II:93–94, 531; III:145–46, 154, 410; IV:350–51
Insurance Post, IV:351*n*
Insurance Press, IV:350
Insurance Register, IV:351*n*
Insurance Report, IV:351*n*
Insurance Reporter, II:94*n*
Insurance Salesman, III:146*n*
Insurance Sun, IV:351*n*
Insurance Times, III:146*n*
Insurance World, III:146
Intellectualist poetry, V:240–41
Intelligence, III:169; IV:287*n*
Intelligencer, II:61
Intercollegiate Law Review, IV:348
Intercollegiate sports, II:203
Interdenominational periodicals, II:75; IV:301–2, 305
Interim (Richardson), V:173
Interior, III:74; IV:293; V:167
Interior decorating, III:482; IV:545
Internal combustion engine, invention of, IV:319
International, IV:224
International affairs
  in magazines before 1865, I:47, 81, 103*n*, 339–40; II:122–28
  after Civil War, II:254–55, 257, 258, 378; III:351–52, 432–34, 441, 475; IV:517, 519, 553, 662, 700, 761, 780, 783–85; V:51, 55–56, 58, 84–85, 333, 336
  See also names of countries and specific international events
International Book Binder, IV:221*n*
International Chess Magazine, IV:382
International Circulation Managers Association, V:64
International Clinics, IV:314
International Confectioner, IV:187*n*
International copyright, I:393; II:128–30, 385–86; III:15–16, 224, 279, 470, 477, 493–94; IV:41–42, 229
International Correspondence School (Scranton, Pa.), V:151*n*
International Dental Journal, III:143*n*
International Engineer, IV:221*n*
International Good Templar, I:210
International Harvester, V:222
International Journal of Ethics, IV:279
International Journal of Medicine and Surgery, IV:314*n*
International Labor Union movement, III:301
International Magazine, II:31, 158, 165, 170, 188
  sketch of, 406–8
International Magazines Company, V:162
International Miscellany, II:400
International Molders' Journal, II:212*n*
International Monthly, IV:73, 225
International Musician, IV:221*n*
International Press, IV:248*n*
International Press Service, V:67
International Quarterly, IV:73, 225
International Record of Charities and Corrections, IV:742
International Review, II:365; III:16–17, 35, 184, 253–54
International Socialist Review, IV:176
International Studio, IV:146
International Trade Developer, IV:186*n*
International Weekly Miscellany, II:406
International Women's Suffrage Alliance, V:134
International Year Book, V:69, 71
Interstate Grocer, IV:187*n*
Interstate School Review, IV:271*n*
Interview, IV:351*n*
Interviews, III:272, 476
Inventions, II:318, 322; III:116–21; IV:319–20, 592–93, 721
  See also specific inventions
Inventive Age, IV:320*n*
Inventor, II:80
Inventor's and Manufacturer's Gazette, III:116
Investigator (Boston), II:78; III:88; IV:278
Investigator (Chicago), III:146
Investigator and General Intelligencer, I:165*n*, 799
Iowa Agriculturist, IV:341*n*
Iowa Churchman, III:75*n*
Iowa City, Iowa, IV:139; V:179*n*
Iowa Engineer, IV:321*n*
Iowa Farmer, III:157
Iowa Farmer and Horticulturist, II:90*n*
Iowa Farmer's Tribune, III:157
Iowa Historical Record, IV:139
Iowa Homestead, III:157; IV:340; V:37
Iowa Homestead and Northwestern Farmer, II:89
Iowa Instructor, II:99*n*
Iowa Journal of History and Politics, IV:139
Iowa Law Review, IV:348*n*

Iowa Medical Journal, II:84; IV:314*n*
Iowa Normal Monthly, III:169
Iowa School Journal, IV:270*n*
Iowa Socialist, IV:176*n*
Iowa State College, periodicals of, IV:321*n*, 341*n*, 348*n*
Iowa State Library, V:349
Iowa Teacher, IV:271
Iowa Tribune, III:157
Ipswich, Mass., III:259
Ireland, III:275, 276, 392; IV:227
Ireland, Archbishop John, IV:72
Irish
  immigration of
    press hostility, III:276
    public reactions, III:338
  periodicals for, IV:227
  satires on, IV:384
Irish-American, II:76*n*
Irish Echo, IV:227*n*
Irish World, IV:298
"Irishism," II:76
Iron Age, II:92; III:128; IV:183
Iron and Machinery World, II:92
Iron Molders' Journal, II:212*n*
Iron periodicals, III:128; IV:183
Iron and Steel, II:92; IV:183*n*
Iron and Steel Magazine, IV:183*n*
Iron Trade Review, III:128; IV:183*n*
Iron-Clad Age, III:89
Iroquois, IV:70
Irrigation Age, IV:339
Irrigation periodicals, IV:339
Irvine, F. Eugene, IV:364
Irving, Mrs. Helen, I:353
Irving, Henry, III:205; IV:256–57
Irving, Howard, III:265*n*
Irving, John Treat, I:608
Irving, Mary, IV:679
Irving, Washington, I:174, 392, 408, 409, 510–11, 608; II:165, 176, 235, 352, 419, 498, 523; III:550
  as editor, I:125, 171–72, 270–81
Irving, William, I:171
Irving Magazine, II:43
Irwin, Bernard John Dowling, IV:384*n*
Irwin, James P., III:46*n*
Irwin, Richard B., II:550*n*, 551
Irwin, Wallace Admah, III:514; IV:106, 458, 565, 585, 604, 606, 693, 713; V:133–34
Irwin, William Henry, IV:459, 465, 466, 600–1, 696; V:75, 80
Isaacs, Abram S., IV:300
Isaacs, Samuel M., II:77
Ishmaelite, IV:390*n*
Islamic periodicals, IV:287
Isolationism, IV:705, 710; V:56
Israelite, II:78*n*
Israelite Alliance Review, IV:300
Italian literature, I:617; III:375
Italian opera, popularity of, I:432–33; II:196
Italy, I:339; II:122
Items of Interest, III:143*n*
Ithaca, N.Y., III:143; IV:303
Ivanowski, Sigismond de, III:475
Ives, Frederick Eugene, IV:153

J. W. Pepper Piano Music Magazine, IV:252–53
Jabs, IV:390
Jaccaci, Auguste, IV:594–95
Jack and Jill, IV:698, 715
Jackman, W. G., I:322, 612
Jacks, Lawrence Pearsall, IV:295
Jackson, Miss., III:73*n*; IV:270*n*
Jackson, Tenn., III:71*n*, 73
Jackson, Alan R., IV:712
Jackson, Andrew, I:340, 679
Jackson, Charles Tenney, IV:114*n*
Jackson, Edward, III:142*n*
Jackson, Francis, II:275*n*, 285
Jackson, George R., III:270*n*
Jackson, Helen Hunt ("H. H."), II:376, 377, 506*n*, 511*n*; III:13*n*, 229, 257, 314, 374, 378, 424, 427, 461–62, 549; IV:111, 765–66
Jackson, Joseph Henry, IV:105*n*
Jackson, Methro, II:115*n*
Jackson, Sheldon, IV:108
Jackson, Mrs. Thomas Jonathan (Stonewall), IV:92
Jackson, William Henry, IV:103
Jacksonville, Fla., IV:92
Jacobs, William L., IV:565
Jacobs, William P., III:74*n*
Jacobs, W. W., IV:49; V:119
Jacobus, Melancthon Williams, I:534*n*
James, Ed (editor of *Sportsman*), II:204
James, Edmund Janes, III:169; IV:52*n*, 192, 263, 331, 499, 662
James, Frank, III:62
James, Frank Lowher, III:134
James, George Payne Rainsford, II:160, 406; IV:679
James, George Wharton, IV:107*n*, 415, 637
James, Henry (the elder), II:207, 505*n*; III:78, 335
James, Henry, II:248, 257, 398, 398*n*, 401, 424, 431, 482, 505, 510; III:16, 35*n*, 199, 223, 224, 227, 228, 232, 238, 257, 279, 335, 369, 372, 375, 397, 398, 461,

471; IV:51, 85, 130–31, 134, 451, 455, 483, 721; V:x, 90, 175, 342
criticism of, III:244–45
James, Jesse, III:62
James, U. P., III:112
James, William, III:335, 386; IV:74, 295, 722, 727
James, William Grant, III:42*n*
James, William Roderick, IV:566
James Boys Weekly, IV:119
Jameson, John Franklin, IV:138
Jameson, Storm, IV:713
Jamestown, N.Y., III:545; IV:188*n*
Jamestown, N.D., IV:341
Jamestown Tercentenary Exposition, IV:782
Jamison, D. F., I:723–24
Janesville, Wis., II:89
Janvier, Thomas Allibone, II:398; III:397; IV:490, 719, 756
Janvrin, Mrs. Mary, I:587, 592
Japan, II:125; IV:232–33
Jastrow, Joseph, III:540
Jastrow, Morris, III:349; IV:303
Jebb, Richard Claverhouse, IV:226
Jeffers, Robinson, IV:730; V:237, 258
Jefferson, Charles Edward, IV:74*n*
Jefferson, Joseph, I:168; III:203, 472; IV:256, 258, 489
Jefferson, Thomas, I:106, 132, 227, 228; V:195–97, 202, 349
Jefferson City, Mo., III:169
Jeffersonian, IV:163*n*
Jeffries, James J., IV:372, 700
Jeffries, John, I:440
Jelliffe, Smith Ely, III:140*n*
Jenkins, Charles Francis, III:153*n*
Jenkins, Charles W., III:425
Jenkins, Edward, III:249
Jenkins, John, II:62*n*, 517*n*
Jenkins, MacGregor, II:513; V:159–62
Jenks, Francis, I:284*n*, 286
Jenks, Tudor, III:503, 549; IV:645
Jenness Miller Magazine, IV:359
Jennings, Robert, I:536*n*, 537
"Jenny June" (Croly, Jane Cunningham), IV:356
Jerome, Jerome Klapka, II:482; IV:66, 228, 458, 689
Jerome, William Travers, IV:459–60, 754; V:78
Jerrold, Douglas, II:495
Jerry Simpson's Bayonet, IV:178
Jersey Bulletin, III:160
Jersey City, N.J., III:145*n*
Jerseyman, IV:138
Jessop, George Henry, III:530, 555
Jester (Boston, 1845), I:425, 807
Jester (Boston, 1891–92), IV:385
Jester (Philadelphia), IV:385
Jesuit, I:373, 800
Jesuit order, III:68
Jewelers' Circular, IV:188
Jewelers' Review, IV:188*n*
Jewelers' Weekly, IV:188*n*
Jewelry magazines, III:136; IV:188
Jewett, John Punchard, II:494
Jewett, Sarah Orne, II:398*n*, 506*n*, 510, III:508, 546, 558; IV:483, 544, 721, 767
Jewish Advocate, III:80*n*
Jewish Charity, IV:744
Jewish Christian, IV:300*n*
Jewish Comment, IV:300*n*
Jewish Criterion, IV:300*n*
Jewish Era, IV:300*n*
Jewish Evangelist, IV:300*n*
Jewish Exponent, IV:300
Jewish Home, IV:300
Jewish Ledger, IV:300*n*
Jewish magazines, II:77–78; III:80–81; IV:300
Jewish Messenger, II:77; IV:300
Jewish Progress, III:80
Jewish Review, IV:300*n*
Jewish Review and Observer, IV:300*n*
Jewish Spectator, IV:300
Jewish Times, III:80
Jewish Voice, III:80
Jews
press comments on, II:252; IV:565
satires of, IV:383
Jiménez, Juan Ramon, V:243
Jingles, advertising, IV:30–31, 133
Job, Herbert Keightley, IV:637
Jodl, Franz, IV:279
John Crerar Library, V:349
John-Donkey, I:426, 780–83; II:181
John Englishman, I:25*n*, 787
"John Paul," *see* Webb, Charles Henry
John Swinton's Paper, III:300; IV:220
John Three Sixteen, IV:238*n*
Johns Hopkins University, periodicals of, III:66; IV:128
Johns, Orrick, IV:654; V:266
Johnson, Alfred Sidney, IV:71
Johnson, Alva, IV:709, 713
Johnson, Alvin Saunders, V:191*n*, 200, 210, 333
Johnson, Andrew, II:373, 476, 532; III:285, 339–40, 477
Johnson, Burges, III:552*n*
Johnson, C. Stuart, IV:610, 617
Johnson, Charles Howard, IV:47*n*, 385, 564

Johnson, Clifton, III:429
Johnson, Eastman, IV:144
Johnson, Emory Richard, IV:193
Johnson, F. Hilliard, IV:98*n*
Johnson, Francis Howe, IV:398
Johnson, Gerald W., V:12, 222–23
Johnson, Helen Kendrick, IV:354
Johnson, Helen Louise, V:138
Johnson, Henry Lewis, IV:247
Johnson, Hiram, IV:107*n;* V:5, 8
Johnson, Hugh Samuel, IV:709; V:57
Johnson, James J., IV:50*n*
Johnson, James Weldon, V:12, 96
Johnson, Lionel, IV:425, 434
Johnson, Lyndon B., V:323*n*
Johnson, Martin, IV:785
Johnson, Martyn, III:541, 542
Johnson, Oliver, II:141, 282, 284, 285, 286, 372, 373; III:424
Johnson, Owen, III:489; IV:601, 604; V:85
Johnson, Robert L., V:304
Johnson, Robert Underwood, III:457*n*, 461–63, 469–70, 477
Johnson, Rossiter, III:420
Johnson, Samuel (contributor to *Radical*), III:78
Johnson, Samuel William, II:433
Johnson, Stanley Phillips, V:100*n*, 101, 109
Johnson, Thomas M., III:89
Johnson, Tom L., V:152
Johnson, Walter Alexander, IV:214*n*
Johnson, William (lawyer), I:115
Johnson, William Martin, III:388*n*
Johnson, Willis Fletcher, II:259
Johnston, Joseph Eggleston, III:469
Johnston, Mary, II:402, 512; IV:441
Johnston, Myrna, V:45
Johnston, P. P., IV:343
Johnston, Richard Malcolm, II:398*n;* III:46, 400*n*, 465, 503; IV:482
Johnston, Sir Harry, IV:626; V:118
Johnston, W. J., III:122*n*
Jolly Hoosier, III:268*n*
Jolly Joker, II:185*n;* IV:387*n*
Jones, Alexander, II:448
Jones, Charles A. ("Dick Tinto"), III:441
Jones, Charles Henry, III:417*n*, 419
Jones, E. Penrose, II:114*n*
Jones, Garth, V:256
Jones, Harry C., IV:154
Jones, Howard Mumford, IV:730; V:96, 98, 184–85, 264, 345
  Foreword by, V:ix–xiv
Jones, Idwal, V:12
Jones, Ione L., IV:121
Jones, J. Hannum, I:580*n*
Jones, James, II:204*n*
Jones, Jenkin Lloyd, III:78
Jones, Jesse H., III:299
Jones, John A., I:331
Jones, John W. (founder of *Southern Cultivator*), I:444*n*
Jones, John William, III:262
Jones, Kiler K., I:389*n*
Jones, Leonard Augustus, III:144*n*
Jones, Llewellyn, V:168
Jones, Lombard C., V:19
Jones, Richard Lloyd, IV:464
Jones, Roger M., III:535*n*
Jones, Rufus Matthew, I:773*n*, 774; IV:296, 520, 746
Jones, Thomas, Jr., II:94*n*
Jones, Thomas P., I:445, 556–57
Jones, William Alfred
  as contributor, I:680, 712, 719, 726, 760, 770
  quoted, I:348, 406, 415, 427, 490, 719–20
Jones, W. S., I:444*n*
Jordan, David Starr, III:78, 498, 540; IV:73*n*, 105, 106*n*, 107, 262, 494, 662; V:288
Jordan, Elizabeth, III:388*n*, 390
Jordan, William George, IV:127, 506–7, 671*n*, 682
Joseph, Arthur, IV:752
Joslin, Theodore, IV:787
Journal, defined, I:8
Journal (Indianapolis), I:443
Journal (Philadelphia), III:81
Journal of Agriculture, I:442, 808; II:89
Journal of the American Asiatic Association, IV:233
Journal of the American Chemical Society, III:110; IV:309
Journal of the American Electrical Society, III:121
Journal of American Ethnology and Archaeology, IV:140
Journal of American Folk-Lore, IV:128
Journal of the American Foundrymen's Association, IV:183*n*
Journal of the American Geographical Society of New York, II:413
Journal of the American Medical Association, III:141, 317; IV:246, 313
  sketch of, IV:524–35
Journal of American Orthoepy, IV:212
Journal of the American Osteopathic Association, IV:316

Journal of the American Statistical Association, IV:192, 310*n*
Journal of the American Temperance Union, II:210
Journal of the American Unitarian Association, III:436
Journal of the American Veterinary Medical Association, III:143
Journal of Analytical and Applied Chemistry, IV:309
Journal of Applied Chemistry, III:110
Journal of the Arkansas Medical Society, IV:313*n*
Journal of the Association of Engineering Societies, III:114
Journal of Banking Law, III:145*n*
Journal of Belles Lettres, I:191, 207, 796
Journal of Biblical Literature, III:84*n*
Journal of the Boston Society of Medical Sciences, IV:314
Journal of Commerce, II:370
Journal of Commercial Education, IV:352*n*
Journal of Comparative Literature, IV:128
Journal of Comparative Neurology, IV:314
Journal of Cutaneous Diseases Including Syphilis, III:142*n*
Journal of Education, I:490, 804; III:168; IV:268
Journal of Electricity, IV:322
Journal of English and Germanic Philology, IV:128
Journal of Experimental Medicine, IV:315
Journal of Experimental Zoology, IV:310
Journal of Foreign Medical Science and Literature, I:151*n*, 796
Journal of Forestry, IV:343*n*
Journal of the Franklin Institute, I:445, 556–58; II:80; III:115, 121
Journal of Geography, IV:224
Journal of Geology, IV:309
Journal of Germanic Philology, IV:128
Journal of Health, I:440, 800; IV:676
Journal of Hygiene, I:441*n*
Journal of Hygiene and Herald of Health, IV:316
Journal of Infectious Diseases, IV:315
Journal of Internal Medicine, IV:528
Journal of Jurisprudence, see: American Law Journal
Journal of the Kansas Medical Society, IV:314*n*
Journal of the Knights of Labor, III:300*n;* IV:220
Journal of Magnetism, IV:284
Journal of Materia Medica, II:92
Journal of Medical Reform, II:85
Journal of Medical Research, IV:314
Journal of Medicine and Science, IV:313*n*
Journal and Messenger, II:65*n;* IV:292
Journal of the Michigan State Medical Society, IV:314*n*
Journal of the Minnesota Medical Association, III:141*n*
Journal of the Missouri State Medical Association, IV:313*n*
Journal of Morphology, IV:314
Journal of the National Association of Railway Surgeons, III:141*n*
Journal of the New Jersey Medical Society, IV:313*n*
Journal of the New York Microscopical Society, IV:310*n*
Journal of Ophthalmology, Otology and Laryngology, IV:315–16
Journal of Osteopathy, IV:316
Journal of Pedagogy, IV:269*n*
Journal of Philadelphia College of Pharmacy, I:539–40
Journal of Philosophy, Psychology, and Scientific Methods, IV:303
Journal of Physical Chemistry, IV:309
Journal of Physical and Colloidal Chemistry, IV:309*n*
Journal of Political Science, IV:180–81
Journal of Practical Metaphysics, IV:413
Journal of Prison Discipline and Philanthropy, II:212; III:314
Journal of Psycho-Asthenics, IV:315*n*
Journal of Railway Appliances, III:126*n*
Journal of the Rhode Island Institute of Instruction, I:492, 808
Journal of School Education, III:169*n*
Journal of School Geography, IV:224
Journal of Science (Chicago), III:109
Journal of Science (New Haven), *see: American Journal of Science*
Journal of Social Forces, V:284
Journal of Social Science, III:313; IV:192
Journal of the Society of Biblical Literature and Exegesis, III:84
Journal of Sociologic Medicine, IV:313*n*
Journal of Speculative Philosophy, sketch of, III:385–87
Journal of Surgery, Gynecology and Obstetrics, III:143
Journal of the Switchmen's Union, IV:221*n*

Journal of the Telegraph, III:121
Journal of the Times, I:163; II:275
Journal of United Labor, III:300
Journal of the Western Society of Engineers, IV:321
Journal of the Worcester Polytechnic Institute, IV:306*n*
Journalism
  courses on, III:273–74
  histories of, V:66
  literature and, IV:110
  popular, IV:454–55
  See also Newspapers
Journalist, IV:243; V:62–63, 66
Journalists' periodicals, III:273–74; IV:243–44
Journeyman Barber, Hairdresser and Cosmetologist, IV:221*n*
Journeyman Mechanics' Advocate, I:445, 799
Joyce, James, V:94, 173–75, 178, 241, 266
Jubilee Days, III:266
Judd, David W., I:731; III:99*n*
Judd, Henry W., I:731
Judd, Neil Merton, IV:629
Judd, O. B., II:64*n*
Judd, Orange, I:728, 730–32; III:23
Judd, Sylvester, I:488
Judge, II:463, 465, 481; III:199, 268, 328, 525, 552–56; IV:383, 386, 568; V:262
  sketch of, 552–56
Judge, William Quan, IV:287
Judge's Library, III:554
Judge's Quarterly, III:554
Judicious Advertising, IV:247*n*
Judson, Adoniram, I:252
Judson, Edward Z. C. ("Ned Buntline"), I:388, 609; II:37; III:16, 43
Judy, I:425–26, 808; V:248
Juengling, Frederick, II:477; III:188, 191, 411, 466; IV:719
Julien, Louis Antoine, II:195
Juling, Ray Greene, IV:268
Junction City, Kan., IV:97
Junior Cook Book, V:47
Junior Garden Clubs, V:43
Junior Munsey, IV:117*n*, 273
Junior Naturalist Monthly, IV:275
Junior Republic, IV:275
Jury, John G., IV:126
Jusserand, Jean Jules, IV:629
Just Fun, IV:386
Juvenile departments in magazines, III:424, 487
Juvenile Instructor, III:180
Juvenile Magazine, I:144, 792
Juvenile magazines
  early (1789–90), I:29
  in nationalist era (1794–1825), I:144–45
  in expansionist era (1825–50), I:622–23
    illustrations, I:522
    quality and types, II:492–93
  in Civil War era (1850–65)
    engravings, II:193
    trends, II:100 1
    weeklies, II:34, 266–67
  in post-Civil War era (1865–85)
    monthlies, III:500–502, 508–9
    quality and types, III:174–80
    religious juveniles, III:180
    rural, III:179
    weeklies, II:267–68, 270
  in Gilded Age (1885–1905), IV:764–65
    all-fiction magazines, IV:116
    Catholic periodicals, IV:275
    institutional periodicals, IV:275
    leading periodicals, IV:273–74
    mail order periodicals, IV:417–20
    monthlies, III:502–4, 509
    school supplements, IV:275
    Sunday School periodicals, IV:274–75
    weeklies, II:268–73
  modern (1905–), II:274
    monthlies, III:504–5
Juvenile Miscellany, I:492, 799
Juvenile Monitor, I:148, 704
Juvenile novels, III:247–48
Juvenile Olio, I:144, 792
Juvenile Port Folio, I:144, 794

Kaempffert, Waldemar, II:316*n*, 322; III:495*n*, 499; IV:494, 604; V:55
Kahler, Hugh McNair, IV:471, 473
Kahn, Otto Hermann, IV:519; V:171
Kalamazoo, Mich., IV:345*n*
Kaleidoscope, II:59; III:265
Kalischer, Peter, IV:478
Kallen, Horace Meyer, III:542
Kandinsky, Vasili, V:178
Kane, Elisha Kent, II:79, 208, 413, 414, 455
Kane, William R., 428*n*, IV:431
Kaneko, Kentaro, IV:225, 780
Kansas, Civil War era magazines on, II:120–21
Kansas, University of, magazines published by, IV:74, 348*n*

Kansas Breeze, IV:340*n*
Kansas Christian Advocate, IV:291*n*
Kansas Churchman, III:75n
Kansas City, Kan., III:55
Kansas City, Mo.
post-Civil War magazines in (1865–85)
agricultural, III:158
general science, III:109
manufacturers' periodical, III:128
religious, III:73*n,* 80
magazines after 1885
agnostic, IV:277
agricultural, IV:340
all-fiction, IV:117*n*
amateur, IV:390*n*
dental, IV:317
general, IV:47
insurance, IV:351*n*
legal, IV:347*n*
manufacturing, IV:186*n,* 188*n*
medical, III:141*n;* IV:315
music, IV:254
poultry, IV:345*n*
real estate, III:148
religious, II:67*n;* IV:285–86, 292*n*
trade, IV:188*n*
urban weeklies, IV:97–98, 117*n*
Kansas City Bar Monthly, IV:347*n*
Kansas City Jeweler and Optician, IV:188*n*
Kansas City Lancet, III:141*n*
Kansas City Medical Index, III:141*n*
Kansas City Medical Record, III:141*n*
Kansas City Review of Science and Industry, III:109
Kansas Educational Review, II:99*n*
Kansas Farmer, II:90; III:158; IV:340
Kansas Industrialist, III:127*n*
Kansas Knocker, IV:387*n*
Kansas Lawyer, IV:348*n*
Kansas Magazine, III:55
Kansas Medical Index, III:141*n*
Kansas Methodist, III:71*n*
Kansas Telephone, III:77*n*
Kansas University Quarterly, IV:74
Kansas-Nebraska Bill (1854), II:133–34 242
Kantor, MacKinlay, IV:713
Kaplan, H. Eliot, III:296*n*
Kapp, Friedrich, III:336
Kappa Tau Alpha, V:347
Karst, John, III:191
Kasson, Frank H., III:168*n;* IV:268
Kastle, Martin, IV:89
Kate Field's Washington, IV:61–62
Kaufman, Herbert, IV:367*n,* 493, 589*n,* 605
Kauffman, Reginald Wright, V:264
Kazin, Alfred, V:218
Kean, Edmund, I:169
Keane, John Joseph, III:69*n*
Kearney, Francis, I:209
Kearney, Martin J., II:77
Keating, John W., III:141*n*
Keating, William Hypolitus, I:557
Keats, John, I:661
Keeler, Harry Stephen, III:270*n*
Keeler, James Edward, IV:308
Keeler, Ralph, III:359–60
Keenan, Henry Francis, III:248
Keene, Laura, III:204
Keepapitchinin, III:266
Keer, Charles H., IV:204
Keese, George Pomeroy, II:425
Keet, Alfred Ernest, IV:511*n,* 517
Kefauver, Estes, V:319
Kehoe, Lawrence, III:329*n*
Keimer, Samuel, IV:683
Keith's Magazine on Home Building, IV:324
Kelland, Clarence Budington, III:515; IV:503, 616, 695, 709, 713, 771
Kellen, William V., III:295*n*
Keller, A. R., IV:751*n*
Keller, Albert Calloway, V:329*n*
Keller, Helen, IV:546
Kelley, Florence, IV:744, 745, 747
Kelley, James, I:389*n*
Kelley, William Valentine, I:299*n,* 301
Kellock, Harold, V:88*n,* 94
Kellogg, Alice M., III:177
Kellogg, Ansel Nash, III:53, 125*n,* 273
Kellogg, Arthur P., IV:743
Kellogg, Clara, IV:98
Kellogg, Clara Louise (opera singer), II:195
Kellogg, E. M., III:177
Kellogg, Edward Leland, IV:269
Kellogg, F. Beulah, IV:361
Kellogg, Gertrude, IV:256
Kellogg, Paul U., IV:741*n,* 743–50
Kellogg, Vernon, V:85
Kellogg, Warren F., 79*n*
Kelly, A. O. J., I:566*n*
Kelly, Elisha W., IV:651
Kelly, Eugene, IV:85
Kelly, John C., III:158*n*
Kelly, Myra, IV:601; V:30
Kelly, Thomas, IV:85
Kelly, Thomas Howard, IV:607; V:246*n,* 271
Kelly, William Valentine, IV:291
Kelmscott Press, V:182
Kelsey, Charles E., 262*n,* 273

Kemble, Edward Winsor, III:268, 473, 504, 552; IV:26, 29, 151, 456, 484, 496, 561
Kemble, Frances Ann, II:506*n*
Kemp, Harry, V:266
Kemp, Oliver, IV:698
Kemper, Mary Jean, IV:761
Kendall, Otis H., III:34*n*
Kendallville, Ind., III:161
Kendrick, Charles, II:335, 402; III:267, 268; IV:561
Kenealy, A. J., IV:636
Kennan, George, II:414, 429; III:398, 430, 473; IV:40, 231–32, 342, 620
Kennebec Farmer, I:444*n*
Kennedy, Crammond, III:422–23
Kennedy, James Harrison, III:262*n*
Kennedy, John B., IV:470, 472
Kennedy, John F., V:315–17, 320, 323*n*
Kennedy, John Pendleton, I:155, 204; II:424, 425, 497*n*
  as contributor, I:295, 651, 726, 751
  es editor, I:171, 172
  evaluations of, I:408, 409
Kennerley, Mitchell, IV:511*n,* 518, 652
Kensett, John Frederick, II:188; III:187
Kent, Frank Richardson, IV:728, 730; V:10
Kent, Ira Rich, 262*n,* 273
Kent, James, I:115, 255, 748
Kent, Mabel, B:154*n*
Kent, Rockwell, III:479, 489; IV:748
Kentucky Abolition Society, I:164
Kentucky Church Chronicle, III:75*n*
Kentucky Family Journal, II:59
Kentucky Freemason, II:215*n*
Kentucky Garland, II:58
Kentucky Law Reporter, III:144*n*
Kentucky Livestock Record, III:159
Kentucky Medical Journal, IV:33*n*
Kentucky Stock Farm, III:159; IV:343
Kenyon, F. C., III:108*n*
Keogh, James, III:69
Keokuk, Iowa, II:84; III:169; IV:254*n*
Keppler, Joseph, II:462, 523; III:191, 267, 268, 286, 521–30, 552
Keppler, Joseph, Jr., III:530, 531
Ker, David, IV:482
Keramic Studio, IV:147
Kerfoot, John Barrett, IV:501, 565; V:84
Kern, Richard A., I:566*n*
Kernot, Henry, II:41*n*
Kerr, Alvah Milton, IV:45*n*
Kerr, Joe, 48*n,* 196
"Kerr, Orpheus C.," *see* Newell, Robert Henry
Kerr, Sophie, IV:471, 472, 604, 709, 729, 769
Ketcham, Silas, III:36*n*
Kettell, Samuel, I:601, 713
Kettell, Thomas Prentice, I:678*n,* 681–82 696*n*
Key, I:790
Key, Francis Scott, I:204
Key, Ted, IV:714
Key, Thomas J., III:155
Keyes, Frances Parkinson, V:134
Keyes, George T., III:296*n*
Keyes, Henry W., V:134
Keynes, John Maynard, IV:521; V:211, 336
Keynote, III:197
Keys, Clement Melville, IV:776–78
Keyser, Harriette A., IV:221*n*
Keyserling, Count Hermann Alexander, II:404
Keystone (jewelry), III:136; IV:188*n*
Keystone (Masonic), III:314; IV:222*n*
Keystone (women's clubs), IV:356*n*
Khayyám, Omar, *see* Omar Khayyám
Khrushchev, Nikita, V:323*n*
Kiefer, Daniel, IV:62
Kieffer, Henry Martyn, III:502
Kihn, William Langdon, IV:630
Kilbourne, Fannie, III:488
Kildal, Arne, III:350
Kilgallen, Dorothy, IV:504
Kilgo, John Carlisle, IV:213; V:274, 276–77, 281–82
Killion, John Joseph (Jake Kilrain), II:333; IV:371
Kilmer, Joyce, III:330; IV:438; V:236, 258
Kilpatric, Guy, IV:473, 709
Kilrain, Jake (John Joseph Killion), II:333; IV:371
Kimball, Arthur Reed, IV:113*n,* 150, 614
Kimball, Fred M., IV:344*n,* 345
Kimball, Grace Atkinson, V:154*n*
Kimball, Ingalls, IV:450–51; V:156, 200
Kimball, Mrs. Lou H., III:52
Kimball, Richard Burleigh, II:171, 420, 429, 462, 542; III:18, 511
Kimball's Dairy Farmer, IV:344*n*
Kindergarten Magazine, IV:272
Kindergarten Messenger, III:163
Kindergarten Messenger and New Education, III:163
Kindergarten News, IV:272
Kindergarten periodicals, III:163; IV:272
Kindergarten Review, IV:272

King, Basil, II:431; IV:604, 695
King, Ben, V:118
King, Charles, III:178*n*, 400, 533; IV:49*n*, 116*n*
King, Clarence, II:506*n*; III:405
King, Clyde Lyndon IV:193*n*
King, Edward S., III:48, 398, 464–65
King, Finlay M., II:215
King, Francis Scott, III:188
King, Grace Elizabeth, I:535; II:398*n*; III:400, 465
King, Mrs. H. C., II:490
King, Herbert Booth, IV:247
King, Horatio Collins, III:422*n*
King, John, II:45
King, Joseph, IV:397
King, Martin Luther, V:323*n*
King, Mitchell, I:724; II:488
King, Rufus, III:260
King, William P., II:66*n*
Kingdom, IV:283
Kingdon & Boyd, III:411
Kingsland, William G., IV:121
Kingsley, Charles, II:377; III:249
Kingsley, Elbridge, IV:719
Kingsley, Florence Morse, V:33
Kingsley, James Luce. II:233
Kingsley, Rev. William L., II:312*n*, 313, 315; V:329–30
Kinmont, Alexander, I:491
Kinnaman, J. O., III:112*n*
Kinney, Coates, II:114
Kinnosuke, Adachi, IV:662
Kinsley, Apollos, I:122*n*
Kip, William Ingraham, I:669; II:365
Kipke, Harry, IV:700
Kipling, Rudyard, II:269, 482; III:400, 472, 486, 494, 503, 550; IV:132–33; V:51, 73, 117, 342
  as contributor, IV:7, 41, 49*n*, 114*n*, 456, 457, 490, 501, 544, 546, 591–92, 593, 601, 689, 692, 721, 722, 781
  discussion of, IV:37, 141, 226, 230, 433, 641–43
Kipling Note Book, IV:133
Kiplingiana, IV:133
Kiplinger, Willard Monroe, IV:730
Kirby, Rollin, IV:566
Kirby, Dr. S. R., II:85*n*
Kirchner, Raphael, III:531
Kirchwey, Freda, III:331*n*, 354–56
Kirk, Edward C., II:91*n*
Kirk, John Foster, III:33–34, 396–99
Kirk, Thomas, I:132*n*
"Kirke, Edmund," *see* Gilmore, James Roberts
Kirkland, Mrs. Caroline Matilda Stansbury, II:309, 310, 425, 543; IV:385
  as contributor, I:546, 585, 609, 720, 743, 760
  as editor, I:347, 769–70
  quoted, I:414, 420
Kirkland, John Thornton, I:255, 571
Kirkland, Joseph, III:540
Kirkpatrick, J. D., II:62*n*
Kirkpatrick, T. J., IV:763*n*, 764, 766, 768
Kirksville, Mo., IV:316
Kirtland, Jared Potter, II:115*n*
Kirtland, Ohio, II:74
Kiser, Samuel Ellsworth, III:554; IV:713
Kitchen Ideas, V:47
Kittle, William, IV:415
Kittredge, E. A., I:441
Kittredge, George Lyman, III:236*n*, 347, 536
Klapp, Eugene, IV:324; V:154*n*, 155–57
Klauber, M. L., 175*n*
Klaw, Marc, IV:255
Klee, Paul, V:178
Klein, Charles, IV:410, 493
Kline, Henry Blue, V:116*n*
Klondike gold rush, IV:1, 108–9, 322
Klopsch, Louis, V:286, 288
Knapp, Arnold, III:142*n*
Knapp, George R., IV:65*n*
Knapp, Herman, III:141, 142
Knapp, Isaac, II:275*n*, 278, 283, 284
Knapp, Joseph Palmer, IV:70, 468–77, 768
"Knapp, Mrs. Louisa," *see* Curtis, Louisa Knapp
Knapp, O. H., II:115*n*
Knapp, Samuel Lorenzo, I:127*n*, 343
Knapp's Liberator, II:285
Knaufft, Ernest, III:185*n*; IV:148*n*
Kneeland, Abner, III:88*n*
Knerr, Col. Hugh J., V:23
Knibbs, Henry Herbert, IV:114*n*, 116*n*, 365*n*
Knickerbocker, William Skinkle, IV:733*n*, 737–38
"Knickerbocker literature," III:28
Knickerbocker Magazine, I:274–75, 393, 424, 432–33, 446–47, 449–50, 505–6, 510, 515, 523, 618, 704–5; II:5, 14, 21, 30, 149, 165, 177, 388, 396, 426, 524*n*, 540, 541
  founding of, I:345
  sketch of, II:606–14
Knight, Albion Williamson, IV:736
Knight, Frank Hyneman, IV:181*n*

Knight, Franklin, II:75*n*
Knight, H. Ralph, IV:712*n*
Knight, John S., V:222*n*
Knights of Honor Reporter, III:315
Knights of Labor, III:298–300, 302–3
Knights of Pythias, III:37*n*; IV:221
Knipe, Alden Arthur, III:504
Knipe, Emily Benson, IV:496
Knister, Raymond, V:179*n*, 184
Knocker, IV:300*n*
Knopf, Alfred A., V:4, 13, 17, 19, 270
Knopf, Samuel, V:17
Knott, Richard Wilson, III:47
Knott, Thomas, V:344
Knowledge, IV:64
Knowles, James Davis, I:666
Knox, J. Armory, III:270
Knox, Thomas Wallace, II:462
Knoxville, Tenn., III:71*n*, 154; IV:324, 341
Kobbe, Gustav, IV:261*n*
Koch, Kenneth, V:244
Koch, Robert, IV:311
Kock, Charles Paul de, I:359, 362
Koehler, Hugh W., IV:785
Koehler, Sylvester Rosa, III:185
Koeppen, Adolph Louis, II:28
Koestler, Arthur, IV:478
Kohlsaat, Herman Henry, IV:697
Kollmar, Richard, IV:504
Kollock, Shepard, I:112–13
Komroff, Manuel, III:543
Kopelin, Louis, IV:206*n*
Kopkind, Andrew, V:191*n*
Kossuth, Louis, II:123–5, 290, 373
Kotzebue, August Friedrich Ferdinand von, I:168, 248; IV:121*n*
Koves, Helen, V:135
Kraemer, Henry, I:539*n*
Krapp, George Philip, V:7
Krauth, August, II:37*n*
Krauth, Charles Philip, II:73
Krehbiel, Henry Edward, III:197*n*; IV:261*n*
Kretchmar, Ella M., IV:767
Kroeber, Alfred L., IV:308
Kroeger, Adolph Ernst, III:386
Kroll, Henry Harrison, IV:606
Kroneberger, Louis, V:306
Kropotkin, Peter Alexevich, IV:232, 517
Krout, John Allen, IV:180*n*
Kruell, George, II:477; III:188, 466; IV:719, 720
Krumbhaar, E. B., I:556*n*
Krupp, John, I:185*n*
Krutch, Joseph Wood, III:331*n*, 354–55; IV:737
Ku Klux Klan, V:6, 212, 284
Kuhn, Ferdinand, IV:749*n*
Kunitz, Stanley, V:243
Kunkel's Musical Review, III:198*n*; IV:251
Kuprin, Alexander, V:98
Kurtz, Charles M., III:185
Kurtz, W., 58*n*
Kyle, Melvin Grove, I:739*n*, 742
Kyne, Peter B., III:489; IV:116*n*, 466, 471, 498, 694, 695

L.A.W. Magazine, IV:379*n*
L. B. Case's Botanical Index, III:111
L. J. Callanan's Monthly, IV:187*n*
Labor, *see* Anarchism; Socialism; Strikes; Trade union periodicals; Trade unions; Working class
Labor Balance, III:299
Labor Enquirer, III:300
Labor Herald, IV:220
Labor Standard, III:300
Labouchère, Henry, II:255
La Bree, Benjamin, IV:139
Labree, Lawrence, I:365
Lace Maker, IV:185*n*
Lackaye, Wilton, IV:133, 357
La Cossitt, Henry, IV:453*n*, 475–76
LaCrosse, Wis., IV:199
Ladd, George Trumbull, IV:262, 396
Ladd, Joseph Brown, I:40, 102
Ladd, William, II:211*n*
Ladies' Companion, I:352, 515
  sketch of, I:626–28; II:384
Ladies' Floral Cabinet, III:161
Ladies' Garland, I:517, 804
  sketch of, I:672
Ladies' and Gentlemen's Weekly Literary Museum and Musical Magazine, I:173, 796
Ladies' Home Companion, IV:763*n*, 765–66
Ladies' Home Journal (Philadelphia), II:434; III:137, 505; IV:4, 15, 16, 17, 21, 29, 31, 32, 35, 37, 39, 41, 87, 229, 245, 360, 363, 460, 504, 528, 587, 597*n*, 681–82, 687, 688, 693, 694, 698, 708, 715, 770; V:37, 43–44, 74, 131, 140, 150
  advertising in, III:11
  circulation of, III:7
  founding of, III:100; IV:536–37
  sketch of, IV:536–55
Ladies' Home Journal (San Francisco), III:101
Ladies' Home Topics, IV:367*n*

Ladies' Illustrated Magazine, I:555
Ladies' Illustrated Newspaper, III:99
Ladies' Journal, IV:89
Ladies' Literary Cabinet, I:139, 796
Ladies' Literary Port Folio, I:354, 800
Ladies' Magazine (Boston), I:349–50, 606, 799
Ladies' Magazine (Chicago), IV:367*n*
Ladies' Magazine (Philadelphia), I:353, 362, 449, 733*n*, 734
Ladies' Magazine and Musical Repository, I:173, 791
Ladies' Messenger, IV:357*n*
Ladies' Museum, I:791
Ladies' Own Magazine, III:95
Ladies' Pearl, I:354, 805; II:58
Ladies' Quarterly Report of Broadway Fashions, III:481
Ladies' Repository (Boston), II:57; III:98
Ladies' Repository (Cincinnati), I:388, 522, 805; II:57, 65, 192; III:55, 70, 98, 184, 186
  sketch of, II:301–5
Ladies' Review, IV:222
Ladies' World, III:99; IV:360, 366, 603
Ladies' Wreath, I:353, 513, 522, 808; II:14, 57*n*
Lady and Gentleman's Pocket Magazine, I:35, 122*n*, 790
"Lady or the Tiger?" (Stockton), III:20, 228, 472
Lady's Bazar, III:98*n*
Lady's Book, see: Godey's Lady's Book
Lady's Companion, II:301
Lady's Dollar Newspaper, I:354, 582, 809
Lady's Friend, II:59
Lady's Home Magazine, II:416*n*
Lady's Magazine, I:37, 65–66, 789
Lady's Weekly Miscellany, I:139, 792
Lady's Western Magazine, I:389–90, 809
Lady's World, II:306*n*, 308
Lady's World of Literature and Fashion, II:306*n*
La Farge, C. Grant, V:7
La Farge, John, III:182, 472; IV:144, 151, 225, 455, 602, 726
La Farge, Oliver, IV:701
Lafayette, Ind., III:149*n*; IV:184*n*
  music journal in, IV:251
La Follette, Robert Marion, III:352, 514; V:90, 212
La Follette, Suzanne, V:88*n*, 90, 92, 98–99
La Follette, William Leroy, V:90
Lagarde, Ernest, II:113*n*
Lagate, Henry R., IV:203
Lagerlöf, Selma, V:133
La Gorce, John Oliver, IV:620*n*, 622*n*, 632
La Guardia, Fiorello, V:24
Lakeside Monthly, III:53, 184, 234, 539
  sketch of, 413–16
Lakeside Publishing Company, III:415
Lakey, Charles D., III:130
Lamade, Dietrick, IV:68*n*, 69
Lamade, George R., IV:68*n*
Lamade, Howard J., IV:68*n*
Lamb, Arthur Becket, III:110*n*
Lamb, Martha J., III:260
Lambdin, Alfred Cochran, III:320
Lambert, Alexander, IV:532
Lambert, Mrs. James H., IV:538
Lambert, Louis A., III:69; IV:298
Lambert, Mary, IV:117*n*
Lambert Pharmacal Co., V:15, 16
Lambing, A. A., III:261*n*
Lamoni, Iowa, III:81
Lamont, Hammond, III:331*n*, 348
Lamont, Thomas William, IV:466–68
Lamp, III:236*n*
Lamphear, Emory, IV:315
Lampman, Archibald, IV:722
Lampoons, *see* Satires and lampoons
Lamprecht, Karl, IV:225
Lampson, J. L., III:168
Lampton, William James, III:554; IV:38, 66, 80, 186, 328; V:251
Lamson, Alvan, I:284*n*, 288
Lamson, Edwin Ruthven, IV:125
Lancaster, Frank H., IV:244
Lancaster, Pa., II:99*n*
Lancaster Law Review, III:144*n*
Land and Freedom, IV:179–80
Land of Sunshine, IV:107
Land We Love, III:46
Landis, Robert W., II:537, 538
Landon, Alfred M., IV:533, 577, 660
Landon, C. W., III:197
Landon, Letitia E., I:400–401
Lane, Charles, I:709
Lane, Franklin Knight, IV:617, 629, 785
Lane, Gertrude Battles, IV:763*n*, 768–70
Lane, Laurence William, IV:105*n*, 106*n*
Lane, Rose Wilder, IV:700, 709
Lane, Samuel W., IV:365
Lane, Winthrop D., IV:747
Lang, Andrew, I:535, II:255, 377, 399, 401; III:511, 551; IV:36, 61, 112, 426, 433, 451, 490, 513, 722
Lang, Ossian H., IV:517
Langdon, William C., II:510*n*
Langley, Samuel Pierpont, IV:334, 487
Langner, Lawrence, V:171
Langton, William M., IV:109

Langtree, Samuel Daly, I:346, 606*n*, 606–07, 678–80
Langtry, Lily, III:205; IV:259
Language, American
satires on, I:235–36
stylistic criticisms of, I:147–48
See also Style, literary
Langworthy, I. P., II:71*n*
Lanham, Edwin, IV:475
Lanier, Albert Gallatin, III:500*n*
Lanier, Charles Day, IV:129, 369, 484; V:118, 122
Lanier, Henry Wysham, IV:637, 774–75, 783; V:117*n*, 118, 122–24
Lanier, Lyle, V:116*n*
Lanier, Sidney, II:377, 498, 508; III:46, 46*n*, 47, 231, 238, 241, 374, 397, 398, 463; V:278–80
Lanigan, George T., III:20; IV:559
Lankes, Julius J., IV:748
Lanman, Charles, I:611–12, 626, 644
Lanman, James H., I:697
Lannan, J. Patrick, V:243–44
Lansdale, Pa., III:140*n*
Lansing, Mich., III:169; IV:314*n*, 345, 390
Lansing, Robert, IV:617
Lantern, see: Diogenes hys Lanterne
Lantern (New Orleans), IV:93
Lantern (Portland), IV:107–08
Lapham, William Berry, III:259
Laprade, William T., V:273*n*, 282–83
Laramie, Wyo., III:269
Larcom, Lucy, II:22, 377, 417, 505*n*; III:100, 175, 229, 501; IV:44*n*, 80, 292
Lardner, John, IV:712
Lardner, Ring, III:504, 555; IV:469, 498, 567, 693, 695; V:121, 134
Lark, IV:388
Larkin, Aimee, IV:470
Larned, Augusta, III:394, 395
Larned, William Augustus, II:312*n*, 313, 314
Larrabee, Charles B., IV:246*n*
Larrabee, William Clark, II:301*n*
Larsen, Roy E., V:304, 322
Laryngoscope, IV:315*n*
Lash, Joseph P., V:218
Lasker, Albert D., V:298
Lasker, Bruno, IV:747
Lasker's Chess Magazine, IV:382
Laski, Harold J., II:404; III:542; IV:438; V:92, 203, 206, 208, 211, 336
Last Sensation, III:44
Latham, O'Neill, III:530
Lather, IV:221*n*
Lathrop, George Parsons, I:683, 691; II:493*n*, 506*n*, 511*n*; III:51*n*, 186, 465*n*; IV:60, 78, 83, 154, 299, 559, 633
Lathrop, John, I:84, 85
Lathrop, John, Jr., I:122*n*
Latin America
American interest in, IV:236–37
imperialist plans for, II:127
See also Cuba; Spanish-American War
Latrobe, Benjamin Henry, I:156
Latrobe, John Hazlehurst Boneval, I:204, 294
Latter-Day Saints, *see* Mormon periodicals
Lattimore, Owen, IV:631
Lattin, Frank H., III:111
Latzke, Paul, IV:690, 691
Lauder, Harry, IV:697
Laugel, Auguste, III:336, 347
Laughlin, James Laurence, III:498; IV:180, 181, 500, 662, 728
Laundry magazines, III:132
Laut, Agnes C., IV:637
Lauzanne, Stéphane, III:434; IV:519
Laval, Pierre, V:323*n*
La Varre, William, V:3*n*, 25–26
Law, William, I:172*n*
Law Bulletin, IV:348*n*
Law Intelligencer, I:451, 800
Law Journal, III:144
Law journals
before 1865, I:154–55, 342*n*, 451–52; II:34, 93
in post-Civil War era (1865–85) III:145*n*, 336
circulation, III:144
medico-legal journals, III:142
mid-western, III:51
number and quality, III:144
in Gilded Age (1885–1905), IV:346–48
circulation, IV:346–47
law schools and, IV:347–48
medico-legal periodicals, IV:348
number, IV:346
Law Notes, IV:347
Law schools, IV:346–48
Law Student's Helper, IV:348*n*
Lawes, Lewis E., IV:787
Lawn Tennis, IV:377
Lawn tennis periodicals, IV:377
Lawrence, D. H., III:543; IV:729; V:230, 258
Lawrence, David, IV:707
Lawrence, Henry W., III:37*n*
Lawrence, Isaac, I:678*n*; II:28*n*
Lawrence, J. J., III:140

Lawrence, Joseph Stagg, IV:663
Lawrence, Kan., IV:97, 215*n*
Lawrence, Sir Thomas, I:620
Lawrence, Thomas Edward, IV:787
Lawrence, William Beach, II:234
Laws of Health, III:139
Laws of Life, II:53
Lawson, Alexander, I:209
Lawson, Helen, I:243
Lawson, John Davison, III:144*n*
Lawson, Theodore W., IV:476
Lawson, Thomas William, IV:47, 126*n,* 168, 208, 651, 778; V:75–83, 87
Lawson, W. B., IV:274
Lawton, William Cranston, II:510*n*
Lawyers
  early magazines and (1741–94)
    editors, I:71, 78
    satires on, I:58
    feelings against, I:58–59
  nationalist era magazines and (1794–1825)
    contributors, I:139, 154–56
    editors, I:154, 282, 297, 332
    literary clubs, I:243
    praise of, I:155–56
expansionist era magazines and (1825–50)
    editors, I:551, 601–2, 664
    publishers, I:388
  Civil War era magazines and (1850–65)
    contributors, II:224, 227–28, 470
    editors, II:224
  post-Civil War magazines and (1865–85), III:454
  Gilded Age magazines and (1885–1905), IV:346, 569
  professional magazines of, *see* Law journals
Lazarus, Emma, III:374, 397, 463, 549
Lazarus, Marx E., II:535
Lea, Henry Charles, II:542; III:34*n,* 337; IV:192
Leach, Anna, IV:612
Leach, Henry Goddard, IV:511*n,* 519–22
Leacock, Stephen, III:514, 532; V:121
Leader (Boston music journal), III:197*n*
Leader (New York single-tax paper), IV:179
Leader (New York week-end paper), II:38
League of American Penwomen, V:9
League of Nations
  press comment on, IV:663; V:208
  support for, II:377, 378; IV:785
Leander Richardson's Illustrated Dramatic Weekly, IV:260*n*
Lease, Mary Elizabeth, IV:204
Leather Gazette, III:127*n*
Leather industry periodicals, IV:185, 188, 189*n*
Leather Manufacturer, III:127; IV:185
Leather and Shoes, IV:189*n*
Leaves of Healing, IV:286
Leavis, F. R. and Q. D., IV:739
Leavitt, John McDowell, II:364*n,* 365; III:35*n*
Leavitt, Joshua, I:373, 457; II:369, 371, 372
Lebanon, Pa., IV:138, 295*n*
Lebrun, Ricco, III:489
Lechlitner, Ruth, V:187
Lecky, William Edward Hartpole, IV:226, 513
Le Conte, Joseph, III:406, 407; IV:74
Lecturers
  Chautauqua movement, III:173, 544–47
  earnings, III:171–72
  European, III:249–51; IV:226
  leading lecturers, III:172, 446, 450–51
  scientific, III:250
  women lecturers, III:93
  See also Lyceum lectures
Lederer, Charles A., II:325*n,* 328
Ledger, see: New York Ledger
Ledger Monthly, II:356*n,* 363
Lee, Albert, IV:464
Lee, Algernon, IV:175*n*
Lee, Bee Virginia, III:402*n*
Lee, Charles, I:27–28, 42
Lee, Gerald Stanley, II:431; III:549
Lee, Henry, I:184
Lee, James Melvin, III:552*n,* 555; V:67
Lee, Joseph, IV:744
Lee, Mary Elizabeth, I:700
Lee, Muna, V:266
Lee, Olive B., IV:94
Lee, Richard, I:53, 122*n*
Lee, General Robert Edward, III:383; V:275, 280
Lee, Sarah Tomerlin, V:154*n,* 165
Lee, William, II:495*n*
Lee, William F., II:70*n*
Lee's Texas Magazine, IV:94
Leeser, Isaac, II:77
Leet, Glen, IV:749
Lefèvre, Edwin, IV:117*n,* 691, 693; V:81
Leffel, James, III:116*n*
Leffel's Illustrated Mechanical News, III:116
Leffingwell, Charles Wesley, III:75; IV:294
Legal Advisor, II:93; III:144

Legal Bibliography, III:144*n*
Legal and Insurance Reporter, II:94*n*
Legal Intelligencer, II:93*n;* III:144
Legal Journal, III:144
Legal News, III:144
Legal periodicals, *see* Law Journals
Le Gallienne, Richard, III:485, 487; IV:37, 125, 360*n*, 426–27, 490, 492, 618, 645–46; V:133, 251, 258
Legaré, Hugh Swinton, I:155, 205, 383, 573–75, 699
Legaré, J. D., I:442*n*
Legaré, J. M., I:756
Legaré, James W., II:345
Léger, Fernand, V:178
Leggett, T. B., II:45
Leggett, William, I:323, 326, 355–56, 611
Legion of Honor (of France), V:64
Legion for the Survival of Freedom, Inc., V:3*n*, 26*n*
Legislative reports, I:72, 75, 78, 93, 109, 143, 158; III:441
  See also Congress
Leibnitz, Gottfried Wilhelm von, III:386
Leisure, III:39*n*
Leisure, increase in, III:209
Leisure Hours (New York), III:39*n*
Leisure Hours (Philadelphia), IV:44
Leisure Hours (Pittsburgh), III:31*n*
Leland, Charles Godfrey, I:544*n*, 554–55, 587*n*, 606*n*, 609, 612–13, 771; II:24, 30, 33, 44, 87, 184, 407, 551; III:13*n*, 41*n*, 211, 257, 264, 397; IV:87
  as editor, 520*n*, 524, 527, 540–43
Lemley, Walter H., III:83*n*
Lend a Hand, IV:193, 742
Leney, William Satchwell, I:209
Lengel, William Charles, V:246*n*, 271
Lenin, Vladimir Ilyich, V:97
Lenson, Robert H., I:426
Lenz, Frank G., IV:376, 636
Lenz, Sidney S., III:555
Leonard, Albert, IV:269*n*
Leonard, Baird, IV:567
Leonard, Ella S., IV:61
Leonard, Harry, IV:567
Leonard, P. A., IV:104, 322*n*
Leonard, William Ellery, V:184
Leonard Scott & Company, II:129
Le Queux, William, IV:84
Lerner, Max, III:331*n*, 355; V:218, 222
Lescarboura, Austin C., II:316*n*, 323
Leslie, Eliza, I:353, 584, 612, 733–34
Leslie, Frank, I:771; II:31, 44, 130, 409–12, 437–41, 452–65; III:24, 35–36, 44, 269*n*, 510
  background of, II:452–53
Leslie, Mrs. Frank ("Miriam Florence Squier"), II:439*n*, 440–441, 452, 462–63; III:510*n*, 511; IV:44, 57
Leslie, Shane, IV:440
Leslie's Monthly Magazine, III:510*n*, 512
Leslie's Weekly, II:44, 110, 144, 146, 150, 156, 198, 386*n*, 474; IV:10, 39, 57, 686; V:xiii
  circulation of, II:10, 102
  illustration in, II:54, 193
  relationship to *Harper's Weekly,* II:470, 476
Leslie's Weekly (*Frank Leslie's Illustrated Newspaper*), III:16, 28, 40, 269*n*, 274, 286, 294, 554, 555
  advertising in, III:10
Lessing, Bruno, III:532; IV:493
Lessing, Gotthold Ephraim, II:164
Le Sueur, Meridel, IV:729
Letters on Brewing, IV:186*n*
"Letters from Prison" (Emma Goldman), V:169
Leupp, Francis Ellington, III:296*n*
Leveque, Joseph Mark, IV:91, 93
Lever, III:310
Lever, Charles James, II:384, 385, 454, 476; III:224
Levering, Albert, III:484, 531; IV:565
Levien, Sonya, IV:605
Levison, M. A., II:184
Levison, W. H., II:179
Lewis, Alfred Henry, IV:46, 186, 386, 414, 492–93, 495, 496, 500
"Lewis, Amelia," *see* Freund, Mrs. John C.
Lewis, Charles Bertrand ("M. Quad"), II:180; III:271*n;* IV:59*n*, 384*n*
Lewis, Charlotte, V:154*n*
Lewis, Charlton Thomas, II:430
Lewis, David, II:398
Lewis, Dean, IV:533
Lewis, Enoch, I:773
Lewis, Grace Hegger, III:489
Lewis, H. N. F., I:444*n;* II:90; III:52, 179
Lewis, Henry Alfred, V:75
Lewis, Henry Harrison, IV:775
Lewis, Howard J., IV:417*n*
Lewis, John L., V:299
Lewis, Mrs. Juan, III:96
Lewis, Samuel H., II:77
Lewis, Sinclair, IV:471, 498, 503, 695, 769; V:12, 81, 95, 136, 264, 309–11

Lewis, Taylor, II:389, 445
Lewis, Wyndham, IV:739; V:173, 178
Lewis and Clark Exposition, IV:266, 782
Lewisohn, Ludwig, III:355; IV:438, 737; V:249, 258
Lewiston Journal, IV:70
Lexington, Ky., I:32, 206–7, 311, 389, 439; III:155; IV:93–94, 278
Leyendecker, Francis Xavier, III:484; IV:456, 689, 694, 767
Leyendecker, Joseph Christian, III:484; IV:456, 689, 698
Leypoldt, Frederick, III:235, 491–94, 517, 518, 519
Leypoldt's Monthly Book Trade Circular, III:492
Libbey, John M., I:529*n*, 534
Libel suits
 in nationalist era (1794–1825), I:127, 150, 163, 170, 229–30, 243, 330
 in expansionist era (1825–50), I:426
 in Gilded Age (1885–1950), IV:459–61
Liberal, IV:442*n*, 449
Liberal Christian, I:373, 807; II:72; III:77, 394–95
Liberal Freemason, III:315
Liberal Review, IV:277
Liberalism, 19th-century European, I:339
Liberator, I:164, 456, 457, 460, 801; II:125, 133, 140, 146, 152, 372; III:332–33
 sketch of, II:275–96
Liberia, IV:238
Libertarians, II:78, 252, 286–87
 See also Anarchism
Liberty, III:301; V:xvi
Liberty Boys of '76, IV:119*n*
Libraries, IV:143
Libraries, I:188; III:170–71; IV:142–43
 library periodicals, III:170–71, 517–19; IV:142–43
Library (Pittsburgh), IV:88
Library of Congress, V:348
Library Journal, III:171, 493; IV:142–43
 sketch of, III:517–19
Library Magazine, III:256
Library Notes, IV:143
Library Publishing Company, V:27
Library Table, III:233
Libro d'oro, V:117
Liddell, Mark Harvey, IV:774
Lieber, Francis, I:640, 723, 778; II:134, 425, 497*n*
Lies, IV:752
Lies, Eugene, II:197
Life (New York, 1883–1936), III:199, 268, 317, 555, 556; IV:100, 152, 207, 383, 385
 sketch of, IV:556–68
Life (New York, founded 1936), V:30, 303, 308, 321–22
Life en Español, V:322*n*
Life and Health, IV:210
Life Illustrated, II:42
Life insurance, II:255; IV:777
 See also Insurance companies; Insurance periodicals
Life Insurance Courant, IV:351*n*
Life and Light for Heathen Women, III:77*n*
Light (Buffalo), IV:184*n*
Light (Columbus), IV:387*n*
Light (La Crosse), IV:199–200
Light, Heat and Power, IV:184*n*
Light of Dharma, IV:287
Light for Thinkers, III:82*n*
Lighton, William R., IV:695
Lilienthal, Dr. Samuel, II:85*n*
Lillard, Benjamin, III:110*n*; IV:318
Lillie, John, II:399
Lily, II:50
Lily Dale, N.Y., IV:304
Linage reports on newspapers, V:69–70
Lincoln, Neb., III:77*n*, 158, 169; IV:162, 176, 270*n*, 271*n*, 390*n*
Lincoln Clarion, II:137
Lincoln, Abraham, II:152, 153, 156, 245, 292, 295, 372, 474, 475, 501, 523, 524, 531, 537, 538, 543, 544–45, 548; V:5, 8, 205
 campaign of 1860, II:135–37
Lincoln, Joseph C., II:435; III:488, 530; IV:49*n*, 471; V:30, 80, 133
Lincoln, Natalie Sumner, IV:140*n*, 583
Lind, I. Robert, IV:738
Lind, Jenny, II:180, 194–95, 452
Lindbergh, Anne, IV:626
Lindbergh, Charles Augustus, IV:626; V:307, 323
Lindemann, Eduard C., V:211
Lindley, Ernest K., V:55
Lindsay, Mrs. H. C., II:58
Lindsay, (Nicholas) Vachel, III:430; IV:518, 654; V:12, 121, 168, 176, 210, 228–29
Lindsey, Benjamin Barr, IV:744; V:83
Lindsley, J. Berrien, IV:531
Linen, James A., V:320–31, 324*n*, 327
Line-of-Battle Ship, II:411*n*
Lingle, Caroline Gray, IV:61
Linn, John Blair, I:123, 155

Linotype Bulletin, IV:248
Linsley, D. S., II:91
Linson, Corwin Knapp, IV:602
Linton, Henry, III:187, 411
Linton, William James, I:524; II:194; III:185, 187, 189–90, 191, 359, 379, 411, 466
Lipchitz, Jacques, V:178
Lippard, George, II:29, 212
Lippincott, Leander K., II:100
Lippincott, Sara Jane Clarke (Grace Greenwood), I:553, 585, 770; II:36, 100, 352; III:99*n*, 424; IV:542
Lippincott's Magazine, II:396; III:33–34, 47–48, 90, 184, 226, 231, 280, 293, 295, 307, 313, 403; IV:3–4, 13, 21, 44, 87
 advertising in, III:10
 payments to contributors, III:14
 sketch of, III:396–401
Lippmann, Walter, IV:769; V:17, 191*n*, 193, 196–97, 204–9, 212, 333
Lipscomb, Andrew Adgate, II:389
Lipton, Thomas, IV:690, 700
Liquor advertising, IV:27
Liquor magazines, III:135; IV:189*n*
Lissueris, Meyer, IV:107*n*
Lister, Joseph, IV:310–11
Litchfield, A., III:269*n*
Litchfield, Paul, I:134*n*
Literary Advertiser (Cincinnati), II:158
Literary Advertiser (New York), II:158
Literary American, II:40
Literary Budget, II:115
Literary Bulletin, II:235, 491
Literary Cabinet, I:172, 793
Literary Casket, I:390, 805
Literary Club (Walpole, N.H.), I:194
Literary clubs, I:194, 254–57, 254*n*, 287; II:226–28; III:231, 233
 See also Anthology Society; Delphian Club; Examiner Club; Friendly Club, Literary Club (of Walpole); Transcendentalist Club; Tuesday Club
Literary Collector, IV:127
Literary criticism
 in early magazines (1741–94), I:44, 54, 74, 106
 in nationalist era magazines (1794–1825), I:280, 282; II:230
  antiromanticism, I:257
  attacks on critics, I:186–87
  classicism, I:230
  general magazines, I:226, 230–33, 239, 241–42, 321, 328–29
  literary magazines, I:257–58, 293–95
  low quality, I:182
  nationalist bias, I:183–92, 275
  novels and short stories, I:321, 328–29
  poetry, I:178–82, 273–75, 280, 295, 312
  politics and, I:182
  religious magazines, I:300, 315
  trends, I:124, 128, 185–86
  women's magazines, I:321, 328–29
 in expansionist era magazines (1825–50), I:397–405, 408–427
  evaluations, I:408–20
  general magazines, I:577, 610; II:237–38, 240
  indictments of critics, I:405–8
  literary magazines, I:563, 624, 635–37, 640–42, 660–61, 712, 723–24, 757, 777–78
  political magazines, I:751
  religious periodicals, I:563, 624
  trends, I:345
  women's magazines, I:547, 586, 700–1, 736–37
 in Civil War era magazines (1850–65), II:243, 343, 365, 407
  classicism, II:532
  English literature, II:159–62
  French literature, II:162–64
  general magazines, II:451
  German literature, II:164–65
  novels, II:159–60, 165–69, 171–72
  poetry, II:166–71
  quality, II:157–59, 425
  short stories, II:173
  women authors, II:170–71
 in post-Civil War magazines (1865–85), III:237–56
  current events magazines, III:343–44, 347
  defects, III:233–34
  general magazines, III:421
  literary magazines, II:253; III:232–237, 320, 375, 416, 455, 548–50
  religious magazines, II:518
  specialized periodicals, III:233–34, 539
 in Gilded Age magazines (1885–1905), IV:121–36, 613
  booksellers' periodicals, IV:436–437, 439
  Chautauqua magazines, III:546
  comic periodicals, IV:560–61
  literary immorality, IV:122–24
  review periodicals, IV:513

specialized periodicals, III:540–41
trends, IV:121–24
urban periodicals, IV:85
in modern magazines (1905–), IV:780–81
general magazines, V:10–11, 90, 96, 280
poetry magazines, V:105–7
specialized periodicals, III:541–543
Literary Digest, IV:3, 10, 64, 120, 509, 664; V:50, 55, 294, 296, 298, 307, 324
sketch of, IV:569–79
Literary Era, IV:125
Literary Examiner, I:390, 804
Literary Gazette and American Athenaeum, I:128, 185
Literary Gazette, or Journal of Criticism, I:279*n*
Literary Journal, II:58, 151*n*, 396–98, 747–49; V:196
Literary Life, III:234; IV:125
Literary Locomotive and Phonetic Paragon, II:212
Literary Magazine and American Register, I:124, 150, 192
sketch of, I:220–21
See also Brown, Charles Brockden
Literary magazines
of nationalist era (1794–1825), I:279–283; II:220–34
in expansionist era (1825–50)
book review magazines, I:766–68
monthlies, I:343–48, 544–55, 559–61, 577–79, 595–614, 618–21, 629–57, 664–65, 677–84, 692–93, 711–12, 718–20, 735–38, 769–72
number, I:342*n*
quarterlies, I:573–77, 669–71, 721–27, 775–79; II:234–41
weeklies, I:354–58, 747–49, 757–62, 766–68; IV:672–78
in Civil War era (1850–65)
advertising, II:13–14
high-circulation, II:10–11
monthlies, II:29–33, 383–94, 419–28, 494–504
payments to contributors, II:20–21
quarterlies, II:27–29, 242–45
weeklies, II:407–8; IV:678–80
in post-Civil War era (1865–85), II:245–54
biweeklies, III:548–50
college magazines, *see names of specific colleges and universities*
monthlies, II:394–99, 428–30, 505–11; III:32–37, 361–81, 396–99, 402–6, 454, 539
Southern, III:47
weeklies, III:40–42, 319–24; IV:680–81
Western, III:56–57
in Gilded Age (1885–1905), II:254–58
fortnightlies, III:455–56, 540–41
mail-order periodicals, IV:365
monthlies, II:399–402, 430–31, 511–13; III:399–401, 407–8, 550–51; IV:90, 92, 94, 96–97, 99, 104–5, 124–26, 129, 424–27, 429*n*
quarterlies, IV:71–72, 733–35
semi-monthlies, III:540; IV:424*n*
trends, IV:124–26
weeklies, IV:89, 93, 99, 100–1, 681–91
modern (1905–), II:258–61; V:29
monthlies, II:402–5, 431, 513–15; III:401, 408–9, 541–43, 551; IV:424*n*, 499–505; V:117–24, 166–90
quarterlies, IV:735–40; V:100–16
weeklies, IV:691–716
Literary Miscellany, I:125, 277, 793
Literary Museum, I:790
Literary and Musical Review, III:233*n*
Literary News, III:235, 247, 492, 519; IV:126–27
Literary News Letter, I:408*n*, 807
Literary Northwest, IV:96
Literary Review, III:233; IV:125; V:110
Literary and Scientific Repository, I:130, 140, 185
sketch of, I:313–14
Literary and Scientific Review, I:804
Literary and Theological Review
founding of, I:371
sketch of, I:624–25
Literary West, IV:126
Literary World, I:766–68; II:143, 158; III:233, 240, 254, 551; IV:79, 124
sketch of, III:454–56
Literature, *see* Essays; Literary criticism; Novels; Plays; Romanticism; Short stories
Literature, IV:229*n*
Lithograph, III:186
Lithographs
before 1865, I:282, 343*n*, 520, 521, 656, 672, 684; II:116*n*, 441
after Civil War, III:483, 522, 528
See also Engravings

Littauer, Kenneth, IV:470, 477
Littell, Eliakim, I:130, 151*n*, 396–98, 747–49; V:196
Littell, Philip, V:191*n*, 196–201
Littell, Robert S., I:747*n*, 748–49; IV:761; V:191*n*, 196, 337
Littell's Living Age, I:747*n*
See also: Living Age
Little Chronicle, IV:64
Little Corporal, III:175, 176
Little Folks, III:176, IV:212
Little Folks Reader, III:177
Little Joker, III:268*n*
Little Magazine, V:171*n*
Little Ones at Home, IV:764
Little Pilgrim, II:100; III:175
Little Review, V:xv
sketch of, V:166–78
Little Review Anthology (Margaret Anderson), V:176–77
Little Rock, Ark., III:71*n*, 155; IV:271*n*, 313*n*, 341
Little Silver, N.J., III:162
Littlehales, George Washington, II:415
Live Wire, IV:617*n*
Livermore, D. P., II:73*n*
Livermore, Mary Ashton Rice, III:93, 94, 172; IV:45*n*, 354, 355, 405; V:287
Livernash, Edward J., IV:105
Live-Stock Indicator, III:159
Live Stock Journal, III:159
Live Stock and Western Farm Journal, III:157
Livestock magazines, III:159–61, IV:343–44
Living Age, I:308, 397; II:129, 425, IV:56, 64, 79; III:256, 360; IV:56, 64; V:196
sketch of, I:747–49
Living Church, III:75; IV:294
Living Epistle, III:72
Living Issue, III:310*n*
Living pictures, IV:153, 259
Livingston, Robert R., I:48
Livingstone, David, II:414, 455
Livonia, Pa., IV:342
Lloyd, D. R., III:402*n*
Lloyd, Henry Demarest, IV:204, 205
Lloyd, John Uri, IV:299*n*, 435
Lloyd, Sam, IV:769
Locke, Alain, IV:749*n*
Locke, David Ross ("Petroleum V. Nasby"), II:178, 182*n*, 481; III:55, 78, 271*n*
Locke, Justin, IV:630
Locke, William John, III:487; IV:49*n*, 694; V:83, 134
Locker, Frederick, II:377
Lockridge, Patricia, IV:771
Lockwood, Belva Ann, IV:353
Lockwood, Howard, III:128; IV:247
Lockwood, Ingersoll, IV:127
Locomotive, III:126*n*
Locomotive Fireman's Magazine, III:125*n*
Lodge, Dr. Edwin A., II:85*n*
Lodge, Henry Cabot, II:220*n*, 248, 401; III:21, 31, 35*n*, 455; IV:398, 494, 514, 617, 721; V:28
Lodge, Paul, V:62
Lodge, Sir Oliver, III:434
Lodges, *see specific lodges and fraternal organizations*
Loeb, Hanau Wolf, IV:315
Log Cabin, IV:120
Logan, Harlan de Baun, IV:717*n*, 730–31
Logan, John Alexander, IV:496
Logan, Mrs. John Alexander, IV:360, 496
Logan, Olive, III:33*n*, 93, 172, 375, 393
Logan, W. C., 62*n*
Logansport, Ind., IV:254*n*, 335
Lomax, Jane T., I:644
Lomax, John Avery, IV:736
Lombroso, Cesare, 73, 514
London, Charmian, III:479
London, Jack, II:271; III:408, 471; IV:40, 49, 105, 106, 142, 429, 457, 458, 490, 493, 497, 501, 601, 637, 662, 690, 692, 767; V:80, 119, 148, 249
London Graphic, III:190*n*, 359
London Illustrated News, II:409, 452, 470
London Journal, III:279
London Quarterly, II:130
London Saturday Review, see: Saturday Review (London)
Long, Haniel, V:184
Long, John Davis, III:512
Long, John Luther, III:400*n*, 485; V:290
Long, Percy Waldron, III:236*n*
Long, Ray, IV:480*n*, 497–98, 502–3
Long, Tudor Seymour, IV:733*n*, 737–38
Long Island Magazine, I:122*n*, 790
Longacre, James Barton, I:208, 210, 520
Longevity of magazines, I:13, 21, 70, 114, 120, 214, 341–42, 528; II:4–5, 218; III:318; IV:4–5, 15
Longfellow, Henry Wadsworth, I:390, 392–93, 759–60; II:494, 510;

III:59, 175*n*, 237, 238, 241, 548; V:ix, 280
as contributor, I:128, 129, 331–32, 335, 546, 547, 586, 600, 609, 615, 627, 642, 711, 734, 771; II:24, 175, 235, 237, 271, 377, 420, 423, 424, 495, 504
criticism of, I:409, 506–7; II:167–68, 290, 361; III:239, 321
Longfellow, William Pitt Preble, III:129; IV:145
Longley, Alcander, III:300
Longstreet, Augustus Baldwin, I:644, 700; III:46*n*, 483
Longstreet, James, III:469
Looking Backward, IV:110, 201–2, 280
Loomis, Charles Battell, III:530; IV:66, 98
Loomis, Pascal, III:265
Loomis' Musical and Masonic Journal, III:197*n*
Lord, David Nevins, I:372–73; II:75*n*
Lord, Henry G., IV:185
Lord, R. Halkett, IV:127
Lord, Samuel, Jr., II:488
Lord, William S., IV:647
Lord & Taylor, V:165*n*
Lord & Thomas, V:298
Lorenz, E. S., IV:254
Lorgnette or Studies of the Town by an Opera Goer, II:41
Lorimer, Emila Stuart, V:228
Lorimer, George Horace, IV:35, 59, 166, 536*n*, 552, 671*n*, 685, 686–708, 713
Lorimer, Graeme, IV:708
Loring, Ellis Gray, II:275*n*, 280, 285
Loring, James, II:265
Los Angeles, Cal.
post-Civil War magazines in (1865–85), III:158
Gilded Age magazines in (1885–1905)
advertising journal, IV:247*n*
agnostic periodical, IV:277
agricultural periodicals, IV:341, 345*n*
antitrust periodical, IV:178
five cent weeklies, IV:107
medical journal, IV:314*n*
regional periodicals, IV:107
religious periodicals, IV:285*n*, 301
socialist periodicals, IV:176*n*, 206
modern magazines in (1905–)
agnostic periodical, IV:277
agricultural magazines, III:158
dental journal, IV:317
labor periodical, IV:221*n*
manufacturing journals, IV:186*n*
medical journal, IV:314*n*
religious periodicals, IV:304*n*
socialist periodical, IV:176*n*
Los Angeles Socialist, IV:176*n*
Los Angeles Times, V:257
Lossing, Benson John, I:364*n*, 364, 522, 523, 524; II:175*n*, 387, 390, 178*n*, 260, 465*n*
Lost Cause, IV:139,
Loth, Paul V., IV:48*n*
Lothrop, Daniel, III:177, 508
Lothrop, George Parsons, III:69*n*
Lotos (New York), IV:356
Lottery advertisements, IV:675
Lotus (Kansas), IV:98, 390*n*
Loughbridge, J., I:469
Louisiana Planter and Sugar Manufacturer, IV:339
Louisiana Purchase, I:161
Louisiana Purchase Exposition (1903), IV:101, 266, 489, 655, 782
Louisiana School Review, IV:270n
Louisville, Ky.
nationalist era magazines in (1794–1825), I:137
expansionist era magazines in (1825–50), I:389
literary magazine, I:658–61
medical journal, I:439
religious periodical, I:372
Civil War era magazines in (1850–65)
home magazine, II:59
religious periodicals, II:63*n*, 66, 68*n*
post-Civil War magazines in (1865–85), III:47
agricultural magazines, III:155–56
general magazines, III:47
grange magazine, III:149
historical magazine, III:47
insurance periodical, IV:351*n*
medical journals, III:141*n*
religious magazines, III:75*n*, 80
trade magazine, IV:189*n*
Gilded Age magazines in (1885–1905)
agricultural periodicals, IV:337–38, 341
brick periodical, IV:325*n*
education periodical, IV:271*n*
general periodical, IV:93
historical periodical, IV:139
home periodical, IV:764
medical periodical, IV:313*n*
religious periodicals, IV:292–93
ten-cent periodical, IV:93
modern magazines in (1905–)
agricultural magazine, IV:341
trade magazine, IV:189*n*

Louisville Female College, II:46
Louisville Journal of Medicine and Surgery, I:439*n*, 804
Louisville Monthly Journal of Medicine and Surgery, IV:313*n*
Louisville Monthly Magazine, III:47
Louisville Review, I:439*n*
Lounsbury, Thomas Raynesford, I:488*n*, 535; II:315, 402; III:236*n*, 347, 549
Love, Alfred Henry, III:312
Love, Robertus, IV:53*n*, 101
Lovejoy, Elijah Parish, I:458, 660; II:285
Lovejoy, Owen P., IV:745, 767
Lovelorn advice, I:85; II:361
Lovett, J. T., III:162
Lovett, Robert Morss, III:539*n*, 542; IV:273; V:191*n*, 196, 210
Low, Alfred Maurice, IV:517
Low, David, III:355
Low, Seth, II:269; III:165
Low, Will Hickok, III:557; IV:151, 544, 720
Lowe, Charles, III:506*n*, 507
Lowe, Martha Ann, III:507
Lowell, Abbott Lawrence, IV:193
Lowell, Amy, II:260; III:479, 543; IV:436, 438, 440; V:136, 210, 228, 230, 242, 280, 336
Lowell, Charles, I:285, 571
Lowell, Francis Cabot, II:512
Lowell, James Russell, I:412, 490, 757–58; III:13, 23, 31, 166*n*, 175, 231, 232, 236, 241, 264, 277, 335, 337, 339, 418–19, 550; IV:61, 129, 483, 680
  as contributor, I:506, 510, 535, 711, 718–19, 751, 758, 764, 767, 771, 778; II:124, 127, 148, 156, 167, 168, 175, 193, 240, 280, 373, 420, 423, 504, 507, 510
  criticism of, III:237, 238, 239
  as editor, I:347, 488, 735–38; II:21, 24, 32, 220*n*, 243–47, 260, 426, 493*n*, 494–503
Lowell, John, I:176, 258, 318
Lowell, Orson, III:484; IV:565, 604
Lowell, Robert, V:243
Lowell Offering, I:471, 805
Lowie, Robert H., V:98
Lowndes, Arthur, III:75*n*
Lowndes, Marie Bellow, IV:604
Lowrey, Frederick C., V:290–91
Lubbock, Sir John, II:271
Lucca, Pauline, III:193
Luccock, Naphtali, IV:291
Luce, Henry Robinson, V:293–304, 309, 315, 318, 322, 326–27, 328*n*
Luce, Robert, V:224*n*
Lucifer, the Light-Bearer, III:301; IV:277
"Luck of Roaring Camp, The" (Bret Harte), III:403–4
Luckey, Samuel, I:299*n*
Lucky Dog, IV:390*n*
Lüders, Charles Henry, IV:722
Ludlow, Fitz-Hugh, I:613; II:117, 121, 173, 395, 477, 505*n*, 527
Ludwig, Emil, IV:521
Ludwig, Otto, II:164; III:255
Luggage and Leather Goods, IV:189*n*
Luks, George Benjamin, IV:386, 747
Lull, Richard Swan, III:108*n*
Lum, Dyer D., IV:173
Lumber, IV:325*n*
Lumber Review, IV:325*n*
Lumber Trade Journal, III:130
Lumber World, III:130; IV:325*n*
Lumbering magazines, III:130; IV:325
Lumberman, IV:325*n*
Lumberman's Gazette, III:130
Lumley, Arthur, II:45, 332
Lummis, Charles Fletcher, III:530; IV:105, 107
Luncheon, I:171, 795
Lundorg, Florence, IV:388
Lundy, Benjamin, I:162–64; II:275
Lunn, George R., V:196
Lunt, George, I:578
Lupton, Frank L., IV:141, 366
Lurid magazines
  before 1865, II:185–87, 325–28
  after Civil War, II:328–37; III:43–45
"Lusitania" (ship), V:51, 156, 206
Lutes, Della Thompson, IV:364
Luther, Mark Lee, IV:493; V:246*n*, 256, 259
Luther, Martin, III:330
Luther League Review, IV:295*n*
Lutheran, II:73
Lutheran (Lebanon, Pa.), IV:295*n*
Lutheran (Philadelphia), IV:295
Lutheran (York, Pa.), IV:295*n*
Lutheran Church Quarterly, II:73
Lutheran Church Review, II:73*n*; III:79
Lutheran Church Visitor, IV:295n
Lutheran Companion, IV:295*n*
Lutheran Evangelist, IV:295
Lutheran magazines, II:73; III:79; IV:295
Lutheran and Missionary, II:73
Lutheran Observer, I:742*n*; II:73; IV:295

Lutheran Quarterly, II:73*n;* IV:295
Lutheran Review, I:742
Lutheran Standard, II:73
Lutheran Witness, III:79
Lutheran World, IV:295*n*
Lutz, C. Arthur, IV:48*n*
Lyceum Banner, III:52
Lyceum lectures, I:489, 542, 620; II:97–98; III:171–73; IV:265–66
Lyceumite, IV:266
Lyle, Eugene P., IV:782; V:149
Lyman, Joseph Bardwell, III:99
Lynch, Anne C., I:680, 687, 745; II:352
Lynch, Frederick, III:83*n*
Lynch, John Joseph, III:69*n*
Lynch, Patrick Nieson, II:76; III:69*n*
Lynchburg, Va., III:197
Lynchings, IV:213, 445, 668
Lynde, Francis, III:400*n,* 483; IV:80, 361*n,* 767
Lynn, Mass., II:59; IV:361, 366
Lyon, Harris Merton, IV:654; V:147–48
Lyon, John, I:122*n*
Lyon, Mary, I:485
Lyons, Daniel, IV:453*n,* 454
Lyons, Eugene, V:3*n,* 20–25
Lyons & Carnahan, V:47
Lytle, Andrew, V:116*n*

"M. Quad," *see* Lewis, Charles
"Maartens," V:258
Mabie, Hamilton Wright, III:422*n,* 427–28, 432–33; IV:110, 398, 551; V:28, 282
MacAdam, George, IV:784, 785
McAdoo, William (congressman), IV:202
McAdoo, William Gibbs, IV:549, 776
MacAfee, Helen, V:329*n,* 339
MacAlister, Merle, IV:82*n*
McAllister, Ward, IV:201, 562, 563
McAndrew, William, IV:785
McAneny, George, III:296*n*
McArdle, Kenneth, IV:453*n,* 479
Macaroni and Noodle Manufacturers' Journal, IV:186*n*
MacArthur, C. L., IV:68
MacArthur, James, IV:432–36
MacArthur, Peter, IV:49
MacArthur, Robert Stuart, III:72*n*
Macaulay, D., I:384
Macaulay, Thomas Babington, I:1, 399, 615
McBride, Robert Medill, III:478
McBride's Magazine, III:396*n,* 401
McBryde, John McLaren, Jr., IV:733*n,* 736–37
McBurney, John, III:169
McCabe, James D., Jr., I:112, 200
McCabe, John Collins, I:651
Maccabeean, IV:300
McCaine, Alexander, I:722
McCall, Anne Bryan, IV:709
McCall, James, IV:580–81
McCall, Samuel Walker, IV:461–62
McCall's Magazine, IV:17, 770; V:44, 140, 142
  sketch of, IV:580–88
McCallum, Andrew, II:475
McCann, John A., IV:184*n*
McCarter, Henry, IV:19
McCarthy, Joseph, V:25–26, 223, 314
McCarthy, Justin, II:255, 270, 375, 393, 477; III:13, 35*n,* 224, 249, 278, 369, 372, 376, 389, 421, 429
McClellan, George Brinton, III:469
McClenahan, Howard, I:556*n,* 558
McClintock, John, I:299*n,* 300
McClintock, John N., III:36*n;* IV:69*n*
McCloud, Norman C., IV:95
McClure, Alexander Kelly, IV:53*n,* 689
McClure, H. H., IV:595, 603
McClure, John, V:5, 266
McClure, Samuel Sidney, III:214, 512; IV:5, 6, 7–8, 35, 169, 208, 273, 319, 589–607, 633–34, 641
McClure Publications, II:486
McClure's Magazine, II:513; III:512, IV:5, 6, 17, 19, 21, 27, 41, 46 152, 331, 489; V:266, 288, 341
  sketch of, IV:589–607
McClure's Quarterly, IV:597
McClurg, Alexander Caldwell, III:539, 540
McCluskey, William, I:328
McCord, D. J., I:575, 725, II:345
McCord, Louisa S., II:49
McCormick, Cyrus Hall, III:74; IV:293, V:226
McCormick, Eliot, III:427
McCormick, William B., IV:147*n*
McCosh, James, I:535; II:517; IV:281
McCrackan, William Denison, II:257; IV:178, 407
MacCracken, Henry, IV:74*n*
McCulloch, Hugh, IV:238, 721
McCulloch, James H., I:294
McCullough, John, III:204; IV:81*n*
McCune, Thomas C., IV:88*n*

McCutcheon, George Barr, III:489; IV:435, 618; V:158
McCutcheon, John I., V:32
McCutcheon, John Tinney, IV:456, 497
McDonald, E. H., III:47*n*
McDonald, E. M., III:89
Macdonald, George, III:249, 423, 439, 460
McDonald, W. N., III:47*n*
MacDonald, William, III:355
McDonnell, J. P., III:301
McDonough, Frank Wheatley, V:36*n*, 44
Macdougall, David, IV:227
McDougall, William, IV:520
McDowall, John R., II:211*n*
McDowell, Albert, IV:362
McDowell, Anna, II:52
McEachin, Hec A., IV:665*n*, 669
Macedonian, II:64
McElheney, Jane ("Ada Clare"), II:39, 117, 520, 521
McElrath, Thomas, II:386*n*
McElroy, John, IV:69*n*
McEvoy, George E., II:335
McEvoy, Joseph Patrick, IV:473, 709
McEwen, Arthur, IV:107, 615
Macfadden, Bernarr, IV:316
McFarland, John Horace, III:430, IV:338*n*, 776
McFarland, John Thomas, III:180
McFarlane, Arthur Emerson, IV:691
Macfarlane, Clark, IV:465
McFee, William, IV:439
McGaffey, Ernest, IV:654
McGee, Thomas D'Arcy, II:77
McGee, W J, IV:306, 308, 620*n*, 622
McGee's Illustrated Weekly, III:69*n*
MacGibbons, John, I:26*n*
McGlynn, Edward, IV:179
M'Govern, Chauncey Montgomery, V:72*n*
McGovern, John, III:54*n*; IV:99
MacGowan, Grace, II:431
McGowan, John P., IV:652*n*
MacGrath, Harold, IV:46*n*, 691; V:148
McGrath, James Howard, III:126*n*; IV:321, 333, 714; V:288
McGraw-Hill Publishing Co., V:322*n*
McGraw-Marden Co., V:288
McGregor, Hugh, III:300
Macgregor, James, I:531
McGuffey, William Holmes, I:491
McGuire, J. A., IV:381*n*
Machamer, Jefferson, III:555
Macharg, William B., V:148
McHenry, James, I:129, 274–75, 610
Machinery, IV:321, 333*n*
Machinery periodicals, IV:321
Machinist periodicals, III:115
Machinists' Monthly Journal, IV:221*n*
McIntosh, John, III:301
McIntosh, Maria J., II:171
McIntyre, John D., IV:412
McIntyre, Oscar Odd, IV:498, 607
McJilton, John N., I:381*n*
McKay, Charlotte E., III:96
McKay, J. A., II:355
McKay, James, I:361
McKay, James T., III:22, 465*n*
McKay, John Angus, IV:87
McKay, Robert, IV:617
Mackay, Robert, III:486; V:288, 291
MacKaye, James Steele, III:202
Mackaye, Percy, IV:518
McKee, Thomas H., V:146
Mackeever, Samuel A. ("Prowler Paul"), II:330, 331
Mackenzie, Cameron, IV:589*n*, 601–4
Mackenzie, Compton, III:390
Mackenzie, Hector, I:568
Mackenzie, Robert Shelton, I:609; II:159, 532
McKeogh, Arthur, IV:589*n*, 606, 708
McKeon, Almira Guild, III:402*n*
Mackey, Albert Gallatin, II:215; III:315
Mackey's National Freemason, III:315
Mackie, John M., II:425
McKim, James Miller, III:332, 333
McKinley, William, II:377, 485; III:346; IV:161, 227, 234, 235, 278, 413, 572, 644, 660, 782
McKnight, Charles, III:299
"Maclaren, Ian," *see* Watson, John
McLaughlin, Andrew Cunningham, IV:138*n*
McLaughlin, William G., IV:243*n*
McLean, Emily Pratt, III:248
McLean, George Agnew, IV:116
Maclean, John, I:530
McLean, John Emery, IV:284, 287*n*, 401*n*, 414
MacLeish, Archibald, V:210, 237, 241, 305, 338
McLenan, John, II:182*n*, 183, 454, 523
"MacLeod, Fiona," *see* Sharp, William
MacLeod, Norman, IV:738
McLuitock, F. S., IV:519
Maclure, William, I:537
McMaster, James Alphonsus, II:77; IV:297
McMaster, John Bach, I:535; II:414; III:472; IV:87, 138, 516
McMichael, Morton, I:580*n*, 582, 734; IV:671*n*, 674

MacMillan, Donald Baxter, IV:625
McMillan, Emilie, V:91, 95*n*
McMillan, H. C., III:158*n*
Macmillan's Magazine, II:505
McMillen, Wheeler, IV:63*n*
McMurtry, Lewis S., IV:530
McNamee, Theodore, II:367*n*, 368
McNutt, William Slavens, IV:405
Macon, Ga., I:699; III:73, 143*n*, 176
McPeak, Ival, V:179*n*, 180
Macpherson, Jay, V:244
McQuilkin, Albert H., III:132*n*
Macready, John A., IV:626
Macune, C. W., IV:176
McVeagh, Wayne, III:290
McVickar, Harry W., IV:561, 756, 757
McVicker, James Hubert, III:206
Macy, Jesse, IV:659, 662
Macy, John, II:262*n*, 273; III:354, 541; IV:440, 441; V:96, 265
Madame, IV:361*n*
Madison, Ind., I:491
Madison, Wis., II:89; III:111, 157, 262*n*; IV:339, 340
Madison, J. O., IV:187
Maeterlinck, Maurice, II:257; IV:121, 501, 520
Magazine, defined, I:6–7, 40–41, 92–93
Magazine of American History, III:260
Magazine of Art, III:185
Magazine boy-merchants, IV:691
Magazine of Christian Literature, IV:301
Magazine of the Daughters of the Revolution, IV:139
Magazine of Fun, III:554*n*
Magazine of New England History, IV:140*n*
Magazine of Poetry, IV:121
Magazine-starting "mania" in post-Civil War era (1865–85), III:5
Magazine supplements in Gilded Age (1885–1905), IV:69–70
Magazine of Useful and Entertaining Knowledge, I:363, 800
Magazine of Western History, III:262; IV:139
Magazinists, recognition of, II:26; III:17–18
Magee, J. L., II:185*n*
Magee, Thomas, IV:239
Magenta, III:165*n*
Magicians' magazines, IV:391
Magnolia (Charleston) I:383, 699–701; II:112*n*
Magnolia (Hudson, N.Y.), II:112*n*
Magnolia (Richmond, 1851), II:110*n*, 112*n*
Magnolia (Richmond, 1862–64), *see Magnolia Weekly,* II
Magnolia Weekly, II:112, 200,
Magoun, George Frederick, II:374, 518*n*, 519; IV:52*n*
Magoun, H. W., I:741
Magruder, Julia, II:463; III:400; IV:45, 50, 544, 767
Mahaffy, Sir John Pentland, III:545; IV:226
Mahan, Alfred Thayer, IV:596, 721, 722, 725
Mahogany Tree, IV:389
Mahony, Walter Butler, II:220*n*, 259
Mail and Breeze, IV:340*n*
Mail-order advertising, III:37–39, 101
Mail Order Journal, IV:247*n*
Mail-order magazines
  in post-Civil War era (1865–85), III:37–39, 54, 99, 101
  in Gilded Age (1885–1905), IV:16, 21, 50–51, 65, 67, 76, 118, 364–68, 417–20
  modern (1905–), IV:421–23
Mail Order Monthly, IV:367
Mails
  early magazines and (1741–94), I:16–19
  in nationalist era (1794–1825), I:19–20
    Western, I:207
  expansionist era magazines and (1825–50), II:266
    handicaps in distribution, I:519
    private transportation, I:518
    rate variations, I:517–18
    West, I:518
  Civil War era magazines and (1850–65), II:3
    effects of war, II:8
  Gilded Age magazines and (1885–1905), IV:20, 368
  See also Postal regulations
Maine Central, IV:333*n*
Maine Farmer, I:444*n*, 801; III:259
Maine Genealogist and Biographer, III:259
Maine Historical and Genealogical Recorder, III:259; IV:137*n*
Maine Historical Magazine, IV:138
Maine Horse Breeders' Monthly, III:215*n*
Maine Journal of Education, III:168*n*
Maine Mining Journal, III:115*n*
Maine Monthly Magazine, I:352*n*, 803
Maine Normal, III:168*n*
Maine Sportsman, IV:381*n*
Maintenance Engineering, III:122*n*

Maisch, John Michael, I:539*n*, 540
Major, Charles, V:73
Mallarmé, Stéphane, IV:451
Mallon, Isabel A., IV:540
Mallory, Bolton, IV:556*n*, 568
Mallory, George S., IV:294
Mallory, M. H., II:364*n*, 365
Malloy, Charles D. O., IV:94*n*
Malone, Dumas, IV:180*n*; V:345–46
Malone, Kemp, III:535*n*
Malone, Walter, V:118
"Mammoth" papers, I:358–63, 446, 520
Man, I:445*n*; IV:287*n*
"Man with the Good Face, The" (Mott), V:xiii
Man of the World, IV:86
Manassas, Va., IV:92
Manchester, N.H., II:90*n*; III:259; IV:185*n*, 382
Manchester, William, V:4*n*
Mancur, J. H., I:507*n*, 546
Mandigo, John H., IV:374
Manet, Édouard, IV:145
Manford, Erasmus, II:73*n*
Manford's Magazine, II:73*n*; III:79; IV:296
Manhattan, III:37, 191
Manhattan, Kan., III:77*n*; IV:310
Manhattan Monthly, III:68
Manière, Alfred, IV:434
Manifest destiny, doctrine of, IV:10–11, 163–65
Manifesto, III:81
Manley, James R., I:215*n*, 216
Mann, E. D., IV:751*n*, 752–53
Mann, Henry, V:151*n*
Mann, Horace, I:441, 490, 491; II:98, 445
Mann, Prestonia, IV:204*n*
Mann, Thomas, III:542; V:336–37
Mann, Col. William D'Alton, IV:46, 459, 751*n*, 752–55; V:246–48, 251, 255, 257, 261
Mann, William W., I:652; I:89
Manners, *see* Social customs and manners
Manners, Mary, V:74
Manning, Alice, IV:580*n*, 583–84
Manning, Henry Edward, II:252; III:69*n*
Manning, John H., I:425; II:409
Manning, Walter W., IV:167*n*
Mansfield, Edward Deering, I:560, 597
Mansfield, Katherine, IV:439; V:119
Mansfield, 1st Earl of (William Murray), V:316
Mantle, Burns, III:199*n*
"Manton, May," *see* Bladworth, Mrs. George H.
Manual Training Magazine, IV:272*n*
Manufacturer, IV:183
Manufacturer and Builder, III:127
Manufacturers, I:60–61; II:319, 449
  manufacturing journals, III:127–29; IV:182–85
  See also specific manufacturing industries and specific industrial magazines
Manufacturers' Chronicle, III:130
Manufacturers' Gazette, III:127
Manufacturers' Record, III:127; IV:183
Manufacturers' Review and Industrial Record, III:127
Manufacturing Chemist, IV:184*n*
Manufacturing Jeweler, III:136
Manumission Intelligencer, I:162
Manumission Journal, I:162*n*
Mao Tse-tung, V:301
Mapes, James Jay, I:556*n*
Maps and charts, IV:621
  colored, IV:574
  of Klondike, IV:109
Maquire, J. R., V:3*n*, 25–26
Marble, Earl, III:267*n*
Marblehead, Mass., III:300
March, Francis Andrew, IV:212
March, William, V:136, 182
"March of Time, The," V:322–23
Marconi, Guglielmo, IV:592
Marcossin, Isaac Frederick, IV:500; 614, 616, 617, 692, 693, 696, 776–77, 780
Marcotte, Anna M., IV:92
Marcousis, Louis, V:178
Marden, Orison Swett, IV:168–69, 416; V:286, 288–91
Marie, Queen of Roumania, IV:700
Marine Biological Laboratory (Woods Hole), IV:309
Marine Engineering, IV:334
Marine engineering periodicals, IV:333–34
Marine Journal, III:126; IV:334
Marine Record, IV:334
Mariners' Advocate, V:194*n*
Mario, Giuseppe, III:193
Mario, Jessie White, III:36, 347
Marion, Ala., II:65*n*
Marion, Ind., IV:270*n*
Marion, S.C., III:155
Mariotti, L., II:23
Maris, Albert Branson, II:93*n*
Maritain, Jacques, IV:739
Market-advertising patterns, IV:22–28
Market Basket, III:153

Markham, (Charles) Edwin, III:408, 485; IV:105, 107, 130, 216, 415, 458, 493, 495, 690, 722; V:133
Marks, Jeanette, V:96, 184, 265
Marks, Montague, III:185
Marley, Harold P., V:284
Marot, Helen, III:542
Marple, Allen, IV:476
Marple, F. T., IV:448
Marquand, John Philips, IV:472, 476, 504, 585, 696, 697, 709; V:136
Marquis, Don, II:41; IV:472; V:118
Marquis, J. Clyde, II:432*n*
Marriage, I:85, 90; II:440; III:449, 452, 486; V:268
Marriner, William M., III:47*n*
Marrion, James, IV:387
Marriott, Frederick, II:118*n;* IV:105, 106
Marriott, Frederick, Jr., II:118*n*
Marriott, Frederick Alfred, II:118*n;* III:56, 402*n*, 408
Marryat, Frederick, I:325, 359, 395
Marryatt, Florence, IV:117
Marsh, Mrs. Anne, II:384
Marsh, George (editor of *Suburban*), IV:82
Marsh, George Perkins, I:751, 753; III:336
Marsh, Harry W., III:296
Marsh, Henry, III:188
Marsh, J. T. B., III:76*n*
Marsh, James, II:229
Marsh, Ngaio, IV:713
Marshall, Charles Clinton, II:514
Marshall, Edison, IV:421, 607
Marshall, Edward, IV:485
Marshall, George C., V:323*n*
Marshall, Ill., III:69*n*
Marshall, James B., I:595*n*, 597
Marshall, James Wilson, II:118
Marshall, Margaret, III:355
Marshall, Thomas Riley, IV:500
Marshall, W. H., II:297*n*, 299
Marshalltown, Iowa, municipal affairs periodical in, IV:198
Martin, Alexander, I:108*n*, 111
Martin, Artemas, III:110
Martin, Ben Ellis, II:551
Martin, Charles, IV:628
Martin, Edward Sanford, II:402, 483, 485; IV:271, 556*n*, 557–68, 722; V:30
Martin, George Madden, III:504; IV:366*n*, 601
Martin, Harold, II:483
Martin, Helen Reimensnyder, IV:601
Martin, John Stuart, V:293*n*, 303–5
Martin, Lannie Hayes, IV:107*n*
Martin, Thomas Commerford, III:122*n*
Martin, W. Thornton, IV:708, 712
Martineau, Harriet, I:395, 576
Martineau, James, III:438
Martyn, Henry, IV:154
Martyn, Mrs. Sarah Towne, I:353
Marvell, Andrew, V:115
Marvin, E. P., II:518*n*
Marvin, George, IV:783
Marvin, Joseph B., III:78*n*
Marx, Karl, IV:110, 174–76, 191, 202, 205, 206, 785
Marxian socialists, influence of, IV:191
Marxist periodicals, II:207; IV:174–76
Maryland, public education in, I:145
Maryland Churchman, IV:294*n*
Maryland Farmer, II:90*n;* III:154
Maryland Law Record, III:144
Maryland Medical Record, III:140*n*
Mascagni, Pietro, IV:544
Mascot, III:45, 268; IV:93
Masefield, John, V:119, 336
Mason, A. I., I:322
Mason, Alfred Edward Woodley, IV:607
Mason, Charles, II:319
Mason, Daniel Gregory, III:429; IV:253; V:95
Mason, Gregory, III:432, 433; IV:787
Mason, James M., I:439n
Mason, Jerry, IV:417*n*, 422
Mason, Lowell, II:197; III:196
Mason, Perry, & Co., II:262*n*, 266, 272, 274
Mason, R. B., III:74*n*
Mason, Thomas, I:299*n*
Mason, Van Wyck, IV:422
Mason, Walt, III:514
Mason, William. IV:250
Mason, William Powell, II:224, 226*n*
Mason's Coin and Stamp Collectors' Journal, III:113*n*
Masonic journals, II:214–15; III:314–15; IV:221–22, 222*n*
Masonic Miscellany and Ladies' Literary Magazine, I:312, 797
Masonic Review, II:215; IV:222*n*
Masonic Voice-Review, IV:222*n*
Massachusetts, number of magazines in, I:202*n*, 375
Massachusetts Abolition Society, I:457
Massachusetts Abolitionist, I:457, 804; II:287
Massachusetts Antislavery Society, II:284, 288
Massachusetts Baptist Missionary Magazine, I:251
Massachusetts Centinel, I:162, 345

Massachusetts Editor, IV:244
Massachusetts Historical Society, V:344
Massachusetts Institute of Technology, IV:308, 309
Massachusetts Magazine, I:6, 34, 37, 43, 55, 65
  founding of, I:30
  sketch of, I:108–11
Massachusetts Missionary Magazine, I:133–34, 263, 792
Massachusetts Ploughman, I:442, 805
Massachusetts Quarterly Review, I:368, 775–79; II:28, 494*n*
Massachusetts Teacher, I:492, 809; II:99*n;* III:168*n*
Masseck, Clinton Joseph, III:539*n,* 541
Masses, V:203
Massey, Gerald, III:249; IV:680
Masson, Thomas Lansing, III:530; IV:66, 542, 556*n,* 561, 562, 566, 708, 786; V:133, 251
Mast, Phineas Price, III:156; IV:337, 468, 763*n,* 764, 768
Masters, E. Woodworth, III:198
Masters, Edgar Lee, IV:654, 656; V:12, 176, 228, 336
Masters in Art, IV:147
Masters in Music, IV:253
Masterson, Kate, V:249
Mathematical Magazine, III:110
Mathematical Monthly, II:79
Mathematics, I:295, 303
Mathematics periodicals, III:110–11; IV:310
Mather, Cotton, II:221
Mather, Frank Jewett, III:349; IV:517, 781
Mathew, Theobald, II:290
Mathews, Charles, I:169
Mathews, Cornelius
  comment on, I:610, 781
  as contributor, I:347, 546*n,* 669, 767
  as editor, I:346, 425, 711–12, 780
  quoted, I:390–91, 453, 479
Mathews, Jason, V:3*n,* 25
Mathews, John L., II:262*n;* V:149
Mathews, Shailer, II:379; III:84*n;* IV:192, 499
Mathews, William (founder of *Yankee Blade*), II:36
Mathews, William Smith Babcock, II:197*n;* IV:253
Mathews' Quarterly Journal, IV:313*n*
Mathias, Benjamin, IV:671*n,* 675
Matisse, Henri, III:542; V:178
Matrimonial advertising in Civil War era magazines, II:440
Matsell, George Washington, I:481*n;* II:325*n,* 327, 328
Matteson, Tompkins Harrison, I:524
Matteson, W. T., I:417
Matthews, Cornelius, II:180
Matthews, G. C., III:54*n*
Matthews, James, II:537*n,* 538
Matthews, J. Brander, I:535; II:398*n,* 400, 482; III:16, 35*n,* 37*n,* 199, 200, 225–26, 347, 375, 397, 399, 421, 465*n,* 503, 511; IV:37, 38, 73*n,* 74, 83, 113, 225, 229, 434, 438, 482, 483, 516, 517, 557, 559, 612, 618, 641, 722, 728; V:28, 338
Matthews, Marcia C. J., V:3*n*
Matthews, Thomas Stanley, V:293*n,* 303–5, 312
Matthews, William, III:416; IV:265–66
Mattison, Anna C., II:51
Maugham, Somerset, IV:498, 697; V:134, 264–65
Maule, Harry E., IV:114*n*
Maupassant, Guy de, IV:114*n,* 135; V:119
Maurice, Arthur Bartlett, IV:432*n,* 436–37
Maurois, André, IV:476, 521, 522, 729; V:336
Maury, Matthew Fontaine, I:469, 629*n,* 642–43, 651, 726; II:345, 413
Maverick, Augustus, II:420
Maverick, Peter, I:106, 210
Maxim, Hiram S., IV:334, 483, 487
Maxwell, Clair, IV:567
Maxwell, Lee Wilder, IV:469, 763*n*
Maxwell, Perriton, IV:145, 154, 261*n*
Maxwell, William, I:382
May, Emily H., II:308, 416*n,* 418
"May, Sophie," *see* Clarke, Rebecca Sophia
Mayer, Albert, IV:749*n*
Mayer, Brantz, I:726; II:345
Mayer, Henry, III:531; IV:66, 564
Mayer, Milton, IV:711
Mayes, Herbert Raymond, IV:480*n;* V:125*n,* 136, 143
Mayflower, IV:342
Mayflower Descendant, IV:140
Maynard, Theodore, III:330
Mayo, Caswell O., III:133*n*
Mayo, Earl Williams, IV:117*n*
Mayo, Frank, IV:256
Mead, Charles, I:177
Mead, Darius, I:743*n,* 744, 745; II:57*n*
Mead, Edwin Doak, III:386; IV:70–80
Mead, Margaret, IV:554, 761; V:12

Meade, William, II:68*n*
Meadville, Pa., III:544*n*, 545
Meat trade magazines, IV:187*n*
Mebane, Daniel, V:210, 220
Mechanic, I:445
Mechanic-Apprentice, I:445, 807
Mechanical Engineer, III:115–16
Mechanical engineering periodicals, III:113; IV:320–21
Mechanical magazines, *see specific mechanical crafts*
Mechanical News, III:116*n*
Mechanics, III:116
Mechanics, I:61, 90, 96, 124, 139, 445–46, 524
  cotton gin, I:304
  steamboat, I:96
Mechanic's Advocate, I:445, 808
Mechanic's Magazine, I:445, 800
Mechanic's Magazine and Journal of the Mechanic's Institute, I:445, 801
Mechanicsburg, Pa., III:149*n*, 300
Mechem, Floyd Russell, IV:348
Mecom, Benjamin, I:26*n*
Medes, W. J., III:169
Medford, Mass., IV:345
Media Records, Inc., V:70
Medical Advance, III:143
Medical Brief, III:140
Medical Bulletin of the Jefferson Medical Association, III:140*n*
Medical Century, IV:315
Medical Council, IV:314*n*
Medical education, III:138
Medical Examiner, I:439*n*, 804
Medical Fortnightly, IV:313*n*
Medical Herald and Physio-Therapist, III:141*n*
Medical information
  in magazines before 1865, I:61–62, 84–85, 102, 115, 149–51, 221, 254, 426, 440–41, 539–90; II:214, 228, 319
  after Civil War, III:137–38, 376; IV:310–12; V:7, 143
  See also Doctors
Medical Investigator, II:85
Medical Journal and Record, I:439*n*
Medical journals
  in nationalist era (1794–1825), I:139, 149, 215–17
    circulation, I:199
  in expansionist era (1825–50), I:342*n*, 566–68
    contributors, I:494, 567
    proliferation, I:438–40
  in Civil War era (1850–65)
    trends, II:84–88
    weeklies, II:34
  in post-Civil War era (1865–85), III:51, 138
    circulation, III:140
    longevity, III:140
    number, III:139
    quality and type, III:139–43
  in Gilded Age (1885–1905)
    leading periodicals, IV:313–15, 524–29
    number, IV:312
    patent medicine advertising, IV:245
    public health periodicals, IV:316–17
    shortcomings, IV:312–13
    specialized periodicals, IV:314–16
  modern (1905–), IV:313*n*–15*n*, 529–35
Medical Libraries, IV:143
Medical Life, IV:313*n*
Medical Missionary, IV:238
Medical News, I:439n, 568, 806; II:84*n*; IV:313
Medical and Physical Recorder, I:293, 793
Medical profession, *see* Doctors
Medical Progress, III:141*n*
Medical Record, III:140; IV:313
Medical Register, III:140*n*
Medical Repository, I:149, 194, 199
  sketch of, I:215–17
Medical Review of Reviews, IV:314*n*
Medical schools, III:138
Medical Sentinel, IV:314*n*
Medical Summary, III:140
Medical and Surgical Reporter, II:84
Medical World, III:140
Medicine, advertising of, IV:27, 437
  see also Patent medicine advertising
Medicine, IV:313*n*
Medico-Legal Journal, III:142; IV:348
Medico-legal journals, III:142
Medill, James, IV:212
Medina, Ohio, III:161
Medley, or Monthly Miscellany, I:32, 206, 792
Meehan, Patrick J., II:76
Meehan, Thomas, II:90; IV:342
Meehan's Monthly, IV:342
Meek, Alexander Beaufort, I:651, 700, 726; II:113, 343
"Meet the Press," V:24
Megargee, Louis N., IV:390*n*
Meigs and Dana, I:31*n*
Mekeel, Charles Haviland, IV:391
Mekeel's Weekly Stamp News, IV:391

Melba, Nellie (Helen Porter Mitchell), IV:546
Melcher, Frederick Gershom, III:491*n*, 494, 517*n*, 519
Meline, James Florant, I:692; III:363, 375
Mellen, Grenville, I:323, 326, 331, 355, 409, 587*n*, 620, 623, 679
Mellett, Lowell, IV:468
Melliss, David M., III:392
Mellquist, Proctor, IV:106*n*
Meloney, Marie Mattingley (Mrs. William Brown), III:481*n*, 489; IV:361
Melrose, Mass., IV:299
Meltzer, Charles Henry, IV:501, 519
Melville, Herman, I:416, 587*n*; II:169, 173, 395, 420, 423, 424, 508; V:9
Memoirs, *see* Autobiography; Reminiscences
Memphis, Tenn., II:65*n*, 111; III:69*n*, 137, 141*n*; IV:185*n*, 300, 339
Memphis Medical Monthly, III:141*n*
Men, IV:287*n*
Men and Matters, IV:93
Men of New York, IV:287
Men and Women, IV:299
Menace, IV:416, 641
Menamin, R. S., III:131
Mencken, Henry Louis, III:355, 487; IV:6, 66, 169, 518, 656; V:3–26, 104, 190, 197, 246*n*, 251–54, 256–58, 259*n*, 260–72, 308–11, 313, 333, 338, 348
Mendell, Seth, II:262*n*, 272, 273
Mendenhall, James W., I:299*n*, 301
Mendum, Josiah P., II:78; III:88*n*
Mennonite periodicals, III:81
Menorah Monthly, IV:265, 300
Men's magazines, I:673–76; IV:422–23
Men's Outfitter, IV:187
Men's Wear, IV:187*n*
Mental disease journals, III:142
Mentor, IV:194
Mercantile Library Association, I:437
Mercer, Asa S., III:61
Mercer, Willis, V:185–88
Mercersburg Review, I:809; II:73*n*; III:79
  sketch of, II:380–82
Merchant World, III:134*n*
Merchant's Ledger and Statistical Record, II:356
Merchant's Magazine, see: Hunt's Merchant's Magazine
Merchant's Magazine and Commercial Review, I:696–98
Merchant's Record and Show Window, IV:187*n*
Merchant's Review, III:147; IV:186, 349
Merck's Archives, IV:314*n*
Merck's Report, IV:318*n*
Mercury Publications, Inc., V:22, 24
Meredith, Edwin Thomas, III:157; IV:340; V:36–42
Meredith, Edwin Thomas, Jr., V:42
Meredith, George, IV:424, 433, 518
Meredith, Mrs. Gertrude, I:244
Meredith, Thomas, II:65*n*
Meredith Publishing Company, V:42, 44–48
Meriden, Conn., IV:140, 270*n*
Merimée, Prosper, V:119
Meritt, Benjamin Dean, III:535*n*, 538
Merriam, Charles Edward, IV:192*n*
Merriam, Clinton Hart, IV:621
Merriam, Edmond Franklin, III:39*n*
Merriam, George Spring, III:422*n*, 425, 426
Merrick, Leonard, IV:501, 604, 694; V:83, 119, 258
Merrill, Albert J., III:153
Merrill, Estelle M. H., IV:364
Merrill, Frank Thayer, III:441
Merrill, James, V:243
Merriwell, Frank, IV:119
Merry Masker, III:269*n*
Merry and Wise, III:268*n*
Merryman's, III:267
Merryman's Monthly, II:185*n*
Merry's Museum, II:100, 270; III:174
  founding of, I:492
  sketch of, I:713–15
  wood-cuts in, I:522
Merwin, Henry Bannister, IV:64*n*, 617
Merwin, James Burtis, II:59; III:169
Merwin, Samuel, III:488, 512; IV:389, 584, 604, 605, 690; V:86, 286, 288
Merz, Charles, V:191*n*, 209, 212
Mesmerism, I:447, 700
Message Bird, II:197
Messenger, II:73; III:68*n*; IV:254*n*
Messenger of Peace, III:312
Messenger of the Sacred Heart, III:68; IV:298
"Messer Marco Polo" (Byrne), V:119
Metal Finishing, IV:183*n*
Metal Industry, IV:183*n*
Metal products industry, IV:183*n*
Metal Worker, Plumber and Steam Fitter, III:130*n*
Metal World, IV:183*n*

Metallographist, IV:183*n*
Metaphysical Magazine, IV:287
Metcalf, H. H., III:36*n*
Metcalf, James, IV:66
Metcalf, Lorettus Sutton, II:250; IV:51, 511*n*, 512–15
Metcalf, Theron, II:228, 229
Metcalfe, James Stetson, IV:556*n*, 564–65
Meteorology, I:91, 97, 254, 303, 557; II:414; IV:621
Meteorology periodicals, III:112
Methodist, II:67
Methodist Advocate, III:71*n;* IV:291
Methodist Advocate Journal, II:67*n*
Methodist Book Concern, II:301
Methodist controversies, I:369
Methodist Journal, IV:291
Methodist Magazine, I:132, 790
Methodist magazines
  in nationalist era (1794–1825), I:136, 138, 299–301
  in expansionist era (1825–50), I:370, 373, 389, 699–700
    slavery issue, I:458, 460
    women's magazines, II:301–3
  in Civil War era (1850–65), II:31, 57, 65–68
    women's magazines, II:301–3
  in post-Civil War era (1865–85), III:70–72
    circulation, III:67, 70
    juvenile periodicals, III:180
    missionary magazines, III:70
    Negro-oriented, III:71
    number, III:68
    southern, III:70, 382–84
    women's magazine, II:304; III:70
  in Gilded Age (1885–1905), IV:290–91
    missionary periodicals, IV:305
    Southern periodicals, IV:291
    Sunday School periodicals, IV:274
Methodist Protestant, II:68
Methodist Protestant-Recorder, II:68
Methodist Quarterly Review, II:66*n*
Methodist Recorder, II:68
Methodist Review, II:65*n;* III:70; IV:291
  founding of, I:132
  sketch of, I:299–301
  in third period, I:370
  transportation of, I:519
Methodist Review (South), *see: Quarterly Review of the Methodist Church South*
Metronome, IV:254
Metropolitan, II:76; III:97, 481
Metropolitan Fashions, III:98*n*
Metropolitan Magazine, IV:46–47, 152, 393; V:145, 229
Metropolitan Philatelist, IV:391*n*
Metropolitan Pulpit, III:83; IV:569
Metropolitan Record, II:77*n*
Metropolitan and Rural Home, IV:367*n*
Mexican politics, press comment on, III:352
Mexican War, I:454–56, 464, 478, 757–58, 764, 777, 781; II:314, 326–27
Meyer, A. C., III:47
Meyer, Henry C., III:113*n*
Meyer Brothers' Druggist, III:133
Meyers, Augustus A., I:646
Meynell, Alice, III:330, 484
Mezzotints, I:545, 753
  in nationalist era magazines (1794–1825)
    in *Eclectic,* I:309
  in expansionist era magazines (1825–50)
    in annuals, I:421
    in *Campbell's,* I:398
    in *Columbian Lady's and Gentleman's,* I:744
    in *Democratic Review,* I:684
    in Eclectic, I:520–21
    fashion plates in, I:521
    in *Gentleman's,* I:675
    in *Graham's,* I:548, 592
    in *Sartain's,* I:521
    in *Union Magazine,* I:771
Miami, Fla., IV:270*n*
Mich, Daniel D., IV:587
Michels, John, IV:307
Michelson, Gustav, III:532
Michigan Alumnus, IV:75
Michigan Banker, IV:349*n*
Michigan Christian Advocate, III:71
Michigan Christian Herald, III:73*n*
Michigan Churchman, IV:294*n*
Michigan Farmer, I:444*n*, 806; IV:340
Michigan Investor, IV:350*n*
Michigan Law Review, IV:348
Michigan Maccabee, IV:222
Michigan Political Science Association Publications, IV:181
Michigan Poultry Breeder, IV:345*n*
Michigan Presbyterian, IV:293*n*
Michigan School Moderator, III:169
Michigan Technic, IV:321*n*
Michigan University, periodicals of, IV:321*n*
  alumnus magazine, IV:75
  legal periodical, IV:348
  student periodical, IV:273

Microcosm, III:89
Microscope, III:112
Microscopical Bulletin and Science News, III:112
Microscopy
interest in, III:465
periodicals, III:111–12; IV:310*n*
Midas Criterion, IV:189*n*
Mid-Continent (Indianapolis), IV:96
Mid-Continent Banker, IV:350*n*
Mid-Continent Jeweler, IV:188*n*
Mid-Continent Magazine (Louisville), IV:93
Mid-Continent Review, IV:97
Middle West, III:4
agriculture in, II:434
comment on, II:120–21
growing importance of, III:49
magazine centers in, II:113–16; III:50–55; IV:94–100
See also specific mid-western towns and cities
Middleton, Conn., III:84
Middleton, George, IV:437
Middleton, James, IV:783
Middletown, N.Y., II:52
Midland, V:172*n*
sketch of, V:179–90
Midland (United Presbyterian periodical), IV:294
Midland Christian Advocate, IV:291*n*
Midland Druggist, IV:318*n*
Midland Farmer, III:157
Midland Industrial Gazette, III:127
Midland Magazine (St. Louis), IV:101
Midland Monthly (Des Moines), IV:96–97
Midland Municipalities, IV:198
Midland Schools, IV:270*n*
Midmonthly Survey, IV:741*n*, 748–50
Mid-Week Pictorial, V:50–51
Mifflin, Houghton, V:131
Mifflin, J. Houston, I:436
Milburn, George, V:9
Miles, Gen. Nelson A., II:256, 271; IV:485, 488, 494; V:288
Milestones, IV:195*n*
Milholland, Inez, IV:604
Military Gazette, II:150
Military Magazine, I:456, 804
Military Monitor, I:125, 794
Military and Naval Magazine, I:456, 802
Military and naval periodicals
in Civil War era (1860–65), II:7, 150–51, 545–48, 550–51
in post-Civil War era (1865–85), II:548–49; III:132
in Gilded Age (1885–1905), II:549
modern (1905–), II:549
Military technology, magazines on, II:548
Milk Reporter, III:135
Milk Review, IV:186*n*
Mill, John Stuart, III:253
Millard, Bailey, IV:480*n*, 492–94; V:75
Millard, H., III:215*n*
Millay, Edna St. Vincent, III:504, 543; IV:518, 654; V:136, 237
Milledgeville, Ga., II:63*n*
Millennial Harbinger, II:74; III:80
Miller, Alice Duer, II:431; III:400*n*; V:247
Miller, Andrew, IV:556*n*, 557–66
Miller, Charles William Emil, III:535*n*, 538
Miller, Cincinnatus Heine ("Joaquin"), II:117, 377; III:54, 100, 229, 244, 373, 406, 409, 416, 463, 511; IV:105, 107, 125, 186, 408, 415, 646
Miller, Edward, I:115, 149, 215
Miller, Elizabeth Duer, IV:49*n*; V:30
Miller, Emily Huntington ("Olive Thorne"), II:511*n*; III:175, 501, 502, 509; IV:45*n*
Miller, Francis Trevelyan, IV:82; V:291
Miller, Harlan, IV:553; V:43
Miller, Horace B., III:115*n*
Miller, J. Bruen, II:297*n*, 299
Miller, J. J., III:155
Miller, Joaquin, *see* Miller, Cincinnatus Heine
Miller, John E., III:175*n*
Miller, John W., I:355
Miller, Joseph Dana, IV:168, 179
Miller, Lewis, III:173
Miller, Lischen M., IV:108
Miller, Mark, II:89
Miller, Ned, II:523
Miller, Olive Thorne, *see* Miller, Emily Huntington
Miller, Roswell, IV:689
Miller, S. A., III:109
Miller, Samuel, I:115
Miller, Samuel, Jr., I:530, 533
Miller, Truman W., 524*n*
Miller's Journal, III:128
Miller's Review, III:128; IV:185*n*
Millet, Josiah B., IV:719
Millikan, Robert Andrews, IV:520, 728
Milliken, D. L., III:100

Milliner, IV:188*n*
Millinery magazines, III:134
Millinery Trade Review, III:134
Milling and Grain News, IV:185*n*
Milling World and Chronicle of the Grain and Flour Trade III:128*n*
Millis, Walter, V:294, 333
Mills, Clark, II:189
Mills, Enos Abijah, IV:695
Mills, J. Warner, IV:407
Mills, Roger Quarles, II:254
Millstone, III:128*n*
Milmine, Georgine, IV:602
Milne, Alan Alexander, III:489, 504
Milnes, Monckton, III:250
Milton, John, I:178
Milwaukee, Wis.
  post-Civil War magazines in (1865–85)
    general magazine, III:55
    kindergarten magazine, III:163
    manufacturing periodical, III:128
    religious magazine, III:69*n*
  Gilded Age magazines in (1885–1905), IV:38*n*
    archeological periodical, IV:140*n*
    educational periodicals, IV:271*n*, 272
    manufacturing periodicals, III:128; IV:184*n*
    medical periodicals, IV:314*n*
    religious periodicals, III:69*n*; IV:298
    society periodical, IV:96
    temperance periodical, IV:210
    trade magazine, IV:189*n*
    travel periodical, IV:224
  modern magazines in (1905–)
    archeological periodical, IV:140*n*
    education periodicals, IV:271*n*, 272
    manufacturing periodicals, III:128; IV:184*n*
    medical periodical, IV:315*n*
    music periodical, IV:254*n*
    religious periodicals, III:69*n*; IV:298*n*
    trade magazine, IV:189*n*
    travel periodical, IV:224
  newspapers in, III:269
Milwaukee Magazine, IV:101
Mims, Edwin, IV:785; V:101, 106, 117, 123, 273*n*, 278, 282
Mind, IV:284, 414
Miner, E. N., IV:352
Miner, Edward Herbert, IV:627
Miner, George Roberts, IV:484
Mineral Collector, IV:391
Mineral collectors' magazines, IV:391
Mineralogy, *see* Geology
Minerals, IV:391
Minerva, I:127–28, 797
Minerva and Saturday Post, I:380*n*
Miniatures, I:209–10
Mining America, IV:322*n*
Mining and Contracting Review, IV:322*n*
Mining and Engineering World, IV:322*n*
Mining Herald, III:115*n*
Mining Industry, IV:322*n*
Mining Journal, II:81; III:114
Mining journals, II:80–81; III:114–15; IV:322
Mining Magazine, II:81; IV:322*n*
Mining and Metallurgical Journal, III:114
Mining Reporter, IV:322*n*
Mining Review, III:114
Mining Review and Metallurgist, III:114
Mining and Scientific Press, II:80
Mining and Scientific Review, III:114
Mining in West, III:62
Minneapolis, Minn.
  post-Civil War magazines in
    agricultural magazines, III:157
    construction periodicals, III:129, 130
    grange magazine, III:149*n*
    home magazine, III:101
    manufacturers' periodical, III:128
    medical journal, III:141*n*
    religious magazines, III:73*n*, 77*n*
    temperance periodical, III:310*n*
    women's magazine, III:101
  Gilded Age magazines in (1885–1905)
    agricultural periodicals, III:157; IV:341
    construction periodicals, III:129, 130; IV:323, 324
    education periodical, III:169*n*
    financial periodical, IV:350*n*
    grange periodical, III:149*n*
    home magazine, II:101
    horse-racing periodical, IV:343
    mail-order periodical, IV:318*n*
    manufacturers' periodical, III:126
    medical journal, III:141*n*
    pharmacy periodicals, IV:318*n*
    photography periodical, IV:150*n*
    religious periodicals, III:75*n*, 77*n*; IV:291*n*, 293*n*
    single-tax periodical, IV:179
    socialist periodical, IV:283

Minneapolis, Minn.—*Continued*
temperance periodicals, III:310*n;* IV:210
trade magazine, IV:188*n*
urban weekly, IV:96
women's periodicals, III:101; IV:367
modern magazines in (1905–)
agricultural periodicals, III:157; IV:341
construction periodicals, III:130; IV:323, 324
financial periodical, IV:350*n*
grange periodical, III:149*n*
home magazine, III:101
medical journal, III:141*n*
pharmacy periodical, IV:318*n*
sports periodical, IV:381
temperance periodical, IV:210
trade magazine, IV:188*n*
women's periodicals, III:101; IV:361, 367
muckraking articles on, IV:599
Minneapolis Review, III:310*n*
Minnesota Engineer, IV:321*n*
Minnesota Farmer and Stockman, III:157
Minnesota Journal of Education, III:169
Minnesota University, IV:321*n*
Minor, Benjamin Blake, I:629*n,* 639, 644–47; II:345
Minor, D. Kimball, II:297
Minor, Lucian, I:459, 632, 651
Minor, Mrs. Virginia Otey, I:646
Minot, George Richards, I:28
Minot, John Clair, II:262*n,* 273
Minstrel shows, I:433–34; II:196; III:195, 208–9; IV:259
Minton, Maurice M., IV:58*n*
Miranda, Fernando, II:464
Miró, Joan, V:178
Mirror, see: New York Mirror
Mirror (St. Louis), *see: Reedy's Mirror*
Mirror Club, I:254*n*
Mirror and Farmer, II:90*n*
Mirror of Fashion, II:45
Mirror of Fashions, III:97, 325
Mirror of Taste and Dramatic Censor, I:166, 260, 793
Miscellaneous Notes and Queries with Answers, III:259*n*
Mishewaka, Ind., IV:321
Miss Leslie's Magazine, I:352–53, 733–34
Mission Bulletin, IV:195*n*
Mission Dayspring, III:77*n*
Mission Field, IV:238*n*
Mission Gleaner, III:79
Missionary, III:74
Missionary activities, I:369
magazine comment on, II:257; IV:397
in West, I:386
Missionary Herald, I:134, 263; II:71, 233
Missionary magazines
before 1865, I:133–34, 199, 200, 252; II:62–64, 71
after Civil War, III:70, 72, 74, 76*n,* 77*n,* 84; IV:108, 237–38, 304–5
Missionary Messenger, IV:238*n*
Missionary Monthly, IV:238*n*
Missionary Reporter, IV:238*n*
Missionary Review of the World, III:84; IV:237, 305, 569
Missionary Tidings, III:80
Missions, I:252
Mississippi School Journal, IV:270*n*
Mississippi Valley Lumbermen, III:130
Mississippi Valley Medical Monthly, III:141*n*
Missouri Baptist, III:73*n*
Missouri Compromise (1820), I:162, 164
Missouri and Kansas Farmer, III:158
Missouri Ruralist, IV:340
Missouri School Journal, III:169
Missouri Socialist, IV:176*n*
Missouri Valley Farmer, IV:349
Mitchel, Ormsby MacKnight, III:111*n*
Mitchell, Arthur J., III:128*n*
Mitchell, D. D., I:632
Mitchell, David Inscho, IV:63*n*
Mitchell, Donald Grant ("John Timon"), I:488*n,* 651; II:41, 171, 173, 389, 420, 505*n;* III:23, 99, 151, 224, 465*n,* 501, 557
Mitchell, Edward Page, IV:727
Mitchell, George Dean, IV:63
Mitchell, Harley B., III:128*n*
Mitchell, John, IV:494
Mitchell, John Ames, IV:556–66
Mitchell, John J., IV:187
Mitchell, S. D., IV:96, 270*n*
Mitchell, Silas Weir, II:506*n;* III:34*n,* 397, 400*n,* 471; IV:87
Mitchell, Stewart, III:543
Mitchell, Walter, II:505
Mitchell, William L., IV:626, 630
Mitchill, Samuel Latham, I:115, 149, 215–17, 266, 298
Mix, J. Rowland, IV:723
Mixed Drinks, IV:210
Mixer and Server, IV:221*n*
M'lle New York, IV:77, 86

Mobile, Ala., II:111
Model Farmer, III:155
Moderator-Topics, III:169
Modern Age, III:39*n*
Modern Art, IV:147
Modern Cemetery, IV:343*n*
Modern Farmer and Busy Bee, IV:345
Modern Grocer, IV:187*n*
Modern Homes, V:159
Modern Housekeeping, IV:364*n*
Modern Language Association, V:345
Modern Language Notes, IV:128
Modern Maccabee, IV:222
Modern Machinery, IV:321
Modern Medical Science, IV:314*n*
Modern Medicine, IV:313*n*
Modern Mexico, IV:237
Modern Miller, III:128
Modern Philology, IV:128
Modern Poetry Association, V:244
Modern Poultry Breeder, IV:345*n*
Modern Priscilla, IV:361
Modern Stories, IV:367*n*
Modern View, IV:300
Modern Women, IV:366
Modern Woodman, IV:222
Moderwell, Hiram K., V:97
Modes and Fabrics, IV:367*n*
Modes and Fashions, IV:363*n*
Modigliani, Amedeo, V:178
Modjeska, Mme. Helena, III:205; IV:256, 410
Moffett, Cleveland Langston, II:463; IV:319, 329, 330, 429, 592–93, 596, 604, 662
Moffett, Samuel Erasmus, IV:489
Moffitt, Mabel, III:402*n*
Mohawk & Hudson Railroad, I:467
Moholy-Nagy, Laszlo, V:178
Moley, Raymond, IV:709
Moline, Ill., III:128, 156
Molly Maguires, III:303
Mommsen, Theodore, IV:227
Momus, II:136, 179, 184, 188, 206
Monahan, Michael, IV:390, 448, 645–46, 655
Monet, Claude, IV:145
Monette, J. W., II:345
Money, IV:349
Money Management Book, V:48
Moneychangers, The (Sinclair), V:254
Monist, IV:303
Monitor (Cincinnati), IV:48
Monitor (New York), II:94*n*
Monopolies, economic, *see* Trusts
Monroe, Harriet, V:105, 225–312, 237–43, 258
Monroe, J. R., III:89
Monroe, Lucy, III:550
Monroe, Paul, IV:192
Monroe Doctrine, I:162
Montana Christian Advocate, III:71*n*
Montana Churchman, III:75*n*
Montessori, Maria, IV:604
Montgomery, Ala., II:65*n*, 89, 110*n*
Montgomery, Alexander, II:194
Montgomery, C. E., IV:385
Montgomery, Charles A., IV:415
Montgomery, George Edgar. IV:60
Montgomery. H. F., III:481*n*, 482
Montgomery, James, I:135*n*
Montgomery County Law Reporter, IV:347*n*
Monthlies
- in nationalist era (1794–1825), I:122–29
- in expansionist era (1825–50)
  - number, I:342*n*, 387
  - quality and trends, I:343–48
- in Civil War era (1850–65)
  - advertising, II:13–14
  - anonymity, II:25
  - average circulation, II:10
  - number, II:4*n*
  - payments to contributors, II:19–21
  - trends, II:29–33
- in Gilded Age (1885–1905)
  - number, IV:11
  - trends, IV:43–56
- *See also monthlies by name and topic*

Monthly Abstract of Medical Science, I:568
Monthly American Journal of Geology, I:446, 801
Monthly Anthology, I:147, 164, 165, 167, 175, 176, 184, 186, 198, 200, 277, 278; II:218
- founding of, I:124
- sketch of, I:253–59

Monthly Anthology Club, V:103
Monthly Book Trade Circular, III:491
Monthly Bulletin of the American Republics, IV:237
Monthly Cyclopedia of Practical Medicine, IV:314*n*
Monthly Echo, III:314
Monthly Illustrator, IV:154
Monthly Journal of the American Unitarian Association, II:72
Monthly Journal of Insurance Economics, IV:351*n*
Monthly Journal of the Unitarian Association, III:77

Monthly Law Reporter, II:93
Monthly Literary Miscellany, II:116*n*
Monthly Magazine and American Review, I:14, 54, 164, 167, 168, 187, 192
founding of, I:124
sketch of, I:218–22
See also Brown, Charles Brockden
Monthly Military Repository, I:122*n*, 790
Monthly Miscellany, I:31*n*, 288, 789
Monthly Miscellany of Religion and Letters, I:804
Monthly Offering, II:287*n*
Monthly Petroleum Trade Report, III:131
Monthly Register and Review, I:167, 176, 191, 194–95, 205
sketch of, I:260–61
Monthly Religious Magazine, I:372, 807; II:72; III:77
Monthly Review, V:73*n*
Monthly Review and Literary Miscellany, see: Monthly Register and Review
Monthly Serial Supplement, I:360
Monthly Trade Gazette, II:159
Montpelier, Vt., III:77*n*
Monumental News, IV:189
Moods, IV:518*n*
Moody, Charles Amadon, IV:107*n*
Moody, Dwight Lyman, III:86, 87; IV:301, 544
Moody, John, IV:600
Moody, William Vaughn, II:513; IV:273; V:228
Moody's Monthly, IV:301
Moon, George Washington, III:309, 323
Moon, Parker Thomas, IV:180*n*
Mooney, Herbert R., I:481*n*; II:325*n*, 328
Moore, A., II:58
Moore, Arthur S., IV:603
Moore, Charles B., III:260*n*
Moore, Charles C., IV:277–78
Moore, Charles Herbert, III:336
Moore, Charles Leonard, III:541
Moore, Charles W., II:215; III:314
Moore, Clement Clarke, II:364
Moore, Cornelius, II:215
Moore, D. D. T., II:89; III:23, 152
Moore, Don, IV:417*n*
Moore, George, III:543; V:5, 258
Moore, Mrs. H. G., II:58
Moore, J. Quitman, II:155, 346
Moore, John Bassett, III:351; IV:180, 225, 662
Moore, John Foot, IV:395*n*
Moore, John M., I:359
Moore, Marianne, III:539*n*, 543; IV:739; V:173, 176, 237
Moore, Merrill, IV:738; V:100*n*, 108, 115
Moore, Myrna Drake, IV:360*n*
Moore, N. Hudson, III:485
Moore, S. H., III:99
Moore, Mrs. S. V., IV:100*n*
Moore, T., I:520
Moore, Thomas, I:180, 190, 231, 278; II:230–31
Moore, W. H., IV:229
Moore, W. Robert, IV:630, 632
Moore, William Thomas, III:80
Moore, Willis Luther, IV:622*n*
Moore's Rural New Yorker, III:153
Moorhead, Minn., V:179*n*
Morality
early magazines on (1714–94), I:66
expansionist era magazines on (1825–50)
smoking, I:474–75
swearing, I:475
temperance, I:473–74
in post-Civil War era (1865–85)
decline of puritanism, III:4, 305
scientific criticism, III:305–6
theater, III:206–8
in Gilded Age (1885–1905)
literary criticism and, IV:122–24
theater and, IV:257
Moran, Edward Percy, IV:19
Moran, John Leon, IV:19
Moran, Thomas, III:411
Morand, Paul, III:542
Moravian, II:74
More, Paul Elmer, III:331*n*, 348; IV:225, 295, 738
Morehouse, Linden Husted, III:75
Morgan, Appleton, III:237
Morgan, H. H., III:51
Morgan, J. P., and Company, V:197
Morgan, John Pierpont, II:401, 548; IV:489, 690, 776
Morgan, John Tyler, II:254; IV:163
Morgan, Matt, II:335, 462; III:269*n*; IV:385
Morgan, Robert E., III:270*n*
Morgan, Tom P., III:530
Morgantown, W. Va., IV:390*n*
Morgenthau, Henry, IV:784, 785
Morison, John Hopkins, II:72*n*; III:506*n*, 507
Morley, Christopher, IV:425, 438, 439, 521; V:136
Morley, Frank, III:110*n*

Morley, John, III:472
Morley, Sylvanus Griswold, IV:629
Mormon periodicals
  in Civil War era (1850–65), II:74–75
  in post-Civil War era (1865–85), III:57, 57*n*, 81
    juvenile periodicals, III:180
  in Gilded Age (1885–1905), IV:104, 296–97
    education periodical, IV:272
    juvenile periodical, IV:275
Mormon Tribune, III:57*n*
Mormons, III:275, 313; IV:495
Morning Star (Boston), II:65; IV:291
Morning Star (Carlisle), IV:215
Morphology journals, IV:314
Morphy, Edward R., III:57*n*
Morrill, Joseph S., II:254
Morris, Charles (archaeologist), II:532
Morris, Charles D'Urban, III:536, 537
Morris, Clara, III:204; IV:602
Morris, Edward, V:89
Morris, Frank Daniel, IV:476
Morris, George Perry, IV:289
Morris, George Pope, I:128, 320–21, 366, 546, 585, 627; II:57, 150, 349, 350, 352, 354, 360; III:102
Morris, Gouverneur, I:123, 155; IV:497, 504, 637
Morris, Harrison Smith, III:396*n*, 400
Morris, Helen Swift, V:89–90, 96–99
Morris, Joe Alex, IV:476
Morris, Malcolm, I:568
Morris, Robert, I:354, 546*n*; II:215
Morris, William, III:549; IV:110, 131, 132, 148, 425, 646; V:182
Morrison, Arthur, IV:196, 685
Morrison, J. P., III:46*n*
Morrison, Theodore, IV:75*n*
Morrison-Fuller, J., IV:62
Morristown, Tenn., III:73*n*; IV:270*n*
Morrow, Honoré Willsie, III:481*n*, 487, 488; V:85
Morrow, Hugh, IV:712*n*
Morrow, Marco, IV:645
Morse, Charles W., V:82*n*
Morse, James Herbert, III:549
Morse, Jedediah, I:262–65
Morse, John Torrey, Jr., II:532; III:35*n*
Morse, Richard, I:373
Morse, Samuel Finley Breese, II:318
Morse, Samuel H., III:78
Morse, Sidney Edwards, I:373
Morse, Sidney H., III:301
Morse, Mrs. T. Vernette, IV:148*n*
Morse, Willard H., IV:376
Mortimer, C., I:726
Mortimer, Lee, V:24
Morton, David, IV:519, 522, 724, 738; V:113, 266
Morton, Henry, I:556*n*, 558
Morton, Frederick W., IV:147
Morton, Julius Sterling, IV:178–79
Morton, Mrs. Sarah Wentworth, I:109, 203; IV:80
Morton Park, Ill., IV:200
Mortuary trade magazines, IV:189
Moses, George H., II:260
Moses, Montrose Jonas, III:235*n*
Mosher, Thomas Bird, IV:424–27
Mosher's Magazine, IV:265
Moslem periodicals, IV:287
Moslem World, IV:287
Mossadegh, Mohammed, V:323*n*
Mossman, William Templeton, IV:88*n*
Motherhood, IV:364
Motherhood, I:65; III:482
Mothers' and Daughters' Magazine, II:58*n*
Mothers' Friend, IV:364
Mother's Journal, IV:363*n*
Mother's Journal and Family Visitant, II:57
Mothers' Magazine, II:57*n*, 58*n*
Motion pictures
  controversies over, V:121
  early shorts in, IV:260
  invention of, IV:320
  reviews of
    comic magazines, III:555; IV:567
    current events magazines, V:322–23
    family magazines, III:434; IV:504
    general magazines, III:555
    illustrated periodicals, IV:567
    women's magazines, IV:552
Motive Power, IV:33*n*
Motley, John Lathrop, I:401, 578; II:163, 175, 240, 243, 494, 495
Moton, Robert Russa, IV:780; V:278
Motor, IV:331
Motor Age, IV:331
Motor Boat, IV:373
Motor Vehicle Monthly, III:216*n*
Motor Vehicle Review, IV:331
Motor Way, IV:331
Motor World, IV:331
Motorcycle, IV:330
Motorcycle Illustrated, III:213*n*
Motor-Cycle Magazine, III:213*n*
Motorman and Conductor, IV:221*n*
Mott, Ed, III:528
Mott, H. S., III:260*n*
Moulton, Charles Welles, IV:55*n*, 121
Moulton, Louise Chandler, II:267, 309, 395, 417, 506*n*; III:37*n*, 373, 393, 424, 508, 558; IV:481, 680

Moundsville, W. Va., III:81
Mount, Mrs. P. W., IV:93
Mount Morris, Ill., III:81; IV:345*n*
Mount Vernon, Iowa, II:51; IV:343*n*
Mountain Cove, Va., II:210
Mountain Cove Journal and Spiritual Harbinger, II:210
Mowry, William Augustus, III:168*n*
Mrs. Devereux' Tips, IV:95
Mrs. Grundy, III:265–66
Mrs. Stephens' Illustrated New Monthly, II:32
Mrs. Whittelsey's Magazine for Mothers, II:58
Muckraking
  in post-Civil War magazines (1865–85), III:427, 430, 447, 471, 513–14
  in Gilded Age magazines (1885–1905), IV:207–9, 415
    family magazines, IV:494
    general magazines, III:512–13; IV:406–8, 597–601
    literary magazines, II:512
    social sources, IV:11, 207
  in modern magazines (1905–), IV:494–95; V:149
"Mug" features, IV:77
Muggeridge, Malcolm, IV:762
Muilenburg, Walter J., V:183, 186
Muir, Edwin, V:96
Muir, John, III:56*n*, 463, 465
Muir, Ward, IV:604
Mukerji, Dhan Gopal, IV:520
Muldoon, William, II:332
Mulford, Prentice, III:406
Mullaly, John, II:77*n*
Mullen, Edward F., II:523; III:265*n*
Müller, Friedrich Max, II:271; IV:302*n*
Müller, G. F., IV:88
Muloch, Dinah M., *see* Craik, Dinah Maria Muloch
Mulroney, Joseph S., IV:171*n*
Mumford, Ethel Watts, IV:390*n*, 607
Mumford, Lewis, IV:730; V:12, 90–91, 93–95, 211
Mumler, William H., III:267*n*
Munday, Eugene H., IV:683–84
Mundé, Paul Fortunatus, III:141
Mundy, Talbot, V:85
Municipal Affairs, IV:198
Municipal affairs periodicals, IV:198
Municipal corruption
  in post-Civil War era (1865–85), III:26–27
    Tweed ring, II:478–80; III:4, 290–91, 320, 342, 440–42; IV:124
  in Gilded Age, IV:197–98, 406–7
    muckraking articles, IV:599, 600
    reform campaigns, IV:406–7
  in modern magazines, IV:776
Municipal Engineering, IV:322*n*
Municipal engineering periodicals, IV:322*n*–23*n*
Municipal Journal, IV:198
Municipality, IV:198*n*
Munkittrick, Richard Kendall, III:528, 554; IV:98, 480, 634, 768; V:248
Munn, Charles Allen, II:316, 321, 322, 323
Munn, Charles Clark, IV:187
Munn, Orson Desaix, II:316*n*, 317, 322, 323
Munn & Company, II:316*n*, 318, 321, 323
Munro, Dana Carleton, IV:138
Munro, David A., II:220*n*, 254, 256
Munro, George, III:43, 98, 223, 256; IV:117–18
Munro, Norman L., III:178, 223; IV:117–18
Munroe, Frederick Mitchell, IV:87
Munroe, Kirk, III:178*n*, 509; IV:224
Munsey, Frank Andrew, I:352; II:311; III:178, 268
Munsey's, IV:615
  in *Public Opinion,* IV:651
  in *Review of Reviews,* IV:662
  in *Scribner's,* IV:724
  in *World's Work,* IV:775–76
Munsey's Illustrated Weekly, IV:608*n*
Munsey's Magazine, IV:4–6, 15–19, 21, 46, 152, 420, 422, 485, 596
  sketch of, IV:608–19
Munsey's Weekly, III:268*n*; IV:39, 420, 608–9
Munson, Gorham Bert, IV:441, 738; V:98, 113
Munson Photographic News and Teacher, IV:352
Münsterberg (Muensterberg), Hugo, IV:604; V:5, 51, 134
Munyon's Illustrated World, IV:87
Munyon's Magazine, IV:87–88
Murayama, Hashime, IV:628
Murdock, Fridge, III:46
Murdock, Gertrude M., 115*n*
Murdock, John Nelson, I:666*n*
Murdock, Victor, IV:117*n*
Murfree, Mary Noailles ("Charles Egbert Craddock"), II:398, 506*n*, 510; III:48, 228, 508; IV:689
Murphy, Lady Blanche, III:398, 511
Murphy, Daniel, IV:92
Murray, George, I:209
Murray, Grace Peckham, III:484

Murray, Judith, I:109
Murray, Nicholas, III:537
Murray, Sir Gilbert, III:351
Murray, William Henry Harrison, IV:403, 408
Murray-Aaron, Eugene, IV:55
Murrell, John A., II:326
Murrow, Edward R., IV:478
Muse (chapbook), IV:390*n*
Muse (music periodical), IV:253
Museum of Foreign Literature and Science, I:130, 272
  sketch of, I:307–9
Music
  in magazines before 1825, I:110, 172–73, 296, 303, 358
  in magazines 1825–50, I:403, 481, 589, 592, 623, 627, 714, 719, 744, 745
    Negro influence, I:433–34
    popularity, I:431–35
  in Civil War era magazines, II:45, 303, 308, 352, 416–17, 437, 507*n*
    popularity, II:194–97
  after Civil War, II:376, 428; III:195–98, 416; IV:250–54, 544
    Negro music, I:433–34
    popularity, III:195
    trends, III:192–95
  symphonic, IV:249–50
  See also Opera; Songs
Music box advertising, IV:24
Music comment and criticism
  before 1850, I:172–73, 227, 431–35, 589, 610, 682, 736, 757–59, 764, 766, 771
  in magazines 1850–85, II:425, 451; III:233, 337, 347, 368, 416, 528
  in magazines after 1885, III:429, 542; IV:87, 613, 675; V:95
Music and Drama, III:198*n*, 199; IV:251, 261
Music magazines
  early, I:29, 139, 172, 427, 434–35; II:197
  after Civil War, III:195–98; IV:250–54
Music Trade Indicator, III:198*n*
Music Trade Journal, III:196
Music Trade Review, III:196
Music Trades, IV:254*n*
Musical Age, IV:251
Musical America, IV:251–52
Musical Bulletin, III:198*n*
Musical Cabinet, I:435, 805
Musical concerts, II:194–95; IV:249–50
Musical Courier, III:196; IV:251–52
Musical Echo, IV:254*n*
Musical Enterprise, V:254*n*
Musical Harp, III:197*n*
Musical Herald of the United States, III:197*n*
Musical Leader, IV:254
Musical Magazine (Boston), I:435, 804
Musical Magazine (Cheshire, Baltimore, and Philadelphia), I:172*n*
Musical Magazine (New York), I:434–35, 803
Musical Messenger, IV:254*n*
Musical Million, II:198*n*
Musical People, III:197*n*
Musical Record, IV:253
Musical Record and Review, III:197*n*
Musical Review, IV:253
Musical Review and Gazette, III:196
Musical and Sewing Machine Gazette, III:196
Musical Times, II:197; III:198*n*; IV:254
Musical World (Cleveland), II:198*n*
Musical World (New York), II:197
Musician, 197*n*; IV:253
Musser, John H., Jr., I:556*n*
Mussey, Henry Raymond, III:350; IV:80*n*
Mussey, Mabel H. B., III:355
Mussolini, Benito, V:312
Mustard, Wilfred Pirt, III:535*n*
Mutual Underwriter, III:146*n*
Muzzey, David S., V:56
Muzzey, Mrs. Harriet, I:326
My Better Homes and Garden Cook Book, V:42–43, 47
My Thirty Years' War (Anderson), V:174
Mycology, Journal of, IV:310
Myers, Gustavus, IV:494; V:54
Myers, William B., I:656
Myrick, Herbert, I:728*n*, 732; IV:337*n*
Mystic Worker, IV:222*n*
"Myth of a Guilty Nation" (Nock), V:97

N.A.R.D. Notes, IV:318
Nadal, Ehrman Syme, III:463
Nahl, Charles, III:265
Naidu, Padmaja, IV:555
Nankivall, Frank Arthur, III:530
Nansen, Fridtjof, II:402; IV:593
Napoleon Bonaparte, II:389, 390; IV:137, 230, 485, 590–91, 719
Narcross, C. P., IV:48*n*
Narragansett Historical Register, III:260
"Nasby, Petroleum V.," *see* Locke, David Ross

Nash, Ogden, IV:713; V:136
Nashville, Tenn., II:107
medical and dental journals, II:84*n;* III:141*n,* 143*n;* IV:315*n*
poetry magazine, V:100–16
religious periodicals, II:64, 68; III:71, III:71, 73*n,* 80; IV:229*n,* 294, 305
other magazines II:57*n,* 110*n;* III:155, 168; IV:305
Nashville Journal of Medicine and Surgery, II:84*n*
Nashville and Louisville Christian Advocate, II:57*n*
Nashville Tennesseean, V:111
Nason, Elias, II:176*n*
Nassau Literary Magazine, I:489, 806; III:165
Nassau Monthly, I:489; 806; II:99
Nast, Condé, II:45, 184, 454, 474–82, 523; III:40, 53*n,* 99*n,* 265, 281, 286, 389, 524; IV:58n, 61, 66, 387*n*
Nast's Weekly, IV:387*n*
Nathan, George Jean, III:531, 532, 555; IV:390*n,* 731; V:3–7, 13–17, 21, 23, 26*n,* 99*n,* 246*n,* 251, 254, 256–258, 259*n,* 260–72, 348
Nathan, Henry C., IV:184
Nation, I:613; II:379; III:17, 19, 40, 47, 64–65, 123, 124, 184, 190, 199, 227, 232, 255, 272, 279, 281, 283–84, 286, 288, 307, 309, 314, 324, 369, 464–65; IV:10, 60; V:19, 30*n,* 89, 96, 99, 207, 214, 306
sketch of, III:331–56
Nation, Carrie, IV:210
National Academy of Design, founding of, I:437
National advertising, IV:22–29
National Advertising, IV:247*n*
National Advocate, I:203
National Agriculturist, III:152
National Agriculturist and Working Farmer, III:153
National Anti-Slavery Standard, I:458; II:141, 175, 285; III:310
National Baker, IV:186*n*
National Bank controversy, I:52, 454, 575, 679, 697
National Baptist, III:72; IV:291
National Baptist Union Review, IV:292*n*
National Barber and Druggists' Gazette, IV:180*n*
National Bimetallist, IV:163*n*
National Builder, IV:324–25
National Car Builder, II:300; III:126*n*
National Citizen and Ballot Box, III:94
National Conference on Building, V:43
National Co-Operator and Farm Journal, III:160
National Cooper's Journal, IV:184*n*
National Corporation Reporter, IV:182
National Democrat, IV:69*n*
National Democratic Quarterly, II:116*n*
National Democratic Quarterly Review, II:28, 134
National Druggist, III:134
National Eclectic Medical Association Quarterly, IV:316
National Economist, IV:176
National Editorial Journalist, III:274*n*
National Educator, II:99*n*
National Electrical Contractor, IV:322
National Era, I:381, 457–58, 808; II:22, 134, 139, 140, 142, 146, 175
National Farmer and Home Magazine, IV:365
National Farmer and Stockgrower, IV:341
National Fireman's Journal, III:118
National Food and Drug Act of 1906, V:137–38, 143
National Food Magazine, IV:363*n*
National Gazette, I:272
National Geographic Magazine, IV:109, 224, 233, 307
sketch of, IV:620–32
National Glass Budget, III:127; IV:184*n*
National Grange Monthly, III:149*n*
National Harness Review, III:216
National Hay and Grain Reporter, IV:189*n*
National Hibernian, IV:227
National Housing Act, V:43
National Humane Journal, III:312
National Intelligencer, I:160; II:139, 449; IV:60*n*
National Journal of Finance, II:96
National Journalist, III:274*n*
National Labor Relations Board, V:20*n*
National Labor Tribune, III:299
National Labor Union, III:299, 393
National Laundry Journal, III:132
National Live Stock Journal, III:159
National Magazine, I:771; II:31, 66; III:262*n*
National Magazine (Boston), IV:40, 80–81
National Magazine, (Chicago), IV:55*n*
National Magazine or Cabinet of the United States, see: National Magazine, or a Political, Histo-

rical, Biographical, and Literary Repository
National Magazine, or Lady's Emporium, I:381, 800
National Magazine, or a Political, Historical, Biographical, and Literary Repository, I:204–205, 791
National Monthly Farm Press, III:156*n*
National Nurseryman, IV:343*n*
National Philanthropist, I:165, 473; II:275
National Police Gazette, I:481, 808; II:187, 190; III:44, 198, 209, 218, 309; IV:199, 372, 384; V:xiii, 346–47
advertising rate of, III:11, 28
circulation of, III:7
sketch of, II:325–337
National Post, V:290
National Preacher, I:798; III:83
National Presbyterian, III:74
National Press, I:330
See also: Home Journal
National Printer-Journalist, III:274; IV:243
National Provisioner, IV:186*n*
National Quarterly Review, II:28, 93, 149, 158, 164; III:31, 103, 281
sketch of, II:530–33
National Real Estate Index, III:148
National Reciprocity, IV:166–67
National Recorder, I:130, 306
National Recovery Administration, V:20*n*, 71, 139, 284
National Repository, II:304; III:70
National Republican, IV:69*n*
National Rural, I:444*n*
National School Digest, III:169*n*
National Single-Taxer, IV:179
National Socialist, III:301
National Sportsman, IV:381
National Standard, II:141; III:310
National Stenographer, IV:352
National Stockman and Farmer, III:160
National Sunday School Teacher, III:84
National Temperance Advocate, III:310
National Tribune, IV:69
National Underwriter, IV:351*n*
National university project, I:146
National View, IV:69*n*, 163
National Watchman, IV:163*n*
National Women's Rights Convention, (1853), II:291
Nationalism, IV:200–203, 280, 406
in early magazines, I:23
colonial, I:22
economic nationalism, I:60
Revolution period, I:22–23, 48–49
in magazines after 1794
literary goals, I:183–88
paper war with England, I:188–90
specific examples, I:275, 322
in expansionist era magazines, I:390–91, 413
Bellamy, IV:191, 202–03
Nationalist, IV:202–03
Native American movement, I:752
Natural History, IV:309
Natural history, I:39, 82, 112, 363, 493, 623, 714, II:228, 408, 439–40; III:211, 460
See also Nature writing
Natural resources, IV:622–23
Naturalist Advertiser, III:109*n*
Naturalist and Fancier, III:109*n*
Naturalists' Agency Monthly Bulletin, III:109*n*
Naturalists' Leisure Hour, III:109*n*
Nature Guard, IV:341*n*
Nature writing, II:243; III:426, 503; IV:309, 725
See also Natural history
Nautical Gazette, III:126; IV:333–34
Nautilus (collectors' periodical), IV:391
Nautilus (New Thought periodical), IV:284
Naval Magazine, I:456, 803
Navigation, I:303
Navy, U.S., I:125, 280, 282, 456, 478, 643; IV:726–27
Navy periodicals, *see* Military and naval periodicals
Naylor, Aubrey W., V:273*n*
Naziism, press opposition to, III:352
Neagle, John, I:436
Neagle, John B., I:521
Neal, Alice B., *see* Haven, Alice Bradley Neal
Neal, John, I:127*n*, 169–70, 177, 201, 204, 241–42, 269, 272, 418, 490; II:467; IV:677
as contributor, I:293–96, 352, 359, 498–99, 506, 743, 770
as editor, I:293–96, 397, 355, 361
Neal, Joseph Clay, I:378, 546, 582, 585, 602, 609, 680, 737
Neale, Walter, IV:73
Neall, Adelaide W., IV:708, 711
Neal's Saturday Gazette and Ladies' Literary Museum, II:36–37
Nebraska, magazines on, II:120–21
Nebraska Bee-Keeper, IV:345
Nebraska Blue Print, IV:321*n*
Nebraska City, Neb., IV:179
Nebraska Congregrational News, III:77*n*

Nebraska Cultivator and Housekeeper, III:158
Nebraska Farmer, III:158
Nebraska Legal News, IV:347*n*
Nebraska Teacher, IV:270*n*
Nebraska University, IV:321*n*
Neef, Francis J. N., I:537
Neely, Kate J., II:394
Neely, Thomas Benjamin, III:180
Negro art, magazines on, IV:86
Negro minstrel shows, I:433–34; II:196; III:195, 208–9; IV:259
Negro music, I:433–34; III:195
Negro periodicals, II:141; III:71, 73; IV:214
Negro slavery, *see* Slavery debate
Negroes
  expansionist-era magazines on
    education, I:537–564
    literary sketches, I:653
  Civil War magazines on (1850–65), II:524
  post-Civil War magazines on (1865–85), III:71, 73, 75*n*
  Gilded Age magazines on (1885–1905), IV:384, 445
    civil rights, IV:212–14
  modern magazines on (1905–), IV:780; V:9, 218, 274–77, 284–85
  satire on, II:179
  settlement-house periodical for, IV:195*n*
  See also Freedman
Neighbor, IV:195*n*
Neighborhood House, IV:195*n*
Neihardt, John Gneisenau, II:431; III:408, 514; IV:518; V:185, 251
Neil, Marion Harris, IV:364*n*
Neill, William, I:136, 315, 316
Neilson, Francis, V:88–90, 93, 96–98
Nelson, Charles Brown, V:187
Nelson, Edward William, IV:627
Nelson, Frederick, IV:712
Nelson, Henry Loomis, II:469*n*, 484; IV:163*n*, 456
Neohumanism, IV:441, 738
Nervous disease journals, III:142; IV:314
Nesbit, Wilbur Dick, III:554
Nethersole, Olga, IV:257–58
Nettleship, Henry, III:536
Nevada Magazine, IV:108
Nevill, Samuel, I:26
Nevin, John Williamson, II:380, 381
Nevins, Allan, IV:478; V:55
Nevinson, Henry Woodd, II:402; IV:196; V:97
New Age, III:315
New Age Illustrated, V:292
New Age Magazine, IV:222*n*
New Albany Medical Herald, III:141n
New American Magazine, I:26, 33*n*, 48, 53, 787
New Amsterdam Gazette, III:260; IV:137*n*
New Argosy, IV:417*n*, 422
New Bedford, Mass., III:31, 300
New Bohemian, IV:95
New Brighton, Pa., III:210*n*
New Brunswick, N.J., I:31*n*
New Century (Catholic), IV:298
New Century (theosophical), IV:287
New Century Path, IV:287
New Charter, IV:175
"New Chicago Movement," V:172
New Christian Quarterly, IV:295
New Christianity, IV:296
New-Church Independent and Monthly Review, II:74
New Church Life, III:82; IV:296
New Church Messenger, II:74; IV:296
New-Church Review, II:74; IV:296
New Covenant, II:73*n*
New Cycle (New Thought periodical), IV:287*n*
New Cycle (women's clubs periodical), IV:356
New Deal, press comment on, III:353; IV:663; V:216, 284
New Democracy, The (Weyl), V:196
New Earth (single tax), IV:180
New Earth (Swedenborgian), IV:296
New Eclectic, III:46, 256
New Education, III:163; IV:269*n*
New England, I:346
  early economy of (1791), I:60–61
  factory system, I:471
  periodicals in, IV:78–82
  public education in, I:145
  See also specific towns and cities
New-England Anti-Slavery Society, II:281
New England Art-Union, II:191
New England Bibliopolist, III:259
New England Conservatory Quarterly, IV:253
New England Druggist, IV:318
New England Editor, IV:244
New England Family Magazine, I:517–18, 523
New England Farmer (Fessenden's; 1822–46), I:154, 442
  sketch of, 317–19
New England Farmer (1848–71), I:319, 442, 809

New England Farmer (1865–1913), III:152; IV:339
New England Farms, III:152
New-England Galaxy, I:127, 169, 169*n*, 199, 795
New England Genealogical and Historical Register IV:137
New England Grocer, IV:187
New England Grocery and Market, III:134
New England Historical and Genealogical Register, I:422, 808; II:175; III:259
New England Homestead, I:731; III: 152; IV:337
New England Insurance Gazette and Monthly Financial Record, II:94*n*
New England Journal of Education, III:163, 168
New England Journal of Medicine, II:84*n*
New England Journal of Medicine and Surgery, I:151*n*, 794
New England Kitchen Magazine, IV:363–64
New England Magazine, I:344, 448, 505; II:494; III:137; V:79–80
  sketch of, I:599–603
New England Magazine of Knowledge and Pleasure, I:26*n*, 33*n*, 41, 787
New England Mechanic, I:445, 808
New England Medical Gazette, III:143
New England Medical Monthly, III:140*n*
New England Medical Review and Journal, I:151*n*, 799
New-England Quarterly Magazine, I:129, 178, 792
New England Shoe and Leather Industry, IV:185*n*
New England Spiritualist, II:210*n*
New England Sportsman, IV:381
New Englander, I:269, 371, 806; II:70, 498, 519; III:76, 164, 166, 281, 312; V:329
  sketch of, II:312–15
New Era, III:80*n*
New Era Magazine, IV:293*n*
New Freeman, V:99
New Genesee Farmer, I:443, 805
New Hampshire Genealogical Record, IV:140*n*
New Hampshire Journal (Congregational weekly), III:77*n*
New Hampshire Journal: Or The Farmer's Weekly Museum, see: Farmer's Museum
New Hampshire Journal of Agriculture, II:90*n*
New Hampshire Journal of Medicine, II:84*n*
New Hampshire Magazine, I:31*n*, 789
New Hampshire and Vermont Magazine, I:790
New Harmony community, I:536–37
New-Harmony Gazette, I:536–37
New Haven, Conn.
  early magazines in (1741–94), I:29, 31*n*, 104
  nationalist era magazines in (1794–1825), I:135, 204, 302
  expansionist era magazine in (1825–50), I:371
  Civil War era magazines in (1850–65)
    education magazine, II:100
    religious magazines, II:68, 69, 364–65
    utopian communist magazines, II:207*n*
  post-Civil War magazines in (1865–85)
    agricultural magazines, III:152
    banking periodical, III:147*n*
    educational periodical, III:168*n*
    historical journal, III:262*n*
    music journal, III:197*n*
    women's magazine, III:100
  Gilded Age magazines in, (1885–1905)
    agricultural magazine, III:152
    banking periodical, III:147*n*
    general magazines, IV:82, V:329*n*
    music journal, III:197*n*
    philology journal, IV:128
    socialist periodical, IV:174
    women's periodical, IV:363*n*
  modern magazines in (1905–)
    agricultural magazine, III:152
    banking periodical, III:147n
    general magazine, V:329*n*
    philology journal, IV:128
    regional periodical, IV:82
New Haven Gazette, I:31*n*, 788
New Haven Railway, V:149, 151*n*
New Iberia, La., III:155
New Idea, III:486
New Idea Women's Magazine, IV:361
New Ideal Magazine, IV:283
New Illustrated Magazine, IV:228
New Jersey Baptist Bulletin, IV:292*n*
New Jersey Forester, IV:342
New Jersey Historical Society Proceedings, II:176*n*
New Jersey Law Journal, I:347*n*

New Jersey Magazine, I:31*n,* 788; III:33*n*
New Jersey Mechanic, I:445
New Jersey Review of Charities and Corrections, IV:193–94
New Jersey Temperance Gazette, III:310*n*
New Jerusalem Magazine, II:74; IV:296
New Lebanon, N.Y., II:92
New McClure's Magazine, IV:589*n,* 607; V:271–72
New Man, IV:285*n*
New Mexico Journal of Education, IV:270*n*
New Mirror, I:327–30, 328–29
New Monthly Family Magazine, I:364, 806
New Music Review, IV:254
New Nation, IV:203
New National Era, II:140n; III:283
New Northwest, III:95
New Occasions, IV:204
New Orleans, La.
  expansionist era magazines in (1825–50), I:377
    business magazine, II:339
    literary magazine, I:721–27
    magazine center, I:380, 383–84
    medical journal, I:439–40
    number, I:375
  Civil War era magazines in (1850–65)
    literary magazine, I:721*n;* II:30
    magazine center, II:107
    medical journal, I:439*n;* II:8
    religious magazine, II:65*n*
  post-Civil War magazines in (1865–85)
    comic magazine, III:268
    magazine center, III:45
    medical journal, I:439*n*
    music periodical, III:197*n*
    religious magazines, III:71, 75*n*
  Gilded Age magazines in (1885–1905), IV:92–93
    agricultural magazines, III:155; IV:92
    all-fiction magazine, IV:116–17
    business magazines, IV:92–93
    comic periodical, IV:387*n*
    education periodical, IV:270*n*
    general magazines, IV:93
    Jewish periodicals, IV:300
    medical journal, II:84*n*
    religious magazine, II:75*n*
  modern magazine in (1905–), medical journal, II:84*n*
  cholera epidemic in (1873), III:137
  theater in, I:169
  yellow fever epidemic in (1853–54), II:86
New Orleans Advocate, III:71*n*
New Orleans Christian Advocate, II:68*n*
New Orleans Journal of Medicine, I:439*n*
New Orleans Medical and Surgical Journal, I:439, 807; II:8, 84*n*
New Orleans Miscellany, I:384, 809
New Orleans Monthly Review, III:45
New Orleans Quarterly Review, III:45
New Outlook, III:422*n,* 434–35
New Peterson Magazine, II:306*n,* 310
New Philosophy, IV:296
New Pictorial, I:364*n*
New Pictorial Family Magazine, I:364*n*
New Preparations, III:141*n*
New Princeton Review, I:529*n,* 535
New Remedies, III:133
New Republic, II:379; V:xiii, 7–8, 20*n,* 91, 303
  sketch of, V:191–224
New School Presbyterians, III:74
New Science Review, IV:308
New Star (Concord), I:790
New Star (Hartford), I:122*n,* 790
New Success: Marden's Magazine, V:291
New Testament, A (Anderson), V:177
New Thought, IV:284
New Thought cult, IV:283–85
  periodicals of, IV:304*n*
New Time, IV:204, 413
New Varieties, III:266
New Vienna, Ohio, III:81
New Voice, III:310*n*
New Western Magazine, II:114*n*
New World (Catholic), IV:298*n*
New World ("mammoth" paper), I:359–61, 396, 513, 523–24, 805
New World (Unitarian), III:507; IV:295
New York, New York
  early magazines in (1741–94)
    general magazines, I:29, 47–48, 104
    literary magazine, I:114–16
    magazine center, I:31
    mail regulations and, I:19
  nationalist era magazines in
    comic and satiric periodicals, I:170–72
    education magazines, I:148
    general magazines, I:121, 127–29, 168, 174, 218, 260
    literary clubs, I:194
    literary magazines, I:333–35

magazine center, I:202
medical journal, I:215–17
religious magazines, I:131, 133, 135, 299
scientific magazine, I:149
theater periodicals, I:165–66
women's magazines, I:139, 321–22
expansionist era magazines in (1825–50)
abolitionist periodicals, I:457, 458
agricultural magazine, I:444, 728–32
business magazine, I:696–98
comic magazine, I:780–83
crime periodical, I:481–82; II:325–27
family magazine, II:349–55
juvenile magazine, II:264*n*
"knowledge" magazines, I:363–64
legal periodicals, I:451
literary magazines, I:343, 345–48, 354–55, 367–68, 606*n*, 619, 669–71, 711, 743*n*, 757, 766–68, 769*n*
magazine center I:361, 375–77, 379
"mammoth" papers, I:358–63
medical journals, I:439
music magazines, I:434–35
number of periodicals, I:375*n*
political magazines, I:750*n*; II:325–27
railroad journal, II:297–99
religious magazines, I:368–71, 372, 373, 624, 666*n*, 739, 745*n*; II:313, 367*n*
scientific magazine, II:316–24
temperance magazine, I:473
theatrical criticism, I:427–28
vocational magazines, I:445–46
women's magazines, I:321–22, 352, 626–28
Civil War era magazines in (1850–65)
abolitionist periodicals, I:458; II:141*n*
agricultural magazines, I:728*n*; II:90*n*, 91
art journals, II:193–94
"blue laws," II:34
business magazine, I:696–98
comic magazines, II:179–83, 520–29
"Copperhead" magazine, II:544–46
crime periodical, II:187, 325–28
education journals, II:99*n*, 443*n*
family magazines, II:59, 349*n*, 469*n*
financial journals, II:94*n*, 95*n*, 96
general magazines, II:448–51, 530–33
geographical periodical, II:79, 413–15
illustrated weeklies, II:7, 452*n*
insurance periodicals, II:94*n*
juvenile magazines, II:100–1
literary magazines, II:29, 31, 37–38, 42, 158–59, 383*n*, 406*n*, 419*n*
magazine center, II:103–5
"mammoth pictorals," II:58
Masonic journal, II:197
medical journals, I:439; II:85
military periodicals, II:547–51
music journals, II:197
Odd Fellows magazine, II:215
pharmacy journals, II:92
printers' magazine, II:93
police gazettes, II:187, 325
railroad journals, I:297*n*; II:81, 83
religious periodicals, II:7, 63, 65*n*, 66, 68, 72, 73, 74, 75, 76, 77, 365, 366*n*, 516
scientific periodicals, II:79, 316*n*
socialist periodicals, II:207
spelling-reform periodicals, II:212
spiritualist periodicals, II:209–10
sports magazines, II:204
stenographic periodicals, II:212
theatrical periodicals, II:198
trade magazines, II:92–93
women's magazines, II:58, 437–41, 466*n*
post-Civil War magazines in (1865–85
agricultural magazines, I:728*n*; III:152
art journals, III:185, 410–12
artificial gas periodical, III:131
biographical journals, III:260, 262*n*
booksellers' periodicals, III:235
chromolithographic journals, III:186
comic magazines, III:265–67, 268*n*–69*n*, 520*n*, 553*n*
construction periodicals, III:129, 130
crime periodicals, II:325*n*; III:44
current events magazines, III:332
drama periodicals, III:198–99
educational periodicals, II:99*n*; III:163, 167, 168
engineering periodicals, III:114–15
family magazines, II:349*n*, 469*n*; III:422*n*
fashion magazines, III:97–98, 481–90
financial publications, II:94*n*, 96, III:147

New York, New York—*Continued*
freedmen's journal, III:283
gardening magazines, III:161
general magazines, II:250, 530*n;* III:256, 417–21
geographical periodical, II:413*n*
health magazines, III:139
historical journals, III:260
home magazines, III:98–99
insurance journals, II:94*n;* III:145, 146*n*
juvenile magazines, II:100–1; III:176–79, 500–5
kindergarten magazine, III:163
library periodical, III:517–19
literary magazines, II:383*n,* 419*n;* III:31, 33, 35, 37, 39*n,* 233–35, 319, 361
lurid publications, II:325*n;* III:44
magazine center, III:25–29
mail-order papers, III:39
manufacturers' periodicals, III:127–28
medical journals, II:85*n;* III:140–43
military periodicals, II:547*n;* III:132, 533–34
mining periodicals, III:114–15
music journals, II:197; III:196
philosophical journal, III:385–87
photography periodical, III:186
printers' magazines, II:93; III:131
railroad magazines, I:297*n;* III:125*n,* 126*n*
religious magazines, II:367*n;* III:64, 67–77, 79–85, 89, 422–23
scientific periodicals, II:316*n,* III:109*n,* 495*n*
secret societies, III:315
socialist periodicals, III:301
society notes, III:101–2
sports periodicals, III:209–11, 213, 215, 218, 220
technical periodicals, III:115, 117–18, 122
temperance periodicals, III:310
trade magazines, III:133–36
trade-union magazines, II:92; III:300; IV:220
vocational magazines, III:132
women's magazines, III:99, 388–90
women's rights magazines, III:94, 443–53
Gilded Age magazines in (1885–1905)
advertising journals, IV:247, 337
agricultural periodicals, I:728*n;* IV:337
all-fiction magazines, IV:115, 117, 417*n,* 608*n*
amateur periodicals, IV:390, 391
Anglo-American periodicals, IV:228
architectural periodicals, IV:323
art periodicals, III:185; IV:146–47, 233
automobile periodicals, IV:330–31
booksellers' magazines, III:235; IV:127, 434*n*
charity magazines, IV:382
chess magazines, IV:382
child-care periodicals, IV:364
comic periodicals, III:270, 520*n,* 553*n;* IV:385, 387*n*
construction periodicals, III:129, 130*n;* IV:325*n*
crime periodicals, II:325*n;* IV:199
current-events magazine, IV:64, 649–51
education periodicals, III:168, 170; IV:265, 269, 272*n*
engineering periodicals, III:122*n;* IV:320–23
family magazines, II:349*n,* 469*n;* III:422*n;* IV:480*n;* V:154*n*
fashion periodicals, III:98, 481*n;* IV:363*n,* 580*n,* 756, 763*n*
financial periodicals, II:96; III:147*n;* IV:349
flower periodicals, III:161; IV:342*n*
general magazines, III:510*n;* IV:45, 506*n,* 589–99, 608*n,* 717*n;* V:145*n,* 286*n*
geographical periodicals, II:413*n;* IV:225
health periodicals, III:139; IV:316, 317
historical journals, III:260; IV:138, 139
hobby periodicals, IV:391
illustrated magazines, II:452*n;* IV:58, 153, 453*n*
insurance periodicals, II:94*n;* III:145, 146*n;* IV:350–51
Irish-American periodical, IV:227
Jewish periodicals, IV–300
journalists' periodicals, IV:243–44
juvenile periodicals, III:500*n;* IV:273–75
low-priced magazines, IV:4, 46–47, 49
lecture periodicals, IV:266
legal periodicals, IV:347, 348
library periodical, III:517*n*
literary magazines, II:383*n,* 419*n*
local topics, IV:84–86

magazine center, IV:82–83
mail-order periodicals, IV:367
manufacturing periodicals, III:127–28; IV:183–85, 186*n*, 325*n*
marine periodicals, IV:333–34
medical periodicals, III:140–43; IV:313*n*, 314–16
military magazines, II:547*n*; III:533*n*
mining periodicals, III:114–15
missionary periodicals, IV:238, 305
municipal affairs periodicals, IV:198
music journals, IV:251–52, 254
office-practice periodicals, IV:352
outdoor magazines, IV:633*n*
penmanship periodicals, III:170
pet periodical, IV:382
pharmacy periodicals, IV:317–18
philology journals, IV:128
philosophical journal, IV:303
photography periodicals, IV:149–50
political magazines, IV:171, 178
political science journals, IV:180–81
printers' periodicals, III:131; IV:248*n*
psychology journal, IV:303
railroad periodicals, I:297*n*; III:126*n*; IV:333*n*
real-estate periodical, IV:325
religious periodicals, II:367*n*; IV:284, 285*n*, 287–88, 290–91, 293*n*, 295*n*, 296–98, 300, 301
review periodicals, IV:52, 60, 62, 66, 511*n*, 657*n*, 773*n*
scientific periodicals, II:316*n*, III:109*n*, 495*n*; IV:307, 309, 310*n*
Scottish-American periodical, IV:227
settlement-house periodicals, IV:195*n*, 196*n*
single-tax periodicals, IV:176, 204, 206
socialist periodicals, IV:176, 204, 206
social-work periodicals, IV:194
society magazines, IV:65–66, 756–62
spelling-reform periodical, IV:212
spiritualist periodicals, IV:304
sports periodicals, III:210, 213, 215, 218, 220, IV:372–74, 376, 379–81
success periodical, IV:169
Sunday papers, IV:69
tariff periodicals, IV:166
theater periodicals, IV:260–61
theosophical periodicals, IV:287
trade periodicals, III:117, 118*n*, 131, IV:186–87, 189*n*; 236
trade union periodicals, IV:220
urban magazines, IV:77–78, 83–87
vegetarian periodicals, IV:317
women's club periodicals, IV:356
women's periodicals, I:580*n*; III:388*n*; IV:360–62, 364, 366, 763–72
YMCA periodicals, IV:287
modern magazines in (1905–)
advertising journal, IV:247, 337
all-fiction magazines, IV:115, 417*n*, 608*n*
architectural periodicals, IV:323
art journals, V:166*n*
automobile periodicals, IV:331
charity magazines, IV:741*n*
comic magazines, III:520*n*, 552*n*
crime periodicals, II:325*n*; IV:199
current-events magazines, V:49*n*, 191*n*, 293*n*, 649*n*
dental journal, IV:317
drama magazines, IV:741*n*
family magazines, II:349*n*, 469*n*; III:422*n*; IV:480*n*; V:125*n*, 154*n*
fashion magazines, III:481*n*; IV:580*n*, 756*n*
financial journals, II:96, III:147*n*
general magazines, III:510*n*; IV:453*n*, 506*n*, 599–607, 608*n*, 717*n*; V:3*n*, 72, 88–89, 154*n*, 286*n*
geographical publication, II:413*n*
health periodicals, IV:316, 317
hobby periodicals, IV:391
home periodicals, IV:324*n*
illustrated weekly, II:452*n*
Indian periodical, IV:215
insurance periodicals, III:145, 146*n*; IV:350–51
journalists' periodicals, IV:244
juvenile magazines, III:500*n*, IV:273–74
lecture periodical, IV:266
legal periodicals, III:144*n*, IV:348
libertarian magazine, V:88–99
library periodical, III:517*n*
literary magazines, III:383*n*. 419*n*; V:117–24, 165–78
medical journals, III:140–43, IV:313*n*, 314–16
military periodicals, II:547*n*; III:533*n*
municipal-affairs periodical, IV:198

New York, New York—*Continued*
music periodical, IV:253*n*
newspaper trade magazines, V:59*n*
office-practice periodicals, IV:352
outdoor magazines, IV:633*n*
pet periodical, IV:382
pharmacy periodicals, IV:317–18
philosophical journal, IV:303
photography periodical, IV:150
psychology journal, IV:303
publishers' magazine, V:59*n*
railroad journals, I:297*n*; III:126*n*; IV:333*n*
real-estate periodical, IV:325
religious magazines, II:69, 367*n*; III:84; IV:194, 285*n*, 287–88, 290–91, 293*n*, 295*n*, 297–98, 300, 305
review periodicals, IV:510*n*, 657*n*, 754, 773*n*
scientific periodicals, II:316*n*; III:495*n*; IV:309, 310*n*
settlement-house periodicals, IV:195*n*, 196*n*
socialist periodical, IV:176, 206
society magazine, IV:756*n*
sports magazines, III:210; IV:373, 376, 380, 381
success magazine, V:286–92
technical magazines, III:117, 118*n*, 122*n*; IV:321, 323, 334
theosophical periodicals, IV:287
trade magazines, II:92–93; III:131*n*; IV:186–87, 189*n*, 236
women's magazines, III:388*n*, IV:360–62, 364, 763*n*; V:125*n*
athletic clubs in, III:221
burlesque theaters in, III:206
crime in, II:27–28
growth of, I:375
homeless children in, IV:200
municipal corruption in, II:478–80; III:4, 26–27, 290–91, 320, 342, 345–46, 440–42, 524–25, 553; IV:124, 197–98
muckraking articles, IV:600
municipal reform in, III:313
music in, I:434; IV:249
newspapers in, I:160, 465; II:205; III:266
opera in, I:173
population of, I:202; II:103–4
postal regulations (1792) and, I:19
prostitution in, III:27–28
as publishing center, II:103–4, 496
public school system in, II:96
theater in, I:55–56, 169, 427–28
yellow fever epidemics in, I:149

New-York American, II:297
New York Amusement Gazette, IV:260
New York Anti-Slavery Society, I:457
New York Aquarium Journal, III:111
New York-Atheneum Association, I:335
New York Baptist Advocate, II:64*n*
New York *Book-Lover*, V:29
New York Boys' Weekly, III:179
New York City Mission Monthly, IV:195*n*
New York Chronicle, II:64, 547
New York Citizen and Round Table, III:324
New York Clipper, II:198, 203, 204; III:198, 209, 211, 218, 220; IV:260
New York Colonization Journal, II:141
New York Colored Mission, IV:195*n*
New York Commercial Advertiser Pictorial Review, IV:70
New York Daily Democrat, III:269*n*
New York Dramatic Mirror, III:198*n*; IV:255, 260
New York Dramatic News, III:198, 199; IV:260
New York Eclectic Medical and Surgical Journal, III:143
New York Evangelist, see: Evangelist (New York)
New York Evening Mail, III:323
New York Evening Mirror, see: New York Mirror
New York Evening Post, II:205, 420, 426, 428, 448; III:344–50
New York Examiner, II:64, 547
New York Family Story Paper, IV:117, 118*n*
New York Farmer, I:442*n*, 799; III:153
New York Genealogical and Biographical Record, III:260; IV:137*n*
New York Graphic, III:126
New York Graphic Society, V:328*n*
New York Herald, II:291, 530; III:273, 548
See also Bennett, James Gordon
New York Herald Tribune, V:15
New York Humorist, III:269*n*
New York Illustrated Magazine, I:808
New York Illustrated News, II:14, 15; III:325
New York Illustrated Times, III:198
New York Insurance Journal, II:94*n*
New York Journal of the Deaf, IV:194
New York Journal of Education, I:492*n*
New York Journal of Homoeopathy, II:85*n*
New York Journal of Medicine, I:807; II:84*n*

New York Journal of Romance, General Literature, Science and Art, see: Frank Leslie's New York Journal of Romance, General Literature, Science and Art
New York Leader, II:526
New York Ledger, II:38, 130, 149, 206, 527; III:6, 7*n*, 224, 279, 528; IV:4, 39, 65
 advertising in, II:14–16
 circulation of, II:10, 102
 payment to contributors, II:23–24
 sketch of, II:356–63
New York Legal Observer, I:451, 806; II:93*n*
New York Literary Gazette, I:128, 798
New York Lumber Trade Journal, IV:325
New York Lyceum, I:490
New-York Magazine, I:19, 34, 37–38, 55–56
 founding of, I:30
 sketch of, I:114–16
New York Magazine of Mysteries, IV:304
New York Mechanic, II:317
New York Medical Gazette, II:84*n*
New York Medical Journal, I:439*n*, 568; III:140; IV:313; V:29
New York Medical and Physical Journal, I:151*n*, 797
New York Mercury, III:209
New York Mining Record, III:114
New York Mirror (nineteenth-century magazine), I:210, 354, 393, 427–30, 431, 449, 477, 520, 522, 578; II:540, 349, 356, 426; III:179, 198, 220*n*; IV:676
 founding of, I:127
 sketch of, I:320–30
New-York Missionary Magazine, I:133, 199, 200*n*, 791
New York Monthly Magazine, I:242
New York Musical Gazette, III:196
New York Musical Pioneer and Chorister's Budget, II:198*n*
New-York Musical Review and Gazette, II:197
New York News Library, IV:117
New York Observer, see: Observer (New York)
New York Picayune, I:426, 808; II:179, 181
New-York Quarterly, II:28
New York Railroad Men, IV:333*n*
New York Review, I:367, 669–71
New-York Review and Atheneum Magazine, I:172–73, 184–85, 199, 332
 founding of, I:128
 sketch of, I:334–35
New York Saturday Review, IV:85
New York Society for the Suppression of Vice, V:174
New York Sportsman, III:215*n*
New York State
 number of magazines in, I:202*n*, 375*n*
 public education in, I:145
 See also specific towns and cities
New York State College of Agriculture, IV:341*n*
New York State Journal of Medicine, IV:314
New York State Mechanic, I:445, 805
New York State Reporter, IV:347*n*
New York Suffrage Newsletter, IV:356
New York Sun, II:44; III:190, 511, V:269
New York Time-Piece, II:183
New York Times, I:730, 747; II:392, 426, 509, 530; III:117, 190, 290, 363, 369; V:49–51, 55–58, 114, 212–13, 307
New York Times Current History of the European War, V:50
New York Times Supplement, IV:70, 126
New York Tribune, II:144, 205, 386, 407, 426; III:107, 151, 196, 338; V:202, 248
 See also Greeley, Horace
New York Tribune Illustrated Supplement, IV:70
New York Underwriter, II:94*n*; III:145
New York Voice, III:310*n*
New York Weekly, II:10, 38; IV:4, 119
 advertising rate of, III:11, 16, 39, 224
 circulation of, III:6
New York Weekly Magazine, I:121, 164, 167, 172, 174, 790
New York Weekly Museum, I:127, 795
New York Weekly Review, II:197; III:196
New York World, III:319, 411, 529; V:209, 294
New-Yorker (1834–41), I:345, 357, 358–59 515, 620, 803; IV:86
New Yorker, IV:568; V:19, 162, 315
New Yorker Staats-Zeitung, V:51
Newark, N.J., I:31*n*; III:33, 146*n*; IV:178, 221*n*, 269*n*, 292*n*, 401*n*
Newbern, N.C., III:261*n*
Newberry Library, V:349
Newburgh, N.Y., II:212; III:80, 98
Newcomb, Harry Turner, IV:332; V:330

Newcomb, Simon, I:535; II:79*n*, 248; III:110, 337
Newell, Peter, II:400; IV:546, 720
Newell, Robert Henry, II:37, 117; III:441, 558
Newell, William Wells, IV:128
Newman, Harry, III:556
Newman, Thomas G., III:81
Newmarket, N.H., IV:391*n*
Newnan, Ga., II:111
Newnes, George, IV:658
Newport, R.I., IV:140*n*
Newport Historical Magazine, III:259
News, V:59
News articles, *see* Current events; Current events magazines; Newspapers; Review-type magazines
News companies, III:8; IV:610–11
News depots, III:9
News-Letter, III:101; IV:106
News and Observer, V:275–77
News periodicals, *see* Current events magazines; Newspapers; Review-type magazines
News photography, IV:455
  See also Half-tones
News from the Spirit World, III:82*n*
Newsman, IV:127
Newspaper Maker, IV:244
Newspaperdom, IV:244; V:62, 66
Newspapers, I:9
  defined, I:6, 8*n*
  early (1741–94)
    taxes on, I:92
  in nationalist era (1794–1825)
    agricultural, I:153–54
    circulation, I:161
    daily, I:159, 329
    growth, I:160
    independent development, I:162
    literary qualities, 156–58
    political, I:158–62
    popularity, I:156, 160
  in expansionist era (1825–50), I:683
    circulation, I:465–66
    mail privileges I:517–18
    number, I:342*n*, 375*n*, 465
    quality and type, I:465–66
  in Civil War era (1850–65)
    average circulation, II:10
    circulation, II:205
    growth, II:204–6
    news pictures, II:43
    quality and type, III:271–74
  in post-Civil War era (1865–85), III:5*n*
    advertising, III:272–73
    circulation, III:6
    comic, III:269
    increasing number, III:272
    popularity, III:271
    religious, III:66
  in Gilded Age (1885–1905), IV:2, 10, 110
    magazine comment, IV:240–42
    magazine competition, IV:8
    magazine supplements, IV:69–70
    merger with magazines, IV:8–9
  modern (1905–)
    colored illustrations, V:70
    linage reports, V:69–70
  as social interpreters, IV:2
  style of writing in, V:xi–xii
  telephone and, IV:242
  trade magazines for, V:59–71
  typewriter and, IV:242–43
Newsstand sales, I:77; III:8–9; IV:18–20, 586, 622
Newsweek, IV:577, 587
Newton, H. E., III:157
Newton, John, II:92*n*
Newton, L. V., II:92*n*
Newton, Richard Heber, IV:282, 299
Newton, William Wilberforce, III:34*n*
Nicaraguan Canal, IV:237
Nichola, Lewis, I:26*n*
Nichols, Edward Leamington, IV:309
Nichols, James R., III:110*n*
Nichols, John W., II:36; IV:79*n*
Nichols, Samuel, II:37*n*
Nichols, Thomas, I:425
Nichols, Thomas L., II:186
Nichols, W. A., II:518*n*
Nichols, Wade Hampton Jr., V:125*n*, 143
Nichols, Walter S., II:94*n*; IV:350
Nichols, William Ichabod, IV:105*n*
Nicholson, Meredith, IV:46*n*, 390*n*, 466
Nick Carter Library, IV:120
Nick Nax, III:267
Nick-Nax for All Creation, II:183
Nickell Magazine, IV:48
Nichol, John, IV:149
Nicholary, John George, II:542; III:470; IV:40, 43, 137
Nicoll, William Robertson, IV:433
Nicolson, Harold, IV:761
Niebuhr, Reinhold, IV:738
Nietzsche, Friedrich, V:123, 168
Nightingale, I:122*n*, 790
Niles, Hezekiah, I:268–69
Niles, Samuel, I:134*n*
Niles, William Ogden, I:268, 268*n*
Niles' Weekly Register, I:160; II:43
  delinquent subscribers of, I:200
  sketch of, I:268–70

Nilsson, Christine, III:192, 193
Nims, John Frederick, V:225*n*
"9019, The," V:274
Nineteenth Century, IV:228
Nirdinger, Albert H., III:132
Nirdlinger, C. F., IV:58*n*
Nirdlinger, Charles J., IV:66
Nirdlinger Samuel F., IV:255
Nixon, H. C., V:116*n*
Nixon, Richard, V:317, 319
No Name Magazine, IV:90
Noah, Mordecai Manuel, I:326, 490
Noble, Alden Charles, IV:389
Noble, David W., V:209
Noble, Edmund, II:510*n*
Noble, Frederick Alphonso, III:77*n*
Nock, Albert Jay, III:354; V:21, 88–99, 203
Noeggerath, Emil, III:141
Noguchi, Yone, IV:106, 654; V:237
Nolan, Mary, III:95
Nolen, John, IV:263
Noll, Arthur Howard, IV:12
Non-Conformist, IV:163*n*
Nondenominational periodicals, III:82–85
Non-Resistance Society, II:285
Non-Resistant, II:286
Norcross, W. F., III:315
Nordau, Max, IV:73, 123, 196–97
Nordhoff, Charles, II:303, 395
Nordhoff, Charles Bernard, IV:701, 709
Nordica, Lillian, II:271; IV:546
Normal, Illinois, III:169*n*
Normal Instructor, IV:53*n*, 269
Normal Seminar, IV:272*n*
Norman, John, I:37
Norman, Okla., IV:270*n*
Norris, Charles G., V:291
Norris, Edward James, IV:269
Norris, Frank, IV:106, 112, 456, 457, 690, 780–81; V:73, 293*n*
Norris, J. Parker, III:237*n*
Norris, Kathleen, III:489; IV:471, 498, 584, 604, 769; V:83, 134
Norristown, Pa., IV:345
Norristown Herald, III:270*n*
North, Jessica Nelson, V:225*n*, 239, 241, 243
North, William, II:183, 185, 420, 424
North American (Philadelphia), I:552
North American Archives of Medical and Surgical Science, I:439*n*, 802
North American Journal of Homoeopathy, II:85; IV:315
North American Magazine, I:345, 801
North American Medical and Surgical Journal, I:438, 798
North American Medico-Chirurgical Review, I:439*n*
North American Miscellany, I:348; II:129
North American Quarterly, see: *North American Magazine*
North American Review, I:130, 148, 164, 173, 176, 177, 187, 188–89, 192, 197–98, 200, 203, 204, 213, 259, 278, 367, 421, 422, 514, 756; II:27–28, 102, 134, 137, 138, 149, 158, 530, 533; III:18, 19, 21, 31, 35, 85, 88, 90–91, 96, 163, 166, 206, 263, 271, 277, 281, 282, 314, 436; IV:2, 10, 21, 51, 78, 216, 403, 512; V:332
  political questions in, III:290–95, 298
  sketch of, II:218–61
North American Review's War Weekly, II:259
North British Review, II:130
North Carolina Christian Advocate, II:61
North Carolina Farmer, III:154
North Carolina Presbyterian, II:63*n*
North Carolina Teacher, III:168
North Exit, III:75*n*
North Pacific Coast, III:57
North Pacific Rural Spirit, III:158
North and South, IV:93
North Star, I:458; II:140*n*; IV:108
North and West, IV:293*n*
North Western Reporter, IV:347
Northampton, Mass., IV:265
Northend, Charles, I:694*n*, 695
Northern Budget, IV:68
Northern Christian Advocate, II:67*n*
Northern Independent, II:67, 140, 146
Northern Magazine, III:33
Northern Presbyterian, IV:293*n*
Northern World, V:26*n*
Northport, N.Y., IV:347
Northrup, F. W., II:312*n*, 313
Northwest, IV:96
Northwest Dairyman and Farmer, IV:344*n*
Northwest Farm Equipment Journal, IV:188
Northwest Journal of Education, IV:271*n*
Northwest Magazine, III:55, 148; IV:96*n*
Northwest Medicine, IV:314
Northwest-Pacific Farmer, III:158
Northwestern, II:67
Northwestern Agriculturist, IV:341

Northwestern Architect, III:129
Northwestern Banker, IV:349*n*
Northwestern Christian Advocate, II:66–7, 97; III:70; IV:217, 291
Northwestern Chronicle, III:69*n*
Northwestern Church, II:69
Northwestern Congregationalist, IV:283
Northwestern Dental Journal, IV:317
Northwestern Druggist, IV:318*n*
Northwestern Farmer (Indianapolis), II:89
Northwestern Farmer (Fargo), III:158
Northwestern Farmer (Portland, Ore.), III:158
Northwestern Farmer and Horticultural Journal, II:89
North-Western Home Journal, II:59
North-Western Home and School Journal, II:59
Northwestern Horseman and Stockman, IV:343
Northwestern Journal of Education, IV:271
Northwestern Journal of Homoeopathia, II:85*n*
Northwestern Lancet, III:141*n*
Northwestern Medical and Surgical Journal, II:84*n*
Northwestern Miller, III:128; IV:185
Northwestern Presbyterian, III:75*n*
Northwestern Prohibitionist, III:310*n*
Northwestern Review, III:146*n*
Northwestern Shoe and Leather Journal, IV:185*n*
Northwestern Sportsman, IV:381*n*
Northwestern University, IV:317
Norton, Andrews, I:124, 138, 255, 277–78, 287, 401, 410, 535, 571, 615–17; II:220, 227, 243
Norton, Charles B., II:158, 159; III:491–92
Norton, Charles Eliot, II:146–147, 220*n*, 243, 245, 260, 424, 495, 508; III:23, 31, 186, 232, 332, 335, 347
Norton, Charles Ledyard, III:422*n*, 425, 426, 557
Norton, George Lowell, IV:334
Norton, Jacob, I:134*n*
Norton's Literary Advertiser, II:158; III:492
Norton's Literary Gazette and Publishers' Circular, III:492
Norton's Literary Letter, II:159
Notes and Queries, III:259
Notices of Recent Publications, III:259
Notion, I:361
Notre Dame, University of, IV:298
Notre Dame Scholastic, III:166
Nott, Charles Cooper, III:337
Nott, Josiah Clark, I:575, 723, 726; II:138, 345
Novelettes, I:620; II:308, 509; III:400; IV:118, 586, 610, 618, 713; V:136
Novelist, III:54
Novels
  in early magazines (1741–94), I:103
    moral novels, I:96
    prejudices against, I:42, 63
  in nationalist era magazines (1794–1825), I:173, 249–50, 323, 414–19
    defense of, I:175
    popularity, I:178–79
    prejudices against, I:174
    serials, I:122, 174, 219, 307, 312, 323, 359, 547, 616, 619, 643–44, 646, 650, 748
  in expansionist era magazines (1825–50), I:616
    cheap novels, I:418–19
    critical evaluations, I:411
    English influence, I:398–99, 415
    French influence, I:404, 415
    German influence, I:403, 415
    historical, I:416
    juvenile, I:714–15
    opposition to, I:416–18
    pirated, I:348
    quality and type, 414–19
    serials, I:360; II:352
  in Civil War era magazines (1850–65), II:384–87
    condemnations, II:186, 387
    literary criticism, II:159–60, 165–69
    popularity, II:172
    women novelists, II:21–22, 170–71
  in post-Civil War magazines (1865–85), III:400
    best sellers, III:247–48
    juveniles, III:247–48
    popular authors, III:242–46
    serialized, III:357–58
  in Gilded Age magazines (1885–1905), IV:610, 673, 725
    best sellers, IV:141
    digests, IV:658
    foreign, IV:134–36
    leading novelists, IV:130–31
    serialized, II:257
  in modern magazines (1905–), IV:618; V:22, 133
  dime, *see* Dime novels
  foreign, *see* English literature; French literature; German literature;

Russian literature; Scandinavian literature
realist versus romantic, IV:111–12
reviews of, *see* Book reviews
thematic trends, IV:110–13
Now, IV:285*n*
Now and Then, IV:137*n*
Noyes, Alexander Dana, III:347; IV:517, 726
Noyes, Alfred, IV:438, 713; V:96, 136, 336
Noyes, George Rapall, I:292*n*
Noyes, George W., II:207*n*
Noyes, James Oscar, I:606*n*
Noyes John Humphrey, II:78, 207, 286, 328
Noyes, William Albert, III:110*n*
Noyes, William H., IV:400
Nude and semi-nude illustrations, IV:46–47, 152–53; 611; V:145–46
See also Sex magazines
Nugget, IV:120
Nullification, I:458, 575; II:234–35
Number of magazines, IV:11–12
early (1741–94), I:24, 24*n,* 29, 35*n*
chronological relationship (chart), I:70
in nationalist era (1794–1825), I:120–21, 202*n*
monthlies, I:128–29
religious, I:136–39
short-lived, I:199
weeklies, I:126–28
in expansionist era (1825–50), I:341–42
by cities and states, I:375*n*
increase in publications, I:340–42
in Civil War era (1850–65)
agricultural, II:88
comic, II:179
educational, II:98
historical, II:176
Masonic, II:214
political magazines, II:131
religious, II:60–62, 76
statistical trends, II:4–5
women's, II:56
in post-Civil War era (1865–85)
agricultural, III:151
college, III:165
educational periodicals, III:167
insurance periodicals, III:146
legal periodicals, III:144
medical journals, III:139
mining, III:114
musical journals, III:195
religious periodicals, III:66–68, 76
scientific periodicals, III:104–5
statistical trends, III:5
temperance, III:309
in Gilded Age (1885–1905)
agricultural periodicals, IV:336
high-circulation, IV:17
insurance periodicals, IV:350
low-cost, IV:6
legal periodicals, IV:346
statistical trends, IV:11–12
depressions and, IV:159–60
Numismatic periodicals
in post-Civil War era (1865–85), III:113
in Gilded Age (1885–1905), IV:391
Nursery, III:176
Nursing World, IV:315
Nye, Bill, V:121
Nye, Edgar Wilson ("Bill"), III:269; IV:507

O.K., II:185*n*
Oak Park, Ill., III:169; IV:274, 275
Oakland, Cal., III:141*n;* IV:296, 304*n,* 345*n,* 390*n*
Oaksmith, Alvin, II:450
Oaksmith, Appleton, II:450
Oaksmith, Edward, II:450
Oaksmith, Sidney, II:450
Oberholtzer, Ellis Paxon, IV:183, 197
Oberlin, Ohio, IV:293
Oberlin College, III:166
Oberlin Evangelist, II:63*n*
Oberlin Review, III:166
Obituaries, II:222
O'Brien, Edward Joseph Harrington, IV:436; V:182–83, 187, 265
O'Brien, Fitz-James, I:613; II:20, 39, 173, 181, 183, 388, 395, 420, 424, 471, 505*n,* 520, 525; III:229
O'Brien, Frank Michael, IV:617
O'Brien, Frederick, III:479
O'Brien, Harry R., II:435; V:43
O'Brien, Robert Lincoln, IV:546, 777
Obscene pictures, I:475
See also Sex magazines
Observer (Baltimore), I:204, 793
Observer (New York religious periodical, 1823–1912), I:373, 797; II:63, 388; III:74, 320; IV:288, 293
Observer (St. Louis), I:458; III:75*n*
Obstetrics journals, III:141; IV:315*n*
Oceanography, articles on, IV:621
Occasional Reverberator, I:25*n,* 787
Occident (Chicago), III:80; IV:300
Occident (San Francisco), III:74

Occident and American Jewish Advocate, II:77
Occidental Medical Times, IV:314*n*
Occult and Biological Journal, IV:304*n*
Occupations, magazines on, IV:774
Ocean, IV:617
Ochs, Adolph S., V:50
Ochs-Oakes, George Washington, V:49*n*, 51, 54, 56
O'Connell, Daniel, II:290
O'Conner, James, III:69*n*
O'Connell, John J., IV:480*n*
O'Conner, Thomas Power, III:69*n*
O'Conner, William Douglas, II:429
"Octave Thanet," *see* French, Alice
Odd Fellows' Companion, III:315
Odd Fellows magazines, II:215; III:37*n*, 315; IV:221
Odd Fellows' Talisman, III:315
O'Dell, Edith, V:117*n*, 122–23
Odell, George Clinton Densmore, IV:126
Odell, Joseph Henry, III:433
O'Donnell, Jack, IV:469
O'Donoghue, John J. W., III:147
Odontographic Journal, III:143*n*
O'Dwyer, William, III:31*n*
Office, IV:351
Office appliance magazines, IV:352
Office Appliances, IV:352
Office practice journals, IV:351–52
Office of Price Administration, V:139
Office Workers' Union, strike of (1935), V:20
Official Railway Equipment Register, III:126*n*
Ogburn, William Fielding, IV:192*n*, 748
Ogden, Herbert Gouverneur, IV:621
Ogden, Robert Curtis, IV:689; V:72
Ogden, Rollo, III:346, 349
Ogg, Frederick Austin, IV:618
O'Gorman, Ned, V:244
O'Hagen, Anne, IV:618
O'Higgins, Harvey J., III:512; IV:602, 604, V:83
Ohio
  educational and publishing facilities in, I:205–6
  mailing time to, I:207
  number of periodicals in, I:375*n*
  periodicals, IV:95
Ohio Common School Director, I:490, 804
Ohio Cultivator, I:444, 809
Ohio Educational Monthly, II:99*n*; IV:270
Ohio Farmer, I:444, 809; II:89; III:156; IV:340
Ohio Journal of Education, II:99*n*
Ohio Journal of Science, IV:308
Ohio Law Bulletin, III:145*n*
Ohio Law Bulletin and Reporter, III:145*n*
Ohio Law Journal, III:145*n*
Ohio Law Reporter, III:145*n*; IV:347*n*
Ohio Legal News, IV:347*n*
Ohio Medical and Surgical Journal, I:439, 809; II:84*n*
Ohio Medical Repository, I:803
Ohio Medical Repository of Original and Selected Intelligence, I:439*n*, 798
Ohio Mining Journal, III:115*n*
Ohio Poultry Journal, III:161*n*
Ohio State Archaeological and Historical Quarterly, IV:14*n*
Ohio State Journal of Dental Science, III:143*n*
Ohio State University, IV:341*n*
Ohio Teacher, III:169
Oil, Paint and Drug Reporter, III:133
Oil City, Pa., III:130–31
Oil City Derrick, III:131
Oil and Gas Journal, IV:184*n*, 350*n*
Oil industry, IV:184
  investment in, IV:350*n*
  muckraking articles on, IV:598
Oil Investor's Journal, IV:184*n*, 350*n*
Oil periodicals, III:130–31; IV:184
Oklahoma City, Okla., IV:313*n*; V:3*n*
Oklahoma Law Journal, IV:347*n*
Oklahoma School Herald, IV:270*n*
O'Laughlin, John Callan, II:547*n*, 549
Old Cap Collier, IV:119
Old Dominion, III:47
Old Dominion Journal of Medicine and Surgery, IV:313*n*
Old Flag, II:151
Old Guard, II:147, 154, 177; III:281
  sketch of, II:544–46
Old King Brandy, IV:119
Old and New, I:291; II:249; III:34, 77, 232, 280, 506
  sketch of, III:436–39
Old and New Testament Student, III:84*n*
Old Northwest Genealogical Quarterly, IV:140*n*
Old Oaken Bucket, II:211
Old Sleuth, IV:119
"Old Sleuth" Library, III:43*n*
Old Testament Student, III:84*n*
Old Times, III:259
Olden Times, I:422, 808
O'Leary, James, V:333
Oleographs, fashion, III:483
Oler, Wesley Marion, IV:649, 650

Oliphant, Laurence, II:249
III:418, 460, 502
Oliphant, Margaret Wilson, II:510; III:418, 460, 502
Olive Branch, II:74
Olive Tree, IV:238*n*
Oliver, Andrew, I:48
Oliver, Warner, IV:712
"Oliver Optic," *see* Adams, William Taylor
Oliver Optic's Magazine, III:176
Ollivant, Alfred, IV:783
Olmstead, John Wesley, II:262*n,* 266
Olmsted, Denison, II:314, 315
Olmsted, Frederick Law, III:331
Olney, Richard, IV:219
O'Loughlin, Daniel, IV:204
O'Loughlin, Robert S., III:481*n,* 482
Omaha, Neb.
Western Magazine, III:53
other periodicals in
agricultural, III:158
medical, IV:314*n*
religious, III:75*n;* IV:291, 300
other, IV:97, 163*n,* 185*n,* 275, 391*n*
Omaha Bee, IV:70
Omaha Christian Advocate, IV:291*n*
Omaha Illustrated, IV:97
Omahan, IV:97
Omar Khayyám, IV:37, 133–34, 141, 491
Omega, I:441*n*
Once a Month, III:256
Once a Week (Collier's periodical), IV:453
Once a Week (Leslie's periodical), II:441; III:98
Onderdonk, Benjamin Tredwell, I:135, 329
Onderdonk, William H., II:69
Oneal, James, V:5
Oneida Circular, see: Circular
Oneida community, II:207*n;* III:300
O'Neill, Eugene, V:13, 121, 236, 266
O'Neill, Moira, IV:602
O'Neill, Rose, III:489; V:136
Onward, III:176, 219
Oölogist (Albion, N.Y.), III:111
Oölogist (Rockville, R.I.), III:111
Opal, II:100
Open Court, III:78*n;* IV:302
Open Shop, IV:183*n*
Open Shop Review, IV:183*n*
Opera, I:172–73, 325, 403, 432–33, 610; II:196
after Civil War, III:192–96; IV:249
Opera Glass, I:427, 800; IV:94, 261
Operative Miller, IV:185*n*
Operator, III:121, 122*n*
Ophthalmic Record, IV:315*n*
Opthalmology, IV:315*n*
Ophthalmology journals, III:141–42; IV:315
Oppenheim, E. Phillips, IV:471, 493, 501, 607, 618, 694, 695; V:86, 249, 291
Oppenheim, James, III:487; V:290
Oppenheimer, Franz, V:92
Opper, Frederick Burr, II:464; III:504, 525–26, 528, 531
Opportunity, IV:169
"Optic, Oliver," *see* Adams, William Taylor
Optical Journal, IV:315*n*
Optimist (Philadelphia), 285*n*
Optimist (St. Louis), IV:101
Orange, N.J., IV:296
Orange County Farmer, III:153
Orange Judd American Agriculturist, I:728*n*
Orange Judd Farmer, I:731; IV:337
Oratory, I:184–85, 423
Orchard, Harry, IV:600
Orchard and Garden, III:162
Orchardry journals, III:162
Orcutt, C. R., III:109
Orcutt, Edward, IV:700
Orczy, Baroness Emmusca, V:72
Ordeal, I:160*n,* 793
Ordinance of 1782, I:17
Orear, J. Davis, IV:386
Oregon Agriculturist, III:158
Oregon Churchman, III:75*n*
Oregon City, Ore., III:72
Oregon Farmer, II:90; IV:341
Oregon Historical Quarterly, IV:139
Oregon Merchants' Magazine, IV:186
Oregon Teachers' Monthly, IV:270*n*
Oregon Territory issue, I:463–64
O'Reilly, John Boyle, III:69*n;* IV:297, 633
"O'Reilly, Miles," *see* Halpine, Charles Graham
"O'Rell, Max," *see* Blouet, Paul
Ores and Metals, IV:322*n*
Orff, Frank ,V:151–53
Orff, Samuel, IV:361
Organists' Quarterly Journal and Review, 197*n*
Oriental and Biblical Journal, III:84, 112*n*
Oriental religion, I:709
Oriental Series, IV:233*n*
Oriental tales, I:42, 44, 109, 122
Oriental World, IV:233
Orion, I:383, 806

Ormond, John Raper, V:281
Orne, Caroline, I:529; II:410
Ornithologist and Oölogist, III:111
Ornithology, II:449
periodicals, III:111; IV:310
Orphans, magazines on, IV:200
Orphan's Cry, IV:200
Orpheus, III:197*n*
Orr, John William, II:43, 215, 410, 449, 454; III:37
Orr, Lyndon, IV:616
Orr, Nathaniel, I:522, 714; II:43, 390, 449
Orr, T. E., IV:89
Orris, John, I:764
Orth, Samuel Peter, IV:778, 779
Orvis, John, III:300; IV:203
Osborn, Charles, I:162
Osborn, Clifton Carlisle, IV:430
Osborn, Thomas Mott, IV:199
Osborne, Charles Francis, IV:324*n*
Osborne, Duffield, II:253; IV:371
Osbourne, Lloyd, IV:616, 692, 720; V:30, 83
Osceola, Mo., III:89
Osgood, Mrs. Frances Sargent, I:412, 499, 508, 546, 584, 743, 760, 770; II:35, 308
Osgood, James R., & Co., II:249, 386
Osgood, Kate Putnam, II:469, III:463
Osgood, Samuel, I:292*n,* 663; II:28, 389
O'Shaughnessy, Arthur, IV:425
Oskaloosa, Iowa, III:77*n,* 80
Oskison, John M., IV:464, 783
Ostenso, Margaret, IV:585
Ossining, N.Y., IV:199
Osteopathic journals, IV:316
O'Sullivan, John L., I:346, 678–81
Oswald, Felix, III:558
Oswald, John Clyde, IV:244, 247
Other Side, IV:181
Otis, Bass, I:208, 210
Otis, Elita Proctor, IV:85
Otis, Harrison Gray, II:280
Otis, James, III:503; IV:765
Otology journals, III:141–42; IV:315
Ottawa, Illinois, III:128*n*
Ottley, James Henry, IV:580*n,* 581–83
Ottolengui, Rodrigues, III:143*n*
"Ouida," *see* De la Ramée, Marie Louise
Our Banner, III:74
Our Boys, III:179
Our Boys and Girls, III:176*n*
Our Boys' and Girls' Own, IV:298
Our Church Paper, III:79
Our Continent, III:557
Our Country, III:262*n*
Our Country Home, III:152
Our Daily Fair, II:87
Our Day, IV:52, 284
Our Dumb Animals, III:312
Our Enemy the State (Nock), V:92
Our Fireside Friend, III:8*n,* 101
Our Fireside Journal, III:39
Our Grange Homes, III:152
Our Home Companion, IV:82
Our Home Field, IV:305
Our Home and Fireside Magazine, III:39*n;* IV:305
Our Home Journal, III:155
Our Homes and Our Homeless, IV:200
Our Language, IV:212
Our Little Granger, III:179
Our Little Men and Women, III:177
Our Little Ones and the Nursery, III:176
Our Living and Our Dead, III:261, 262*n*
Our Monthly (Clinton, S.C.), III:74*n*
Our Monthly (Philadelphia), III:74
Our Neighborhood, III:99
Our Players' Gallery, IV:261*n*
Our Rest and Signs of the Times, III:81
Our Schoolday Visitor, II:101
Our Second Century, III:100
Our Times, IV:53, 64, 270
Our Union, III:310
Our Young Folks, III:175, 191, 501
Our Young People, IV:764
Our Youth, IV:275
Out of the Night (Valtin), V:23
Out West, IV:107
Out West Magazine, III:409
Outcault, Richard Felton, III:554; IV:90
Outdoor Life, IV:381*n*
Outdoor magazines, III:210–11; IV:633–38
Outdoor Recreation, IV:381*n*
Outdoor sketches, I:547, 620
Outdoor World and Recreation, IV:381*n*
Outdoors, IV:376
Outer's Book, IV:381
Outing, III:210, 211, 214*n,* 317; IV:39; V:254
sketch of, IV:633–38
Outlaws, western, III:62
Outlook (originally *Christian Union*), II:355, 379; III:65, 66, 76, 82, 192, 224, 281, 295, 308; IV:10, 59, 301; V:205, 294
sketch of, III:422–35
Outlook (*Sabbath Quarterly*), III:85*n*
Outpost, IV:117*n*
Overall, John W., II:112

Overland Monthly, III:10, 14*n,* 56, 184, 228, 280; IV:5, 104–5
sketch of, III:402–9
Overland Trail, comment on, II:121
Overseer, III:315
Overstreet, Harry Allen, IV:750; V:56
Overton, Grant, IV:440
Oviatt, Edwin, V:338
Ovid, Mich., III:214*n*
Owen, Catherine, V:131
Owen, F. A., IV:52–53
Owens, John W., V:5
Owen, Robert, I:536, 561
Owen, Robert Dale, I:536*n,* 537; II:506*n;* III:52, 263, 397, 439
Owen, S. M., III:157
Owen, Samuel, I:451
Owen, William, I:536*n,* 537
Owens, R. B., I:556*n*
Owl (Boston), IV:48, 117
Owl (Chicago), III:233
Owl (Columbus and Chicago), IV:387*n*
Owne, Sidney M., IV:341
Owsley, Frank Lawrence, V:116*n*
Oxenham, John, V:30
Oyen, Henry, IV:777
Oysterman, IV:186*n*

Pach, Walter, V:95
Pacific, II:71*n*
Pacific Advertising, IV:147*n*
Pacific Banker, IV:349*n*
Pacific Baptist, III:72; IV:291
Pacific Christian Advocate, II:67
Pacific Churchman, III:75*n*
Pacific Coast Miner, IV:322*n*
Pacific Dairy Review, IV:344*n*
Pacific Dental Gazette, IV:317
Pacific Drug Review, IV:318*n*
Pacific Electrician, III:121*n*
Pacific Empire, IV:108
Pacific Fanciers' Monthly, IV:345*n*
Pacific Farmer, III:158
Pacific Friend, IV:296
Pacific Index, II:80
Pacific Life, III:210
Pacific Lumber Trade Journal, IV:325*n*
Pacific Magazine, IV:108
Pacific Marine Review, IV:334
Pacific Medical Journal, II:84
Pacific Methodist Advocate, II:68*n*
Pacific Miner, IV:322*n*
Pacific Monthly (Los Angeles), IV:107
Pacific Monthly (Portland), IV:107
Pacific Municipalities and Counties, IV:198*n*
Pacific Musical Review, IV:254*n*
Pacific Outlook, IV:107
Pacific Poultrycraft, IV:345*n*
Pacific Poultryman, IV:345*n*
Pacific Printer, III:131
Pacific Rural Press, III:158
Pacific States Watchman, III:315
Pacific Tree and Vine, III:159
Pacific Underwriter and Banker, IV:351*n*
Pacific Union, IV:203*n*
Pacific Unitarian, IV:294
Pacifism, *see* Peace magazines; Peace societies
Packages, IV:184*n*
Packaging industry, IV:184
Packard, Alpheus Spring, III:108*n*
Packard, Arthur Vance, V:317
Packard, Francis R., I:566*n*
Packard, Winthrop, IV:79*n*
Packard's Monthly, III:176
Packer, IV:186*n*
Paderewski, Ignace Jan, IV:149–50, 544
Page, Arthur Wilson, IV:773*n,* 776, 779, 783–87
Page, Cyrus A., III:102*n;* IV:81*n*
Page, David Perkins, IV:569*n,* 578
Page, Howard W., II:93
Page, Thomas Nelson, II:398*n,* 399, 400; III:48, 228, 428, 465, 471, 502; IV:129, 511*n,* 514–16, 720, 721; V:133
Page, Walter Hines, II:493*n,* 512; IV:13, 35, 39, 44, 51, 53, 165, 168, 236, 514–16, 785; V:73–74, 277
as editor, IV:9, 773–83
Page, William, I:757,
Page, William A., IV:123
Pageant, V:23
Paige, Eldbridge G., II:37*n*
Pain, Barry, IV:228; V:249
Paine, Albert Bigelow, III:400*n,* 504; IV:45*n,* 98, 117*n,* 360*n,* 584
Paine, George D., IV:602
Paine, Martin, II:68*n*
Paine, Ralph Delahaye, IV:116*n,* 729
Paine, Robert Treat, I:203, 232, 280; IV:744
Paine, Thatcher, I:185, 334
Paine, Thomas, I:26–27, 87–91, 102, 132, 159, 227; II:534
Paine Family Records, III:262
Paine's Photographic Magazine, IV:150*n*
Paint, Oil and Chemical Review, III:133
Paint Industry Magazine, IV:188*n,* 318*n*
Paint industry magazines, IV:188

Painter, E. O., III:155
Painter and Decorator, IV:221*n*
Painters' Magazine, III:133
Painting, *see* Art; Art criticism and comment
Painting and Decorating, IV:188*n*
Palazzo, Tony, IV:476, 477
Paleontological Bulletin, III:112
Paleontologist, III:112
Palfrey, John Graham, I:135, 284*n,* 285–86, 367; II:218*n,* 220*n,* 226*n,* 227, 234, 237
Palgrave, Francis A., II:248
Palm, Andrew J., IV:181
Palmer, Alexander Mitchell, V:212
Palmer, A. N., III:170
Palmer, Albert, II:42
Palmer, C. A., II:94*n*
Palmer, Frank Herbert, III:168*n;* IV:268
Palmer, Frederick, IV:455, 458, 465, 787; V:84
Palmer, George Herbert, IV:398
Palmer, Harry C., IV:380
Palmer, John James Ellis, IV:733*n,* 739–40; V:329*n,* 340
Palmer, John McAuley, III:346
Palmer, John Williamson, II:121, 505*n*
Palmer, Joseph, I:477
Palmer, Loren, III:481*n;* IV:453*n,* 469
Palmer, Paul, V:3*n,* 19, 20*n,* 21
Palmer, Potter, V:226
Palmer, Thomas, I:536
Palmyra, Mo., III:73*n*
Palmyra, N.Y., IV:382
Pamphlets, I:39
Pan-American Exposition, IV:266, 489, 782
Pan-American Magazine, IV:237
Pan-Americanism, IV:786
Panama Pacific Exposition, IV:782
Panics, *see* Depressions
Panoplist, I:134, 262–65
Panorama, V:322*n*
Panoramas, II:191–92
Panorama of Life and Literature, II:129
Pansy, III:177
Pan-Therapist, II:85*n*
Papashvily, George and Helen, IV:554
Paper
  defined, I:8
  See also Newspapers
Paper, printing
  early (1741–94)
    quality, I:35, 656
    shortage, I:20
    taxes, I:92–93
  in Civil War era (1850–65)
    rising costs, II:6, 8
    effects of war, II:6
  in post-Civil War era, III:117
  in Gilded Age, IV:5
Paper Makers' Journal, IV:221*n*
Paper Mill and Wood Pulp News, III:128
Paper and Paper Products, IV:184*n*
Paper and Press, IV:248*n*
Paper and Pulp Makers' Journal, IV:221*n*
Paper Trade, III:135
Paper Trade Journal, III:128, 135
Paper war with England, I:394; II:222
Paper World, III:128; V:126, 131
Paper-industry periodicals, III:128; IV:184*n,* 188
Papyrus, IV:390*n*
Paradise of the Pacific, IV:109
Paragon Monthly, IV:367
Pardoe, Julia, I:359
Parents' Magazine, V:142
Paris, Illinois, III:315
Paris, Tex., III:73*n*
Paris Commune (1871), IV:718
Paris Press Association, V:326
Parish, Elijah, I:134*n*
Parisian, IV:231
Parisian Illustrated Review, IV:231*n*
Parisienne, V:261
Park, Edwards Amasa, I:372, 532, 739–40; III:76
Park, John, I:160*n*
Park, Robert Emory, IV:192*n*
Park College, IV:74
Park Review, IV:74
Parker, Alton Brooks, III:349, 531; IV:706; V:206
Parker, C. Gray, *see* Gray-Parker, C.
Parker, Dorothy, IV:49*n,* 440, 566, 568; V:121
Parker, Eliza R., IV:765
Parker, Frank, IV:67
Parker, George, I:322
Parker, George Frederick, IV:62, 85, 157, 170, 602
Parker, Gilbert, II:273, 402, 463, III:400; IV:451, 497, 584, 592, 618, 689, 692; V:51
Parker, Harold, IV:612, 617
Parker, Henry G., II:35*n;* IV:69*n*
Parker, James, I:25*n*
Parker, Joel, II:62*n,* 148, 545
Parker, John, 31*n*
Parker, Theodore, I:288*n,* 289, 368, 402, 455, 659, 703–8, 775–79; II:28, 169, 239, 494, 534; III:78
Parker, Thomas F V·282

Parker, William Belmont, II:493
Parkersburg, W. Va., IV:292*n*
Parkhurst, Charles Henry, III:486; IV:282, 397
Parkinson, James W., III:100
Parkman, Francis, I:292*n*, 609, 659; II:239, 248, 252, 272, 387, 505*n*, 510*n*; III:90, 91, 242, 337; IV:136
Parkman, Francis (the elder), I:285
Park's Floral Magazine, IV:342
Parkville, Mo., IV:74
Parkyn, Herbert A., IV:284
"Parley, Peter," *see* Goodrich, Samuel Griswold
Parley's Magazine
  founding of, I:492
  sketch of, I:622–23
  woodcuts in, I:522
Parloa, Maria, V:131
Parlor Magazine, II:115
Parnell, Charles Stewart, III:277
Parochial schools, III:67
Parodies, literary, V:108
Parr, John, V:84
Parran, Thomas, Jr., IV:553
Parrish, Maxfield, III:473, 475; IV:456, 602, 720, 726
Parry, David Maclean, IV:126*n*
Parsons, Albert R., III:302; IV:172–73
Parsons, Charles, II:396, 397, 454
Parsons, Charles West, IV:318
Parsons, Floyd William, IV:785
Parsons, Frank, IV:204, 404, 415
Parsons, George F., II:510*n*
Parsons, George Lathrop, II:505*n*
Parsons, Louella O., IV:504, 606
Parsons, O. F., II:159
Parsons, Theophilus, I:255; II:78, 227
Parsons, Theophilus, Jr., I:127*n*, 332
Parsons, Thomas William, I:719, 736, 737; III:229
Parton, James, II:176, 244, 262*n*, 270, 352, 353, 506*n*; III:33*n*, 52*n*, 55, 290, 311
Parton, Sara Payson Willis ("Fanny Fern"), II:23, 36, 170, 352, 357, 361
Parton, Sara Willia Eldridge, IV:679
Partridge, Charles, II:209
Party magazines, political, III:301; IV:170–71
Pascalis, Felix, I:215*n*, 216
Pascin, Jules, V:178
Pascoe, C. E., III:420
Patent medicine advertising, II:437; IV:27, 31, 245, 526, 530, 543, 675, 681
Patent and Trademark Review, IV:320*n*
Patents, I:557; II:318–19, 323; III:115, 122*n*
Pater, Walter, IV:42
Paterson, N.J., III:301
Path, IV:287
Pathfinder, IV:53*n*, 62–63
Pathfinder Railway Guide, II:181
Patriot (Boston), I:331
Patriot (What Cheer, Iowa), V:x
Patriotism
  in early magazines (1741–94), I:22–28, 45, 48–49, 89, 95
  in nationalist era magazines (1794–1825), I:183–90, 275, 322
  and Mencken, V:268
Patron of Husbandry, III:149*n*
Pattee, Fred Lewis, IV:134; V:12
Patten, Gilbert ("Burt L. Standish"), IV:119
Patten, Simon Nelson, IV:192, 744
Patten, William, III:185*n*
Patternmaker, IV:184*n*
Patterns for sewing (with magazines), II:417–18, 437; III:97–98, 325, 327, 389, 481
Patterson, A. D., I:427, 618–19
Patterson, Catherine M., IV:88*n*
Patterson, Charles Brodie, IV:401*n*, 414
Patterson, Charles S., IV:244
Patterson, Elmore C., IV:464
Patterson, Graham, III:153*n*
Patterson, Joseph Medill, IV:174, 703
Patterson, Samuel D., I:552, 672*n*; IV:671*n*
Patterson, Wright A., III:274*n*
Patti, Adelina, II:195; III:192, 193
Pattie, James Ohio, V:118
Pattison, James William, IV:147
Patton, Alfred Spencer, II:65*n*
Patton, Francis Landey, III:74
Patton, Robert, I:530
Patton, William Weston, II:315; III:76–77
Pattullo, George, IV:693, 696
Paul, Elliot, IV:504
Paul, John Gilman D'Arcey, II:493*n*
Paul, Louis, IV:477
Paul Pry, I:356, 801; II:41; III:186
Paulding, James Kirke, I:177, 189, 408, 409, 429; II:222, 352, 498; IV:677
  as contributor, I:276, 280, 282, 298, 546, 547, 585, 608, 627, 638, 643, 679, 743, 767
  as editor, I:171–72
Paul, Robert Galloway, IV:88

Paving and Municipal Engineering, IV:323*n*
Paxton, Harry T., IV:712*n*
Paxton, John R., I:531
Payments to contributors, I:3
  by early magazines (1789), I:15
  by nationalist era magazines (1794–1825)
    general magazines, II:232
    police gazettes, I:327
    trends, I:197–99
  by expansionist era magazines (1825–50), I:344, 494–95, 504–12
    literary magazines, I:633–34, 725, 738, 771–72
  by Civil War era magazines (1850–65)
    cartoonists, II:182*n*
    general magazines, II:232, 244–45, 368, 385–86, 427
    highest payments, II:23–24
    illustrated periodicals, II:411
    trends, II:19–24
  by post-Civil War era magazines (1865–85), III:368, 469, 470, 515
    general magazines, III:358
    literary magazines, II:509; III:13–16, 364, 371, 372*n*, 377–78
    trends, III:12–17
  by Gilded Age magazines (1885–1905), IV:458
    diversity, IV:39
    highest payments, IV:41, 543, 725
    increases, IV:4
    "standard rates", IV:40
  by modern magazines (1905–)
    general magazines, III:408, 515; IV:698, 705
  See also Salaries of editors
Payn, James, II:482
Payne, George Henry, IV:66, 511*n*, 519
Payne, Henry B., V:192
Payne, Kenneth Wilcox, II:259; III:495*n*, 499; IV:605
Payne, Will, IV:692, 693, 696; V:81
Payne, William Morton, III:540, 541
Payne, William W., III:111
Pauson, Charles Shipman, IV:732
Peabody, Andrew Preston, I:601; II:220*n*, 238, 242; III:386, 507; IV:75, 398, 513
Peabody, Elizabeth Palmer, I:487, 659, 687, 703, 708–9; III:51*n*, 163
Peabody, Ephraim, I:658*n*, 661, 662; II:139, 241
Peabody, Francis Greenwood, IV:742
Peabody, George III:108
Peabody, Josephine Preston, II:402
Peabody, Oliver William Bourn, I:454; II:236
Peabody, William Bourn Oliver, I:287, 398, 411, 416–17, 418; II:235–36
Peace magazines, I:773; II:211, 275, 285–86; III:312
Peace societies, I:285
  press support for, IV:746
Peacemaker, III:312
Peale, Charles Willson, I:208
Peale, Rembrandt, I:295, 436
Pearl Magazine, IV:117*n*
Pearne, Thomas H., II:67*n*
Pearson, Arthur Clemens, IV:184
Pearson, Edmund Lester, III:350
Pearson, George R., IV:88*n*
Pearson, Paul Martin, IV:266
Pearson Publishing Co., V:72
Pearson's, V:151*n*
Pearson's Magazine, IV:228, 393
Peary, Robert E., V:148
Peary, Robert Edwin, II:271, 402, 415; IV:593, 621, 625; V:148
Pease, Joseph Ives, I:520, 521, 592, 684
Pease, Lute, IV:107*n*
Peaslee & Company, III:12*n*
Pechin, William, I:380
Peck, George, I:299*n*
Peck, George Washington, I:435, 750*n*, 753
Peck, George Wilbur, III:269
Peck, Harry Thurston, III:166; IV:49*n*, 124, 250, 432–37, 490, 641, 642,
Peck, John Mason, I:596
Peck's Sun, III:269
Pedagogical periodicals, I:491–92, 541–43, 694–95; II:34, 98–99, 442–45; III:163–64, 167–70; IV:267–71
Pedagogical Seminary, IV:268
Pedestrianism, III:218–19
Pediatrics journals, III:142
Peet, Stephen Denison, III:84, 112
Peffer, William Alfred, III:158; IV:177
Peirce, Benjamin, II:79*n*
Peirce, Charles Sanders, III:337, 386, 497
Peixotto, Benjamin F., IV:300
Peixotto, Daniel Levy Maduro, I:334
Peixotto, Ernest Clifford, IV:388, 720, 725
Pelham, William, I:536*n*
Pell, John H. G., 220*n*, 260
Pellew, George, IV:110, 112, 136–37

Peloubet, Francis Nathan, IV:274
Pelton, E. R., IV:56
Pelton, O., I:520
Pemberton, Max, IV:48*n,* 616; V:249
Pen and Pencil (Chicago), II:194*n*
Pen and Pencil (Cincinnati), II:194*n*
Pendexter, Hugh, V:80
Pendleton, Edmund Monroe, I:669
Pendleton, James Madison, II:63
Pendleton, John, I:323*n*
Pendleton, Philip C., I:699, 700
Pendleton, S.C., II:89
Pendleton, W. K., III:80*n*
Penfield, Edward, IV:19, 725
Penfield, Roderic Campbell, II:306*n,* 310, 416, 418
Peninsula Methodist, III:71*n*
Penman Artist and Business Educator, 352*n*
Penman's Art Journal, III:170
Penman's Gazette and Business Educator, III:170
Penmanship periodicals, III:170
Penn Dental Journal, IV:317
Penn Germania, IV:138*n*
Penn Magazine, I:550, 551*n*
Penn Monthly, III:34–5, 41, 184, 281, 287
Penn State Farmer, IV:341*n*
Pennell, Joseph, III:472, 557; IV:146, 151, 634
Pennsylvania
  number of magazines in, I:202*n,* 375*n*
  See also specific towns and cities
Pennsylvania, University of, IV:317, 348
Pennsylvania Anti-slavery Society, I:457
Pennsylvania Farmer, III:154; IV:340*n*
Pennsylvania Freeman, I:457, 804
Pennsylvania Justices' Law Reporter, IV:347*n*
Pennsylvania Law Journal, I:451, 806; II:93
Pennsylvania Magazine, I:14, 26–27, 37, 49, 61
  sketch of, I:87–91
Pennsylvania Magazine of History, IV:137*n*
Pennsylvania Magazine of History and Biography, III:261
Pennsylvania Medical Journal, IV:313*n*
Pennsylvania Methodist, III:71*n*
Pennsylvania School Journal, II:99*n;* III:167; IV:270
Pennsylvania State College, IV:341*n*
Pennsylvania state convention, I:52
Pennsylvania-German, IV:138, 231
Penny Magazine, IV:50
Penny magazines, IV:50
Penny newspapers, I:466
Pennypacker, Isaac R., V:5
Penology, IV:743
Pensacola, Fla., IV:163
Pentecost, George Frederick, IV:52*n*
Pentecost, Hugh O., IV:178, 215, 646
People, IV:174–75
People's Cause, IV:166
People's Fireside Journal, IV:366*n*
People's Friend, I:260
People's Home Journal, IV:366
People's Illustrated Journal, IV:365
People's Journal (New York), II:80*n*
People's Journal (Philadelphia), III:39*n*
People's Journal (Portland, Maine), III:39*n*
People's Journal (Washington), IV:367
People's Literary Companion, III:7, 37–38; IV:365
People's Magazine, IV:467*n*
People's Monthly, III:299; IV:48
People's party, *see* Populist periodicals; Populist movement
People's Party Paper, IV:178
People's Popular Monthly, IV:367
Peoria, Ill., II:99*n;* III:126*n;* IV:272*n,* 345
Pepper, E. I. D., III:72
Pepper's Musical Times and Band Journal, IV:254
Percival, Harold W., IV:287
Percival, James Gates, I:128, 204, 331, 408, 409, 602, 734
Percy, William Alexander, V:113
Perelman, S. J., III:555
Perfectionist, II:207*n*
Perfectionist community magazines, II:207
Perfume Gazette, IV:184*n*
Perine, George E., I:309; III:46*n*
Period, IV:94
Periodical, defined, I:5–6, 9
Perkins, Charles Callahan, II:197*n*
Perkins, Frances, IV:748
Perkins, Frederic Beecher, II:395, 424 429, 430, 443*n,* 477; III:18, 363, 423, 439, 456, 518
Perkins, George Walbridge, IV:500, 776
Perkins, Granville, III:411
Perkins, James Handasyd, I:658*n,* 661, 662–63; II:238
Perley, Sidney, IV:138
Peron, Juan, V:326
Perrine, William, IV:684
Perry, Bliss, II:493*n,* 512, 513; IV:9, 44, 120, 722; V:282
Perry, Enoch Wood, II:477
Perry, Eugene Ashton, IV:147

Perry, George, II:349*n*, 354
Perry, George H., V:72–73
Perry, Katherine, III:530
Perry, Matthew Calbraith, II:455
Perry, Nora, II:471, 505*n*; III:229, 374
Perry, O. H., IV:719
Perry, Thomas Sergeant, II:220*n*, 148, 506*n*, 507*n*
Perry Magazine, IV:147
Persons, William Frank, IV:741
Pestalozzian system, I:542
Petaluma Poultry Journal, IV:345*n*
Peters, Abraham, I:307*n*, 308, 397*n*
Peters, Absalom, II:444
Peters, Lulu Hunt, IV:472
Peters, Madison Clinton, IV:127*n*
Peters, Margedant, V:225*n*, 243
Petersburg, Va., II:59; III:154
Peterson, Charles Jacobs, I:352, 544*n*, 549, 550; IV:671*n*, 677–78
  as editor, II:306–10
Peterson, Mrs. Charles Jacobs, II:306*n*, 310
Peterson, Elmer T., V:36*n*, 42, 44
Peterson, Henry, II:36; IV:671*n*, 678–80
Peterson's Counterfeit Detector, II:96
Peterson's Magazine (*Peterson's Ladies' National Magazine*), I:351–52; II:11, 14, 57, 102, 192, 417, 418; III:6, 98, 186, 224; IV:5, 87, 152, 359
  sketch of, II:306–11
Petigru, James Lewis, I:205, 575; II:488
Petit Journal des Refusées, IV:387
Petrie, John W., II:94*n*
Petroleum Age, III:131
Petroleum Gazette, IV:184*n*
Petroleum Gazette and Scientific Journal, II:81
Petroleum Monthly, III:131
Petroleum periodicals, *see* Oil periodicals
Pet magazines, IV:382
  pets, IV:627
Petronius, Gaius, V:119
Pettengill, S. M., & Co., III:7*n*, 12*n*, 99
Pettengill's Newspaper Directory, III:7*n*
Pettengill's Reporter, II:17
Pettigrew, John, V:131
Pettingill, Lillian, V:74
Peuzner, Antoine, V:178
Pew, J. Howard, V:26
Pew, Marlen Edwin, V:59*n*, 67, 70
Pfirshing, C., II:213
Phalanx, I:366, 763, 807
Pharmaceutical Era, IV:188*n*, 317
Pharmaceutical Record and Market Review, III:133*n*
Pharmacy journals, I:539–40; II:92; III:133–34; IV:188, 317–18
Phelan, James Duval, IV:494
Phelan, Michael, II:203; III:220
Phelps, Austin, I:740
Phelps, Charles H., III:56*n*, 406
Phelps, E. H., V:131, 137
Phelps, Edward Bunnell, IV:351*n*
Phelps, Elizabeth Stuart, *see* Ward, Elizabeth Stuart Phelps
Phelps, Moses Stuart, II:315
Phelps, William Lyon, IV:437, 518, 520, 550–51, 728; V:117*n*, 119, 337
Phelps Publishing Co., V:131
Phi Beta Kappa Society of Harvard, quarterly of, I:125
Philadelphia, Pa.
  early magazines in (1741–94), I:24–25, 30–31, 47
    general magazines, I:80, 87, 94
    literary magazines, I:100, 104
    political magazines, I:71, 73
  nationalist era magazines in (1794–1825), I:208
    comic and satiric, I:170, 172
    general magazines, I:122–24, 127, 173–74, 223, 260, 306, 308
    juvenile periodicals, I:144
    legal periodical, I:154
    magazine center, I:200–1
    medical journals, I:151
    number of magazines, I:136, 315
    religious magazines, I:136, 315
    rivalry with Boston, I:203
    theatrical magazines, I:166, 167
  expansionist era magazines in (1825–50), I:345–47
    agricultural magazine, I:444*n*
    comic magazine, I:780
    decline, I:377
    general magazines, I:343, 345, 347, 544–55
    legal periodicals, I:451
    literary magazines, I:355, 368
    magazine center, I:376–78
    mammoth paper, I:361
    military periodical, II:7
    medical journals, I:438–39, 566–68
    men's magazine, I:673*n*
    number of periodicals, I:375*n*
    pharmacy periodicals, I:539–40
    railway journal, II:297*n*, 299
    religious periodicals, I:373, 562–65, 773
    scientific periodical, I:556–58
    theatrical criticism, I:427

women's magazines, I:348, 352–54, 580*n*, 672*n*
Civil War era magazines in (1850–65)
agricultural magazines, II:90, 90*n*, 91
Army magazine, II:7
"blue laws," II:34
dental journals, II:91, 92*n*
financial journal, II:94*n*
general magazines, I:544*n*, II:36; IV:671*n*
health magazine, II:87
home magazine, II:57–58
humor magazine, II:185*n*
insurance periodicals, II:94
juvenile magazines, II:101
law journals, II:93*n*
literary magazines, I:355; II:30
magazine center, II:106–7
medical journals, I:566*n*; II:84, 84*n*
pharmacy periodical, I:539*n*
printers' journals, II:93
railroad journal, II:81
religious magazines, I:562*n*; II:62–63, 70, 73–74, 75, 517
scientific periodical, I:556*n*
spiritualist magazine, II:210
Sunday papers, II:35–37
Sunday school magazine, II:101
trade union periodical, II:212
women's periodicals, I:580*n*
post-Civil War era magazines in (1865–85)
agricultural magazines, II:90, 90*n*, 91; III:153–54
biographical journals, III:261
booksellers' periodicals, III:235, 491
dental magazines, II:92*n*; III:143, 143*n*
engineering periodicals, III:113–14
family magazines, III:100
fashion magazines, III:97
financial journal, II:94*n*
freedman's journal, III:283
gardening journal, III:161
general magazines, III:35, 256, 557–59, IV:671*n*
historical journals, III:260–61
hygiene magazine, III:139
insurance periodicals, II:94*n*; III:146, 146*n*
journalists' periodical, III:273–74
juvenile magazines, II:101; III:176
labor periodical, III:300
legal journals, II:93*n*; III:144
literary magazines, III:33, 41, 396–401
magazine center, III:30
mail-order paper, III:39*n*
manufacturers' periodicals, III:128
medical journals, I:566*n*; II:84; III:140, 140*n*
military magazine, III:533*n*
music journal, III:197
peace magazine, III:312
pharmacy periodical, I:539*n*
photography periodicals, III:186
printers' magazines, II:93; III:131
railroad periodicals, II:81; III:126*n*
religious periodicals, I:562*n*; III:69, 71*n*, 72, 73*n*, 74, 75, 81, 85
scientific periodicals, I:556*n*; III:34*n*, 109*n*, 110*n*, 111, 112
secret-society periodical, III:314
sports periodical, III:218
story-paper, III:42
technical periodical, III:116
temperance periodical, II:210; III:310
trade magazines, III:133, 135, 136, 216
vocational magazines, III:132
women's magazines, I:580*n*; III:99–100
women's rights' magazine, III:96
Gilded Age magazines in (1885–1905)
agricultural magazines, II:90*n*, 91; III:153–54; IV:337
amateur periodical, IV:390*n*
Anglo-American periodical, IV:227–28
automobile periodical, IV:331
booksellers' magazine, III:235
comic periodical, IV:385
dental periodical, II:92*n*; III:143*n*
decline, IV:87
education periodicals, IV:263, 269*n*, 271
engineering periodicals, III:113*n*; IV:323*n*
ethical culture periodical, IV:279
fashion periodical, IV:363*n*
financial periodicals, II:94*n*; IV:350*n*
flower periodicals, IV:342
general periodicals, III:396*n*; IV:44, 671*n*
historical journals, III:261; IV:138, 140*n*
home decorating periodical, IV:324
hygiene magazine, III:139

Philadelphia, Pa.—*Continued*
Indian periodical, IV:215
insurance periodicals, II:94*n;* III:146, 146*n;* IV:215
juvenile periodicals, IV:273
Jewish periodicals, IV:300
law journal, II:93*n*
leading periodicals, IV:87–88
lecture periodical, IV:266
legal periodicals, IV:346, 347*n*
literary magazines, IV:125, 129, 671*n*
mail-order periodicals, IV:367
manufacturing periodicals, III:128; IV:183, 184*n*–86*n*
medical periodicals, I:566*n;* II:84; III:140; IV:314–15
military periodicals, II:549; III:533*n*
missionary periodical, IV:305
music journals, IV:251–53
news periodical, IV:64
peace magazine, III:312
pharmacy periodicals, I:539*n,* IV:188*n*
photography periodicals, III:186; IV:149
pigeon periodical, IV:345
poetry magazine, IV:121
political science journal, IV:180, 192–93
populist periodical, IV:178
printers' periodicals, II:93; III:131; IV:248*n*
proportional representation periodical, IV:178
railroad journals, II:81, III:126*n;* IV:333
religious magazines, I:562*n;* III:71*n,* 72, 73*n,* 74; IV:285*n,* 291, 292*n,* 293–96, 298, 299, 301*n*
review magazine IV:60
scientific periodicals, I:556*n;* III:109*n;* IV:310
settlement-house periodicals, IV:195*n,* 196*n*
sports periodicals, III:218; IV:374, 379
technical periodical, III:116
trade periodicals, III:135, 136, 216; IV:186*n*–89*n*
urban weeklies, IV:88
women's magazines, I:580*n;* IV:367, 536*n*
modern magazines in (1905–)
agricultural magazines, II:90*n,* 91; III:153–54, 591*n*
automobile periodical, IV:331
booksellers' magazine, III:235
education periodical, IV:271*n*
engineering periodicals, III:113*n*
fashion periodical, IV:363*n*
financial periodicals, II:94*n;* IV:350*n*
general magazines, III:396*n;* 671*n;* V:27*n*
historical journals, III:261; IV:138
insurance periodicals, III:146*n;* IV:351*n*
law journals, II:93*n;* IV:347*n*
literary magazines, IV:129, 671*n*
manufacturers' periodicals, III:128, IV:185*n*
medical journals, I:566*n;* III:140; IV:314
peace magazine, III:312
pharmacy periodicals, I:539*n;* IV:188*n*
philology journal, IV:128
pigeon periodical, IV:345
poetry magazine, IV:121
political science journal, IV:180, 192–93
railroad journal, II:81
religious periodicals, I:562*n;* III:71*n,* 72, 73*n,* 74; IV:291, 292*n,* 293*n,* 295*n,* 301*n*
review magazines, IV:63*n,* 522
scientific periodicals, I:556*n;* IV:310
settlement-house periodicals, IV:195*n,* 196*n*
sports periodical, III:218; IV:374
trade periodicals, III:135, 136, 216; IV:187*n*–89*n*
women's magazine, IV:536*n*
anti-Catholic riots in, I:371
as cultural center, I:201
muckraking articles on, IV:599
theater in, I:169
yellow fever epidemics in, I:149–50
Philadelphia Builder, V:131
Philadelphia Drug, Oil and Paint Reporter, IV:318*n*
Philadelphia Home Weekly, I:355, 806
Philadelphia Intelligencer, II:94*n*
Philadelphia Journal of the Medical and Physical Sciences, I:151, 566–67
Philadelphia Magazine Review, I:791
Philadelphia Medical Museum, I:151, 792
Philadelphia Medical Times, III:140*n*
Philadelphia Minerva, I:121, 789
Philadelphia Monthly Magazine (1798), I:14, 46, 149, 167, 173, 175, 700

Philadelphia Monthly Magazine (1827–29), I:343, 799
Philadelphia Photographer, II:194*n;* III:186
Philadelphia Press, III:271*n*
Philadelphia Public Ledger, V:51
Philadelphia Record, III:363
Philadelphia Register, I:130, 306, 796
Philadelphia Repository and Weekly Register, I:127, 791
Philadelphia Underwriter, III:146
Philanthropist (anti-vice periodical), IV:199
Philanthropist (Cincinnati), I:162*n,* 457, 803
Philanthropist (Mount Pleasant), I:162, 796
Philatelic Bulletin, IV:391*n*
Philatelic Era, IV:391*n*
Philatelic Journal of America, IV:391
Philatelic Monthly, III:113*n*
Philatelic West, IV:391*n*
Philatelic World, III:113*n*
Philately periodicals, III:113; IV:391
Philbrick, John Dudley, I:694*n,* 695
Philbrick, Samuel, II:275*n,* 285
Philes, George Philip, II:159
Philharmonic, IV:253, 390*n*
Philippine Christian Advocate, IV:236*n*
Philippine Education, IV:236*n*
Philippine Magazine, IV:236*n*
Philippine Observer, IV:236*n*
Philippine Review, IV:236
Philippines, magazine comment on, II:256; IV:237
Philistine, IV:388, 389, 426, 452
  sketch of, IV:639–48
Philleo, Calvin Wheeler, II:424, 495
Phillips, Coles, IV:566
Phillips, David Graham, III:487; IV:494–95, 501, 690, 693–94, 706; V:73
Phillips, George S., II:45
Phillips, Henry Wallace, IV:601–2
Phillips, John Sanborn, III:510*n,* 512, 514*n;* IV:589–600
Phillips, Morris, II:349*n,* 354; III:102
Phillips, Moses Dresser, II:494, 502
Phillips, Ralph E., IV:778
Phillips, Wendell, I:490, 778; II:252, 292, 373, 459; III:90, 172, 333, 338
Phillips, Willard, I:127*n,* 154, 179, 180; II:220, 224, 238, 431
Phillpotts, Eden, II:431; IV:435, 518, 737, 767; V:249
Philobiblion, II:159
Philology, magazine comment on, II:248; III:336, 377, 416
Philology periodicals, III:236–37, 535–38; IV:127–28
Philosopher, IV:390*n*
Philosophical Journal, III:81
Philosophical Review, IV:303
Philosophy
  in magazines, II:233; III:51, 337, 385; V:281
  philosophical periodicals, III:89, 385–87; IV:302–3
Phoebus, George, III:265*n*
Phoebus, William, I:131*n*
"Phoenix, John," *see* Derby, George Horatio
Phonograph, III:120; IV:25, 320; V:34
Phonography, *see* Shorthand; Shorthand periodicals
Phonographic World, IV:352
Photo-American, IV:149
Photo-Beacon, IV:149
Photo Critic, IV:150*n*
Photo-Era, IV:149–50
Photo Miniature, IV:150
Photoengraving
  growing use of, IV:148
  See also Half-tone pictures
Photographic Art Journal, II:194*n*
Photographic and Fine Art Journal, II:194*n*
Photographic Herald and Sportsman, IV:149
Photographic Journal of America, II:194*n*
Photographic Times, III:186
Photographic Topics, IV:150*n*
Photography
  in Civil War magazines (1850–65), II:191, 194, 464
  in post-Civil War magazines (1865–85), III:186, 188
  in Gilded Age magazines (1885–1905), IV:616, 685; V:25, 73, 148–50, 153–54
    amateur contests, II:464
    general periodicals, IV:719–20
    growth, IV:148
  in modern magazines (1905–)
  charity magazines, IV:748
    general periodicals, IV:602, 725, 731
    geographic magazines, IV:626–28
  amateur, IV:149, 634, 636
  color, IV:149
  development of, IV:148
  news, IV:455
    See also Half-tone pictures

Photography—*Continued*
nude, IV:152–53
revolutionary impact of, IV:153
Photography advertising, IV:25
Photography magazines, III:186; IV:149–50
Phrenological Journal, I:447–48, 804; II:42; III:163
Phrenology, I:152, 305, 447–50, 624, 642, 700; II:87–88
Phunniest of Awl, III:268*n*
Phunniest of Phun, III:265
Phunny Phellow, II:184
Physical Culture, IV:316, 393
Physical culture and education
in magazines through Civil War, I:143–44, 440–41, 485, 542, 590; II:201, 445
in magazines after Civil War, III:138; IV:28, 369–70
physical culture magazines, IV:316
Physical Review, IV:309
Physical Training, IV:272n
Physician and Surgeon, III:141*n*
Physicians, *see* Doctors
Physics, comment on, III:107
Physics periodicals, IV:309
Physiology journals, IV:315
Piano advertising, IV:24
Piatt, Donn, III:271, 368; IV:45*n*
Piatt, John James, II:429, 505*n;* III:229, 322, 374
Piatt, Mrs. Sarah Morgan Bryan, II:477, 505*n;* III:229, 508
Picabia, Francis, V:166*n*, 178
Picasso, Pablo, V:178
Piccard, Auguste IV:626
Pick, I:426, II:183; IV:387*n*
Pickard, S. T., II:181*n*
Pickering, John, I:255, 277; II:277
Pickering, Timothy, I:40, 96, 318
Pickett, Albert, I:148
Pickett, Mrs. George Edward, IV:496
Pickett, John Erasmus, II:432*n;* IV:550
Pickett, John W., 148, 491
Pickings from Puck, III:267, 529
Pickrel, Paul, V:329*n*, 340
Pictorial Brother Jonathan, I:362*n*
Pictorial Gallery for Young Folks, III:177
Pictorial magazines, *see* Illustrated periodicals
Pictorial Review, III:490; IV:362, 393, 770; V:136
Pictorial Wag, I:425, 805
Picture and Art Trade, III:136
Picture Gallery, 44*n*
Picture and Gift Journal, III:136
Picturesque America, III:187, 419
Pier, Arthur Stanwood, II:262*n*, 272, 273; IV:75*n*
Pierce, Frank G., IV:198
Pierce, Franklin, II:422
Pierce, George F., I:699
Pierce Harian A., II:297*n*, 299
Pierce, James Melville, IV:340
Pierce, Marvin, IV:587
Pierpont, John, I:177, 203, 204, 293–94, 409
Pierre, S.D., IV:270*n*
Piersol, George Morris, I:566*n*
Pierson, Arthur Tappen, III:84
Pierson, Lydia Jane, I:644, 672; II:308
Pierson Romaine, IV:318*n*
Pierson, Walter G., IV:149*n*
Pigeon, Charles D., I:624*n*, 625
Pigeon Flying, IV:345
Pigeon News, IV:345
Piggot, Robert, I:208, 210
Pike, Albert, I:481, 578, 609, 620, 627 660, 756; II:215
Pike, Manley H., III:528
Pilcher, Lewis Stephen, IV:314–15
Pilgrim (Congregation periodical), III:77*n*
Pilgrim (railroad periodical), IV:333*n*
Pilgrim (women's magazine), IV:362
Pilgrim Missionary, IV:238*n*, 305
Pilgrim of our Lady of Martyrs, III:68*n*
Pilgrim Teacher, IV:272
Pillsbury, Arthur Judson, IV:107*n*
Pillsbury, John Elliott, IV:622*n*
Pillsbury, Parker, II:141, III:94, 391, 393
Pilot, I:373, 800; II:76; III:36*n*, 67, 69; IV:297
Pilsbury, Caroline T., IV:81
Pinchot, Amos, V:98, 203, 206
Pinchot, Gifford, IV: 779
Pine Tree Magazine, IV:82
Pinero, Arthur Wing, IV:257–58
Pingree, Hazen S., IV:407
Pinkerton, William Allan, IV:199
Pinkham, Mrs. Lydia, IV:22–23, 541, 543
Pinkey, Edward Coate, I:204, 408–9
Pioneer, I:347, 508*n;* II:117, 139, 426; III:419
sketch of, I:735–38
Pioneer Farmer, II:89
Pioneer and Women's Advocate, II:52
Piper, Edwin Ford, IV:390*n;* V:179*n*, 180, 184
Pirandello, Luigi, IV:521; V:119

Pirating
by early magazines, I:39–40
by expansionist era magazines (1825–50), I:348, 356–61, 392–93, 502; II:352
by Civil War era magazines (1850–65), II:128–29, 352, 384–85, 421, 424–25, 439, 476*n*
by British magazines, I:392–93
Pitkin, Walter Boughton, III:153*n*, 434
Pitman, Isaac, I:479
Pitman's Journal, IV:352
Pitt, R. H., II:64*n*
Pitt, Theodore L., II:207*n*
Pittsburgh, Pa., I:389
music in, IV:249
industrial and trade periodicals, II:92; III:127, 167; IV:183*n*, 184*n*, 188*n*, 322
labor periodicals, III:299; IV:221*n*
law periodicals, II:93; III:144
medical and dental periodicals, IV:313*n*, 317
religious periodicals, II:63*n*, 67*n*, 68; III:85; IV:294, 298
women's magazines, II:50, 141
other periodicals, III:31*n*, 146, 235–36, 261*n*; IV:88–89, 300*n*, 349, 349*n*; V:193*n*
Pittsburgh Banker, IV:349*n*
Pittsburgh Catholic, II:77; IV:298
Pittsburgh Christian Advocate, II:67*n*
Pittsburgh Chronicle-Telegraph, III:270*n*
Pittsburgh Legal Journal, II:93
Pittsburgh Medical Review, IV:313*n*
Pittsburgh Quarterly Magazine, III:31*n*
Pittsburgh Saturday Visitor, II:50, 141
Pittsburgh Weekly Chronicle, II:100
Pixley, Frank M., III:56–57; IV:77, 106
Plank, George, IV:760
Planned Society (Soule), V:216
Plant World, IV:309, 310
Plantation, II:29, 138; III:154
Platonist, III:89
Platt, Orville Hitchcock, IV:494–95
Platt, S. H., II:467
Platt, Thomas Collier, IV:161, 602
Play, III:199
Plays
antislavery, *see: Uncle Tom's Cabin*
copyright laws on, I:429
in magazines, V:119, 266
one-act, IV:425; V:96
opposition to, I:56, 63, 167
trends in, IV:255–58
See also Drama criticism; Theater
Playthings, IV:184*n*
Plough, the Loom and the Anvil, I:442, 800
Plough Boy, I:154, 796
Plow, I:729
Pluck and Luck, IV:119
Plumber, Gas and Steamfitters' Journal, IV:221*n*
Plumber and Sanitary Engineer, III:113*n*
Plumbers' Trade Journal, III:130*n*
Plunkett, Henry Grattan, I:425
Plymouth Pulpit, III:77*n*, 422, 426; IV:45*n*
Plymouth Rock Monthly, IV:345*n*
Pocket Magazine, IV:115
Poe, Clarence, V:280
Poe, David, I:168–69, 249
Poe, Edgar Allan, I:249, 330, 347, 352, 405, 407, 411, 419, 448, 627, 709, 712, 781–82; II:35, 166, 210, 243, 352, 407, 419, 455, 546; III:196, 225–26, 548; IV: 666, 677, 680; V:9
as contributor, I:329–30, 345, 365, 381, 392, 412, 498, 503, 507–98
as editor, I:498, 512, 544*n*, 549–51, 629*n*, 634–39, 673*n*, 674–75, 757*n*, 758–62
Poems about God (Ransom), V:101
Poet-Lore, IV:121
Poetry, V:188
sketch of, V:225–45
Poetry
in early magazines (1741–94), I:93
didactic, I:109
on education, I:63–64
elegiac, I:89, 115
on fashions, I:67
general magazines, I:109
idolatry of Washington, I:52–53, 97–98
literary magazines, I:115
on love, I:75
lyric, I:109
patriotic, I:45, 48, 89, 95
political, I:51, 89
satiric, I:45
styles, I:45–46, 81–82
on women, I:64, 67
in nationalist era magazines
biblical, I:38
classical, I:125, 257, 312
comic and satiric, I:171
elegiac, I:295, 313–14
on fashions, I:235
general magazines, I:219, 227–28, 232–33, 247, 253–54, 257, 273–

Poetry—*Continued*
75, 280, 295, 312, 320, 323, 335; II:222, 225, 233
juvenile periodicals, I:144–45
literary magazines, I:121, 124–25, 128, 260, 293–95, 311–13, 331–32, 335
on magazines, I:126
political magazines, I:158
on politics, I:161, 228
quality of, I:176–82, 185–87, 194
religious magazines, I:138, 299
scurrilous, I:161
sentimental, I:323
women poets, I:177, 295
women's periodicals, I:139
in expansionist era magazines (1825–50)
on bathing, I:476
devotional, I:716
eclectic magazines, IV:674
English influence, I:399–401
on fashions, I:477
general magazines, I:577, 600, 620, 623, 709, 748
German influence, I:401
juvenile periodicals, II:264
literary magazines, I:355–56, 674, 661–62, 719, 755, 758, 760; IV:674
mammoth papers, I:359
men's magazines, I:674
payments to contributors, I:506–8
political magazines, I:75
quality, I:413–14
religious magazines, I:563
sentimental, I:347, 628
sonnets, I:711
Southern magazines, I:632, 634–35, 644, 650–51
Western magazines, I:666
women poets, I:400–1, 409, 412–13, 583–85, 588–89
women's magazines, I:545, 547, 626, 714
in Civil War-era magazines (1850–65)
criticism, II:166–71
English poems, II:161–62
family magazines, II:360, 417–18, 471
general magazines, II:451, 490
illustrated magazines, II:410
juvenile magazines, II:271–72
literary magazines, II:420, 423, 495, 497*n*, 498–99, 501–2
political poems, II:152–54
satiric magazines, II:523
Southern magazines, II:113, 490
wartime, II:151–52, 174–75
women poets, II:170–71, 174
in post-Civil War magazines (1865–85)
best sellers, III:247
"Copperhead" magazines, II:545
current events magazines, III:335
European, III:252–53
family magazines, III:424
fashion magazines, III:483
general magazines, III:358–59, 466, 462–63, 479, 511
juvenile magazines, III:501, 508
light verse, III:460
literary magazines, III:36, 229–31, 322, 373–74, 403–4, 407, 416, 548, 551
religious magazines, III:377, 439
trends, III:237–42
women's rights issue, III:92, 391
in Gilded Age magazines (1885–1905)
booksellers' magazines, IV:436
comic magazines, III:523
decline, IV:120
elegiac poems, IV:719
family magazines, II:482; IV:483, 490
general periodicals, IV:507, 593, 612, 616, 690, 713–14, 722, 724
illustrated periodicals, IV:457–58
leading poets, IV:128–30
literary magazines, IV:425, 674
satirical, IV:562–63, 666–68
specialized magazines, IV:121
urban weeklies, IV:654–55
women's periodicals, IV:544, 768
in modern magazines (1905–)
aristocrat poetry, V:240–41
booksellers' periodicals, IV:439–40
contests, V:113
current events magazines, V:210
disputes, V:113
domestic themes, V:154–55
family magazines, III:430; IV:498; V:130–32
general periodicals, IV:602, 616, 618, 702–3; V:5, 12–13, 21, 96, 238, 250, 266, 336
imagist, V:230, 239
intellectualist, V:240–41
literary magazines, II:431; III:542–43; IV:737–40; V:119, 121, 184
literary manifestoes, V:105
review periodicals, IV:518, 521
women's magazines, V:130–33

Poetry Journal, V:226
Poetry magazines, IV:121; V:100–16, 225–45
Poetry Society of America, V:234
Poinsett, Joel Roberts, II:345
Point Loma, Cal., IV:287
Police Chronicle of Greater New York, IV:199
Police Gazette, see: National Police Gazette
Police gazettes, II:187, 325–37; III:44; IV:199, 372
Police News, III:44
Political cartoons
in early magazines (1741–94), I:36, 48, 85–86
in expansionist era magazines (1825–50), I:782
in Civil War era magazines (1850–65), II:153, 181, 184, 462, 475–76
in post-Civil War magazines (1865–85), III:267, 269*n*, 286, 288, 441, 522–26, 553
in Gilded Age magazines (1885–1905), III:531, 554, 667, 775
in modern magazines (1905–), III:531
Political Censor, see: Porcupine's Political Censor
Political expansionism, I:339–40
Political magazines
in expansionist era (1825–50), I:775–79; II:325
number, I:342*n*
Whig, I:750–54
in Civil War era (1850–65), II:540–43
ante bellum issues, II:133–49
growing number, II:131
number, II:4*n*
in Gilded Age (1885–1905)
anarchist periodicals, III:301–2; IV:172–73, 176
Democratic party magazines, IV:170–71
Free-Soil periodicals, II:292, 369
Greenback party magazines, III:301
party magazines, IV:170–71
populist magazines, IV:162–63, 205
Republican party magazines, IV:171
socialist periodicals, I:536–38; II:207; III:300–1; IV:172–76; V:93
urban periodicals, IV:89, 100–1
Political Register, see: Cobbett's American Political Register
Political satire, I:51; II:523–24; III:523–25, 527, 529, 531
Political science journals, IV:180–81, 190, 192
Political Science Quarterly, I:535; IV:180
Polk, L. L., IV:176
Polk, Willis, IV:388
Pollard, Alfred William, III:481, 482, 484; IV:248
Pollard, Charles Louis, IV:309
Pollard, Edward Albert, III:397
Pollard, Joseph Percival, IV:101, 125, 385, 389, 390, 451, 645, 654, 754
Pollard, Josephine, III:175*n*
Pollock Channing, V:251–54
Pollock, Edward A., II:117
Pollock, Frederick, IV:347–48
Polls by *Literary Digest,* IV:575–77
Polo articles, IV:634, 636
Polyanthos, I:125, 167, 169, 208, 793
Polygamy, articles on, III:313
Pomerene, Atlee, II:260
Pomeroy, Cashel, IV:116*n*
Pomeroy, Marcus Mills ("Brick"), III:269
Pomeroy's Advance Thought, III:269*n*
Pomeroy's Democrat, III:7*n*, 11, 269
Pond, Enoch, I:569*n*, 571–72, 624
Pond, George Edward, III:281, 363, 376
Pond, James Burton, IV:265, 689
Ponsot, Marie, V:244
Pool, Maria Louise, III:13*n*, 373, 400*n*, 407; IV:450, 481, 765
Pool, S. D., III:261
Pool, Ernest, IV:692; V:85
Pool, William Frederick, III:233, 518, 540
Poole's Index, V:342
Poor, Henry Varnum, I:469; II:297*n*, 299, 413; IV:331
Poor Richard Club, V:324*n*
Poore, Ben Perley, II:410
Poore, Charles, IV:762
Poor's Manual, II:299
Pope, Albert Augustus, III:212, 213*n*
Pope, Alexander, I:6, 178
Pope, Alfred Atmore, IV:590, 633
Pope, F. L., III:122*n*
Pope, Gerald S., V:3*n*
Pope, O. C., III:73*n*
Pope John XXIII, V:312, 323*n*
Popular Astronomy, IV:308–9
Popular Educator, IV:269
Popular Gardening, IV:341
Popular Magazine, IV:116
Popular Mechanics, IV:320

Popular Science, III:110*n*
Popular Science Monthly, III:105, 108, 110*n*, 164, 250, 253, 418, 516*n;* IV:21, 109, 307; V:29
sketch of, III:495–99
Popular Science News, III:110*n*
Popular songs, IV:250
Population, U.S., I:16, 32–33, 208, 342*n*
Populism, IV:176–79
Populist movement, II:484; IV:177, 179, 191, 666
Populist periodicals, IV:162–63, 205
Porcupine, IV:107
"Porcupine, Peter," *see* Cobbett, William
Porcupine's Gazette, I:150, 159
Porcupine's Political Censor, I:158–59, 790
Poritt, Edward, V:330
Port Chester, N.Y., III:139
Port Folio, I:123, 145–46, 155, 161, 166, 168, 173, 174, 176, 177–82, 190, 192, 193*n*, 194, 198–200, 202, 203, 207–8, 209–10; II:221, 426
sketch of, I:223–46
Port Jervis, N.Y., III:153
"Porte Crayon," *see* Strother, David Hunter
Porteous J. Moir, III:249
Porter, Bruce, IV:388
Porter, Charlotte, IV:121
Porter, Eleanor Hallowell, IV:79*n*
Porter, Eliphalet, I:571, 572
Porter, Gene Stratton, IV:584, 687; V:134, 254
Porter, Henry H., I:440
Porter, Horace, III:469, 472
Porter, Joseph W., IV:138
Porter, Katharine Ann, IV:739
Porter, Noah, I:745; II:312*n*, 313, 314; III:85, 164, 321, 336, 558; IV:384
Porter, Robert P., III:35*n*
Porter, Rufus, II:316
Porter, T. D., II:38
Porter, T. O., I:356–57
Porter, William Sidney ("O. Henry"), III:514; IV:36, 40, 49, 421, 443, 457, 592, 602, 616, 617, 665–70, 692; V:73–75, 80, 118–19, 148, 249–50
Porter, William Trotter, I:425, 480
Porterfield, Allen Wilson, III:434; IV:738
Porter's Spirit of the Times, I:480*n*
See also: Spirit of the Times
Portfolio of Home Decorating, V:163
Portico, I:143, 152*n*, 167, 179, 183–84, 191, 193, 208
founding of, I:125–26
sketch of, I:293–96
Portland, Maine
The Bibelot, IV:424–27
Pine Tree Magazine, IV:82
religious magazines, II:65*n*, 71*n*, III:75*n*
Youth's Companion, II:265–66
other periodicals, III:39*n*, 168*n;* IV:186, 313*n*, 341, 387*n*, 391*n*
Portland, Ore., IV:107–8
agricultural magazines, II:90; III:158; IV:341
religious magazines, II:67*n;* III:72, 75*n;* IV:291
other periodicals, III:95, 148; IV:139, 314*n*, 318*n*, 325*n*, 349*n*, 350*n*
Portland Exposition, *see* Lewis and Clark Exposition
Portland Figaro, IV:387*n*
Portland Magazine, I:352, 802
Portland Pleasure Boat, II:36
Portland Transcript, II:36
Portrait of the Artist as a Young Man (Joyce), V:174
Portrait Monthly, II:176
Portraits
in early magazines (1741–94), I:37, 94
in nationalist era magazines (1794–1825), I:209–10, 252, 282, 307, 309
in expansionist era magazines (1825–50), I:347–48, 436–37, 520, 523–24, 545, 620, 683–84, 696, 762
in Civil War era magazines (1850–65), II:176, 192, 303, 428, 551
in post-Civil War magazines (1865–85), III:186, 328, 379–81, 416
in Gilded Age magazines (1885–1905), III:551; IV:22–23, 85, 152, 415, 571, 602, 720
in modern magazines (1905–), III:475; IV:438, 786
Time's covers, V:297–301
Portsmouth, N.H., I:135
Post, Charles William, IV:25, 126*n*, 460–61
Post, George W., IV:417*n*
Post, Israel, I:352, 769
Post, Louis Freeland, IV:62, 179, 204
Post, Lyman D., III:128
Post, Melville Davisson, IV:694, 697
Post, Truman Marcellus, II:374
Post Office, IV:335*n*
Post Office Clerk, IV:335*n*
Postal employee magazines, IV:335
Postal Record, IV:335*n*

Postal regulations
early (1741–94)
franking privileges, I:17
Massachusetts Act (1787), I:92
Postoffice Act (1792), I:18–19, 98, 103
in nationalist era (1794–1825)
costs, I:329
extension of postal routes, I:120
Postal Act (1794), I:19, 119–20
in expansionist era (1825–50), I:19, 361, 517–19; II:19,
in Civil War era (1850–65), II:266
Post Office Act (1850), II:19*n*
Post Office Act (1851), II:19*n*
Post Office Act (1852), II:3, 18–19
Post Office Act (1863), II:19
in post-Civil War era (1865–85), Post Office Act (1874), IV:20
in Gilded Age (1885–1905), IV:20
in modern era (1905–), IV:368
in England
Queen Anne's Act (1710), I:16–17
See also Mails
Poster art, IV:151, 450, 452
in advertising, IV:29
for newsstands, IV:19–20
Postgate, J. P., III:537
"Postman Always Rings Twice" (Cain), V:22
Postmaster Everywhere, IV:335*n*
Postmaster's Advocate, IV:335*n*
Postum Cereals, V:81
Poteat, William Louis, V:281
Potter, Alonzo, I:669; II:365
Potter, David Morris, V:329*n*, 339–40
Potter, Edwin S., IV:63*n*
Potter, Eliphalet Nott, IV:486
Potter, Henry Codman, IV:514
Potter, Isaac B., IV:327
Potter, John E., III:260
Potter, May Guillot, IV:94
Potter, Paul Meredith, IV:751*n*, 752
Potter's American Monthly, III:35, 260
Potter's Herald, IV:221*n*
Pottery, Glass and Brass Salesman, IV:188*n*
Pottery and Glass Salesman, IV:184*n*
Pottery and Glassware Reporter, III:127
Pottery periodicals, III:127–28; IV:184
Pottle, Emery, IV:66
Potts, Mrs. Eugenia Dunlap, IV:93–94
Poultry, IV:345*n*
Poultry Culture, IV:345*n*
Poultry Herald, IV:345*n*
Poultry Item, IV:345*n*
Poultry Keeper, III:161
Poultry magazines, III:161; IV:344–45
Poultry Monthly, III:161
Poultry Raiser, III:161*n*
Poultry Success, IV:345*n*
Poultry Tribune, IV:345*n*
Poultry World, III:161
Pound, Ezra, III:543; IV:654; V:94, 166*n*, 173–78, 228, 230–37, 241–42, 266
Pound, Roscoe, IV:738
Poverty, I:470; IV:10–11, 404
Powderly, Terence Vincent, II:255; III:299, 300
Powel, Harford W. H., Jr., II:262*n*, 274; IV:453*n*, 468
Powell, Aaron, II:141
Powell, Charles S., I:248
Powell, Edward Alexander, IV:638, 726, 728
Powell, Edward Payson, IV:302, 637, 638
Powell, Harford, III:388*n*
Powell, John Wesley, III:465; IV:240*n*, 620
Powell, Thomas, II:181, 182, 184
Powell, Thomas Reed, IV:180*n*
Power, III:116*n*
Power, Ethel B., V:154*n*
Power Engineering, IV:523*n*
Power Farming, IV:188*n*
Power Farming Dealer, IV:188*n*
Power Plant Engineering, IV:323*n*
Power plant engineering periodicals, IV:323*n*
Power and Transmission, IV:321
Powers, Hiram, I:173, 436; II:189; III:183
Powers, Horace Henry, IV:164, 182*n*
Powers, John E., III:12; IV:27
Powers, Thomas E., IV:61, 86
Powys, Llewellyn, V:97
Practical Dairyman, IV:343
Practical Druggist, IV:188*n*
Practical Druggist and Pharmaceutical Review of Reviews, IV:318
Practical Farmer, II:90*n*; III:153
Practical Housekeeper and Ladies' Companion, IV:365
Practical Ideals, IV:356*n*
Practical Printer, IV:248*n*
Practical Teacher, III:168
Prairie Farmer, I:444*n*, 731, 805; III:149, 156, 176, 179; IV:340
Prairie Herald, II:71*n*
Prairie Schooner, The, V:188
Prang, Louis, III:182, 186, 442; III:182, 186, 442; IV:147
Prang, James, I:31*n*
Prang's Chromo, III:186

Pratt, Charles E., III:213
Pratt, Charles Stuart, III:177, 508, 509
Pratt, Cornelia Atwood, III:483; IV:61
Pratt, D. Anson, II:356
Pratt, Frances N., II:506*n*
Pratt, Harry Noyes, III:402*n*
Pratt, Orson, II:75
Pray, Isaac Clark, I:356
Preacher's Assistant, IV:301*n*
Preacher's Helper, IV:301*n*
Preacher's Magazine, IV:301*n*
Prebeck, Florence, IV:367*n*
Preface to Politics (Lippmann), V:196, 205
Prejudices, V:3–4
Premium advertising, IV:368
Premiums, subscription, II:267–68, 273; III:7–8, 110*n*, 174, 437; IV:17–18
  See also Chromolithographs
Prentice, George Denison, I:204; II:362
Prentice, Marion Alcott, II:416
Prentice, Pierrepont Isham, V:312
Presbrey, Frank, IV:517, 649–50
Presbyter, II:63*n*
Presbyterian (Philadelphia), II:63; IV:293
Presbyterian (St. Louis), III:74*n*
Presbyterian Advocate, II:63*n*
Presbyterian Banner, I:138, 795; II:63*n*
Presbyterian Church and Congregational Church, II:367–68
Presbyterian Examiner, IV:293*n*
Presbyterian Excinding Act (1837), I:530
Presbyterian Herald, II:63*n*; IV:293*n*
Presbyterian Home Missionary, III:74
Presbyterian Journal, III:74
Presbyterian Magazine, I:136, 315; II:62; IV:293*n*
Presbyterian magazines
  in nationalist era (1794–1825), I:137–38, 315–16
  in expansionist era, (1825–50), I:370, 372, 373, 624–25
    Old School, I:529–35
    slavery issue, I:458
  in Civil War era (1850–65), II:516–17, 537–39
    trends, II:62–63
  in post-Civil War era (1865–85)
    juvenile periodicals, III:180
    trends, III:73–74
  in Gilded Age (1885–1905), IV:293–94
    juvenile periodical, IV:275
    missionary periodicals, IV:305
    Sunday School periodicals, IV:274
Presbyterian Monthly Record, II:62
Presbyterian Quarterly, I:529–35
Presbyterian Quarterly Review, II:62, 517
Presbyterian and Reformed Review, IV:29
Presbyterian Review, III:74; IV:294
Presbyterian of the South, II:62*n*, 63*n*
Presbyterian Standard, II:63*n*
Presbyterian of the West, II:63*n*
Presbyterian at Work, III:75*n*
Prescott, Eustis, II:38
Prescott, Harriet E., I:613; II:173, 467, 477
Prescott, W. W., III:77*n*
Prescott, William Hickling, I:543, 748, 777; II:175, 228, 232, 233, 237
Present, III:55
Present Age, III:45, 82
President, V:322*n*
Presidential campaigns, *see* Election campaigns
Press, I:791
Press Congresses of the World, V:64
Presser, Theodore, III:197
Presses, *see* Printing presses
Presto, III:198*n*
Preston, John, IV:204*n*
Preston, Mrs. Margaret Junkin, I:651; III:46, 46*n*, 48, 397, 411, 455
Preston, May Wilson, IV:692; V:84
Price, Charles W., III:122*n*
Price, Warren Elbridge, V:29
Price, Wesley, IV:712*n*
Price, William, I:151*n*
Price Current and Live Stock Record, III:159
Prices, agricultural, I:33–34, 318, 513
Prices, general, II:7; III:12–13
Prices, magazine
  early (1741–94), I:33–34, 72, 77, 104, 115
  in nationalist era (1794–1825), I:220, 226, 238, 249, 251, 270
  in expansionist era (1825–50), I:513–14
    abolitionist magazines (1825–50), I:513–14
    agricultural magazines, I:318, 729, 730
    children's periodicals, I:144
    comic paper, I:782
    general magazines, I:602, 607, 612, 615
    "knowledge magazines," I:364
    literary magazines, I:647, 655, 712, 736, 768
    "mammoth" papers, I:360–61

movement for cheap literature, I:348
railway journals, II:297, 298
religious periodical, II:368
women's magazines, I:139, 672; II:307
in Civil War era (1850–65), II:7
agricultural magazines, II:433, 434, 435
business magazines, II:342, 448, 449
comic magazines, II:523, 528
family magazines, II:354, 359, 417–18
in Far West, II:116, 117
general magazines, II:35, 42, 221, 255, 359, 384, 391, 393, 407, 409, 411
home club system, II:11
illustrated weeklies, II:453
juvenile magazines, II:264, 266, 268, 274
literary magazines, II:13, 180, 384, 393, 506
pirated publications, II:129–30
religious magazines, II:535, 537
scientific periodical, II:319, 454, 464–65, 467
in South during War, II:112, 113
typical prices, II:13
weeklies, II:35
women's magazines, II:51*n*, 53, 57, 58, 303, 417, 438, 453, 454, 464–65, 467
in post-Civil War era (1865–85)
agricultural magazines, III:153–54, 156–58, 161
art magazines, III:411
booksellers' magazines, III:492
business magazine, III:146*n*
Chautauqua magazines, III:545
comic magazines, III:441, 552
current events magazines, III:333, 339
family magazines, III:423
fashion magazines, III:481–82
general magazines, III:467, 510–11
home magazines, II:354, 355; III:99
illustrated magazines, III:327
juvenile magazines, III:177, 501
literary magazines, III:319, 321, 323, 454, 540
medical magazine, III:140
military magazines, III:533
outdoor journals, III:210
scientific periodicals, III:497–98
women's rights magazines, II:417; III:394, 448
in Gilded Age (1885–1905)
agricultural magazines, II:434
all-fiction magazines, IV:114–15, 116*n*–17*n*
anarchist periodical, III:301
charity magazines, IV:741, 747
comic magazines, III:554*n*
country-life periodicals, IV:338
current events periodicals, IV:500
digest periodicals, IV:571
family periodicals, IV:485; V:126, 131, 133
fashion periodicals, IV:363, 581–82
general periodicals, IV:20, 453, 507, 590, 609–11, 689, 718, 723; V:286–87
geographic magazines, IV:624
illustrated periodicals, IV:453
juvenile periodicals, IV:419, 764
legal periodicals, IV:347
library periodicals, III:519
literary magazines, II:315; III:540; IV:101, 425–26, 429–30; V:186
military magazines, II:549; III:534
outdoor magazines, IV:634, 638
political magazines, IV:101
populist periodicals, IV:412
religious magazines, II:315
review periodicals, IV:52*n*–53*n*
scientific periodicals, IV:308
society magazines, IV:106
urban weeklies, IV:106
women's periodicals, II:310, 418; IV:367, 536, 538, 545, 582, 587, 766, 771; V:126, 131, 133
in modern period (1905–)
agricultural magazines, II:434
all-fiction magazines, IV:608
amateur periodicals, IV:451
booksellers' magazines, III:494
current events magazines, V:112–13, 228
family magazines, II:355; IV:497
fashion periodicals, IV:759–60, 762
gardening magazines, V:38
general magazines, III:555; IV:605, 617–18; V:4, 24–25, 29*n*, 81, 86, 217, 290, 291, 339
home magazines, V:38
illustrated weeklies II:465; IV:46
juvenile magazines, III:504
literary magazines, III:543; IV:500, 502, 738
poetry magazines, V:112–13, 228
publishers' magazines, V:71
review periodicals, IV:663

Prices, magazine—*Continued*
scientific magazine, II:323
society periodicals, IV:759–60, 762
women's magazines, III:487–88, 490; IV:551, 554, 587, 771
lowering of, IV:3–10, 47–51
advent of ten-cent magazine, IV:3–6
British magazines, IV:4
effects of ten-cent magazine, IV:7–10
five-cent weeklies, IV:4
movement for cheap literature, I:348
nature of ten-cent magazine, IV:6–7
Priestley, John Boynton, IV:439, 478
Prieth, Benedict, IV:390*n*
Primary Education, IV:269, 272
Primary Plans, IV:269*n*
Primary School, IV:269
Primary Teacher, III:163
Prime, Samuel Irenaeus, I:531; II:63*n*, 388; III:271; IV:293
Prime, William Cowper, III:185
Primitive Baptists, II:65
Primitive Catholic, IV:300
Prince, John Tilden, IV:231, 263
Prince, Thomas, II:221
"Prince Otto" (Stevenson), V:119
Prince of Wales (Edward VII), II:126, 473, 525
Princeton, Mass., III:301
Princeton, N.J., III:84, 110*n;* IV:389
Princeton Review, I:136; II:6, 62, 155, 517; III:72, 164, 166, 281, 292, 312; IV:194
sketch of, I:529–35
Princeton Theological Review, I:535; IV:294
Princeton University, I:427, 489
magazines in, I:370, 530; II:99; III:73, 165; IV:74
Princeton University Bulletin, IV:74
Principia, II:141
Pringle, Henry Fowles, IV:473, 713, 730, 787; V:12
Printer, II:93
Printer and Publisher, III:274
Printers' Circular, III:131
Printers' Guide, III:132*n*
Printers' Ink, IV:146
Printers' magazines, II:93; III:131–132, 411; IV:247–48
early problems of, I:13, 20, 85–86
Literary Digest strike, IV:574
Printing Art, IV:247–48
Printing Gazette, III:131
Printing presses, I:20, 37; III:117, 189
Printing Trade News, III:131
Prison reform, II:207, 211–12; III:314; IV:513
Prisoner's Friend, II:212
Prisoners' periodicals, III:314; IV:199
Pritchett, Henry S., IV:738, 744
Prize fighting, I:481–82
in Civil War era (1850–65), II:201, 458–459
popularity, II:201–202
woodcuts, II:459
in post-Civil War era (1865–85)
defense, II:253
famous matches, II:331–33; III:218
illegality, II:331
magazine reportage, II:331–34
popularity, III:218
in Gilded Age (1885–1905)
famous matches, IV:371
magazine reportage, IV:372–73
popularity, IV:371
modern (1905–), II:336
Prizes, by magazines, I:15, 327, 500, 597; IV:39, 115, 429, 457, 487; V:43, 113
Process engraving, III:191
Proctor, J. Harris, V:273*n*
Proctor, Richard Anthony, III:249
Proctor, William, Jr., I:539
Produce Review, IV:186*n*
Producer and Builder, IV:325*n*
Profanity, I:57, 475
Professional and Amateur Photography, IV:150*n*
Profits of Religion, The (Sinclair), V:151*n*
Progress (home study periodical), IV:55
Progress (women's suffrage periodical), IV:356
Progress of the World, IV:55–56
Progressive Age, III:131
Progressive Age—Gas, Electricity, Water, IV:184
Progressive Bee-Keeper, IV:345
Progressive Farmer, III:155; IV:176, 341; V:280
Progressive Medicine, IV:314
Progressive Party, V:204–6, 211–12
Progressive Printer, IV:248*n*
Progressive Pulpit, IV:283
Progressive Springfield, V:131*n*
Progressive Teacher, IV:270*n*
Progressive Union Club, II:207
Progressive Woman, IV:205*n*
Progressivism, IV:706, 746; V:202, 204–5
See also Populist movement

Prohibition movement, IV:530, 569
in expansionist era (1825–50), I:473
in Civil War era (1850–65), II:210
in post-Civil War era, III:309–311
press support, III:545
in Gilded Age, IV:210
periodicals, IV:189*n*
press and, III:259, 336; IV:513
liquor advertising restrictions, IV:27
opposition, III:555; IV:210, 470, 568
polls on repeal, IV:576
See also Temperance; Temperance magazines
Promise of American Life (Croly), V:192–196, 205, 207
Promotional magazines, IV:96, 105, 106*n*, 108
Proof Sheet, III:132*n;* IV:212, 683
Prophetic and Mission Record, IV:238*n*
Proportional representation, magazine comment on, III:334, 342
Proportional representation magazines, IV:178
Proportional Representation Review, IV:178
Prose poems, IV:425
Prospect from the Congress Gallery, see: Porcupine's Political Censor
Prosperity, III:475; IV:1, 167–69
See also Depressions
Prostitution, III:27–28, 313, 445; IV:200, 405, 600
Protectionist, IV:166
Protestant American, IV:300
Protestant Churchman, II:70*n*
Protestant Episcopal periodicals, *see* Episcopalian magazines
Protestant Episcopal Quarterly and Church Register, II:68
Protestant Episcopal Review, IV:294
Protestant Standard, IV:299
Prout, H. E., IV:326
Providence, R.I.
educational magazine, III:168*n*
literary magazines, III:234, 262*n;* IV:127
trade magazine, III:136
other periodicals, II:52, 64; III:186; IV:247*n*, 366
Providence Medical Journal, IV:313*n*
"Prowler Paul," *see* Mackeever, Samuel A.
Prud'homme, John Francis Eugene, I:322, 522
Prussia, II:122; III:275, 279–80
Pryor, Mrs. Roger Atkinson (Sarah A. Rice), III:483; IV:86
Psyche, III:111
Psychiatric Bulletin of New York State Hospitals, IV:315*n*
Psychiatric journals, II:85
Psychic phenomena, IV:407; V:152
Psychical periodicals, IV:304
Psychical Review, IV:304
Psychological Bulletin, IV:303
Psychological journals, IV:303
Public, IV:62, 204
Public affairs, *see* Current events
Public Health Journal, IV:316
Public health magazines, I:440–41; II:86; IV:316
Public Leader, III:311
Public Ledger, III:492
Public Libraries, IV:143
Public Opinion, IV:3, 10, 64, 573, 649–51; V:79
Public Ownership, IV:178
Public Ownership Review, IV:178
Public Policy, IV:181
Public-School Journal, III:169*n*
Public schools, I:487; II:96; III:163–64, 486
See also Education
Public Works, IV:198
Publication, defined, I:5
Publications of the American Dialect Society, IV:128*n*
Publications of the American Economics Association, IV:181–82, 331
Publications of the American Statistical Association, IV:310*n*
Publications of the Modern Language Association of America, III:236; IV:128
Publications of the Southern Historical Association, IV:139
Publishers' Auxiliary, III:273; IV:243
Publishers New Company, V:82
Publishers' periodicals, III:135, 235–36, 491–94; IV:125–27, 243–44, 432–41; V:59–71
Publishers' Press Association, V:59
Publishers' and Stationers' Weekly Trade Circular, III:491
Publishers' Weekly, III:171, 235, 517
sketch of, III:491–94
Puck, II:481; III:87, 91–92, 125, 191, 192, 199, 267, 268, 272, 288, 292, 552, 555; IV:10, 29, 383
sketch of, III:520–32
Puck (German language periodical), III:521, 522, 524*n*

Puck: The Pacific Pictorial, III:265
Puck on Wheels, III:267, 529
Puck's Library, III:528
Pueblo, Colo., IV:204
Puffing, I:478–79
Pugh, Edwin, IV:196
Pulitzer, Joseph, III:527; IV:410, 428
Pulitzer Prize to Mott, V:xv, 347
Pullam, Marian M., II:352
Pullman, George Mortimer, III:53
Pulp and Paper Magazine, IV:184*n*
Pulpit, IV:301*n*
Pulpit Herald and Altruistic Review, IV:28
Pulpit Treasury, III:84
Pulsifer, Harold Trowbridge, III:422*n,* 433–34
Punch (London), II:521; III:441, 521
Punch and Judy, III:269*n*
Punchinello, III:91, 266, 279
  sketch of, III:440–42
Puns in magazines, I:236; V:312
Pupin, Michael, IV:727
Purdy, Ken W., IV:417*n*
Pure food, campaign for, IV:460; V:137–38
Purington, Julia M., III:95
Puritan, IV:361, 614
Puritan Recorder, II:71
Puritanism, III:4, 305
Purity Journal, IV:200
Pushing to the Front (Marden), V:286
Putnam, Allen, I:317*n,* 318–19
Putnam, George (editor of *Christian Examiner*), I:284*n,* 289, 703
Putnam, George Haven, II:248
Putnam, George Palmer, I:375, 393; II:419, 428
Putnam, J. Bishop, II:429
Putnam, Mary Lowell, II:124, 241
Putnam, Nina Wilcox, IV:606
Putnam & Mellen, II:36*n*
Putnam's Historical Magazine, IV:140
Putnam's Monthly Magazine, I:648; II:31–32, 102, 104, 121, 130, 172, 389, 396, 449–50, 495*n;* III:17, 29, 33–34, 184, 192, 231, 279, 281, 284, 307, 311, 458, 551; IV:46
  criticism in, II:158, 188, 198
  payment to contributors, II:20; III:14, 15
  politics in, II:135, 138, 140, 148
  sketch of, II:419–31
Putney, Vt., II:207*n*
Puzzles in magazines, II:417, 440
  crossword, III:555; IV:567
Pygmalion (Shaw), V:85
Pyle, Howard, II:397, 401, 402, 483; III:473, 503, 504, 509, 557; IV:151, 484, 545, 719, 726; V:341
Pyles, Joseph Gilpin, IV:782
Pyne, John, II:532
Pythian Journal, III:315

Quackenbos, G. P., II:40
"Quad, M.," *see* Lewis, Charles Bertrand
Quaker, IV:117, 273, 614
Quaker magazines, I:562, 652–65, 773–74; II:140; III:81; IV:296, 305
Quakers
  early magazine on (1757–58), I:61
  expansionist era magazines on
    criticisms, I:472
    water cure, I:441, 475, 700; II:87; IV:316
  Civil War era magazines on, II:48, 319
  Gilded Age magazines on, IV:245, 528, 543
  modern magazines on, IV:530–31
"Quality magazines," IV:7–9
Quampeag Coyote, II:185*n*
Quarterlies
  in nationalist era (1794–1825), I:129–30
  in expansionist era (1825–50)
    number, I:342*n*
    quality, I:366–69
  in Civil War era (1850–65), II:61, 103, 150
    anonymity, II:25
    average circulation, II:10
    growth, II:27–29
    number, II:4*n,* 27–29
  in post-Civil War era (1865–85), III:31–32
  See also specific quarterlies
Quarterly Bulletin of the American Institute of Architects, IV:323
Quarterly Christian Spectator, I:310
Quarterly Illustrator, IV:154
Quarterly Journal (Jenness Miller), IV:359
Quarterly Journal of Economics, IV:182
Quarterly Journal and Review, I:388 808
Quarterly Register of Current History, IV:71
Quarterly Reporter of Y.M.C.A.'s in North America, II:75
Quarterly Review, IV:228
Quarterly Review of the Evangelical Lutheran Church, II:73*n;* III:79

Quarterly Review of the Methodist Church South, II:66*n;* III:70, 384
Quarterly Review of the United Brethren, IV:296
Quarterly of the Texas State Historical Association, IV:139
Quartley, Frederick William, III:187, 411, 420
Quatrefages de Bréau, Jean Louis Armand de, III:496
Queen, II:418; IV:580–81
"Queen, Ellery" (Frederic Dannay and Manfred Bennington Lee), IV:503
Queen, Frank, II:203, 204; IV:260
Queen Anne's Act (1710), I:16–17
Queen Bee, III:95
Queen of Fashion, IV:582
Queen Victoria (Strachey), V:211
Quequelle, Frederick, I:31*n*
Queries, IV:55
Quick, Herbert, II:431; III:156*n;* IV:46*n,* 490, 550, 697, 779
Quigg, J. Travis, III:196*n*
Quiller-Couch, Arthur Thomas, IV:114*n,* 451, 720, 726
Quinby, D. F. II:116*n,*
Quincy, Edmund, II:275*n,* 285, 289, 424
Quincy, Illinois, III:161; IV:254*n,* 345
Quincy, Josiah, I:244, 255; IV:161, 407
Quinn, Arthur Hobson, III:235*n;* IV:728
Quinn, Frank, V:72*n,* 86
Quinn, Thomas C., IV:50
Quint, Alonzo Hall, II:71*n*
Quirk, James R., IV:589*n,* 607; V:271
Quiver, IV:220*n*
Quo Vadis, IV:141, 260

R. F. D. News, IV:355*n*
R. R. Donnelly and Sons, V:327–28
Racer and Driver, IV:373*n*
Rachel, Elisa, II:199
Racine, Wis., II:89*n,* 99*n;* III:157
Racine Agriculturist, III:157
Racing boat, *see* Boat racing
Racing, horse, *see* Horse racing
Radford Review, IV:325*n*
Radiant Centre, IV:285*n*
Radical, III:78, 91
Radical Abolitionist, II:141
Radical Review, III:31, 301
Radio, IV:319, 592
  Radio reviews, III:555; IV:567
Raemakers, Louis, III:532; IV:566
Rafinesque, Constantine Smalz, I:297, 311, 312*n,* 312
Ragland, Sam, V:248
Rago, Henry, V:225*n,* 243–44
Raguet, Condy, I:235, 245
Railroad Advocate, II:81
Railroad Brakeman's Journal, III:126*n*
Railroad Car Journal, IV:333*n*
Railroad Conductors' Brotherhood Monthly, III:125*n*
Railroad and Engineering Journal, II:297*n*
Railroad Gazette, III:125
Railroad Herald, IV:333*n*
Rail-road Journal, I:469; II:297*n*
Railroad journals, II:81–83, 297–300; III:125–26; IV:332–33
  See also: American Railroad Journal
Railroad Magazine, IV:422
Railroad Men's Magazine, IV:422, 617*n*
Railroad Record, II:81
Railroad Record and Investment Guide, III:126*n*
Railroad Trainman, III:126*n*
Railroads
  through Civil War era, I:206–8, 466–69; II:144–45, 297, 340, 343, 414, 531
  post-Civil War era (1865–85), III:149–50
    agrarian discontent and, III:124
    complaints against service, III:123
    expansion, III:3
    press hostility, III:342
    railroad strike (1877), III:124–25, 303
    speculation, III:122–23, 296
  in Gilded Age (1885–1905), IV:326, 331–332, 782
    advertising, IV:27
    articles on, IV:487–88, 593
    press accounts, IV:689, 721
    rate regulation, IV:464
    strike of 1894, IV:218
    trusts, IV:156
  modern (1905–), V:83
    criticism, V:149–50
Railway Age, III:125
Railway Age Gazette, II:297*n,* 300
Railway Carmen's Journal, IV:221*n*
Railway Clerk, IV:221*n*
Railway Conductor, III:125*n*
Railway Conductor's Monthly, III:125*n*
Railway Earnings Record, III:147*n*
Railway and Industrial Compendium, III:147*n*
Railway Journal, IV:333*n*
Railway and Locomotive Engineering, IV:333*n*

Railway Master Mechanic, III:126
Railway Mechanical Engineer, II:297*n,* 300
Railway Post Office, IV:335*n*
Railway Purchasing Agent, III:126*n*
Railway Register, III:126*n*
Railway Review, III:125
Railway Telegrapher, IV:221*n*
Railway Times, IV:175
Railway World, IV:333
Raine, Norman Reilly, IV:701 713
Raine, William McLeod, IV:79*n,* 421
Raleigh, Henry, IV:695
Raleigh, N.C., II:65*n,* 113; III:154–55, 168, 261*n,* 262*n;* IV:176
Ralph, Julian, II:482; IV:66, 226, 233, 489, 662, 689, 721; V:28
Ramage, Burr James, IV:733*n,* 735
Rambler, III:268
Rambler and Dramatic Weekly, III:199
Rambler's Magazine, I:166, 793
Ramée, Marie Louise de la ("Ouida"), II:255, 439; III:91, 252, 397; IV:51, 514, 679
Ram's Horn, IV:301
Ramsay, William, III:402
Ramsden, T., III:270*n*
Ranch, IV:341
Rand, Asa, II:262*n,* 263–64
Rand, McNally & Co.'s Bankers Monthly, III:147
Rand McNally Bankers' Monthly, IV:349
Randall, James G., V:280
Randall, George M., II:69
Randall, Samuel S., I:491*n*
Randall, Theodore A., III:130
Randall-Diehl, Anna, IV:125
Randolph, John, I:184
Rankin, Jeremiah Earmes, II:518*n;* IV:52*n*
Rankin, John, II:282
Ransom Beverly C., III:71*n*
Ransom, John Crowe, IV:737, 739, 749; V:100*n,* 101–7, 110–12, 114–16, 222, 336
Rascoe, Burton, IV:432*n,* 440–41; V:257*n,* 259
Ratchford, B. U., V:273*n*
Rathom, John R., IV:783
Ratner, Joe E., V:36*n,* 44
Rauch, Friedrich August, II:380n
Raumer, Karl von, II:445
Raven, IV:117*n*
Raven, Anton A., II:414
Rawlings, Augustus, II:110, 458
Rawlings, Charles A., IV:712
Rawlings, Marjorie Kinnan, IV:729
Ray, Man, V:178
Raymond, Henry Jarvis, I:329, 358, 753, 779; II:361, 383*n,* 391
Raymond, James H., I:490
Raymond, John T., III:204
Raymond, Robert L., III:425
Raymond, Rossiter Worthington, III:114*n*
Rayne, Martha L., III:95, 416
Reactionary periodicals, IV:442–49; V:26
Read M. C., II:115*n*
Read, Opie, II:311; III:54, 238, 270; IV:48*n,* 93, 100, 114*n,* 115*n,* 167*n,* 390, 654, 767
Read, Thomas Buchanan, II:308, 410, 505*n;* III:237, 374, 397
Reade, Charles, II:270, 386, 393, 454, 471, 476, 482, 506*n,* 508; III:224, 251, 322–23, 358, 372; IV:679
Reade, Frank, III:179
Readel, John D., I:294
Reader, II:431; IV:46
Readers Guide to Periodical Literature, V:342
Readers, magazines, I:13
See also Subscriptions
Reader's Digest, IV:587; V:xvi
Reading, Pa., III:139; IV:301*n*
Reading-course magazines, III:153, 173, 177, 544–47; IV:54–55
Real Democracy, IV:283
Real estate periodicals, III:147–48; IV:325
Real Estate and Record Building Guide, IV:325
Realf, Richard, IV:65
Realist novels, romantic versus, IV:111–12
Reason, IV:304*n*
Reavis, Holland S., IV:184*n*
Reavis, L. U., IV:261*n*
Receipts, I:33–35, 72, 82, 103, 111; II:35, 42
See also Circulation; Subscriptions
Recipes, I:589; II:440, 466; III:511; IV:537; V:45–6
Reckoning, The (Chambers), V:30
Reconstruction Period, II:245; III:4, 283–84, 333–34, 340
Record, II:113*n*
Record of Christian Work, III:86
Recorder, II:263
Records of the American Catholic Historical Society of Philadelphia, IV:138

Records of the Past, IV:140
Recouly, Raymond, IV:727, 728
Recreation, IV:381
Red Book, I:172, 706; IV:116, 393; V:30, 143
Red Man, IV:215
Red Men, Improved Order of, III:37*n*
Red River Rover, II:151
Redding, Mrs. Josephine, IV:756*n*, 758–59
Redfield, W. D., I:322, 522
Redfield, William Cox, IV:617
Redman, Peggy Dowat, IV:712*n*
Redmond, Daniel George, IV:511*n*, 523; V:49*n*, 58
Redmond, Daniel George, Jr., V:58
Redpath, James, II:251
Reed, C. McF., IV:671*n*
Reed, Edward Bliss, V:339
Reed, Gideon F. T., IV:412
Reed, H. V., III:413*n*, 414
Reed, Isaac G., Jr., III:269
Reed, Joseph P., II:416, 418; IV:48*n*, 671*n*
Reed, Myra G., IV: 580*n*, 584
Reed, Myrtle, IV:117*n*, 436, 612, 767–68
Reed, T. Smith, II:45
Reed, Thomas Brackett, II:255, 269; IV:166, 612, 689
Reed, Thomas Buchanan, I:366, 540, 585, 743, 767, 771
Reed, William B., II:238
Reed's Isonomy, IV:94
Reedy, William Marion, IV:77, 101, 130–31, 132, 135, 164, 168, 278, 390, 427, 447–78, 646, 652–56
Reedy's Mirror, IV:77, 101
  sketch of, IV:652–56
Rees, Albert, IV:181*n*
Reese, Lizette Woodworth, V:185, 266
Reeve, Arthur Benjamin, IV:493, 497, 604, 651
Reeve, James Knapp, IV:117
Referee, IV:379
Referendum, IV:178
Reform Advocate, IV:300
Reform bill (1832), I:339
Reform movements, III:308–12; IV:194–214
  press attention to, IV:513
  variety of, IV:209–12
  See also specific reforms and reform movements
Reformed Church Review, I:809
  sketch of, II:380–82
Reformed Judaism, magazines of, III:80
Reformed Quarterly Review, II:380; III:79
Refrigerating industry periodicals, IV:183*n*
Refrigerating Review, IV:183*n*
Regional Labor Board, V:20*n*
"Reid, Christian," *see* Tiernan, Frances Fisher
Reid, John Morrison, II:31*n*
Reid, Mayne, III:16, 43, 175*n*, 176, 179, 219, 502; IV:680
Reid, Whitelaw, III:332*n*; IV:74
Reifsnider, Mrs. Calvin Kryder, IV:413–14
Reilly, Henry Joseph, II:547*n*, 549
Reilly, Louis W., IV:297
Reinhart, Charles Stanley, II:397, 399, 477; III:189, 504
Reinsch, Paul Samuel, IV:499
Reliable Poultry Journal, IV:345
Religion
  early magazines and (1741–94)
    articles on religion, I:56, 75
    clergy called useless extravagance, I:58
    religious controversies I:75–77
    school curriculum, I:62–64, 105
  nationalist era magazines and (1794–1825), I:258, 297
    controversy, I:562–64
    emphasis, I:124
    progressive views, I:258
  expansionist era magazines and (1825–50), I:560–61
    controversy, I:369
    science and, I:447, 611; II:314
    slavery issue, I:369, 373, 458, 461
  Civil War era magazines and (1850–65)
    slavery issue, II:138–39
    theater and, II:200
  post-Civil War era magazines and (1865–1885), II:252; III:320, 463–64, 526–27, 545
    controversy, III:63–66
    debate on free-thinking, II:252
    declining influence, III:305–6
    juveniles, III:180
    newspapers, III:66
    prohibition, III:310
    statistics, III:66–67
    Sunday School topics, III:424
    theater and, III:206
    theological issues, III:85–89
    trends, III:4
  in Gilded Age (1885–1905)
    church membership, IV:276
    New Thought cult, IV:283–85, 304*n*

Religion—*Continued*
press discussions, IV:403–4, 444, 513
socialist ideas and, IV:176, 190–191, 280–83
trends, IV:276
modern magazines and (1905–30)
digest periodicals, IV:570
general magazines, V:32, 281
literary magazines, II:513
review periodicals, IV:520
See also specific religious denominations
Religion in Life, II:66*n*
Religio-Philosophical Journal, III:81
Religious Cabinet, I:716
Religious Herald (Hartford), II:71*n*
Religious Herald (Richmond), II:64
Religious Magazine, III:506, 507
Religious Magazine and Monthly Review, II:72*n*
Religious Monitor, I:791
Religious periodicals
early (1789–90), I:29
in nationalist era (1794–1825), I:310
editing, I:198
increase in, I:210
quality and variety, I:131–39
in expansionist era (1825–50), II:312–15
conflict with science, I:447
didactic, I:745–46
number, I:342*n*
quality and variety, I:369–74
in Civil War era (1850–65), II:60–78, 380–82
advertising, II:15, 368, 372
circulation, II:370–71, 381
criticism, II:60
distribution, II:61
education, II:97
high-circulation, II:10
number, II:4*n*
trends, II:60–78
weeklies, II:34
in post-Civil War era (1865–85), II:382; III:422–23
advertising, II:375
circulation, II:315, 376; III:7, 67, 70, 76*n*, 422, 436, 507
juvenile magazines, III:180
newspapers, III:66
number, III:66–68
science periodicals, and, III:497
weeklies, III:63–67
in Gilded Age (1885–1905)
monthlies, IV:395–400
See also specific religious denominations
Religious Remembrancer, see: Christian Observer
Religious revivals, I:300
Religious Telescope, II:68*n*, 74; III:81
Remarque, Erich Maria, IV:475
Remarques, IV:87
Remembrancer, I:122*n*, 123*n*, 790
Remington, A. G., II:28
Remington, Frederick, II:482; III:473; IV:151, 456, 458, 484, 496, 635, 637, 726
Reminiscences, III:433, 475; IV:474, 513, 586–87, 713
See also Autobiography
Remsen, Ira, II:271; III:109
Renoir, Pierre Auguste, IV:145
Renwick, James, I:276; III:182
Repertory of Papers on Literature and Other Topics, I:167, 794
Reporter (Washington), IV:90
Repository and Ladies' Weekly Museum, see: Philadelphia Repository and Weekly Register
Repplier, Agnes, II:511*n*; III:330, 428; IV:490; V:251, 337–38
Representative, IV:178
Representative Americans, V:247
Reprints in magazines, I:360–61
See also Condensations
Republic, II:44*n*, 123, 125; III:281; IV:89
Republican-Chronicle, I:320
Republican Magazine, IV:171
Republican party
early program of, II:423
elephant as symbol of, II:480
periodicals of, IV:171
See also names of Republican presidents
Retail Coalman, IV:189*n*
Retail Druggist, IV:188*n*
Retail Grocers' Advocate, III:134; IV:187*n*
Retail trade periodicals, *see* Trade periodicals
Retailers' Association, V:113
Reuterdahl, Henry, IV:100*n*, 456
Reuther, Walter, IV:478
Reveille, II:180
Revere, Paul, I:26, 36, 85, 86, 250
Review, defined, I:7–8
Review of American Chemical Research, IV:309
Review of the Churches, IV:301
Review and Expositor, IV:292

Review of Missions, IV:238*n,* 305
Review periodicals, *see* Book reviews; Condensations; Current-events magazines
Review of Reviews, IV:10, 17, 21, 35, 52, 216, 228, 508, 570, 571, 578, 775, 788; V:50–51, 55, 341
sketch of, IV:657–64
Review of Reviews for Australasia, IV:658*n*
Review of Reviews Corporation, V:117–18, 123
Review of Telegraph and Telephone, III:122*n*
Revista del Mundo, IV:786
Revolution, II:207; III:94, 445–46
sketch of, III:391–95
Revolution, American
histories, I:97, 98, 103, 176, 188, 260
reportage, I:83–85, 89–90
Revolving Book Publication Fund, V:345
Revue des Revues, IV:659*n*
Revue Mondiale, IV:659*n*
Rexford, Eben Eugene, I:592; II:362, 468; III:416, 511; IV:80, 115, 360, 361, 542, 637, 765
Reynolds, Ignatius Aloysius, II:76
Reynolds, J. N., I:611
Reynolds, John, III:315
Reynolds, John Parker, III:159
Reynolds, Quentin, IV:470, 472, 476
Reynolds, Thomas C., I:646
Reynolds, William M., II:73*n*
Rhead, Louis, IV:26
Rhoads, James E., I:773*n,* 774
Rhoads, Margaret W., I:565
Rhoads, Samuel, I:773
Rhode Island Advertiser, IV:247*n*
Rhode Island College of Agriculture, IV:341*n*
Rhode Island Historical Magazine, III:259
Rhode Island Schoolmaster, III:168
Rhodes, Albert, III:18, 465*n*
Rhodes, Anne, II:463
Rhodes, Bradford, II:94*n*
Rhodes, Eugene Manlove, IV:694, 695
Rhodes, James Ford, III:262, 347
Rhodes, Harrison Garfield, IV:451
Rhodes, James Allen, V:317
Rhodes Journal of Banking, II:94*n;* III:147
Rhodes Journal of Banking and the Banker's Magazine, II:94*n*
Rhodora, IV:310
Rhys, Dynevor, III:489
Rhys, Ernest, IV:425
Ricci, Rolandi, IV:519
Rice, Alice Hegan, III:471, 504; IV:429
Rice, Allen Thorndike, II:218*n,* 220*n,* 249–50, 254, 260; III:23, 31, 35; IV:51
Rice, Arthur L., III:116*n*
Rice, George, IV:107
Rice, Grantland, IV:465, 466, 470, 478, 604
Rice, Isaac Leopold, IV:511–19
Rice, John H., II:155
Rice, Joseph Mayer, IV:517–18
Rice, Philip Blair, V:240
Rice, Wallace, V:236
Rice Industry, IV:186*n*
Rice Journal, IV:339
Rice periodicals, IV:339
Rich, H. S., III:135
Rich, H. Thompson, IV:511*n,* 519
Richard, Joseph W., 73*n*
Richard, Mary Ellen, IV:744
Richards, Frederick Thompson, IV:456
Richards, George Livingston, IV:82, 366
Richards, George W., II:380*n*
Richards, I. W., IV:322*n*
Richards, Joseph H., III:331*n,* 332
Richards, Laura Elizabeth, III:503
Richards, Thomas Addison, II:390
Richards, Walker C., II:110*n*
Richards, Willard, II:75
Richardson, Albert Deane, II:468, 546
Richardson, Allen H., IV:583
Richardson, Anna Steese, IV:604, 769
Richardson, C. B., II:175
Richardson, Charles B., II:550
Richardson, Charles F., II:376; IV:398
Richardson, Dorothy, V:173
Richardson, Fred, IV:452
Richardson, Frederick A., IV:225
Richardson, Henry Hobson, III:182, 183
Richardson, James H., II:390
Richardson, Leander, IV:243*n,* 260*n*
Richardson, Lou, IV:105*n*
Richardson, Nathaniel Smith, I:372; II:68, 364*n,* 365
Richardson, Solon, II:186
Richardson, William H., IV:90
Richmond, Cora L. V., III:82*n*
Richmond, Ind., II:51; III:111, 312
Richmond, Va.
nationalist era magazines in (1794–1825), I:204–5
expansionist era magazines in (1825–50)
agricultural magazines, I:444*n;* II:88*n*

Richmond, Va.—*Continued*
literary magazine, I:629–57
magazine center, I:380, 382
religious periodicals, II:64, 68*n*
Civil War era magazines in (1850–65)
agricultural magazine, II:88*n*
comic magazine, II:112
literary magazines, I:629*n;* II: 112–13
medical journal, II:87
religious periodicals, II:64, 68, 88*n*
post-Civil War magazines in (1865–85)
agricultural magazines, II:88*n;* III:154
comic magazine, III:269*n*
"Copperhead" magazine, II:545
education magazine, III:168*n*
general magazines, III:46–47
historical journal, III:261–62
legal journal, III:145*n*
medical journals, III:140*n*
religious magazines, II:64*n,* 68*n;* III:74
spiritualist magazine, III:82*n*
Gilded Age magazines in (1885–1905)
education periodicals, III:168*n;* IV:270*n*
family periodicals, IV:92
historical periodical, IV:139
legal journal, III:145*n*
medical journals, III:140*n;* IV:313*n*
religious periodicals, II:64*n,* 68*n*
modern magazines in (1905–)
agricultural magazine, II:88*n*
family periodical, IV:92
historical periodical, IV:139
insurance periodical, III:146*n*
medical journals, III:140*n;* IV:313*n*
religious periodical, II:64*n*
anti-abolitionist activities in, I:461
in Civil War, II:112–13, 155
theater in, I:169
Richmond Christian Advocate, I:382, 801; II:68*n*
Richmond Eclectic, III:46
Richmond Examiner, III:537
Richmond and Louisville Medical Journal, III:141*n*
Richmond Medical Journal, III:140*n*
Richter, Francis C., IV:374
Richter, Henry, IV:567
Richter, Jean Paul Friedrich, I:401; II:164
Riddel, Samuel Hopkins, I:491*n*
Ridder, Herman, IV:298
Rideing, William Henry, II:254, 262*n,* 270, 272; III:550
Rideout, E. G., IV:418
Rideout's Monthly Magazine, III:36
Rider, Fremont, III:519
Rider, Sidney, III:234
Rider-Taylor, Henry, IV:665*n,* 669
Ridge, W. Pett, IV:196
Ridgeway, James, V:191*n*
Ridgewood, New Jersey, amateur periodical in, IV:390*n*
Ridgway, Erman J., III:487, 488
Ridgway, Erman Jesse, IV:47; V:72*n,* 74–75, 78–87
Ridgway Publishing Company, V:82
Ridgway's Weekly, V:81–82
Riding, Laura, V:241
Ridley's Fashion Magazine, III:98*n*
Ridpath, John Clark, III:546; IV:164, 401*n,* 412
Rifle, IV:381*n*
Riggs, Arthur Stanley, IV:629
Riggs, James A., V:36*n,* 48*n*
Riis, Jacob Augustus, II:512; III:430, 432, 486; IV:662, 721, 744
Riley, James Whitcomb, II:377, 400; III:54, 508; IV:61, 95, 456, 544, 561, 765; V:73
Riley, Woodbridge, V:5
"Rime of the Ancient Mariner" (Coleridge), V:122
Rinehart, Mary Roberts, III:401, 487; IV:421, 471, 552, 584, 604, 605, 616, 693, 695, 697, 700, 771; V:83, 134, 254
Rinehart, Stanley Marshall, Jr., IV:440, 696
Ripley, George, I:289–90, 366, 687, 690, 703, 704–7, 764; II:163–64, 239, 373*n,* 425, 426; IV:787
Ripley, William Zebrina, II:514
Risk, T. F., II:116*n*
Ristori, Adelaide, III:205
Ritchie, Albert Cabell, II:260; IV:707
Ritchie, Alexander Hay, II:444
Ritchie, Mrs. Anna Cora, II:360
Rittenhouse, David, I:90, 201
Rittenhouse, Jessie Belle, IV:440; V:113
Rivers, William James, II:491
Riverside Bulletin, III:360
Riverside Magazine for Young People, III:176, 191, 458
Rives, Amélie, II:398*n;* III:400, 550; IV:50, 123, 465, 497, 754
Rivington, James, I:27
Roadmaster and Foreman, IV:333*n*
Roads, I:16, 120
Robb, Arthur T., V:59*n,* 70

Robbins, J. J., I:451*n*
Robert Elsmere (Mrs. Ward), IV:110, 141, 280–81
Robert Merry's Museum, I:713*n*
Roberts, Charles George Douglas, III:400*n*, 483; IV:46*n*, 71*n*, 421, 450, 612, 637, 689; V:80, 251
Roberts, Edward P., I:154*n*
Roberts, George, I:361, 507*n*; II:45
Roberts, Harold C., II:93*n*
Roberts, Kenneth Lewis, IV:696, 709
Roberts, Michael, V:237
Roberts, Morley, IV:49*n*, 737
Roberts, Theodore, IV:616
Roberts, Willa, IV:763*n*, 770
Roberts, William, II:449
Robertson, Morgan, IV:116*n*, 685, 689, 692, 767
Robertson, Nugent, IV:78
Robertson, Thomas William, III:204
Robey, John, IV:63*n*
Robie, Virginia, V:154*n*, 159
Robins, Elizabeth, II:511*n*
Robinson, Boardman, IV:456
Robinson, Charles Mulford, IV:744
Robinson, Corinne Roosevelt, IV:727
Robinson, David Moore, III:535*n*
Robinson, Doane, IV:96
Robinson, E. H., III:144*n*
Robinson, Edward, I:739
Robinson, Edwin Arlington, III:543; IV:125, 434, 654, 724, 735; V:210, 228–29, 336
Robinson, Ezekiel Gilman, I:666*n*, 668
Robinson, Geroid Tanquary, V:88*n*, 90, 97
Robinson, H. D., I:536*n*
Robinson, Harriet Jane Hanson, II:471*n*
Robinson, Harry Perry, IV:218
Robinson, J. H., II:37, 38, 410
Robinson, James Harvey, II:404; III:351; IV:138, 180, 193; V:204, 338
Robinson, Nugent, IV:85, 453*n*, 454
Robinson, Ralph D., II:325*n*, 336
Robinson, Solon, I:729, 730; III:28, 151
Robinson, Therese A. L. von J., II:238
Robinson, Walter C., IV:757, 758
Robinson's Epitome of Literature, III:455–56
Rochacker, J. H., III:269*n*
Roche, Arthur Somers, IV:421, 469, 471, 477, 503, 584
Roche, James Jeffrey, IV:297
Rochester, Minn., III:169*n*
Rochester, N.Y., I:443, 458
 agricultural and gardening magazines, II:88*n*, 89; III:152, 153, 162; IV:343*n*
 insurance periodicals, III:146*n*; IV:351*n*
 other periodicals, III:69*n*, 132; IV:143*n*, 221*n*, 269*n*, 304*n*, 480*n*
"Rochester Knockings," I:472
Rock, Joseph Francis Charles, IV:630
Rock Island, Illinois, IV:295*n*
Rock Products, IV:325*n*
Rock-collecting magazines, IV:391
Rockafellow, Ralph, V:117*n*
Rockefeller, John Davison, IV:208, 448, 489, 495, 644, 689, 748, 767, 777–78
Rockford, Ill., IV:188*n*
Rockville, R.I., III:111
Rockwell, Norman, IV:698
Rocky Mountain Christian Advocate, III:71*n*; IV:291*n*
Rocky Mountain Druggist, IV:318*n*
Rocky Mountain Husbandman, III:158
Rocky Mountain Magazine, IV:108
Rocky Mountain Medical Journal, IV:314*n*
Rocky Mountain Presbyterian, III:75*n*
Rod, Edouard, IV:73
Rod and Gun and American Sportsman, III:210*n*
Rode, Charles R., II:159; III:492
Roderick, S. V., V:72*n*, 86
Roderick, Virginia, III:94*n*
Rodker, John, V:166*n*
Rodolf, Charles Clark, IV:406
Roe, Edward Payson, II:66*n*; III:54, 76*n*, 99, 223, 224, 248, 426, 502, 550, 558; IV:131, 293, 481, 513
Roentgen rays, IV:592
Rogers, Bruce, V:159
Rogers, Cameron, IV:787
Rogers, Edward H., III:299
Rogers, Lindsay, V:57
Rogers, Nathaniel Peabody, I:458
Rogers, Will, IV:566, 696, 716
Rogers, William Allen, II:481, 483, 484; III:185*n*; IV:561
Rogers and Fowle, I:25, 78, 78*n*
Rohmer, Sax, IV:465, 471, 477, 604
Rolfe, William James, III:110*n*, 237*n*, 455, 549, 550; IV:121
Roller Mill, III:128
Roller Monthly, IV:95
Roller-skating, III:220; IV:380, 634
Rolling Stone, IV:665–70
Rollins, Mabel, V:154*n*
Romains, Jules, III:543; V:166*n*
Roman, Anton, III:56, 402–6

Roman Catholic Church, *see* Catholicism; Catholic magazines; Catholic Total Abstinence Union
Romance, IV:114–15; V:86
Romanticism, I:339, 257
See also names of Romantic authors, composers, and artists
Rome, N.Y., III:216
Romer, John Irving, IV:246*n*
Roode, Albert de, III:296*n*
Rooney, John Jerome, IV:645
Roosevelt, Alice, IV:459, 754
Roosevelt, Eleanor, IV:503, 552–53, 586–87, 769
Roosevelt, Franklin Delano, III:153*n*, 353, 355; IV:474, 475, 503, 549, 576, 578, 660, 707, 726–27; V:20, 71, 216, 218–19, 318, 323, 333
Roosevelt, Kermit, IV:728
Roosevelt, Robert Barnwell, III:324
Roosevelt, Theodore, I:535; II:271, 401, 485, 511, 512, 513; III:296, 349, 470, 478, 503, 531, 546; IV:67, 72, 100, 169–70, 213, 235, 338, 339, 458, 462–63, 509, 615, 636, 655, 660, 705–6, 782; V:80, 84, 204–5, 342
as commentator on muckraking, IV:207, 209, 494–95, 778
as contributor, III:429–32; IV:44, 61, 75, 271, 483, 516, 546, 612, 626, 635, 662, 685, 722, 724–25, 727, 734–35, 767
quoted, IV:133, 236
Roosevelt, Theodore, Jr., II:260
Root, Elihu, IV:495
Root, George Frederick, II:197
Root, Louis Carroll, IV:163*n*
Root, O. T., II:79*n*
Ropes, John Codman, IV:230, 719
Rorer, Sarah Tyson, IV:363, 546
Rosary, IV:275, 298
Roscoe, Theodore, IV:422
Rose, Philip Sheridan, II:432*n*
Rose, Robert H., I:245
Rose, Stuart, IV:712
Rose, Will, IV:728
Rose of Sharon, II:57*n*
Roseboro, Viola, IV:595, 605
Rosecrans, E. J., III:129*n*
Rosen, Lew, IV:387*n*
Rosenberg, Adolphus, IV:86
Rosenberg, Charles, II:182
Rosenberg, Felix, IV:95
Rosenfield, Genie H., IV:64*n*
Rosenfield, Sydney, III:199, 520*n*, 521, 522
Rosenkranz, Karl, III:386
Rosenthal, Abe, IV:300
Ross, Albert, IV:124
Ross, Edward Alsworth, III:478; IV:191
Ross & Tousey, II:184
Rossetti, Christina, III:439; IV:131
Rossetti, Dante Gabriel, III:253
Rossetti, William Michael, II:503; III:277
Rossi, Ernesto, III:205
Rostand, Edmond, IV:256; V:148
Rostrum, IV:53
Roswell, Harold H., II:325*n*
Rotary clubs, V:268–69
Rothermel, Peter Frederick, I:521, 592
Rothwell, R. P., III:114*n*
Rough Notes, III:146*n*
Rough Rider, IV:117
Rough Rider Weekly, IV:120
Rouiller, C. A., III:109*n*
Round Table (Dallas), IV:94
Round Table (New York), II:21, 509; III:40–41, 184, 199, 233, 272, 281, 307, 309, 332
sketch of, III:319–24
Round's Printer's Cabinet, II:93
Rounseville, William R., I:389
Rourke, Constance, V:98
Rouse, E. S. S., II:51
Rousseau, Jean-Jacques, V:123
Routh, James, V:280
Rover, I:365, 806; II:449
Rowe, Gilbert T., II:66*n*
Rowe, Nicholas, II:543
Rowell, Chester Harvey, IV:107*n*
Rowell, George Presbrey, II:13; III:6, 7*n*, 12*n*, 38; IV:16, 246, 741
Rowing, III:222; IV:634, 636
Rowland, Henry Cottrell, IV:116*n*
Rowson, Mrs. Susanna, I:127*n*, 203, 250
Royal, Mrs. Ann, I:356
Royal American Magazine, I:35, 36, 48–49, 53, 62
founding of, I:26
sketch of, I:83–86
Royal Magazine, V:72
Royal Spiritual Magazine, I:26*n*, 788
Royal Templar, IV:210
Royall, Anne, II:40
Royce, Josiah, III:347, 386, 407, 507; IV:73, 225, 279, 295; V:179–80
Roycroft Quarterly, IV:72
Royer, John S., III:169
Roys-Gavit, E. M., IV:315
Rubber industry periodicals, IV:184
Rubin, Louis D., V:116
Rubinstein, Anton, III:193, 416

Rückert, Friedrich, II:164
Rudder, IV:373
Rudeness, magazine comment on, I:475
Rudyard, Charlotte, V:200
Ruffin, Edmond, II:345
Ruffner, Henry, I:642
Ruhl, Arthur, IV:464
Rukeyser, Muriel, V:243
Runkle, John D., II:79*n*
Runyon, Alfred Damon, IV:470, 472, 476
Rupp, William, II:380*n*
Ruppell, Louis, IV:453*n*, 477–79
Rural American, II:90*n*; IV:338
Rural Californian, III:158
Rural Carolinian, III:155
Rural Farmer, III:153
Rural Free Delivery, IV:20
Rural Magazine, I:790
Rural Magazine, or Vermont Repository, I:122*n*, 789
Rural Messenger, III:154
Rural New Yorker, II:89; III:152; IV:340
Rural Northwest, IV:341
Rural Repository, I:195
Rural Southland, III:155
Rural and Workman, III:155
Rural World, I:444
Rush, Benjamin, I:40, 49, 61–62, 90, 98, 102, 216
  as contributor, I:40, 49, 61–62, 63, 90, 98, 102, 216
Rush, James, I:609
Rush, Richard, I:123, 155, 244
Rush-Light, I:150, 791
Ruskin, John, III:182*n*; IV:130, 148, 646
Russell, Bertrand, II:404; III:479; IV:73, 520, 748, 761; V:211
Russell, Charles Edward, IV:492, 495, 496, 509; V:81, 149, 151*n*, 152–53, 288
Russell, Charles Taze, III:409
Russell, E. F., III:155
Russell, Elijah, I:31*n*
Russell, Ernest, IV:649*n*, 650
Russell, Ezekiel, I:26*n*, 29*n*
Russell, George William, IV:425
Russell, Irwin, III:463
Russell, J. T., I:316
Russell, Jacob, II:272
Russell, John (publisher of *Russell's Magazine*), II:488, 489
Russell, John B., I:317*n*, 318
Russell, Lillian, II:335; IV:259
Russell, Walter, IV:58*n*, 465
Russell, William, I:541–42; II:445
Russell, William Clark, IV:490
Russell's Magazine, II:33, 110, 138–39, 145, 172, 188, 423
  sketch of, II:488–92
Russia
  American interest in, IV:231–32
  magazines on, III:473
  Soviet, V:22, 93, 97, 99, 212–13
    prediction of U.S. war with, IV:478
Russian literature, III:255–56, 347, 357, 373; IV:135–36, 232; V:95–96, 119
Russian Revolution, III:351–52; IV:785; V:80, 85
Russo-Japanese War, IV:232, 780
Rust, George W., III:159
Rutgers College Quarterly, II:99
Rutgers Literary Miscellany, I:489, 806
Rutgers University, I:489; II:99
Rutherford, Rutledge, IV:363*n*
Rutland, Vt., III:269*n*
Rutland Times, III:269*n*
Rutledge, Archibald, V:284
Rutter's Political Quarterly, III:282
Ryan, Clendenin J., V:24–25, 26*n*
Ryan, Paddy, II:331–32
Ryan, Archbishop Patrick John, II:69; IV:72, 298
Ryan, Thomas Fortune, V:25
Ryckman, John W., IV:125
Ryder, Albert Pinkham, IV:144
Ryder, William Hering, IV:395*n*

Sabatini, Raphael, IV:498, 767; V:72, 82, 119
Sabbath Quarterly, III:85*n*
Sabbath School Visitor, III:8*n*
Sabbatarianism, II:34, 221, 252, 286–87; III:86–87
Sabin, Edwin Legrand, III:530; IV:96, 115*n*, 224, 618, 692
Sabin, Joseph, III:235
Sabine, Lorenzo, II:241
Sacco-Vanzetti case, II:514; III:353
Sack, A. J., IV:785
Sackville-West, Victoria, II:260
Sacramento, Cal., IV:314*n*
Sacred Circle, II:209
Sacred Heart Review, IV:298*n*
Sadd, H. S., I:548, 684, 744
"Safety" bicycle, popularity of, IV:377
Safety Maintenance, IV:351*n*
Safety Maintenance and Production, IV:322*n*
Safety razor advertising, IV:26
Sagebrush Philosophy, IV:387*n*
Sail and Paddle, III:211

Sailors' Aid, IV:194
Sailors' magazines, I:135; IV:104
St. Andrews' Cross, IV:294*n*
Saint-Gaudens, Augustus, III:182, 467
St. George's Journal, IV:227
St. John, John Pierce, III:427
St. John, Samuel, II:115*n*
St. Joseph, Mich., IV:188*n*
St. Joseph, Mo., III:141*n,* 312; IV:341, 345
St. Joseph Medical Herald, III:141*n*
St. Louis, Mo.
expansionist era magazines in (1825–50)
antislavery magazine, I:458
magazine center, I:389
Civil War era magazines in (1850–65)
agricultural magazines, II:88*n,* 89
industrial magazine, II:92
religious periodical, II:67
post-Civil War magazines in (1865–85)
agricultural magazines, II:88*n,* 89; III:157
communist periodicals, III:300
education periodicals, III:168–69
engineering periodical, III:114
historical journal, III:262*n*
home magazine, II:58
insurance periodicals, III:146*n*
journalists' periodical, III:274
legal journals, III:144
manufacturers' periodical, III:127, 127*n*
medical journals, II:85*n;* III:140, 141*n,* 142
music periodicals, III:198*n*
philosophical periodical, III:51, 89, 384–87
photography periodicals, III:186
railroad periodicals, III:126*n*
religious periodicals, III:69*n,* 71, 73*n,* 74*n,* 75*n,* 80
scientific periodical, III:112
secret-society periodical, III:315
spelling magazine, III:312
trade magazines, III:133–34, 136
women's rights magazines, III:95
Gilded Age magazines in (1885–1905)
agricultural periodicals, II:88*n,* 89; III:157
comic magazine, III:269*n*
communist periodical, III:300
construction periodical, III:130
education periodicals, III:168–69, IV:270
financial periodicals, IV:350*n*
hobby periodical, IV:391
horse-show periodical, IV:343
humorous periodical, IV:385
insurance periodical, III:146*n*
juvenile periodical, IV:275
legal periodicals, III:144, IV:346
literary magazines, IV:65–66, 72, 98, 100–1
lumber periodical, IV:325*n*
mail-order periodical, IV:367
marine periodical, IV:334
medical periodicals, III:140, 141*n,* 142; IV:313*n,* 314–15
music journals, III:198*n;* IV:251
philosophy periodical, IV:101
printers' periodicals, IV:248*n*
religious periodicals, III:69*n,* 74*n,* 75*n,* 80; IV:292, 295, 299–300
secret-society periodical, III:315
single-tax periodical, IV:179
socialist periodical, IV:175
spiritualist periodical, IV:414*n*
sports periodicals, IV:374, 381*n*
trade periodicals, III:133–34, 136; IV:186*n,* 187, 188, 189*n*
trade union periodical, IV:221*n*
urban weeklies, IV:77, 652–56
women's periodicals, IV:361, 363*n,* 367
modern magazines in (1905–), IV:652*n*
agricultural magazines, II:88*n,* 89, IV:338, 340
communist periodical, III:300
education periodical, III:168–69
financial periodical, IV:350*n*
hobby periodical, IV:350*n*
insurance periodical, III:146*n*
legal journals, III:144
lumber periodical, IV:325*n*
manufacturers' journal, IV:183
marine periodical, IV:334
medical journals, III:140, 142; IV:313*n,* 315
religious periodicals, III:69*n,* 75*n,* 80, IV:295
sports periodical, IV:374
trade periodicals, III:133–34, 136; IV:186*n,* 187, 189*n*
trade union periodical, IV:221*n*
urban weeklies, IV:100, 652–56
women's periodical, IV:361
growth of, III:50
economic, III:30
magazine comment on, III:50–51
muckraking articles on, IV:599
philosophy school in, III:385

St. Louis and Canadian Photographer, III:186
St. Louis Christian Advocate, II:68*n*
St. Louis Drug Market, III:133
St. Louis Druggist, III:134
St. Louis Exposition, *see* Louisiana Purchase Exposition
St. Louis Furniture News, IV:188*n*
St. Louis Grocer, III:135*n*
St. Louis Illustrated Magazine, IV:101
St. Louis Labor, IV:175
St. Louis Ladies' Magazine, III:95
St. Louis Life, IV:65, 100
St. Louis Lumberman, IV:95; IV:363*n*
St. Louis Magazine, III:95; IV:363*n*
St. Louis Medical and Surgical Journal, II:84*n*
St. Louis Mirror, IV:652*n*
  See also: Reedy's Mirror
St. Louis Post-Dispatch, V:304, 346
St. Louis Practical Photographer, III:186
St. Louis Sportsman and Amateur Athlete, IV:381*n*
St. Nicholas, II:269; III:99*n*, 175, 176, 188, 191, 508; IV:152, 229, 273; V:341
  sketch of, III:500–6
St. Paul, Minn., magazines in
  agricultural and gardening magazines, III:157, 158; IV:341, 344*n;* V:45
  educational, III:169
  free-silver, IV:163*n*
  general, III:55
  legal, IV:347–48
  medical, IV:314*n*
  pharmacy, IV:318*n*
  populist, IV:178
  poultry, IV:345*n*
  promotional, IV:96
  real estate, III:148
  religious, III:69*n*
  sports, IV:381
  stock-breeding, IV:344
  trade, IV:188*n*–89*n*
  women's club, IV:356*n*
St. Paul Farmer, III:158
St. Paul Medical Journal, IV:314*n*
St. Vincent de Paul Quarterly, IV:194
Saints' Herald, II:74; III:81; IV:296
Saintsbury, George Edward Bateman, IV:112, 124, 433
Sajous, Charles Euchariste de M., III:140*n*
"Saki" (Hector Hugh Munro), V:119
Sala, George Augustus, III:250
Salaries of editors
  early (1775), I:87
  nationalist era (1794–1825), I:198–99, 239, 272*n*, 279
  expansionist era (1825–50), I:512–13, 549*n*, 612, 627, 634, 635, 707, 725, 764
  in Civil War era (1850–65), II:24–25
  in post-Civil War era (1865–85), III:12, 332, 339, 405
  in Gilded Age (1885–1905), IV:35, 687; V:146
modern (1905–), III:431; IV:469, 497, 549, 768; V:302
Salem, Mass., II:176*n;* III:108, 109*n*, 259; IV:140
Salem, Ohio, I:458
Salem, Ore., II:67*n;* III:82, 158; IV:139, 270*n*
Salesmanship, IV:187*n*
Salina, Kan., IV:97
Salinger, Herman, V:273*n*
Salmagundi, I:171–72, 197; II:41
Salon of Dilettanti, IV:147*n*
Salt Lake City, Utah
  agricultural magazine, IV:339
  antipolygamy magazine, III:313
  education periodical, IV:272
  literary magazine, III:57
  mining periodical, IV:322*n*
  religious periodicals, III:71*n;* IV:297
  urban weeklies, IV:104
  See also Mormon periodicals
Salt Lake Mining Review, IV:322*n*
Salter, Sir Arthur, V:338*n*
Salter, William Mackintire, IV:279
Saltus, Edgar Evertson, III:400; IV:45, 49*n*, 84, 123, 501; V:28, 147, 247
Saltus, Francis Saltus, III:269*n;* IV:385, 685
Salvation, IV:300*n*
Salvation Army, IV:287–88
Salvini, Tommasso, III:205
Sam the Scaramouch, IV:387*n*
Sample Case, IV:186–87
Sampson, Lewis D., IV:115*n*
Sampson, William Thomas, III:475
Samuel Bowles and Company, V:126
Samuels, Arthur H., III:388*n*, 390; V:154*n*, 162
San Antonio, Tex., IV:298*n*, 390, 665*n*
San Diego, Cal., III:109
San Francisco, Cal.
  Civil War era magazines in (1850–65), II:116–17
    agricultural magazine, II:90

San Francisco, Cal.—*Continued*
home magazine, II:59
humor magazine, II:185*n*
magazine center, II:116–18
medical journal, II:84
police gazette, II:187
religious periodical, II:67*n*
sports magazine, II:204
technical journals, II:80
post-Civil War magazines in (1865–85)
agricultural magazines, II:90; III:158
anarchist periodical, III:302
comic magazines, III:265–66
drama periodical, III:199
education magazine, II:99*n*
financial periodical, III:147*n*
gardening magazine, III:162
grange magazine, III:149*n*
insurance periodical, III:146*n*
literary magazines, III:402–9
magazine center, III:56–57
medical journals, II:84
mining periodical, III:114
music periodical, III:198*n*
police gazette, II:187
printers' magazine, III:131
religious magazines, II:67*n*; III:74, 75*n*, 80–81
secret-society periodical, III:315
society weekly, III:101
sports periodicals, III:215
trade magazine, III:136
women's magazine, III:101
Gilded Age magazines in (1885–1905)
agricultural periodical, III:158; IV:342
Anglo-American periodical, IV:228
banking periodical, III:147
booksellers' magazine, IV:127
education periodical, IV:271*n*
electrical periodical, IV:322
financial periodicals, III:147*n*; IV:349*n*
hobby periodical, IV:391
home-finding periodical, IV:200
insurance periodicals, III:146*n*, IV:351*n*
Jewish periodical, IV:300
literary magazines, III:402*n*; IV:104–5, 126
manufacturing periodical, IV:186*n*
Masonic journal, IV:222*n*
medical journals, II:84; III:141*n*; IV:314
photography periodical, IV:150*n*
promotional magazines, IV:105–7
religious periodicals, II:67*n*; III:75*n*, 80–81, IV:287, 294
secret-society periodical, III:315
socialist periodicals, IV:175, 204
sports periodical, III:215
theater periodicals, IV:261
urban weeklies, IV:77, 105–7
women's club periodical, IV:356*n*
modern magazines in (1905–)
agricultural magazines, III:158, 159; IV:342
banking periodical, III:147*n*
education periodical, IV:277*n*
electrical periodical, IV:322
export magazine, IV:233
general magazine, IV:105–6
insurance periodicals, III:146*n*; IV:351*n*
literary magazine, III:402*n*
manufacturing periodical, IV:184*n*
marine periodical, IV:334
Masonic journal, IV:222
medical journals, II:84; III:141*n*
music periodical, IV:254*n*
photography periodical, IV:150*n*
religious periodicals, II:67*n*; III:81; IV:294
trade magazine, IV:254*n*
earthquake in (1906), IV:493–94
San Francisco Chronicle, II:198
San Francisco News-Letter, II:118*n*; III:56
San José, Cal., IV:175
San José Tribune, IV:175*n*
Sanborn, Edward H., III:127; IV:203
Sanborn, Edwin D., III:36*n*
Sanborn, Franklin Benjamin, II:99, 141, 535; III:36*n*, 313*n*, 439, 551; IV:73*n*, 80, 390*n*
Sanborn, Herbert Charles, V:102
Sanborn, Kate, III:368; IV:45*n*
Sancton, Thomas, IV:749*n*; V:218
Sand, George, I:404; II:162, 163–64, 240; III:254
Sandburg, Carl, IV:440, 607, 654; V:12, 96, 176, 228–29, 236, 244
Sanders, Alvin Howard, III:159; IV:344, 627
Sanders, Cora Francis, IV:367*n*
Sanders, George N., I:678*n*, 682
Sanders, James H., III:159
Sanderson, Albert, IV:175*n*
Sanderson, John, I:614
Sandow, Eugene, IV:316
Sandow's Magazine, IV:316
Sands, Robert C., I:128–29, 326, 334–35, 608
Sands, Samuel, I:154*n*

Sands, William, II:64*n*
Sands, William B., I:154*n*
Sandys Edwin William, IV:636
Sanford, Arthur B., I:299*n*
Sanford, David, I:134*n;* V:191*n*
Sanford, Winifred, V:12
Sanger, Joseph P., III:533
Sanger, Margaret, V:169
Sangster, Margaret Elizabeth, III:327, 388*n*, 390; IV:45, 360, 542, 768, 769; V:246*n*, 272
Saniel, Lucien, IV:174
Sanitarian, III:139
Sanitary Commission Bulletin, II:86
Sanitary Engineer, III:113*n*
Sanitary Era, IV:314*n*
Sanitary fairs, II:86–87
Sanitary and Heating Age, III:130*n*
Sanitary and Heating Engineering, III:130*n*
Sanitary Inspector, IV:316
Sanitary Plumber, III:130*n*
Sanitation, II:86–87
Santa Clara Valley, III:159
Santa Fe, N.M., IV:270*n*, 285*n*
Santayana, George, III:479, 543; IV:73*n*, 79*n*, 295; V:91–92, 196
Saphier, William, IV:438
Sapho, IV:257–58
Sappho, V:119
Sarcey, Francisque, IV:490
Sardou, Victorien, IV:122
Sarett, Lew, V:119, 237
Sarg, Tony, III:531
Sargent, Epes, I:232, 320*n*, 326, 352, 587*n*, 601, 608, 781; II:505*n*
Sargent, John Osborne, I:490, 599*n*, 601
Sargent, John Singer, IV:144–46
Sargent, Nathan, I:363
Sargent, Winthrop, II:163
Sargent's New Monthly Magazine, I:352, 806
Sarjent, Abel, I:31*n*
Saroni, Herman S., II:197
Saroni's Living Pictures, IV:153
Saroni's Musical Times, I:435, 809; II:197
Saroyan, William, IV:473, 729; V:321, 337
Sartain, John, I:309, 347, 421, 521, 550, 592, 675, 769–72; II:444; III:186
Sartain's Union Magazine, see: Union Magazine
Sartorial Art Journal, IV:187
Sartorial Art Review, III:134
Sartre, Jean-Paul, IV:761
Sassoon, Siegfried, II:260
"Satanic Press," I:361, 419
Satires and lampoons
  in early magazines (1741–94)
    political articles, I:51
    poetry, I:45
    on professional classes, I:58–59
  in nationalist era magazines (1794–1825), I:170–72, 233–34
    anticlerical, I:133
    fashions, I:140
  in expansionist era magazines (1825–50)
    literary topics, I:395
    phrenology, I:456
  in Civil War era magazines (1850–65)
    art, II:188
    customs, II:422, 426, 521–23
    drugs, II:528
    female boarding schools, II:46–47
    literature, II:527
    personalities, II:525
    politics, II:523–24
    puns, II:527–28
    quality, II:179
    war, II:524–26
    women's fashions, II:53–56
  in post-Civil War magazines (1865–85), III:268, 440–42
    literary magazines, III:365–67, 380–81
    politics, III:523–25, 527, 529
    women's suffrage, III:91–92
  in Gilded Age magazines (1885–1905), IV:639–46, 665–70
    illustrated periodicals, IV:562–63
    politics, III:531
    urban periodicals, IV:84
  in modern magazines (1905–), IV:646–48
    general magazines, V:4, 7, 28, 267
  See also Comic magazines; Humor magazines
Satirist, I:170, 794
Satterlee, Herbert Livingston, IV:560
Saturday Blade, IV:18, 67–68
Saturday Bulletin (Philadelphia), IV:67
Saturday Chronicle (Philadelphia), I:355, 803; IV:675
Saturday Courier, I:355
Saturday Evening Gazette, II:35, 121, 196, 198; III:42*n*, 199; IV:69*n*, 81
Saturday Evening Herald, III:101
Saturday Evening Herald (Chicago), IV:100
Saturday Evening Mail, II:37; IV:70

Saturday Evening Post, I:127, 213, 343, 352, 355, 546, 797; II:14, 36; III:11, 317, 553; IV:6, 16, 17, 18, 21, 29, 35, 59, 67, 87, 207, 464, 475, 501–2, 551, 574
  sketch of, IV:671–716
Saturday Gazette (Philadelphia), IV:678
Saturday Globe, IV:62, 85, 170
Saturday Journal, III:43
Saturday Magazine, I:130, 306–7
Saturday Morning Visitor, I:380*n*
Saturday News, I:582
Saturday News (Philadelphia), IV:677
Saturday Night, IV:87, 117
Saturday Night (Cincinnati), III:55
Saturday Night (Philadelphia), III:8*n,* 42
Saturday press, II:38–40
Saturday Press, II:38–40, 353; III:228
Saturday Review (Baltimore), IV:90*n*
Saturday Review (London), III:190*n,* 365
Saturday Review (New York, 1889–1891), IV:85
Saturday Review (Pittsburgh), IV:88
Saturday Review of Books (in *New York Times*), IV:8, 9, 126
Saturday Review of Literature, V:234–35, 327, 339
Saturday Standard, IV:47, 67
Saturday Visiter, I:380–81, 801
Saucy Stories, V:261
Sauveru, Albert, IV:183*n*
Savage, G. S. F., II:518*n,* 519
Savage, James, I:253*n,* 255*n,* 257
Savage, Minot Judson, IV:224, 276, 407
Savannah, Ga., I:700; III:141*n,* 197*n;* IV:254*n*
Savell, Morton, IV:569*n,* 578
Sawyer, Walter Leon, II:262*n,* 272
Saxe, John Godfrey, I:553, 609, 771; II:116, 180, 360; III:264, 374, 463
Saxe-Weimar, Grand Duke of, I:537
Saxon, Lyle, III:479
Saxton, C. M., II:90
Saxton, Eugene, IV:440
Sayer, Lydia, II:52
Scandals, III:448–50
  periodicals devoted to, II:187
  See also Crime magazines
Scandinavia
  American interest in, IV:231
  literature of, III:255, 540
Scandinavia, IV:231
Schaal, Albert A., V:138
Schabelitz, R. F., III:489
Schackleton, Ernest Henry, IV:623
Schade, Louis, IV:69*n*
Schaeffer, George C., II:297*n,* 298
Schaerf & Brother, II:116*n*
Schaff, Philip, II:380, 543; III:84*n*
Schell, F. Cresson, II:401, 464
Schelling, Friedrich Wilhelm Joseph von, III:386
Schemm, J. C., IV:751*n*
Schenck, Leopold, III:521
Schenectady, N.Y., IV:322
Schevitsch, Serge, IV:179
Schieren, Charles Adolph, IV:690
Schiller, Johann Christoph Friedrich von, I:191, 192; II:164
Schindler, Solomon, IV:202, 415
Schlegel, A. W. von, I:192
Schlegel, K. W. F. von, I:192
Schleicher, John A., II:452*n,* 464; III:554
Schlesinger, Arthur Meier, Jr., IV:738; V:218
Schlich, Paul J., IV:480–81
Schloss, Murray S., IV:116
Schmidt, Karl, III:520*n*
Schnabel, Dudley, V:184
Schneider, Otto J., III:531
Schnell, Harry J., II:92*n*
Schnitzler, Arthur, V:121, 258
Schoff, Stephen Alonzo, I:522
Schonfaber, J. G., IV:221*n*
School, IV:270
School and College, IV:268
School and Home, IV:275
School and Home Education, III:169*n*
School Arts Book, IV:272*n*
School Bulletin and New York State Educational Journal, III:168
School Economy, IV:272*n*
School Education, III:169*n*
School Executives' Magazine, III:169
School Journal, III:168; IV:269
School juvenile magazines, IV:275
School of Mines Quarterly, III:112, 115
School Music, IV:254*n*
School music periodicals, IV:254
School News and Practical Education, IV:271*n*
School Review, IV:268–69
School Science, IV:272*n*
School Visitor, III:169
School Weekly, IV:275
School World, IV:269*n*
Schoolcraft, Henry Rowe, I:609, 624; II:175*n*
Schoolday Magazine, II:101; III:169
Schoolmate, II:100
Schools, *see* Colleges and universities; Public schools
Schopenhauer, Arthur, III:386

Schramm, R. von Horrum, IV:354*n*
Schramm, Wilbur, IV:713
Schriener, Olive, IV:354, 485
Schroeder, Rilla, IV:749
Schroeder, Theodore, IV:405
Schuler, Loring Ashley, II:432*n;* IV:536*n*, 551–52
Schultz, Gladys Denny, V:44
Schultz, John H., II:297*n*, 299
Schumann-Heink, Ernestine, IV:546; V:297–98
Schurman, Jacob Gould, IV:10, 171, 268–69, 303
Schurz, Carl, II:271, 469*n*, 484, 503; III:296*n*, 342, 344; IV:60, 193
Schuyler, Eugene, III:465*n*, 472
Schuyler, George S., V:9
Schuyler, Montgomery, II:469*n*, 484
Schuyler, Robert Livingston, IV:80*n*, 138*n*
Schwab, Charles M., IV:776
Schwab, Fred, IV:752
Schwab, John Christopher, V:329*n*
Schwartz, Delmore, V:243
Schwarzmann, A., III:521, 522, 552
Science
  in early magazines (1741–94), I:61–62, 90–91
    agricultural periodicals, I:112
    general periodicals, I:39, 82
  in nationalist era magazines (1794–1825), II:151–52, 230, 233, 302–5, 311–12
    general magazines, I:219–20, 247, 297, 446–47
    "knowledge" magazines, I:363
    religion and, I:447, 611; II:314
    religious magazines, I:300, 563
    trends, I:124
    women's magazines, I:139
  in expansionist era magazines (1825–50), II:301, 446–50, 556–58, 566–68, 574
  in Civil War era magazines (1850–65)
    conflict with religion, II:68, 78–79, 314
    general magazines, II:222, 243, 384
    literary magazines, II:534
  in post-Civil War magazines
    Chautauqua periodicals, III:545
    general magazines, II:107–9, 248, 253, 395
    illustrated magazines, III:376, 460, 465
    literary magazines, III:398, 418
    morality and, III:305–6
    popular interest, III:104–7
    review-type magazines, III:337
  in Gilded Age magazines (1885–1905)
    Chautauqua magazines, II:401
    eclectic periodicals, IV:592
    geographic periodicals, IV:621
    literary magazines, II:401
    popular interest, IV:306
    religion and, IV:396
  in modern magazines (1905–), IV:785; V:134
    general magazines, IV:713; V:6
    literary magazines, II:402, 513
  lecturers on, III:250
Science, III:108, 317, 498; IV:307–8
Science and Industry, IV:320*n*
Science fiction, IV:489–90
Science News, III:109*n*
Scientific American, I:446, 808; II:80; III:107, 108, 115, 117, 121, 211, 499; IV:306–7, 320
  sketch of, II:316–24
Scientific American Building Monthly, II:321; IV:324
Scientific American Monthly, II:323
Scientific American Supplement, II:321; III:117
Scientific books, growing number of, III:105
Scientific Commercial, III:109*n*
Scientific Machinist, III:116
Scientific Methods, IV:303
Scientific Monthly, III:109, 499
Scientific News, III:110
Scientific Observer, III:109n
Scientific periodicals
  in nationalist era (1794–1825), I:151–52
    editing, I:198
    general, I:293, 302–5, 313
  in expansionist era (1825–50), I:524
  in Civil War era (1850–65)
    conflict with religion, II:78–79
    trends, II:78–79
  in post-Civil War era (1865–85)
    circulation, II:322
    general science magazines, III:34*n*, 107–9
    number, III:104
    popular science magazine, III:494–98
  in Gilded Age (1885–1905)
    circulation, II:322, 498; IV:308*n*
    general periodicals, IV:306–8
    popular science magazine, 498
  modern (1905–), IV:309*n*
    popular science magazine, III:498–99
  See also Natural history; *and specific sciences*

Scientific Record, III:109*n*
Scientific Tracts, I:489
Scoggins, Charles Elbert, IV:696, 709
Scoles, Isaac, I:37, 115
Scollard, Clinton, III:54, 407; IV:45*n*, 66, 120, 436, 612, 634, 690, 737, 768; V:248
Scopes trial, IV:785
Score, III:197*n*
Scott, Evelyn, IV:729; V:337
Scott, Frank Hall, III:475, 477; IV:15
Scott, Henry, E., II:176*n*
Scott, John W., I:127*n*, 137, 697
Scott, Julian, II:477
Scott, Leonard, IV:228
Scott, Leroy, V:80
Scott, Michael, II:406
Scott, Robert F., V:84
Scott, Tom, V:244
Scott, Sir Walter, I:178, 231, 280, 323–24, 398, 415, 417; II:230
Scott, W. J., III:45*n*
Scott's Monthly, III:45–46
Scottish-American Journal, II:128
Scottish-American periodicals, II:128; IV:227
Scottish Review, IV:228
Scourge (Baltimore), I:170, 794
Scourge (Boston), I:170, 794
Scourge of Aristocracy, I:791
Scoville, Joseph A., I:426; II:179, 183
Scoville, Samuel, Jr., III:504
Scranton, Pa., IV:320*n*
Scrap Book, IV:617*n*
Scribner, Charles, III:457–58, 467–68
Scribner's, V:30, 118, 341–42
Scribner's Commentator, IV:717*n*, 731–32
Scribner's Magazine, III:468; IV:4, 9, 14, 15, 17, 19, 21, 35, 229, 331
sketch of, IV:717–32
Scribner's Monthly, see: Century Illustrated Monthly Magazine
Scripp, Charles, I:389*n*
Scripps-Howard, V:56
Scripps-McRae Press Association, V:59
Scriptural Interpreter, I:288*n*, 801
Scroggs, William Oscar, III:434
Scudder, Horace Elisha, II:71, 493*n*, 501, 511, 512; III:176, 502
Scudder, M. L., IV:61
Scudder, (Miss) Preston, II:511*n*
Scudder, Samuel Hubbard, III:108; IV:307
Scudder, Vida Dutton, IV:281, 398, 746; V:338
Sculpture, I:303; II:189; IV:145
Scurrilous literature, I:27–28, 159–60, 329, 426; II:60
Sea Breeze, IV:194
Seaboard, IV:333–34
Seabury, Samuel, II:69
Seals, John H., III:46*n*; IV:92
Seamens' aid periodicals, IV:194
Search-Light, IV:64
Searcher, IV:64
Searing, Laura Catherine Redding ("Howard Glyndon"), III:229, 374, 416
Sears, Barnas, I:666–67, 740
Sears, E. G., I:666*n*, 667
Sears, Edmund Hamilton, II:72*n*
Sears, Edward I., II:28, 165, 530ff; III:24, 31, 281
Sears, Henry, II:396
Sears, Joseph H., V:29
Sears, Robert, I:364
Sears' Pictorial, I:523
"Sears' Review," *see: National Quarterly Review*
Seaside Library, III:256
Season, III:98*n*
Seattle, Wash., magazines in
advertising journal, IV:247*n*
dairy, IV:344*n*
educational, V:271*n*
financial, IV:349*n*
fishing, IV:186*n*
lumber, IV:325*n*
marine, IV:334
medical, IV:315*n*
poultry, IV:345*n*
promotional, IV:108
trade, IV:186*n*, 187*n*, 325*n*
urban, IV:108
Seaver, Horace, II:78, III:88
Seaver, William A., II:396, 399
Seavers, Fanny P., III:176
Seawell, Molly Elliot, III:483
Secession, *see* Confederate States of America
Second Adventist magazines, III:81
Secret Service, IV:119
Secret societies, II:214–15; III:314–15; IV:221–22
Seddon, T., I:94
Sedgwick, Anne Douglas, IV:521
Sedgwick, Arthur George, II:507*n*, 509; III:144, 281, 336, 347
Sedgwick, Catherine, I:408, 409, 585, 680, 743, 770
Sedgwick, Ellery, I:747*n*, 749; II:262*n*, 272, 274, 493*n*, 513–14; III:510*n*, 512; V:27*n*, 30, 154, 159–62

Sedgwick, Henry Dwight, IV:781
Sedgwick, Theodore, II:389, 469*n*, 470
Sedley, Henry, III:319*n*, 323–24
See, Richard H., II:37
Seeger, Alan, II:256
Seeley, Howard, III:270*n*
Seely, Howard, II:310
Seely, Walter Hoff, V:291
Seely-Brown, Horace, Jr., V:317
Seen and Heard by Megargee, IV:390*n*
Seer, II:74
Seghers, Charles John, III:69*n*
Segonzac, André, V:178
Segregation, school, V:285
Seignobos, Charles, IV:225
Selassie, Haile, V:323*n*
Seldes, George, IV:730
Seldes, Gilbert, III:542, 543; IV:730, 731; V:211
Select Journal of Foreign Periodical Literature, I:397, 615–17
Select Reviews, I:130, 279–80
Self Culture (Chicago), IV:54–55
Self Culture (St. Louis), IV:54*n*
Self-Instructor and Journal of the Universal Lyceum, I:489, 806
Seligman, DeWitt, IV:60
Seligman, Edward Robert Anderson, IV:180, 494, 746; V:330
Sell, Henry Blackman, III:388*n*, 390
Sellersville, Pa., IV:345*n*
Sellew, Edwin P., I:562*n*, 565
Sellin, Thorstein, IV:193*n*
Sembrich, Marcella, II:271
Semiannuals, I:124, 331
Semimonthlies, number of, I:342*n*
Seminary Magazine, III:47
Semi-Tropic California, III:158
Senate
  direct election to, IV:462
  See also Congress
Seneca Falls, N.Y., II:50–51
Senn, Nicholas, IV:527
Senner, Joseph Henry, IV:239
Sensational magazines, II:185–87, 325–37; III:43–45
Sentimental and Literary Magazine, see: New York Weekly Magazine
Sentimentality
  in magazines to about 1850, I:42–44, 57, 103, 323, 349, 351, 500, 587–88, 628, 641, 770
  in later magazines, II:192, 394–95, 418, 490; III:226–29, 231, 239, 373
  in chromolithographs, IV:18
  in novels, I:415
Sentinel (Washington), IV:69*n*
Sentinel of the Blessed Sacrament, IV:298*n*
Sergel, Roger L., V:179*n*, 180
Serial fiction
  in nationalist era magazines (1794–1825), novels, I:122, 174, 219, 307, 312
  in expansionist era magazines (1825–50)
    general magazines, I:547, 764; IV:675
    juvenile magazines, I:714; II:265
    literary magazines, IV:675
    mammoth papers, I:359
    novels, I:360; II:352
  in Civil War era magazines (1850–65), II:172, 265, 268, 273, 304, 308, 309, 393, 404, 406, 439, 450, 462
    eclectic magazines, II:490; IV:679
    family magazines, II:416, 471
    illustrated weeklies, II:410, 453, 462
    literary magazines, II:384–86, 393, 406, 424, 495; IV:679–80
    military magazines, II:551
    women's magazines, II:439–40
  in post-Civil War magazines (1865–85), III:54, 420
    family magazines, III:476–77; III:423
    general magazines, III:357–58, 460–61, 471, 511, 558
    illustrated weeklies, II:463
    juvenile magazines, III:501–2, 509
    literary magazines, II:398, 508–9; III:40, 223–25, 369, 371–72, 377, 397
    military magazines, III:533
    religious magazines, III:439
    women's magazines, III:389–90
  in Gilded Age magazines (1885–1905)
    booksellers' periodicals, IV:435–36
    family magazines, IV:481, 490
    general periodicals, IV:454, 591–92, 609, 614, 616, 681, 689–91, 719–20, 723
    illustrated periodicals, IV:58*n*, 454
    juvenile magazines, III:502–3
    literary magazines, IV:681, 689
    novels, II:257
    outdoor magazines, IV:636
    women's periodicals, IV:537, 543, 765
  in modern magazines (1905–)
    family periodicals, IV:497, 502–4; V:133–34

Serial fiction—*Continued*
general magazines, IV:601–2, 604, 606, 694–97, 700–1, 709; V:22, 80, 86
illustrated periodicals, IV:465, 471, 473
literary magazines, II:402; IV:501
women's magazines, III:487, 489; IV:546, 552–54, 583–85, 769; V:22, 80, 86
Serial nonfiction, II:534; III:472, 479; IV:439, 490, 554, 602, 606, 612, 616, 713, 721; V:72, 75–78, 80–81, 84, 131
Sermon, IV:304*n*
Sermons, I:252–53, 262; III:426
Sessions, Archibald, IV:49*n*
Set, Alan, V:25
Seth, James, IV:303*n*
Seton, Ernest Thompson, IV:224, 721, 724, 725
Settlement-house magazines, IV:195, 196*n*
Settlement Journal, IV:195*n*
Setzler, Frank Maryl, IV:629
Seven Arts, V:90
Severance, Mary Harriman, IV:96
Sewall, Alfred L., III:175
Sewall, Samuel E., II:280
Sewall, Thomas, I:642
Sewanee, Tenn., IV:734
Sewanee Review, IV:73
sketch of, IV:733–38
Seward, William Henry, II:532, 541
Sewell, Anna, III:248
Sewall, Elizabeth, II:57
Sewing, *see* Patterns for sewing
Sewing Machine Advance, IV:184*n*
Sewing Machine Advocate, III:117
Sewing Machine Journal, III:117
Sewing Machine News, III:117
Sewing machine periodicals, III:117; IV:184*n*
Sewing Machine Times, IV:184*n*
Sex
in advertising, IV:32
education in, IV:547
freedom in, III:305
press discussions of, IV:405, 440–45; V:24
sex magazines, III:43–44; IV:611
sketch of *National Police Gazette,* II:324–37
See also Girl covers; Police gazettes
Seymour, Charles, II:181
Seymour, Henry James, III:262*n*
Seymour, Horatio, II:413, 545
Seymour, Mary F., IV:354
Seymour, Ralph Fletcher, V:228
Shafer, Robert, IV:441
Shafter, William Rufus, III:475
Shairp, John Campbell, I:534
Shaker, III:81
Shaker magazines, III:81
Shaker and Shakeress, III:81
Shakespeare, William, I:178; III:330, 368, 430, 433, 548; IV:121, 131–32, 256
Shakespeare Magazine, IV:125
Shakesperiana, III:237
Shale, James B., IV:244; V:59–63
Shaler, Nathaniel Southgate, II:511*n;* III:347, 456, 507, 549; IV:73*n,* 212, 225, 234, 398, 722
Shallus, Francis, I:106
Shanghai, II:185*n*
Shanly, Charles Dawson, II:39, 184, 520*n,* 527, 528; III:265, 266, 322, 374, 411, 421, 440
Shannon, W. P., IV:751*n*
Shapiro, Karl, V:225*n,* 236, 243
Sharon, Mass., IV:390
Sharp, Dallas Lore, II:262*n,* 273; IV:776; V:158, 338
Sharp, Margery, IV:473, 554, 709
Sharp, William ("Fiona MacLeod"), IV:425, 451
Shattuc, W. B., II:114*n*
Shattuck, George B., III:139
Shaw, Adele Marie, IV:776, 781
Shaw, Albert, IV:35, 52, 161, 172, 180, 197, 236, 264, 434, 569*n,* 578, 657*n,* 659–64, 775; V:117*n,* 118, 122–23
Shaw, Albert, Jr., IV:569*n,* 578, 657*n,* 663
Shaw, Anna, IV:181
Shaw, Arch Wilkinson, IV:352
Shaw, Charles Emory, IV:385
Shaw, Francis G., I:764
Shaw, George Bernard, IV:501, 503, 584, 642, 643; V:50, 84–5
Shaw, Henry Wheeler ("Josh Billings"), II:37, 40; III:248, 264
Shaw, Howard, V:158
Shaw, John, I:245
Shaw, Lemuel, I:164; II:228
Shaw, Roger, IV:578, 663
Shaw, Wilfred Byron, IV:75*n*
Shaw, William Smith, I:253*n,* 255
Shay (Edward) Felix, IV:630, 648
Shays' Rebellion, I:50, 93

"She" (Haggard), V:119
Shea, John Dawson Gilmary, II:175; III:69*n*, 330, 511
Shears, IV:184*n*
Sheboygan Falls, Wis., IV:186*n*
Shedd, William Greenough Thayer, I:531, 740; II:517
Sheean, Vincent, V:57
Shehan, Henry I:747*n*, 749
Shekinah, II:209
Shelbyville, Ky., I:164
Sheldon, Alexander E., III:362
Sheldon, Arthur Frederick, IV:187*n*
Sheldon, Charles Monroe, IV:110, 281, 293
Sheldon, Electra, II:58
Sheldon, Frederick, III:93,
Sheldon's Business Philosopher, IV:187*n*
Shell-collectors' magazines, IV:391
Shelley, Percy Bysshe, V:91
Shelton, William Henry, IV:151
Shepard, Thomas W., I:317
Shephard, P. W., IV:88*n*
Shepherd, Forrest, II:115*n*
Shepherd, William Gunn, IV:465, 470, 472; V:85
Shepherd of the Valley, II:77
Shepherd's Criterion, IV:344
Shepherdson, Francis W., IV:264
Sheppard, William L., III:359, 441
Sherard, Robert, IV:434, 591
Sheridan, Philip Henry, IV:44*n*
Sherin, George A., V:145–46
Sherlock, Chesla, III:500*n*, 505; V:36*n*, 37, 42
Sherman, Frank Dempster, IV:560, 612, 634, 766
Sherman, John, IV:448
Sherman, Lucius Adelno, IV:121
Sherman, Richard, IV:472
Sherman, Stuart Pratt, III:349; IV:439; V:117*n*, 119, 268
Sherman, William Tecumseh, II:548; IV:44*n*
Sherman antitrust law, V:203
Sherrill, Charles Hitchcock, IV:520, 663
Sherrod, Robert Lee, IV:712
Sherwin, Lewis, V:266
Sherwood, James Manning, I:529*n*, 740; II:517; III:32*n*
Sherwood, Mary Elizabeth Wilson, III:420
Sherwood, Robert Emmet, IV:439, 478, 556*n*, 567; V:121
Sherwood, Sidney, IV:182*n*
Shields, G. O., IV:381
Shields, Mrs. S. A. (S. Annie Frost), I:580*n*, 592
Shillaber, Benjamin Penhallow, II:35, 180, 181*n*
Shinn, Charles Howard, III:56*n*, 402*n*, 407; IV:107
Shinn, Earl, III:336
Shinn, Everett, III:489
Shinn, Milicent Washburn, III:56*n*, 402*n*, 407
Shipman, George E, II:85*n*
Shipman, Louis Evan, IV:556*n*, 566
Shippen, Joseph, I:81
Shippey, Henry Lee, IV:464–65
Shipping periodicals, IV:333–34
Shiras, George, IV:628
Shirlaw, Walter, II:477
Shirley, Dana, II:117
Shober, Charles Ernest, IV:93
Shoe and Leather Gazette, III:127*n*
Shoe and Leather Reporter, II:93; IV:185
Shoe and Leather Review, III:127*n*
Shoe periodicals, III:127; IV:185, 189*n*
Shoe Retailer, IV:189*n*
Shoe Trade Journal, IV:189*n*
Shonts, Theodore Perry, IV:626
Shorey, John L., III:176
Shorey, Paul, III:537, 540; IV:53*n*, 520
Short, Charles, III:536
Short, Charles Wilkins, I:439
Short, Luke, IV:422
Short stories
- in early magazines (1741–94)
  - general magazines, I:96–97
  - literary magazines, I:103
  - trends, I:42–44
- in nationalist era magazines (1794–1825), I:219–21
  - general magazines, I:237, 249
  - literary magazines, I:173–74, 334
- in expansionist era magazines (1825–50), I:561, 596
  - college magazines, I:535
  - critical evaluation, I:412, 419–20
  - general magazines, I:577, 596
  - juvenile magazines, I:714
  - literary magazines, I:355, 602, 611, 634–35, 641, 643–44, 650–51, 674–75, 679–80, 736–37
  - men's magazines, I:674
  - trends, I:344
  - women's magazines, I:547, 549–50, 587–88, 627; II:308–9, 437
- in Civil War era magazines (1850–65), II:343, 398, 401, 404
  - eclectic magazines, II:490

Short stories—*Continued*
family magazines, II:360, 416–17
illustrated weeklies, II:462
literary magazines, II:384, 387–88, 393–95, 429, 495
popularity, II:173
in post-Civil War magazines (1865–85), III:54
comic magazines, III:523
eclectic magazines, III:420–21, 461–62, 471–72, 511–12
family magazines, II:359, 471
juvenile magazines, II:269; III:501–2
literary magazines, II:398, 420, 507–8; III:225–28, 372–73, 397, 403–5, 408, 416, 420
popular authors, III:243–44
story-papers, III:42–43
in Gilded Age magazines (1885–1905)
all-fiction magazines, IV:114–17, 425, 428–30
comic periodicals IV:566, 668
eclectic magazines, IV:507, 509, 592, 616, 673–74, 685, 689, 692
family magazines, II:482; IV:489, 493; V:126
illustrated periodicals, IV:456, 457, 566
juvenile magazines, III:502–4
later decline, IV:113–14
literary magazines, II:401; IV:425, 428–30, 673–74, 685, 689
outdoor magazines, IV:636
popularity, IV:113
satiric magazines, IV:668
"short short" stories, IV:472
urban periodicals, IV:84, 654
women's magazines, IV:537, 765, 767; V:126
in modern magazines (1905–), II:259, 405
booksellers' periodicals, IV:439
family magazines, IV:493, 497; V:133–34, 136
general magazines, IV:601–2, 604, 618, 695, 697, 701, 709, 713, 720–21, 729; V:5, 29–30, 74, 95, 148
illustrated periodicals, IV:471
juvenile magazine, III:504
literary magazines, V:119, 121, 123, 182–84
review periodicals, IV:518, 521
women's magazines, III:489; IV:583, 769, 772; V:133–34, 136
Short Stories, IV:114
Shorter, Clement K., III:550; IV:433
Shorthand, praise of, I:479
Shorthand Educator, III:170
Shorthand periodicals, II:212; III:169–70; IV:352
Shoup, Francis A., IV:735
Showalter, W. D., V:62
Showalter, William Joseph, IV:632
Showerman, Grant, IV:737; V:184
Shrader, Frederick F., III:199*n*
Shrady, George Frederick, III:140; IV:311, 313
Shreve, Thomas H., I:660, 662
Shreveport, La., III:137; IV:292*n*
Shroud, III:133
Shults, A. B., III:528
Shuman, Frederick L., V:58
Shurtleff, Nathaniel Bradstreet, II:175*n*
Shuster, William Morgan, III:457*n*, 478; IV:500
Shute, Nevil, IV:475, 554
Shuttleworth, Jack, III:552*n*, 556
Sibley Journal of Engineering, IV:321
Sibyl, II:52–53, 56, 135, 150
Siddall, John MacAlpine, III:510*n*, 513, 514, 515; IV:595, 600
Sidereal Messenger (Cincinnati), III:111*n*
Sidereal Messenger (Northfield, Minn.), III:110
Sidgwick, Ethel, V:168
Sidney, Margaret, III:177, 248, 509; IV:71*n*; V:126
Sienkiewicz, Henryk, IV:141
Sigel, Franz, IV:56
Sigma Delta Chi, V:70, 347
Sigmund, Jay G., V:184
Signal, I:360; III:310
Sigourney, Lydia Huntley, I:409, 412, 413; II:35, 116, 117, 170, 222, 265, 302, 308, 356, 410
as contributor, I:177, 347, 350, 353, 388, 499, 546, 578, 602, 623, 637, 651, 672, 679, 692, 734, 743, 745, 770
as editor, 580*n*, 584, 585, 626*n*, 627
Sill, Edward Rowland, I:488*n*; III:14*n*, 56*n*, 78, 374, 406, 407
Sillman, Benjamin, I:152, 255, 267, 302–5
Sillman, Benjamin, Jr., I:302*n*, 304; III:105, 261; IV:306
Siloam Springs, Ark., IV:215*n*
Silsbee, William, I:288*n*
Silver, John, III:269*n*
Silver issue, III:4, 294–95, 346, 525, 529; IV:160–63, 406, 516

Silver Knight, IV:163
Silverman, Sime, V:308
Silversmith, Julius, III:80
Silverton, Ore., IV:277
Silverware advertising, IV:24
Simmons, Edward Alfred, III:125*n;* IV:583
Simmons, George Henry, IV:524*n,* 527–30
Simmons, James Wright, I:382
Simmons-Boardman Company, II:300
Simms, William Gilmore, I:155, 376, 382, 408, 416, 461, 610, 637, 646, 649; III:32*n,* 46, 48, 238, 397
as contributor, I:499, 553, 585, 627, 640, 646, 650, 651, 679, 692, 723, 760, 767, 770
as editor, I:512, 664–65, 699*n,* 700, 721*n,* 725–26, 755–56
Simms's Magazine, see: Southern and Western Monthly Magazine and Review
Simon, Herman, IV:636
Simonds, Frank Herbert, IV:663, 783; V:211
Simons, Algie Martin, IV:175*n,* 176, 205*n*
Simpich, Frederick, Jr., IV:631, 632
Simpson, Edmund, I:168*n*
Simpson, Jerry, IV:178, 666
Simpson, Matthew, III:92
Simpson, Stephen, I:126, 293–94
Simpson, Wallis Warfield, V:323*n*
Simpson College, III:166
Simpsonian, III:166
Sims, Philip Hal, III:555
Sims, Adm. William S., II:515; IV:784; V:54
Sinclair, Angus, IV:333*n*
Sinclair, May, II:513; III:471; IV:49*n,* 466
Sinclair, Upton, III:514; IV:116*n,* 174, 421, 436, 440, 463, 493, 520, 578, 702, 778; V:18, 151*n,* 254
Sinclair, William, I:294
Sing Sing Bulletin, IV:199*n*
Singerly, Benjamin, III:215*n*
Single-Tax Courier, IV:179
Single-tax issue, III:4; IV:179–80, 406; V:93
Single-Tax Review, IV:179
Singmaster, Elsie, III:489; IV:439
Singmaster, J. A., II:73*n*
Sioux City, Iowa, III:158*n*
Sioux Falls, S.D., III:158*n;* IV:96
Sir Hopkins' Own Book, IV:386
"Sirius," arrival of, I:396
Sisson, Edgar Grant, IV:48*n,* 464, 492
Sister Carrie (Dreiser) V:147
Siviter, William Henry, III:270*n*
Size of magazines, *see* Format and size
Sjolander, John P., IV:94
Skelly, Robert, II:135
Sketch, IV:228*n*
Sketch Book, I:172, 796; IV:148*n*
Skiing articles, IV:634
Skilman, Thomas T., I:206
Skin disease journals, III:142*n*
Skinner, Frederick Gustavus, III:215
Skinner, John Stuart, I:153, 479
"Skinner, Mose," *see* Brown, James E.
Skinner, Richard Dana, II:260
Skyscrapers, comment on, IV: 197
Slang terms, sources of, IV:384–85
Slater, H. D., IV:650
Slauson, Harold Whiting, IV:638
Slavery debate
in early magazines (1741–94), I:89*n*
anti-slavery writings, 1:57–58, 102
in nationalist era magazines (1794–1825)
antislavery writings, I:138, 162–64, 300–301, 764
colonization views, I:310
proslavery writings, I:312, 781
in expansionist era magazines (1825–50), I:524, 589, 597, 611–13, 640–41, 764
antislavery writings, I:456–58, 563
constitutional issues, I:458–59
Mexican war and, I:455
middle-of-the-road, I:681, 756; II:255
persecution of abolitionist press, I:457–58, 460–61
proslavery writings, I:369, 458–62, 632, 634, 648–50, 664, 681, 683, 722–23, 725
religious periodicals, I:369, 373, 458, 532, 564, 659–60, 668, 773–74, 777
in Civil War magazines (1850–65), II:29, 108–9, 131–33, 137–42, 235, 275, 344, 345, 459, 489–90, 523, 524, 534
antislavery periodicals, II:140–42
antislavery writings, I:456–57, 773, 777, 794; II:67, 72*n,* 133, 140–42, 148, 207, 242, 245, 312, 314, 368, 500, 540–41
biblical arguments, I:613; II:138–39
colonization arguments, II:139

Slavery debate—*Continued*
Compromise of 1850, II:3
importance, III:131
proslavery arguments, II:138–40, 161, 242, 344–45, 489–90, 537
racial arguments, II:138
religious periodicals, II:67*n*, 368–72
Uncle Tom literature, II:142–44; *see also: Uncle Tom's Cabin*
war years, II:131
women and, II:48, 50
clergy and, II:314, 368
See also Abolitionist periodicals, Abolitionists; Freedmen
Sleeping cars, advent of, II:83
Slesinger, Tess, IV:729
Sloan, John, IV:451
Sloan, Oscar B., II:115
Sloanaker, William, I:770
Sloane, William Milligan, I:529*n*, 535; III:472; IV:230
Sloan's Garden City, II:115
Slosson, Anne Trumbell, II:398*n*
Slosson, Edwin Emery, II:378, 379; IV:53*n*, 472, 785
Slums, III:313; IV:10, 195–97, 404, 462
Small, Albion Woodbury, III:72*n*; IV:191–92
Small, F. O., II:401
Smalley, Eugene Virgil, III:55, 272, 273; IV:96
Smalley, George Washburn, IV:602
Smalley, P. J., IV:96
Smallpox epidemics, III:137
Smallpox inoculation, I:150
Smart Set, IV:98, 607; V:3–4, 7, 12, 183, 348
sketch of, V:246–72
Smedley, William Thomas, II:401, 483; II:509, 557; III:151, 545, 720
Smile, Samuel, V:286
Smiley, Charles Wesley, III:112
Smillie, James, I:548, 745
Smith, Alex R., IV:334
Smith, Alfred Emanuel, II:514; III:352, 422*n*, 434; IV:707; V:212, 318
Smith, Austin, IV:524*n*, 535
Smith, Benjamin Bosworth, I:138
Smith, Beverly, IV:712*n*
Smith, C. C., I:292*n*; III:507
Smith, Charles (editor of *Monthly Military Repository*), I:122
Smith, Charles Henry ("Bill Arp"), II:178, 186
Smith, Charlotte, III:95
Smith, Daniel B., I:539*n*
Smith, Mrs. E. V., II:243
Smith, Elias, I:137
Smith, Elihu Hubbard, I:115, 149, 215–16
Smith, Elizabeth Oakes, I:349, 366, 376, 505, 546, 585, 642, 644, 743; II:308, 406, 449, 450, 468; III:35*n*, 261
Smith, Francis Hopkinson, II:398*n*, 400; III:428, 485; IV:49*n*, 93, 154, 489, 546, 719, 721, 723; V:148
Smith, Francis S., II:38; IV:65
Smith, Frank P., IV:480
Smith, Gean, IV:636
Smith, George, IV:49*n*, 65
Smith, Gideon B., I:153*n*, 154*n*, 480
Smith, Goldwin, II:244, 253, 503; III:249; IV:602; V:28
Smith, H. Allen, IV:504
Smith, Mrs. H. M. F., III:52
Smith, Harrison, V:234
Smith, Mrs. Harrison, I:641
Smith, Harry Bach, III:268; IV:61
Smith, Harry James, II:493*n*
Smith, Helen Huntington, IV:771
Smith, Henry Boynton, I:529*n*, 533, 740; II:516–17
Smith, Henry Justin, IV:389
Smith, Henry M., II:85*n*
Smith, Henry Worthington, IV:351*n*
Smith, Hoke, IV:210
Smith, Huntington, III:102*n*; IV:81*n*
Smith, J. F., II:130, 357
Smith, James Walter, IV:125
Smith, Jerome van Crowninshield, I:489; II:84*n*
Smith, Jessie Wilcox, II:402; IV:456, 546, 602, 726, 767; V:136
Smith, John, I:106, 645
Smith, John Jay, I:307*n*
Smith, John Talbot, III:70; IV:298, 406
Smith, Joseph T., II:537*n*, 538
Smith, Judson, I:739*n*
Smith, Kingsbury, V:23
Smith, Mildred C., III:491*n*
Smith, Ormond Gerald, IV:49*n*, 65
Smith, Paul Clifford, IV:453*n*, 479, 763*n*, 771
Smith, Rebecca, I:295
Smith, Richard Penn, I:378, 587*n*
Smith, Robert, 3rd., I:562–64
Smith, Robert Pearsall, II:90*n*
Smith, Robert S., V:273*n*
Smith, Roswell, III:457–58, 467–68, 475, 500
Smith, Samuel Francis, I:499, 666*n*, 667
Smith, Samuel Harrison, I:122*n*, 160
Smith, Sarah Louisa Hickman, I:412

Smith, Sarah Towne, II:211*n*
Smith, Seba, I:365–66, 376, 675; II:32, 448–51
Smith, Sidney Goodsir, V:244
Smith, Mrs. Sydney, IV:94*n*
Smith, Thomas, II:69
Smith, Mrs. Thomas K., IV:57
Smith, Thomas R., III:457*n*
Smith, Tom Wash., IV:90
Smith, W. Granville, IV:84
Smith, W. Hazleton, IV:270
Smith, William, I:25, 80
Smith, William A. J., II:112*n*
Smith, William B., III:45
Smith, William Henry, III:541
Smith and Barrow's Monthly, II:112*n*
Smith's Magazine, III:486; V:146–47
Smithville, N.J., I:445
Smithwick, John G., II:401; III:188
Smoking, I:165, 474–75; II:53, 212–13; III:311
Smoot, Reed, IV:520
Smyth, Albert Henry, III:553
Smyth, Egbert Coffin, IV:395–400
Smyth, Joseph Hilton, IV:732; V:56
Smyth, Thomas H., II:155
Smythe, Andrew E., IV:671*n*, 680, 684
Smythe, William Ellsworth, IV:104
Snappy Stories, V:261
Snaps, IV:385
Sneed, A. C., IV:736
Snelling, William Joseph, I:601
Snider, Denton Jaques, III:51, 385, 386
Snively, John H., II:92*n*
Snodgrass, J. E., I:381*n*
Snodgrass, Rhey T., IV:69*n*
Snow, Carmel, III:388*n*, 390
Snow, Edgar, IV:709, 712, 713
Snow, George K., II:181
Snow, R. A., II:85*n*
Snowden, Isaac Clarkson, I:343
Snowden, William W., I:352, 626–28; II:301
Snyder, Charles M., IV:39
Snyder, Henry N., V:280–81
Snyder, W. P., IV:767
Soap advertising, IV:25, 29
Soap Gazette and Perfumer, IV:188*n*
Sobolewski, E., III:386
Social classes, *see* Business; Wealth; Working class
Social Crusader, IV:283
Social customs and manners
  magazines on, I:57–59, 103, 234, 348, 472–79; II:104–5, 350–51, 429; III:307–9; IV:567; V:24–25, 93
  press as interpreter of, IV:2–3
  See also Morality
Social Democrat, IV:175
Social Democratic Herald, IV:175
Social-Democratic Working-Men's Party, III:301
Social Economics, IV:171
Social Economist, IV:204
Social expansion, I:339–40
Social Gospel, IV:283
Social Progress, IV:194
Social Republic, II:207
Social Service, IV:194
Social Visitor, IV:366
Social welfare magazines, II:241, 313–14; IV:193–94, 195, 741–50
Socialism
  expansionist era magazines on (1825–50), I:366, 388, 470, 471, 688, 763–65
  Gilded Age magazines on (1885–1905), IV:513, 719
    press opposition, IV:173–74
    press support, IV:174, 190–91
  modern magazines on (1905–), IV:703, 746, 788; V:284
  Christian, IV:176, 190–91, 280–83
  Fabian, IV:191, 203, 204
  free-lance, IV:204–7
  Guild, V:93
  Marxian, IV:91
  utopian, IV:202–3
Socialist (New York), III:300; IV:175*n*
Socialist (San Francisco), IV:204
Socialist party, IV:174–76, 191; V:92–93, 152–53, 314
Socialist periodicals
  in expansionist era (1825–50), I:536–38
  in Civil War era (1850–65), II:207
  in post-Civil War era (1865–85), III:300–301
  in Gilded Age (1885–1905), IV:203*n*, 204–7, 283*n*
    Haymarket bombing and, IV:172
    trends, IV:173–76
  modern (1905–), V:93
Socialist Review, IV:203*n*
Socialist Spirit, IV:283*n*
Socialist Woman, IV:205*n*
Socialized medicine, IV:531–34
Social-work periodicals, IV:193–94
Société des Gens de Lettres, V:250, 258
Society, IV:88
Society of Friends, *see* Quakers
Society magazines, III:101–2; IV:89, 96–97, 756–62
Society notes in magazines, III:101–2, 425; IV:77–78, 84

Sociology journals, IV:191–93
  See also Political science
Socrates, V:99
Soda Fountain Magazine, IV:188*n*
Soil of the South, II:89
Solberg, Thorvald, IV:143
Somerby, Charles P., IV:204
Somers, Frederick M., III:56, 406; IV:114, 506–7
Somerset, Ohio, IV:298
Something, I:171, 793
Sommers, Martin, IV:709, 712
Sommerville, Mass., III:82
Song Friend, III:198*n*
Songs, II:196–97, 352, 437, 551; III:195; IV:250
Sontag, Henriette, II:195
"Sophie May," *see* Clarke, Rebecca Sophia
Sorensen, Grace, IV:275
Sorokin, Pitirim, IV:520
Sorosis, III:95
Sorosis Club, III:326–27
Sothern, Edward Hugh, IV:725
Sothoron's Magazine, IV:48
Soule, George, V:168, 191*n*, 210, 214–16, 219
Soule, J. H., IV:90
Soule, Joshua, I:299*n*
Soule and Bugbee's Legal Bibliography, III:144*n*
Sound Currency, IV:163*n*
Sound Waves, IV:335
Soundings, IV:108
Sousa, John Philip, IV:544, 697; V:32
South, I:729; II:97–99, 110, 251, 425, 472–74; III:47–49, 277, 284, 383, 464–65; IV:780; V:10, 281
  See also Civil War; Confederate States of America; Southern magazines
South America, *see* Latin America
South Atlantic, III:47
South Atlantic Publishing Co., V:274
South Atlantic Quarterly, IV:73, 213, 393; V:332
  sketch of, V:273–85
South Carolina Historical and Genealogical Magazine, IV:139
South Carolina Weekly Museum, I:32, 122, 205, 790
South Dakota Educator, IV:270*n*
South Dakotan, IV:96
South Illustrated, IV:92
South and West, III:157
Southard, Samuel Lewis, I:490
Southeastern Christian Advocate, II:72*n*
Southeastern Underwriter, IV:351*n*
Southern Agriculturist (Charleston), I:442*n*, 799
Southern Agriculturist (Corinth, Miss.), III:155
Southern Banker, IV:349*n*
Southern Baptist Review and Eclectic, II:63
Southern Bivouac, III:47
Southern Botanico-Medical Reformer, II:85
Southern Cabinet of Agriculture, I:422*n*
Southern California Practitioner, IV:314*n*
Southern Christian Advocate, II:68*n*
Southern Churchman, II:69
Southern Clinic, III:140*n*
Southern Cultivator, I:444*n*, 806; II:8, 88*n*, 435*n*; III:154
Southern Dental Journal, III:143*n*
Southern Eclectic, II:110*n*
Southern Educational Journal, IV:270*n*
Southern Engineer, IV:321
Southern Episcopalian, II:70*n*
Southern Farmer, III:154
Southern Field and Fireside, I:652; II:89
Southern Hardware and Implement Journal, III:136
Southern Herald, II:146*n*
Southern Historical Monthly, III:262*n*
Southern Historical Society Papers, III:261–62
Southern Illustrated News (Atlanta), II:112*n*
Southern Illustrated News (Richmond), I:652*n*; II:112, 200
Southern Ladies' Book, I:383, 699–700
Southern Lady's Companion, II:57*n*
Southern Literary Companion, II:111
Southern Literary Gazette, I:382, 800; II:110*n*
Southern Literary Journal, I:383, 664–65; II:110
Southern Literary Messenger, I:422, 505, 512, 515; II:8, 24–25, 30, 54, 110, 123, 138, 149, 169, 172, 206, 423, 492; IV:92
  founding of, I:382
  sketch of, I:629–57
Southern Lumberman, III:130
Southern Magazine (Baltimore), III:256
Southern Magazine (Louisville), IV:93*n*
Southern Magazine (Manassas, Va.), IV:92
Southern Magazine (Richmond), III:46
Southern magazines
  early (1741–94), I:155
  in nationalist era, I:204–5
  in expansionist era (1825–50), I:380–84
    business magazines, II:339–42

free-school demands, I:487
general magazines, I:573–76, 755–56
literary magazines, I:629–57, 664–65, 721–27
quality, I:380–84
women's magazines, I:660–701
in Civil War era (1850–65), II:29
agricultural magazines, II:88*n*, 89
business magazines, II:342–46
comic, II:112–13, 155, 185
conflicts with northern magazines, II:108
dramatic criticism, II:200
eclectic magazines, II:488–92
effects of war, II:8–9, 22–23
on immigration, II:123
literary magazines, II:30, 33, 110*n*, 111
medical journals, II:84*n*, 87
Panic of 1857, II:145
payments to contributors, II:22–23
poetry, II:113
proslavery writings, II:138–39, 143–44, 344–45
regional centers, II:107, 110–11
religious magazines, II:61, 63–65, 68
social role of women, II:48–49
trends, II:107–13
wartime magazines, II:111–13, 154–56, 346*n*
women's magazines, II:59
in post-Civil War era (1865–85), II:545
agricultural magazines, III:154–55
attitude toward North, III:284–85
business magazines, II:346–48
eclectic magazines, III:46–47
family magazines, III:46
historical journals, III:261–62
literary magazines, III:47
magazine centers, III:45
medical journals, III:140*n*–41*n*
religious magazines, III:70, 73, 382–84
trends, III:45–47
in Gilded age (1885–1905)
attitudes toward magazines, IV:91–92
historical magazines, IV:139
literary flowering, IV:91
magazine centers, IV:92–94
religious periodicals, IV:291
Southern Medical Record, III:141*n*
Southern Medical and Surgical Journal, II:8, 339
Southern Medicine, III:141*n*
Southern Medicine and Surgery, IV:314
Southern Messenger, IV:209*n*
Southern Methodist Itinerant, II:61
Southern Methodist Review, II:66*n*
Southern Monthly, II:111
Southern Musical Advocate, II:198*n*
Southern Musical Journal, III:197*n*
Southern Pacific Railroad, V:149–50
Southern Parlour Magazine, II:111
Southern Planter, I:444*n*, 805; II:88*n*, 435*n*; III:154
Southern Planter and Grange, III:149*n*
Southern Power and Industry, IV:321
Southern Practitioner, III:141*n*
Southern Presbyterian, II:63*n*, 155
Southern Presbyterian Review, II:8, 62; III:74; IV:294
Southern Punch, II:112, 155, 185
Southern Quarterly Review, I:512, 646; II:28, 110, 165, 339; III:45
founding of, I:383
sketch of, I:721–27
Southern Review, I:382–83, 573–76; II:66*n*; III:70; V:340
sketch of, III:382–84
Southern Rose, I:383, 801
Southern Rosebud, I:383, 801
Southern Ruralist, IV:341
Southern School Journal, IV:270*n*–271*n*
Southern Society, III:47
Southern Teacher, IV:271*n*
Southern Times, II:110*n*
Southern Tobacco Journal, IV:339
Southern Underwriter, III:146*n*; IV:351*n*
Southern and Western Literary Messenger and Review, I:629*n*, 646
Southern and Western Monthly Magazine and Review, I:383, 755–56
Southern and Western Textile Excelsior, IV:185*n*
Southern Women's Magazine, IV:363*n*
Southern Workmen, III:127*n*
Southey, Robert, I:278
Southland (Negro periodical), IV:214*n*
Southland (railroad periodical), IV:93
Southland Queen, IV:363*n*
Southwest Hardware and Implement Journal, IV:188*n*
Southwest Journal of Medicine and Surgery, IV:313*n*
Southwest Review, V:188
Southwestern Baptist, II:65*n*
Southwestern Baptist Chronicle, II:65*n*
Southwestern Christian Advocate, II:68*n*; III:71
Southwestern Freemason, IV:222*n*
Southwestern Historical Quarterly, IV:139

Southwestern Journal of Education, III:168
Southwestern Miller, III:128; IV:185
South-Western Monthly, II:110*n*
Southwestern Presbyterian, IV:75*n*
Southwick, Solomon, I:154
Southworth, Alvan S., II:414*n*
Southworth, Mrs. Emma Dorothy Eliza Nevitte, II:36, 38, 171, 309, 358, 360, 362; III:224, 246; IV:678–79
Sovereign, James R., III:300*n*
Sovereigns of Industry Bulletin, III:299
Soviet Russia Pictorial (1922–23), V:22
Soviet Union, *see* Russia
Spaeth, Sigmund, IV:578
Spahr, Charles Barzillai, III:428, 430; IV:506*n*, 508
Spain, I:339, 617
  See also Spanish-American War
Spalding, John Lancaster, IV:217
Spalding, Martin John, III:69*n*
Spanish treaty of 1819, I:161
Spanish-American War
  events leading to, IV:234–35
  magazines on, II:256, 401; IV:59, 517, 565, 572, 722
    medical journals, IV:527
    pictorial reports, II:464, 483, IV:613
    press opposition, IV:235
    press support, III:346
    reportage, II:549; IV:235–36, 455, 485, 596, 613, 661; V:287
  popularity of, IV:235
  prosperity following, III:475
  West and, IV:94
Spann, Mrs. Eleanor, II:59
Spargo, John, II:379; IV:494, 767, 785
Sparhawk, Edward V., I:629*n*, 634
Sparkes, Bovden, IV:713
Sparks, Jared, I:130, 138, 175, 204, 367, 415; II:175*n*, 218*n*, 220*n*
  as editor, 223–25, 231, 233–34
Spaulding, Charles D., IV:583
Spaulding, Eugene W., IV:491
Speakeasies, press comment on, IV:567
Spear, Samuel Thayer, II:347, 376
Speare, Dorothy, III:489
Spearman, Frank Hamilton, IV:115*n*, 691, 767
Spears, John Randolph, II:483; IV:722
Spears, Monroe K., IV:733*n*, 740
Spectator (London), III:279; V:91
Spectator (New York), III:145
Spectator (New York insurance periodical), IV:350
Speech, III:308–9, 377
  See also Dictionaries
Speed, James Gilmore, IV:66
Speed, John Gilmer, IV:49, 154, 329
Speed in transportation, IV:325–26
Spelling, IV:212
Spelling magazines, III:312
Spelling reform, II:212; IV:212, 573
Spencer, Anna W., II:52
Spencer, Arthur, IV:347*n*
Spencer, Bella Z., IV:671*n*, 680
Spencer, Benjamin Townley, IV:738
Spencer, Herbert, III:108, 250, 253, 495, 496, 497; IV:131, 396
Spencer, Lorillard, IV:58
Spencer, Mary V., II:308
Spencer, Stephen M., IV:712*n*
Spencer, Theodore, IV:738
Spender, Stephen, IV:740; V:242
Spengler, Joseph John, IV:730
Spengler, Oswald, III:543
Speranza, Gino, IV:786
Speyer, Leonora, V:96, 266
Sphinx, IV:391
Spice Mill, III:134
Spicer, Anne Higginson, V:157
Spielhagen, Friedrich, III:255
"Spike, Ethan," *see* Whittier, Matthew
Spiller, Robert Ernest, IV:738
Spingarn, Joel Elias, III:349; IV:126, 128
Spink, Albert H. and Charles C., IV:374
Spirit of the Age, II:207, 210
Spirit of the Fair, II:87
Spirit Messenger and Harmonial Guide, II:210*n*
Spirit of Missions, II:70*n*
Spirit of the XIX Century, I:381, 806
Spirit of the Pilgrims, I:264, 265, 569–72
Spirit of '76, III:262*n*
Spirit of the Times, I:480, 801; II:203–4, 121, 173, 178, 195, 198, 201, 206, 327; III:11, 18, 209, 215, 218, 220; IV:373
Spiritual Magazine, II:207*n*, 210*n*
Spiritual Record, III:82*n*
Spiritual Republic, III:82*n*
Spiritual Telegraph, II:209
Spiritualism and spiritualist periodicals, I:472–73; II:208–10; III:81–82, 446, 447, 452; IV:304, 414
Spivak, Lawrence E., V:xvii, 3*n*, 15*n*, 18*n*, 19, 20*n*, 22–25, 26*n*
Splint, Fred C., V:246*n*, 251, 256
Splint, Sarah Field, III:486
Spofford, Harriett Prescott, II:26, 37, 395, 462, 505*n*; III:33*n*, 99*n*,

373, 397, 411, 461, 511, 546; IV:44*n*, 367*n*, 481, 538, 765
Spokane, Wash., III:148; IV:341
Spokesman of the Carriage and Associate Trades, IV:189*n*
Sport Life, III:218*n*
Sporting Goods Dealer, IV:189*n*
Sporting Goods Gazette, IV:189*n*
Sporting goods magazines, IV:189*n*
Sporting Life, III:218, 220; IV:374
Sporting News, IV:374
Sporting Review, III:210; IV:380–81
Sporting and Theatrical Journal, III:198, 210
Sporting Times, III:209, 218
Sports, I:479–82, 673
  in Civil War era magazines (1850–65), II:37, 201–3
  buffalo massacre, III:60
  illustrated weeklies, II:453
  police gazettes, II:327, 331–33
  in Gilded Age magazines (1885–1905)
    eclectic magazines, IV:689
    family magazines, II:483
    illustrated weeklies, II:464
    juvenile magazines, III:503
    outdoor periodicals, IV:634, 636
    urban periodicals, IV:84, 87
  in modern magazines (1905–)
    comic magazines, III:555
    eclectic magazines, III:555; IV:700, 713
    illustrated magazines, IV:470, 478
  clubs devoted to, III:213, 219–22
  college, *see* College sports
  criticisms of, III:222
  popularity of, II:201–3, 209, 211–20; IV:369–71
    baseball, IV:374
    bicycling, IV:377–78
    boxing, IV:371
    racing, IV:373
    whist craze, IV:381
  women and, III:219; IV:370–71, 378
  See also Sports magazines; *specific sports*
Sports Afield, IV:381
Sports and Games, III:210
Sports Illustrated, V:322
Sports, Music, and Drama, IV:47*n*
Sports and Pastimes, III:209
Sports magazines, I:427, 479–80; II:203–4, 328, 455; III:209–22; IV:47*n*, 373, 380–81, 384
Sports of the Times, I:480*n*; IV:373, 384
Sportsman (New York; 1863), II:204
Sportsman (New York; 1901–5), IV:381
Sportsman (St. Louis), IV:381*n*
Sportsmen's Review, IV:380
Spotswood, William, I:94, 94*n*, 95
Sprague, Charles, I:203, 326, 409, 412, 601
Sprague, Mary Aplin, III:248
Sprague, Timothy Dwight, I:347
Sprague, William Cyrus, IV:347
Spread the Light, IV:179
Sprigg, D. A., 70*n*
Spring, Samuel, I:134*n*
Springer, Gertrude, IV:750
Springer, John, V:186
Springer, Marguerite Warren, IV:115*n*
Springfield, Ill., IV:314*n*
Springfield, Mass.
  agricultural magazines, III:149*n*; IV:337
  Good Housekeeping, IV:360; V:125, 131–32
  other periodicals, II:210*n*; III:152; IV:187, 272, 379, 389
Springfield, Ohio
  agricultural and flower periodicals, III:156, 161*n*; IV:337, 342, 345*n*
  Collier's, IV:453*n*, 467–68
  Woman's Home Companion, III:100; IV:763*n*, 764–65
  other periodicals, III:116, 544*n*; IV:188*n*, 390*n*
Springfield Republican (Mass.), V:125–26, 132
Springfield Union, V:13
Spurgeon, Charles Haddon, III:83
Square and Compass, IV:222*n*
Squatter Sovereign, II:135
Squibb, Edward Robinson, IV:245
Squier, Ephraim George, II:452*n*, 456, 461
Squier, Miriam Florence, *see* Leslie, Mrs. Frank
Stacpoole, Henry de Vere, IV:101
Stage, IV:199; IV:261
Stagg, Amos Alonzo, IV:697
Stahr John S., II:380*n*
Stalin, Joseph, V:22, 323*n*
Stallings, Laurence V:20
Stamford, Connecticut, photography periodical in, IV:149
Stamp Act (1765), I:26, 72
Stamp-collectors' periodicals IV:391
Standard (Boston), III:146*n*
Standard (Chicago), III:72; IV:291
Standard (New York), V:145
Standard (single tax periodical), IV:179
Standard Delineator, IV:363
Standard Oil Corp., V:75, 288
  antitrust suit, II:257

Standard Quarterly, IV:47*n*
"Standish, Burt L.," *see* Patten, Gilbert
Stanlaws, Penrhyn, III:487, 554; IV:49*n*, 496, 501, 564
Stanley, Arthur Penrhyn, III:250
Stanley, Henry Morton, II:271, 414; III:171, 258, 465*n*; IV:226, 342, 721; V:312
Stanley, Hiram M., III:541
Stansbury, Charles Frederick, IV:50
Stanton, Elizabeth Cady, II:51, 252; III:90, 91, 93, 172, 391–92, 394, 445–46, 448; IV:200, 480
Stanton, Frank Lebby, IV:93, 456, 458, 690, 713
Stanton, Robert Livingston, II:537*n*
Stanton, Theodore, IV:302*n*
Stanwood, Edward, II:262*n*, 270, 272, 273
Star Bulletin, IV:199*n*
Star of Hope, IV:199
Star Journal, II:468; III:43, 210
Star Monthly, IV:274
Star Route Trials, III:289
Star in the West, II:72
Star of Zion, III:71
Starbuck, C. C., IV:398
Starchroom Laundry Journal, IV:184*n*
Starey, A. B., III:178*n*
Starr, Alfred, V:100*n*, 110
Starr, Ella, II:463
Starr, Frederick, IV:302*n*
Starrett Helen Elkin, III:53
Starrett, Vincent, IV:654
Starrett, William A., III:53
Stars, theatrical, II:199; III:203–5
Stars and Stripes, IV:69*n*
State, IV:108
State and Municipal Compendium, III:147*n*
State Normal Monthly, IV:270*n*, 272*n*
State Rights Register, I:683
State's Duty, IV:380
States' rights, I:722
Stationery magazines, III:135
Statistical periodicals, IV:310*n*
Staunton, Va., III:148
Stead, William Thomas, IV:52, 158, 201, 281, 403, 406, 517, 657–60, 719
Stead's Review, IV:658*n*
Steam, III:115
Steamships, I:642
Stearns, George Luther, III:332, 338
Stearns, Harold, III:541, 542; V:90
Stearns, John Newton, I:713*n*, 714
Stedman, Edmund Clarence, I:535; II:21–22, 26, 106, 271, 377, 419*n*, 428, 429, 430, 497, 506*n*, 525; III:21, 37*n*, 229, 232, 237, 238, 322, 360, 361, 362, 374, 463, 503, 540, 549; IV:83*n*, 271, 410, 451, 483
  criticism of, III:240
Stedman, Thomas Lathrop, II:272
Steeger, Henry, IV:417*n*, 422
Steel, III:128; IV:183*n*
Steel and Iron, IV:183*n*
Steel periodicals, III:128; IV:183*n*
Steele, Wilbur Daniel, II:402, 404; V:134
Steel-plate engravings
  earliest, I:106
  in expansionist era magazines (1825–50), I:353, 519–21, 547, 592, 628, 675
  in Civil War era magazines (1850–65), II:192–93, 303, 308, 551
  in post-Civil War magazines (1865–85), II:309; III:41, 186–89, 420, 425
  in Gilded Age magazines (1885–1905), II:310; IV:134
  declining use of, III:186; IV:134
Steep, George Wail, IV:107*n*
Stefansson, Vilhjalmur, II:402, 415; IV:625
Steffens, Lincoln, II:260; III:479, 510*n*, 512, 513, 514; IV:49*n*, 208, 518, 593–600, 603; V:83, 85
Stegner, Wallace, IV:476
Stein, Gertrude, III:543; IV:703; V:173, 176, 243
Steiner, Edward Alfred, III:430, IV:768
Steinitz, William, IV:382
Stella, Joseph, IV:747; V:178
Stellar Ray, IV:284
Stengel, Alfred, I:566*n*
Stenographic magazines, II:212
Stephen, Leslie, III:337
Stephens, Alexander Hamilton, I:751
Stephens, Alice Barber, IV:602, 685
Stephens, Mrs. Ann Sophia, I:352, 353, 499, 544*n*, 549, 584, 627; II:32, 172, 306*n*, 307, 437; III:224, 246; IV:336
Stephens, Charles Asbury, II:262*n*, 268–69; III:174, 465*n*, 504
Stephens, Edward, II:32
Stephens, Harriet Marion, I:586
Stephens, Henry Louis, II:397, 520*n*, 521ff; III:265, 266, 440, 441
Stephens, James, III:542

Stephens, John Lloyd, II:420
Stephens, Louis Henry, II:520
Stephens, W. H., II:184
Stephens, William Allen, II:520; III:440
Stephenson, Gilbert T., V:280
Sterling, George, III:408; IV:106, 702; V:12–13, 258
Sterling, James, I:81
Sterling Magazine, V:151*n*
Sterne, Laurence, V:331
Sterner, Albert Edward, II:401; III:473
Stetson, Charlotte Perkins, *see* Gilman, Charlotte Perkins
Stetson, G. Henry, V:159
Stetson, John, III:266
Stetson's Dime Illustrated, III:44
Steuart, George S., IV:90
Stevens, Abel, I:301; II:31*n*, 67, 139
Stevens, Albert William, IV:626, 630
Stevens, Ashton, IV:106
Stevens, Beatrice, III:475
Stevens, George Alexander, I:132
Stevens, James, V:9, 12
Stevens, John Austin, III:260*n*
Stevens, Mortimer I., IV:104*n*
Stevens, Otheman, IV:493
Stevens, Thomas, IV:379, 634, 636
Stevens, Thomas Wood, IV:389
Stevens, Wallace, IV:739; V:173, 176, 237, 241
Stevens, William Dodge, IV:720
Stevens Indicator, III:114*n*
Stevenson, Adlai Ewing, IV:714–15; V:221, 222*n*, 319
Stevenson, Alec Brock, V:100*n*, 101, 103–5, 111
Stevenson, Elizabeth, V:285
Stevenson, Lionel, V:273*n*
Stevenson, Robert Louis, II:377; III:250, 252, 328, 503; IV:7, 43, 112, 134, 141, 230, 451, 490, 591, 592, 720; V:117, 119, 154–55, 342
Stewart, A. T., V:72
Stewart, B. Anthony, IV:628
Stewart, Charles Samuel, I:456
Stewart, Donald Ogden, IV:439, 607
Stewart, George A., IV:373
Stewart, George Rippey, IV:554
Stewart, Henry, I:731
Stewart, Ruth McEnery, II:398*n*
Stewart, T. A., I:389*n*
Stewart, William Morris, IV:163, 413
Stewart, William Rhinelander, IV:489
Stickley, Gustave, IV:148
Stieglitz, Alfred, IV:149, 150
Stiles, Henry Reed, II:175*n*
Stiletto, IV:390–91
Stillé, Charles Janeway, I:488
Stillman, James, III:427
Stillman, William James, II:193, 505*n*; IV:73*n*
Stillwell, Sarah S., II:402
Stimson, Frederic Jesup, II:398*n*; IV:560, 721; V:30
Stimson, George, III:39*n*
Stimson, Henry Lewis, IV:727
Stimson, N. R., II:154
Stinson, George, IV:365
Stipple engravings, I:209–10, 314, 675; II:192
Stirling, Matthew W., IV:629, 630
Stock, John E., I:244
Stock Exchange, II:514–15; III:3–4; IV:567
Stockbridge, Frank Parker, IV:705, 784; V:54
Stockham, Alice Bunker, IV:272
Stockholder, II:82
Stockton, Frank Richard, II:402, 429, 467; III:20, 99, 228, 397, 512; IV:61, 483, 543, 612, 712; V:342
in *Saint Nicholas,* III:20, 99, 228, 397, 512
in *Scribner's Monthly,* III:457*n*, 461, 462, 472
Stockton, Louise, III:400
Stoddard, Charles Augustus, IV:293
Stoddard, Charles Warren, II:117, 118, 506*n*; III:405, 407, 511; IV:105
Stoddard, Elizabeth Barstow, II:429, 497, 502, 505*n*; III:397
Stoddard, Henry L., II:310, 311
Stoddard, Joseph, Jr., IV:125
Stoddard, Lothrop, III:478, 479; IV:728, 730, 784
Stoddard, Richard Henry, I:553, 587*n*, 608, 613, 651, 745, 771; II:26, 39, 116, 353, 377, 406, 424, 430, 497, 505*n*, 524, 527; III:13*n*, 37*n*, 232, 237, 257, 321, 397, 410*n*, 411, 418, 421, 460, 463, 541, 549; IV:45, 60, 482; V:97
Stoddart, Henry, III:396*n*, 400
Stoddart, Joseph Marshall, IV:64, 308
Stoddart's Review, III:41–42
Stoever, Martin L., II:73*n*
Stokes, Rose Pastor, IV:405
Stolberg, Benjamin, IV:685; V:21
Stone, IV:325*n*
Stone, A. J., IV:775
Stone, Herbert Stuart, IV:324, 450–52; V:154*n*, 156–57, 159

Stone, John Augustus, I:429
Stone, Lucy, II:252; III:90, 91, 94; IV:355
Stone, Melville E., IV:450–51; V:60, 66, 156
Stone, Ormond, III:110
Stone, William Leete, I:490, 311, 637; II:282
Stong, Philip Duffield, IV:701
Storey, Moorfield, III:144
Storrs, Richard Salter, II:367*n*, 368, 369; III:76*n*
Story, Joseph, I:155, 198, 255, 600, 748; II:227, 228, 232
Story, William Wetmore, I:410, 546*n*, 718, 737, 764; II:505*n*
Story-papers, III:42, 53–54
Story-Teller, IV:115
Stouch, Clarence Edgar, IV:478
Stoughton, Edwin Wallace, II:251; III:286
Stout, E. H., IV:658
Stout, Rex, IV:697, 701
Stout, Wesley Winans, IV:671*n*, 708–11, 714
Stoves and Hardware Reporter, III:136
Stowe, Calvin Ellis, I:624
Stowe, Harriet Beecher, I:510, 585, 586, 597; II:22, 267, 361, 370, 373, 495, 504, 505, 506, 510; III:92, 99, 101, 175*n*, 224, 246, 308, 393, 423, 426, 439, 558
  See also: Uncle Tom's Cabin
Stowell, Charles Henry, III:112
Stowell, Kenneth K., V:154*n*, 163
Stowell, Louisa Reed, III:112
Strachey, Lytton, V:211
Strahan, Alexander, III:278
Strahan, Edward, III:398
Straight, Dorothy Whitney, V:192–97, 210, 213–14, 216
Straight, Michael Whitney, V:191*n*, 217, 219–23
Straight, Willard, V:191–97, 214
Strait, H., I:467
Strand, IV:4, 228
Stratemeyer, Edward, IV:274
Stratospheric photography, IV:629
Stratton-Porter, Gene, *see* Porter, Gene Stratton
Straus, Nathan Jr., III:520*n*, 531
Straus, Roger W., Jr., V:57
Strauss. Anna Lord, III:457*n*
Strauss, Eduard, IV:544
Strauss, Theodore, IV:763*n*, 771
Strausz-Hupé, Robert, V:57
Straw votes, by *Literary Digest,* IV:575–77
Straznicky, Edward R., II:414*n*
Street, Alfred Billings, I:347, 546, 487*n*, 614, 620, 679, 743; II:406, 429, 468, 543; III:374
Street, Francis, II:38
Street, Julian, IV:466, 604
Street & Smith, II:184; III:223; IV:116, 118, 119, 141, 274
Street-gamin fiction, IV:196
Street Railway Gazette, IV:333
Street Railway Journal, III:126; IV:333
Street Railway Review, IV:333
Streeter, Edward, IV:477
Strell, George W., III:210*n*
Stribling, Thomas Sigismund, IV:422, 618
Strickland, W. P., II:194*n*
Strickland, William, I:208, 209
Strikes
  in Civil War era (1850–65), II:51, 378
    shoemakers' strike, II:145
  in post-Civil War era (1865–85), III:297, 342
    coal miners' strike (1869), III:303
    general strike (1877), III:303
    press support, III:447
    railroad strike (1877), III:124–25, 303
    violence and, III:302–4
  in Gilded Age (1885–1905), IV:218–19
    coal strike (1894), IV:219
    Homestead strike, IV:218
    press opposition, IV:217
    railroad strike (1894), IV:218
  modern (1905–), IV:746: V:212
    coal strike (1919), III:352
    general, V:93
    on *Literary Digest,* IV:574
    office workers (1935), V:20
    press opposition, IV:778–79, 786
    steel strike (1919), III:352
Strindberg, August, V:258
Stringer, Arthur John Arbuthnot, IV:101, 436, 458, 689, 695, 714; V:251
Stringer & Townsend, II:41, 406
Stringfellow, J. H., II:135
Strobel, Marion, V:225*n*, 239, 243
Strong, Anna Louise, IV:520
Strong, Jonathan, I:134*n*
Strong, Leonard Alfred George, V:113, 337
Strong, T. W., II:43, 44, 182
Strong, William Duncan, IV:629
Strong, William L., IV:197
Strong, William M., III:346

Strother, David Hunter ("Porte Crayon"), II:110, 338, 390, 472; III:48
Strother, French, IV:783
Stryker, James, I:368; II:28
Stryker's American Register, I:368
Stuart, Carlos, II:209
Stuart, Charles T., V:70
Stuart, Gilbert, I:436
Stuart, James, IV:554, 730
Stuart, Kenneth, IV:712
Stuart, Moses, I:446, 532, 572, 740; II:233
Stuart, Ruth McEnery, I:535, III:400, 465; IV:390*n*
Student, II:100
Student Army Training Corps, V:294
Student and Family Miscellany, II:100*n*
Student and Schoolmate, II:100; III:174
Studio, IV:146
Studley, George W., II:31
Study magazines, *see* Information periodicals; Reading course magazines
Sturgis, Russell, III:184, 185, 336; IV:73*n*, 499, 517, 720
Sturtevant, Julian Monson, II:372
Style, III:7*n*, 98
Style, literary
  in nationalist era magazines (1794–1825)
    bombastic, I:194–95
    criticism, I:147–48, 196, 235–36
    heaviness, I:195
    stilted, I:144–45
  in expansionist era (1825–50), I:705
  in post-Civil War magazines (1865–85), II:17–18, 337–38
  in Gilded Age magazines (1885–1905), IV:13–14; V:76, 115
  sentimentality in, *see* Sentimentality
Subscriptions
  to early magazines (1741–94), I:100–1
    delinquent, I:13, 19–20, 82, 101*n*, 103
    to nationalist era magazines (1794–1825), II:264
  delinquent, I:200, 237–38, 242, 326, 359
    mailing costs and, I:119–20
  to expansionist era magazines (1825–50)
    book review magazines, I:768
    canvassing, I:345
    children's magazines, I:754
    club system, I:516
    delinquent, I:514–15, 561, 598, 628, 644–45, 647–48, 655, 700, 722, 724
    exchange list, I:515–16
    number, I:514
    political magazines, I:754
    prospectuses, I:516
    women's magazines, I:351, 581
  to Civil War era magazines (1850–65), II:535
    effects of war, II:6–7
    illustrated weeklies, II:453
    literary monthlies, II:453
    religious magazines, II:370
    trends, II:9–13
  to post-Civil War magazines (1865–85), II:50–56
  to Gilded Age magazines (1885–1905), II:355
  to modern magazines (1905–30)
    family magazines, II:355
    juvenile, II:274
  premiums with, *see* Premiums, subscription
  rates for, *see* Prices, magazine
  See also Circulation
Subterranean, II:325
Suburban, IV:82
Suburban Life, II:378; IV:82, 338
Suburban magazines, II:378; IV:82, 338
Subways, II:320–21; III:26–27
Success (Didier's), IV:169
Success (Marden's), IV:38, 169, 393
  sketch of, V:286–92
Success with Flowers, IV:342*n*
Success Magazine and the National Post, V:290
"Success" theme, IV:10, 167–69, 208; V:286–92
Successful American, IV:169
Successful Farming, IV:340, V:36
Succession (Sidgwick), V:168
Successward, IV:169
Suckow, Ruth, II:404; IV:729; V:5, 12, 179*n*, 183, 263
Suderman, Hermann, IV:121, 136, 256; V:121
Suffolk County Journal, III:101
Suffrage, women's, *see* Women's suffrage
Sugar Beet, III:154
Sugar Beet News, III:158
Sugar Bowl and Farm Journal, III:155
Sugar periodicals, III:154, 155, 158; IV:339
Sugar Planter, III:155
Suggestion, IV:284
Suggestive Therapeutics, IV:284
Sullivan, Sir Arthur, III:195; IV:544

Sullivan, Frank, IV:568
Sullivan, Jack, IV:77, 656
Sullivan, John L., II:332–34; III:218; IV:371
Sullivan, Mark, IV:208, 453*n*, 460, 461, 465, 543, 785
Sullivan, T. S., IV:496, 564
Sully, Thomas, I:436
Summary, III:314
Summers, Thomas Osmond, II:66*n*
Summy, Clayton F., IV:253
Sumner, Charles, I:451, 490, 776; II:212, 503; III:172
Sumner, John Saxon, IV:501; V:174–75
Sumner, William Graham, II:463; III:292, 337; IV:191, 518; V:330, 332
Sumter, Fort, firing on, I:149
Sun, New York, I:781
Sun and Shade, IV:150*n*
Sunday, William Ashley ("Billy"), IV:449
Sunday Afternoon, III:39*n*
Sunday Capital, IV:89
Sunday Courier (New York), IV:69
Sunday Democrat (New York), IV:69
Sunday Dispatch (Philadelphia), II:37; IV:69*n*
Sunday Flash, IV:67
Sunday Gazette, III:46; IV:69*n*
Sunday Herald, IV:69*n*
Sunday Magazine, III:278
Sunday Magazine of Intelligence and Entertainment, IV:70
Sunday Mercury (New York), II:11, 37, 38, 203; IV:69
Sunday Mercury (Philadelphia), IV:69*n*, 88
Sunday Mirror, see: Reedy's Mirror
Sunday Morning Times, II:37
Sunday papers, II:56; IV:2, 6, 8, 57
"blue laws" and, II:34
criticisms of, IV:242
trends in, II:34–38
See also specific Sunday periodicals
Sunday School Advocate, III:180
Sunday School Journal, II:75; III:8*n*, 67, 70
Sunday School Magazine, III:71*n*
Sunday school movement, I:144
Sunday school periodicals, II:75, 101, 263, 265; III:67, 70, 71*n*, 77*n*, 84, 174, 177, 180; IV:274–75
Sunday School Times, II:75; III:67; IV:274
Sunday School World, II:75
Sunday Telegram, IV:90*n*
Sunday Times, II:38
Sunday Times and Messenger, IV:69
Sunday Transcript, II:37; IV:69*n*
Sunderland, J. Y., III:79*n*
Sunflower, IV:304*n*
"Sunny Jim," IV:25, 30
Sunny Lands, IV:62*n*
Sunny South, III:8*n*, 46; IV:92
Sunnyside, III:132; IV:189
Sunset, IV:105–6
Sunshine, IV:365
Sunshine for Youth, IV:274
Superintendent and Foreman of the Shoe Manufacturing Trade, IV:185
Superior, Neb., IV:391*n*
Superstition in magazines, I:82
Supplee, H. H., IV:517
Supplement to the Popular Monthly, III:498
Surgery journals, III:143; IV:314–15
Survey, sketch of, IV:741–50
mentioned, IV:193
Survey Graphic, sketch of, IV:748–50
Surveyor, IV:351*n*
Sussex, N.J., III:135
Sutherland, Anne, IV:143*n*
Sutherland, J. T., IV:294
Sutherland, John Bain (Jack), IV:700
Sutherland, Mason, IV:630, 632
Sutherlin, R. N., III:158
Sutter, John Augustus, II:118
Sutton, James, Jr., III:410*n*, 411
Swackhamer, Conrad, I:678*n*, 683
Swain, George F., II:297*n*, 299
Swamp Angel, II:151
Swanee Review, V:332, 340
Swart, Annie L. Y., IV:361
Swearing, comment on, I:475
Swedenborgian periodicals, II:74; IV:296
Swedish literature, I:415
Sweek, Alexander, IV:107
Sweeny, Peter B., III:4, 440
Sweet, Alex E., III:270
Sweetser, Arthur, IV:783
Sweetser, Charles Humphreys, III:319, 323
Sweetser, Henry Edward, III:319, 322, 323
Swetland, H. L., III:116*n*
Swetland, H. M., IV:334
Swett, John, II:117
Swett, Sophie, II:268, 273; III:178*n*; IV:360, 481, 533, 765
Swift, Morrison I., IV:157
Swinburne, Algernon Charles, II:256; III:252–53; IV:61, 122–23, 132, 425
Swine Breeders' Journal, III:160

Swing, David, III:53, 54*n*, 76*n*, 83
Swing, Raymond Gram, III:331*n*, 555; IV:749
Swinnerton, Frank, IV:439
Swinton, William, II:425, 426
Swisshelm, Jane Grey, II:50, 141; III:53
Swords, Thomas and James, I:30, 114–16, 122*n*, 133*n*, 135, 215*n*, 218*n*, 219*n*
Sycamore, Illinois, III:71
Sydnor, Charles Sackett, V:273*n*
Sykes, Charles Henry, IV:566
Syllabi, IV:346–47
Sylvester, E. H., IV:84*n*
Sylvester, Frederick O., II:272
Sylvester, J. J., III:110
Symonds, John Addington, IV:112
Symons, Arthur, IV:519, 520; V:251
Symposia, II:251–52, 254, 256, 259; III:282, 295, 298; IV:14
Symposium, IV:265
Syndicalism, V:93
Synge, John Millington, IV:425; V:121
Synon, Mary, IV:724
Syphilis, campaigns against, IV:553
Syracuse, N.Y.
  education periodicals, III:168; IV:147, 268, 269*n*
  trade periodicals, IV:186, 189*n*
  other periodicals, II:67*n*; III:94; IV:254*n*, 344*n*, 362
System, IV:352

T.P.A. Magazine, IV:187
Tabard Inn Corporation, V:27
Tabard Inn Libraries, V:27
Tabasco, IV:391
Tabb, John Banister, II:511*n*; IV:297, 436
Taber, Gladys, IV:533
Taber, Harry Persons, IV:639*n*, 641, 644–45
Taber, William R., II:488
Table and Home Magazine, IV:364*n*
Table Talk, IV:363
Tablet (Boston), I:212, 225, 789
Tablet (Charleston), I:382
Tablet (New York), II:77; III:69
Tabor, Grace, IV:769
Tacoma, Wash., IV:108
Taft, Edward A., III:114
Taft, Lorado, IV:145, 147
Taft, Robert Alfonso, IV:714
Taft, William Howard, II:378; III:349, 475, 487, 531; IV:549, 626, 660, 769, 782; V:32, 56, 333
Taggard, Genevieve, IV:440, 739
Taggart's Sunday Times, IV:69*n*
Tagore, Rabindranath, V:228, 237
Tailor's Review, III:134*n*
Taine, Hippolyte Adolphe, II:272
Talbot, Dean Marion, V:158
Talbot, Henry, IV:257
Talbot, J. J., III:34*n*
Talbott, E. H., III:125*n*
Talent, IV:266
Tales from Town Topics, IV:754; V:246
Talmage, Thomas DeWitt, III:27, 28, 77, 82, 83, 84, 87, 365, 526, 527; IV:217, 301, 542
Tammany Hall
  attacks on, III:342, 345–46, 524–25, 553
  corruption in, III:290–91
  muckraking articles on, IV:600
  periodicals subsidized by, III:266, 440; IV:170–71
  Tweed ring, II:478–79, III:4, 342; IV:124
  See also New York, New York—municipal corruption in
Tammany Times, IV:170
Tammen, Heye Harry, IV:103
Tanner, Benjamin, I:209
Tanner, Benjamin Tucker, III:71*n*
Tanner, John, I:445
Tapley, D. J., III:109*n*
Tappan, Arthur, I:457
Tappan, Lewis, II:371
Tappan, William Bingham, I:177
Tapper, Thomas, III:197*n*
Tarbell, Arthur Winslow, IV:80, 82*n*
Tarbell, Ida Minerva, III:510*n*, 512, 513; IV:35, 208, 465, 503, 590–91, 594, 595, 598, 600, 606; V:342
Tarbox, Increase N., II:314
Tardieu, André, IV:785
Tariff issue, I:463, 575, 723; II:233; III:292, 334, 342, 345, 513, 529; IV:165–67
Tariff League Bulletin, IV:166*n*
Tariff Reform, IV:166
Tariff Review, IV:166*n*
Tariff-Trust Letters, IV:166
Tarkington, Booth, II:402; IV:457, 466, 497, 498, 552 601, 605, 692, 694, 769, 785; V:30, 80, 83, 134
Tarver, Micajah, II:116*n*
Tasistro, Louis Fitzgerald, I:361
Tasker, Dana, V:293*n*
Tassin, Algernon, IV:389, 435, 437
Tate, Allen, IV:733*n* 738–39, 740

Tate, John Orley Allen, V:100*n*, 102–12, 155–56, 222, 231, 238, 241
Tatler of Society in Florida, IV:92
Tattler, I:360
Tatum, Josiah, I:444*n*
Taussig, Frank William, III:337; IV:182, 500
Taussig, Lucy, V:91
Tax burdens of magazines, I:26, 92–93; II:7
Tax reform, *see* Single-tax issue
Tax Reformer, IV:179
Taylor, Bayard, II:37, 166, 253, 373, 377, 406, 424, 429, 430, 464, 505*n;* III:14*n*, 237, 238, 240–41, 255, 257, 374, 378, 421
Taylor, Benjamin Franklin, I:390; II:115; III:231, 416, 464*n*
Taylor, Bert Leston, III:531, 532
Taylor, Charles Fayette, III:140
Taylor, Charles Jay, III:528, 530
Taylor, E. H., II:435
Taylor, Edward Thompson, I:708
Taylor, Eli, I:206*n*, 597
Taylor, Frank J., IV:709, 713
Taylor, George Boardman, I:666*n*
Taylor, Graham, IV:743, 745, 746, 747
Taylor, Graham Romeyn, IV:744, 745
Taylor, H. R., III:132
Taylor, Hannis, III:144*n;* IV:234
Taylor, Hobart C. Chatfield, *see* Chatfield-Taylor, Hobart C.
Taylor, Horace, IV:386
Taylor, J. Bayard, I:512, 544*n*, 551, 585, 609, 771
Taylor, J. E., II:462
Taylor, J. Orville, I:491
Taylor, John Phelps, IV:395*n*, 397
Taylor, Mary Imlay, IV:224, 583
Taylor, Nathaniel William, I:571
Taylor, Ned, IV:120
Taylor, Samuel Harvey, I:739*n*, 740
Taylor, V. V., III:402*n*
Taylor, W. B., II:90
Taylor, William Ladd, IV:544–45, 546, 720
Taylorsville, Ill., IV:27
Tchelietchev, Pavel, V:178
Tea and Coffee Trade Journal, IV:187*n*
Teacher (New York), IV:269*n*
Teacher (Philadelphia), IV:271
Teachers, magazines and, I:139, 155, 198, 288, 487
Teacher's College Record, IV:272
Teachers' Institute, III:168; IV:269
Teachers' Journal, IV:270*n*
Teachers' Magazine, IV:269
Teachers' Offering, see: Youth's Friend and Scholars' Magazine
Teachers' trade papers, IV:269–70
Teachers' World, IV:269
Teall, Edward N., III:504
Teall, Gardner, IV:501
Teasdale, Sara, IV:436, 440, 654, 748; V:258, 336
Tebbel, John, V:23, 25
Technical journals, *see* Engineering periodicals; *and other specific technologies*
Technical World, IV:320
Technologist, III:114*n*
Technology
  industrial, IV:782
  magazine comment on, IV:592–93; V:72
  military, II:549
  See also Inventions
Technology Architectural Review, IV:323
Technology periodicals, IV:308
Technology Quarterly, IV:308
Teen-age departments, IV:552
Teetotalism, *see* Temperance
Tefft, Benjamin Franklin, II:301*n*, 302
Telegram (Baltimore), III:102
Telegram (Boston), IV:90
Telegraph Age, III:121*n*
Telegraph and Telephone Age, III:121*n*
Telegrapher, II:92
Telegraphers' Advocate, III:121*n*
Telephone Journal, IV:335
Telephone Magazine, IV:335
Telephones
  invention of, III:121
  importance to newspapers, IV:242
Telephony, IV:335
Telford, Thomas, III:299*n*
Teller, Henry Moore, IV:161
Temperance, I:165; II:210, 276, 281, 314; III:463
  expansionist era magazines on (1825–50), I:473–74, 563
    satires, I:781
  Civil War era magazines on (1850–65), II:50–51, 53, 211
  See also Temperance magazines
Temperance Advocate, IV:676
Temperance Benefit, III:310*n*
Temperance Cause, III:310*n*
Temperance magazines, II:210–11, 275, 286; III:309–11
Temperance societies, *see* Prohibition movement
Templar's Magazine, II:210; III:310
Temple, IV:413

Templeton, Herminie, IV:601
Ten-cent magazines, IV:3–10, 46–47
10 Story Book, IV:115, 390
TenBrook, Andrew, II:543
Tenderloin, IV:67
Tenements, III:470
Tennessee Baptist, II:64; III:73*n;* IV:292*n*
Tennessee Farmer, I:444*n,* 802
Tennis, III:219; IV:377
Tennyson, Alfred Lord, I:399; II:159, 161, 271, 361, 377, 509; III:249, 252, 548, 549, 550; IV:131
Terhune, Albert Payson, III:489; IV:49*n,* 186, 421, 471; V:257*n,* 258
Terhune, Mrs. Edward Payson, IV:356, 364, 537, 680
Terhune, Mary Virginia ("Marion Harland"), I:592, 651, 653; III:224, 372, 400*n,* 558; V:130
Terpsichorean, IV:254*n*
Terre Haute, Ind., II:92; IV:342*n*
Terrell, Frank G., IV:101
Terrestrial Magnetism, IV:309
Terrific Register, I:481*n*
Terry, Ellen, III:205; IV:226, 256–57
Terry, Rose, *see* Cooke, Rose Terry
Texas, I:453, 560, 681
  annexation of, I:723
  magazines, IV:94
  Mexican War and, I:455–56
  See also specific Texan towns and periodicals
Texas, University of, IV:74
Texas Baptist, III:73
Texas Baptist Herald, III:73*n*
Texas Christian Advocate, II:68*n*
Texas Courier-Record of Medicine, III:141*n*
Texas Dental Journal, III:143*n*
Texas Farmer, III:155
Texas Medical and Surgical Record, III:141*n*
Texas Monthly Magazine, IV:94
Texas School Journal, III:168
Texas School Magazine, IV:270*n*
Texas Sifter, IV:387*n*
Texas Siftings, III:7, 269; IV:229, 387*n*
Texas Stock and Farm Journal, III:160
Texas Stockman, III:160
Texian Monthly Magazine, II:59
Textile Advance News, IV:185*n*
Textile American, IV:185*n*
Textile Colorist, III:127; IV:185*n*
Textile Manufacturer, IV:185*n*
Textile Manufacturers' Journal, IV:185*n*
Textile Manufacturers' Review, IV:185*n*
Textile periodicals, III:127; IV:185*n*
Textile Record of America, III:127; IV:185*n*
Textile World, IV:185
Thackara, James, I:37, 98
Thackeray, Anne, II:393; III:224, 358
Thackeray, William Makepeace, I:357; II:159, 160, 385, 386, 387, 390, 406; III:224; IV:720
"Thanet, Octave," *see* French, Alice
Thanksgiving Day, national celebration of (1864), I:584
Thatcher, Peter O., I:255*n*
Thatcher, Samuel Cooper, I:253*n,* 255*n,* 285
Thaxter, Adam Wallace, II:35
Thaxter, Celia, II:377, 505*n;* III:229, 465*n,* 501
Thayer, Alexander Wheelock, II:197*n*
Thayer, Gideon F., II:445
Thayer, John Adams, II:511; III:484; IV:21, 29, 47, 545; V:74–75, 78, 80–82, 87, 255–60, 263
Thayer, Kathleen, V:284
Thayer, Scofield, III:539*n,* 542, 543
Thayer, Thomas B., II:72*n*
Thayer, William M., IV:168–69
Thayer, William Roscoe, III:347; IV:75, 773–74
Theatre, IV:260–61
Theater
  early, I:55–56, 63, 127, 139, 427–31, 481
  in Civil War era (1850–65), II:145, 198–200
  in post-Civil War era (1865–85), III:198–209
  in Gilded Age, IV:255–61
  See also Burlesque; Drama criticism and comment; Negro minstrel shows; Plays; Theater magazines
Theatre Arts, V:214
Theatre Magazine, IV:261*n*
Theater magazines, I:427; II:198–200; III:198–200; IV:260–61; V:145–53
Theatrical Censor, I:166, 793
Theatrical Censor and Critical Miscellany, I:166, 793
Theatrical Censor and Musical Review, I:427, 800
Theological Eclectic, I:741; II:75
Theological and Literary Journal, I:373; II:75
Theological Magazine, I:131, 790
Theological Medium, II:62*n*
Theological Quarterly, IV:295
Theology, *see* Religion; Religious magazines

Theophilanthropist, I:132, 794
Theosophical Forum, IV:287*n*
Theosophical Path, IV:287*n*
Theosophical periodicals, IV:286–87
Theosophy, IV:287
Therapeutic Gazette, III:141*n*
Therapeutic Notes, IV:314*n*
Thespian Mirror, I:166, 166*n*, 793
Thespian Monitor, I:166, 793
Thespian Oracle, I:165, 790
Thinker, IV:301
Thirteenth Amendment, II:295
Thistle, I:427, 802; III:269*n*
Thistleton, George, III:267*n*
Thistleton's Jolly Giant, III:266
Thomas, A. A., IV:90
Thomas, Augustus, IV:564, 697
Thomas, Calvin, IV:74
Thomas, Dorothy, IV:713
Thomas, Dylan, V:243–44
Thomas, Edith Matilda, II:511*n;* III:483, 549; IV:71*n*, 482, 722
Thomas, Frank M., II:66*n*
Thomas, Frederick William, I:660
Thomas, Ifor, IV:476
Thomas, Isaiah, I:88, 106, 156*n*
as editor, I:26, 30, 83, 86, 92–93 108–10, 156*n*
Thomas, John, I:524
Thomas, John J., I:443; II:432*n*, 433, 434
Thomas, Lowell, IV:477, 478, 732, 787
Thomas, Norman, III:352, 355; V:92, 216
Thomas, R. H., III:300
Thomas, Rowland, IV:457
Thomas, Theodore, III:193, 194, 416; IV:249
Thomas, William I., IV:191
Thomas' Musical Journal, III:197*n*
Thomason, John W., IV:727; V:21
Thomes and Talbot, II:31*n*, 35*n*, 36*n*
Thompson, Alfred, IV:752
Thompson, Carol L., V:49*n*, 58
Thompson, Charles Miner, II:262*n*, 272
Thompson, Clifford, IV:350
Thompson, David Decamp, III:72*n*
Thompson, Denman, III:27
Thompson, Dorothy, IV:553, 700
Thompson, Edward (legal publisher), IV:347
Thompson, Edward William, II:262*n*, 272
Thompson, Francis, IV:450
Thompson, Frank J., II:520, 529
Thompson, George (abolitionist), II:284, 291
Thompson, George F., III:500*n*, 504
Thompson, Harry Arthur, II:432*n;* IV:692
Thompson, Holland, IV:662
Thompson, John (banker), II:95
Thompson, John Q., IV:69*n*
Thompson, John Reuben, I:629*n*, 647–52; II:30, 89, 112, 407, 545; III:46*n*, 397, 411, 420, 421
Thompson, Joseph Parrish, I:488; II:312*n*, 313, 314, 315, 368, 369
Thompson, Lydia, II:328; III:207–8
Thompson, Maurice, II:377, 398, 506*n;* III:46, 47, 397, 400, 421, 502; IV:93, 216*n*, 390*n*, 451, 634
Thompson, Mary Wolfe, V:185
Thompson, Otis, I:136*n*
Thompson, Porter, III:47
Thompson, Ralph, V:55
Thompson, Robert Ellis, III:34*n*, 35, 41, 281
Thompson, S. D., III:144*n*
Thompson, Slason, IV:60–61
Thompson, Vance, IV:77, 80, 86, 100*n*, 101, 125, 637; V:80
Thompson's American Book Report, II:95*n*
Thompson's Bank Note and Commercial Reporter, II:95; III:146
Thompson's Weekly Reporter, II:95*n*
Thoms, William M., III:196
Thomson, Clifford, III:118*n*
Thomson, Edward, II:301*n*, 302
Thomson, James, IV:424
Thomson, Sir Joseph John, II:402
Thomson, Mortimer ("Philander Doesticks"), I:426; II:45, 179, 182, 456
Thoreau, Henry David, I:704, 707, 775, 778, II:167, 239, 420, 423, 424, 501, 505*n*
Thorne, Harley, II:100
"Thorne, Olive," *see* Miller, Emily Huntington
Thorne, William Henry, IV:72, 235
Thornton, Francis G., IV:101
Thornwell, James Henley, I:721*n*, 726–27; II:346
Thoroughbred Record, III:159
Thoroughbred Stock Journal, III:160
Thorp, Willard, IV:738
Thorpe, Frederick, IV:763–64
Thorpe, S. L., IV:763
Thorpe, Thomas Bangs, I:481; II:173, 456; III:35*n*, 420
Thought, IV:286
Threshermen's Review, IV:188*n*, 339
Thrift, IV:351*n*
Thrift, magazine comment on, I:56–60

Thruelson, Richard, IV:709, 712
Thrum, J. F., III:199
Thulstrup, Thure de, II:481; IV:84, 151, 456, 719
Thurber, Charles Herbert, IV:269
Thurber, George, I:728*n*, 731
Thwaites, Reuben Gold, III:262
Thwaites, William H., II:438, 471
Thwing, Charles Franklin, I:741; II:315; III:77*n*, 455, 464*n*; IV:52*n*
Tichenor, Frank A., III:422*n*, 434
Tickler, I:170, 793
Ticknor, Francis Orray, III:46*n*
Ticknor, George, I:192, 255, 543; II:227, 232
Ticknor & Fields, II:245, 502–3
Tidball, W. D., II:114*n*
Tid-Bits, III:268; IV:383
Tide, V:322
Tidings, III:72
Tiebout, Cornelius, I:209
Tiernan, Francis Fisher ("Christian Reid"), I:502; II:546; III:398, 400*n*
Tietjens, Eunice, IV:583, 654; V:171, 231–34, 237, 239
Tiffany, O., II:496, 497*n*
Tigert, John James, II:66*n*
Tilden, Freeman, III:531; IV:787
Tilden, George H., II:92
Tilden, Samuel Jones, III:525; IV:85
Tile-trade magazines, III:130
Tilghman, Benjamin C., III:117
Tilley, R. H., III:259
Tillotsen, Daniel, I:203*n*
Tilton, Elizabeth R., III:393
Tilton, Ralph, III:481*n*
Tilton, Theodore, II:148, 367*n*, III:41, 63–65, 76, 229, 233, 325, 393, 394, 426, 448
  as editor, II:371–74
Timberman, IV:325*n*
Time (Baltimore), IV:90
Time (1888–1890), III:268*n*
Time (Luce's), IV:577; V:117–18, 218, 269
  sketch of, V:293–328
Time Air Express, V:327
Time and the Hour, IV:390
Time, Inc., V:302–4, 315, 321–22, 327–28
Time-Life Books, V:328*n*
Time-Life International, V:322, 325, 326*n*, 328
Time Piece; and Literary Companion, I:121, 790
"Timon, John," *see* Mitchell, Donald Grant
Timrod, Henry, I:651; II:112, 488, 490, 498
Tin and Terne and the Metal World, IV:183*n*
Tingley, Katherine, IV:287
Tinker, Chauncey B., V:337
"Tinto, Dick," *see* Jones, Charles A.
Tip-Top Library, IV:119
Tip-Top Weekly, IV:119
Tire Review, IV:184
Titchener, Edward Bradford, IV:303*n*
Titherington, Richard Handfield, IV:420, 608*n*, 609–10, 612, 613, 617
Tittle, Walter, III:479; IV:786
Tittman, Otto Hilgard, IV:620, 622
Titusville, Pa., IV:184*n*
Titzell, John M., II:389*n*
Toal, D. C., IV:323*n*
Tobacco, IV:189*n*
Tobacco
  magazines on, I:440; II:212–13; III:311; IV:210–11
  chewing of, I:474; II:213
  restrictions against, II:474–75
  See also Smoking
Tobacco industry magazines, III:135; IV:189*n*, 339
Tobacco Leaf, II:213; III:135; VI:189*n*
Tobacco World, III:135; IV:189*n*
To-Day (Boston), II:158, 159, 165, 196
To-Day (Melbourne), IV:658*n*–659*n*
To-Day (New York), IV:752
To-Day (Philadelphia), IV:88, 296
Today's Secretary, IV:352*n*
Todd, Burt Kerr, IV:630
Todd, F. Dundas, IV:149
Todd, John, I:771
Toilettes, III:98
Toksvig, Signe, V:191*n*, 200, 209
Toledo, Ohio, III:55
  Ballot Box, III:94
  Blade, III:53*n*, 55, 94, 270*n*; IV:68
  medical and dental periodicals, III:141*n*, 143*n*; IV:315
  other periodicals, III:78, 109, 112*n*, 197*n*
Tolstoy, Count Leo, II:256; III:32*n*; IV:37, 112, 123, 130, 135, 232, 281, 291, 641, 658, 781; V:117, 266
Tomahawk, II:462
Tomlinson, Charles, V:244
Tomlinson, Paul, IV:604
Tomlinson, Theodore E., II:204*n*
Tompkins, Abel, II:72*n*
Tompkins, John F., II:89

Tompkins, Juliet Wilber, IV:117*n*, 360*n*, 361, 388, 584, 612; V:75
Tooker, Lewis Frank, III:457*n*, 468
Tooth paste and powder advertising, IV:26
Topeka, Kansas
  agricultural magazines, II:90; III:158; IV:340
  general magazines, III:55; IV:97
  religious magazines, III: 71*n*, 75*n*; IV:291*n*
  other magazines, III:301*n*; IV:271*n*, 314*n*, 362, 387*n*
Torch of Reason, IV:277
Torgeson, Edwin Dial, IV:728
Tornow, Max L., IV:236
Torrance, Cal., V:3*n*
Torrey, Bradford, II:263*n*, 270
Torrey, Reuben Archer, IV:301*n*
Tostée, Mlle., III:194
Tosti, Francesco Paolo, IV:544
Totten, J. R., III:260*n*
Tourgée, Albion Winegar, II:254; III:42, 248, 281, 284, 426, 557–59; IV:110, 171, 490, 513
Tourgee, Eben, III:196
Tousey, Frank, III:179, 552
Tower, James Eaton, III:489; V:125*n*, 131–33
Tower, Roy A., V:179*n*
Towle, George Makepeace, II:262*n*, 270; III:18, 397, 418, 424, 511
Town and Country, II:349*n*, 355
Town Topics (Cleveland), IV:95
Town Topics (New York), III:102; IV:85, 459–60; V:246–47, 255, 257
  sketch of, IV:751–55
Town Topics Financial Bureau, V:246
Towne, Alfred, V:24
Towne, Charles Hanson, III:388*n*, 390, 479, 486, 531; IV:38, 46, 484, 589*n*, 603, 714, 768; V:246*n*, 248
Towne, E. C., III:89
Towne, Edward C., IV:54*n*
Towne, Elizabeth, IV:284
Townley, Daniel O'Connell, III:184, 463
Townsend, A. J., II:40
Townsend, Edward Waterman, IV:196
Townsend, James Bliss, IV:147, 757
Townsend, R. D., III:428
Townsend, Virginia Frances, I:587; II:267, 268, 303, 416–417; III:224, 325; IV:680
Towse, John Ranken, III:347, 549; IV:261*n*
Toy, Crawford Howell, II:376; III:337, 536; IV:73*n*, 295
Tracy, Frank Basil, IV:177,
Tracy, Louis, IV:618
Tracy, Merle Elliott, V:49*n*, 56
Tracy, Paul Aubrey, IV:670
Trade, III:134
Trade Bureau, III:136*n*
Trade and Export Journal, IV:186*n*
Trade-marks and advertising, IV:33–34
Trade periodicals
  in Civil War era (1850–65), II:34, 92
  in post-Civil War era (1865–85), III:133–36
  in Gilded Age (1885–1905), IV:186–89
  See also specific retail trades
Trade Register, IV:187*n*
Trade and Transportation, IV:333*n*
Trade Union Advocate, IV:220*n*
Trade union periodicals, II:212; III:125, 126*n*, 129*n*, 299–301; IV:172, 220, 221*n*
Trade unions
  in expansionist era (1825–50), I:471
  in post-Civil War era (1865–85), III:4
    growth, III:298
    press opposition, III:529
    violence and, III:302–4
  in Gilded Age (1885–1905)
    Christian socialism and, IV:282
    press opposition, III:529; IV:126*n*, 217–20
    press support, IV:408
    muckraking articles, IV:599
  modern (1905–)
    press opposition, IV:778–79, 786
    press support, V:212
  forerunners of, I:340
  syndicalist, V:93
  See also Strikes; *and specific trade union organizations*
Trade of the West, II:92
Tradesman, III:136
Trafton, Alice, III:461
Trafton, E. H., III:186
Train, Arthur, III:489; IV:520, 602, 691, 693; V:83
Train, George Francis, III:392, 449–51
Trained Motherhood, IV:364
Trained News and Hospital Review, IV:315
Trains of dresses, II:56
Tramps, III:297–98
Transatlantic Tales, IV:754*n*; V:246

Transcendentalism, II:238, 313
in magazines, I:289–90, 368–69, 402, 410–11, 610, 764; II:48; III:237; IV:283–85
Transcendentalist Club, I:703, 706
Transcendentalist magazines, I:369, 702–10
Transcontinental railroad, projects for, II:81–82
Transcript (Boston), I:290, 781
Transit, IV:321*n*
Transit Journal, III:126*n*
Translations, I:282; II:352, 406, 490, 535; III:254–55, 357, 373; IV:655; V:95, 119
Trans-Mississippi Exposition, IV:266, 489
Transportation, II:319, 320; III:123, 125–26; IV:487–88
See also Automobiles; Aviation; Railroads; Subways
Transylvania Journal of Medicine, I:439, 799
Transylvania University (Lexington, Ky.), I:206
Trask, William Blake, II:176*n*
Traubel, Horace L., IV:129, 148, 279–80, 410
Travel articles
in early magazines (1741–94)
general magazines, I:39, 97
literary magazines, I:115
in nationalist era magazines (1794–1825), I:176
in expansionist era magazines (1825–50)
general magazines, I:221, 235, 239, 241, 282, 325, 611, 623; II:225, 228, 233
literary magazines, I:124, 282, 295, 357, 563, 597, 600–601, 620, 632, 650, 726
religious magazines, I:563
trends, I:4, 22–23, 176
women's magazines, I:325; II:303, 440, 589
in Civil War era magazines (1850–65), II:30
commercial magazines, II:343
family magazines, II:471
general magazines, II:449, 451
illustrated weeklies, II:409–10, 455
popularity, II:176–77
women's magazines, II:439
in post-Civil War magazines (1865–85), III:258
family magazines, II:477
general magazines, II:429; III:418, 420, 465, 511
literary magazines, II:395, 398, 401; III:375*n*
religious magazines, II:518
Southern magazines, II:347
women's magazines, III:483
in Gilded Age magazines (1885–1905)
Chautauqua magazines, III:546
family magazines, IV:625–26
general magazines, IV:685, 720, 724–25
geographic magazines, IV:625–26
illustrated weeklies, II:464
literary magazines, IV:685
outdoor magazines, IV:636
specialized periodicals, IV:224
trend, IV:223–24
women's periodicals, IV:765
in modern magazines (1905–)
family magazines, III:430
general magazines, IV:725; V:32
geographic magazines, IV:626, 630
literary magazines, II:402, 431
Travel books, III:257–58
Travel Magazine, IV:224
Traveler's Record, III:146
Traveling salesmen's magazines, IV:186–87
Traveller, I:480
Traver, G. A., II:464
Traynor, W. J. H., IV:299
Trayser, Lewis W., IV:710
Treadwell, Daniel, I:152*n*
Treasure Trove, III:177
Treat, Selah B., I:307*n*, 397*n*
Tree, Herbert Beerbohm, IV:226
Trego, Charles B., I:556*n*
Tremaine, F. Orlin, V:246*n*, 271
Trenchard, John, I:30, 37, 94, 94*n*, 95
Trent, Harrison, II:204*n*
Trent, William Peterfield, I:574*n*; III:349; IV:73, 126, 225, 263, 516, 517, 593, 733–35; V:342, 344
Trenton, N.J., III:39*n*; IV:184*n*, 401*n*
Trescot, William Henry, I:725
Trestle Board, IV:222*n*
Tribune (Chicago), I:389
Tribune (New York), I:359
Tribune Farmer (New York), IV:70
Tribune and Farmer (Philadelphia), IV:536
Tricycles, *see* Bicycles
Trifet's Monthly Galaxy of Music, IV:254*n*
Triggs, Oscar L., IV:121

"Trilby" (du Maurier), IV:43, 133; V:122
Trimble, Henry, I:539*n*
Trinity College (Duke University), magazines published by, IV:73; V:274, 276–78, 282–83
Trinity Park School, V:274
Triumph of the Egg (Anderson), V:177
Triweeklies, I:121
Trollope, Anthony, II:253, 385, 387, 393, 462; III:224, 251, 358, 378, 397, 439
Trombly, Albert Edmund, V:280
Trotsky, Leon, IV:700; V:337
Trotter and Pacer, IV:373*n*
Trousey, Maud, V:131
Trow, John F., II:540*n*
Trowbridge, David, II:532
Trowbridge, John Townsend, II:173, 180, 270, 271, 308, 395, 495, 505*n;* III:53*n,* 99*n,* 175, 175*n,* 178, 465*n,* 501, 509, 558; IV:71
Troy, N.Y., III:132; IV:68
True, IV:422
True, George, II:114
True American, IV:300
True Catholic, II:69
True Commonwealth, IV:178
True Flag, II:36, 411*n;* IV:79*n*
True Presbyterian, II:63*n*
True Story, V:xvi
True Woman, III:96
Truman, Harry S, IV:714; V:25, 219, 221, 314, 319, 323*n*
Trumble, Alfred, IV:751*n,* 752, 753
Trumbull, Charles G., II:75*n*
Trumbull, Henry Clay, II:75*n;* IV:274
Trumbull, John (painter), I:436
Trumbull, John (poet), I:102, 105, 186, 232
Trumpet and Universalist Magazine, II:72
Trunks and Leather Goods Record, IV:189*n*
Trust Companies, IV:182
Trusts
  growth of, IV:156–57
  press opposition to, III:292–93, 525, 527, 529; IV:166, 177–78, 406, 489, 615; V:149
  press support for, III:554; IV:706, 775
  protective tariff and, IV:165–66
  as threat to advertising, IV:33
Truth (Detroit), IV:210
Truth (New York), IV:19, 29, 39, 83–85, 152, 383
Truth (St. Louis), III:85*n*
Truth (Salt Lake City), IV:104
Truth (San Francisco), III:302
Truth-Seeker, III:89
Truth-Teller, II:76
Tryon, George W., Jr., III:111
Tuberculosis
  control of, IV:311
  research on, III:138
Tucker, Benjamin Ricketson, III:31, 301
Tucker, George, I:409, 697
Tucker, Gilbert, I:443
Tucker, Gilbert Milligan, II:432*n,* 434
Tucker, Henry Holcombe, II:64*n*
Tucker, Henry St. George, I:640
Tucker, Joshua Thomas, II:518
Tucker, Luther, I:442–3; II:89, 90, 432, 433, 434; III:153; IV:339–40
Tucker, Luther H., II:432*n,* 433, 434
Tucker, Luther H., Jr., II:432*n,* 434
Tucker, Nathaniel Beverly, I:409*n,* 632, 637, 642, 645–6, 648, 726
Tucker, Perley, II:527
Tucker, William E., I:209, 521, 548, 592
Tucker, William Jewett, IV:395
Tuckerman, Henry Theodore, I:292*n,* 546, 587*n,* 602, 644, 651, 680, 718*n,* 720, 726, 743, 753, 767, 770; II:238, 429, 542; III:32*n,* 257; IV:677
Tuckerman, Joseph, I:255, 285
Tuckett's Insurance Journal, II:94
Tudor, William, I:130, 179, 184, 188, 255; II:218*n,* 220ff, 238
Tues, C. E., III:54
Tuesday Club, I:194, 243–44
Tuesday Evening Club, II:233
Tufts, James Hayden, IV:279*n*
Tugwell, Rexford Guy, V:56, 139, 211
Tullidge, Edward W., IV:104
Tully, Jim, V:9, 12
Tulsa, Oklahoma, oil journal in, IV:184*n,* 350*n*
Tunis, John R., IV:730
Tunney, James Joseph (Gene), IV:607
Turano, Anthony M., V:20
Turf, Farm and Home, III:215*n*
Turf, Field and Farm, III:215, 220; IV:373
Turf Register, III:215
Turgenev (Turgeniev), Ivan S., III:255, 357, 373; IV:114*n,* 135; V:119
Turnbull, Lawrence, III:46
Turnbull, Robert, I:666*n*
Turnbull, Robert James, I:575
Turner, Arlin, V:273*n*
Turner, Frederick Jackson, IV:138
Turner, George Kibbe, IV:600–1

Turner, H. L., III:76*n*
Turner, Henry E., III:259
Turner, James, I:36
Turner, John Kenneth, III:514
Turner, Joseph Addison, II:29, 111, 138
Turnure, Arthur B., II:401; III:185; IV:756–59
Turnvereins, III:221
Tuskegee, Ala., II:65*n*
Tuskegee Institute, V:278
Tuttle, A. S., II:13
Tuttle, E. C., III:413*n*
Tuttle, George, II:364*n*
Tuttle, Herbert, II:510*n*
Tuttle, Hurson, IV:403
Tuttle, Julius Herbert, IV:138
Tuttle, Morehouse & Taylor, V:338
Tuttle, Wilber C., IV:114*n*, 422
"Twain, Mark," *see* Clemens, Samuel Langhorne
Tweed, William Marcy, II:478–80; III:4, 290–91, 320, 342, 440–42; IV:58*n*
  See also Tammany Hall
Twelve Men (Dreiser), V:148
Twelve Times a Year, III:47
Twentieth Century, IV:178, 204
Twentieth Century-Fox, V:322–23
Twentieth Century Homes, IV:491
Twentieth Century Magazine, IV:416
Twentieth Century Monthly, IV:284
Twentieth Century Pastor, IV:301*n*
Twentieth Century Review, IV:54
Twining, Kinsley, II:376, 377
Twinkles, IV:70, 385–86
Two-cent magazines, IV:117
Two-Step, IV:254
Two Tales, IV:117*n*
Tyler, Bennett, I:571
Tyler, Edward Royall, II:312, 314, 315
Tyler, Gus, V:218
Tyler, John, I:640, 647
Tyler, John, Jr., II:346
Tyler, Lyon Gardiner, IV:139
Tyler, Moses Coit, III:416, 424
Tyler-Keystone, IV:V222*n*
Tyler, Royall, I:55, 125, 155, 156, 225, 232, 371
Tyler, Samuel, I:533
Tynan, Katharine, III:330
Tyndall, John, II:270; III:107, 172, 249, 250, 253, 496; IV:513, 514
Tyner, Paul, IV:174, 401*n*, 413–14
Type, printing, I:20, 35–36, 85, 321
  See also Typography
Type-metal cuts, I:72, 86
Type of the Times, II:212
Typesetting machines, III:117
Typewriter advertising, IV:22
Typewriter Trade Journal, IV:352
Typewriters
  importance to newspapers, IV:242–43
  importance to writers, III:118
  typing, IV:351–52
Typographic Advertiser, II:93
Typographical Journal, IV:221*n*
Typography, II:267; III:339, 466–67; IV:29, 543
  See also Format and size of magazines
Tyrrell, Henry, IV:46*n*, 517

U. S. Egg and Poultry Magazine, IV:345
Uhle, Charles P., I:589–90
Ulmann, Doris, IV:727
Ulyat, William C., I:666*n*
Ulysses (Joyce), V:173–75, 178
Umbastaetter, Herman Daniel, IV:27, 428–31
Una, II:52
Uncle Remus Home Magazine, IV:361*n*
Uncle Remus Magazine, III:46*n*
Uncle Sam, III:269*n*
Uncle Sam's Magazine, III:533
Uncle Tom's Cabin, I:458, 553–54, 649; II:130, 142–44, 171, 242, 291, 370, 494, 505
  songs and plays, II:143
Under Cover (Carlson), V:23
Undertakers' magazines, III:132–33; IV:189
Underwood, Benjamin Franklin, III:78, 107; IV:302
Underwood, Clarence F., IV:695
Underwood, Francis Henry, II:424, 493*n*, 494, 499, 500, 508
Underwood, William E., IV:351*n*
Underwood's United States Counterfeit Reporter, III:147*n*
Underwriters' Review, IV:351*n*
Unemployment, II:5; III:297
  See also Depressions
Union, V:126
Union Agriculturist, I:444*n*, 805
Union Gospel News, IV:295*n*
Union Labor Advocate, IV:221*n*
Union Magazine, I:347, 510, 521; II:30, 53, 188, 192
  sketch of, I:769–72
Union Printer, III:300; IV:220
Union Signal, III:310
Union University, IV:74
Union University Quarterly, IV:74
Unionist, IV:221*n*
Unions, *see* Trade unions
Uniontown, Pa., I:372

Unique Monthly, IV:50
Unitarian, I:288, 799; IV:294
Unitarian controversies, I:131, 264, 286, 369, 569, 571
Unitarian magazines
in nationalist era (1794–1825), I:135, 138, 277–78, 284–92
in expansionist era (1825–50), I:372, 373–74, 387, 658–63
number, I:369
in Civil War era (1850–65), II:223
trend, II:71–72
in post-Civil War era (1865–85), III:77–79, 436–39, 506–7
in Gilded Age (1885–1905), III:507; IV:294–95
Unitarian Miscellany, I:204, 287*n*, 797
Unitarian Review, II:72*n*; III:77; IV:295
sketch of, III:506–7
Unitarian Word and Work, IV:204
United Brethren, magazines of, II:74, III:81
United Brethren Review, IV:296
United Mine Workers' Journal, IV:221*n*
United Presbyterian, II:63*n*; IV:294
United Presbyterian Quarterly Review, II:63
United Press, V:59, 66
United Press Associations, V:59
United Service, III:132
sketch of, III:533–34
United States Army and Navy Journal, II:150; III:132
United States Bank, *see* National-bank controversy
United States Catholic Historical Magazine, IV:138
United States Catholic Intelligencer, I:373
United States Catholic Magazine, I:371, 716–17
United States Catholic Miscellany, I:136, 797; II:76; III:69
United States Christian Magazine, I:122*n*, 790
United States Democratic Review, II:30–31
United States and Dollar Newspaper, IV:677
United States Economist and Dry Goods Reporter, II:93; III:134
United States Gazette, IV:90
United States Insurance Gazette and Magazine, II:94*n*; III:146*n*
United States Investor, IV:349*n*
United States Journal, II:448, 449
United States Law Intelligencer and Review, I:451*n*, 800
United States Law Review, III:144*n*
United States Literary Gazette, I:128, 331–33
United States Magazine (New York), II:32, 132, 198, 428
advertising in, II:13–14
sketch of, II:448–51
United States Magazine (Newark), I:31*n*, 789
United States Magazine (Philadelphia), I:27, 45–46, 49
United States Magazine and Democratic Review, see: Democratic Review
United States Medical Investigator, II:85*n*
United States Medical and Surgical Journal, II:85*n*
United States Miller, III:128*n*
United States Monthly Magazine, III:53
United States Paper Maker, IV:184*n*
United States Post Office Department, V:14
United States Railway and Mining Register, II:81
United States Review, I:677*n*, 682; III:146*n*
United States Review and Literary Gazette, I:129, 333
United States Saturday Post, IV:671*n*, 677–78
United States Service Magazine, II:550–51
United States Tobacco Journal, III:135, IV:189*n*
United States Weekly Journal, II:448
Unity, III:78, 79; IV:286
Universal Asylum, I:53, 60–61
Universal Lyceum, I:489
Universal Truth, IV:285*n*
Universalist (Boston), II:72, 73*n*; III:79*n*; IV:296
Universalist (Cincinnati), II:57*n*
Universalist controversies, I:369
Universalist Herald, II:73*n*; III:79
Universalist and Ladies' Repository, II:57*n*
Universalist Leader, I:138, 796; III:79; IV:296
Universalist Magazine, I:7; III:79*n*
Universalist magazines, I:370, 372; II:7, 57, 72; III:79; IV:296
Universalist Quarterly, I:372, 807; III:79
Universalist Quarterly and General Review, II:72, 409

Universalist Watchman, II:72
Universe, III:53, 89; IV:64*n*
Universities, *see* Colleges and universities
University, IV:55*n*
University of California Chronicle, IV:74
University Extension, IV:263
University Extension Magazine, IV:263–64
University Extension World, IV:264
University Law Review, IV:348
University Literary Magazine, II:99
University of Pennsylvania Law Review and American Law Register, II:93
University quarterlies, IV:73–74
  See also specific university magazines
University Quarterly, II:99
University Record, IV:74
University of the South Magazine, IV:733
University of Texas Record, IV:74
University of Virginia Magazine, II:99
Untermeyer, Louis, IV:439, 654; V:12, 98, 113, 258, 336
Untermeyer, Samuel, IV:468, 738
Up de Graff, T. S., III:142
Up to Date, IV:61
Up from Methodism (Asbury), V:13
Upham, Charles Wentworth, I:463; II:228
Upholstery magazines, III:136
Upshur, Abel Parker, I:640, 643
Upson, William Hazlitt, IV:709, 713
Upton, Francis R., III:119
Urban America Inc., V:322*n*
Urban problems
  growth of, IV:194–203
  See also Municipal corruption; Prostitution; Slums
Urban weeklies
  in Baltimore, IV:90
  in Boston, IV:81
  in Chicago, IV:77–78, 83
  in Kansas City, IV:97–98
  in Minneapolis, IV:96
  nature of, IV:77–78
  in New York, IV:77–78, 83
  in Philadelphia, IV:88
  in Pittsburgh, IV:88
  in St. Louis, IV:653–56
  in Salt Lake City, IV:104
  in Seattle, IV:108
  in Washington, IV:89–90
Urbana, Illinois, IV:296
Utah Farmer, IV:339
Utah Magazine, III:57
Utica, N.Y., II:64*n*–65*n*, 75, 85, 90*n*, 100; IV:68, 322
Utica Saturday Globe, IV:68

Vacationing, IV:779–80
Vachel, Horace Annesley, III:408
Vaile, E. O., III:169
Valdés, Palacio, IV:135, 490
Valentine, B. B., III:521, 528
Valentine, Edward A. Uffington, IV:92
Valentine, Lawson, III:422*n*, 426–28
Valentine, Milton, II:73*n*
Vallance, John, I:37, 98
Vallandingham, Clement Laird, II:545
Valley Falls, Kan., III:301
Valley Farmer, I:444, 809; II:88*n*; III:157
Valley Magazine, IV:101
Valtin, Jan, IV:554; V:23
Van Alen, Eleanor, V:57
Van Arsdale, R. M., II:299
Van Buren, Martin, I:679
Van Cleave, James Wallace, IV:183
VanCleve, John S., III:197*n*
"Van Dine, S. S.," *see* Wright, Willard Huntington
Van Doren, Carl, III:353, 354, 457*n*, 470; V:5, 251, 344
Van Doren, Dorothy Graffe, III:355
Van Doren, Irita, III:354
Van Doren, Mark, III:354; IV:739; V:185
Van Duzer, C. D., IV:108
Van Dyke, Henry, IV:546, 584, 724, 727
Van Dyke, Paul, III:430
Van Etten, Nathan B., IV:534
Van Evrie, Dr. J. H., II:545
Van Ingen, W. B., IV:725
Van Loan, Charles Emmet, IV:50, 466, 616, 694
Van Loon, Henrik Willem, III:354; IV:522; V:266
Van Norden's Magazine, IV:510
Van Nostrand, David, III:113*n*
Van Nostrand's Eclectic Engineering Magazine, III:113
Van Nostrand's Engineering Magazine, II:299
Van Oost, John W., III:185*n*
Van Renssalaer, Mrs. Schuyler, III:472
Van Schaick, S. W., IV:564
Van Vechten, Carl, V:147
Van Vorst, Bessie, V:73
Van Vorst, Mrs. John, IV:691
Van Vorst, Marie, III:400*n*; V:30
Van Zile, Edward Sims, IV:754
Vance, Arthur Turner, IV:185, 361, 362, 763*n*, 767–68

Vance, Louis Joseph, IV:421, 471, 473, 584, 616
Vancouver, Wash., III:75*n*
Vandalia, Ill., I:595
Vandenberg, Arthur Hendrick, IV:709
Vanderbilt, Consuelo, IV:758
Vanderbilt, Cornelius, III:4, 444; IV:756
Vanderbilt, William Henry, III:214
Vanderbilt University, V:100–2, 106–7
  magazine published at, IV:74
Vanderbilt University Quarterly, IV:74
Vanderlip, Frank Arthur, IV:519, 689
Vanderpoel, John Henry, IV:147
Vanguard, IV:176*n*
Vanity, IV:78, 85
Vanity Fair, II:104, 148, 150, 152, 179, 184, 188, 205; III:265*n*, 440; IV:47, 373, 760; V:171
  sketch of, II:520–29
Vardaman, Governor, V:280
Varney, Harold Lord, V:21, 25
Vassar Female College, III:102–3
Vázquez de Ayllón, Lucas, IV:121*n*
Veblen, Thorstein Bunde, III:542; IV:192; V:95
Vedder, Elihu, III:411; IV:144, 781
Vedder, Henry Clay, III:72*n*, 182
Vedette, III:132
Vegetarian, IV:317
Vegetarian Magazine, IV:317
Vehicle Monthly, III:216*n*
Velocipedist, III:211
Venable, Edward Carrington, IV:729
Venable, Richard M., III:383
Venable, William Henry, III:262*n*; IV:140*n*
Venereal disease, campaigns against, IV:553
Verdict, IV:386
Verdon, Ida, IV:502
Verlaine, Paul, IV:451
Vermont Chronicle, II:71*n*
Vermont Medical Monthly, IV:313*n*
Vermonter, IV:82
Verne, Jules, II:270; III:254, 460; IV:513, 685
Verplanck, Gulian Crommelin, I:280, 326, 608
Verrill, Addison Emory, I:304
Versailles
  conference, II:259
  treaty, V:208
Verse, *see* Poetry
Very, Jones, I:650, 662, 736
Veterans' magazines, III:132; IV:69
Veterinary journals, III:143
Vice, *see* Comstock, Anthony; Crime; Crime stories and reports; Municipal corruption; Prostitution
Vice-control periodicals, IV:199–200
Vick, E. C., III:483–84
Vick, James, II:90*n*
Vickery, P. O., III:38
Vickery's Fireside Visitor, III:38
Vickroy, T. R., III:312
Vick's Illustrated Monthly Magazine, III:162; IV:342
Vicksburg Daily Citizen, II:151
Victor, Metta Victoria Fuller, I:587; II:114, 172, 302, 466, 467; III:224; IV:366
Victor, Orville James, I:587; II:114, 193, 467
Victor Talking Machine, V:81
Victoria, Queen of England, I:397; IV:226, 685
Viereck, George Sylvester, IV:509–10, 654
Views, IV:351*n*
Vigilance committees (1865), II:120
Vigilant, IV:350
Villard, Henry, III:344; V:330
Villard, Oswald, V:89, 207
Villard, Oswald Garrison, III:331*n*, 346; IV:726, 748
  as editor, III:350–56
Villon, François, IV:425; V:118
Vincent, George Edgar, III:545; IV:181, 191, 748
Vincent, John Heyl, III:173, 545; IV:514
Vindicator, III:146*n*
Violin World, IV:254
Violinist, IV:254
Virginia
  early handicrafts in (1791), I:60
  secession of (1861), I:654
  See also specific cities and towns
Virginia, University of, I:648
  magazines published at, I:489; II:99
Virginia City, Mont., III:75*n*
Virginia Evangelical and Literary Magazine, I:205, 795
Virginia Historical Register and Literary Companion, I:382, 809
Virginia Law Journal, III:145*n*
Virginia Law Register, IV:347*n*
Virginia Literary Museum, I:489, 800
Virginia Magazine of History and Biography, IV:139
Virginia Medical Monthly, III:140*n*
Virginia School Journal, IV:270*n*
Virginia Seminary Magazine, IV:294

"Virginian, The" (Wister), V:119
Virginias, III:148
Virginius affair (1873), III:280
Vision, IV:296
Visitor, I:205*n,* 793
Vitchesbain, J. H., III:299*n*
Vivas, Éliseo, IV:739, 740
Vivisection, campaign against, IV:562
Vizetelly, Frank Horace, IV:573
Vizetelly, Henry, II:410
Vocalist, IV:254*n*
Vogue, V:165*n*
  sketch of, IV:756–62
Voice (temperance journal), III:310
Voice (Werner's), III:170; IV:251
Voice of Angels, III:82
Voice of Freedom, see: Emancipator
Voice magazines, musical, III:170
Voice of Masonry, II:215; IV:222*n*
Voice of Missions, IV:238
Voice of the Negro, IV:214*n*
Voice from the Old Brewery, III:314
Voidato-Patcevitsch, Iva Sergie, IV:756*n,* 761
Volcanology, IV:621
Volk, Leonard Wells, IV:114
Volstead Act, V:212
Von Hutten zum Stolzenberg, Baroness (Bettina Riddle), V:249
Von Kotzebue, August, V:121
Voorhees, Daniel, II:545
Vorse, Mary Heaton, IV:584; V:133
Vosburgh, Frederick G., IV:630, 632
Vose, John D., I:426; II:179
Vox Humana, III:198*n*
Vrooman, Frank Buffington, III:478

W. B. A. Review, IV:222
Waco, Tex., IV:292, 443
Wade, John Donald, V:116*n*
Wadsworth, F. L., III:82*n*
Wag, III:268*n*
Wages, I:33–34; III:12–13
  See also Salaries; Strikes; Trade unions; Working class
Waggoner, J. Fred, II:235
Wagner, Harr, IV:1–6
Wagner, Richard, II:253; III:192–93; IV:249
Wagner, Robert (artist), IV:66, 451
Wagner, Robert Ferdinand, IV:749
Wagner, Samuel, II:91
Wahl, William H., I:556*n;* III:127
Wait, Thomas B., I:541
Waite, Henry Randall, IV:181
Wakeman, Edgar L., III:54
Wakeman, Thaddeus Burr, IV:277
Waldie's Literary Omnibus, I:361, 803
Waldo, James E., III:45
Waldo, Richard H., V:137
Wales, George E., II:464
Wales, James Albert, III:268, 525, 528, 552
Wales, Salem Howe, II:316*n,* 319
Waley, Arthur, V:237
Walford, L. B., III:550
Walker, Charles Rumford, II:493*n*
Walker, E. C., III:301
Walker, E. D., IV:480, 481–84
Walker, Edwin, IV:219
Walker, General Edwin A., V:3*n,* 316
Walker, Francis Amasa, I:535; III:465*n,* 470; IV:173, 719, 721; V:330
Walker, Frank, IV:423
Walker, Harry Wilson, IV:86
Walker, Helen D., IV:708
Walker, Howell, IV:630
Walker, J. Bernard, II:323
Walker, James (editor of the *Christian Examiner*), I:284*n,* 286–87, 289
Walker, James John, IV:472
Walker, John Brisben, IV:35, 37, 169, 216, 218, 234, 319, 480*n,* 482–91, 600; V:342
Walker, Mrs. M. L., III:95
Walker, Mary, III:91, 96
Walker, Robert J. C., IV:671*n*
Walker, Robert John, II:540*n,* 542, 543
Walker, Roy, III:505
Walker, Ryan, IV:205, 415
Walker, T. Dart, IV:100*n*
Walker, Timothy, I:452, 601
Walker, W. D., III:533*n,* 534
Walker, Wareham, II:65*n*
Walker, William, I:752, 753
Walking matches, III:218–19
Wall, James Walter, II:545
Wall Street
  magazine comment on, I:472
  See also Stock Exchange
Wall Street Underwriter and the Joint Stock Register, II:94*n*
Wallace, Alfred Henry, IV:407
Wallace, Benjamin J., II:62*n*
Wallace Edgar, III:489; IV:466; V:85
Wallace, Francis, IV:478
Wallace, Henry (founder of *Wallace's Farmer*), IV:340
Wallace, Henry (legal editor), I:451*n*
Wallace, Henry Agard, IV:730; V:191*n,* 216, 219–21
Wallace, Henry Cantwell, III:157

Wallace, J. M. Power, II:93*n*
Wallace, John H., III:215
Wallace, John S., I:427
Wallace, Lew, III:248; IV:141
Wallace, Ray, IV:367*n*
Wallace, T. C., I:575
Wallace, Walter W., IV:214
Wallace, William, II:93*n*
Wallace's Farmer, II:90*n;* III:157; IV:340
Wallace's Monthly, III:215
Wallach, Rita Teresa, IV:744
Wallack, Lester, III:204; IV:256, 721
Wallack, Mrs. Lester, IV:127*n*
Wallin, Samuel, II:454
Wallingford, Conn., II:207
Wall-Paper News and Interior Decorator, IV:323*n*
Walpole, Hugh, III:489; IV:436, 438; V:86, 117*n,* 123, 265, 337
Walpole, N.H., I:194
Walsh, Francis, Jr., I:44*n*
Walsh, Henry Collins, V:248
Walsh, Richard John, IV:453*n,* 469
Walsh, Robert, I:146, 155, 189, 409; II:221
as editor, I:129, 222, 271–76, 307
quoted, I:184, 185, 436
Walsh, Thomas, IV:436
Walsh, William Shepard, IV:64, 125
Walsh, William Shepherd, III:396*n,* 399–400
Waltmer's Magazine, IV:285*n*
Walton, Francis, III:422*n,* 434–35
Walton, Joseph, I:562*n,* 564–65
Waltz, popularity of, I:479
Wanamaker, John, II:75*n;* III:235; IV:246; V:72, 74
Wang Doodle, II:185*n*
Wannamaker, William Hane, V:273*n,* 283
War Cry, III:85; IV:288
War Medicine, IV:531
War reporting, *see specific wars*
War of 1812, I:125, 161, 188, 240–41, 243, 272, 280, 285
Warbler, IV:310*n*
Ward, Artemus, *see* Browne, Charles Farrar
Ward, C. J., III:161
Ward, Elizabeth Stuart Phelps, II:267, 395, 505*n;* III:99*n,* 247, 508; IV:257, 292, 304, 350, 514, 538, 593, 768
Ward, Herbert, IV:726
Ward, Mrs. Humphry, II:402; III:471; IV:110, 141, 280–81, 295, 601, 720
Ward, John Quincy Adams, III:182, 183
Ward, Julius Hammond, II:249
Ward, Kirk, IV:106
Ward, Lauriston, IV:126*n*
Ward, Leo L., V:183–85
Ward, Lester Frank, IV:191, 514
Ward, William Hayes, II:367*n,* 374, 376, 377, 378; III:465*n;* IV:719
Ware, Eugene Fitch, IV:97
Ware, Henry, I:134, 262, 288, 570–71
Ware, Henry, Jr., I:135, 138, 285
Ware, John, I:152*n,* 288; II:228
Ware, William (editor of *Christian Examiner*), I:284*n,* 287–88, 401, 609
Ware, William Robert, III:129*n;* IV:323
Ware's Valley Monthly, III:51
Warfield, Benjamin Breckinridge, III:74
Waring, George Edwin, I:732; II:413, 506*n;* III:461
Warman, Cy, IV:50, 224, 331, 593, 651, 692
Warne, Colston E., V:58
Warner, Arthur, III:355
Warner, Charles Dudley, I:535; II:398, 399, 402, 424, 425, 506*n,* 511*n;* III:238, 257, 314, 424, 439, 463, 503; IV:61, 255, 267, 513
Warner, Eltinge F., V:260–62, 265, 270
Warner, Francis Lester, II:493*n*
Warner, Glen Scobey (Pop), IV:700
Warner, H. J., I:292*n*
Warner, Susan, II:171; III:100
Warner, William Bishop, IV:584
Warren, A. C., II:409
Warren, A. W., II:475
Warren, Earl, IV:476
Warren, Fred D., IV:205, 206*n*
Warren, J. L. L. F., II:90
Warren, John Collins, II:139
Warren, Joseph, II:432*n,* 433
Warren, Mrs. Mercy, I:203
Warren, O. G., II:209
Warren, Robert Penn, IV:730, 740; V:100*n,* 107, 110–16, 242
Warren, Ohio, IV:356
Warrington's Musical Review, III:197*n*
Washburn, Edward Abiel, II:551
Washburn, Elihu Benjamin, IV:719
Washburn, Emory, II:235
Washburn, L. K., III:88*n;* IV:278
Washington, Booker Taliaferro, II:271; III:430; IV:213, 214, 743, 780; V:275–76, 278, 287
Washington, George, I:52–53, 97–98, 101, 102, 116, 263, 553

Washington, D.C.
nationalist era magazines in, I:164
expansionist era magazines in
abolitionist periodical, I:457
general magazines, I:268, 346
literary magazines, I:356, 677*n*, 678
Sunday school magazine, II:101
Civil War era magazines in (1850–65)
military periodical, II:150
Sunday school magazine, II:101
post-Civil War magazines in
Masonic periodical, III:315
military periodicals, III:132
scientific periodicals, III:109*n*, 112
temperance periodical, III:310*n*
urban weeklies, IV:89
women's rights magazine, III:96
Gilded Age magazines in (1885–1905)
amateur periodical, IV:390*n*
family veterans' periodical, IV:69
Florence Crittenton periodical, IV:200
forestry periodical, IV:343
free-silver periodicals, IV:163
geographic periodicals, IV:620–32
governmental magazines, IV:90
health periodical, III:139
historical publication, III:140
insurance periodical, IV:351*n*
labor periodical, III:300
legal periodical, IV:347*n*
literary magazines, IV:89, 92
military periodical, III:132
news periodical, IV:648*n*
political periodicals, IV:73, 89, 178
populist periodical, IV:176
religious magazines, IV:285*n*, 298
review magazine, IV:61
scientific periodicals, III:112; IV:308
settlement-house periodical, IV:195*n*
society magazines, IV:89–90
temperance periodicals, III:310*n*; IV:210
trade-union periodicals, IV:220
urban weeklies, III:89–90
women's periodical, IV:361
women's suffrage periodicals, III:95; IV:355
modern magazines in (1905–)
anthropological journal, IV:308
current events periodical, V:191*n*
forestry periodical, IV:343
geographic magazine, IV:620*n*
Indian periodical, IV:215*n*
insurance periodical, IV:351*n*
legal periodical, IV:347*n*
Masonic periodical, IV:222*n*
medical journal, IV:313*n*
military periodical, III:132
religious magazines, II:65, 67*n*
rifle periodical, IV:381*n*
temperance periodical, IV:210
trade-union periodical, IV:220
Washington, Idaho and Oregon Farmer, IV:341
Washington, N.C., III:80
Washington Christian Advocate, II:67*n*
Washington Confidential (Mortimer), V:24–25
Washington Hatchet, IV:89
Washington Law Reporter, III:144*n*; IV:347*n*
Washington Life, IV:90
Washington Medical Annals, IV:313*n*
Washington Mirror, IV:89
Washington Newsletter, IV:285*n*
Washingtonian, III:310*n*
Wasp, I:170, 792; II:118*n*, III:56–57, 101; IV:77, 106
Wasson, David Atwood, I:290; II:152, 503, 505; III:18, 35*n*, 78, 230, 301, 302
Watch Tower, III:85*n*
Watch and Ward Society, Mencken's conflict with, V:13–15
Watchman (Boston), IV:291
Watchman (Chicago), III:82; IV:287*n*
Watchman (Washington), III:80
Watchman-Examiner, I:138, 796
Watchman of the Prairies, II:65*n*
Watchman and Reflector, II:64, 266; III:72
See also Watchman-Examiner
Watchword, III:85*n*
Water cure, I:441, 475, 700; II:87; IV:316
Water-Cure Journal, I:441, 808; II:87; III:139; IV:316
Water-Cure Monthly, II:87
Water-Cure World, II:87
Water-Gas Journal, III:131
Water and Gas Review, IV:323*n*
Water sports, III:211; IV:634, 636
Water Works Engineering, IV:323*n*
Water Works and Sewerage, IV:323*n*
Waterloo, Iowa, IV:186*n*, 344*n*, 345
Waterloo, Stanley, IV:115*n*, 767
Waterman, Nixon, IV:224, 390*n*
Waterman's Journal, IV:62
Watertown, N.Y., IV:221*n*
Waterville, Maine, II:36*n*; III:215*n*; IV:363*n*
Watervillonian, see: Yankee Blade
Waterways Journal, IV:334
Watkins, Tobias, I:126, 293–96

Watrous, A. E., III:528
Watson, Dawson, IV:451
Watson, Donald, IV:629
Watson, Egbert P., III:116*n*
Watson, Elizabeth, III:82; IV:304*n*
Watson, Elmo Scott, III:274*n*
Watson, Henry Brereton Marriott, IV:116*n*, 691
Watson, Henry C., I:366, 757*n*, 758; II:452*n*, 455; III:196
Watson, J. F., I:279*n*
Watson, James Sibley, Jr., III:542
Watson, James V., II:67
Watson, John ("Ian Maclaren"), III:429; IV:49*n*, 134, 226, 230, 435, 544, 593, 685
Watson, John Broadus, V:121
Watson, John Whitaker, II:472
Watson, Stephen Marion, III:259
Watson, Thomas Edward, IV:178
Watson, Thomas John, IV:147*n*
Watson, Warren, III:109*n*
Watson, William, II:211*n*; 132, 141, 451
Watson, William Perry, III:142
Watson's Art Journal, III:196
Watson's Weekly Art Journal, II:197
Watters, James, I:122
Watterson, Henry, II:251; III:477; IV:164*n*
Wattles, John D., II:75*n*
Waud, Alfred R., II:45, 397, 409, 449, 466, 474, 481; III:187, 359–60, 420
Waud, William, II:474
Waugh, Arthur, III:550; IV:121
Waugh, Beverly, I:299*n*
Waugh, Evelyn, V:136
Waugh, William W., IV:81*n*
Wausau, Wis., IV:390*n*
Waverly, Iowa, IV:345*n*
Waverly Library, IV:118
Waverly Magazine, II:41–42, 100; IV:79*n*
Way of Faith, IV:296
Wayland, Francis, I:461; II:154
Wayland, Julius Augustus, IV:204–6
Wayland's Monthly, IV:205–6
Wayne, Hamilton, III:402*n*
Wayside Monthly, IV:115
Wealth
  magazines on, I:470; III:293; IV:489, 495, 614, 662; V:75–78, 149
  increase in, IV:10–11
Weapons, development of, IV:319
Weatherby, George W., III:53*n*
Weaver, James Baird, III:157; IV:177, 406
Weaver, John Van Alstyn, III:390; IV:440
Weaver, Richard M., IV:738
Weaver, William Dixon, III:122*n*
Webb, Alfred, III:337
Webb, Charles Henry ("John Paul"), II:118
Webb, George J., I:435
Webb, James Watson, II:282
Webb, Mohammed Alex Russell, IV:287
Webb, Sidney, IV:746
Webb Publishing Company, V:45
Webbe, John, I:24, 71, 72, 73–74
Webber, Charles Wilkins, I:752–53
Weber, Charles, II:464
Webster, Daniel, I:255, 318, 423, 751, 753, 781; II:227, 290
Webster, David, I:451*n*
Webster, Frank B., III:111
Webster, Franklin, IV:350
Webster, Harrie, IV:233
Webster, Henry Kitchell, IV:690; V:85, 290
Webster, Jean, IV:546
Webster, John White, I:152*n*; II:228
Webster, Noah
  attacked, I:147–48, 186, 257, 235–36
  as contributor, I:62–64, 600
  as editor, I:29–30, 104–7, 156
  as member of Friendly Club, I:115
Webster-Hayne debate (1830), II:234
Webster's Collegiate Dictionary, V:43*n*
Webster's Dictionary, II:177
Wedekind, Franz, V:258
Wedel, Mildred Mott, V:344–45
  Editorial Note by, V:xv–xvii
Wee Wisdom, IV:286
Weed, Clarence Moores, V:158
Weed, Thurlow, III:376
Weeden, William Babcock, III:436
Week, III:256
Weeklies
  in nationalist era (1794–1825), I:121–29
    religious, I:136–38
  in expansionist era (1825–50), I:354–66
  in Civil War era (1850–65), II:33–45, 150, 178, 206
    home, I:57–58
    library, II:172
    religious, II:61, 103
  average circulation of, II:10
  earliest (1771), I:92
  increase in, I:210
  in movement for cheap literature, I:348
  as newspaper supplements, IV:69–70

number of, I:341–42, 387; II:4*n*
payments to contributors, II:21–22
trends, II:33–45
variety, II:33–34
See also Urban weeklies; *specific weeklies*
Weekly, V:74
Weekly Budget, III:45
Weekly Export Bulletin, IV:186*n*
Weekly Journal of Free Opinion, II:367*n*
Weekly Magazine, III:53; IV:55*n*
Weekly Magazine of Original Essays, I:122, 149, 173, 174, 790
Weekly Messenger, I:355, 674, 803
Weekly Mirror, I:320*n*, 329–30
Weekly Museum, I:122, 790
Weekly News and Southern Literary Gazette, II:110*n*
Weekly Novelette, II:36, 411*n*, 468
Weekly People, IV:175
Weekly Recorder, II:63*n*
See also: Presbyterian Banner
Weekly Register, see: Niles' Weekly Register
Weekly Review, II:379
Weekly Sports, IV:47*n*, 372–73
Weekly Trade Circular, III:491, 492
Weekly Underwriter, IV:350
Weekly Underwriter and the Insurance Press, II:94*n*
Weekly Weather Chronicle, III:112
Weeks, Edward Augustus, Jr., II:493*n*, 515
Weeks, Raymond, V:182–83, 185
Week's Progress, IV:64
Weir, Robert Walter, I:520; II:475
Weiss, John, I:292*n*, 775, 776, 778; III:78, 91, 301, 386
Weitenkampf, Frank, IV:720
Welby, Mrs. Amelia B. Coppuck, I:553, 692
Welch, Deshler, IV:260
Welch, Thomas B., I:208, 521; III:143*n*
Welch, W. Henry, IV:68*n*
Welcome Friend, IV:367*n*
Welcome Guest, II:411
Weld, Ezra W., I:108*n*
Weld, Horatio Hastings, I:127*n*, 359, 360*n*, 361, 546*n*, 587; II:410
Weld, Mason C., I:731
Weldon, Charles Dater, II:397
Welford, B. R., II:346
Well-Spring, II:101
Welles, Gideon, III:376
Welliver, Judson Churchill, IV:601, 615, 616, 617, 662; V:149, 288
Wellman, Walter, III:270*n*; IV:456, 593, 625
Wellman's Literary Miscellany, II:116
Wells, Anna Marie, I:412
Wells, Benjamin Willis, IV:733*n*, 734
Wells, Carolyn, II:431; III:400*n*, 401, 485, 504, 530, 532, 555; IV:46*n*, 49*n*, 50, 388, 389, 436, 438, 646, 692; V:251
Wells, Charles H., IV:92
Wells, David Ames, III:292, 498
Wells, Herbert George, II:257; III:478; IV:466, 474, 490, 498, 501, 552; V:51, 84, 211, 336
Wells, John, I:115
Wells, Samuel Roberts, I:441, 447
Wells, Thomas Bucklin, II:383*n*, 403
Wells, William, III:465*n*
Wells, William Bittle, IV:107
Wells, William Harvey, II:303
Wells and Lilly, II:221, 227
Wellstood, William, I:328, 522; II:303; III:187
Welsh, Herbert, IV:60
Welty, Eudora, IV:739; V:284
Wenham, Mass., III:161
Wentworth, E., II:301*n*
Wenzell, Albert Beck, IV:455, 564, 692
Werfel, Franz, IV:553
Werk, Emil, IV:381
Werner, Edgar S., III:170
Werner's Voice Magazine, III:170; IV:251
Wertenbaker, Thomas Jefferson, IV:737
Wertheim, Maurice, III:355–56
Wertheimer, Rose M., IV:656
Wessel, E. L., IV:64*n*
West, II:119–21, 206, 548–49; III:58–60, 414–15, 473
agriculture in, II:434
cattle-raising in, III:61–62
culture in, I:432; III:242–44
expansionist spirit in, IV:94–95
politics, I:342
development of, III:49–50; IV:102–3
general press accounts of
early (1741–94), I:32
nationalist era (1794–1825), I:207, 241, 275
expansionist era (1825–50), I:355, 384–86, 422–23, 609, 674, 725
Civil War era (1850–65), II:118–21, 425, 434
Post-Civil War era (1865–85), III:61–62, 376
Gilded Age, III:473; IV:102–3
literary talent in, III:242–44
music in, III:242–44
outlawry in, III:62
political changes in, I:340

West—*Continued*
problems of, III:60–62; IV:103
religion in, I:369
wildlife in, III:60–61
West, Benjamin, I:201, 436
West, Henry Litchfield, IV:432*n*, 438, 517
West, James H., IV:283
West, Jessamyn, IV:476
West, Rebecca, IV:441, 503; V:211
West, Robert (Congregational editor), III:77*n*
West, Robert A., I:743*n*, 744
West American Monthly, II:115*n*
West American Review, II:115*n*
West American Scientist, III:109
West Coast and Puget Sound Lumberman, IV:325*n*
West Grove, Pa., IV:342*n*
West Meriden, Conn., III:210*n*
West Shore, III:57, 148
West Virginia Bar, IV:348*n*
West Virginia School Journal, III:168
Westcott, Edward Noyes, IV:141
Westcott, Thompson, I:450
Western Academician, I:491, 803
Western Architect, IV:323
Western Architect and Builder, III:129
Western Art Journal, II:194*n*
Western Art-Union, II:191
Western Baptist, IV:292
Western Baptist Review, II:63
Western Bookseller, III:235
Western Breeders' Journal, III:158
Western Brewer, III:135
Western Camera Notes, IV:150*n*
Western Christian, II:65*n*
Western Christian Advocate, I:389, 802; II:66; III:70
Western Christian Monitor, I:120*n*
Western Confectioner and Baker, III:135
Western Continent, I:362, 808
Western Creamery, IV:186*n*
Western Cyclist, III:214*n*
Western Democratic Review, II:116
Western Dental Journal, IV:317
Western Destiny, V:26*n*
Western Druggist, III:133
Western Economist, IV:351*n*
Western Educational Review, III:51
Western Electrician, IV:322
Western Empire, IV:341
Western Episcopalian, II:70*n*
Western Examiner, I:659, 802
Western Farm Life, IV:341
Western Farmer, I:444*n*; II:90; III:157
Western Farmer and Gardener (Cincinnati), I:443*n*, 805
Western Farmer and Gardener (Indianapolis), I:444*n*, 807
Western Field, IV:381*n*
Western Finance and Trade, III:147*n*
Western Friend, III:81
Western Fruit-Grower, IV:341
Western Galaxy, IV:104
Western General Advertiser, II:114*n*
Western Granger and Home Journal, III:149*n*
Western Graphic, IV:107
Western Herald, II:71*n*
Western Home, III:101
Western Home Journal, III:157
Western Home Visitor, II:51
Western Homoeopathic Observer, II:85*n*
Western Horseman, III:215*n*
Western Hotel Reporter, III:136
Western Insurance Review, III:146*n*
Western Journal, III:116*n*
Western Journal and Civilian, II:389, 809; II:116
Western Journal of Education, II:117; IV:271*n*
Western Journal of the Medical and Physical Sciences, I:439*n*
Western Journal of Medicine and Surgery, I:439, 439*n*, 805
Western Journal of Surgery, Obstetrics, and Gynecology, IV:314*n*
Western Jurist, III:145*n*
Western Lady's Book, II:52, 58
Western Law Journal, I:452, 807; II:93*n*
Western Literary Cabinet, II:58
Western Literary Journal and Monthly Magazine, I:388, 807
Western Literary Journal and Monthly Review, I:387, 803
Western Literary Magazine, II:115
Western Literary Messenger, II:20, 116
Western Luminary, I:206, 798
Western Machinist, III:116
Western Magazine, I:389, 808; III:53
Western Magazine and Review, *see: Western Monthly Review*
Western magazines
far-Western, II:116–18
mailing difficulties of, I:120*n*
predictions of, I:208
problems of, I:120*n*, 193, 207, 518
publishing centers of, I:205–7; II:114–16; III:56–57; IV:103–8
quality of, I:208, 384–90
resources of, I:205
trends, II:113–21
See also specific magazines, cities, and towns

Western Manufacturer, III:127
Western Medical and Physical Journal, I:439*n,* 799
Western Medical Review, IV:314*n*
Western Medical Times, III:141*n*
Western Messenger, I:387, 658–63
Western Methodist, III:71*n*
Western Minerva, I:797
Western Mining World, IV:322*n*
Western Monitor, I:311
Western Monthly, III:413*n,* 414–15
Western Monthly Magazine, I:387, 595–98, 515
Western Monthly Review, I:120*n,* 146, 175, 191, 514–15
sketch of, I:559–61
Western Musical Review, III:197*n*
Western Musician, IV:254*n*
Western News Company, III:8
Western Paper Trade, III:135
Western Penman, III:170
Western Pioneer, II:65*n*
Western Plowman, III:156
Western Poultry Journal, IV:345*n*
Western Presbyterian, III:74*n;* IV:293*n*
Western Quarterly Reporter of Medical, Surgical and Natural Science, I:207, 797
Western Railroad Gazette, II:81
Western Railroader, III:126*n*
Western Recorder, II:64, 65*n;* IV:292
Western Reserve Library, V:349
Western Review, II:116*n*
Western Review and Miscellaneous Magazine, I:146, 164–65, 191, 193, 205–6
founded, I:207
sketch of, I:311–12
Western Review of Science and Industry, III:109*n*
Western Rural, I:444*n;* II:90; III:149, 156; IV:176
Western School Journal, IV:271*n*
Western Soldiers' Friend, III:52
Western Spirit, III:135
Western Sportsman and Live Stock News, III:215*n*
Western Standard, III:74
Western Star, III:82*n*
Western Stationer, III:135, 235
Western Stock Journal, III:159
Western Teacher, IV:271*n*
Western Tobacco Journal, III:135
Western Undertaker, III:133
Western Underwriter, IV:351*n*
Western Unitarian Association, I:659
Western Watchman, III:69*n*
Western Weekly, IV:104*n*
Western World, IV:104
Westerner, IV:108
Westfield, N.Y., III:168
Westminster, III:74
Westminster Lesson Leaf, III:8*n*
Westminster Review, II:130; IV:228
Westmoreland, Gen. William C., V:323*n*
Weston, III:51, 184
Weston, Bertine E., III:517*n,* 519
Weston, Christine, IV:554
Weston, H. G., III:72
Weston, John W., III:113
Weston, S. E., II:35*n*
Weston, Samuel Burns, IV:27
Westrum, Adrian Schade van, IV:127
Wet Dog, IV:391
Wetjen, Albert Richard, IV:473
Wetmore, Alexander, IV:627, 628
Wetmore, Claude H., IV:101
Wetmore's Weekly, IV:101
Wevill, George, II:523; III:441
Weybright, Victor, IV:749
Weydemeyer, Joseph, II:207
Weyl, Walter Edward, V:191*n,* 196–97, 209
Weyman, Stanley John, II:482; IV:456, 592, 616, 685
Weyman, William, I:25*n*
Wharton, Don, IV:731
Wharton, Edith, II:506*n;* III:489; IV:409, 434, 457, 490, 721, 723, 724, 726, 727, 728; V:336
Wharton, Francis, I:697
Wharton, Thomas Isaac, I:279*n,* 282
What Cheer, Iowa, V:x
What to Eat, IV:363
What's the Use? IV:390*n*
Wheatley, Phillis, I:89
Wheatley, Richard, III:545
Wheaton, Henry, II:228
Whedon, Daniel Denison, I:299*n,* 300–301, 741; III:23, 70, 383
Wheel, III:213
Wheel and Cycle Trade Review, III:213*n;* IV:379
Wheeler, Andrew Carpenter ("Nym Crinkle"), III:199*n,* 200; IV:66, 410, 434
Wheeler, Benjamin Ide, IV:74
Wheeler, Cora Stuart, II:36*n*
Wheeler, Edward Jewitt, IV:506*n,* 509–510, 569*n,* 571–73
Wheeler, Ella, *see* Wilcox, Ella Wheeler
Wheeler, Everett Pepperell, II:512
Wheeler, Howard, V:72*n,* 85
Wheeler-Lea Act (1938), V:140
Wheeling, W. Va., III:168

Wheelman, III:212, 213*n,* 219, IV:633–34
Wheelman's Gazette, III:213; IV:379
Wheelock, John Gall, IV:654; V:258
Wheelwoman, IV:378
Wheelwright, John Tyler, IV:559
Wheelwright, Philip, IV:739
Whelpley, F. M., I:753
Whelpley, James Davenport, I:750*n,* 752
Whidden, Hamlin, IV:645
Whig Review, see: American Whig Review
Whigham, Henry James, II:349*n,* 355; IV:147*n,* 458
Whim, I:166, 795; IV:390*n*
Whip, III:269*n*
Whipple, Chandler H., IV:417*n*
Whipple, Charles K., II:292
Whipple, Edwin Percy, I:406 423, 490, 553, 720; II:26, 240, 243, 389, 503, 505*n;* III:172, 232
Whipple, Leander Edmund, IV:287*n*
Whipple, Leon, IV:747*n,* 748, 749
Whiskey Ring scandal, III:4, 289
Whist, IV:382
Whist, growth of, IV:381–82
Whistler, James Abbott McNeill, III:182*n;* IV:144
Whitaker, Daniel Kimball, I:383, 664–65, 721–25; II:110*n,* 339; III:45
Whitaker's Magazine, I:383*n;* II:110*n*
Whitaker's Southern Magazine, I:383*n;* II:110*n*
Whitcher, Mrs. Frances Miriam, I:585–86
White, Andrew Dickson, II:271, 414; III:164, 439, 498; IV:514
White, Charles Ignatius, I:371, 716–17
White, Frank Marshall, III:528; IV:556*n,* 563
White, George G., II:335
White, Horace, III:297, 337, 344, 346, 349; IV:163*n,* 171, 180
White, J. D., II:91
White, J. M., IV:108
White, Leander Mitchell, 104*n*
White, Matthew, Jr., IV:117*n,* 362, 417*n,* 420–21, 609, 612, 617
White, Maunsell, II:340–41
White, Nelia Gardner, IV:771; V:184, 273*n*
White, Owen P., IV:470
White, Richard Grant, I:425, 613, 753, 771; II:26, 424, 505*n,* 510*n;* III:13*n,* 21, 32, 207, 231, 238, 272, 273, 309, 363, 368–69, 375, 376, 419, 456
White, Stanford, III:467; IV:481, 718
White, Stewart Edward, II:273; III:430, 512; IV:105, 601, 637, 638, 695; V:80, 119
"White, Thom," *see* Elliott, Charles Wyllys
White, Thomas Willys, II:629–44
White, Trumbell, IV:116, 499, 636; V:27*n,* 30, 32, 72*n,* 84–85
White, William Allen, II:512; III:510*n,* 512, 513, 514, 555; IV:97, 107*n,* 210, 472, 592, 600, 685, 692, 696, 703, 706, 721, 728; V:333
White, William Chapman, IV:730
White, William N., III:154
White Banner, II:29, 212
White Elephant, IV:117
White Owl, IV:117*n*
White River Junction, N.H., IV:82
White Springs, Mont., III:158
Whitefield, George, I:76–77
Whitefield controversy (1741), II:75–77
Whitehead, John, IV:296
White's Sayings, IV:247*n*
Whiting, Frances, IV:480*n*
Whiting, Henry, II:233
Whiting, Lillian, III:42*n;* IV:45*n,* 81
Whitlock, Brand, III:488; IV:46*n;* V:85, 88
Whitlock, L. L., III:82
Whitman, Bernard, I:571
Whitman, Edmund Allen, IV:728
Whitman, Leroy, II:547*n,* 549
Whitman, Walt, II:359, 366, 433, 680; II:39, 42, 168–9, 253, 254, 271, 429, 498, 501, 508; III:41, 230, 231, 238, 241, 278, 305, 344, 373–74, 473, 548; IV:87, 121, 129, 279–80; V:8–9, 238, 342
Whitney, Adeline Dutton Train, II:505*n;* III:463, 508; IV:538
Whitney, Caspar, II:483; IV:458, 633*n,* 637–38
Whitney, Eli, I:304
Whitney, Flora, V:192
Whitney, Harry Payne, IV:466, 467
Whitney, J. H., III:188
Whitney, J. L., III:518
Whitney, Thomas R., II:123
Whitney, William C., V:192
Whitney, William Dwight, II:248; III:536, 537
Whitney's Musical Guest, III:197*n*
Whiton, James Morris, III:429
Whitson, Thomas, IV:53*n*
Whittaker, Charles, IV:101
Whittaker's Milwaukee Magazine, III:55
Whittelsey, Mrs. A. G., II:57*n*
Whittelsey, S., II:57*n*

Whittemore, George, IV:184
Whittier, Cal., IV:296
Whittier, John Greenleaf, I:412; II:134, 168, 175, 197*n*, 211, 221, 275, 373, 496, 501, 502, 504, 510; IV:129, 398
criticism of, III:455
as contributor, I:355, 563, 600–2, 609, 679, 680, 737, 764
as editor, I:457
Whittier, Matthew ("Ethan Spike"), II:527
Whittingham, William Rollinson, II:365
Whole Family, IV:48
Wholesale Grocery Review, IV:187*n*
Whyte-Melville, George John, II:439
Wichita, Kan., III:55; IV:178
Wickerman, Charles I., IV:671*n*
Wickersham, George Woodward, IV:500
Wickware, Francis G., V:344
Widdemer, Margaret, IV:440; V:236, 266
Wide Awake, III:175, 177
sketch of, III:508–9
Wide Awake Library, III:179; IV:119
Wide West, II:118*n*
Wieland, C. M., I:192
Wieniawski, Henri, III:193, 416
Wiese, Otis, V:140
Wiese, Otto Lee, IV:580*n*, 585–88
Wiggam, Albert Edward, IV:787
Wiggin, Frank A., IV:81*n*
Wiggin, Kate Douglas, II:400; III:503; IV:544, 546, 724, 768
Wigglesworth, Michael, I:570
Wikoff, Henry, I:681
Wikoff (Chevalier) Henry, II:44*n*
Wilber, John, I:564
Wilber, Ray Lyman, IV:533
Wilcox, Ella Wheeler, II:309, 417 462; III:53, 100, 229–30, 511; IV:49*n*, 84, 98, 120, 123, 359, 361, 408, 496, 537, 542, 612, 765; V:136, 248
Wild Oats, III:265, 266*n*
Wild West shows, III:209
Wild West stories, IV:120
Wild West Weekly, IV:119
Wilde, Oscar, III:250, 400; V:247
Wilde, Richard Henry, I:546*n*, 630, 633
Wilde, Willie, IV:57–58
Wilder, B. F., III:484
Wilder, C. D., III:484
Wilder, George Warren, III:482, 484; IV:47; V:74–75, 81–82
Wilder, Jones Warren, III:481 483, 484
Wilder, Marshall Pinckney, IV:57
Wilder, Royal G., III:84
Wilder, Silas W., II:180, 181
Wilder, Thornton, V:337
Wildlife
destruction of, III:60–61
illustrations of, IV:627, 725
magazines on, IV:593, 627
Wildman, Edwin, IV:511, 519
Wildman, Rounsevelle, III:402*n*, 407–8
Wile, Simeon, III:132
Wile, William C., III:140*n*
Wiley, David, I:152–53
Wiley, Harvey Washington, IV:651; V:134, 138
Wiley, Isaac William, II:301*n*
Wiley, John, I:375, 551
Wiley's Literary Telegraph, III:492
Wilford's Microcosm, III:89
Wilhelm II (German Kaiser), IV:231
Wilkes, George, I:480*n*, 481; II:203, 325
Wilkes, John, V:316
Wilkes-Barre, Pa., IV:139
Wilkes' Spirit of the Times, II:203–4
See also: Spirit of the Times
Wilkins, Mary Eleanor, II:398*n*; III:389, 487; IV:71*n*, 480, 544, 769; V:73
Wilkins, Milan William, IV:175
Wilkins, William E., III:147
Wilkinson, Florence, IV:100*n*, 602
Wilkinson, Harold, I:580*n*, 593
Wilkinson, Marguerite, IV:440
Wilkinson, William Cleaver, III:465*n*
Will, Thomas Elmer, IV:415
Will Rossiter Monthly, IV:253–54
Willamette Farmer, III:158
Willard, C. D., IV:107*n*
Willard, Emma, I:495
Willard, Frances Elizabeth Caroline, II:303; III:416; IV:72, 181, 358; V:287
Willard, Josiah Flynt, IV:115*n*, 125, 496
Willard, Mary B., III:310
Willard, Sidney, I:255*n*, 257, 344, 604–5; II:227
Willets, Gilson, II:464
William and Mary College Quarterly Historical Magazine, IV:139
Williams, Albert Rhys, IV:749
Williams, B. Lawton, IV:733
Williams, Ben Ames, II:435; III:489; IV:366*n*, 693, 709; V:85
Williams, Blanche Colton, V:117, 123
Williams, Byron, IV:367*n*
Williams, Churchill, IV:708
Williams, David, III:128*n*, 129; IV:183
Williams, Eleazar, II:421, 422*n*

Williams, Gluyas, IV:475, 502, 566
Williams, Gurney, IV:476
Williams, Henry T., II:90*n;* III:161
Williams, J. H., III:270*n*
Williams, Jesse Lynch, IV:271, 389, 466, 721
Williams, John S., I:422
Williams, John W., I:276
Williams, Maynard Owen, IV:628, 632
Williams, Michael, IV:520
Williams, Miles Evans, III:156*n;* IV:340
Williams, Samuel, I:122*n*
Williams, Samuel H., III:53–4
Williams, Sarah Langdon, III:94
Williams, Talcott, II:379; III:235*n*
Williams, Valentine, IV:471
Williams, Walter, V:64
Williams, Whiting, IV:728
Williams, William Carlos, IV:739; V:173, 177–78, 237, 241
Williams, William W., III:262*n*
Williams, Wythe, IV:469
Williamson, A. J., II:37–38
Williamson, Alice Muriel, III:496; V:158
Williamson, Charles Norris, III:486; V:158
Williamsport, Pa., IV:68–69
Willing, Jennie F., III:310
Willis, Julia, II:352
Willis, Nathaniel, I:8, 138, 492
  as editor, II:262–66
Willis, Nathaniel Parker, I:274, 409, 759; II:57, 150, 166, 264, 265, 498; III:17, 102, 229; IV:677
  as contributor, I:129, 138, 335, 392, 495–98, 506, 507, 509, 546, 585, 608, 627, 633, 719
  as editor, I:320*n,* 323, 325, 327–30, 344, 356–58, 360*n,* 366, 577–79; II:349–54
  quoted, I:411, 415, 736–37
Willis, Sara P., *see* Parton, Sara Payson Willis
Willkie, Wendell, IV:476, 711
Wills, Helen, IV:700
Wills, Jesse Ely, V:100*n,* 110, 112
Wills, Ridley, V:100*n,* 107–8
Willsie, Honoré, *see* Morrow, Honoré Willsie
Wilmer, Lambert A., I:380, 587*n,* 639; IV:675–76
Wilmington, Del., II:63*n;* III:31*n,* 71*n,* 143*n*
Wilmington, N.C., III:75*n*
Wilshire, Henry Gaylord, IV:206
Wilshire's Magazine, IV:206
Wilson, Alexander, I:123, 177, 201, 221, 235
Wilson, Allen Benjamin, II:318
Wilson, Clarence True, IV:470
Wilson, Edmund, IV:730; V:191*n,* 211, 214–15
Wilson, Forceythe, II:505*n;* III:237, 238
Wilson, Franklin, I:666*n*
Wilson, George Henry, III:197*n*
Wilson, Harry Leon, III:520*n,* 530; IV:695, 696; V:30
Wilson, Henry D., IV:491, 492
Wilson, James, III:157; IV:494, 779
Wilson, James Grant, II:69, 272, 551; III:260, 376, 397, 416, 418, 429; IV:14*n*
Wilson, John S., I:589
Wilson, Matthew, I:90
Wilson, "Tug," III:218
Wilson, William Lyne, IV:73
Wilson, Woodrow, I:535; II:258–259, 273, 378, 401, 402, 485, 512; III:349, 350, 486, 531, 546; IV:180, 181, 462–63, 465, 478, 509, 516, 549, 617, 655, 662, 705, 707, 769, 782–83, 785; V:36, 71, 92, 197–201, 204–8, 216, 333
Wilson Bulletin, IV:310*n*
Wilson's Photographic Magazine, II:194*n*
Winchell, Newton Horace, IV:309
Winchell, Walter, IV:477, 567; V:308, 313
Winchell's Quarterly, IV:53
Winchester, E., II:215
Winchester, Jonas, I:358–59, 418; II:215
Winchester, Mass., IV:390*n*
Winckelmann, Johann Joachim, III:386
Windle, C. A. and C. Pliny, IV:442*n,* 449
Windle's Liberal Magazine, IV:442*n,* 449
Wine magazines, III:135
Wine and Spirit Bulletin, IV:189*n*
Wine and Spirit Gazette, IV:189*n*
Wine and Spirit Review, III:135
Winer, Jacob, IV:181*n*
Wines, Frederick Howard, IV:742
Winesburg, Ohio (Anderson), V:177
Wing, Dewitt C., V:167*n,* 169
Wing, J. M., III:135
Wing, Joseph E., III:159
Wingate, Charles E. N., III:550

Wingate, Charles Frederick, II:248; III:291
Winged Foot, IV:369
Winger, Albert E., IV:476–78, 763*n*
Winnemucan, Nev., IV:108
Winnetka, Ill., IV:271
Winona, Minn., IV:341
Winship, Albert Edward, IV:268
Winslow, Helen Maria, IV:356
Winslow, Thyra Samter, V:263
Winsmore, Robert, IV:577
Winsor, Justin, III:258, 320, 347, 357, 455, 518; IV:136; V:350
Winston, N.C., IV:214*n*
Winston, Robert Watson, V:274–75
Winston-Salem, N.C., IV:339
Winter, Ella, IV:730
Winter, William, II:35, 39, 376, 462, 482, 527; III:14*n*, 35*n*, 199*n*, 200, 229, 322, 374; IV:108*n*, 261*n*
Winter bathing, II:214
Winters, Yvor, V:241
Winthrop, Maine, I:444*n*
Winthrop, Robert Charles, III:322
Winthrop, Theodore, II:503, 505
Winthrop Press, V:152
Wirsig, Woodrow, IV:763*n*, 771
Wirt, William, I:184, 205, 409
Wirth, Louis, IV:192*n*
Wisconsin Agriculturist, III:157
Wisconsin Archaeologist, IV:140*n*
Wisconsin Engineer, IV:321*n*
Wisconsin Farmer, II:89; IV:340
Wisconsin Farmer (Madison), III:157
Wisconsin Journal of Education, II:99*n*; IV:270
Wisconsin Medical Journal, IV:314*n*
Wisconsin University, IV:321*n*
Wisdom Monthly, IV:50
Wise, Daniel, I:299*n*, 354; II:67
Wise, Herbert C., IV:124*n*
Wise, Isaac Mayer, II:77
Wise-Man, IV:285*n*
Wisherd, Edwin L., IV:628
Wistar Institute, IV:310, 314
Wister, Mrs. Annis Lee, II:506*n*
Wister, Owen, II:398*n*, 482; III:400; IV:105, 142, 457, 637, 691, 706; IV:73, 118–19
Wit, *see* Humor and wit; Humor magazines
Wit and Wisdom, III:269*n*
Witherspoon, John, I:27, 40, 63, 89, 90, 102, 147
Witherstine, Horatio P., IV:171*n*
Witness (New York), III:83; IV:301
Witness (Putney, Vt.), II:207*n*
Witte, Sergius, IV:785
Witter, James Clell, IV:147
Witwer, Harry Charles, IV:114*n*, 116*n*, 469, 470, 471
Wobblies, *see* Industrial Workers of the World
Wodehouse, P. G., IV:604, 618, 695, 709
Wolcott, Frederick, IV:177
Wolf, George Deering, IV:298
Wolf, Henry (engraver), III:188, 466
Wolf, William Almon, IV:469
Wolfe, Henry C., V:57
Wolfe, Thomas, IV:729; V:23
Wolfers, Arnold, V:329*n*
Wolman, Leo, V:211
Woman (Jackson's), IV:92
Woman (Munsey's), IV:617*n*
Woman Citizen, III:94
Woman Suffrage, IV:355–56
Woman's Advocate, II:52
Woman's Campaign, III:94
Woman's Century, III:100
Woman's Cycle, IV:356
Woman's Evangel, III:81
Woman's Home Companion, III:100, 317, 515; IV:21, 468, 473, 479; V:44
  sketch of, IV:763–72
Woman's Home Journal, III:100; IV:366
Woman's Journal, III:91, 94, 96*n*, 394; IV:355–56
Woman's Magazine, III:100, 486, 489
Woman's Magazine (Brattleboro, Vt.), IV:361
Woman's Magazine (St. Louis), IV:367
Woman's Medical Journal, IV:315
Woman's Missionary Friend, III:70; IV:237, 305
Woman's Missionary Record, IV:238*n*
Woman's Temperance Union, III:310
Woman's Tribute, III:95; IV:355
Woman's Welfare, IV:354*n*
Woman's Words, III:96
Woman's Work, IV:238*n*, 305
Woman's World, IV:367, 694*n*
Women
  early magazines and (1741–94)
    education, I:63–64
    literary entertainment for, I:105, 111
    poetry on, I:64–67
    writers, I:15, 66, 109

Women—*Continued*
nationalist era magazines and (1794–1825), I:139–44, 247, 322–23
advice, I:121
education, I:143, 145
poetry, I:295
writers, I:244
expansionist era magazines and (1825–50)
criticisms, I:345
editors, I:350, 356, 484–85, 537, 583–85; II:307
education, I:349–50, 484–85, 583, 672
growing role, I:482–83
writers, I:388, 400–1, 409, 412–13, 482, 499–500, 583–89, 743; II:308
Civil War era magazines and (1850–65), II:46–59
editors, II:50
education, II:46–47
social attitudes, II:48
writers, II:21–22, 46–49, 170–71, 173–74, 352–53, 357, 462, 467–68, 551; IV:679, 680
post-Civil War magazines and (1865–85), III:392
editors, II:463; III:94–96, 177, 390, 404–5, 407, 428–29, 500–1, 508
education, III:102–3, 403
writers, II:357–58, 546; III:90–101, 224–27, 231, 246, 327, 368, 371, 374, 377, 389, 397–400, 403, 423–24, 439, 483, 501–3, 508–12, 549–50
Gilded Age magazines and
criticisms, IV:444–45
editors, IV:142–43, 273, 360–64, 413, 539, 581
education, IV:357–58
medical journal, IV:315
personal columns, IV:540, 542–43
press emphasis, IV:405–6, 513
women's activities, III:546
writers, III:503–4, 546; IV:120, 141, 204, 242, 354, 360–63, 366, 397, 404, 409, 490, 537–38, 542, 612, 616, 654, 765–66
modern magazines and (1905–)
editors, III:354–55, 489, 504, 543; IV:470, 584, 700, 708, 712*n*, 768–71; V:25, 122–23
medical journal, IV:315
photographers, IV:761–62
writers, III:354–55, 479, 489, 514, 543; IV:466, 470–71, 475–76, 503, 584–85, 601–2, 604, 616, 655, 693, 697, 709, 712*n*, 713, 727, 729, 761–62, 768–71; V:20, 23, 28, 73–74, 96, 110, 122–23, 133–34
bicycles and, IV:378
boarding schools for, II:46–47
changing tastes of, IV:353
employment of, IV:354–55
as lecturers, I:743
social prominence of, IV:353
sports and, III:219; IV:370–71, 378
See also Prostitution; Women's magazines; Women's rights; Women's suffrage
Women's clubs, IV:356, 547
Women's magazines
earliest (1792), I:65–66
in nationalist era (1794–1825), I:139–40, 247–48
in expansionist era (1825–50), I:322–29, 348–54, 580–94, 626–28, 672, 733–34; II:306–8
music criticism, I:435
quality, I:348–54, 388
religious periodicals, II:301–3
signed contributions, I:504
in Civil War era (1850–65), II:308–9, 437–41, 453, 466–67
advertising, II:437
circulation, II:51, 303, 441
domestic journals, II:56–59
dress patterns, II:417–18; 437
engravings, II:193
expenses, II:18
high-circulation, II:11
male readers, I:590
payments to contributors, II:21
religious magazines, II:303–4
southern readership, II:109
trends, II:50–53
weeklies, II:34
in post-Civil War era (1865–85), II:304, 309–10; III:98–101, 388–90, 481–82
advertising, III:11, 391, 394, 447
circulation, II:309, 441; III:6–7, 100, 388, 450
fashions, III:97–98, 325, 327, 389, 481
Mid-Western, III:51–55
religious magazines, II:304; III:70
in Gilded Age (1885–1905), II:310–11; III:390, 482–84
advertising, IV:362, 537, 539, 766
biweeklies, V:125–31

circulation, III:484; IV:360, 362, 537, 539, 545, 582, 586–87; V:131–32
leading periodicals, IV:359–64, 536–46
mail-order journals, IV:364–68
major topics, IV:363–64
monthlies, IV:580–83; V:131–32
modern (1905–)
changing trends, IV:551
leading periodicals, IV:546–55
monthlies, IV:583–88; V:132–43
popularity with males, IV:550–51
services offered by, IV:548, 550, 552
Women's rights
abolitionists and, II:291
convention on (1848), I:483
to education, *see* Education
magazine comment on, I:90, 141–43, 483–85; III:377; IV:767; V:149
to vote, *see* Women's suffrage
to work, IV:354
Women's rights magazines, II:50–53; III:94–96, 391–95, 445–53; IV:62, 355–56
Women's suffrage
in expansionist era (1825–50), I:483–84
in Civil War era (1850–65), II:50, 291
in post-Civil War era (1865–85)
female image, III:306–7
lectures, III:93
magazine comment, II:251–52, 373; III:90–93, 391
in Gilded Age (1885–1905)
press opposition, IV:758
press support, IV:462
suffrage movement, IV:355
in modern period (1905–), III:486
magazine comment, III:432; IV:547
Womrath, Kay, V:248
Wood, A. L. S., V:13
Wood, Benjamin, II:545
Wood, Charles Erskine Scott, IV:107*n*
Wood, Clement, IV:748; V:185
Wood, Eugene, IV:49*n*, 604; V:80, 147
Wood, Fernando, II:154, 455, 545
Wood, Frank, II:520, 524
Wood, Mrs. Henry, II:439; IV:420, 680
Wood, Mrs. John, IV:258
Wood, John Seymour, IV:271
Wood, Percy, V:187
Wood, S. S., III:98
Wood, Sam, IV:104*n*
Wood, Stanley, IV:103
Wood, William, III:141; IV:700
Wood-Allen, Mary, IV:364
Wood Craft, IV:184*n*
Wood engraving, *see* Woodcuts
Wood industry periodicals, IV:184
Wood and Iron, III:130
Wood Worker, III:130*n*
Wood's Household Magazine, III:7*n*, 98
Woodberry, George Edward, II:510*n*, 511*n*; III:347; IV:126, 128, 451, 602
Woodbridge, Frederick James Eugene, III:349; IV:303
Woodbridge, N.J., I:26
Woodbridge, William Channing, I:401, 541*n*, 542
Woodbury, Isaac Baker, II:197
Woodbury, J. H., II:263*n*, 270
Woodcock, W. H., III:273
Woodcock's Printers' and Lithographers' Weekly Gazette and Newspaper Reporter, III:273*n*
Woodcuts
in early magazines (1741–94), I:36, 75, 81
in nationalist era magazines (1794–1825)
agricultural periodicals, I:153
general magazines, I:322, 328, 346
literary magazines, I:282
religious magazines, I:252
trends, I:210
women's magazines, I:322, 328
in expansionist era magazines (1825–50), I:493, 545, 567, 611, 656, 672, 714, 731, 745, 748, 781
abolitionist periodicals, II:282
agricultural magazines, I:731
comic magazines, I:425, 771
engravers, I:522
general magazines, I:364, 548, 622–23, IV:675
juvenile magazines, I:714; II:265
literary magazines, I:734, 762, 767, 771; IV:675
"mammoth" papers, I:359
police gazettes, II:325
quality, I:523–24
religious magazines, I:745
scientific periodicals, II:317
trends, I:521
women's magazines, I:592
in Civil War era magazines (1850–65), I:656; II:30, 32, 37, 43, 45, 100, 116*n*, 117, 176, 272, 304, 308, 345, 360, 375, 388,

Woodcuts—*Continued*
399, 400, 406, 433, 439, 476, 546
art magazines, III:410–11
cost, II:193
education magazines, II:445
family magazines, II:417, 471
general magazines, II:449; IV:679
humor magazines, II:180–81, 182–84
illustrated weeklies, II:409
literary magazines, II:390, 428; IV:679
popularity, II:192–93
portraits, II:176
satiric magazines, II:523
universal use, II:193
women's fashions, II:53, 55
women's magazines, II:195, 309
in post-Civil War magazines (1865–85)
art magazines, III:410–11
artistic advances, III:187–90
comic magazines, III:265–66
fashion magazines, III:482–83
general magazines, III:358–60, 420
illustrated magazines, III:118
juvenile magazines, II:272; III:508
literary magazines, II:396, 399; III:41
"new school," III:466
photography and, III:188
police gazettes, II:329–30
religious magazines, III:85
women's magazines, III:325, 410–11
in Gilded Age magazines (1885–1905)
declining use, III:472; IV:5, 154
fashion magazines, IV:581
general periodicals, IV:146, 154, 720
literary magazines, IV:674–75
women's magazines, IV:537
in modern magazines (1905–), III:479
Woodhull, Victoria Claflin, III:93, 95, 172
as editor, III:443–53
Woodhull, Zulu Maud, III:452*n*
Woodhull & Claflin's Journal, III:452
Woodhull & Claflin's Weekly, III:95, 302, 308, 313
sketch of, III:443–53
Woodlock, Thomas F., IV:776
Woodman, C. H., II:530*n*, 533
Woodpulp paper, V:86
Woodridge, George L., II:186
Woodrow, James, II:63*n*
Woodrow, Mrs. Wilson, IV:49*n*, 367*n*, 602; V:86
Woodruff, Clinton Rogers, IV:415
Woodruff, Frank E., IV:395*n*
Woods, Mrs. Frances Armstrong, IV:101
Woods, Frank E., III:199*n*
Woods, Franklin, II:448
Woods, Henry E., II:176*n*
Woods Hole, Mass., IV:309
Woods, Leonard, I:263, 401, 571, 572
Woods, Leonard, Jr., I:624–25
Woods, Robert Archey, IV:744
Woods, William Seaver, IV:569*n*, 574–77
Woodstock, Md., III:68; IV:298
Woodward, Elizabeth, IV:553
Woodward, F. W., II:90*n*
Woodward, George, II:181
Woodward, George A., III:533
Woodward, George E., II:90*n*
Woodward, George Murgatroyd, I:44*n*
Woodward, George Washington, II:545
Woodward, John D., III:411
Woodward, Joseph, II:179
Woodworth, Samuel, I:128, 139, 320–21, 499, 627
Wool Markets and Sheep, IV:344
Woolf, Benjamin, III:202
Woolf, Michael Angelo, III:528; IV:564
Woolf, Philip, IV:69*n*
Woolf, Samuel Johnson, IV:747–48; V:84
Woolf, Virginia, V:211, 336
Woollcott, Alexander, IV:697; V:85
Woolley, Edward Mott, IV:604
Woolsey, James J., I:666*n*
Woolsey, Theodore Dwight, II:312*n*, 313, 314
Woolsey, Theodore Salisbury, IV:227, 232; V:330
Woolson, Constance Fenimore, II:398, 407, 506*n*; III:224, 227, 261, 373, 397, 420–21, 461
Woolworth, Frank Winfield, IV:605
Worcester, Mass., I:92; III:300; IV:184*n*, 268, 272*n*
Worcester, Noah, I:131, 135, 284*n*, 285
Worcester, Samuel, I:134*n*
Worcester Magazine, I:32, 41 49–50, 55
sketch of, 92–93
Worcester's Dictionary, II:177
Word, III:301; IV:287
Word coinage, V:309
Word and Way, IV:292*n*
Word and Works, IV:309
Worden, William L., IV:712, 713

Wordsworth, William, I:180–81, 231, 399; II:161
Work, magazines on, IV:774
Work, Milton C., IV:473
Work and Win, IV:119
Worker, IV:175
Worker's Call, IV:175
Working Christian, III:73*n*
Working class
expansionist era magazines and (1825–50), I:487, 719
antiunion, I:471
factory magazine, I:471
pro-labor, I:470
socialist periodicals, I:536–38
Civil War era magazines and (1850–65)
socialist periodicals, II:207
trade union periodicals, II:212
unemployment, II:5, 145
post-Civil War magazines and (1865–85)
railroad strike (1877), III:124–25
socialist periodicals, II:300–1
trade union periodicals, III:125, 126*n*, 129*n*, 299–301
Gilded Age magazines and (1885–1905), IV:215–21
Chicago anarchists, IV:172
descriptions, IV:721
socialist periodicals, IV:173–76
trade union periodicals, III:300–301; IV:172, 220, 221*n*
See also Anarchism; Communist magazines; Socialism; Strikes; Trade unions
Working Farmer, II:89; III:152
Working Man's Advocate, I:445*n*, 800
Working Men's Party, I:340
Workingmen's Advocate, II:212; III:299
Workman, II:73
Workmen's Advocate, IV:174
World Affairs, II:211*n*
World Magazine, III:102; IV:68*n*
World To-Day, IV:55, 499–500
World Trade, IV:186*n*
World War One (1914–1918), II:323, 336, 403, 404, 549; III:433, 478, 555; V:5, 49, 57, 86, 101, 124, 182, 206–9, 211, 217, 242, 255, 261–63, 290, 338
effects on magazines, IV:770
magazine reportage on, II:258–59, 403; III:350, 488, 532; IV:529, 549–50, 574, 584, 629, 663, 696, 726–27, 770, 783; V:5, 57, 182, 208, 284
pictures, II:378
poetry on, V:242
World War Two (1939–1945), IV:631, 712, 771; V:44, 57, 217–19, 231, 242–43, 284, 307, 325–26, 336
"World War III" *Collier's* article on, IV:478
World-Wide Missions, IV:238*n*, 305
World's Advance, III:499
World's Advance-Thought, III:82
World's Chronicle, IV:64
World's Columbian Exposition Illustrated, IV:99
World's Events, IV:52–53, 269*n*
World's Fair Puck, IV:100
World's Progress, III:116
World's Work, IV:35, 53, 223, 773–88; V:50–51, 54–55, 73*n*, 294
Worman, Ben James, IV:633*n*, 635–37
Worman, James Henry, IV:633*n*, 635–36
Worrall, John M., II:537*n*, 538
Worth, Patience, IV:655
Worth, Thomas, II:477; III:270*n*, 552; IV:385
Worthington, Alfred D., IV:45*n*
Worthington's Illustrated Monthly Magazine, IV:45–56
Wotherspoon, George, IV:751*n*
Wren, Percival Christopher, IV:606
Wright, Carroll Davidson, IV:52*n*, 171, 218, 458
Wright, Chauncey, II:248
Wright, Frances, I:445*n*, 536*n*, 537–38
Wright, Frank Lloyd, V:158, 163
Wright, George Frederick, I:739*n*, 741; III:407; IV:140, 293
Wright, Guy W., I:438*n*
Wright, Harold Bell, IV:584
Wright, I. B., I:736
Wright, J. T., IV:571
Wright, John R., IV:88*n*
Wright, Rawdon, I:548
Wright, Richardson, IV:324*n*
Wright, Roy V., II:298*n*, 300
Wright, Theodore Francis, IV:296
Wright, Willard Huntington ("S. S. Van Dine"), III:515; IV:503, 728; V:246*n*, 256–59, 265–66
Wright, William ("Dan DeQuille"), III:54, 407; IV:105
Wrightington, Sidney R., IV:347*n*
Wrigley, G. M., II:415
Writer, IV:142
Writers for magazines, *see* Contributors
Writers' magazines, IV:142
Writing, *see* Style

Wu Ting-fang, II:271; III:512; IV:89, 193, 233
Wundt, William, IV:303
Wyant, G. G., IV:432*n*, 437
Wyatt, Edith, IV:457–58, 601
Wyatt, Sir Thomas, V:118
Wyckoff, Walter Augustus, IV:721, 724
Wyckoff, William Cornelius, IV:45*n*
Wyeth, Andrew, V:323
Wyeth, Mary E. C., III:175*n*
Wyeth, Newell Convers, II:402; III:475, 487; IV:637, 692; V:84
Wylie, Elinor, V:210, 236
Wylie, Ida Alexa Ross, IV:697, 713; V:134
Wylie, Philip, IV:478, 709, 761
Wylly, W. H., III:45*n*
Wyman, Walter Forestus, IV:783

X-rays, discovery of, IV:311, 319

Y.M.C.A., *see* Young Men's Christian Association
Y.M.C.A. Watchman, III:85
Y.M.C.A.'s, The, IV:287*n*
Yachting, IV:373
Yachting articles, IV:634, 636
Yachting magazines, III:211; IV:373
Yale, Leroy Milton, IV:364
Yale Alumni Weekly, V:338
Yale Divinity Quarterly, IV:293
Yale Law Journal, IV:348
Yale Literary Magazine, I:488, 803; II:99; III:165
Yale News, V:294
Yale Publishing Association, V:338
Yale Review, II:315; IV:73, 293, 393
  sketch of, V:329–40
  See also New Englander
Yale Scientific Monthly, IV:306*n*
Yale Sheffield Monthly, IV:306*n*
Yale University, V:330, 332–33, 337
  faculty contributors, I:348
  general periodicals, IV:73
  legal periodical, IV:348
  literary periodicals, I:172; II:99; III:165–66
  magazines published at, I:151, 488, 571; III:168*n*
  religious periodicals, II:70, 315
  scientific periodicals, III:108*n;* IV:310
  sporting activities at, IV:375–76
Yale University Press, V:339
Yancey, Ben C., III:154
Yankee (New York), I:355*n*
Yankee (Portland), I:355, 799
Yankee Blade, II:36; IV:4, 18, 67, 79*n*
Yankee Doodle, I:425, 808; II:183
Yankee Notions, II:54, 156, 182; III:267
Yankee Privateer, II:36*n*
Yard, Robert Sterling, III:457*n,* 477–78
Yarmolinsky, Abraham, IV:437
Yarros, Victor S., IV:312*n*
Yates, Edmund, III:249, 358
Yates, Giles F., II:215
Yates, James, IV:712
Yazoo Daily Yankee, II:151
Ybarra, Thomas Russell, III:434; IV:787
Ye Giglampz, III:267
Yeats, William Butler, II:256; III:543; IV:121, 297, 425, 451, 602; V:173, 177–78, 228–29, 231, 258
Yellow Book, IV:49, 450
Yellow Dog, IV:391
Yellow fever epidemics, I:122, 149; II:86; III:137
Yellow journalism, IV:196, 242–43
Yellow Kid, IV:48–49, 196
Yellow-Kid characters, IV:384
Yellow Springs, Ohio, II:87
Yenowine's Illustrated News, IV:96
Yeoman Shield, IV:222*n*
Yerby, Frank, IV:477
Yerkes, Charles Tyson, IV:414
Yerkes, Stephen, II:537*n*, 539
Yerrinton, J. B., II:296
Yezierska, Anzia, III:479
Yiddish language periodicals, IV:300
Yoder, Robert M., IV:712*n*
Yohn, Frederick Coffay, IV:727
Yonge, Charlotte, III:32*n*
Yonkers, N.Y., IV:285*n*
York, Neb., IV:345
York, Pa., IV:48, 295*n*
Yorkston, R. P., III:274
Yorkville, S.C., III:73*n*
Youmans, Edward Livingston, III:105, 108, 172, 363, 417–18, 424
  as editor, III:495–98
Youmans, Eliza Ann, III:496
Youmans, J. W., I:533
Youmans, William Jay, III:495, 498
Young, Alexander, III:550
Young, Arthur Henry, III:531, 554; IV:456, 491
Young, Brigham, III:57
Young, Cortland H., IV:116–17; V:145*n;* 146
Young, James, IV:90
Young, Owen D., V:323*n*
Young, Sarsfield, III:441

Young, Stark, IV:729; V:116*n*, 191*n*, 210, 219
Young, Thomas, I:62, 85
Young, W. W., V:145*n*, 152
Young, William, I:94*n*, 98
Young America, I:445*n*, 807; II:182
"Young America" movement, I:682; II:127
Young Catholic, III:70
Young Churchman, III:75
Young Folk's Circle, IV:764
Young Folk's Monthly, III:176
Young Folks' Rural, III:179
Young Idea, IV:275*n*
Young Intellectuals' movement, V:93
Young Italy movement, I:339
Young Klondike, IV:109
Young Ladies' Journal, IV:228*n*
Young Mechanic, I:445, 801
Young Men, IV:287*n*
Young Men of America, III:7*n*, 179
Young Men's Christian Association, III:27*n*, 84–85; IV:272*n*, 287–88, 369–70
Young Men's Christian Journal, II:75
Young Men's Era, IV:287*n*
Young New Yorker, II:468; III:210, 218
Young Oölogist, III:111
Young People, III:180; IV:274
Young People's Magazine, III:176
Young People's Weekly, IV:274
Young Sam, II:182
Young Scientist, III:109*n*
Young Sleuth, IV:119
Young Wild West, IV:119*n*
Young Woman's Journal, IV:297
Young's Magazine, IV:116–17; V:146
Youngman, E. H., II:95*n*
Youth magazines, *see* Juvenile magazines
Youth's Casket, II:100, 466
Youth's Companion, I:492, 799; II:100, 200; III:174, 177, 512; IV:16, 17, 21, 29, 79, 273*n*, 597*n*; V:29
  advertising in, III:11
  circulation of, III:6–8
  sketch of, II:262–74
Youth's Companion (New York), II:264*n*
Youth's Friend and Scholar's Magazine, I:144, 797; II:101
Youth's Home Library, IV:764
Youth's Penny Gazette, II:10
Youth's Temperance Banner, III:8*n*
Ypsilanti, Mich., IV:269*n*
Yukon, IV:108–9

Zabel, Morton Dauwen, V:225*n*, 239, 241
"Zabriski, Olympe," III:228
Zadkine, Ossip, V:178
Zangwill, Israel, II:273, 402, 482; IV:196, 451, 456, 490, 592; V:338
Zaturenska, Marya, V:237
Zell's Monthly Magazine, III:39*n*
Zieber, G. B., I:426, 780
Ziegler, P. W., III:176
Zimmerman, Eugene, III:528, 553; IV:386
Zimmerman, J. Frederick, IV:255
Zingg, Charles J., IV:246*n*
Zion Banner, IV:286
Zion City, Illinois, IV:286
Zionist magazines, IV:300
Zion's Advocate (Portland, Maine), II:65*n*
Zion's Advocate (Washington), II:65
Zion's Herald, I:138, 460, 797; II:67, 140; IV:291*n*
Zion's Hope, III:81
Zion's Watch Tower and Herald of Christ's Presence, III:85*n*
Zion's Watchman, III:83; IV:301
Zogbaum, Rufus Fairchild, I:593; II:483; IV:151, 720
Zola, Émile, III:252, 254; IV:114*n*, 122, 124, 130, 135
Zoology, magazine articles on, I:303–4
Zoology magazines, IV:310
Zueblin, Charles, IV:191
Zuppke, Robert Carl, IV:700
Zwaska, Charles A., V:166*n*, 172